W9-CCD-672

Houghton
Mifflin
Harcourt

Algebra 2

Volume 2

TIMOTHY D. KANOLD

EDWARD B. BURGER

JULI K. DIXON

MATTHEW R. LARSON

STEVEN J. LEINWAND

© Houghton Mifflin Harcourt Publishing Company • Cover/TitlePage (Arches, Moab, UT) holbox/
Shutterstock; (Space Needle, WA) Rruntsch/Shutterstock; (Downtown, Chattanooga, TN) Sean Pavone/
Shutterstock.

Printed in the U.S.A.

ISBN 978-0-544-38590-0

8 9 10 0928 24 23 22 21 20 19 18 17

4500663404   E F G H I

Authors

Timothy D. Kanold, Ph.D., is an award-winning international educator, author, and consultant. He is a former superintendent and director of mathematics and science at Adlai E. Stevenson High School District 125 in Lincolnshire, Illinois. He is a past president of the National Council of Supervisors of Mathematics (NCSM) and the Council for the Presidential Awardees of Mathematics (CPAM). He

has served on several writing and leadership commissions for NCTM during the past decade. He presents motivational professional development seminars with a focus on developing professional learning communities (PLC's) to improve the teaching, assessing, and learning of students. He has recently authored nationally recognized articles, books, and textbooks for mathematics education and school leadership, including *What Every Principal Needs to Know about the Teaching and Learning of Mathematics*.

Edward B. Burger, Ph.D., is the President of Southwestern University, a former Francis Christopher Oakley Third Century Professor of Mathematics at Williams College, and a former vice provost at Baylor University. He has authored or coauthored more than sixty-five articles, books, and video series; delivered over five hundred addresses and workshops throughout the world; and made more than fifty radio and

television appearances. He is a Fellow of the American Mathematical Society as well as having earned many national honors, including the Robert Foster Cherry Award for Great Teaching in 2010. In 2012, Microsoft Education named him a "Global Hero in Education."

Juli K. Dixon, Ph.D., is a Professor of Mathematics Education at the University of Central Florida. She has taught mathematics in urban schools at the elementary, middle, secondary, and post-secondary levels. She is an active researcher and speaker with numerous publications and conference presentations. Key areas of focus are deepening teachers' content knowledge and communicating and justifying mathematical ideas. She is a past chair of the NCTM Student Explorations in Mathematics Editorial Panel and member of the Board of Directors for the Association of Mathematics Teacher Educators.

Matthew R. Larson, Ph.D., is the K-12 mathematics curriculum specialist for the Lincoln Public Schools and served on the Board of Directors for the National Council of Teachers of Mathematics from 2010 to 2013. He is a past chair of NCTM's Research Committee and was a member of NCTM's Task Force on Linking Research and Practice.

He is the author of several books on implementing the Common Core Standards for Mathematics. He has taught mathematics at the secondary and college levels and held an appointment as an honorary visiting associate professor at Teachers College, Columbia University.

Steven J. Leinwand is a Principal Research Analyst at the American Institutes for Research (AIR) in Washington, D.C., and has over 30 years in leadership positions in mathematics education. He is past president of the National Council of Supervisors of Mathematics and served on the NCTM Board of Directors. He is the author of numerous articles, books, and textbooks

and has made countless presentations with topics including student achievement, reasoning, effective assessment, and successful implementation of standards.

Exponential and Logarithmic Functions and Equations

MODULE 12

Sequences and Series

MODULE 13

Exponential Functions

© Houghton Mifflin Harcourt Publishing Company • Image Credits: (t) ©Ron Chapple/Corbis; (b) ©Adam Hart-Davis/Science Photo Library

MODULE 14

Modeling with Exponential and Other Functions

MODULE 15

Logarithmic Functions

MODULE 16

Logarithmic Properties and Exponential Equations

UNIT 7
Volume 2
Trigonometric Functions

MODULE 17
Unit-Circle Definition of Trigonometric Functions

MODULE 18
Graphing Trigonometric Functions

Probability

UNIT ★ 8

Volume 2

MODULE 19 — Introduction to Probability

MODULE 20 — Conditional Probability and Independence of Events

MODULE 21

Probability and Decision Making

Statistics

MODULE 22

Gathering and Displaying Data

MODULE 23

Data Distributions

Making Inferences from Data

MODULE **24**

Exponential and Logarithmic Functions and Equations

MATH IN CAREERS

Nuclear Medicine Technologist
Nuclear medicine technologists use technology to create images, or *scans*, of parts of a patient's body. They must understand the mathematics of exponential decay of radioactive materials. Nuclear medicine technologists analyze data from the scan, which are presented to a specialist for diagnosis.

If you are interested in a career as a nuclear medicine technologist, you should study these mathematical subjects:
- Algebra
- Statistics
- Calculus

Check out the career activity at the end of the unit to find out how **Nuclear Medicine Technologists** use math.

© Houghton Mifflin Harcourt Publishing Company • Image Credits: © Robert Kneschke/Shutterstock

Reading Start-Up

Vocabulary

Review Words

  asymptote
  (*asíntota*)

  inverse function
  (*función inversa*)

✔ translation
  (*traslación*)

✔ vertical compression
  (*compresión vertical*)

✔ vertical stretch
  (*estiramiento vertical*)

Preview Words

explicit formula
  (*fórmula explícita*)

geometric sequence
  (*sucesión geométrica*)

logarithmic function
  (*función logarítmica*)

recursive formula
  (*fórmula recurrente*)

Visualize Vocabulary

Use the ✓ words to complete the graphic.

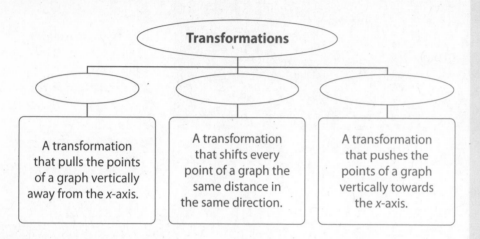

Transformations

A transformation that pulls the points of a graph vertically away from the *x*-axis.

A transformation that shifts every point of a graph the same distance in the same direction.

A transformation that pushes the points of a graph vertically towards the *x*-axis.

Understand Vocabulary

To become familiar with some of the vocabulary terms in the module, consider the following. You may refer to the module, the glossary, or a dictionary.

1. A sequence in which the ratio of successive terms is a constant *r*, where $r \neq 0$ or 1 , is a _____.

2. A _____ is a rule for a sequence in which one or more previous terms are used to generate the next term.

3. A _____ is the inverse of an exponential function.

Active Reading

Booklet Before beginning the unit, create a booklet to help you organize what you learn. Each page of the booklet should correspond to a lesson in the unit and summarize the most important information from the lesson. Include definitions, examples, and graphs to help you recall the main elements of the lesson. Highlight the main idea and use colored pencils to help you illustrate any important concepts or differences.

Sequences and Series

Essential Question: How do sequences and series help to solve real-world problems?

REAL WORLD VIDEO
Fractal geography is the study of fractal patterns that occur in geographic features such as coastlines and watersheds. Check out how geometric series are involved in determining the area and perimeter of fractals.

MODULE PERFORMANCE TASK PREVIEW

How Big Is That Snowflake?

Did you ever make cutout snowflakes in school? If you did, you folded the paper a few times and snipped little triangles from the edges. The more you snipped, the more you decreased the overall area. In this module, you'll explore a fractal pattern called a Koch snowflake that starts with a triangle and adds smaller and smaller triangles to the edges. So, what is the total area of a Koch snowflake? The answer to this will crystalize later in the module.

Are YOU Ready?

Complete these exercises to review skills you will need for this module.

Real Numbers

Example 1

Add: $\dfrac{5}{6} + \dfrac{5}{7} + \dfrac{5}{8}$

$\dfrac{5}{2 \cdot 3} + \dfrac{5}{7} + \dfrac{5}{2^3}$

$\dfrac{5(2^2 \cdot 7)}{2 \cdot 3(2^2 \cdot 7)} + \dfrac{5(2^3 \cdot 3)}{7(2^3 \cdot 3)} + \dfrac{5(3 \cdot 7)}{2^3(3 \cdot 7)}$

$\dfrac{365}{168}$

Use prime factors in denominators.

Use the LCD to rewrite fractions.

Simplify and add numerators.

- Online Homework
- Hints and Help
- Extra Practice

Add.

1. $\dfrac{1}{2} + \dfrac{2}{3} + \dfrac{3}{4}$

2. $\dfrac{2}{3} + \dfrac{1}{2} + \dfrac{2}{5}$

3. $\dfrac{1}{8} + \dfrac{3}{10} + \dfrac{5}{12}$

Exponential Functions

Example 2

Write the values for $f(x)$ for $x = \{3, 4, 5\}$, if

$f(x) = \dfrac{1}{8}(4)^x$

$f(3) = \dfrac{1}{8}(4)^3 = \dfrac{1}{8}(64) = 8$

$f(4) = \dfrac{1}{8}(4)^4 = \dfrac{1}{8}(256) = 32$

$f(5) = \dfrac{1}{8}(4)^5 = \dfrac{1}{8}(1024) = 128$

The solution set is $\{8, 32, 128\}$.

Write the solution set for $f(x)$ for $x = \{3, 4, 5\}$.

4. $f(x) = 0.2(5)^x$

5. $f(x) = \dfrac{2}{3}(3)^x$

6. $f(x) = 0.75(2)^x$

12.1 Arithmetic Sequences

Essential Question: What are algebraic ways to define an arithmetic sequence?

 Explore   **Investigating Arithmetic Sequences**

Consider a staircase where the vertical distance between steps is 7.5 inches and you must walk up 14 steps to get from the first floor to the second floor, a total vertical distance of 105 inches. Define two functions: $B(s)$, which models the distance from the bottom of the staircase (the first floor) to the bottom of your foot, and $T(s)$, which models the distance from the bottom of your foot to the top of the staircase (the second floor). For both functions, the independent variable s represents the number of steps that you have walked up.

(A) Complete the table. Show your calculations.

s	B(s)	T(s)
0	0	105
1	$0 + 7.5 = 7.5$	
2	$0 + 2(7.5) = 15$	
3		
4		

(B) Based on the patterns in the table, write rules for the two functions in terms of s.

$B(s) = \boxed{}$

$T(s) = \boxed{}$

(C) Identify the domain and range of $B(s)$.

- The domain of $B(s)$ is

$$\left\{ 0, 1, 2, 3, 4, \boxed{\ }, \boxed{\ }, \boxed{\ }, \boxed{\ }, \boxed{\ }, \boxed{\ }, \boxed{\ }, \boxed{\ }, \boxed{\ }, \boxed{\ } \right\}.$$

- The range of $B(s)$ is

$$\left\{ 0, 7.5, 15, \boxed{\ }, \boxed{\ }, \boxed{\ }, \boxed{\ }, \boxed{\ }, \boxed{\ }, \boxed{\ }, \boxed{\ }, \boxed{\ }, \boxed{\ }, \boxed{\ } \right\}.$$

Ⓓ Graph $B(s)$.

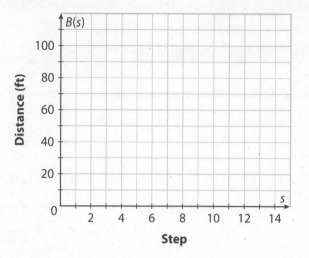

Ⓔ Identify the domain and range of $T(s)$.

- The domain of $T(s)$ is

$$\left\{0, 1, 2, 3, 4, \boxed{}, \boxed{}, \boxed{}, \boxed{}, \boxed{}, \boxed{}, \boxed{}, \boxed{}, \boxed{}\right\}.$$

- The range of $T(s)$ is

$$\left\{105, \boxed{}, \boxed{}, \boxed{}, \boxed{}, \boxed{}, \boxed{}, \boxed{}, \boxed{}, \boxed{}, \boxed{}, \boxed{}, \boxed{}\right\}.$$

Ⓕ Graph $T(s)$.

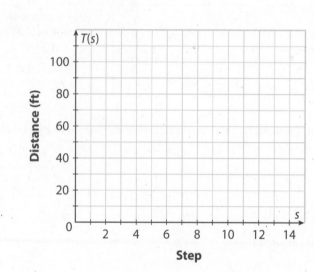

Reflect

1. Both $B(s)$ and $T(s)$ are linear functions, but their graphs consist of discrete points. Why?

_____

_____

2. How are $B(s)$ and $T(s)$ different? Why?

_____

_____

_____

Explain 1 Writing Explicit and Recursive Rules for Arithmetic Sequences

A **sequence** is an ordered list of numbers. Each number in the list is called a *term* of the sequence. You can think of a sequence as a function with a subset of the set of integers as the domain and the set of terms of the sequence as the range. An **explicit rule** for a sequence defines the term in position n as a function of n. A **recursive rule** for a sequence defines the term in position n by relating it to one or more previous terms.

An **arithmetic sequence**, also known as a *discrete linear function*, is a sequence for which consecutive terms have a *common difference*. For instance, the terms of the sequence 0, 7.5, 15, 22.5, 30, 37.5, 45, 52.5, 60, 67.5, 75, 82.5, 90, 97.5, 105, which are the values of the function $B(s)$ from the Explore, have a common difference of 7.5. Likewise, the terms of the sequence 105, 97.5, 90, 82.5, 75, 67.5, 60, 52.5, 45, 37.5, 30, 22.5, 15, 7.5, 0, which are the values of the function $T(s)$ from the Explore, have a common difference of -7.5. Both sequences are arithmetic.

You can write different explicit and recursive rules for a sequence depending on what integer you use as the position number for the initial term of the sequence. The most commonly used starting position numbers are 0 and 1. The table shows rules for the sequences that you examined in the Explore.

	Sequence	
	0, 7.5, 15, 22.5, 30, 37.5, 45, 52.5, 60, 67.5, 75, 82.5, 90, 97.5, 105	105, 97.5, 90, 82.5, 75, 67.5, 60, 52.5, 45, 37.5, 30, 22.5, 15, 7.5, 0
Explicit rule when starting position is 0	$f(n) = 0 + 7.5n$ for $0 \le n \le 14$	$f(n) = 105 - 7.5n$ for $0 \le n \le 14$
Explicit rule when starting position is 1	$f(n) = 0 + 7.5(n-1)$ for $1 \le n \le 15$	$f(n) = 105 - 7.5(n-1)$ for $1 \le n \le 15$
Recursive rule when starting position is 0	$f(0) = 0$ and $f(n) = f(n-1) + 7.5$ for $1 \le n \le 14$	$f(0) = 105$ and $f(n) = f(n-1) - 7.5$ for $1 \le n \le 14$
Recursive rule when starting position is 1	$f(1) = 0$ and $f(n) = f(n-1) + 7.5$ for $2 \le n \le 15$	$f(1) = 105$ and $f(n) = f(n-1) - 7.5$ for $2 \le n \le 15$

In general, when 0 is the starting position for the initial term a of an arithmetic sequence with common difference d, the sequence has the explicit rule $f(n) = a + dn$ for $n \ge 0$ and the recursive rule $f(0) = a$ and $f(n) = f(n-1) + d$ for $n \ge 1$. When 1 is the starting position of the initial term, the sequence has the explicit rule $f(n) = a + d(n-1)$ for $n \ge 1$ and the recursive rule $f(1) = a$ and $f(n) = f(n-1) + d$ for $n \ge 2$.

Example 1 Use the given table to write an explicit and a recursive rule for the sequence.

Ⓐ

n	0	1	2	3	4	5
$f(n)$	2	5	8	11	14	17

First, check the differences of consecutive values of $f(n)$:

$5 - 2 = 3$, $8 - 5 = 3$, $11 - 8 = 3$, $14 - 11 = 3$, and $17 - 14 = 3$

The differences are the same, so the sequence is arithmetic.

The initial term a of the sequence is 2, and its position number is 0. As already observed, the common difference d is 3.

So, the explicit rule for the sequence is $f(n) = 2 + 3n$ for $0 \le n \le 5$. The recursive rule is $f(0) = 2$ and $f(n) = f(n-1) + 3$ for $1 \le n \le 5$.

(B)

n	1	2	3	4	5	6
f(n)	29	25	21	17	13	9

First, check the differences of consecutive values of $f(n)$:

$25 - 29 =$ ☐ , $21 - 25 =$ ☐ , $17 - 21 =$ ☐ , $13 - 17 =$ ☐ , and $9 - 13 =$ ☐

The differences are the same, so the sequence [is/is not] arithmetic.

The initial term a of the sequence is _____, and its position number is _____. As already observed, the common difference d is _____.

So, the explicit rule for the sequence is $f(n) =$ ☐ for ☐ $\leq n \leq$ ☐ . The recursive rule

is $f\left(\boxed{}\right) = \boxed{}$ and $f(n) = f(n-1) +$ ☐ for ☐ $\leq n \leq$ ☐ .

Your Turn

Use the given table to write an explicit and a recursive rule for the sequence.

3.

n	0	1	2	3	4	5
f(n)	−7	−2	3	8	13	18

4.

n	1	2	3	4	5	6
f(n)	11	5	−1	−7	−13	−19

🔑 Explain 2 Graphing Arithmetic Sequences

As you saw in the Explore, the graph of an arithmetic sequence consists of points that lie on a line. The arithmetic sequence 3, 7, 11, 15, 19 has a final term, so it is called a *finite* sequence and its graph has a countable number of points. The arithmetic sequence 3, 7, 11, 15, 19, … does not have a final term (indicated by the three dots), so it is called an *infinite* sequence and its graph has infinitely many points. Since you cannot show the complete graph of an infinite sequence, you should simply show as many points as the grid allows.

Example 2 Write the terms of the given arithmetic sequence and then graph the sequence.

(A) $f(n) = -1 + 2n$ for $0 \leq n \leq 4$

Make a table of values.

n	f(n)
0	$-1 + 2(0) = -1$
1	$-1 + 2(1) = 1$
2	$-1 + 2(2) = 3$
3	$-1 + 2(3) = 5$
4	$-1 + 2(4) = 7$

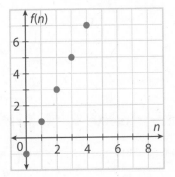

So, the sequence is $-1, 1, 3, 5, 7$.

Graph the sequence.

(B) $f(1) = 4$ and $f(n) = f(n-1) - 0.25$ for $n \geq 2$

Make a table of values, bearing in mind that the table could be extended because the sequence is infinite.

n	f(n)
1	4
2	$f(2) = f(1) - 0.25 = 4 - 0.25 = \boxed{}$
3	$f(3) = f(2) - 0.25 = \boxed{} - 0.25 = \boxed{}$
4	$f(4) = f(3) - 0.25 = \boxed{} - 0.25 = \boxed{}$
5	$f(5) = f(4) - 0.25 = \boxed{} - 0.25 = \boxed{}$

So, the sequence is _____.

Graph the sequence.

© Houghton Mifflin Harcourt Publishing Company

Write the terms of the given arithmetic sequence and then graph the sequence.

5. $f(n) = 8 - \frac{2}{3}(n-1)$ for $1 \le n \le 7$

6. $f(0) = -3$ and $f(n) = f(n-1) - 1$ for $n \ge 1$

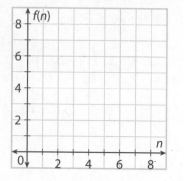

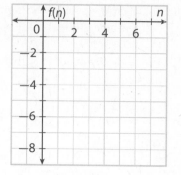

🔧 Explain 3   Modeling with Arithmetic Sequences

Some real-world situations, like the situation in the Explore, can be modeled with an arithmetic sequence. You can then use a rule for the sequence to solve problems related to the situation.

Example 3   **Write a recursive rule and an explicit rule for an arithmetic sequence that models the situation. Then use the rule to answer the question.**

(A)   There are 19 seats in the row nearest the stage of a theater. Each row after the first one has 2 more seats than the row before it. How many seats are in the 13th row?

Let n represent the row number, starting with 1 for the first row. The verbal description gives you a recursive rule: $f(1) = 19$ and $f(n) = f(n-1) + 2$ for $n \ge 2$. Since the initial term is 19 and the common difference is 2, an explicit rule is $f(n) = 19 + 2(n-1)$ for $n \ge 1$.

To find the number of seats in the 13th row, find using the explicit rule.

$f(13) = 19 + 2(13 - 1) = 43$

So, there are 43 seats in the 13th row.

(B) A student with a part-time job borrowed money from her parents to purchase a bicycle. The graph shows the amount the student owes her parents as she makes equal weekly payments. The amount owed is shown only for the first 5 weeks.

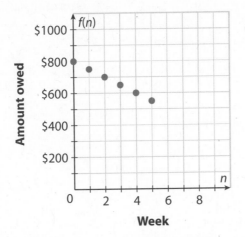

In how many weeks after purchasing the bicycle will the loan be paid off?

Let n represent the number of weeks since the loan was made, starting with _____ for the time at which the loan was made. The sequence of amounts owed is arithmetic because the weekly payments are _____ . To determine the amount of the weekly payment, let $f(n)$ represent the amount owed at week n, and observe from the graph that $f(0) =$ [ ] and $f(2) =$ [ ] . The general explicit rule for the sequence is $f(n) = a + dn$. Substituting 2 for n, the value of $f(0)$ for a, and the value of $f(2)$ for $f(n)$ in $f(n) = a + dn$, you can solve for the common difference d:

$$f(2) = f(0) + 2d$$

$$\boxed{} = \boxed{} + 2d$$

$$\boxed{} = 2d$$

$$\boxed{} = d$$

So, the amount of the weekly payment is _____ , and an explicit rule for the

sequence is $f(n) = \boxed{} + \left(\boxed{} \right)n$. A recursive rule for the sequence is

$f(0) = \boxed{}$ and $f(n) = f(n-1) + \boxed{}$ for $n \geq 1$.

To determine when the loan will be paid off, you want to find the value of n for which $f(n) = 0$. Use the explicit rule.

$$f(n) = 0$$

$$\boxed{} + \left(\boxed{} \right)n = 0$$

$$\boxed{}\, n = \boxed{}$$

$$n = \boxed{}$$

So, the loan will be paid off in _____ weeks.

Write a recursive rule and an explicit rule for an arithmetic sequence that models the situation. Then use the rule to answer the question.

7. The starting salary for a summer camp counselor is $395 per week. In each of the subsequent weeks, the salary increases by $45 to encourage experienced counselors to work for the entire summer. If the salary is $710 for the last week of the camp, for how many weeks does the camp run?

8. The graph shows the length, in inches, of a row of grocery carts when various numbers of carts are nested together. What is the length of a row of 25 nested carts?

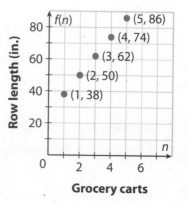

Elaborate

9. **Discussion** Is it easier to use an explicit rule or a recursive rule to find the 10th term in an arithmetic sequence? Explain.

_____

_____

_____

_____

10. What do you know about the terms in an arithmetic sequence with a common difference of 0?

_____

_____

_____

11. Describe the difference between the graph of an arithmetic sequence with a positive common difference and the graph of an arithmetic sequence with a negative common difference.

_____

_____

_____

12. Essential Question Check-In Does the rule $f(n) = -2 + 5n$ for $n \geq 0$ define an arithmetic sequence, and is the rule explicit or recursive? How do you know?

_____

_____

_____

_____

☆ Evaluate: Homework and Practice

- Online Homework
- Hints and Help
- Extra Practice

1. Consider the staircase in the Explore. How would the functions $B(s)$ and $T(s)$ change if the staircase were a spiral staircase going from the first floor to the third floor, with the same step height and distance between floors?

Use the given table to write an explicit and a recursive rule for the sequence.

2.

n	0	1	2	3	4
f(n)	−6	1	8	15	22

$f(n-1)+7=f(n)$

3.

n	0	1	2	3	4
f(n)	8	5	2	−1	−4

$f(n-1)-3=f(n)$

Given the recursive rule for an arithmetic sequence, write the explicit rule.

4. $f(0) = 6$ and $f(n) = f(n-1) + 5$ for $n \geq 1$

$n \geq 1$

$f(n) = (n)(5) + 5$

5. $f(1) = 19$ and $f(n) = f(n-1) - 10$ for $n \geq 2$

$f(0) = 29$

$f(n-1) - 10$

Given the explicit rule for an arithmetic sequence, write the recursive rule.

6. $f(n) = 9.6 - 0.2(n-1)$ for $n \geq 1$

$f(1) = 9.6$

$f(n-1) + 0.2 = f(n)$

7. $f(n) = 14 + 8n$ for $n \geq 0$

$f(0) = 14$

$f(n-1) + 8 = f(n)$

Write the terms of the given arithmetic sequence and then graph the sequence.

8. $f(n) = 7 - \frac{1}{2}n$ for $n \geq 0$

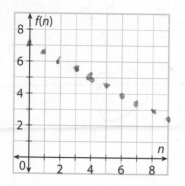

9. $f(n) = 3 + 2(n-1)$ for $1 \leq n \leq 5$

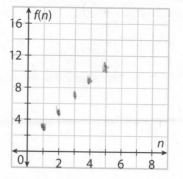

10. $f(1) = -0.5$ and $f(n) = f(n-1) - 0.5$
for $n \geq 2$

11. $f(0) = -5$ and $f(n) = f(n-1) + 3$
for $1 \leq n \leq 4$

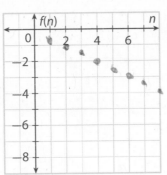

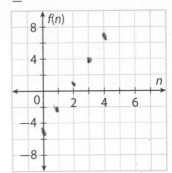

Write a recursive rule and an explicit rule for an arithmetic sequence that models the situation. Then use the rule to answer the question.

12. Thomas begins an exercise routine for 20 minutes each day. Each week he plans to add 5 minutes per day to the length of his exercise routine. For how many minutes will he exercise each day of the 6th week?

$$20 = f(1)$$
$$f(n-1) + 20 = f(n)$$
$$6 \cdot 7 = 42 \times 20 = \boxed{840}$$

13. The Louvre pyramid in Paris, France, is built of glass panes. There are 4 panes in the top row, and each additional row has 4 more panes than the previous row. How many panes are in the 17th row?

$$f = (1) = 4$$
$$f(n-1) + 4 \text{ for } n \geq 2$$
$$f(n-1)4 + 4 \text{ for } n \geq 1$$
$$68, \quad 4 + (4 \times 16)$$
$$4 + 64$$
$$68$$

14. Clarissa is buying a prom dress on layaway. The dress costs $185. She makes a down payment of $20 to put the dress on layaway and then makes weekly payments of $15. In how many weeks is the dress paid off?

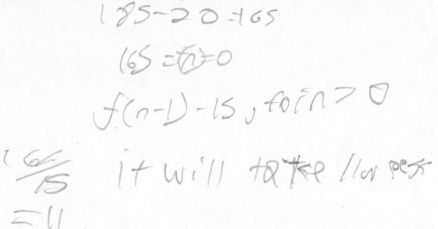

$185 - 20 = 165$

$165 = ?$

$f(n-1) - 15, \text{ for } n > 0$

$\frac{165}{15}$ it will take 11 weeks

$= 11$

15. The graph shows the height, in inches, of a stack of various numbers of identical plastic cups. The stack of cups will be placed on a shelf with 12 inches of vertical clearance with the shelf above. What number of cups can be in the stack without having a tight fit?

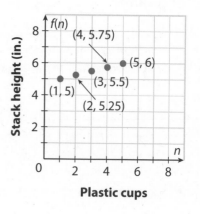

$f(n-1) + .25 = f(n)$

$5 = 6$

$6 = 6.25$

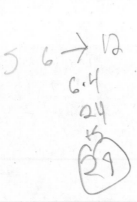

$5 \quad 6 \rightarrow 12$

6.4

24

$\boxed{29}$

16. Determine whether or not each of the following sequences is arithmetic. Select the correct response for each lettered part.

A. 1, 1, 2, 3, 5, 8, 13, 21, 34 — ☐ Arithmetic   ☑ Not arithmetic

B. 1, 4, 7, 10, 13, 16, 19 — ☑ Arithmetic   ☐ Not arithmetic

C. 1, 2, 4, 9, 16, 25 — ☐ Arithmetic   ☑ Not arithmetic

D. −4, 3, 10, 17, 24, 31 — ☑ Arithmetic   ☐ Not arithmetic

E. $\frac{1}{2}, \frac{2}{3}, \frac{3}{4}, \frac{4}{5}, \frac{5}{6}, \frac{6}{7}, \frac{7}{8}, \frac{8}{9}$ — ☐ Arithmetic   ☑ Not arithmetic

F. 18.5, 13, 7.5, 2, −3.5, −9 — ☑ Arithmetic   ☐ Not arithmetic

17. Multiple Representations The graphs of two arithmetic sequences are shown.

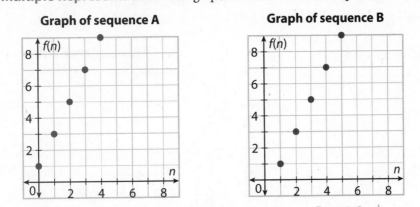

Graph of sequence A   Graph of sequence B

a. Are the sequences the same or different? Explain. _different_

b. Write an explicit rule for each sequence. $2r(n-1)+1 = f(n)$, $(f(n+1)-1)2 = f(n)$

c. How do the explicit rules indicate the geometric relationship between the two graphs?

yes, they have the same slope

18. Communicate Mathematical Ideas You know that if $\left(x_1, f(x_1)\right)$ and $\left(x_2, f(x_2)\right)$ are two points on the graph of a linear function, the slope of the function's graph is $m = \dfrac{f(x_2) - f(x_1)}{x_2 - x_1}$. Suppose $\left(n_1, f(n_1)\right)$ and $\left(n_2, f(n_2)\right)$ are two points on the graph of an arithmetic sequence with the explicit rule $f(n) = a + dn$. What does the expression $\dfrac{f(n_2) - f(n_1)}{n_2 - n_1}$ tell you about the arithmetic sequence? Justify your answer.

It tells you that your lines are similar

19. Construct Arguments Show how the recursive rule $f(0) = a$ and $f(n) = f(n-1) + d$ for $n \geq 1$ generates the explicit rule $f(n) = a + dn$ for $n \geq 0$.

Lesson Performance Task

The graph shows how the cost of a personal transporter tour depends on the number of participants. Write explicit and recursive rules for the cost of the tour. Then calculate the cost of the tour for 12 participants.

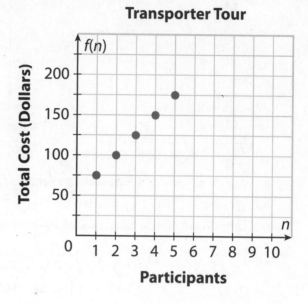

Transporter Tour

12.2 Geometric Sequences

Essential Question: How can you define a geometric sequence algebraically?

⊘ Explore　Investigating Geometric Sequences

As a tree grows, limbs branch off of the trunk, then smaller limbs branch off these limbs and each branch splits off into smaller and smaller copies of itself the same way throughout the entire tree. A mathematical object called a *fractal tree* resembles this growth.

Start by drawing a vertical line at the bottom of a piece of paper. This is Stage 0 of the fractal tree and is considered to be one 'branch'. The length of this branch defines 1 unit.

For Stage 1, draw 2 branches off of the top of the first branch. For this fractal tree, each smaller branch is $\frac{1}{2}$ the length of the previous branch and is at a 45-degree angle from the direction of the parent branch. The first four iterations, Stages 0-3, are shown.

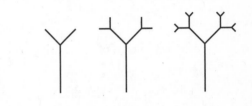

Ⓐ In Stage 2, there are 2 branches drawn on the end of each of the 2 branches drawn in Stage 1. There are ☐ new branches in Stage 2. Each one of these branches will be $\frac{1}{2}$ the length of its predecessors or ☐ unit in length.

Ⓑ For Stage 3, there are 8 new branches in total. To draw Stage 4, a total of ☐ branches must be drawn and to draw Stage 5, a total of ☐ branches must be drawn. Thus, each stage adds ☐ times as many branches as the previous stage did.

Ⓒ Complete the table.

Stage	New Branches	Pattern	New Branches as a Power
Stage 0	1	1	2^0
Stage 1	2	$2 \cdot 1$	2^1
Stage 2	4	$2 \cdot 2$	2^2
Stage 3	8	$2 \cdot$	
Stage 4	16	$2 \cdot$	
Stage 5	32	$2 \cdot$	
Stage 6	64	$2 \cdot$	

(D) The procedure for each stage after Stage 0 is to draw _____ branches on _____ branch added in the previous step.

(E) Using the description above, write an equation for the number of new branches in a stage given the previous stage. Represent stage s as N_s; Stage 3 will be N_3.

$N_4 = \boxed{} \cdot \boxed{}$

$N_6 = \boxed{} \cdot \boxed{}$

$N_5 = \boxed{} \cdot \boxed{}$

$N_s = \boxed{} \cdot \boxed{}$

(F) Rewrite the rule for Stage s as a function $N(s)$ that has a stage number as an input and the number of new branches in the stage as an output.

$N(s) = \boxed{}$

(G) Recall that the domain of a function is the set of all numbers for which the function is defined. $N(s)$ is a function of s and s is the stage number. Since the stage number refers to the _____ the tree has branched, it has to be _____.

Write the domain of $N(s)$ in set notation.

$\left\{ s \mid s \text{ is a } \underline{} \text{ number} \right\}$

(H) Similarly, the range of a function is the set of all possible values that the function can output over the domain. Let $N(s) = b$, the _____.

The range of $N(s)$ is $\left\{ 1,2,4 \boxed{}, \boxed{}, \boxed{}, \ldots \right\}$.

The range of $N(s)$ is $\left\{ N \mid N = 2^s, \text{ where } s \text{ is } \underline{} \right\}$.

(I) Graph the first five values of $N(s)$ on the axes provided. The first value has been graphed for you.

(J) As s increases, $N(s)$ _____.

$N(s)$ is _____ function.

(K) Complete the table for branch length.

(L) Write $L(s)$ expressing the branch length as a function of the Stage.

$$L(s) = \left(\dfrac{1}{\boxed{}}\right)^{\boxed{}}$$

(M) Write the domain and range of $L(s)$ in set notation.

The domain of $L(s)$ is $\left\{s \mid s \text{ is a } \underline{\hspace{2cm}} \text{ number}\right\}$.

The range of $L(s)$ is $\left\{1, \dfrac{1}{2}, \dfrac{1}{4}, \boxed{}, \boxed{}, \boxed{}, \cdots\right\}$.

The range of $L(s)$ is $\left\{L \mid L = \left(\dfrac{1}{2}\right)^{s}, \text{ where } s \text{ is } \underline{\hspace{3cm}}\right\}$.

(N) Graph the first five values of $L(s)$ on the axes provided. The fifth point has been graphed for you.

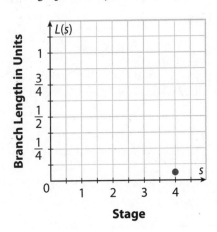

Stage

(O) As s increases, $L(s)$ _____. $L(s)$ is _____ function.

Stage Number	Number of Branches	Branch Length
0	1	1
1	2	$\dfrac{1}{2}$
2	4	$\dfrac{1}{4}$
3	8	$\dfrac{1}{\boxed{}}$
4	16	$\dfrac{1}{\boxed{}}$
5	32	$\dfrac{1}{\boxed{}}$
⋮	⋮	⋮
n	2^{n}	$\dfrac{1}{\boxed{}}$

Reflect

1. What is the total length added at each stage?

_____

_____

_____

2. Is the total length of all the branches a sequence? If so, identify the sequence.

_____

Writing Explicit and Recursive Rules for Geometric Sequences

A sequence is a set of numbers related by a common rule. All sequences start with an initial term. In a **geometric sequence**, the ratio of any term to the previous term is constant. This constant ratio is called the **common ratio** and is denoted by r $(r \neq 1)$. In the **explicit form** of the sequence, each term is found by evaluating the function $f(n) = ar^n$ or $f(n) = ar^{n-1}$ where a is the initial value and r is the common ratio, for some whole number n. Note that there are two forms of the explicit rule because it is permissible to call the initial value the first term or to call ar the first term.

A geometric sequence can also be defined recursively by $f(n) = r \cdot f(n-1)$ where either $f(0) = a$ or $f(1) = a$, again depending on the way the terms of the sequence are numbered. $f(n) = r \cdot f(n-1)$ is called the **recursive rule** for the sequence.

Example 1 Write the explicit and recursive rules for a geometric sequence given a table of values.

Ⓐ

n	0	1	2	3	4	...	$j-1$	j	...
$f(n)$	3	6	12	24	48	...	$ar^{(j-1)}$	ar^{j}	...

Determine a and r, then write the explicit and recursive rules.

Find the common ratio: $\dfrac{f(n)}{f(n-1)} = r.$ $\dfrac{f(1)}{f(0)} = \dfrac{6}{3} = 2 = r$

Find the initial value, $a = f(0)$, from the table. $f(0) = 3 = a$

Find the explicit rule: $f(n) = ar^n$. $f(n) = 3 \cdot (2)^n$

Write the recursive rule. $f(n) = 2 \cdot f(n-1), n \geq 1$ and $f(0) = 3$

The explicit rule is $f(n) = 3 \cdot (2)^n$ and the recursive rule is $f(n) = 2 \cdot f(n-1), n \geq 1$ and $f(0) = 3$.

Ⓑ

n	1	2	3	4	5	...	$j-1$	j	...
$f(n)$	$\dfrac{1}{25}$	$\dfrac{1}{5}$	1	5	25	...	$ar^{(j-1)}$	ar^{j}	...

Determine a and r, then write the explicit and recursive rules.

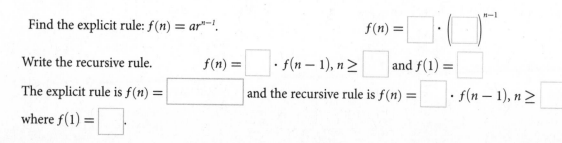

Find the common ratio: $\dfrac{f(n)}{f(n-1)} = r.$ $\dfrac{f(\boxed{})}{f(\boxed{})} = \dfrac{\boxed{}}{\boxed{}} = \boxed{} = r$

Find the initial value, $a = f(1)$, from the table. $f(1) = \boxed{} = a$

Find the explicit rule: $f(n) = ar^{n-1}$. $f(n) = \boxed{} \cdot \left(\boxed{}\right)^{n-1}$

Write the recursive rule. $f(n) = \boxed{} \cdot f(n-1), n \geq \boxed{}$ and $f(1) = \boxed{}$

The explicit rule is $f(n) = \boxed{}$ and the recursive rule is $f(n) = \boxed{} \cdot f(n-1), n \geq \boxed{}$ where $f(1) = \boxed{}$.

3. **Discussion** If you were told that a geometric sequence had an initial value of $f(5) = 5$, could you write an explicit and a recursive rule for the function? What would the explicit rule be?

_____

_____

_____

_____

Your Turn

Write the explicit and recursive rules for a geometric sequence given a table of values.

4.

n	0	1	2	3	4	5	6	$\cdots$
f(n)	$\frac{1}{27}$	$\frac{1}{9}$	$\frac{1}{3}$	1	3	9	27	$\cdots$

5.

n	1	2	3	4	5	6	7	$\cdots$
f(n)	0.001	0.01	0.1	1	10	100	1000	$\cdots$

🔍 Explain 2 Graphing Geometric Sequences

To graph a geometric sequence given an explicit or a recursive rule you can use the rule to generate a table of values and then graph those points on a coordinate plane. Since the domain of a geometric sequence consists only of whole numbers, its graph consists of individual points, not a smooth curve.

Example 2 Given either an explicit or recursive rule for a geometric sequence, use a table to generate values and draw the graph of the sequence.

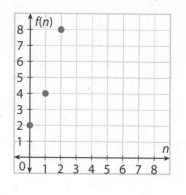

(A) Explicit rule: $f(n) = 2 \cdot 2^n$, $n \geq 0$

Use a table to generate points.

n	0	1	2	3	4	5	...
f(n)	2	4	8	16	32	64	...

Plot the first three points on the graph.

(B) Recursive rule: $f(n) = 0.5 \cdot f(n-1)$, $n \geq 1$ and $f(0) = 16$

Use a table to generate points.

n	0	1	2	3	☐	☐	☐	...
f(n)	☐	☐	☐	☐	☐	☐	☐	...

Your Turn

Given either an explicit or recursive rule for a geometric sequence, use a table to generate values and draw the graph of the sequence.

6. $f(n) = 3 \cdot 2^{n-1}$, $n \geq 1$

n	1	2	3	4	5	...
f(n)						...

7. $f(n) = 3 \cdot f(n-1)$, $n \geq 2$ and $f(1) = 2$

n	1	2	3	4	5	...
f(n)						...

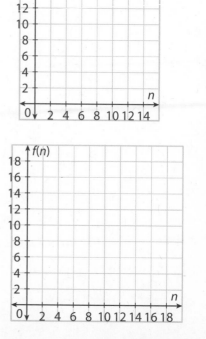

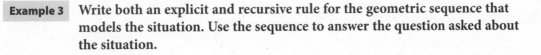 **Explain 3 Modeling With a Geometric Sequence**

Given a real-world situation that can be modeled with a geometric sequence, you can use an explicit or a recursive rule to answer a question about the situation.

Example 3 Write both an explicit and recursive rule for the geometric sequence that models the situation. Use the sequence to answer the question asked about the situation.

(A) The Wimbledon Ladies' Singles Championship begins with 128 players. Each match, two players play and only one moves to the next round. The players compete until there is one winner. How many rounds must the winner play?

 Analyze Information

Identify the important information:
- The first round requires _____ matches, so $a = \boxed{}$.

- The next round requires half as many matches, so $r = \boxed{}$.

Formulate a Plan

Let n represent the number of rounds played and let $f(n)$ represent the number of matches played at that round. Create the explicit rule and the recursive rule for the

tournament. The final round will have _____ match(es), so substitute this value into the explicit rule and solve for n.

 Solve

The explicit rule is $f(n) = \boxed{}$, $n \geq 1$.

The recursive rule is $f(n) = \boxed{} \cdot f(n-1)$, $n \geq 2$ and $f(1) = \boxed{}$.

The final round will have 1 match, so substitute 1 for $f(n)$ into the explicit rule and solve for n.

$$f(n) = 64 \cdot \left(\frac{1}{2}\right)^{n-1}$$
$$\boxed{} = 64 \cdot \left(\frac{1}{2}\right)^{n-1}$$
$$\boxed{} = \left(\frac{1}{2}\right)^{n-1}$$
$$\left(\frac{1}{2}\right)^{\boxed{}} = \left(\frac{1}{2}\right)^{n-1}$$

Two powers with the same positive base other than 1 are equal if and only if the exponents are equal.

$$\left(\frac{1}{2}\right)^{\boxed{}} = \left(\frac{1}{2}\right)^{n-1}$$
$$\boxed{} = n - 1$$
$$\boxed{} = n$$

The winner must play in _____ rounds.

Justify and Evaluate

The answer of 7 rounds makes sense because using the explicit rule gives

$f(7) =$ [ ] and the final round will have 1 match(es). This result can be checked

using the recursive rule, which again results in $f(7) =$ [ ].

Your Turn

Write both an explicit and recursive rule for the geometric sequence that models the situation. Use the sequence to answer the question asked about the situation.

8. A particular type of bacteria divides into two new bacteria every 20 minutes. A scientist growing the bacteria in a laboratory begins with 200 bacteria. How many bacteria are present 4 hours later?

Elaborate

9. Describe the difference between an explicit rule for a geometric sequence and a recursive rule.

   _____

   _____

10. How would you decide to use $n = 0$ or $n = 1$ as the starting value of n for a geometric sequence modeling a real-world situation?

   _____

   _____

   _____

11. **Essential Question Check-In** How can you define a geometric sequence in an algebraic way? What information do you need to write these rules?

   _____

   _____

   _____

   _____

   _____

   _____

You are creating self-similar fractal trees. You start with a trunk of length 1 unit (at Stage 0). Then the trunk splits into two branches each one-third the length of the trunk. Then each one of these branches splits into two new branches, with each branch one-third the length of the previous one.

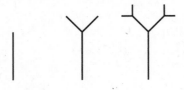

1. Can the length of the new branches at each stage be described with a geometric sequence? Explain. If so, find the explicit form for the length of each branch.

2. Can the number of new branches at each stage be described with a geometric sequence? Explain. If so, find the recursive rule for the number of new branches.

3. Can the total length of the new branches at each stage be modeled with a geometric sequence? Explain. (The total length of the new branches is the sum of the lengths of all the new branches.)

Write the explicit and recursive rules for a geometric sequence given a table of values.

4.

n	0	1	2	3	4	...
f(n)	0.1	0.3	0.9	2.7	8.1	...

geo

$f(n) = 0.1, \quad n = 0$

$f(n) = (n)0.2 + 0.1$

$f(n) = f(n-1) + 0.2$

5.

n	0	1	2	3	4	...
f(n)	100	10	1	0.1	0.01	...

geo

$f(n) = 100, \quad n = 0$

$f(9) = \sqrt[n]{n} + 10n$

$f(n) = f(n-1) \cdot n$

6.

n	1	2	3	4	5	...
f(n)	1000	100	10	1	0.1	...

Arith.

$f(n) = \sqrt[n]{n} + 100$

7.

n	1	2	3	4	5	...
f(n)	10^{50}	10^{47}	10^{44}	10^{41}	10^{38}	...

Arith

$f(n) = 10^{59}, \quad n = 1$

$f(n) = n10^{-3} + 10^{50}$

$f(n) = f(n-1)10^{-3}$

Given either an explicit or recursive rule for a geometric sequence, use a table to generate values and draw the graph of the sequence.

8. $f(n) = \left(\frac{1}{2}\right) \cdot 4^n, n \geq 0$

$25\frac{6}{2} = 1\overline{58}$

n	0	1	2	3	4	$\cdots$
$f(n)$	$\frac{1}{2}$	2	8	32	128	$\cdots$

Geo

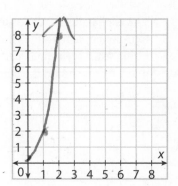

9. $f(n) = 2 \cdot f(n-1), n \geq 1$ and $f(0) = 0.5$

n	0	1	2	3	4	$\cdots$
$f(n)$	0.5	1	2	4	8	$\cdots$

Geo

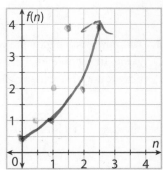

10. $f(n) = 0.5 \cdot f(n-1), n \geq 2$ and $f(1) = 8$

n	1	2	3	4	5	$\cdots$
$f(n)$	8	4	2	1	0.5	$\cdots$

Ar.

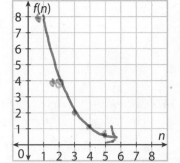

11. $f(n) = \frac{2}{3} \cdot f(n-1), n \geq 2$ and $f(1) = 1$

n	1	2	3	4	5	$\cdots$
$f(n)$	1	$\frac{2}{3}$	$\frac{4}{9}$	$\frac{8}{27}$	$\frac{16}{81}$	$\frac{32}{243}$

Ar.

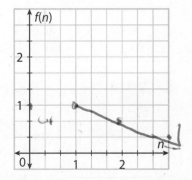

Write both an explicit and recursive rule for the geometric sequence that models the situation. Use the sequence to answer the question asked about the situation.

12. The Alphaville Youth Basketball committee is planning a single-elimination tournament (for all the games at each round, the winning team advances and the losing team is eliminated). The committee wants the winner to play 4 games. How many teams should the committee invite?

$2^4 = 16$

13. An online video game tournament begins with 1024 players. Four players play in each game. In each game there is only one winner, and only the winner advances to the next round. How many games will the winner play?

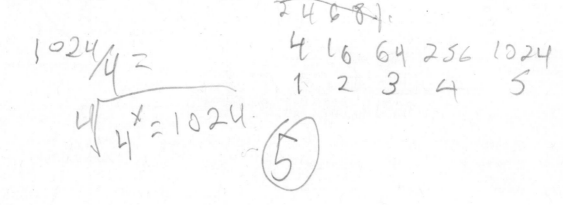

$1024/4 =$

$4\overline{\smash{)}\,4^x = 1024}$

2	4	6	8	.
4	16	64	256	1024
1	2	3	4	5

⑤

14. **Genealogy** You have 2 biological parents, 4 biological grandparents, and 8 biological great-grandparents.

   a. How many direct ancestors do you have if you trace your ancestry back 6 generations? How many direct ancestors do you have if you go back 12 generations?

   $2^6 = 64$

   $2^{12} = 4048$

   b. **What if...?** How does the explicit rule change if you are considered the first generation?

   $n=1$

   $f(N) = 2^{n-1}, f(N)=1$

© Houghton Mifflin Harcourt Publishing Company • Image Credits: ©Ocean/Corbis

15. Fractals Waclaw Sierpinski designed various fractals. He would take a geometric figure, shade it in, and then start removing the shading to create a fractal pattern.

a. The Sierpinski triangle is a fractal based on a triangle. In each iteration, the center of each shaded triangle is removed.

Given that the area of the original triangle is 1 square unit, write a sequence for the area of the nth iteration of the Sierpinski triangle. (The first iteration is the original triangle.)

$(3/4 \times n)$

b. The Sierpinski carpet is a fractal based on a square. In each iteration, the center of each shaded square is removed.

Given that the area of the original square is 1 square unit, write a sequence for the area of the nth iteration of the Sierpinski carpet. (The first iteration is the original square.)

$(8/9 \cdot n)$

c. Find the shaded area of the fourth iteration of the Sierpinski carpet.

3
2 . :
1
0 0 0 0
4

$\frac{8}{9} \cdot \frac{4}{4} = \frac{32}{36}$

⊔ ⊔ ⊔ ⊔ ⊔
1 2 3 4 5

0 000, 2 • 0 • 0, 33 ••00

234 ••••, 2341 0•••

23413 0••• 2341 35

16. A piece of paper is 0.1 millimeter thick. When folded, the paper is twice as thick.

a. Find both the explicit and recursive rule for this geometric sequence.

$f(n) = 2n + 0.8$

$f(n) = f(n-1)2, f(1) = 0.1$

b. Studies have shown that you can fold a piece of paper a maximum of 7 times. How thick will the paper be if it is folded on top of itself 7 times?

0.1×2^7

0.1×128

$12.8 \, mm$

c. Assume that you could fold the paper as many times as you want. How many folds would be required for the paper to be taller than Mount Everest at 8850 meters? (*Hint:* Use a calculator to generate two large powers of 2 and check if the required number of millimeters is between those two powers. Continue to refine your guesses.)

?

© Houghton Mifflin Harcourt Publishing Company • Image Credits: ©imagefactory/Shutterstock

17. Justify Reasoning Suppose you have the following table of points of a geometric sequence. The table is incomplete so you do not know the initial value. Determine whether each of the following can or cannot be the rule for the function in the table. If a function cannot be the rule for the sequence, explain why.

n	$\cdots$	4	5	6	7	$\cdots$
$f(n)$	$\cdots$	6	12	24	48	$\cdots$

A. $f(n) = 2^n$

B. $f(n) = \dfrac{3}{8} \cdot (2)^n$

C. $f(n) = 2 \cdot f(n-1), n \geq 1$ and $f(0) = 6$

D. $f(n) = \dfrac{3}{4} \cdot (2)^{n-1}$

E. $f(n) = 2 \cdot f(n-1), n \geq 1$ and $f(0) = \dfrac{3}{8}$

F. $f(n) = 2 \cdot f(n-1), n \geq 1$ and $f(1) = \dfrac{3}{4}$

G. $f(n) = (1.5) \cdot (2)^{n-2}$

H. $f(n) = 3 \cdot (2)^{n-3}$

18. Communicate Mathematical Ideas Show that the rules $f(n) = ar^n$ for $n \geq 0$ and $f(n) = ar^{n-1}$ for $n \geq 1$ for a geometric sequence are equivalent.

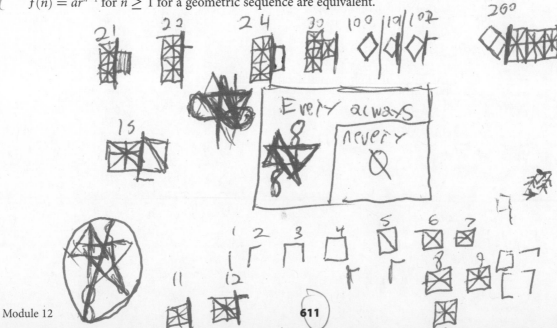

Lesson Performance Task

Have you ever heard of musical octaves? An octave is the interval between a musical note and the same musical note in the next higher or lower pitch. The frequencies of the sound waves of successive octaves of a note form a geometric sequence. For example, the table shows the frequencies in hertz (Hz), or cycles per second, produced by playing the note D in ascending octaves, D_0 being the lowest D note audible to the human ear.

Scale of D's	
Note	Frequency (Hz)
D_0	18.35
D_1	36.71
D_2	73.42
D_3	146.83

a. Explain how to write an explicit rule and a recursive rule for the frequency of D notes in hertz, where $n = 1$ represents D_1.

b. The note commonly called "middle D" is D_4. Use the explicit rule or the recursive rule from part **a** to predict the frequency for middle D.

c. Humans generally cannot hear sounds with frequencies greater than 20,000 Hz. What is the first D note that humans cannot hear? Explain.

12.3 Geometric Series

Essential Question: How do you find the sum of a finite geometric series?

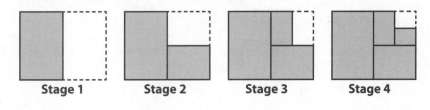 **Explore 1** **Investigating a Geometric Series**

A **series** is the expression formed by adding the terms of a sequence. If the sequence is geometric and has a finite number of terms, it is called a **finite geometric series**. In this Explore, you will generate several related finite geometric series and find a formula for calculating the sum of each series.

(A) Start with a rectangular sheet of paper and assume the sheet has an area of 1 square unit. Cut the sheet in half and lay down one of the half-pieces. Then cut the remaining piece in half, and lay down one of the quarter-pieces as if rebuilding the original sheet of paper. Continue the process: At each stage, cut the remaining piece in half, and lay down one of the two pieces as if rebuilding the original sheet of paper.

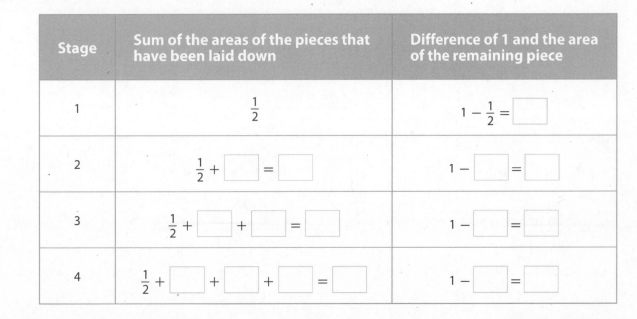

| Stage 1 | Stage 2 | Stage 3 | Stage 4 |

(B) Complete the table by expressing the total area of the paper that has been laid down in two ways:

- as the sum of the areas of the pieces that have been laid down, and
- as the difference between 1 and the area of the remaining piece.

Stage	Sum of the areas of the pieces that have been laid down	Difference of 1 and the area of the remaining piece
1	$\dfrac{1}{2}$	$1 - \dfrac{1}{2} = \boxed{}$
2	$\dfrac{1}{2} + \boxed{} = \boxed{}$	$1 - \boxed{} = \boxed{}$
3	$\dfrac{1}{2} + \boxed{} + \boxed{} = \boxed{}$	$1 - \boxed{} = \boxed{}$
4	$\dfrac{1}{2} + \boxed{} + \boxed{} + \boxed{} = \boxed{}$	$1 - \boxed{} = \boxed{}$

1. Write the sequence formed by the areas of the individual pieces that are laid down. What type of sequence is it?

_____

_____

2. In the table from Step B, you wrote four related finite geometric series: $\frac{1}{2}, \frac{1}{2} + \frac{1}{4}, \frac{1}{2} + \frac{1}{4} + \frac{1}{8}$, and $\frac{1}{2} + \frac{1}{4} + \frac{1}{8} + \frac{1}{16}$. One way you found the sum of each series was simply to add up the terms. Describe another way you found the sum of each series.

_____

3. If the process of cutting the remaining piece of paper and laying down one of the two pieces is continued, you obtain the finite geometric series $\frac{1}{2} + \frac{1}{4} + \ldots + \left(\frac{1}{2}\right)^n$ at the nth stage. Use your answer to the previous question to find the sum of this series.

_____

⊘ Explore 2 Deriving a Formula for the Sum of a Finite Geometric Series

To find a general formula for the sum of a finite geometric series with n terms, begin by writing the series as $S(n) = a + ar + ar^2 + \ldots + ar^{n-1}$.

Ⓐ Find an expression for $rS(n)$.

$$rS(n) = ar + ar^2 + ar^{\boxed{}} \ldots + ar^{\boxed{}}$$

Ⓑ Find an expression for $S(n) - rS(n)$ by aligning like terms and subtracting.

$$S(n) = a + ar + ar^2 + \ldots + ar^{n-1}$$
$$rS(n) = ar + ar^2 + \ldots + ar^{n-1} + ar^n$$
$$S(n) - rS(n) = a + \boxed{} + \boxed{} + \ldots + \boxed{} - ar^n$$

Ⓒ Simplify the expression for $S(n) - rS(n)$.

$$S(n) - rS(n) = \boxed{}$$

Ⓓ Factor the left and right sides of the equation in Step C.

$$S(n) \boxed{} = \boxed{} (1 - r^{\boxed{}})$$

Ⓔ Divide both sides of the equation in Step D by $1 - r$.

$$S(n) = a \left(\frac{\boxed{} - \boxed{}}{1 - r} \right)$$

Reflect

4. Check to see if the formula in Step E gives the same result as the answer you wrote for Reflect 3.

5. What restrictions are there on the values of r that can be used in the formula for the sum of a finite geometric series? Explain.

Explain 1 Finding the Sum of a Finite Geometric Series

The formula $S(n) = a\left(\dfrac{1 - r^n}{1 - r}\right)$ for the sum of a geometric series requires knowing the values of a, r, and n.

Recall that you learned how to find a and r for a geometric sequence, and the technique is no different for a series: a is the value of the first term, and r is the ratio of any two successive terms. To find n, you can simply count the terms if they are all listed. For instance, for the finite geometric series $3 + 6 + 12 + 24 + 48$, you can see that $a = 3, r = 2$, and $n = 5$.

If some of the terms of a finite geometric series have been replaced by an ellipsis, as in $2 + 6 + 18 + \ldots + 1458$, you obviously can't count the terms. One way to deal with this situation is to generate the missing terms by using the common ratio, which in this case is 3. The next term after 18 is $3(18) = 54$, and repeatedly multiplying by 3 to generate successive terms gives $2 + 6 + 18 + 54 + 162 + 486 + 1458$, so the series has 7 terms.

Another way to find the number of terms in $2 + 6 + 18 + \ldots + 1458$ is to recognize that the nth term in a geometric series is ar^{n-1}. For the series $2 + 6 + 18 + \ldots + 1458$ whose nth term is $2(3)^{n-1}$, find n as follows:

$2(3)^{n-1} = 1458$	Set the nth term equal to the last term.
$(3)^{n-1} = 729$	Divide both as power of 3
$(3)^{n-1} = 3^6$	Write 729 as a power of 3
$n - 1 = 6$	When the bases are the same, you can equate the exponents.
$n = 7$	Add 1 to both sides

Find the sum of the finite geometric series.

(A) $5 + 15 + 45 + 135 + 405 + 1215$

   Step 1 Find the values of a, r, and n.

   The first term in the series is a. $a = 5$

   Find the common ratio r by dividing two successive terms. $r = \dfrac{15}{5} = 3$

   Count the terms to find n. $n = 6$

© Houghton Mifflin Harcourt Publishing Company

Step 2 Use the formula $S(n) = a\left(\dfrac{1 - r^n}{1 - r}\right)$.

Substitute the values of a, r, and n.

$$S(6) = 5\left(\dfrac{1 - 3^6}{1 - 3}\right)$$

Evaluate the power in the numerator.

$$= 5\left(\dfrac{1 - 729}{1 - 3}\right)$$

Simplify the numerator and denominator.

$$= 5\left(\dfrac{-728}{-2}\right)$$

Simplify the fraction.

$$= 5(364)$$

Multiply.

$$= 1820$$

Ⓑ $\dfrac{1}{4} + \dfrac{1}{8} + \dfrac{1}{16} + \cdots + \dfrac{1}{512}$

Step 1 Find the values of a, r, and n.

The first term in the series is a.

$a = \boxed{}$

Find the common ratio by dividing two successive terms.

$r = \dfrac{\frac{1}{8}}{\boxed{}} = \boxed{}$

Set the nth term, $\dfrac{1}{4}\left(\dfrac{1}{2}\right)^{n-1}$, equal to the last term to find n.

$\dfrac{1}{4}\left(\dfrac{1}{2}\right)^{n-1} = \boxed{}$

Multiply both sides by $\boxed{}$.

$\left(\dfrac{1}{2}\right)^{n-1} = \dfrac{1}{128}$

Write $\dfrac{1}{128}$ as a power of $\dfrac{1}{2}$.

$\left(\dfrac{1}{2}\right)^{n-1} = \left(\dfrac{1}{2}\right)^{\boxed{}}$

Equate the exponents.

$n - 1 = \boxed{}$

Add 1 to both sides.

$n = \boxed{}$

Step 2 Use the formula $S(n) = a\left(\dfrac{1 - r^n}{1 - r}\right)$.

Substitute the values of a, r, and n.

$$S(8) = \boxed{}\left(\dfrac{1 - \left(\boxed{}\right)^{\boxed{}}}{1 - \boxed{}}\right)$$

Evaluate the power in the numerator.

$$= \dfrac{1}{4}\left(\dfrac{1 - \boxed{}}{1 - \frac{1}{2}}\right)$$

Simplify the numerator and denominator.

$$= \dfrac{1}{4}\left(\dfrac{\frac{\boxed{}}{256}}{\frac{1}{2}}\right)$$

Simplify the fraction.

$$= \dfrac{1}{4}\left(\boxed{}\right)$$

Multiply.

$$= \boxed{}$$

Find the sum of the finite geometric series.

6. $1 - 2 + 4 - 8 + 16 - 32$

7. $\dfrac{1}{2} - \dfrac{1}{4} + \dfrac{1}{8} \cdots - \dfrac{1}{256}$

© Houghton Mifflin Harcourt Publishing Company

Solving a Real-World Problem Involving a Finite Geometric Series

Some financial problems can be modeled by a geometric series. For instance, an *annuity* involves equal payments made at regular intervals for a fixed amount of time. Because money can be invested and earn interest, comparing the value of money today to the value of money in the future requires accounting for the effect of interest. The *future value* of an annuity is how much the annuity payments will be worth at some point in the future. The *present value* of an annuity is how much the annuity payments are worth in the present.

Although an interest rate is typically expressed as an annual rate, it can be converted to a rate for other periods of time. For instance, an annual interest rate of r% results in a monthly interest rate of $\frac{r}{12}$%. In general, if interest is earned n times per year, an annual interest rate of r% is divided by n.

Example 2

(A) Niobe is saving for a down payment on a new car, which she intends to buy a year from now. At the end of each month, she deposits $200 from her paycheck into a dedicated savings account, which earns 3% annual interest that is applied to the account balance each month. After making 12 deposits, how much money will Niobe have in her savings account?

Niobe is interested in the future value of her annuity (savings plan). A 3% annual interest rate corresponds to a $\frac{3}{12}$% = 0.25% monthly interest rate.

First, calculate the sequence of end-of-month account balances. Recognize the recursive nature of the calculations:

- The end-of-month balance for month 1 is $200 because the first deposit of $200 is made at the end of the month, but the deposit doesn't earn any interest that month.

- The end-of-month balance for any other month is the sum of the previous month's end-of-month balance, the interest earned on the previous month's end-of-month balance, and the next deposit.

So, if $B(m)$ represents the account balance for month m, then a recursive rule for the account balances is $B(1) = 200$ and $B(m) = B(m - 1) + B(m - 1) \cdot 0.0025 + 200$. Notice that you can rewrite the equation $B(m) = B(m - 1) + B(m - 1) \cdot 0.0025 + 200$ as $B(m) = B(m - 1) \cdot 1.0025 + 200$ by using the Distributive Property.

Month	End-of-month balance of account
1	200
2	$200 \cdot 1.0025 + 200$
3	$[200(1.0025) + 200] \cdot 1.0025 + 200 = 200(1.0025)^2 + 200(1.0025) + 200$
4	$[200(1.0025)^2 + 200(1.0025) + 200] \cdot 1.0025 + 200 = 200(1.0025)^3$ $+ 200(1.0025)^2 + 200(1.0025) + 200$
⋮	⋮
12	$[200(1.0025)^{10} + \cdots + 200] \cdot 1.0025 + 200 = 200(1.0025)^{11} + \cdots + 200(1.0025) + 200$

Next, find the sum of the finite geometric series that represents the end-of-month balance after 12 deposits. You may find it helpful to use the commutative property to rewrite $200(1.0025)^{11} + \cdots + 200(1.0025) + 200$ as $200 + 200(1.0025) + \cdots + 200(1.0025)^{11}$ so that it's easier to see that the initial term a is 200 and the common ratio r is 1.0025. Also, you know from the recursive process that this series has 12 terms. Apply the formula for the sum of a finite geometric series in order to obtain the final balance of the account.

$$S(12) = 200\left(\frac{1 - 1.0025^{12}}{1 - 1.0025}\right)$$

To evaluate the expression for the sum, use a calculator. You may find it helpful to enter the expression in parts and rely upon the calculator's Answer feature to accumulate the results. (You should avoid rounding intermediate calculations, because the round-off errors will compound and give an inaccurate answer.)

```
1-1.0025^12
        -.0304159569
Ans/(1-1.0025)
         12.16638277
Ans*200
          2433.276553
```

So, Niobe will have $2433.28 in her account after she makes 12 deposits.

(B) Niobe decides to postpone buying a new car because she wants to get a new smart phone instead. She can pay the phone's full price of $580 up front, or she can agree to pay an extra $25 per month on her phone bill over the course of a two-year contract for phone service.

What is the present cost to Niobe if she agrees to pay $25 per month for two years, assuming that she could put the money for the payments in a savings account that earns 3% annual interest and make $25 monthly withdrawals for two years?

As in Part A, a 3% annual interest rate becomes a 0.25% monthly interest rate. If Niobe puts an amount M_1 in the savings account and lets it earn interest for 1 month, then she will have $M_1 + 0.0025M_1$, or $1.0025M_1$, available to make her first phone payment. Since she wants $1.0025M_1$ to equal $25, M_1 must equal $\frac{\$25}{1.0025} \approx \$24.94$. This means that the present cost of her first phone payment is $24.94, because that amount of money will be worth $25 in 1 month after earning $0.06 in interest.

© Houghton Mifflin Harcourt Publishing Company

Similarly, if Niobe puts an additional amount M_2 in the savings account and lets it earn interest for 2 months, then she will have $1.0025M_2$ after 1 month and $1.0025(1.0025M_2)$, or $(1.0025)^{\boxed{}} M_2$, after 2 months. Since she wants $(1.0025)^{\boxed{}} M_2$ to equal \$25, M_2 must equal $\dfrac{\$25}{(1.0025)^{\boxed{}}} \approx \$\boxed{}$.

This means that the present cost of her second phone payment is \$$\boxed{}$. It also means that she must deposit a total of $M_1 + M_2 = \$24.94 + \$\boxed{} = \$\boxed{}$ in the savings account in order to have enough money for her first two phone payments.

Generalize these results to complete the following table.

Number of Payments	Present Cost of Payments
1	$\dfrac{25}{1.0025}$
2	$\dfrac{25}{1.0025} + \dfrac{25}{(1.0025)^2}$
3	$\dfrac{25}{1.0025} + \dfrac{25}{(1.0025)^2} + \dfrac{25}{(1.0025)^{\boxed{}}}$
⋮	⋮
24	$\dfrac{25}{1.0025} + \dfrac{25}{(1.0025)^2} + \cdots + \dfrac{25}{(1.0025)^{\boxed{}}}$

Find the sum of the finite geometric series that represents the present cost of 24 payments.

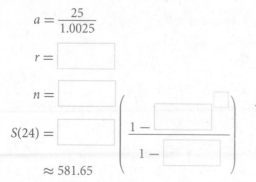

$a = \dfrac{25}{1.0025}$

$r = \boxed{}$

$n = \boxed{}$

$S(24) = \boxed{} \left(\dfrac{1 - \boxed{}^{\boxed{}}}{1 - \boxed{}} \right)$

≈ 581.65

Although Niobe will end up making total payments of $\$25 \cdot 24 = \$\boxed{}$, the present cost of the payments is \$581.65, which is only slightly more than the up-front price of the phone.

8. A lottery winner is given the choice of collecting $1,000,000 immediately or collecting payments of $6000 per month for the next 20 years. Assuming the lottery money can be invested in an account with an annual interest rate of 6% that is applied monthly, find the present value of the lottery's delayed-payout plan in order to compare it with the lump-sum plan and decide which plan is better.

 Elaborate

9. An alternative way of writing the formula for the sum of a finite geometric series is $S(n) = \dfrac{a - r \cdot ar^{n-1}}{1 - r}$. Describe in words how to find the sum of a finite geometric series using this formula.

_____

_____

10. Describe how to find the number of terms in a finite geometric series when some of the terms have been replaced by an ellipsis.

_____

_____

_____

_____

11. **Discussion** When analyzing an annuity, why is it important to determine the annuity's present value or future value?

_____

_____

_____

_____

12. **Essential Question Check-In** What is the formula for the sum of the finite geometric series
$a + ar + ar^2 + \cdots + ar^{n-1}$?

_____

☆ Evaluate: Homework and Practice

1. Suppose you start with a square piece of paper that you divide into four quarters, cutting out an L-shaped piece using three of the quarters and laying it down to create the first term of a geometric series. You then use the remaining quarter to repeat the process three more times, as shown.

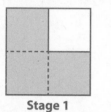 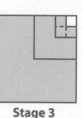 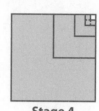 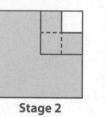

Stage 1　　　**Stage 2**　　　**Stage 3**　　　**Stage 4**

a. Complete the table.

Stage	Sum of the areas of the pieces that have been laid down	Difference of 1 and the area of the remaining piece
1	$\frac{3}{4}$	$1 - \frac{1}{4} = \frac{3}{4}$
2		
3		
4		

b. Generalize the results in the table: At stage n, the second column gives you the finite geometric series $\frac{3}{4} + \frac{3}{16} + \cdots + 3\left(\frac{1}{4}\right)^n$. The third column gives you a way to find the sum of this series. What formula does the third column give you?

c. Show that the general formula for the sum of a finite geometric series agrees with the specific formula from part b.

2. In a later lesson you will learn how to use polynomial division to show that $\frac{x^n - 1}{x - 1} = x^{n-1} + x^{n-2} + \cdots + x^2 + x + 1$ for any integer n greater 0. Use this identity as an alternative method of deriving the formula for the sum of a finite geometric series with n terms. That is, given the series $a + ar + ar^2 + \cdots + ar^{n-1}$, show that its sum is $a\left(\frac{1 - r^n}{1 - r}\right)$.

Find the sum of the finite geometric series.

3. $-3 + 6 - 12 + 24 - 48 + 96 - 192 + 384$

4. $6 - 4 + \dfrac{8}{3} - \dfrac{16}{9} + \dfrac{32}{17}$

Determine how many terms the geometric series has, and then find the sum of the series.

5. $-12 - 4 - \dfrac{4}{3} - \cdots - \dfrac{4}{243}$

6. $0.3 + 0.03 + 0.003 + \cdots + 0.000003$

7. $6 + 30 + 150 + \cdots + 468{,}750$

8. $-3 + 9 - 27 + \cdots - 177{,}147$

Write the finite geometric series from its given description, and then find its sum.

9. A geometric series that starts with 2, ends with -6250, and has a common ratio of -5

10. A geometric series with 5 terms that begins with 1 and has a common ratio of $\dfrac{1}{3}$.

11. A geometric series with 7 terms that begins with 1000 and successively decreases by 20%

12. A geometric series where the first term is −12, the last term is −972, and each term after the first is triple the previous term

13. **Chess** The first international chess tournament was held in London in 1851. This single-elimination tournament (in which paired competitors played matches and only the winner of a match continued to the next round) began with 16 competitors. How many matches were played?

14. A ball is dropped from an initial height and allowed to bounce repeatedly. On the first bounce (one up-and-down motion), the ball reaches a height of 32 inches. On each successive bounce, the ball reaches 75% of its previous height. What is the total vertical distance that the ball travels in 10 bounces? (Do not include the initial height from which the ball is dropped.)

15. Medicine During a flu outbreak, health officials record 16 cases the first week, 56 new cases the second week, and 196 new cases the third week.

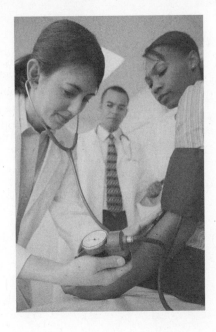

   a. Assuming the pattern of new cases continues to follow a geometric sequence, what total number of new cases will have been recorded by the fifth week?

   b. How many weeks will it take for the total number of recorded cases to exceed 40,000?

16. Finance A person deposits $5000 into an investment account at the end of each year for 10 years. The account earns 4% interest annually. What is the future value of the annuity after the 10th deposit?

17. Business A business wants to buy a parcel of land in order to expand its operations. The owner of the land offers two purchase options: Buy the land today for $100,000, or buy the land in five equal payments of $22,000 where the payments are due a year apart and the first payment is due immediately. The chief financial officer for the business determines that money set aside for the purchase of the land can be invested and earn 5.4% interest annually. Which purchase option is the better deal for the business? Explain.

18. Match each finite geometric series on the left with its sum on the right.

A. $2 + 6 + 18 + \cdots + 1458$ _____ 1094

B. $2 - 6 + 18 - \cdots + 1458$ _____ -2186

C. $-2 + 6 - 18 + \cdots - 1458$ _____ 2186

D. $-2 - 6 - 8 - \cdots - 1458$ _____ -1094

19. Represent Real-World Problems The formula for the future value FV of an annuity consisting of n regular payments of p dollars at an interest rate of i (expressed as a decimal) is $FV = p\left(\dfrac{(1 + i)^n - 1}{i}\right)$, which is valid for any payment rate (such as monthly or annually) as long as the interest rate has the same time unit. The formula assumes that the future value is calculated when the last payment is made. Show how to derive this formula.

20. Represent Real-World Problems The formula for the present value PV of an annuity consisting of n regular payments of p dollars at an interest rate of i (expressed as a decimal) is $PV = p\left(\dfrac{1 - (1+i)^{-n}}{i}\right)$, which is valid for any payment rate (such as monthly or annually) as long as the interest rate has the same time unit. The formula assumes that the present value is calculated one time unit before the first payment is made. Show how to derive this formula.

21. Draw Conclusions Consider whether it's possible for the infinite geometric series $a + ar + ar^2 + \cdots$ to have a finite sum. Since the formula $S(n) = a\left(\dfrac{1 - r^n}{1 - r}\right)$ gives the sum of the first n terms of the series, a reasonable approach to finding the sum of all terms in the series is to determine what happens to $S(n)$ as n increases without bound. Use this approach on each of the following series and draw a conclusion.

a. $1 + 2 + 4 + 8 + \cdots$

b. $1 + \dfrac{1}{2} + \dfrac{1}{4} + \dfrac{1}{8} + \cdots$

Lesson Performance Task

You've finally purchased your dream home after saving for a long time. You've made a nice down payment, and your mortgage loan is $150,000. It is a 30-year loan with an annual interest rate of 4.5%, which is calculated monthly. Find a formula for calculating monthly mortgage payments. Then find the monthly payment needed to pay off your mortgage loan.

Let P be the principal, r be the monthly interest rate expressed as a decimal, and m be the monthly payment.

Sequences and Series

Essential Question: How can you use exponential functions to solve real-world problems?

Key Vocabulary
arithmetic sequence *(sucesión arithmética)*
explicit rule *(regla explicita)*
finite geometric series *(serie geométrica finito)*
geometric sequence *(sucesión geométrica)*
recursive rule *(regla recurrente)*
sequence *(sucesión)*
series *(regla recurrente)*

KEY EXAMPLE *(Lesson 12.2)*

Write the explicit rule for the sequence described by the points $(0, 4), (1, -2), (2, -8), (3, -14), \ldots$

$f(0) = 4 \rightarrow a = 4$ Use the fact that $f(0) = a$ to find a.
$f(1) = a + d$ Use $f(1) = a + d$ to find d.
$f(1) = 4 + d$
$-2 = 4 + d$
$d = -6$
$f(n) = 4 - 6n$ Substitute a and d into $f(n) = a + dn$

The explicit rule for the sequence is $f(n) = 4 - 6n$.

KEY EXAMPLE *(Lesson 12.2)*

Find the 12th term of the geometric sequence 5, 15, 45,…

$r = \dfrac{15}{5} = 3$ Find the common ratio of the sequence.
$a_n = a_1 r^{n-1}$ Write the formula for a geometric sequence
$a_{12} = 5(3)^{12-1}$ Substitute in a, r, and n.
$a_{12} = 5(177,147)$ Use a calculator to solve for a_{12}.
$a_{12} = 885,735$ Simplify.

The 12th term of the geometric sequence is 885,735.

KEY EXAMPLE *(Lesson 12.3)*

Find the sum of the geometric series $2 - 4 + 8 - 16 + 32 - 64$.

$a = 2, r = \dfrac{-4}{2} = -2, n = 6$ Find the values of a, r, and n.

$S(n) = 2\left(\dfrac{1 - r^n}{1 - r}\right)$

$S(6) = 2\left(\dfrac{1 - (-2)^6}{1 - (-2)}\right)$ Use the sum formula

$S(6) = -42$

The sum for the geometric series is -42.

EXERCISES

1. If the first three terms of a geometric sequence are 3, 12, and 48, what is the seventh term? *(Lesson 12.2)*

Write the explicit rule for the algebraic sequence. In every sequence, the first term is the $f(0)$ term. *(Lesson 12.1)*

2. 5, 7, 9, 11, 13 ...

3.

x	0	1	2	3	4
y	−3	1	5	9	13

Find the sum of the geometric series. *(Lesson 12.1)*

4. $4 + 16 + 64 + 256 + ... + 16{,}384$

5. $3 - 6 + 12 - 24 + ... - 1536$

6. $-2 - 6 - 18 - 54 - 162$

7. $-2 + 8 - 32 + ... + 2048$

MODULE PERFORMANCE TASK

How Big Is That Snowflake?

The Koch snowflake is a special kind of shape called a fractal. It begins with an equilateral triangle. In the first iteration, each side of the triangle is divided into thirds. The middle third of each side becomes the base of a new equilateral triangle. In the second iteration, each of the sides is divided into thirds, forming the base of a new equilateral triangle. To make the full snowflake, this process continues infinitely. The first two iterations and the original triangle are shown.

What is the area of the Koch triangle after three iterations? By what factor is the area of the original triangle increased? Start on your own paper by listing the information you will need to solve the problem. Be sure to write down all your data and assumptions. Then use graphs, numbers, tables, words, or algebra to explain how you reached your conclusion.

(Ready) to Go On?

12.1–12.3 Sequences and Series

• Online Homework
• Hints and Help
• Extra Practice

Write a recursive rule and an explicit rule for each sequence.
(Lessons 12.1, 12.2)

1. 9, 27, 81, 243,…

2. 4, −3, −10, −17, …

Find the stated term of the geometric sequence. *(Lesson 12.2)*

3. −3, −6, −12, −24, …; 9th term

4. 4, −12, 36, −108, …; 11th term

Find the sum of the geometric series. *(Lesson 12.3)*

5. $10 − 20 + 40 − 80 + 160 − ... + 2560$

6. $−1 + 3 − 9 + 27 − ... − 6561$

7. $2 + 12 + 72 + 432 + 2592 + 15{,}552$

8. $7 − 7 + 7 − 7 + 7 − ... + 7$

ESSENTIAL QUESTION

9. How can you tell whether a sequence is geometric or algebraic?

Assessment Readiness

1. Consider each sequence. Is the sequence geometric? Select Yes or No for A–D.

   A. 10, 15, 20, 25,…   ○ Yes   ○ No

   B. 5, 15, 45, 135,…   ○ Yes   ○ No

   C. 1, 3, 5, 7,…   ○ Yes   ○ No

   D. 2, 4, 8, 16,…   ○ Yes   ○ No

2. Consider the series 1, 5, 9, 13, 17, …. Choose True or False for each statement.

   A. If n represents the position in the
      sequence, the algebraic expression
      for the sequence is $4n - 3$.   ○ True   ○ False

   B. If n represents the position in the
      sequence, the algebraic expression
      for the sequence is $n + 4$.   ○ True   ○ False

   C. There is no algebraic expression for
      the sequence, because it is a geometric
      sequence.   ○ True   ○ False

3. Give the first five terms of the sequence $2n + 1$, and then create an example of a real
   world situation that could match the arithmetic sequence. If the sequence were plotted
   on a coordinate plane, what kind of function would it be?

4. Solve $\frac{3}{4}|x + 3| - 8 = 4$ for x. Explain your method.

5. Explain the difference between a geometric sequence and a geometric series.

Exponential Functions

Essential Question: How can you use exponential functions to solve real-world problems?

REAL WORLD VIDEO
Check out how exponential functions can be used to model the path of a bouncing ball and other real-world patterns.

MODULE PERFORMANCE TASK PREVIEW
That's the Way the Ball Bounces

The height that a ball reaches after bouncing off a hard surface depends on several factors, including the height from which the ball was dropped and the material the ball is made of. The height of each successive bounce will be less than the previous bounce. How can mathematical modeling be used to represent a bouncing ball? Let's find out!

© Houghton Mifflin Harcourt Publishing Company • Image Credits: ©Adam Hart-Davis/Science Photo Library

Are YOU Ready?

Complete these exercises to review skills you will need for this module.

Real Numbers

Personal Math Trainer
- Online Homework
- Hints and Help
- Extra Practice

Example 1

Write the multiplicative inverse of 0.3125.

$$0.3125 = \frac{3125}{10,000}$$ Write the decimal as a fraction.

$$= \frac{5}{16} \rightarrow \frac{16}{5}$$ Simplify, then take the reciprocal.

The multiplicative inverse of 0.3125 is $\frac{16}{5}$.

Write the multiplicative inverse.

1. 1.125

2. −0.6875

3. 0.444

Exponential Functions

Example 2

Evaluate $12(1.5)^{x-5}$ for $x = 8$.

$12(1.5)^{8-5}$ Substitute.

$12(1.5)^3$ Simplify.

$12(3.375) = 40.5$ Evaluate the exponent. Multiply.

Evaluate each expression.

4. $30(1.1)^{5x}$; $x = 0.4$

5. $8(2.5)^{\frac{x}{3}}$; $x = 12$

6. $2(x)^{2x+9}$; $x = -3$

Geometric Sequences

Example 3

List the first four terms of the sequence if $t_1 = 2$ and $t_n = -3t_{n-1}$.

$t_2 = -3t_{2-1} = -3t_1 = -3 \cdot 2 = -6$ Find the second term.

$t_3 = -3t_{3-1} = -3t_2 = -3 \cdot (-6) = 18$ Find the third term.

$t_4 = -3t_{4-1} = -3t_3 = -3 \cdot 18 = -54$ Find the fourth term.

The first four terms are 2, −6, 18, and −54.

List the first four terms of the sequence.

7. $t_1 = 0.02$

$t_n = 5t_{n-1}$

8. $t_1 = 3$

$t_n = 0.5t_{n-1}$

13.1 Exponential Growth Functions

Essential Question: How is the graph of $g(x) = ab^{x-h} + k$ where $b > 1$ related to the graph of $f(x) = b^x$?

Explore 1 Graphing and Analyzing $f(x) = 2^x$ and $f(x) = 10^x$

An **exponential function** is a function of the form $f(x) = b^x$, where the base b is a positive constant other than 1 and the exponent x is a variable. Notice that there is no single parent exponential function because each choice of the base b determines a different function.

(A) Complete the input-output table for each of the parent exponential functions below.

x	$f(x) = 2^x$
−3	
−2	
−1	
0	
1	
2	
3	

x	$p(x) = 10^x$
−3	
−2	
−1	
0	
1	
2	
3	

(B) Graph the parent functions $f(x) = 2^x$ and $p(x) = 10^x$ by plotting points.

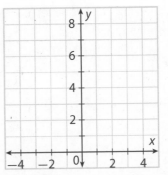

(C) What is the domain of each function?

Domain of $f(x) = 2^x$: $\left\{ x \mid \underline{\hspace{3cm}} \right\}$

Domain of $p(x) = 10^x$: $\left\{ x \mid \underline{\hspace{3cm}} \right\}$

(D) What is the range of each function?

Range of $f(x) = 2^x$: $\left\{ y \mid \underline{\hspace{3cm}} \right\}$

Range of $p(x) = 10^x$: $\left\{ y \mid \underline{\hspace{3cm}} \right\}$

(E) What is the y-intercept of each function?

y-intercept of $f(x) = 2^x$: [ ]

y-intercept of $p(x) = 10^x$: [ ]

(F) What is the trend of each function?

In both $f(x) = 2^x$ and $p(x) = 10^x$, as the value of x increases, the value of y increases/decreases.

Reflect

1. Will the domain be the same for every exponential function? Why or why not?

_____

_____

2. Will the range be the same for every exponential function in the form $f(x) = b^x$, where b is a positive constant? Why or why not?

_____

_____

_____

3. Will the value of the y-intercept be the same for every exponential function? Why or why not?

_____

_____

Explain 1 — Graphing Combined Transformations of $f(x) = b^x$ Where $b > 1$

A given exponential function $g(x) = a(b^{x-h}) + k$ with base b can be graphed by recognizing the differences between the given function and its parent function, $f(x) = b^x$. These differences define the parameters of the transformation, where k represents the vertical translation, h is the horizontal translation, and a represents either the vertical stretch or compression of the exponential function and whether it is reflected across the x-axis.

You can use the parameters in $g(x) = a(b^x - h) + k$ to see what happens to two reference points during a transformation. Two points that are easily visualized on the parent exponential function are $(0, 1)$ and $(1, b)$.

In a transformation, the point $(0, 1)$ becomes $(h, a + k)$ and $(1, b)$ becomes $(1 + h, ab + k)$. The asymptote $y = 0$ for the parent function becomes $y = k$.

The graphs of $f(x) = 2^x$ and $p(x) = 10^x$ are shown below with the reference points and asymptotes labeled.

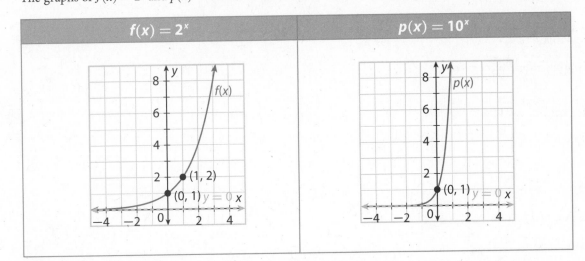

$f(x) = 2^x$	$p(x) = 10^x$

Example 1 State the domain and range of the given function. Then identify the new values of the reference points and the asymptote. Use these values to graph the function.

(A) $g(x) = -3(2^{x-2}) + 1$

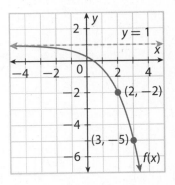

The domain of $g(x) = -3(2^{x-2}) + 1$ is $\left\{ x \mid -\infty < x < \infty \right\}$.

The range of $g(x) = -3(2^{x-2}) + 1$ is $\left\{ y \mid y < 1 \right\}$.

Examine $g(x)$ and identify the parameters.

$a = -3$, which means that the function is reflected across the x-axis and vertically stretched by a factor of 3.

$h = 2$, so the function is translated 2 units to the right.

$k = 1$, so the function is translated 1 unit up.

The point $(0, 1)$ becomes $(h, a + k)$.

$(h, a + k) = (2, -3 + 1)$

$\qquad = (2, -2)$

$(1, b)$ becomes $(1 + h, ab + k)$.

$(1 + h, ab + k) = (1 + 2, -3(2) + 1)$

$\qquad = (3, -6 + 1)$

$\qquad = (3, -5)$

The asymptote becomes $y = k$.

$y = k \quad \rightarrow \quad y = 1$

Plot the transformed points and asymptote and draw the curve.

637

(B) $q(x) = 1.5(10^{x-3}) - 5$

The domain of $q(x) = 1.5(10^{x-3}) - 5$ is $\{x|\underline{\hspace{3cm}}\}$.

The range of $q(x) = 1.5(10^{x-3}) - 5$ is $\{y|\underline{\hspace{2cm}}\}$.

Examine $q(x)$ and identify the parameters.

$a = \boxed{}$ so the function is stretched vertically by a factor of 1.5.

$h = \boxed{}$ so the function is translated 3 units to the right.

$k = \boxed{}$ so the function is translated 5 units down.

The point $(0,1)$ becomes $(h, a + k)$.

$(h, a + k) = (3, 1.5 - 5) = \underline{\hspace{3cm}}$

$(1, b)$ becomes $(1 + h, ab + k)$.

$(1 + h, ab + k) = (1 + 3, 1.5(10) - 5) = \underline{\hspace{3cm}}$

The asymptote becomes $y = k$.

$y = k \quad \rightarrow \quad y = \boxed{}$

Plot the transformed points and asymptote and draw the curve.

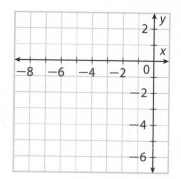

Your Turn

4. $g(x) = 4(2^{x+2}) - 6$

RED
PROBLU

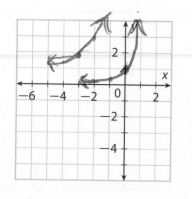

5. $q(x) = -\frac{3}{5}(10^{x+2}) + 3$

$y \quad = \frac{-3}{5} x$

x	y
-1	1/10
0	1

$\rightarrow$

x	y
-3	9/5
-2	12/5

$y = 10^x$

Module 13   638   Lesson 1

Writing Equations for Combined Transformations of $f(x) = b^x$ Where $b > 1$

Given the graph of an exponential function, you can use your knowledge of the transformation parameters to write the function rule for the graph. Recall that the asymptote will give the value of k and the x-coordinate of the first reference point is h. Then let y_1 be the y-coordinate of the first point and solve the equation $y_1 = a + k$ for a.

Finally, use a, h, and k to write the function in the form $g(x) = a\left(b^{x-h}\right) + k$.

Example 2 Write the exponential function that will produce the given graph, using the specified value of b. Verify that the second reference point is on the graph of the function. Then state the domain and range of the function in set notation.

(A) Let $b = 2$.

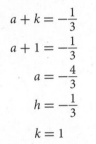

The asymptote is $y = 1$, showing that $k = 1$.

The first reference point is $\left(-\frac{1}{3}, -\frac{1}{3}\right)$. This shows that $h = -\frac{1}{3}$ and that $a + k = -\frac{1}{3}$.

Substitute $k = 1$ and solve for a.

$$a + k = -\frac{1}{3}$$

$$a + 1 = -\frac{1}{3}$$

$$a = -\frac{4}{3}$$

$$h = -\frac{1}{3}$$

$$k = 1$$

Substitute these values into $g(x) = a\left(b^{x-h}\right) + k$ to find $g(x)$.

$$g(x) = a\left(b^{x-h}\right) + k$$

$$= -\frac{4}{3}\left(2^{x+\frac{1}{3}}\right) + 1$$

Verify that $g\left(\frac{2}{3}\right) = -\frac{5}{3}$.

$$g\left(\frac{2}{3}\right) = -\frac{4}{3}\left(2^{\frac{2}{3}+\frac{1}{3}}\right) + 1$$

$$= -\frac{4}{3}\left(2^1\right) + 1$$

$$= -\frac{4}{3}(2) + 1$$

$$= \frac{3}{3} - \frac{8}{3}$$

$$= -\frac{5}{3}$$

The domain of $g(x)$ is $\left\{x \mid -\infty < x < +\infty\right\}$.

The range of $g(x)$ is $\left\{y \mid y < 1\right\}$.

Ⓑ Let $b = 10$.

The asymptote is $y = \boxed{}$, showing that $k = \boxed{}$.

The first reference point is $(-4, 4.4)$. This shows that $h = \boxed{}$ and

that $a + k = \boxed{}$. Substitute for k and solve for a.

$a + k = \boxed{}$

$a + \boxed{} = \boxed{}$

$a = \boxed{}$ $\qquad h = \boxed{}$ $\qquad k = \boxed{}$

Substitute these values into $q(x) = a\left(b^{x-h}\right) + k$ to find $q(x)$.

$q(x) = a\left(b^{x-h}\right) + k = \boxed{}\left(10^{x-\boxed{}}\right) + \boxed{}$

Verify that $q(-3) = -10$.

$q(-3) = \boxed{}\left(10^{-3-\boxed{}}\right) + \boxed{}$

$= \boxed{}\left(10^{\boxed{}}\right) + \boxed{}$

$= \boxed{} + \boxed{}$

$= \boxed{}$

The domain of $q(x)$ is _____. The range of $q(x)$ is _____.

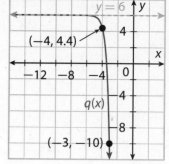

Your Turn

Write the exponential function that will produce the given graph, using the specified value of b. Verify that the second reference point is on the graph of the function. Then state the domain and range of the function in set notation.

6. $b = 2$

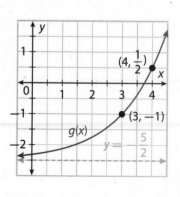

🎸 Explain 3   Modeling with Exponential Growth Functions

An **exponential growth function** has the form $f(t) = a(1 + r)^t$ where $a > 0$ and r is a constant percent increase (expressed as a decimal) for each unit increase in time t. That is, since $f(t + 1) = (1 + r) \cdot f(t) = f(t) + r \cdot f(t)$, the value of the function increases by $r \cdot f(t)$ on the interval $[t, t + 1]$. The base $1 + r$ of an exponential growth function is called the **growth factor**, and the constant percent increase r, in decimal form, is called the **growth rate**.

Example 3   **Find the function that corresponds with the given situation. Then use the graph of the function to make a prediction.**

(A)   Tony purchased a rare guitar in 2000 for $12,000. Experts estimate that its value will increase by 14% per year. Use a graph to find the number of years it will take for the value of the guitar to be $60,000.

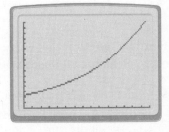

Write a function to model the growth in value for the guitar.

$$f(t) = a(1 + r)^t$$

$$= 12,000(1 + 0.14)^t$$

$$= 12,000(1.14)^t$$

Use a graphing calculator to graph the function.

Use the graph to predict when the guitar will be worth $60,000.

Use the TRACE feature to find the t-value where $f(t) \approx 60,000$.

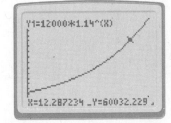

So, the guitar will be worth $60,000 approximately 12.29 years after it was purchased.

(B)   At the same time that Tony bought the $12,000 guitar, he also considered buying another rare guitar for $15,000. Experts estimated that this guitar would increase in value by 9% per year. Determine after how many years the two guitars will be worth the same amount.

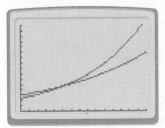

Write a function to model the growth in value for the second guitar.

$$g(t) = a(1 + r)^t$$

$$= \boxed{} \left(1 + \boxed{}\right)^t$$

$$= \boxed{} \left(\boxed{}\right)^t$$

Use a graphing calculator to graph the two functions.

Use the graph to predict when the two guitars will be worth the same amount.

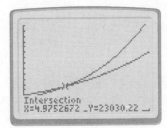

Use the intersection feature to find the t-value where $g(t) = \boxed{}$.

So, the two guitars will be worth the same amount _____ years after 2000.

7. In part A, find the average rates of change over the intervals $(0, 4)$, $(4, 8)$, and $(8, 12)$. Do the rates increase, decrease, or stay the same?

_____

_____

_____

_____

Your Turn

Find the function that corresponds with the given situation. Then graph the function on a calculator and use the graph to make a prediction.

8. John researches a baseball card and finds that it is currently worth $3.25. However, it is supposed to increase in value 11% per year. In how many years will the card be worth $26?

Elaborate

9. How are reference points helpful when graphing transformations of $f(x) = b^x$ or when writing equations for transformed graphs?

_____

_____

_____

_____

10. Give the general form of an exponential growth function and describe its parameters.

_____

11. **Essential Question Check-In** Which transformations of $f(x) = b^x$ change the function's end behavior? Which transformations change the function's y-intercept?

_____

_____

_____

_____

Describe the effect of each transformation on the parent function. Graph the parent function and its transformation. Then determine the domain, range, and *y*-intercept of each function.

1. $f(x) = 2^x$ and $g(x) = 2(2^x)$

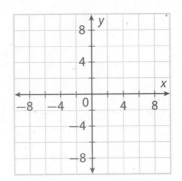

2. $f(x) = 2^x$ and $g(x) = -5(2^x)$

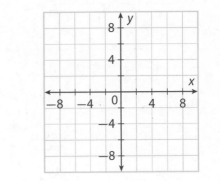

3. $f(x) = 2^x$ and $g(x) = 2^{x+2}$

4. $f(x) = 2^x$ and $g(x) = 2^x + 5$

5. $f(x) = 10^x$ and $g(x) = 2(10^x)$

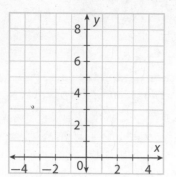

6. $f(x) = 10^x$ and $g(x) = -4(10^x)$

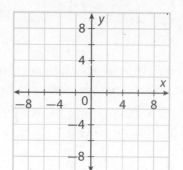

7. $f(x) = 10^x$ and $g(x) = 10^{x-2}$

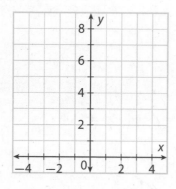

8. $f(x) = 10^x$ and $g(x) = 10^x - 6$

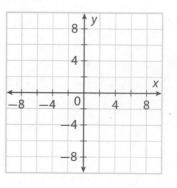

9. Describe the graph of $g(x) = 2^{(x-3)} - 4$ in terms of $f(x) = 2^x$.

10. Describe the graph of $g(x) = 10^{(x+7)} + 6$ in terms of $f(x) = 10^x$.

State the domain and range of the given function. Then identify the new values of the reference points and the asymptote. Use these values to graph the function.

11. $h(x) = 2(3^{x+2}) - 1$

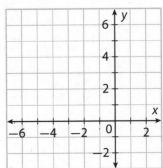

12. $k(x) = -0.5(4^{x-1}) + 2$

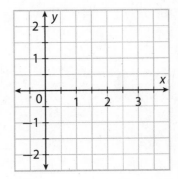

13. $f(x) = 3(6^{x-7}) - 8$

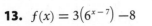

14. $f(x) = -3\left(2^{x+1}\right) + 3$

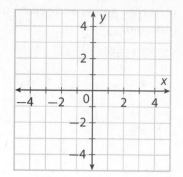

15. $h(x) = -\dfrac{1}{4}\left(5^{x+1}\right) - \dfrac{3}{4}$

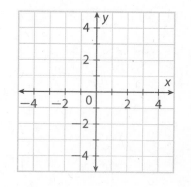

16. $p(x) = 2\left(4^{x-3}\right) - 5$

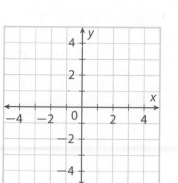

Write the exponential function that will produce the given graph, using the specified value of *b*. Verify that the second reference point is on the graph of the function. Then state the domain and range of the function in set notation.

17. $b = 2$

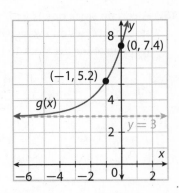

18. $b = 10$

Find the function that corresponds with the given situation. Then graph the function on a calculator and use the graph to make a prediction.

19. A certain stock opens with a price of $0.59. Over the first three days, the value of the stock increases on average by 50% per day. If this trend continues, how many days will it take for the stock to be worth $6?

20. Sue has a lamp from her great-grandmother. She has it appraised and finds it is worth $1000. She wants to sell it, but the appraiser tells her that the value is appreciating by 8% per year. In how many years will the value of the lamp be $2000?

21. The population of a small town is 15,000. If the population is growing by 5% per year, how long will it take for the population to reach 25,000?

22. Bill invests $3000 in a bond fund with an interest rate of 9% per year. If Bill does not withdraw any of the money, in how many years will his bond fund be worth $5000?

23. Analyze Relationships Compare the end behavior of $g(x) = 2^x$ and $f(x) = x^2$. How are the graphs of the functions similar? How are they different?

24. Explain the Error A student has a baseball card that is worth $6.35. He looks up the appreciation rate and finds it to be 2.5% per year. He wants to find how much it will be worth after 3 years. He writes the function $f(t) = 6.35(2.5)^t$ and uses the graph of that function to find the value of the card in 3 years.

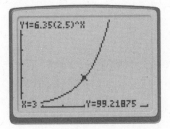

According to his graph, his card will be worth about $99.22 in 3 years. What did the student do wrong? What is the correct answer?

© Houghton Mifflin Harcourt Publishing Company • Image Credits: ©RisingStar/Alamy

Lesson Performance Task

Like all collectables, the price of an item is determined by what the buyer is willing to pay and the seller is willing to accept. The estimated value of a 1948 Tucker 48 automobile in excellent condition has risen at an approximately exponential rate from about \$500,000 in December 2006 to about \$1,400,000 in December 2013.

  a. Find an equation in the form $V(t) = V_0 \left(1 + r\right)^t$, where V_0 is the value of the car in dollars in December 2006, r is the average annual growth rate, t is the time in years since December 2006, and $V(t)$ is the value of the car in dollars at time t. (Hint: Substitute the known values and solve for r.)

  b. What is the meaning of the value of r?

  c. If this trend continues, what would be the value of the car in December 2017?

13.2 Exponential Decay Functions

Resource
Locker

Essential Question: How is the graph of $g(x) = ab^{x-h} + k$ where $0 < b < 1$ related to the graph of $f(x) = b^x$?

⊘ Explore 1 Graphing and Analyzing $f(x) = \left(\frac{1}{2}\right)^x$ and $f(x) = \left(\frac{1}{10}\right)^x$

Exponential functions with bases between 0 and 1 can be transformed in a manner similar to exponential functions with bases greater than 1. Begin by plotting the parent functions of two of the more commonly used bases: $\frac{1}{2}$ and $\frac{1}{10}$.

(A) To begin, fill in the table in order to find points along the function $f(x) = \left(\frac{1}{2}\right)^x$. You may need to review the rules of the properties of exponents, including negative exponents.

x	$f(x) = \left(\frac{1}{2}\right)^x$
−3	8
−2	
−1	
0	
1	
2	
3	

(B) What does the end behavior of this function appear to be as x increases?

_____

(C) Plot the points on the graph and draw a smooth curve through them.

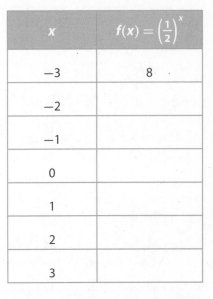

(D) Complete the table for $f(x) = \left(\frac{1}{10}\right)x$.

x	$f(x) = \left(\frac{1}{10}\right)^x$
−3	1000
−2	
−1	
0	
1	
2	
3	

(E) Plot the points on the graph and draw a smooth curve through them.

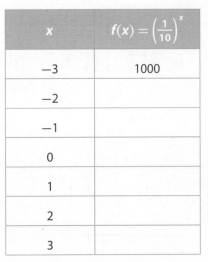

(F) Fill in the following table of properties:

	$f(x) = \left(\frac{1}{2}\right)^x$	$f(x) = \left(\frac{1}{10}\right)^x$
Domain	$\{x \mid -\infty < x < \infty\}$	$\{x \mid \boxed{}\}$
Range	$\{y \mid \boxed{}\}$	$\{y \mid \boxed{}\}$
End behavior as $x \to \infty$	$f(x) \to \boxed{}$	$f(x) \to \boxed{}$
End behavior as $x \to -\infty$	$f(x) \to \boxed{}$	$f(x) \to \boxed{}$
y-intercept	$\boxed{}\,\boxed{}$	$\boxed{}\,\boxed{}$

(G) Both of these functions [decrease/increase] throughout the domain.

(H) Of the two functions, $f(x) = \left(\frac{1}{\boxed{}}\right)^x$ decreases faster.

Reflect

1. **Make a Conjecture** Look at the table of properties for the functions. What do you notice? Make a conjecture about these properties for exponential functions of the form $f(x) = \left(\frac{1}{n}\right)^x$, where n is a constant.

_____

_____

⚿ **Explain 1** **Graphing Combined Transformations of $f(x) = b^x$ Where $0 < b < 1$**

When graphing transformations of $f(x) = b^x$ where $0 < b < 1$, it is helpful to consider the effect of the transformation on two reference points, $(0, 1)$ and $\left(-1, \frac{1}{b}\right)$, as well as the effect on the asymptote, $y = 0$. The table shows these reference points and the asymptote $y = 0$ for $f(x) = b^x$ and the corresponding points and asymptote for the transformed function, $g(x) = ab^{x-h} + k$.

	$f(x) = b^x$	$g(x) = ab^{x-h} + k$
First reference point	$(0, 1)$	$(h, a + k)$
Second reference point	$\left(-1, \dfrac{1}{b}\right)$	$\left(h - 1, \dfrac{a}{b} + k\right)$
Asymptote	$y = 0$	$y = k$

Example 1 The graph of a parent exponential function is shown. Use the reference points and the asymptote shown for the parent graph to graph the given transformed function. Then describe the domain and range of the transformed function using set notation.

(A) $g(x) = 3\left(\dfrac{1}{2}\right)^{x-2} - 2$

Identify parameters: $\qquad a = 3 \qquad b = \dfrac{1}{2} \qquad h = 2 \qquad k = -2$

Find reference points:

$$(h, a + k) = (2, 3 - 2) = (2, 1)$$

$$\left(h - 1, \dfrac{a}{b} + k\right) = \left(2 - 1, \dfrac{3}{\frac{1}{2}} - 2\right) = (1, 4)$$

Find the asymptote: $y = -2$

Plot the points and draw the asymptote. Then connect the points with a smooth curve that approaches the asymptote without crossing it.

Domain: $\left\{x \mid -\infty < x < \infty\right\}$

Range: $\left\{y \mid y > -2\right\}$

(B) $g(x) = -\left(\dfrac{1}{10}\right)^{x+2} + 8$

Identify parameters:

$a = \boxed{} \qquad b = \boxed{} \qquad h = \boxed{} \qquad k = \boxed{}$

Find reference points:

$$\left(h, \boxed{}\right) = (-2, -1 + 8) = (-2, 7)$$

$$\left(h - 1, \dfrac{a}{b} + k\right) = \left(-2 - 1, \dfrac{\boxed{}}{\boxed{}} + 8\right) = \left(\boxed{}, \boxed{}\right)$$

© Houghton Mifflin Harcourt Publishing Company

Find the asymptote:

$y = \boxed{}$

Plot the points and draw the asymptote. Then connect the points with a smooth curve that approaches the asymptote without crossing it.

Domain: $\left\{ x \mid \boxed{} \right\}$

Range: $\left\{ y \mid \boxed{} \right\}$

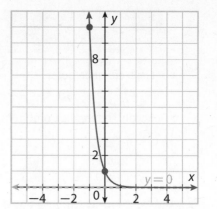

2. Which parameters make the domain and range of $g(x)$ differ from those of the parent function? Write the transformed domain and range for $g(x)$ in set notation.

_____

_____

_____

_____

Your Turn

Graph the given transformed function. Then describe the domain and range of the transformed function using set notation.

3. $g(x) = 3 \left(\dfrac{1}{3} \right)^{x+2} - 4$

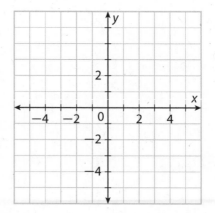

⚙ Explain 2 Writing Equations for Combined Transformations of $f(x) = b^x$ where $0 < b < 1$

Given a graph of an exponential function, $g(x) = ab^{x-h} + k$, the reference points and the asymptote can be used to identify the transformation parameters in order to write the function rule.

Example 2 Write the function represented by this graph and state the domain and range using set notation.

(A)

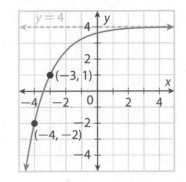

Find k from the asymptote: $k = 4$.

The first reference point is at $(-3,1)$.

Equate point value with parameters-based expression. $\qquad (-3, 1) = (h, a + k)$

Use the x-coordinate to solve for h. $\qquad h = -3$

Use the y-coordinate to solve for a. $\qquad a = 1 - k$

$\qquad = -3$

The second reference point is at $(-4, -2)$.

Equate point value with parameters-based expression. $\qquad (-4, -2) = \left(h - 1, \frac{a}{b} + k\right)$

Equate y-coordinate with parameters. $\qquad \frac{-3}{b} + 4 = -2$

Solve for b. $\qquad \frac{-3}{b} = -6$

$\qquad b = \frac{-3}{-6}$

$\qquad = \frac{1}{2}$

$g(x) = -3\left(\frac{1}{2}\right)^{x+3} + 4$

Domain: $\left\{x \mid -\infty < x < \infty\right\}$

Range: $\left\{y \mid y < 4\right\}$

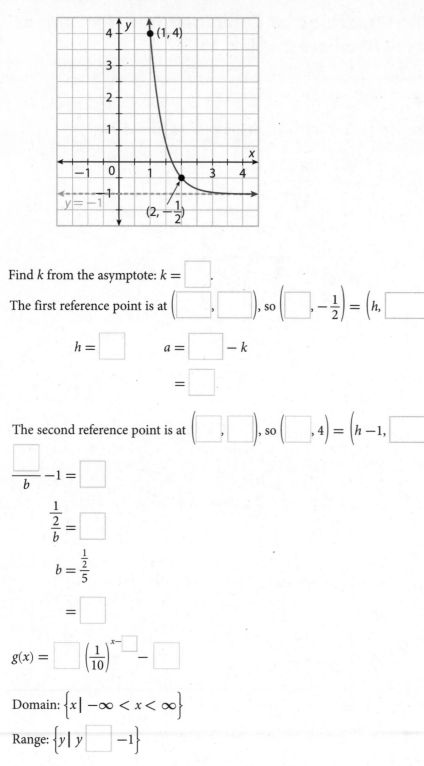

Find k from the asymptote: $k = \boxed{}$.

The first reference point is at $\left(\boxed{}, \boxed{} \right)$, so $\left(\boxed{}, -\frac{1}{2} \right) = \left(h, \boxed{} \right)$

$h = \boxed{}$ $a = \boxed{} - k$

$ = \boxed{}$.

The second reference point is at $\left(\boxed{}, \boxed{} \right)$, so $\left(\boxed{}, 4 \right) = \left(h - 1, \boxed{} \right)$

$\dfrac{\boxed{}}{b} - 1 = \boxed{}$

$\dfrac{\frac{1}{2}}{b} = \boxed{}$

$b = \dfrac{\frac{1}{2}}{5}$

$ = \boxed{}$

$g(x) = \boxed{} \left(\dfrac{1}{10} \right)^{x - \boxed{}} - \boxed{}$

Domain: $\left\{ x \mid -\infty < x < \infty \right\}$

Range: $\left\{ y \mid y \boxed{} -1 \right\}$

Reflect

4. Compare the *y*-intercept and the asymptote of the function shown in this table to the function plotted in Example 2A.

x	−5	−4	−3	−2	−1	0	1	2
g(*x*)	−10	−4	−4	$\frac{1}{2}$	$1\frac{1}{4}$	$1\frac{5}{8}$	$1\frac{13}{16}$	$1\frac{29}{32}$

5. Compare the *y*-intercept and the asymptote of the function shown in this table to the function plotted in Example 2B.

x	−3	−2	−1	0	1	2
g(*x*)	49	4	−0.5	−0.95	−0.995	−0.9995

Your Turn

Write the function represented by this graph and state the domain and range using set notation.

6.

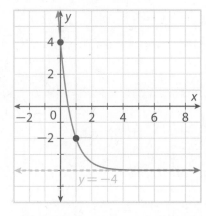

An **exponential decay function** has the form $f(t) = a(1 - r)^t$ where a > 0 and r is a constant percent decrease (expressed as a decimal) for each unit increase in time t. That is, since $f(t + 1) = (1 - r) \cdot f(t) = f(t) - r \cdot f(t)$, the value of the function decreases by $r \cdot f(t)$ on the interval $[t, t + 1]$. The base 1 − r of an exponential decay function is called the **decay factor**, and the constant percent decrease r, in decimal form, is called the **decay rate**.

Example 3 Given the description of the decay terms, write the exponential decay function in the form $f(t) = a(1 - r)^t$ and graph it with a graphing calculator.

(A) The value of a truck purchased new for $28,000 decreases by 9.5% each year. Write an exponential function for this situation and graph it using a calculator. Use the graph to predict after how many years the value of the truck will be $5000.

"Purchased new for $28,000..." $a = 28{,}000$

"...decreases by 9.5% each year." $r = 0.095$

Substitute parameter values. $V_T(t) = 28{,}000(1 - 0.095)^t$

Simplify. $V_T(t) = 28{,}000(0.905)^t$

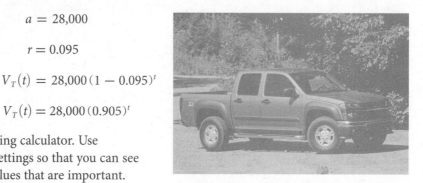

Graph the function with a graphing calculator. Use WINDOW to adjust the graph settings so that you can see the function and the function values that are important.

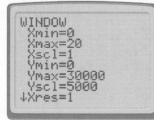

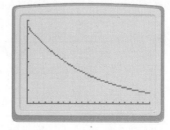

Find when the value reaches $5000 by finding the intersection between $V_T(t) = 28{,}000(0.905)^t$ and $V_T(t) = 5000$ on the calculator.

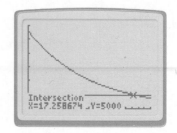

The intersection is at the point $(17.26, 5000)$, which means after 17.26 years, the truck will have a value of $5000.

(B) The value of a sports car purchased new for $45,000 decreases by 15% each year. Write an exponential function for the depreciation of the sports car, and plot it along with the previous example. After how many years will the two vehicles have the same value if they are purchased at the same time?

"Purchased new for $45,000..." $\boxed{}$ = 45,000

"...decreases by 15% each year." $r = \boxed{}$

Substitute parameter values. $V_c(t) = \boxed{}\left(1 - \boxed{}\right)^t$

Simplify. $V_c(t) = 45,000\left(\boxed{}\right)^t$

Add this plot to the graph for the truck value from Example A and find the intersection of the two functions to determine when the values are the same.

The intersection point is $\left(\boxed{}, \boxed{}\right)$.

After $\boxed{}$ years, the values of both vehicles will be

$\$\boxed{}$.

Reflect

7. What reference points could you use if you plotted the value function for the sports car on graph paper? Confirm that the graph passes through them using the calculate feature on a graphing calculator.

_____

_____

_____

8. Using the sports car from example B, calculate the average rate of change over the course of the first year and the second year of ownership. What happens to the absolute value of the rate of change from the first interval to the second? What does this mean in this situation?

_____

_____

_____

_____

_____

_____

9. On federal income tax returns, self-employed people can depreciate the value of business equipment. Suppose a computer valued at $2765 depreciates at a rate of 30% per year. Use a graphing calculator to determine the number of years it will take for the computer's value to be $350.

Elaborate

10. Which transformations of $f(x) = \left(\frac{1}{2}\right)^x$ or $f(x) = \left(\frac{1}{10}\right)^x$ change the function's end behavior?

_____

_____

_____

11. Which transformations change the location of the graph's y-intercept?

_____

_____

12. **Discussion** How are reference points and asymptotes helpful when graphing transformations of $f(x) = \left(\frac{1}{2}\right)^x$ or $f(x) = \left(\frac{1}{10}\right)^x$ or when writing equations for transformed graphs?

_____

_____

_____

_____

13. Give the general form of an exponential decay function based on a known decay rate and describe its parameters.

_____

_____

_____

_____

14. **Essential Question Check-In** How is the graph of $f(x) = b^x$ used to help graph the function $g(x) = ab^{x-h} + k$?

_____

_____

Describe the transformation(s) from each parent function and give the domain and range of each function.

1. $g(x) = \left(\dfrac{1}{2}\right)^x + 3$

2. $g(x) = \left(\dfrac{1}{10}\right)^{x+4}$

3. $g(x) = -\left(\dfrac{1}{10}\right)^{x-1} + 2$

4. $g(x) = 3\left(\dfrac{1}{2}\right)^{x+3} - 6$

Graph the given transformed function. Then describe the domain and range of the transformed function using set notation.

5. $g(x) = -2\left(\dfrac{1}{2}\right)^{x-1} + 2$

6. $g(x) = \left(\dfrac{1}{4}\right)^{x+2} + 3$

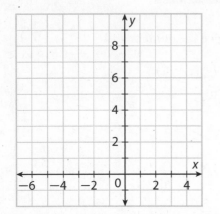

7. $g(x) = \dfrac{1}{2}\left(\dfrac{1}{3}\right)^{x-\frac{1}{2}} + 2$

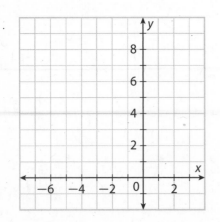

8. $g(x) = -3\left(\dfrac{1}{2}\right)^{x+2} + 7$

Write the function represented by each graph and state the domain and range using set notation.

9.

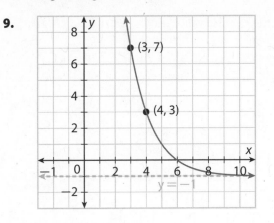

10.

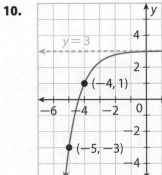

Write the exponential decay function described in the situation and use a graphing calculator to answer each question asked.

11. **Medicine** A quantity of insulin used to regulate sugar in the bloodstream breaks down by about 5% each minute after the injection. A bodyweight-adjusted dose is generally 10 units. How long does it take for the remaining insulin to be half of the original injection?

12. **Paleontology** Carbon-14 is a radioactive isotope of carbon that is used to date fossils. There are about 1.5 atoms of carbon-14 for every trillion atoms of carbon in the atmosphere, which known as 1.5 ppt (parts per trillion). Carbon in a living organism has the same concentration as carbon-14. When an organism dies, the carbon-14 content decays at a rate of 11.4% per millennium (1000 years). Write the equation for carbon-14 concentration (in ppt) as a function of time (in millennia) and determine how old a fossil must be that has a measured concentration of 0.2 ppt.

13. **Music** Stringed instruments like guitars and pianos create a note when a string vibrates back and forth. The distance that the middle of the string moves from the center is called the amplitude (a), and for a guitar, it starts at 0.75 mm when a note is first struck. Amplitude decays at a rate that depends on the individual instrument and the note, but a decay rate of about 25% per second is typical. Calculate the time it takes for an amplitude of 0.75 mm to reach 0.1 mm.

14. **Analyze Relationships** Compare the graphs of $f(x) = \left(\dfrac{1}{2}\right)^x$ and $g(x) = x^{\frac{1}{2}}$. Which of the following properties are the same? Explain.

    a. Domain

    b. Range

    c. End behavior as x increases

    d. End behavior as x decreases

15. **Communicate Mathematical Ideas** A quantity is reduced to half of its original amount during each given time period. Another quantity is reduced to one quarter of its original amount during the same given time period. Determine each decay rate, state which is greater, and explain your results.

16. **Multiple Representations** Exponential decay functions are written as transformations of the function $f(x) = b^x$, where $0 < b < 1$. However, it is also possible to use negative exponents as the basis of an exponential decay function. Use the properties of exponents to show why the function $f(x) = 2^{-x}$ is an exponential decay function.

17. **Represent Real-World Problems** You buy a video game console for $500 and sell it 5 years later for $100. The resale value decays exponentially over time. Write a function that represents the resale value, R, in dollars over the time, t, in years. Explain how you determined your function.

Lesson Performance Task

Sodium-24 is a radioactive isotope of sodium used as a diagnostic aid in medicine. It undergoes radioactive decay to form the stable isotope magnesium-24 and has a half-life of about 15 hours. This means that, in this time, half the amount of a sample mass of sodium-24 decays to magnesium-24. Suppose we start with an initial mass of 100 grams sodium-24.

a. Use the half-life of sodium-24 to write an exponential decay function of the form $m_{Na}(t) = m_0(1 - r)^t$, where m_0 is the initial mass of sodium-24, r is the decay rate, t is the time in hours, and $m_{Na}(t)$ is the mass of sodium-24 at time t. What is the meaning of r?

b. The combined amounts of sodium-24 and magnesium-24 must equal m_0, or 100, for all possible values of t. Show how to write a function for $m_{Mg}(t)$, the mass of magnesium-24 as a function of t.

c. Use a graphing calculator to graph $m_{Na}(t)$ and $m_{Mg}(t)$. Describe the graph of $m_{Mg}(t)$ as a series of transformations of $m_{Na}(t)$. What does the intersection of the graphs represent?

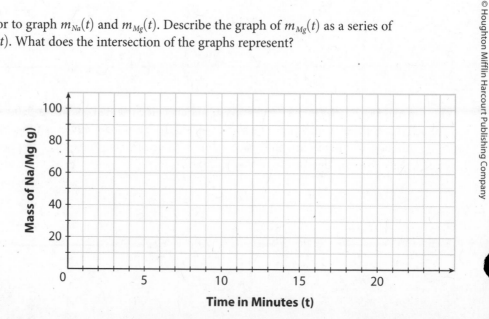

Time in Minutes (t)

13.3 The Base *e*

Essential Question: How is the graph of $g(x) = ae^{x-h} + k$ related to the graph of $f(x) = e^x$?

Resource
Locker

⊘ Explore 1   Graphing and Analyzing $f(x) = e^x$

The following table represents the function $f(x) = \left(1 + \frac{1}{x}\right)^x$ for several values of x.

x	1	10	100	1000	...
f(x)	2	2.5937 ...	2.7048 ...	2.7169 ...	...

As the value of x increases without bound, the value of $f(x)$ approaches a number whose decimal value is 2.718... This number is irrational and is called e. You can write this in symbols as $f(x) \to e$ as $x \to +\infty$.

If you graph $f(x)$ and the horizontal line $y = e$, you can see that $y = e$ is the horizontal asymptote of $f(x)$.

Even though e is an irrational number, it can be used as the base of an exponential function. The number e is sometimes called the natural base of an exponential function and is used extensively in scientific and other applications involving exponential growth and decay.

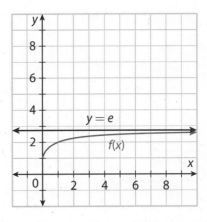

(A) Fill out the table of values below for the function $f(x) = e^x$. Use decimal approximations.

x	−10	−1	−0.5	0	0.5	1	1.5	2
$f(x) = e^x$	4.54×10^{-5}	$\frac{1}{e} = 0.367...$	0.606...		$\sqrt{e} =$			

(B) Plot the points on a graph.

(C) The domain of $f(x) = e^x$ is $\left\{ x \mid \rule{4cm}{0.4pt} \right\}$.

The range of $f(x) = e^x$ is $\left\{ y \mid \rule{3cm}{0.4pt} \right\}$.

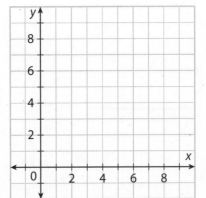

© Houghton Mifflin Harcourt Publishing Company

(D) Is the function increasing or decreasing? For what values of x is it increasing/decreasing?

_____

_____

_____

(E) The function's y-intercept is $\left(0, \boxed{}\right)$ because $f(0) = e^0 = \boxed{}$ and $x = 0$ is in the domain of the function.

(F) Another point on the graph that can be used as a reference point is $\left(1, \boxed{}\right)$.

(G) Identify the end behavior.

$f(x) \to \boxed{}$ as $x \to \infty$

$f(x) \to \boxed{}$ as $x \to -\infty$

There is a horizontal asymptote at $y = \boxed{}$.

Reflect

1. What is the relationship between the graphs of $f(x) = e^x$, $g(x) = 2^x$, and $h(x) = 3^x$? (Hint: Sketch the graphs on your own paper.)

_____

_____

_____

⚙ Explain 1   Graphing Combined Transformations of $f(x) = e^x$

When graphing combined transformations of $f(x) = e^x$ that result in the function $g(x) = a \cdot e^{x-h} + k$, it helps to focus on two reference points on the graph of $f(x)$, $(0, 1)$ and $(1, e)$, as well as on the asymptote $y = 0$. The table shows these reference points and the asymptote $y = 0$ for $f(x) = e^x$ and the corresponding points and asymptote for the transformed function, $g(x) = a \cdot e^{x-h} + k$.

	$f(x) = e^x$	$g(x) = a \cdot e^{x-h} + k$
First reference point	$(0, 1)$	$(h, a + k)$
Second reference point	$(1, e)$	$(h + 1, ae + k)$
Asymptote	$y = 0$	$y = k$

Example 1 Given a function of the form $g(x) = a \cdot e^{x-h} + k$, identify the reference points and use them to draw the graph. State the transformations that compose the combined transformation, the asymptote, the domain, and range. Write the domain and range using set notation.

(A) $g(x) = 3 \cdot e^{x+1} + 4$

Compare $g(x) = 3 \cdot e^{x+1} + 4$ to the general form $g(x) = a \cdot e^{x-h} + k$ to find that $h = -1$, $k = 4$, and $a = 3$.

Find the reference points of $f(x) = 3 \cdot e^{x+1} + 4$.

$(0, 1) \rightarrow (h, a + k) = (-1, 3 + 4) = (-1, 7)$

$(1, e) \rightarrow (h + 1, ae + k) = (-1 + 1, 3e + 4) = (0, 3e + 4)$

State the transformations that compose the combined transformation.

$h = -1$, so the graph is translated 1 unit to the left.

$k = 4$, so the graph is translated 4 units up.

$a = 3$, so the graph is vertically stretched by a factor of 3.

a is positive, so the graph is not reflected across the x-axis.

The asymptote is vertically shifted to $y = k$, so $y = 4$.

The domain is $\left\{ x \mid -\infty < x < \infty \right\}$.

The range is $\left\{ y \mid y > 4 \right\}$.

Use the information to graph the function $g(x) = 3 \cdot e^{x+1} + 4$.

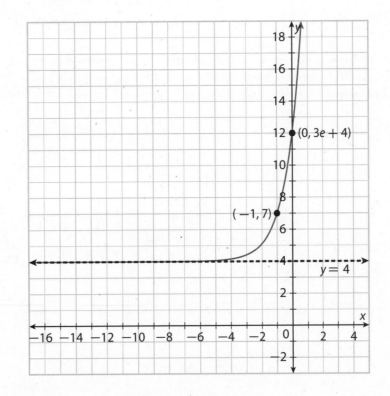

Ⓑ $g(x) = -0.5 \cdot e^{x-2} - 1$

Compare $g(x) = -0.5 \cdot e^{x-2} - 1$ to the general form $g(x) = a \cdot e^{x-h} + k$ to find that $h = \boxed{}$, $k = \boxed{}$, and $a = \boxed{}$.

Find the reference points of $g(x) = -0.5 \cdot e^{x-2} - 1$.

$(0, 1) \rightarrow (h, a + k) = \left(\boxed{}, \boxed{} + \boxed{} \right) = \left(\boxed{}, \boxed{} \right)$

$(1, e) \rightarrow (h + 1, ae + k) = \left(\boxed{} + 1, \boxed{} e + \boxed{} \right) = \left(\boxed{}, \boxed{} \right)$

State the transformations that compose the combined transformation.

$h = \boxed{}$, so the graph is translated $\boxed{}$ units to the _____.

$k = \boxed{}$, so the graph is translated $\boxed{}$ unit _____.

$a = \boxed{}$, so the graph is vertically _____ by a factor of $\boxed{}$.

a is negative, so the graph is reflected across the $\boxed{}$-axis.

The asymptote is vertically shifted to $y = k$, so $y = \boxed{}$.

The domain is $\left\{ x \mid \boxed{} \right\}$.

The range is $\left\{ y \mid \boxed{} \right\}$.

Use the information to graph the function $g(x) = -0.5 \cdot e^{x-2} - 1$.

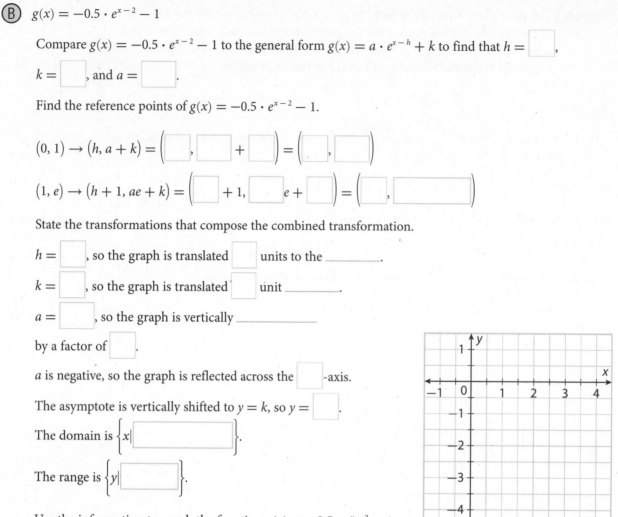

Your Turn

Given a function of the form $g(x) = a \cdot e^{x-h} + k$, identify the reference points and use them to draw the graph. State the asymptote, domain, and range. Write the domain and range using set notation.

2. $g(x) = (-1) \cdot e^{x+2} - 3$

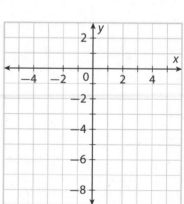

Explain 2 **Writing Equations for Combined Transformations of $f(x) = e^x$**

If you are given the transformed graph $g(x) = a \cdot e^{x-h} + k$, it is possible to write the equation of the transformed graph by using the reference points $(h, a + k)$ and $(1 + h, ae + k)$.

Example 2 Write the function whose graph is shown. State the domain and range in set notation.

(A) First, look at the labeled points on the graph.

$(h, a + k) = (4, 6)$

$(1 + h, ae + k) = (5, 2e + 4)$

Find a, h, and k.

$(h, a + k) = (4, 6)$, so $h = 4$.

$(1 + h, ae + k) = (5, 2e + 4)$, so $ae + k = 2e + 4$.
Therefore, $a = 2$ and $k = 4$.

Write the equation by substituting the values of a, h, and k into the function $g(x) = a \cdot e^{x-h} + k$.

$g(x) = 2e^{x-4} + 4$

State the domain and range.

Domain: $\left\{ x \middle| -\infty < x < \infty \right\}$

Range: $\left\{ y \middle| y > 4 \right\}$

(B) First, look at the labeled points on the graph.

$(h, a + k) = \left(\boxed{}, \boxed{} \right)$

$(1 + h, ae + k) = \left(\boxed{}, \boxed{} \right)$

Find a, h, and k.

$(h, a + k) = (-4, -8)$, so $h = \boxed{}$.

$(1 + h, ae + k) = (-3, -2e - 6)$, so $ae + k = \boxed{}$.

Therefore, $a = \boxed{}$ and $k = \boxed{}$.

Write the equation by substituting the values of a, h, and k into the function $g(x) = a \cdot e^{x-h} + k$.

$g(x) = \boxed{}$

State the domain and range.

Domain: $\left\{ x \middle| \boxed{} \right\}$

Range: $\left\{ y \middle| \boxed{} \right\}$

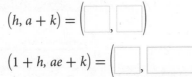

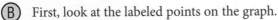

Write the function whose graph is shown. State the domain and range in set notation.

3.

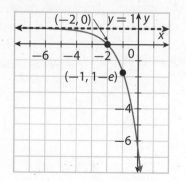

Explain 3 Modeling with Exponential Functions Having Base e

Although the function $f(x) = e^x$ has base $e \approx 2.718$, the function $g(x) = e^{cx}$ can have any positive base (other than 1) by choosing an appropriate positive or negative value of the constant c. This is because you can write $g(x)$ as $(e^c)^x$ by using the Power of a Power Property of Exponents.

Example 3 Solve each problem using a graphing calculator. Then determine the growth rate or decay rate of the function.

(A) The Dow Jones index is a stock market index for the New York Stock Exchange. The Dow Jones index for the period 1980-2000 can be modeled by $V_{DJ}(t) = 878e^{0.121t}$, where t is the number of years after 1980. Determine how many years after 1980 the Dow Jones index reached 3000.

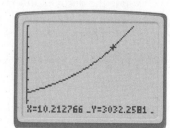

Use a graphing calculator to graph the function.

The value of the function is about 3000 when $x \approx 10.2$. So, the Dow Jones index reached 3000 after 10.2 years, or after the year 1990.

In an exponential growth model of the form $f(x) = ae^{cx}$, the growth factor $1 + r$ is equal to e^c.

To find r, first rewrite the function in the form $f(x) = a(e^c)^x$.

$V_{DJ}(t) = 878e^{0.121t}$

$\qquad = 878(e^{0.121})^t$

Find r by using $1 + r = e^c$.

$1 + r = e^c$

$1 + r = e^{0.121}$

$\quad r = e^{0.121} - 1 \approx 0.13$

So, the growth rate is about 13%.

(B) The Nikkei 225 index is a stock market index for the Tokyo Stock Exchange. The Nikkei 225 index for the period 1990-2010 can be modeled by $V_{N225}(t) = 23{,}500e^{-0.0381t}$, where t is the number of years after 1990. Determine how many years after 1990 the Nikkei 225 index reached 15,000.

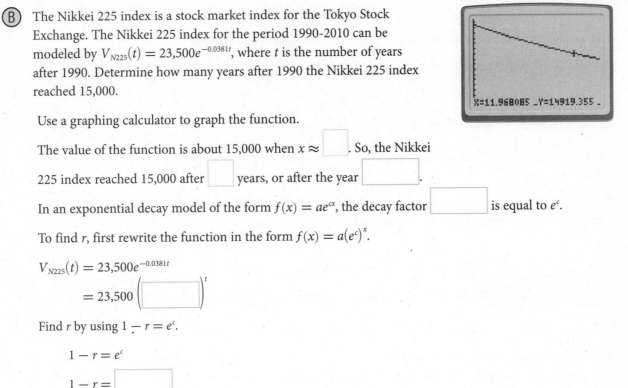

X=11.968085 _Y=14919.355 .

Use a graphing calculator to graph the function.

The value of the function is about 15,000 when $x \approx$ [ ]. So, the Nikkei

225 index reached 15,000 after [ ] years, or after the year [ ].

In an exponential decay model of the form $f(x) = ae^{cx}$, the decay factor [ ] is equal to e^c.

To find r, first rewrite the function in the form $f(x) = a(e^c)^x$.

$V_{N225}(t) = 23{,}500e^{-0.0381t}$

$$= 23{,}500 \left(\boxed{} \right)^t$$

Find r by using $1 - r = e^c$.

$1 - r = e^c$

$1 - r =$ [ ]

$r =$ [ ] $\approx$ [ ]

So, the decay rate is [ ] %.

4. A paleontologist uncovers a fossil of a saber-toothed cat in California. The paleontologist analyzes the fossil and concludes that the specimen contains 15% of its original carbon-14. The percent of original carbon-14 in a specimen after t years can be modeled by $N(t) = 100e^{-0.00012t}$, where t is the number of years after the specimen died. Use a graphing calculator to determine the age of the fossil. Then determine the decay rate of the function.

© Houghton Mifflin Harcourt Publishing Company • Image Credits: ©Julie Dermansky/Corbis

💬 Elaborate

5. Which transformations of $f(x) = e^x$ change the function's end behavior?

_____

_____

6. Which transformations change the location of the graph's y-intercept?

_____

_____

7. Why can the function $f(x) = ae^{cx}$ be used as an exponential growth model and as an exponential decay model? How can you tell if the function represents growth or decay?

_____

_____

_____

_____

8. **Essential Question Check-In** How are reference points helpful when graphing transformations of $f(x) = e^x$ or when writing equations for transformed graphs?

_____

_____

_____

⭐ Evaluate: Homework and Practice

- Online Homework
- Hints and Help
- Extra Practice

1. What does the value of $f(x) = \left(1 + \frac{1}{x}\right)^x$ approach as x increases without bound?

2. Identify the key attributes of $f(x) = e^x$, including the domain and range in set notation, the end behavior, and all intercepts.

Predict the effect of the parameters *h*, *k*, or *a* on the graph of the parent function $f(x) = e^x$. Identify any changes of domain, range, or end behavior.

3. $g(x) = f\left(x - \dfrac{1}{2}\right)$

4. $g(x) = f(x) - \dfrac{5}{2}$

5. $g(x) = -\dfrac{1}{4}f(x)$

6. $g(x) = \dfrac{27}{2}f(x)$

7. The graph of $f(x) = ce^x$ crosses the y-axis at $(0, c)$, where *c* is some constant. Where does the graph of $g(x) = f(x) - d$ cross the *y*-axis?

Given the function of the form $g(x) = a \cdot e^{x-h} + k$, identify the reference points and use them to draw the graph. State the domain and range in set notation.

8. $g(x) = e^{x-1} + 2$

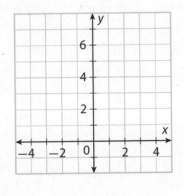

9. $g(x) = -e^{x+1} - 1$

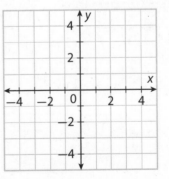

10. $g(x) = \frac{3}{2} e^{x-1} - 3$

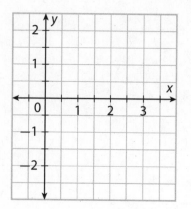

11. $g(x) = -\frac{5}{3} e^{x-4} + 2$

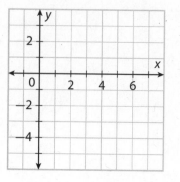

Write the function whose graph is shown. State the domain and range in set notation.

12.

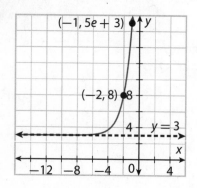

(−1, 5e + 3)   y

(−2, 8) 8

4   y = 3

−12 −8 −4 0   4   x

13.

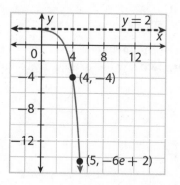

y = 2

y

0   4   8   12   x

−4   (4, −4)

−8

−12

(5, −6e + 2)

Solve each problem using a graphing calculator. Then determine the growth rate or decay rate of the function.

14. Medicine Technetium-99m, a radioisotope used to image the skeleton and the heart muscle, has a half-life of about 6 hours. Use the decay function $N(t) = N_0 e^{-0.1155t}$, where N_0 is the initial amount and t is the time in hours, to determine how many hours it takes for a 250 milligram dose to decay to 16 milligrams.

15. Ecology The George River herd of caribou in Canada was estimated to be about 4700 in 1954 and grew at an exponential rate to about 472,000 in 1984. Use the exponential growth function $P(t) = P_0 e^{0.154t}$, where P_0 is the initial population, t is the time in years after 1954, and $P(t)$ is the population at time t, to determine how many years after 1984 the herd reached 25 million.

16. **Explain the Error** A classmate claims that the function $g(x) = -4e^{x-5} + 6$ is the parent function $f(x) = e^x$ reflected across the y-axis, vertically compressed by a factor of 4, translated to the left 5 units, and translated up 6 units. Explain what the classmate described incorrectly and describe $g(x)$ as a series of transformations of $f(x)$.

17. **Multi-Step** Newton's law of cooling states that the temperature of an object decreases exponentially as a function of time, according to $T = T_s + (T_0 - T_s)e^{-kt}$, where T_0 is the initial temperature of the liquid, T_s is the surrounding temperature, and k is a constant. For a time in minutes, the constant for coffee is approximately 0.283. The corner coffee shop has an air temperature of 70°F and serves coffee at 206°F. Coffee experts say coffee tastes best at 140°F.

   a. How long does it take for the coffee to reach its best temperature?

   b. The air temperature on the patio outside the coffee shop is 86 °F. How long does it take for coffee to reach its best temperature there?

c. Find the time it takes for the coffee to cool to 71°F in both the coffee shop and the patio. Explain how you found your answer.

18. Analyze Relationships The graphing calculator screen shows the graphs of the functions $f(x) = 2^x$, $f(x) = 10^x$, and $f(x) = e^x$ on the same coordinate grid. Identify the common attributes and common point(s) of the three graphs. Explain why the point(s) is(are) common to all three graphs.

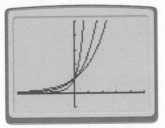

Lesson Performance Task

The ever-increasing amount of carbon dioxide in Earth's atmosphere is an area of concern for many scientists. In order to more accurately predict what the future consequences of this could be, scientists make mathematic models to extrapolate past increases into the future. A model developed to predict the annual mean carbon dioxide level L in Earth's atmosphere in parts per million t years after 1960 is $L(t) = 36.9 \cdot e^{0.0223t} + 280$.

a. Use the function $L(t)$ to describe the graph of $L(t)$ as a series of transformations of $f(t) = e^t$.

b. Find and interpret $L(80)$, the carbon dioxide level predicted for the year 2040. How does it compare to the carbon dioxide level in 2015?

c. Can $L(t)$ be used as a model for all positive values of t? Explain.

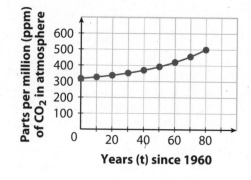

Name_____ Class_____ Date_____

13.4 Compound Interest

Essential Question: How do you model the value of an investment that earns compound interest?

Resource Locker

⊘ **Explore** **Comparing Simple and Compound Interest**

A *bond* is a type of investment that you buy with cash and for which you receive interest either as the bond matures or when it matures. A *conventional bond* generates an interest payment, sometimes called a *coupon payment*, on a regular basis, typically twice a year. The interest payments end when the bond matures and the amount you paid up-front is returned to you.

A *zero-coupon bond*, on the other hand, requires you to invest less money up-front and pays you its maturity value, which includes all accumulated interest, when the bond matures. Over the life of the bond, the interest that is earned each period itself earns interest until the bond matures.

The basic difference between a conventional bond and a zero-coupon bond is the type of interest earned. A conventional bond pays simple interest, whereas a zero-coupon bond pays **compound interest**, which is interest that earns interest.

Ⓐ For $1000, you can buy a conventional bond that has a maturity value of $1000, has a maturity date of 4 years, and pays 5% annual interest. Calculate the interest that the investment earns annually by completing the table. (Bear in mind that interest earned is paid to you and not reinvested.)

	Conventional Bond		
Year	**Value of Investment at Beginning of Year**	**Interest Earned for Year (Paid to the Investor)**	**Value of Investment at End of Year**
0			$1000
1	$1000	$1000(0.05) = $▢	$▢
2	$1000	$1000(0.05) = $▢	$▢
3	$1000	$1000(0.05) = $▢	$▢
4	$1000	$1000(0.05) = $▢	$▢

© Houghton Mifflin Harcourt Publishing Company · Image Credits: ©Treasury Department/AP Images

B For $822.70, you can buy a zero-coupon bond that has a maturity value of $1000, has a maturity date of 4 years, and pays 5% annual interest. Calculate the interest that the investment earns annually by completing the table. (Bear in mind that interest earned is reinvested and not paid to you until the bond matures.)

		Zero-Coupon Bond	
Year	Value of Investment at Beginning of Year	Interest Earned for Year (Reinvested)	Value of Investment at End of Year
0			$822.70
1	$822.70	$822.70(0.05) = $ ____	$822.70 + $ ____ = $ ____
2	$ ____	$ ____ (0.05) = $ ____	$ ____ + $ ____ = $ ____
3	$ ____	$ ____ (0.05) = $ ____	$ ____ + $ ____ = $ ____
4	$ ____	$ ____ (0.05) = $ ____	$ ____ + $ ____ = $1000

Reflect

1. Describe the difference between how simple interest is calculated and how compound interest is calculated.

_____

_____

_____

_____

2. If $V(t)$ represents the value of an investment at time t, in whole numbers of years starting with $t = 0$ and ending with $t = 4$, write a constant function for the last column in the first table and an exponential function for the last column in the second table.

_____

_____

_____

_____

© Houghton Mifflin Harcourt Publishing Company

Modeling Interest Compounded Annually

Recall that the general exponential growth function is $f(t) = a(1 + r)^t$. When this function is applied to an investment where interest is compounded annually at a rate r, the function is written as $V(t) = P(1 + r)^t$ where $V(t)$ is the value V of the investment at time t and P is the *principal* (the amount invested).

Ⓐ A person invests $3500 in an account that earns 3% annual interest. Find when the value of the investment reaches $10,000.

Let $P = 3500$ and $r = 0.03$. Then $V(t) = P(1 + r)^t = 3500(1.03)^t$.

Graph $y = 3500(1.03)^x$ on a graphing calculator. Also graph the line $y = 10,000$ and find the point where the graphs intersect.

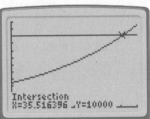

Intersection
X=35.516396 Y=10000

The value of the function is 10,000 at $x \approx 35.5$. So, the investment reaches a value of $10,000 in approximately 35.5 years.

Ⓑ A person invests $200 in an account that earns 6.25% annual interest. Find when the value of the investment reaches $5000.

Let $P =$ _____ and $r =$ _____ . Then $V(t) = P(1 + r)^t =$ _____ (_____)^t .

Graph the function on a graphing calculator. Also graph the line

$y =$ _____ . and find the point of intersection.

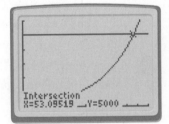

Intersection
X=53.09519 Y=5000

The value of the function is _____ at $x \approx$ _____ . So, the investment reaches a value of $5000 in

approximately _____ years.

Your Turn

3. A person invests $1000 in an account that earns 5.5% annual interest. Find when the value of the investment has doubled.

Modeling Interest Compounded More than Once a Year

Interest may be earned more frequently than once a year, such as semiannually (every 6 months), quarterly (every 3 months), monthly, and even daily. If the number of times that interest is compounded in a year is n, then the interest rate per compounding period is $\frac{r}{n}$ (where r is the annual interest rate), and the number of times that interest is compounded in t years is nt. So, the exponential growth function becomes $V(t) = P\left(1 + \frac{r}{n}\right)^{nt}$.

(A) A person invests $1200 in an account that earns 2% annual interest compounded quarterly. Find when the value of the investment reaches $1500.

Let $P = 1200$, $r = 0.02$, and $n = 4$. Then $V(t) = P\left(1 + \frac{r}{n}\right)^{nt} = 1200\left(1 + \frac{0.02}{4}\right)^{4t} = 1200(1.005)^{4t}$.

Graph the function $y = 1200(1.005)^{4x}$ on a graphing calculator. Also graph the line $y = 1500$ and find the point where the graphs intersect.

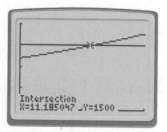

The value of the function is 1500 at $x \approx 11.2$. So, the investment reaches a value of $1500 in approximately 11.2 years.

(B) A person invests $600 in an account that earns 6.25% annual interest compounded semiannually. Find when the value of the investment reaches $1700.

Let $P = \boxed{}$, $r = \boxed{}$, and $n = \boxed{}$.

Then $V(t) = P\left(1 + \frac{r}{n}\right)^{nt} = \boxed{}\left(1 + \dfrac{\boxed{}}{\boxed{}}\right)^{\boxed{}\,t} = \boxed{}\left(\boxed{}\right)^{\boxed{}\,t}$.

Graph the function on a graphing calculator. Also graph the line $y = \boxed{}$ and find the point where the graphs intersect.

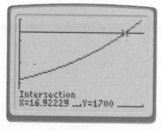

The value of the function is _____ at $x \approx \boxed{}$. So, the investment reaches a value of $1700 in approximately _____ years.

4. A person invests $8000 in an account that earns 6.5% annual interest compounded daily. Find·when the value of the investment reaches $20,000.

🔑 Explain 3 Modeling Interest Compounded Continuously

By letting $m = \frac{n}{r}$, you can rewrite the model $V(t) = P\left(1 + \frac{r}{n}\right)^{nt}$ as $V(t) = P\left(1 + \frac{1}{m}\right)^{mrt}$ because

$\frac{r}{n} = \frac{1}{m}$ and $nt = mrt$. Then, rewriting $V(t) = P\left(1 + \frac{1}{m}\right)^{mrt}$ as $V(t) = P\left[\left(1 + \frac{1}{m}\right)^{m}\right]^{rt}$ and

letting n increase without bound, which causes m to increase without bound, you see that $\left(1 + \frac{1}{m}\right)^{m}$ approaches e, and the model simply becomes $V(t) = Pe^{rt}$. This model gives the value of an investment with principal P and annual interest rate r when interest is compounded *continuously*.

Ⓐ A person invests $5000 in an account that earns 3.5% annual interest compounded continuously. Find when the value of the investment reaches $12,000.

Let $P = 5000$ and $r = 0.035$. Then $V(t) = 5000e^{0.035t}$.

Graph $y = 5000e^{0.035x}$. on a graphing calculator. Also graph the line $y = 12,000$ and find the point where the graphs intersect.

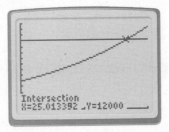

The value of the function is 12,000 at $x \approx 25$. So, the investment reaches a value of $12,000 in approximately 25 years.

(B) The principal amount, $350, earns 6% annual interest compounded continuously. Find when the value reaches $1800.

Let $P =$ ☐ and $r =$ ☐. Then $V(t) =$ ☐ $e^{\boxed{}t}$.

Graph the function on a graphing calculator. Also graph the line $y =$ ☐ and find the point where the graphs intersect.

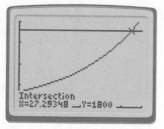

Intersection
X=27.29348 __Y=1800 ___

The value of the function is _____ at $x \approx$ ☐. So, the investment reaches a value of $1800 in approximately _____ years.

Your Turn

5. A person invests $1550 in an account that earns 4% annual interest compounded continuously. Find when the value of the investment reaches $2000.

Explain 4 Finding and Comparing Effective Annual Interest Rates

The value-of-an-investment function $V(t) = P\left(1 + \frac{r}{n}\right)^{nt} = P\left[\left(1 + \frac{r}{n}\right)^{n}\right]^{\wedge}t$, where interest is compounded

n times per year, is an exponential function of the form $f(t) = ab^t$ where $a = P$ and $b = \left(1 + \frac{r}{n}\right)^{n}$. When

the base of an exponential function is greater than 1, the function is an exponential growth function where the

base is the growth factor and 1 less than the base is the growth rate. So, the growth rate for $V(t) = P\left(1 + \frac{r}{n}\right)^{nt}$ is

$b - 1 = \left(1 + \frac{r}{n}\right)^{n} - 1$. This growth rate is called the investment's *effective annual interest rate R*, whereas

r is called the investment's *nominal annual interest rate*.

Similarly, for the value-of-an-investment function $V(t) = Pe^{rt} = P\left[e^{r}\right]^{t}$, where interest is compounded continuously, the growth factor is e^r, and the growth rate is $e^r - 1$. So, in this case, the effective annual interest rate is $R = e^r - 1$.

For an account that earns interest compounded more than once a year, the effective annual interest rate is the rate that would produce the same amount of interest if interest were compounded annually instead. The effective rate allows you to compare two accounts that have different nominal rates and different compounding periods.

(A) Arturo plans to make a deposit in one of the accounts shown in the table. To maximize the interest that the account earns, which account should he choose?

	Account X	Account Y
Nominal Annual Interest Rate	2.5%	2.48%
Compounding Period	Quarterly	Monthly

For Account X, interest is compounded quarterly, so $n = 4$. The nominal rate is 2.5%, so $r = 0.025$.

$$R_X = \left(1 + \frac{r}{n}\right)^n - 1 \qquad \text{Use the formula for the effective rate.}$$

$$= \left(1 + \frac{0.025}{4}\right)^4 - 1 \qquad \text{Substitute.}$$

$$\approx 0.02524 \qquad \text{Simplify.}$$

For Account Y, interest is compounded monthly, so $n = 12$. The nominal rate is 2.48%, so $r = 0.0248$.

$$R_Y = \left(1 + \frac{r}{n}\right)^n - 1 \qquad \text{Use the formula for the effective rate.}$$

$$= \left(1 + \frac{0.0248}{12}\right)^{12} - 1 \qquad \text{Substitute.}$$

$$\approx 0.02508 \qquad \text{Simplify.}$$

Account X has an effective rate of 2.524%, and Account Y has an effective rate of 2.508%, so Account X has a greater effective rate, and Arturo should choose Account X.

(B) Harriet plans to make a deposit in one of two accounts. Account A has a 3.24% nominal rate with interest compounded continuously, and Account B has a 3.25% nominal rate with interest compounded semiannually. To maximize the interest that the account earns, which account should she choose?

For Account A, interest is compounded continuously. The nominal rate is 3.24%, so $r = \boxed{}$.

$$R_A = e^r - 1 \qquad \text{Use the formula for the effective rate.}$$

$$= e^{\square} - 1 \qquad \text{Substitute.}$$

$$\approx \boxed{} \qquad \text{Simplify.}$$

© Houghton Mifflin Harcourt Publishing Company

For Account B, interest is compounded semiannually, so so $n =$ ☐ . The nominal rate is 3.25%,

so $r =$ ☐

$$R_B = \left(1 + \frac{r}{n}\right)^n - 1$$ Use the formula for the effective rate.

$$= \left(1 + \frac{\boxed{}}{\boxed{}}\right)^{\boxed{}} - 1 \quad \text{Substitute.}$$

$$\approx \boxed{}$$ Simplify.

Account A has an effective rate of _____%, and Account B has an effective rate of _____%,

so Account _____ has a greater effective rate, and Harriet should choose Account _____.

Your Turn

6. Jaclyn plans to make a deposit in one of the accounts shown in the table. To maximize the interest that the account earns, which account should she choose?

	Account X	Account Y
Nominal Annual Interest Rate	4.24%	4.18%
Compounding Period	Annually	Daily

© Houghton Mifflin Harcourt Publishing Company • Image Credits: ©David R. Frazier Photolibrary, Inc./Alamy

7. Explain the difference between an investment's nominal annual interest rate and its effective annual interest rate.

8. **Essential Question Check-In** List the three functions used to model an investment that earns compound interest at an annual rate r. Identify when each function is used.

Evaluate: Homework and Practice

- Online Homework
- Hints and Help
- Extra Practice

1. A person invests $2560 in an account that earns 5.2% annual interest. Find when the value of the investment reaches $6000.

2. A person invests $1800 in an account that earns 2.46% annual interest. Find when the value of the investment reaches $3500.

3. Emmanuel invests $3600 and Kelsey invests $2400. Both investments earn 3.8% annual interest. How much longer will it take Kelsey's investment to reach $10,000 than Emmanuel's investment?

4. Jocelyn invests $1200 in an account that earns 2.4% annual interest. Marcus invests $400 in an account that earns 5.2% annual interest. Find when the value of Marcus's investment equals the value of Jocelyn's investment and find the common value of the investments at that time.

5. A person invests $350 in an account that earns 3.65% annual interest compounded semiannually. Find when the value of the investment reaches $5675.

6. Molly invests $8700 into her son's college fund, which earns 2% annual interest compounded daily. Find when the value of the fund reaches $12,000.

7. A person invests $200 in an account that earns 1.98% annual interest compounded quarterly. Find when the value of the investment reaches $500.

8. Hector invests $800 in an account that earns 6.98% annual interest compounded semiannually. Rebecca invests $1000 in an account that earns 5.43% annual interest compounded monthly. Find when the value of Hector's investment equals the value of Rebecca's investment and find the common value of the investments at that time.

© Houghton Mifflin Harcourt Publishing Company • Image Credits: ©Rubberball/Alamy

9. A person invests $6750 in an account that earns 6.23% annual interest compounded continuously. Find when the value of the investment reaches $15,000.

10. A person invests $465 in an account that earns 3.1% annual interest compounded continuously. Find when the value of the investment reaches $2400.

11. Lucy invests $800 in an account that earns 6.12% annual interest compounded continuously. Juan invests $1600 in an account that earns 3.9% annual interest compounded continuously. Find when the value of Lucy's investment equals the value of Juan's investment and find the common value of the investments at that time.

12. Paula plans to make a deposit in one of the accounts shown in the table. To maximize the interest that the account earns, which account should she choose?

	Account X	Account Y
Nominal Annual Interest rate	2.83%	2.86%
Compounding Period	Continuously	Annually

© Houghton Mifflin Harcourt Publishing Company

13. Tanika plans to make a deposit to one of two accounts. Account A has a 3.78% nominal rate with interest compounded daily, and Account B has a 3.8% nominal rate with interest compounded monthly. To maximize the interest that the account earns, which account should she choose?

14. Kylie plans to deposit $650 in one of the accounts shown in the table. She chooses the account with the greater effective rate. How much money will she have in her account after 10 years?

	Account X	Account Y
Nominal Annual Interest Rate	4.13%	4.12%
Compounding Period	Semiannually	Quarterly

15. A person invests $2860 for 15 years in an account that earns 4.6% annual interest. Match each description of a difference in interest earned on the left with the actual difference listed on the right.

    A. Difference between compounding interest   _____ $14.89
         semiannually and annually

    B. Difference between compounding interest   _____ $21.98
         quarterly and semiannually

    C. Difference between compounding interest   _____ $0.25
         monthly and quarterly

    D. Difference between compounding interest   _____ $42.75
         daily and monthly

    E. Difference between compounding interest   _____ $7.27
         continuously and daily

16. Multi-Step Ingrid and Harry are saving to buy a house. Ingrid invests $5000 in an account that earns 3.6% interest compounded quarterly. Harry invests $7500 in an account that earns 2.8% interest compounded semiannually.

    a. Find a model for each investment.

b. Use a graphing calculator to find when the combined value of their investments reaches $15,000.

17. Explain the Error A student is asked to find when the value of an investment of $5200 in an account that earns 4.2% annual interest compounded quarterly reaches $16,500. The student uses the model $V(t) = 5200(1.014)^{3t}$ and finds that the investment reaches a value of $16,500 after approximately 27.7 years. Find and correct the student's error.

18. Communicate Mathematical Ideas For a certain price, you can buy a zero-coupon bond that has a maturity value of $1000, has a maturity date of 4 years, and pays 5% annual interest. How can the present value (the amount you pay for the bond) be determined from the future value (the amount you get when the bond matures)?

Lesson Performance Task

The grandparents of a newborn child decide to establish a college fund for her. They invest $10,000 into a fund that pays 4.5% interest compounded continuously.

   a. Write a model for the value of the investment over time and find the value of the investment when the child enters college at 18 years old.

   b. In 2013, the average annual public in-state college tuition was $8893, which was 2.9% above the 2012 cost. Use these figures to write a model to project the amount of money needed to pay for one year's college tuition 18 years into the future. What amount must be invested in the child's college fund to generate enough money in 18 years to pay for the first year's college tuition?

Essential Question: How can you use exponential functions to solve real-world problems?

Key Vocabulary
exponential decay
  (decremento exponencial)
exponential function
  (función exponencial)
exponential growth
  (crecimiento exponencial)

KEY EXAMPLE   *(Lesson 13.2)*

$g(x) = 3^{x+1}$ is a transformation of the function $f(x) = 3^x$. Sketch a graph of $g(x) = 3^{x+1}$.

$g(x) = 3^{x+1} = f(x + 1)$

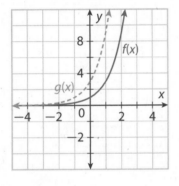

Because $g(x) = 3^{x+1} = f(x + 1)$, the graph of g can be obtained by shifting the graph of f one unit to the left, as shown.

The solid line represents $f(x) = 3^x$.
The dashed line represents $g(x) = 3^{x+1}$.

KEY EXAMPLE   *(Lesson 13.4)*

Which of the following accounts has a greater effective rate?

	Account X	Account Y
Nominal Interest Rate	3.5%	3.49%
Compounding Period	Quarterly	Weekly

$R_x = \left(1 + \dfrac{r}{n}\right)^n - 1$ Use the formula for the effective rate.

$= \left(1 + \dfrac{0.035}{4}\right)^4 - 1$ Substitute.

≈ 0.03546 Simplify.

$R_y = \left(1 + \dfrac{r}{n}\right)^n - 1$ Use the formula for the effective rate.

$= \left(1 + \dfrac{0.0349}{52}\right)^{52} - 1$ Substitute.

≈ 0.0355 Simplify.

Account Y has the higher effective rate.

EXERCISES

Sketch the graphs of the following transformations. *(Lessons 13.1, 13.2, 13.3)*

1. $g(x) = -2(0.5)^x$

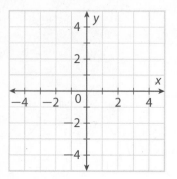

2. $f(x) = \left(\dfrac{1}{2}\right)^{-x}$

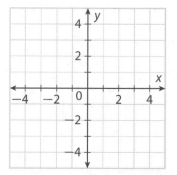

3. $f(x) = 2e^{x-2} + 1$

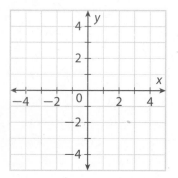

4. $g(x) = \left(\dfrac{3}{5}\right)^x$

MODULE PERFORMANCE TASK

That's The Way the Ball Bounces

Kingston is a chemical engineer who is testing the "bounciness" of two novel materials. He formed each material into two equal-sized spheres. Kingston then dropped each sphere on a hard surface and measured the heights the spheres reached after each bounce. The results are shown in the table.

	Heights (cm)					
	h_0	h_1	h_2	h_3	h_4	h_5
Material A	90	63.0	44.1	30.9	21.6	15.1
Material B	90	49.5	27.2	15.0	8.2	4.5

Use the data to create mathematical models for the heights of the spheres. Compare the two materials. One of the two materials will be used for the tip of a pogo stick. Which material should Kingston recommend and why?

Use your own paper to complete the task. Be sure to write down all your data and assumptions. Then use graphs, numbers, words, or algebra to explain how you reached your conclusion.

13.1–13.4 Exponential Functions

- Online Homework
- Hints and Help
- Extra Practice

State the domain and range for the graphs of the following functions. *(Lessons 13.1, 13.2)*

1. $y = \left(\frac{1}{4}\right)^x$

2. $y = \left(\frac{1}{3}\right)^{(x-2)} + 2$

3. $y = -3 \cdot 2^{x+2}$

4. $y = 3^{x-2} - 1$

Identify the account that has the higher effective rate. *(Lessons 13.4)*

5.

	Account X	Account Y
Nominal Interest Rate	5%	5.2%
Compounding Period	Daily	Annually

6.

	Account A	Account B
Nominal Interest Rate	2.65%	2.6%
Compounding Period	Quarterly	Continuously

ESSENTIAL QUESTION

7. How can you tell whether an exponential function models exponential growth or exponential decay?

Assessment Readiness

1. Consider the base of exponential functions. Will the given base cause exponential growth? Select Yes or No for A–C.

   A. A base between 0 and 1   ◯ Yes   ◯ No

   B. A base greater than 1   ◯ Yes   ◯ No

   C. A base equal to 1   ◯ Yes   ◯ No

2. Consider an investment of $500 compounded annually with 3% interest. Choose True or False for each statement.

   A. After 3 years, if no money is withdrawn, the account will have $546.36   ◯ Yes   ◯ No

   B. The account will gain $15.00 every year.   ◯ Yes   ◯ No

   C. After 5 years, if no money is withdrawn, the account will have $562.75.   ◯ Yes   ◯ No

3. Jordan said that the asymptote of $y = \left(\frac{1}{2}\right)^{x-2} + 3$ is $y = 2$. Describe and correct his mistake.

4. Describe how $f(x) = |x|$ is changed to create $g(x) = \frac{3}{4}|x + 3| - 8$.

5. The graphs of $f(x) = 2^x$, $f(x) = 10^x$ and $f(x) = e^x$ all pass through a common point. Explain why the point $(0, 1)$ is common to all three functions.

Modeling with Exponential and Other Functions

Essential Question: How can modeling with exponential and other functions help you to solve real-world problems?

REAL WORLD VIDEO
Most people have to save up money for a major purchase like a car or new home. Check out some of the factors to consider when investing for long-term goals.

MODULE PERFORMANCE TASK PREVIEW
Double Your Money!

If you had some money to invest, how would you pick the investment option that would let your money grow fastest? The return on an investment depends on factors such as the length of time of the investment and the return rate. How can you use an exponential model to find out when an investment will double in value? Let's find out!

Are (YOU) Ready?

Complete these exercises to review skills you will need for this module.

Writing Linear Equations

- Online Homework
- Hints and Help
- Extra Practice

Example 1   Write an equation for the line that passes
through the points $(2, 3)$ and $(4, -1)$.

$\dfrac{-1-3}{4-2} = \dfrac{-4}{2} = -2$ Find the slope.

So $y = -2x + b$ Substitute slope for *m* in $y = mx + b$.

$3 = -2(2) + b$ Substitute $(2, 3)$ for *x*- and *y*-values.

$b = 7$ Solve for *b*.

The equation is $y = -2x + 7$.

Write an equation for the line that passes through the given points.

1. $(2, -5), (6, -3)$ **2.** $(4, -3), (-2, 15)$ **3.** $(4, 7), (-2, -2)$

Transforming Linear Functions

Example 2   Write the equation of $y = 9x - 2$ after a reflection across the
x-axis followed by a reflection across the *y*-axis.

$y = -1(9x - 2) \rightarrow y = -9x + 2$ Reflection across the *x*-axis

$y = -9(-x) + 2 \rightarrow y = 9x + 2$ Reflection across the *y*-axis

So $y = 9x + 2$ Reflected across both axes is
$y = 9x + 2$.

Write the equation of each function after a reflection across both axes.

4. $y = 2x + 1$ **5.** $y = -3x - 4$ **6.** $y = -0.2x + 6$

Equations Involving Exponents

Example 3   Solve $x^{\frac{2}{3}} = 16$ for *x*.

$\left(x^{\frac{2}{3}}\right)^{\frac{3}{2}} = \pm (16)^{\frac{3}{2}}$ Raise both sides to the same power.

$x = \pm \left(16^{\frac{1}{2}}\right)^3 = \pm (4)^3 = \pm 64$ Evaluate the right side.

So, $x = \pm 64$.

Solve for *x*.

7. $x^6 = 4096$ **8.** $x^{\frac{3}{2}} = 27$ **9.** $\dfrac{1}{3}x^{\frac{2}{5}} = 3$

14.1 Fitting Exponential Functions to Data

Resource Locker

Essential Question: What are ways to model data using an exponential function of the form $f(x) = ab^x$?

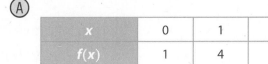 **Explore** **Identifying Exponential Functions from Tables of Values**

Notice for an exponential function $f(x) = ab^x$ that $f(x + 1) = ab^{x+1}$. By the product of powers property, $ab^{x+1} = a(b^x \cdot b^1) = ab^x \cdot b = f(x) \cdot b$. So, $f(x + 1) = f(x) \cdot b$. This means that increasing the value of x by 1 multiplies the value of $f(x)$ by b. In other words, for successive integer values of x, each value of $f(x)$ is b times the value before it, or, equivalently, the ratio between successive values of $f(x)$ is b. This gives you a test to apply to a given set of data to see whether it represents exponential growth or decay.

Each table gives function values for successive integer values of x. Find the ratio of successive values of $f(x)$ to determine whether each set of data can be modeled by an exponential function.

(A)

x	0	1	2	3	4
f(x)	1	4	16	64	256

$\dfrac{f(1)}{f(0)} = \boxed{}$; $\dfrac{f(2)}{f(1)} = \boxed{}$; $\dfrac{f(3)}{f(2)} = \boxed{}$; $\dfrac{f(4)}{f(3)} = \boxed{}$

The data are/are not exponential.

(B)

x	0	1	2	3	4
f(x)	1	7	13	19	25

$\dfrac{f(1)}{f(0)} = \boxed{}$; $\dfrac{f(2)}{f(1)} = \boxed{}$; $\dfrac{f(3)}{f(2)} = \boxed{}$; $\dfrac{f(4)}{f(3)} = \boxed{}$

The data are/are not exponential.

(C)

x	0	1	2	3	4
f(x)	1	4	13	28	49

$\dfrac{f(1)}{f(0)} = \boxed{}$; $\dfrac{f(2)}{f(1)} = \boxed{}$; $\dfrac{f(3)}{f(2)} = \boxed{}$; $\dfrac{f(4)}{f(3)} = \boxed{}$

The data are/are not exponential.

Ⓓ

x	0	1	2	3	4
f(x)	1	0.25	0.0625	0.015625	0.00390625

$\dfrac{f(1)}{f(0)} = \boxed{}$; $\dfrac{f(2)}{f(1)} = \boxed{}$; $\dfrac{f(3)}{f(2)} = \boxed{}$; $\dfrac{f(4)}{f(3)} = \boxed{}$

The data [are/are not] exponential.

Reflect

1. In which step(s) does the table show exponential growth? Which show(s) exponential decay? What is the base of the growth or decay?

_____

_____

2. In which step are the data modeled by the exponential function $f(x) = 4^{-x}$?

_____

3. What type of function model would be appropriate in each step not modeled by an exponential function? Explain your reasoning.

_____

_____

_____

_____

4. Discussion In the introduction to this Explore, you saw that the ratio between successive terms of $f(x) = ab^x$ is b. Find and simplify an expression for $f(x + c)$ where c is a constant. Then explain how this gives you a more general test to determine whether a set of data can be modeled by an exponential function.

_____

_____

_____

_____

🔧 **Explain 1**   **Roughly Fitting an Exponential Function to Data**

As the answer to the last Reflect question above indicates, if the ratios of successive values of the dependent variable in a data set for equally-spaced values of the independent variable are equal, an exponential function model fits. In the real world, sets of data rarely fit a model perfectly, but if the ratios are approximately equal, an exponential function can still be a good model.

Example 1

(A) **Population Statistics** The table gives the official population of the United States for the years 1790 to 1890.

Create an approximate exponential model for the data set. Then graph your function with a scatter plot of the data and assess its fit.

It appears that the ratio of the population in each decade to the population of the decade before it is pretty close to one and one third, so an exponential model should be reasonable.

For a model of the form $f(x) = ab^x$, $f(0) = a$. So, if x is the number of decades after 1790, the value when $x = 0$ is a, the initial population in 1790, or 3,929,214.

One way to estimate the growth factor, b, is to find the population ratios from decade to decade and average them:

Year	Total Population
1790	3,929,214
1800	5,308,483
1810	7,239,881
1820	9,638,453
1830	12,860,702
1840	17,063,353
1850	23,191,876
1860	31,443,321
1870	38,558,371
1880	50,189,209
1890	62,979,766

$$\frac{1.35 + 1.36 + 1.33 + 1.33 + 1.33 + 1.36 + 1.36 + 1.23 + 1.30 + 1.26}{10} \approx 1.32$$

An approximate model is $f(x) = 3.93(1.32)^x$, where $f(x)$ is in millions.

The graph is shown.

The graph looks like a good fit for the data. All of the points lie on, or close to, the curve.

Another way to estimate b is to choose a point other than $(0, a)$ from the scatter plot that appears would lie on, or very close to, the best-fitting exponential curve. Substitute the coordinates in the general formula and solve for b. For the plot shown, the point $(8, 38.56)$ looks like a good choice.

$$38.56 = 3.93 \cdot b^8$$

$$(9.81)^{\frac{1}{8}} \approx (b^8)^{\frac{1}{8}}$$

$$1.33 \approx b$$

This value of b results in a model very similar to the previous model.

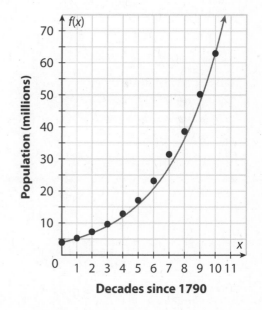

© Houghton Mifflin Harcourt Publishing Company

(B) **Movies** The table shows the decline in weekly box office revenue from its peak for one of 2013's top-grossing summer movies.

Create an approximate exponential model for the data set. Then graph your function with a scatter plot of the data and assess its fit.

Find the value of a in $f(x) = ab^x$.

When $x = 0$, $f(x) =$ _____. So, $a =$ _____.

Find an estimate for b.

Approximate the revenue ratios from week to week and average them:

$$\frac{0.59 + 0.42 + 0.69 + 0.54 + \boxed{}}{\boxed{}} \approx \boxed{}$$

An approximate model is $f(x) = \boxed{}$.

The graph looks like a very good fit for the data. All of the points except one (2 weeks after peak revenue) lie on, or very close to, the curve.

Week	Revenue (in Millions of Dollars)
0	95.3
1	55.9
2	23.7
3	16.4
4	8.8
5	4.8
6	3.3
7	1.9
8	1.1
9	0.6

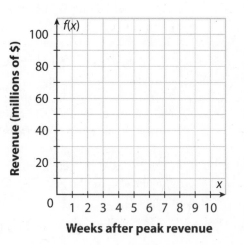

Weeks after peak revenue

5. **Fisheries** The total catch in tons for Iceland's fisheries from 2002 to 2010 is shown in the table.

Year	Total Catch (Millions of Tons)
2002	2.145
2003	2.002
2004	1.750
2005	1.661
2006	1.345
2007	1.421
2008	1.307
2009	1.164
2010	1.063

Create an approximate exponential model for the data set. Then graph your function with a scatter plot of the data and assess its fit.

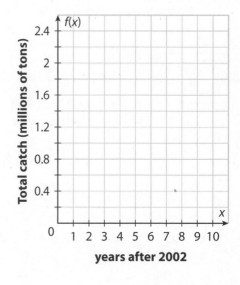

Fitting an Exponential Function to Data Using Technology

Previously you have used a graphing calculator to find a linear regression model of the form $y = ax + b$ to model data, and have also found quadratic regression models of the form $y = ax^2 + bx + c$. Similarly, you can use a graphing calculator to perform exponential regression to produce a model of the form $f(x) = ab^x$.

Example 2

Ⓐ **Population Statistics** Use the data from Example 1 Part A and a graphing calculator to find the exponential regression model for the data, and show the graph of the model with the scatter plot.

Using the STAT menu, enter the number of decades since 1790 in List1 and the population to the nearest tenth of a million in List2.

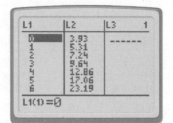

Using the STAT CALC menu, choose "ExpReg" and press ENTER until you see this screen:

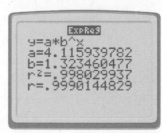

An approximate model is $f(x) = 4.116(1.323)^x$.

Making sure that STATPLOT is turned "On," enter the model into the Y = menu either directly or using the VARS menu and choosing "Statistics," "EQ," and "RegEQ." The graphs are shown using the ZoomStat window:

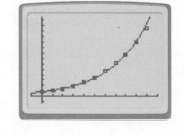

Plotted with the second graph from Example 1 (shown dotted), you can see that the graphs are nearly identical.

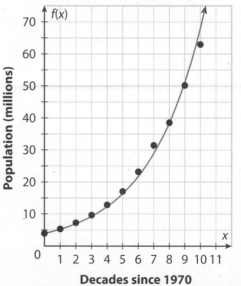

B **Movies** Use the data from Example 1 Part B and a graphing calculator to find the exponential regression model for the data. Graph the regression model on the calculator, then graph the model from Example 1 on the same screen using a dashed curve. How do the graphs of the models compare? What can you say about the actual decline in revenue from one week after the peak to two weeks after the peak compared to what the regression model indicates?

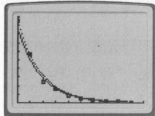

Enter the data and perform exponential regression.

The model (using 3 digits of precision) is $f(x) =$ ☐ .

Reflect

6. **Discussion** The U.S. population in 2014 was close to 320 million people. What does the regression model in Part A predict for the population in 2014? What does this tell you about extrapolating far into the future using an exponential model? How does the graph of the scatter plot with the regression model support this conclusion? (Note: The decade-to-decade U.S. growth dropped below 30% to stay after 1880, and below 20% to stay after 1910. From 2000 to 2010, the rate was below 10%.)

_____

_____

_____

_____

_____

Your Turn

7. **Fisheries** Use the data from YourTurn5 and a graphing calculator to find the exponential regression model for the data. Graph the regression model on the calculator, then graph the model from your answer to YourTurn5 on the same screen. How do the graphs of the models compare?

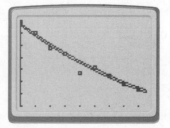

© Houghton Mifflin Harcourt Publishing Company

Solving a Real-World Problem Using a Fitted Exponential Function

In the real world, the purpose of finding a mathematical model is to help identify trends or patterns, and to use them to make generalizations, predictions, or decisions based on the data.

Example 3

Ⓐ The Texas population increased from 20.85 million to 25.15 million from 2000 to 2010.

a. Assuming exponential growth during the period, write a model where $x = 0$ represents the year 2000 and $x = 1$ represents the year 2010. What was the growth rate over the decade?

b. Use the power of a power property of exponents to rewrite the model so that b is the yearly growth factor instead of the growth factor for the decade. What is the yearly growth rate for this model? Verify that the model gives the correct population for 2010.

c. The Texas population was about 26.45 million in 2013. How does this compare with the prediction made by the model?

d. Find the model's prediction for the Texas population in 2035. Do you think it is reasonable to use this model to guide decisions about future needs for water, energy generation, and transportation needs. Explain your reasoning.

a. For a model of the form $f(x) = ab^x$, $a = f(0)$, so $a = 20.85$. To find an estimate for b, substitute $(x, f(x)) = (1, 25.5)$ and solve for b.

$$f(x) = a \cdot b^x$$

$$25.15 = 20.85 \cdot b^1$$

$$\frac{25.15}{20.85} = b$$

$$1.206 \approx b$$

An approximate model is $f(x) = 20.85(1.206)^x$. The growth rate was about 20.6%.

b. Because there are 10 years in a decade, the 10th power of the new b must give 1.206, the growth factor for the decade. So, $b^{10} = 1.206$, or $b = 1.206^{\frac{1}{10}}$. Use the power of a power property:

$$f(x) = 20.85(1.206)^x = 20.85\left(1.206^{\frac{1}{10}}\right)^{10x} \approx 20.85(1.019)^{10x}, \text{ where } x \text{ is measured in decades.}$$

If x is instead measured in years after 2000, the model is $f(x) = 20.85(1.019)^x$. The yearly growth rate is 1.9%.

The model gives a 2010 population of $f(x) = 20.85(1.019)^{10} \approx 25.17$. This agrees with the actual population within a rounding error.

c. Substitute $x = 13$ into the model $f(x) = 20.85(1.019)^x$:

$$f(13) = 20.85(1.019)^{13} \approx 26.63$$

The prediction is just a little bit higher than the actual population.

d. For 2035, $x = 35$: $f(35) = 20.85(1.019)^{35} \approx 40.3$. The model predicts a Texas population of about 40 million in 2035. Possible answer: Because it is very difficult to maintain a high growth rate with an already very large population, and with overall population growth slowing, it seems unreasonable that the population would increase from 25 to 40 million so quickly. But because using the model to project even to 2020 gives a population of over 30 million, it seems reasonable to make plans for the population to grow by several million people over a relatively short period.

(B) The average revenue per theater for the movie in Part B of the previous Examples is shown in the graph. (Note that for this graph, Week 0 corresponds to Week 2 of the graphs from the previous Examples.) The regression model is $y = 5.65(0.896)^x$.

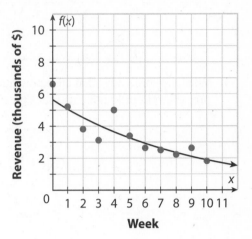

a. From Week 3 to Week 4, there is a jump of over 60% in the average weekly revenue per theater, but the total revenue for the movie for the corresponding week fell by over 30%. What must have occurred for this to be true?

_____

_____

b. A new theater complex manager showing a similar summer movie in a single theater worries about quickly dropping revenue the first few weeks, and wants to stop showing the movie. Suppose you are advising the manager. Knowing that the model shown reflects the long-term trend well for such movies, what advice would you give the manager?

_____

_____

_____

Reflect

8. **Discussion** Consider the situation in Example 3B about deciding when to stop showing the movie. How does an understanding of what other theater managers might do affect your decision?

_____

_____

_____

_____

Your Turn

9. Graph the regression model for the catch in Icelandic fisheries, $f(x) = 2.119(0.9174^x)$, to find when the model predicts the total catches to drop below 0.5 million tons (remember that $x = 0$ corresponds to 2002). Should the model be used to project actual catch into the future? Why or why not? What are some considerations that the model raises about the fishery?

10. How can you tell whether a given set of data can reasonably be modeled using an exponential function?

_____

_____

_____

11. What are some ways that an exponential growth or decay model can be used to guide decisions, preparations, or judgments about the future?

_____

_____

_____

_____

_____

12. Essential Question Check-In What are some ways to find an approximate exponential model for a set of data without using a graphing calculator?

_____

_____

_____

_____

_____

_____

⭐ Evaluate: Homework and Practice

Determine whether each set of data can be modeled by an exponential function. If it can, tell whether it represents exponential growth or exponential decay. If it can't, tell whether a linear or quadratic model is instead appropriate.

1.

x	0	1	2	3	4
f(x)	2	6	18	54	162

2.

x	1	2	3	4	5	6
f(x)	1	2	3	5	8	13

3.

x	0	1	2	3	4
f(x)	2	8	18	32	50

4.

x	5	10	15	20	25
f(x)	76.2	66.2	59.1	50.9	44.6

© Houghton Mifflin Harcourt Publishing Company

Three students, Anja, Ben, and Celia, are asked to find an approximate exponential model for the data shown. Use the data and scatter plot for Exercises 5–7.

x	0	1	2	3	4	5	6	7	8	9	10
f(x)	10	6.0	5.4	3.9	3.7	2.3	1.4	1.0	0.9	0.8	0.5

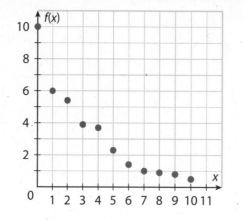

5. To find an approximate exponential model, Anja uses the first data point to find a, and then estimates b by finding the ratio of the first two function values. What is her model?

6. To find his model, Ben uses the first and last data points. What is his model?

7. Celia thinks that because the drop between the first two points is so large, the best model might actually have a y-intercept a little below 10. She uses $(0, 9.5)$ to estimate a in her model. To estimate b, she finds the average of the ratios of successive data values. What is her model? (Use two digits of precision for all quantities.)

8. **Classic Cars** The data give the estimated value in dollars of a
model of classic car over several years.

| 15,300 | 16,100 | 17,300 | 18,400 | 19,600 | 20,700 | 22,000 |

a. Find an approximate exponential model for the car's value
by averaging the successive ratios of the value. Then make
a scatter plot of the data, graph your model with the scatter
plot, and assess its fit to the data.

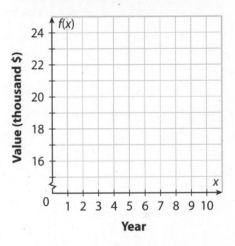

b. In the last year of the data, a car enthusiast spends $15,100 on a car of the given model that is in need
of some work. The owner then spends $8300 restoring it. Use your model to create a table of values
with a graphing calculator. How long does the function model predict the owner should keep the car
before it can be sold for a profit of at least $5000?

9. Movies The table shows the average price of a movie ticket in the United States from 2001 to 2010.

Year	2001	2002	2003	2004	2005	2006	2007	2008	2009	2010
Price ($)	5.66	5.81	6.03	6.21	6.41	6.55	6.88	7.18	7.50	7.89

a. Make a scatter plot of the data. Then use the first point and another point on the plot to find an approximate exponential model for the average ticket price. Then graph the model with your scatter plot and assess its fit to the data.

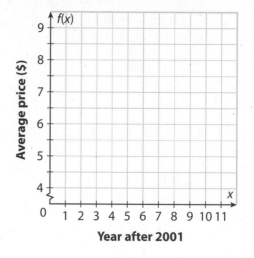

b. Use a graphing calculator to find a regression model for the data, and graph the model with the scatter plot. How does this model compare to your previous model?

c. What does the regression model predict for the average cost in 2014? How does this compare with the actual 2014 cost of about $8.35? A theater owner uses the model in 2010 to project income for 2014 assuming average sales of 490 tickets per day at the predicted price. If the actual price is instead $8.35, did the owner make a good business decision? Explain.

10. Pharmaceuticals A new medication is being studied to see how quickly it is metabolized in the body. The table shows how much of an initial dose of 15 milligrams remains in the bloodstream after different intervals of time.

Hours Since Administration	Amount Remaining (mg)
0	15
1	14.3
2	13.1
3	12.4
4	11.4
5	10.7
6	10.2
7	9.8

a. Use a graphing calculator to find a regression model. Use the calculator to graph the model with the scatter plot. How much of the drug is eliminated each hour?

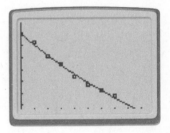

b. The half-life of a drug is how long it takes for half of the drug to be broken down or eliminated from the bloodstream. Using the Table function, what is the half-life of the drug to the nearest hour?

c. Doctors want to maintain at least 7 mg of the medication in the bloodstream for maximum therapeutic effect, but do not want the amount much higher for a long period. This level is reached after 12 hours. A student suggests that this means that a 15 mg dose should be given every 12 hours. Explain whether you agree with the student. (*Hint*: Given the medicine's decay factor, how much will be in the bloodstream after the first few doses?)

11. Housing The average selling price of a unit in a high-rise condominium complex over 5 consecutive years was approximately $184,300; $195,600; $204,500; $215,300; $228,200.

    a. Find an exponential regression model where x represents years after the initial year and $f(x)$ is in thousands of dollars.

    b. A couple wants to buy a unit in the complex. First, they want to save 20% of the selling price for a down payment. What is the model that represents 20% of the average selling price for a condominium?

    c. At the time that the average selling price is $228,200 (or when $x = 4$), the couple has $20,000 saved toward a down payment. They are living with family, and saving $1000 per month. Graph the model from Part b and a function that represents the couple's total savings on the same calculator screen. How much longer does the model predict it will take them to save enough money?

12. Business growth The growth in membership in thousands of a rapidly-growing Internet site over its first few years is modeled by $f(x) = 60(3.61)^x$ where x is in years and $x = 0$ represents the first anniversary of the site. Rewrite the model so that the growth factor represents weeks instead of years. What is the weekly growth factor? What does this model predict for the membership 20 weeks after the anniversary?

13. Which data set can be modeled by an exponential function $f(x) = ab^x$?

    a. $(0, 0.1), (1, 0.5), (2, 2.5), (3, 12.5)$

    b. $(0, 0.1), (1, 0.2), (2, 0.3), (3, 0.4)$

    c. $(0, 1), (1, 2), (2, 4), (4, 8)$

    d. $(0, 0.8), (1, 0.4), (2, 0.10), (3, 0.0125)$

H.O.T. Focus on Higher Order Thinking

14. Error analysis From the data $(2, 72.2), (3, 18.0), (4, 4.4), (5, 1.1), (6, 0.27)$, a student sees that the ratio of successive values of $f(x)$ is very close to 0.25, so that an exponential model is appropriate. From the first term, the student obtains $a = 72.2$, and writes the model $f(x) = 72.2(0.25)^x$. The student graphs the model with the data and observes that it does not fit the data well. What did the student do wrong? Correct the student's model.

15. Critical thinking For the data $(0, 5), (1, 4), (2, 3.5), (3, 3.25), (4, 3.125), (5, 3.0625)$, the ratio of consecutive y-values is not constant, so you cannot write an exponential model $f(x) = ab^x$. But the difference in the values from term to term, 1, 0.5, 0.25, 0.125, 0.0625, shows exponential decay with a decay factor of 0.5. How can you use this fact to write a model of the data that contains an exponential expression of the form ab^x?

16. Challenge Suppose that you have two data points (x_1, y_1) and (x_2, y_2) that you know are fitted by an exponential model $f(x) = ab^x$. Can you always find an equation for the model? Explain.

Lesson Performance Task

According to data from the U.S. Department of Agriculture, the number of farms in the United States has been decreasing over the past several decades. During this time, however, the average size of each farm has increased.

a. The average size in acres of a U.S. farm from 1940 to 1980 can be modeled by the function $A(t) = 174e^{0.022t}$ where t is the number of years since 1940. What was the average farm size in 1940? In 1980?

Farms in the United States	
Year	Farms (Millions)
1940	6.35
1950	5.65
1960	3.96
1970	2.95
1980	2.44
1990	2.15
2000	2.17

b. The table shows the number of farms in the United States from 1940 to 2000. Find an exponential model for the data using a calculator.

c. If you were to determine the exponential model without a calculator, would the value for a be the same as the value from the calculator? Explain your answer.

d. Based on the data in the table, predict the number of farms in the United States in 2014.

e. Using a graphing calculator, determine how many years it takes for the number of farms to decrease by 50%.

f. Using a graphing calculator, determine when the number of farms in the United States will fall below 1 million.

g. Does an exponential model seem appropriate for all of the data listed in the table? Why or why not?

14.2 Choosing Among Linear, Quadratic, and Exponential Models

Resource Locker

Essential Question: How do you choose among, linear, quadratic, and exponential models for a given set of data?

⊘ Explore   Developing Rules of Thumb for Visually Choosing a Model

When you work with data, you may not know whether a linear, quadratic, or exponential model will be a good fit. If the data lie along a curve that rises and then falls or falls and then rises, the data may be well-fitted by a quadratic model. But sometimes it may not be as clear. Consider the following scatter plots.

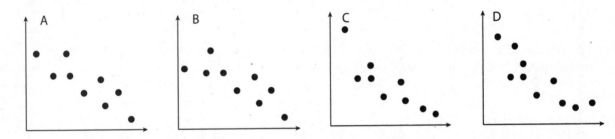

Ⓐ Look at scatter plot A. Do you think a linear model will be appropriate? Explain your reasoning. If you think a linear model is appropriate, what do you know about the lead coefficient?

_____

_____

Ⓑ Look at scatter plot B. What is different now that indicates that another kind of model might be appropriate? What characteristics would this model have?

_____

_____

_____

Ⓒ Look at scatter plot C. What about this plot indicates that yet another kind of model might be appropriate? What characteristics would this model have?

_____

_____

_____

© Houghton Mifflin Harcourt Publishing Company

Look at scatter plot D. This plot is very similar to plot C, but what indicates that a different model would be appropriate? What characteristics would this model have?

_____

_____

_____

Reflect

1. When can it be difficult to distinguish whether a quadratic or an exponential model is most appropriate?

_____

_____

2. Under what circumstances might it be difficult to tell exponential or quadratic data from linear data?

_____

_____

_____

3. For data that do not lie tightly along a curve or line, what is different about the last data point that can make it potentially more misleading than other points?

_____

_____

⊘ Explain 1   Modeling with a Linear Function

As noted in the Explore, it is not always immediately clear what kind of model best represents a data set. With experience, your ability to recognize signs and reasons for choosing one model over another will increase.

Example 1 Examine each scatter plot. Then complete the steps below.

Step 1: Choose the data set that appears to be best modeled by a linear function. Explain your choice, whether you think a linear model will be a close fit, and whether any other model might possibly be appropriate. What characteristics do you expect the linear model will have?

Step 2: Enter the data for your choice into your graphing calculator in two lists, and perform linear regression. Then give the model, defining your variables. What are the initial value and the rate of change of the model?

Step 3: Graph the model along with the scatter plot using your calculator, then assess how well the model appears to fit the data.

© Houghton Mifflin Harcourt Publishing Company · ©L.M. Otero/AP Images

A **Wildlife Conservation** Data sets and scatter plots for populations over time of four endangered, threatened, or scarce species are shown.

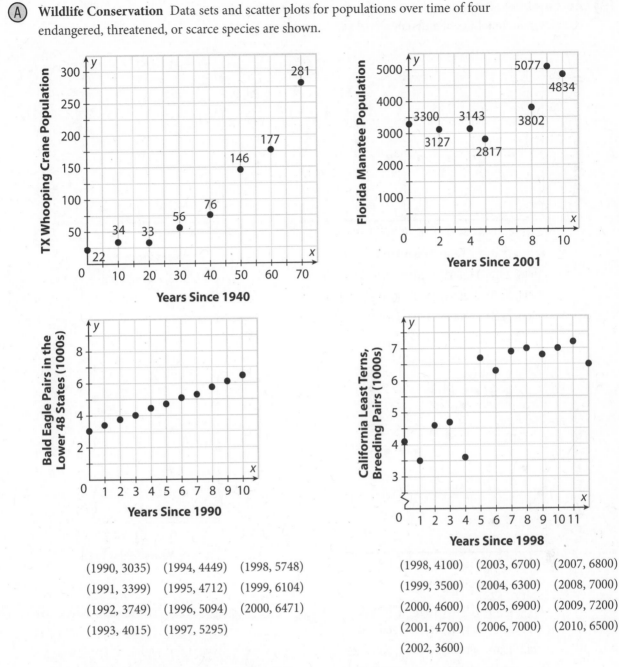

(1990, 3035) (1994, 4449) (1998, 5748)

(1991, 3399) (1995, 4712) (1999, 6104)

(1992, 3749) (1996, 5094) (2000, 6471)

(1993, 4015) (1997, 5295)

(1998, 4100) (2003, 6700) (2007, 6800)

(1999, 3500) (2004, 6300) (2008, 7000)

(2000, 4600) (2005, 6900) (2009, 7200)

(2001, 4700) (2006, 7000) (2010, 6500)

(2002, 3600)

Step 1: The bald eagle population is clearly the one best modeled by a linear function, as the increase in the number of pairs is very steady, with no apparent curving or changes in the trend that might indicate a different model. The model will have a y-intercept of about 3 (in thousands) and will have a slope very close to 0.34, since the rate of change all along the graph remains close to the average rate of change from the first point to the last.

Step 2: A regression model is $y = 338.2x + 3042$ where x is the number of years after 1990 and y is the number of breeding pairs in thousands. The initial value is 3042, and the rate of change is about 338 pairs per year.

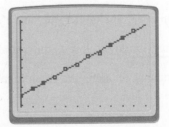

Step 3: The model is a very close fit to the data. It fits both the overall trend and the individual points very closely.

© Houghton Mifflin Harcourt Publishing Company

B **Automobiles** Data sets and scatter plots for various statistics about changes in automobiles of different model years are shown.

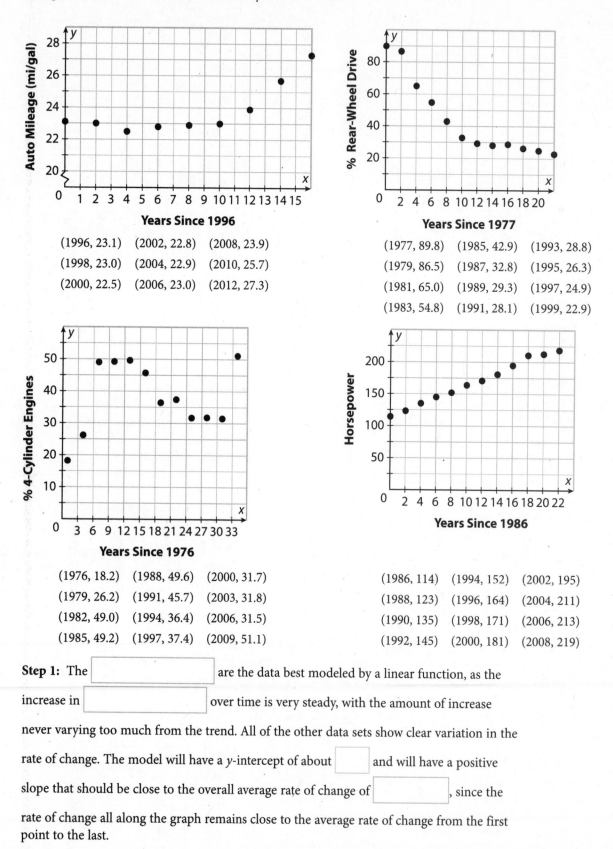

(1996, 23.1)   (2002, 22.8)   (2008, 23.9)

(1998, 23.0)   (2004, 22.9)   (2010, 25.7)

(2000, 22.5)   (2006, 23.0)   (2012, 27.3)

(1977, 89.8)   (1985, 42.9)   (1993, 28.8)

(1979, 86.5)   (1987, 32.8)   (1995, 26.3)

(1981, 65.0)   (1989, 29.3)   (1997, 24.9)

(1983, 54.8)   (1991, 28.1)   (1999, 22.9)

(1976, 18.2)   (1988, 49.6)   (2000, 31.7)

(1979, 26.2)   (1991, 45.7)   (2003, 31.8)

(1982, 49.0)   (1994, 36.4)   (2006, 31.5)

(1985, 49.2)   (1997, 37.4)   (2009, 51.1)

(1986, 114)   (1994, 152)   (2002, 195)

(1988, 123)   (1996, 164)   (2004, 211)

(1990, 135)   (1998, 171)   (2006, 213)

(1992, 145)   (2000, 181)   (2008, 219)

Step 1: The [   ] are the data best modeled by a linear function, as the

increase in [   ] over time is very steady, with the amount of increase

never varying too much from the trend. All of the other data sets show clear variation in the

rate of change. The model will have a *y*-intercept of about [   ] and will have a positive

slope that should be close to the overall average rate of change of [   ], since the

rate of change all along the graph remains close to the average rate of change from the first

point to the last.

Step 2: A regression model is [ ] where x is the number of years after

1986 and y is the [ ] for the model year. The initial value is about 114

horsepower, and the rate of change is about [ ].

Step 3: The model fits both the overall trend and the individual points very closely.

Your Turn

4. **Demographics** Data sets and scatter plots for various changes in the United States population over time are shown. Using these data, complete the three steps described at the beginning of Example 1. Also, tell whether you would expect the trend indicated by your model to continue for a time after the data shown, or whether you expect that it would soon change, and explain your answer.

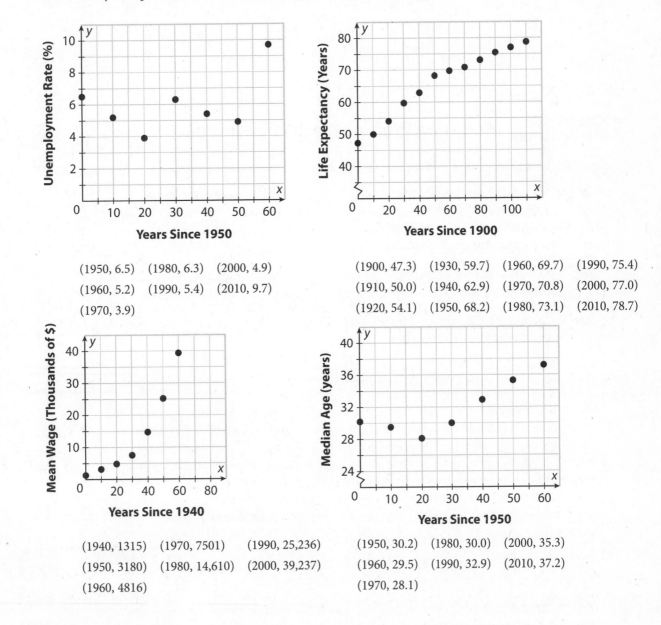

(1950, 6.5)   (1980, 6.3)   (2000, 4.9)
(1960, 5.2)   (1990, 5.4)   (2010, 9.7)
(1970, 3.9)

(1900, 47.3)   (1930, 59.7)   (1960, 69.7)   (1990, 75.4)
(1910, 50.0)   (1940, 62.9)   (1970, 70.8)   (2000, 77.0)
(1920, 54.1)   (1950, 68.2)   (1980, 73.1)   (2010, 78.7)

(1940, 1315)   (1970, 7501)   (1990, 25,236)
(1950, 3180)   (1980, 14,610)   (2000, 39,237)
(1960, 4816)

(1950, 30.2)   (1980, 30.0)   (2000, 35.3)
(1960, 29.5)   (1990, 32.9)   (2010, 37.2)
(1970, 28.1)

4. (continued)

🔑 Explain 2   Modeling With a Quadratic Function

Example 2   Using the groups of data sets and their scatter plots from Example 1:

Step 1: Choose the data set that appears to be best modeled by a quadratic function. Explain your choice, whether you think a quadratic model will be a close fit, and whether any other model might possibly be appropriate. What characteristics do you expect the quadratic model will have?

Step 2: Enter the data for your choice into your graphing calculator in two lists, and perform quadratic regression. Then give the model, defining your variables.

Step 3: Graph the model along with the scatter plot using your calculator, then assess how well the model appears to fit the data.

Ⓐ Use the data about animal populations in Example 1 Part A.

Step 1: The Florida manatee population appears to be the one best modeled by a quadratic function, as its scatter plot is the only one with a clear change in direction, and it clearly would not be well represented by a linear or exponential model. The whooping crane data might also be fit fairly well on one side of a quadratic model, but it might also be exponential. The quadratic model for the manatee population will have a positive leading coefficient since it opens upward, but it is hard to predict what the y-intercept or the vertex will be. Because the graph is not very symmetrical, the fit may not be very close.

Step 2: A regression model is $y = 48.50x^2 - 317.3x + 3411$ where x is the number of years after 2001 and y is the number of manatees

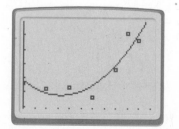

Step 3: The model is not a close fit, but it does look like an appropriate model for the overall trend during the time of the data. It misses the horizontal position for the vertex by a fairly wide margin, but otherwise is not too far from the data.

Ⓑ Use the data about automobiles in Example 1 Part B.

Step 1:

_____

_____

_____

_____

_____

_____

_____

_____

Step 2:

_____

_____

Step 3:

_____

_____

_____

Reflect

5. **Discussion** The Florida manatee has been under consideration for being downgraded from endangered to threatened. Do you believe the graph and model of the manatee population in Part A of this Example support this concept or argue against it? Explain your reasoning.

_____

_____

_____

_____

_____

6. How might the model for miles per gallon affect a decision on when to purchase a car?

_____

_____

_____

7. Using the data in Your Turn Exercise 4, complete the three steps described at the beginning of Example 2. Also, tell whether you would expect the trend indicated by your model to continue for a time after the data shown, or whether you expect that it would soon change, and explain your answer.

🔅 Explain 3 Modeling with an Exponential Function

Example 3 Using the groups of data sets and their scatter plots from Example 1:

Step 1: Choose the data set that appears to be best modeled by an exponential function. Explain your choice, whether you think an exponential model will be a close fit, and whether any other model might possibly be appropriate. What characteristics do you expect the exponential model will have?

Step 2: Enter the data for your choice into your graphing calculator in two lists, and perform exponential regression. Then give the model, defining your variables. What are the initial value, growth or decay factor, and growth or decay rate of the model?

Step 3: Graph the model along with the scatter plot using your calculator, then assess how well the model appears to fit the data.

(A) Use the data about animal populations in Example 1 Part A.

Step 1: The whooping crane population appears to be the one best modeled by an exponential function, as it rises increasingly quickly, but does not reflect a change in direction as a quadratic model can. Though the whooping crane plot is nearly linear in its midsection, the slow initial rise and fast later rise indicate that an exponential model is better. The California least tern data show a significant jump, but no clear pattern. An appropriate whooping crane model shows exponential growth, so the parameter b is greater than 1. Because the growth is not very large considering the time period of 70 years, however, the yearly growth factor will not be much above 1.

Step 2: A regression model is $y = 20.05(1.0374)^x$ where x is the number of years after 1940 and y is the population. The initial value for the model is 20 whooping cranes. The growth factor is 1.0374, and the growth rate is 0.0374, or about 3.74% per year.

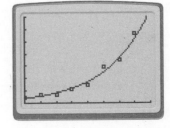

Step 3: The model is very good fit for the data. Some data points are a little above the curve and some a little below, but the fit is close and reflects the trend very well.

(B) Use the data about automobiles in Example 1 Part B.

Step 1:

_____

_____

_____

_____

_____

Step 2:

_____

_____

_____

Step 3:

_____

_____

_____

_____

_____

Reflect

8. **Discussion** What does the model for the whooping crane population predict for the population in 2040? Do you think it is possible that the whooping crane will be removed from the endangered species list any time in the next few decades? Explain.

Your Turn

9. Using the data in YourTurn Exercise 4, complete the three steps described at the beginning of Example 3. Also, tell whether you would expect the trend indicated by your model to continue for a time after the data shown, or whether you expect that it would soon change, and explain your answer.

Elaborate

10. **Discussion** How does making a prediction from a model help make a decision or judgment based on a given set of data?

11. Describe the process for obtaining a regression model using a graphing calculator.

_____

_____

_____

_____

_____

_____

_____

12. Essential Question Check-In How can a scatter plot of a data set help you determine the best type of model to choose for the data?

_____

_____

_____

_____

_____

_____

⭐ Evaluate: Homework and Practice

• Online Homework
• Hints and Help
• Extra Practice

1. Match each scatter plot with the most appropriate model from the following. Do not use any choice more than once.

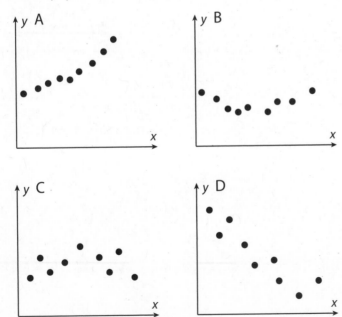

I. quadratic, $a > 0$

II. quadratic, $a < 0$

III. linear, $a < 0$

IV. exponential, $b > 1$

V. exponential, $b < 1$

In Exercises 2–5, for the data set given:

  a. Create a scatter plot of the data. What kind of model do you think is most appropriate? Why? What characteristics do you expect that this model will have?

  b. Use a graphing calculator to find an equation of the regression model. Then interpret the model, including the meaning of important parameters.

  c. Graph the regression model with its scatter plot using a graphing calculator. How well does the model fit?

  d. Answer the question following the data.

2. **Population Demographics** The data set shows the number of Americans living in multigenerational households.

Year	Number (in Millions)
1950	32
1960	27
1970	26
1980	28
1990	35
2000	42
2010	52

What does the model predict for the number in 2020? in 2040? Are these numbers reasonable? Explain.

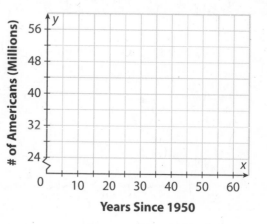

3. **Cycling** The data set shows the inseam length for different frame sizes for road bicycles.

Frame Size (cm)	Inseam Length (cm)
46	69
48	71
49	74
51	76
53	79
54	81
58	86
60	89
61	91

Jarrell has an inseam of 84 cm, but the table does not give a frame size for him. He graphs the model on a graphing calculator and finds that a y-value of 84 is closest to an x-value of 56. He decides he needs a 56 cm frame. Do you think this is a reasonable conclusion. Explain.

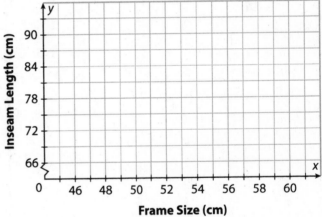

4. **Population Geography** The data set shows the percent of the U.S. population living in central cities.

What does your model predict for the percent of the population living in central cities in 2010? How much confidence would you have in this prediction? Explain. Given that the actual number for 2010 was about 36.9%, does this support your judgment?

Year	% of Population
1910	21.2
1920	24.2
1930	30.8
1940	32.5
1950	32.8
1960	32.3
1970	31.4
1980	30.0

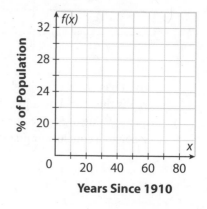

5. **Animal Migration** The data set shows the number of bald eagles counted passing a particular location on a migration route. Predict the number of bald eagles in 2033. How much confidence do you have in this prediction?

Year	Number of Eagles
1973	41
1978	79
1983	384
1988	261
1993	1725
1998	3289
2003	3356

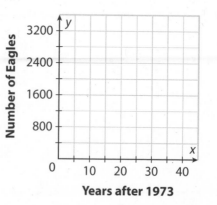

5. (continued)

6. **Smart Phones** For parts a–d, use the data in the table. The data set shows the percent of the world's population owning a smart phone.

a. Create a scatter plot of the data.

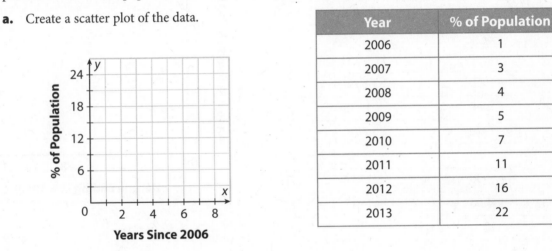

Year	% of Population
2006	1
2007	3
2008	4
2009	5
2010	7
2011	11
2012	16
2013	22

b. Use a graphing calculator to find equations for both exponential and quadratic regression models. Then interpret the models, including the meaning of important parameters.

c. Graph both regression models with the scatter plot using a graphing calculator. Do both models fit the data well? Does one seem significantly better than the other?

d. For how long after the data set do you think either model will be a good predictor? Explain your reasoning.

7. **Stock Market** The data set gives the U.S. stock market's average annual return rates for each of the last 11 decades.

Decade Ending	Annual Return Rate (%)
1910	9.96
1920	4.20
1930	14.95
1940	−0.63
1950	8.72
1960	19.28
1970	7.78
1980	5.82
1990	17.57
2000	18.17
2010	3.1

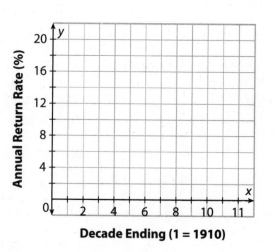

a. Make a scatter plot of the data.

b. What kind of model do you think is most appropriate for the data? Explain your reasoning.

c. Do the data give any kind of prediction about investing in the stock market for the future? Explain.

8. **Explain the Error** Out of curiosity, Julia enters the stock market data from Exercise 7 into her calculator and performs linear and quadratic regression. As she expected, there is almost no fit to the data at all. She then tries exponential regression, and get the message "ERR: DOMAIN." Why does she get this message?

9. **Critical Thinking** A student enters the road bicycle data from Exercise 3, accidentally performs quadratic regression instead of linear, and has the calculator graph the regression model with the scatter plot. The student sees this graph:

   The model graphed by the calculator is $y = -0.001241x^2 + 1.587x - 1.549$. It is obviously a very close fit to the data, and looks almost identical to the linear model. Explain how this can be true. (*Hint*: What happens when you zoom out?)

10. **Critical Thinking** A graphing calculator returns a linear regression equation $y = ax + b$, a quadratic regression equation $y = ax^2 + bx + c$, and an exponential regression equation $y = a \cdot b^x$. For exponential regression, a is always positive, which is not true of the other models. How does an exponential model differ from the other two models regarding translations of a parent function?

11. **Extension** In past work, you have used the correlation coefficient r, which indicates how well a line fits the data. The closer $|r|$ is to 1, the better the fit, and the closer to 0, the worse the fit. When you perform quadratic or exponential regression with a calculator, the *coefficient of determination* r^2 or R^2 serves a similar purpose. Return to the smart phone data in Exercise 6, and perform the quadratic and exponential regression again. (Make sure that "Diagnostics" is turned on in the Catalog menu of your calculator first.) Which model is the closer fit to the data, that is, for which model is R^2 closest to 1?

Lesson Performance Task

A student is given $50 to invest. The student chooses the investment very well. The following data shows the amount that the investment is worth over several years.

x (Years)	y (Dollars)
0	50
1	147
2	462
3	1411
4	4220
5	4431
6	4642

a. Determine an appropriate model for the data. If it is reasonable to break up the data so that you can use different models over different parts of the time, then do so. Explain the reasoning for choosing your model(s).

b. Write a situation that may reflect the given data.

Modeling with Exponential and Other Functions

Essential Question: How can modeling with exponential and other functions help you to solve real-world problems?

Key Vocabulary
exponential regression
(regresión exponencial)

KEY EXAMPLE   *(Lesson 14.1)*

What type of function is illustrated in the table?

x	−1	0	1	2	3
f(x)	9	3	1	$\frac{1}{3}$	$\frac{1}{9}$

Whenever x increases by 1, $f(x)$ is multiplied by the common ratio of $\frac{1}{3}$. Since this ratio is less than 1, the table represents an exponential decay function.

KEY EXAMPLE   *(Lesson 14.2)*

Create a scatter plot for the data in the table. Treat age as the independent variable x and median BMI as the dependent variable y. Then, use a graphing calculator to find an appropriate regression model of the data. Explain why you chose that particular type of function.

Age	2	3	4	5	6	7	8	9	10
Median BMI	16.5	16.0	15.2	15.2	15.6	15.6	15.8	16.0	16.3

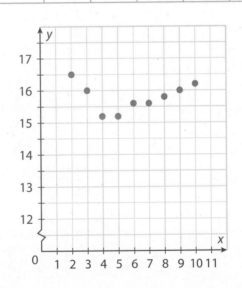

A quadratic regression of the data on a graphing calculator produces the equation $y = 0.0636x^2 - 0.7503x + 17.5867$. A quadratic function was chosen because the data points generally lie on a curve that approximates a parabola.

EXERCISES

Choose the type of function (linear, quadratic, or exponential) you would use to model the data. *(Lesson 14.2)*

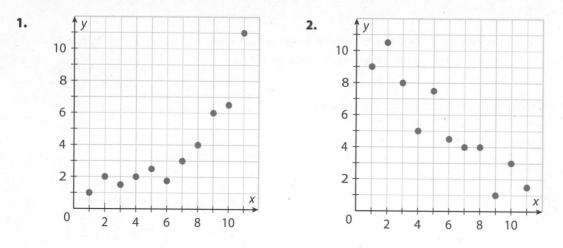

1.

2.

3. How does the Product of Powers Property of Exponents help you in deciding whether a given set of data is exponential? *(Lesson 14.1)*

Double Your Money

Jenna was a game show participant and won $10,000! She eventually wants to use the money as a down payment on a home but is not quite ready for such a big commitment. She decides to invest the money and plans to use it once the amount reaches $20,000. She researches various investment opportunities and would like to choose the one that will let her money double fastest.

Plan	Interest Rate	Compounding
Plan A	5.2%	Quarterly
Plan B	4.8%	Monthly
Plan C	4.25%	Continuously

To the nearest tenth of a year, how long will each plan take to double Jenna's money? Which should Jenna choose? Use your own paper to complete the task. Be sure to write down all your data and assumptions. Then use graphs, numbers, words, or algebra to explain how you reached your conclusion.

14.1–14.2 Modeling with Exponential and Other Functions

• Online Homework
• Hints and Help
• Extra Practice

The isotope X has a half-life of 10 days. Complete the table showing the decay of a sample of X. *(Lessons 14.1, 14.2)*

1.

Number of Half-Lives	Number of Days (t)	Percent of Isotope Remaining (p)
0	0	100
1	10	50
2	20	
3		
4		

2. Write the decay rate per half-life, r, as a fraction.

3. Write an expression for the number of half-lives in t days.

4. Write a function that models this situation. The function $p(t)$ should give the percent of the isotope remaining after t days.

ESSENTIAL QUESTION

5. What are two ways you can find an exponential function that models a given set of data?

Assessment Readiness

1. Look at each exponential function. Does the function pass through (1, 2) and (3, 50)? Select Yes or No for A–C.

   A. $y = \frac{3}{5} \cdot 5^x$ ◯ Yes   ◯ No

   B. $y = \frac{2}{5} \cdot 5^x$ ◯ Yes   ◯ No

   C. $y = \frac{1}{2} \cdot 5^x$ ◯ Yes   ◯ No

2. Consider the function $y = -2 \left(\frac{1}{4} \right)^{x+1} + 7$. Choose True or False for each statement.

   A. The asymptote of the function is $y = 7$.   ◯ True   ◯ False

   B. The asymptote of the function is $x = 7$.   ◯ True   ◯ False

   C. The function has no asymptote.   ◯ True   ◯ False

3. Are there real solutions to the equation $x^3 - 5x^2 = 0$? Explain, then state the roots.

4. Describe the type of function illustrated in the table. Explain.

x	4	5	6	7	8
y	−4	−3	−4	−7	−12

5. How can you use the pattern formed by the points on a scatterplot to determine whether to fit the data to a linear, quadratic, or exponential function?

Logarithmic Functions

Essential Question: How can you use logarithmic functions to solve real-world problems?

REAL WORLD VIDEO
Check out some of the considerations that go into determining the proper dosage of a medication and learn about the role of logarithmic functions in this process.

MODULE PERFORMANCE TASK PREVIEW

What's the Dosage?

Scientists working in the pharmaceutical industry discover, develop, and test drugs for everything from relieving a headache to controlling high blood pressure. One important question regarding a specific drug is how long the drug stays in a person's system. How can logarithmic functions be used to answer this question? Let's find out!

Are YOU Ready?

Complete these exercises to review skills you will need for this module.

• Online Homework
• Hints and Help
• Extra Practice

Exponents

Example 1   Rewrite $x^{-3}y^2$ using only positive exponents.

$$x^{-3}y^2 = \frac{y^2}{x^3}$$

Rewrite each expression using only positive exponents.

1. $x^{-4}y^{-2}$

2. x^8y^{-5}

3. $\dfrac{x^{-1}}{y^{-2}}$

Rational and Radical Exponents

Example 2   Write $\sqrt[4]{a^6b^4}$ using rational exponents.

$\sqrt[4]{a^6b^4} = \left(a^6b^4\right)^{\frac{1}{4}}$ Remove the radical symbol.

$= a^{\frac{3}{2}}b$ Simplify.

Write the expression using rational exponents.

4. $\sqrt[6]{a^3b^{12}}$

5. $\sqrt[3]{ab^2}$

6. $\sqrt[4]{81a^{12}b^8}$

Graphing Linear Nonproportional Relationships

Example 3   Graph $y = -3x + 1$.

Graph the y–intercept of $(0, 1)$.

Use the slope $\frac{-3}{1}$ to plot a second point.

Draw a line through the two points.

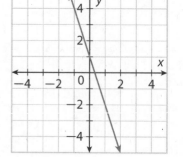

Graph each equation.

7. $y = \frac{2}{3}x - 4$

8. $y = 2x + 3$

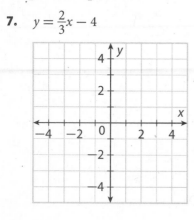

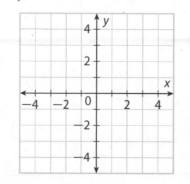

15.1 Defining and Evaluating a Logarithmic Function

Essential Question: What is the inverse of the exponential function $f(x) = b^x$ where $b > 0$ and $b \neq 1$, and what is the value of $f^{-1}(b^m)$ for any real number m?

Explore Understanding Logarithmic Functions as Inverses of Exponential Functions

An exponential function such as $f(x) = 2^x$ accepts values of the exponent as inputs and delivers the corresponding power of 2 as the outputs. The inverse of an exponential function is called a **logarithmic function**. For $f(x) = 2^x$, the inverse function is written $f^{-1}(x) = \log_2 x$, which is read either as "the logarithm with base 2 of x" or simply as "log base 2 of x." It accepts powers of 2 as inputs and delivers the corresponding exponents as outputs.

(A) Graph $f^{-1}(x) = \log_2 x$ using the graph of $f(x) = 2^x$ shown. Begin by reflecting the labeled points on the graph of $f(x) = 2^x$ across the line $y = x$ and labeling the reflected points with their coordinates. Then draw a smooth curve through the reflected points.

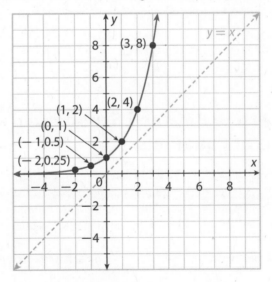

(B) Using the labeled points on the graph of $f^{-1}(x)$, complete the following statements.

$f^{-1}(0.25) = \log_2 \boxed{} = \boxed{}$

$f^{-1}(0.5) = \log_2 \boxed{} = \boxed{}$

$f^{-1}(1) = \log_2 \boxed{} = \boxed{}$

$f^{-1}(2) = \log_2 \boxed{} = \boxed{}$

$f^{-1}(4) = \log_2 \boxed{} = \boxed{}$

$f^{-1}(8) = \log_2 \boxed{} = \boxed{}$

1. Explain why the domain of $f(x) = 2^x$ doesn't need to be restricted in order for its inverse to be a function.

_____

_____

2. State the domain and range of $f^{-1}(x) = \log_2 x$ using set notation.

_____

_____

3. Identify any intercepts and asymptotes for the graph of $f^{-1}(x) = \log_2 x$.

_____

_____

4. Is $f^{-1}(x) = \log_2 x$ an increasing function or a decreasing function?

_____

_____

5. How does $f^{-1}(x) = \log_2 x$ behave as x increases without bound? As x decreases toward 0?

_____

_____

6. Based on the inverse relationship between $f(x) = 2^x$ and $f^{-1}(x) = \log_2 x$, complete this statement:

$f^{-1}(16) = \log_2 \boxed{} = \boxed{}$ because $f\left(\boxed{}\right) = \boxed{}$.

🔑 Explain 1   Converting Between Exponential and Logarithmic Forms of Equations

In general, the exponential function $f(x) = b^x$, where $b > 0$ and $b \neq 1$, has the logarithmic function $f^{-1}(x) = \log_b x$ as its inverse. For instance, if $f(x) = 3^x$, then $f^{-1}(x) = \log_3 x$, and if $f(x) = \left(\frac{1}{4}\right)^x$, then $f^{-1}(x) = \log_{\frac{1}{4}} x$. The inverse relationship between exponential functions and logarithmic functions also means that you can write any exponential equation as a logarithmic equation and any logarithmic equation as an exponential equation.

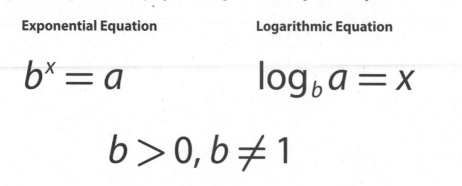

Exponential Equation   **Logarithmic Equation**

$$b^x = a \qquad\qquad \log_b a = x$$

$$b > 0, b \neq 1$$

Example 1 Complete the table by writing each given equation in its alternate form.

Ⓐ

Exponential Equation	Logarithmic Equation
$4^3 = 64$	?
?	$\log_5 \dfrac{1}{25} = -2$
$\left(\dfrac{2}{3}\right)^p = q$	?
?	$\log_{\frac{1}{2}} m = n$

Think of each equation as involving an exponential function or a logarithmic function. Identify the function's base, input, and output. For the inverse function, use the same base but switch the input and output.

Think of the equation $4^3 = 64$ as involving an exponential function with base 4. The input is 3, and the output is 64. So, the inverse function (a logarithmic function) also has base 4, but its input is 64, and its output is 3.

Think of the equation $\log_5 \frac{1}{25} = -2$ as involving a logarithmic function with base 5. The input is $\frac{1}{25}$, and the output is -2. So, the inverse function (an exponential function) also has base 5, but its input is -2, and its output is $\frac{1}{25}$.

Think of the equation $\left(\frac{2}{3}\right)^p = q$ as involving an exponential function with base $\frac{2}{3}$. The input is p, and the output is q. So, the inverse function (a logarithmic function) also has base $\frac{2}{3}$, but its input is q, and its output is p.

Think of the equation $\log_{\frac{1}{2}} m = n$ as involving a logarithmic function with base $\frac{1}{2}$. The input is m, and the output is n. So, the inverse function (an exponential function) also has base $\frac{1}{2}$, but its input is n, and its output is m.

Exponential Equation	Logarithmic Equation
$4^3 = 64$	$\log_4 64 = 3$
$5^{-2} = \dfrac{1}{25}$	$\log_5 \dfrac{1}{25} = -2$
$\left(\dfrac{2}{3}\right)^p = q$	$\log_{\frac{2}{3}} q = p$
$\left(\dfrac{1}{2}\right)^n = m$	$\log_{\frac{1}{2}} m = n$

Ⓑ

Exponential Equation	Logarithmic Equation
$3^5 = 243$	
	$\log_4 \frac{1}{64} = -3$
$\left(\frac{3}{4}\right)^r = s$	
	$\log_{\frac{1}{5}} v = w$

Think of the equation $3^5 = 243$ as involving an exponential function with base 3. The input is ____, and the output is ____. So, the inverse function (a logarithmic function) also has base 3, but its input is ____, and its output is ____.

Think of the equation $\log_4 \frac{1}{64} = -3$ as involving a logarithmic function with base ____. The input is $\frac{1}{64}$, and the output is ____. So, the inverse function (an exponential function) also has base ____, but its input is ____, and its output is $\frac{1}{64}$.

Think of the equation $\left(\frac{3}{4}\right)^r = s$ as involving an exponential function with base ____. The input is ____, and the output is s. So, the inverse function (a logarithmic function) also has base ____, but its input is s, and its output is ____.

Think of the equation $\log_{\frac{1}{5}} v = w$ as involving a logarithmic function with base ____. The input is ____, and the output is ____. So, the inverse function (an exponential function) also has base ____, but its input is ____, and its output is ____.

Reflect

7. A student wrote the logarithmic form of the exponential equation $5^0 = 1$ as $\log_5 0 = 1$. What did the student do wrong? What is the correct logarithmic equation?

_____

_____

Your Turn

8. Complete the table by writing each given equation in its alternate form.

Exponential Equation	Logarithmic Equation
$10^4 = 10,000$	
	$\log_2 \frac{1}{16} = -4$
$\left(\frac{2}{5}\right)^c = d$	
	$\log_{\frac{1}{3}} x = y$

The logarithmic function $f(x) = \log_b x$ accepts a power of b as an input and delivers an exponent as an output. In cases where the input of a logarithmic function is a recognizable power of b, you should be able to determine the function's output. You may find it helpful first to write a logarithmic equation by letting the output equal y and then to rewrite the equation in exponential form. Once the bases on each side of the exponential equation are equal, you can equate their exponents to find y.

Example 2

Ⓐ If $f(x) = \log_{10} x$, find $f(1000)$, $f(0.01)$, and $f\left(\sqrt{10}\right)$.

$f(1000) = y$

$\log_{10} 1000 = y$

$10^y = 1000$

$10^y = 10^3$

$y = 3$

So, $f(1000) = 3$.

$f(0.01) = y$

$\log_{10} 0.01 = y$

$10^y = 0.01$

$10^y = 10^{-2}$

$y = -2$

So, $f(0.01) = -2$.

$f\left(\sqrt{10}\right) = y$

$\log_{10} \sqrt{10} = y$

$10^y = \sqrt{10}$

$10^y = 10^{\frac{1}{2}}$

$y = \frac{1}{2}$

So, $f\left(\sqrt{10}\right) = \frac{1}{2}$.

Ⓑ If $f(x) = \log_{\frac{1}{2}} x$, find $f(4)$, $f\left(\frac{1}{32}\right)$ and $f\left(2\sqrt{2}\right)$.

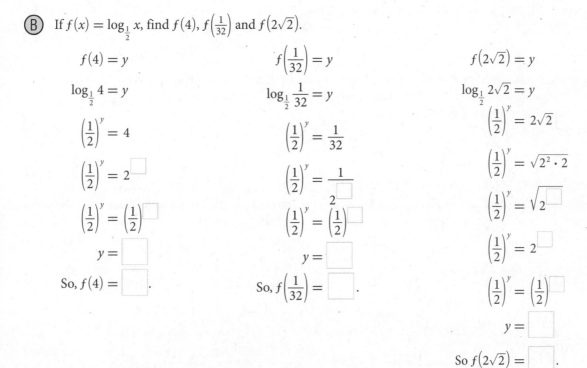

$f(4) = y$

$\log_{\frac{1}{2}} 4 = y$

$\left(\frac{1}{2}\right)^y = 4$

$\left(\frac{1}{2}\right)^y = 2^{\boxed{}}$

$\left(\frac{1}{2}\right)^y = \left(\frac{1}{2}\right)^{\boxed{}}$

$y = \boxed{}$

So, $f(4) = \boxed{}$.

$f\left(\frac{1}{32}\right) = y$

$\log_{\frac{1}{2}} \frac{1}{32} = y$

$\left(\frac{1}{2}\right)^y = \frac{1}{32}$

$\left(\frac{1}{2}\right)^y = \frac{1}{2^{\boxed{}}}$

$\left(\frac{1}{2}\right)^y = \left(\frac{1}{2}\right)^{\boxed{}}$

$y = \boxed{}$

So, $f\left(\frac{1}{32}\right) = \boxed{}$.

$f\left(2\sqrt{2}\right) = y$

$\log_{\frac{1}{2}} 2\sqrt{2} = y$

$\left(\frac{1}{2}\right)^y = 2\sqrt{2}$

$\left(\frac{1}{2}\right)^y = \sqrt{2^2 \cdot 2}$

$\left(\frac{1}{2}\right)^y = \sqrt{2^{\boxed{}}}$

$\left(\frac{1}{2}\right)^y = 2^{\boxed{}}$

$\left(\frac{1}{2}\right)^y = \left(\frac{1}{2}\right)^{\boxed{}}$

$y = \boxed{}$

So $f\left(2\sqrt{2}\right) = \boxed{}$.

Your Turn

9. If $f(x) = \log_7 x$, find $f(343)$, $f\left(\frac{1}{49}\right)$, and $f(\sqrt{7})$.

🔑 Explain 3 Evaluating Logarithmic Functions Using a Scientific Calculator

You can use a scientific calculator to find the logarithm of any positive number x when the logarithm's base is either 10 or e. When the base is 10, you are finding what is called the *common logarithm* of x, and you use the calculator's LOG key because $\log_{10} x$ is also written as $\log x$ (where the base is understood to be 10). When the base is e, you are finding what is called the *natural logarithm* of x, and you use the calculator's LN key because $\log_e x$ is also written as $\ln x$.

Example 3 Use a scientific calculator to find the common logarithm and the natural logarithm of the given number. Verify each result by evaluating the appropriate exponential expression.

(A) 13

First, find the common logarithm of 13. Round the result to the thousandths place and raise 10 to that number to confirm that the power is close to 13.

Next, find the natural logarithm of 13. Round the result to the thousandths place and raise e to that number to confirm that the power is close to 13.

So, $\log 13 \approx 1.114$.

So, $\ln 13 \approx 2.565$.

© Houghton Mifflin Harcourt Publishing Company

Ⓑ 0.42

First, find the common logarithm of 0.42. Round the result to the thousandths place and raise 10 to that number to confirm that the power is close to 0.42.

$\log 0.42 \approx$ ☐

$10^{\square} \approx 0.42$

Next, find the natural logarithm of 0.42. Round the result to the thousandths place and raise e to that number to confirm that the power is close to 0.42.

$\ln 0.42 \approx$ ☐

$e^{\square} \approx 0.42$

Reflect

10. For any $x > 1$, why is $\log x < \ln x$?

_____

_____

Your Turn

Use a scientific calculator to find the common logarithm and the natural logarithm of the given number. Verify each result by evaluating the appropriate exponential expression.

11. 0.25

12. 4

🎸 **Explain 4** **Evaluating a Logarithmic Model**

There are standard scientific formulas that involve logarithms, such as the formulas for the acidity level (pH) of a liquid and the intensity level of a sound. It's also possible to develop your own models involving logarithms by finding the inverses of exponential growth and decay models.

Example 4

(A) The acidity level, or pH, of a liquid is given by the formula $pH = \log \frac{1}{[H^+]}$ where $[H^+]$ is the concentration (in moles per liter) of hydrogen ions in the liquid. In a typical chlorinated swimming pool, the concentration of hydrogen ions ranges from 1.58×10^{-8} moles per liter to 6.31×10^{-8} moles per liter. What is the range of the pH for a typical swimming pool?

Using the pH formula, substitute the given values of $[H^+]$.

$$pH = \log\left(\frac{1}{6.31 \times 10^{-8}}\right)$$

$$\approx \log 15{,}800{,}000$$

$$\approx 7.2$$

$$pH = \log\left(\frac{1}{1.58 \times 10^{-8}}\right)$$

$$\approx \log 63{,}300{,}000$$

$$\approx 7.8$$

So, the pH of a swimming pool ranges from 7.2 to 7.8.

(B) *Lactobacillus acidophilus* is one of the bacteria used to turn milk into yogurt. The population P of a colony of 3500 bacteria at time t (in minutes) can be modeled by the function $P(t) = 3500(2)^{\frac{t}{73}}$. How long does it take the population to reach 1,792,000?

Step 1 Solve $P = 3500(2)^{\frac{t}{73}}$ for t.

Write the model. $\qquad\qquad\qquad\qquad P = 3500(2)^{\frac{t}{73}}$

Divide both sides by 3500. $\qquad \dfrac{P}{\boxed{}} = (2)^{\frac{t}{73}}$

Rewrite in logarithmic form. $\quad \log_2 \dfrac{P}{\boxed{}} = \dfrac{t}{73}$

Multiply both sides by 73. $\quad 73 \log_2 \dfrac{P}{\boxed{}} = t$

Step 2 Use the logarithmic model to find t when $P = 1{,}792{,}000$.

$$t = 73 \log_2 \dfrac{P}{\boxed{}} = 73 \log_2 \dfrac{1{,}792{,}000}{\boxed{}}$$

$$= 73 \log_2 \boxed{} = 73\left(\boxed{}\right) = \boxed{}$$

So, the bacteria population will reach 1,792,000 in _____ minutes, or about _____ hours.

13. The intensity level L (in decibels, dB) of a sound is given by the formula $L = 10 \log \frac{I}{I_0}$ where I is the intensity (in watts per square meter, W/m^2) of the sound and I_0 is the intensity of the softest audible sound, about 10^{-12} W/m^2. What is the intensity level of a rock concert if the sound has an intensity of 3.2 W/m^2?

14. The mass (in milligrams) of beryllium-11, a radioactive isotope, in a 500-milligram sample at time t (in seconds) is given by the function $m(t) = 500e^{-0.05t}$. When will there be 90 milligrams of beryllium-11 remaining?

Elaborate

15. What is a logarithmic function? Give an example.

_____

_____

_____

16. How can you turn an exponential model that gives y as a function of x into a logarithmic model that gives x as a function of y?

_____

_____

_____

_____

17. **Essential Question Check-In** Write the inverse of the exponential function $f(x) = b^x$ where $b > 0$ and $b \neq 1$.

☆ Evaluate: Homework and Practice

1. Complete the input-output table for $f(x) = \log_2 x$. Plot and label the ordered pairs from the table. Then draw the complete graph of $f(x)$.

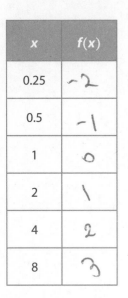

x	f(x)
0.25	~2
0.5	~1
1	0
2	1
4	2
8	3

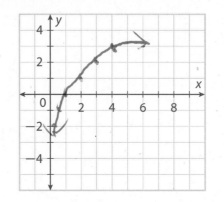

2. Use the graph of $f(x) = \log_2 x$ to do the following.

a. State the function's domain and range using set notation.

b. Identify the function's end behavior.

c. Identify the graph's x- and y-intercepts.

d. Identify the graph's asymptotes.

e. Identify the intervals where the function has positive values and where it has negative values.

f. Identify the intervals where the function is increasing and where it is decreasing

3. Consider the exponential function $f(x) = 3^x$.

Domain: *Range*

$x > 0$

a. State the function's domain and range using set notation.

b. Describe any restriction you must place on the domain of the function so that its inverse is also a function. *none*

c. Write the rule for the inverse function. $\log_3(x) = y$

d. State the inverse function's domain and range using set notation.

Domain $\mathbb{R}$

Range $y > 0$

4. Consider the logarithmic function $f(x) = \log_4 x$.

a. State the function's domain and range using set notation. *D:* $\mathbb{R}$ *R:* $y > 0$

b. Describe any restriction you must place on the domain of the function so that its inverse is also a function. *none*

c. Write the rule for the inverse function. $x^4 = f(x)$

d. State the inverse function's domain and range using set notation.

D: $x > 0$ *R:* $\mathbb{R}$

Write the given exponential equation in logarithmic form.

5. $5^3 = 125$

$\log_5(125) = 3$

6. $\left(\dfrac{1}{10}\right)^{-2} = 100$

7. $3^m = n$

$\log_3(n) = m$

8. $\left(\dfrac{1}{2}\right)^p = q$

Write the given logarithmic equation in exponential form.

9. $\log_6 1296 = 4$

$6^4 = 1296$

10. $\log_{\frac{1}{4}} \dfrac{1}{64} = 3$

11. $\log_8 x = y$

$8^y = x$

12. $\log_{\frac{2}{3}} c = d$

13. If $f(x) = \log_3 x$, find $f(243)$, $f\left(\frac{1}{27}\right)$, and $f\left(\sqrt{27}\right)$.

$3^{(243)} = 5$

$3^{(1/27)} = -3$

$3^{(\sqrt{27})} = 1.5$

14. If $f(x) = \log_6 x$, find $f(36)$, $f\left(\frac{1}{6}\right)$ and $f\left(6\sqrt[3]{6}\right)$

15. If $f(x) = \log_{\frac{1}{4}} x$, find $f\left(\frac{1}{64}\right)$, $f(256)$, and $f\left(\sqrt[3]{16}\right)$

$\log_{1/4}\left(\frac{1}{64}\right) = 3$

$\log_{1/4}(256) = -4$

$\log_{1/4}\left(\sqrt[3]{16}\right) = -\frac{2}{3}$

Use a scientific calculator to find the common logarithm and the natural logarithm of the given number. Verify each result by evaluating the appropriate exponential expression.

16. 19

17. 9

$Ln = 2.197224577$

$log = .954242509$

18. 0.6

19. 0.31

$Ln = -1.171182982$

$log = -.508638306$

20. The acidity level, or pH, of a liquid is given by the formula $pH = \log \frac{1}{[H^+]}$ where $[H^+]$ is the concentration (in moles per liter) of hydrogen ions in the liquid. What is the pH of iced tea with a hydrogen ion concentration of 0.000158 mole per liter?

$\log \dfrac{1}{0.000158 \, mol/L}$

$= \boxed{3.8 \, PH}$

21. The intensity level L (in decibels, dB) of a sound is given by the formula $L = 10 \log \frac{I}{I_0}$ where I is the intensity (in watts per square meter, W/m²) of the sound and I_0 is the intensity of the softest audible sound, about 10^{-12} W/m². What is the intensity level of a lawn mower if the sound has an intensity of 0.00063 W/m²?

$L = 10 \log \dfrac{0.00063}{10^{-12}}$

$L = 87.993$

$L = \boxed{88 \, dB}$

22. Match each liquid with its pH given the concentration of hydrogen ions in the liquid.

Liquid	Hydrogen Ion Concentration	pH
A. Cocoa	5.2×10^{-7}	_____ 3.5
B. Cider	7.9×10^{-4}	_____ 3.3
C. Ginger Ale	4.9×10^{-4}	_____ 2.4
D. Honey	1.3×10^{-4}	_____ 4.5
E. Buttermilk	3.2×10^{-5}	_____ 6.3
F. Cranberry juice	4.0×10^{-3}	_____ 6.4
G. Pinneapple juice	3.1×10^{-4}	_____ 3.1
H. Tomato juice	6.3×10^{-2}	_____ 1.2
I. Carrot juice	4.0×10^{-7}	_____ 3.9

H.O.T. Focus on Higher Order Thinking

23. Explain the Error Jade is taking a chemistry test and has to find the pH of a liquid given that its hydrogen ion concentration is 7.53×10^{-9} moles per liter. She writes the following.

$$pH = \ln \frac{1}{[H^+]}$$
$$= \ln \frac{1}{7.53 \times 10^{-9}}$$
$$\approx 18.7$$

She knows that the pH scale ranges from 1 to 14, so her answer of 18.7 must be incorrect, but she runs out of time on the test. Explain her error and find the correct pH.

24. Multi-step Exponential functions have the general form $f(x) = ab^{x-h} + k$ where a, b, h, and k are constants, $a \neq 0$, $b > 0$, and $b \neq 1$.

   a. State the domain and range of $f(x)$ using set notation.

   b. Show how to find $f^{-1}(x)$. Give a description of each step you take.

   c. State the domain and range of $f^{-1}(x)$ using set notation.

25. Justify Reasoning Evaluate each expression without using a calculator. Explain your reasoning.

   a. $\ln e^2$ since ln is $\log_e$ it's ②

   b. $10^{\log 7}$ $10^{\log 7} = 7$, because $\log(7)$ and $\log_{10}(70) = ⑦$

   c. $4^{\log_2 5}$ $4^{\log_2 5} = 25$, because $4^{\log 2} = x^2$, $x = 5$ so $5^2 = ㉕$

Lesson Performance Task

Skydivers use an instrument called an altimeter to determine their height above Earth's surface. An altimeter measures atmospheric pressure and converts it to altitude based on the relationship between pressure and altitude. One model for atmospheric pressure P (in kilopascals, kPa) as a function of altitude a (in kilometers) is $P = 100e^{-a/8}$.

a. Since an altimeter measures pressure directly, pressure is the independent variable for an altimeter. Rewrite the model $P = 100e^{-a/8}$ so that it gives altitude as a function of pressure.

b. To check the function in part a, use the fact that atmospheric pressure at Earth's surface is about 100 kPa.

c. Suppose a skydiver deploys the parachute when the altimeter measures 87 kPa. Use the function in part a to determine the skydiver's altitude. Give your answer in both kilometers and feet. (1 kilometer ≈ 3281 feet)

15.2 Graphing Logarithmic Functions

Essential Question: How is the graph of $g(x) = a \log_b(x - h) + k$ where $b > 0$ and $b \neq 1$ related to the graph of $f(x) = \log_b x$?

⊘ Explore 1   Graphing and Analyzing Parent Logarithmic Functions

The graph of the logarithmic function $f(x) = \log_2 x$, which you analyzed in the previous lesson, is shown. In this Explore, you'll graph and analyze other basic logarithmic functions.

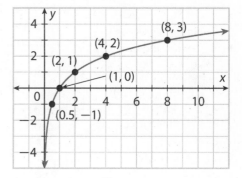

(A) Complete the table for the function $f(x) = \log x$. (Remember that when the base of a logarithmic function is not specified, it is understood to be 10.) Then plot and label the ordered pairs from the table and draw a smooth curve through the points to obtain the graph of the function.

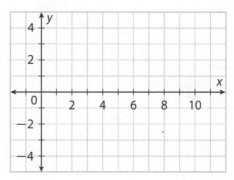

x	$f(x) = \log x$
0.1	
1	
10	

(B) Complete the table for the function $f(x) = \ln x$. (Remember that the base of this function is e). Then plot and label the ordered pairs from the table and draw a smooth curve through the points to obtain the graph of the function.

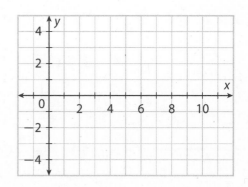

x	$f(x) = \ln x$
$\frac{1}{e} \approx 0.368$	
1	
$e \approx 2.72$	
$e^2 \approx 7.39$	

Ⓒ Analyze the two graphs from Steps A and B, and then complete the table.

Function	$f(x) = \log_2(x)$	$f(x) = \log x$	$f(x) = \ln x$
Domain	$\{x \mid x > 0\}$		
Range	$\{y \mid 0 < y < \infty\}$		
End behavior	As $x \to +\infty$, $f(x) \to +\infty$. As $x \to 0^+$, $f(x) \to -\infty$.		
Vertical and horizontal asymptotes	Vertical asymptote at $x = 0$; no horizontal asymptote		
Intervals where increasing or decreasing	Increasing throughout its domain		
Intercepts	x-intercept at $(1, 0)$; no y-intercepts		
Intervals where positive or negative	Positive on $(1, +\infty)$; negative on $(0, 1)$		

Reflect

1. What similarities do you notice about all logarithmic functions of the form $f(x) = \log_b x$ where $b > 1$? What differences do you notice?

_____

_____

Graphing Combined Transformations of $f(x) = \log_b x$ Where $b > 1$

When graphing transformations of $f(x) = \log_b x$ where $b > 1$, it helps to consider the effect of the transformations on the following features of the graph of $f(x)$: the vertical asymptote, $x = 0$, and two reference points, $(1, 0)$ and $(b, 1)$. The table lists these features as well as the corresponding features of the graph of $g(x) = a \log_b (x - h) + k$.

Function	$f(x) = \log_b x$	$g(x) = a \log_b (x - h) + k$
Asymptote	$x = 0$	$x = h$
Reference point	$(1, 0)$	$(1 + h, k)$
Reference point	$(b, 1)$	$(b + h, a + k)$

Example 1 Identify the transformations of the graph of $f(x) = \log_b x$ that produce the graph of the given function $g(x)$. Then graph $g(x)$ on the same coordinate plane as the graph of $f(x)$ by applying the transformations to the asymptote $x = 0$ and to the reference points $(1, 0)$ and $(b, 1)$. Also state the domain and range of $g(x)$ using set notation.

(A) $g(x) = -2 \log_2 (x - 1) - 2$

The transformations of the graph of $f(x) = \log_2 x$ that produce the graph of $g(x)$ are as follows:

- a vertical stretch by a factor of 2
- a reflection across the x-axis
- a translation of 1 unit to the right and 2 units down

Note that the translation of 1 unit to the right affects only the x-coordinates of points on the graph of $f(x)$, while the vertical stretch by a factor of 2, the reflection across the x-axis, and the translation of 2 units down affect only the y-coordinates.

Function	$f(x) = \log_2 x$	$g(x) = -2 \log_2 (x - 1) - 2$
Asymptote	$x = 0$	$x = 1$
Reference point	$(1, 0)$	$\left(1 + 1, -2(0) - 2\right) = (2, -2)$
Reference point	$(2, 1)$	$\left(2 + 1, -2(1) - 2\right) = (3, -4)$

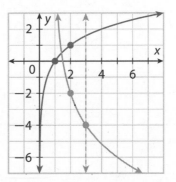

Domain: $\left\{ x \mid x > 1 \right\}$

Range: $\left\{ y \mid \infty < y < +\infty \right\}$

© Houghton Mifflin Harcourt Publishing Company

(B) $g(x) = 2 \log (x + 2) + 4$

The transformations of the graph of $f(x) = \log x$ that produce the graph of $g(x)$ are as follows:

- a vertical stretch by a factor of 2
- a translation of 2 units to the left and 4 units up

Note that the translation of 2 units to the left affects only the x-coordinates of points on the graph of $f(x)$, while the vertical stretch by a factor of 2 and the translation of 4 units up affect only the y-coordinates.

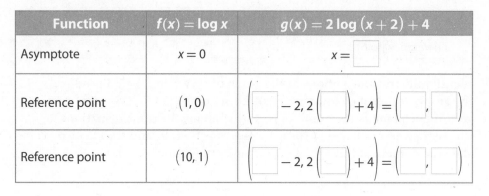

Function	$f(x) = \log x$	$g(x) = 2 \log (x + 2) + 4$
Asymptote	$x = 0$	$x = \boxed{}$
Reference point	$(1, 0)$	$\left(\boxed{} - 2, 2 \boxed{} + 4 \right) = \left(\boxed{}, \boxed{} \right)$
Reference point	$(10, 1)$	$\left(\boxed{} - 2, 2 \boxed{} + 4 \right) = \left(\boxed{}, \boxed{} \right)$

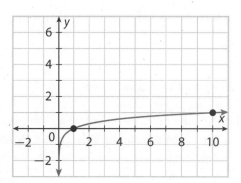

Domain: $\left\{ x \mid x > \boxed{} \right\}$

Range: $\left\{ y \mid -\infty < y < \boxed{} \right\}$

Identify the transformations of the graph of $f(x) = \log_b x$ that produce the graph of the given function $g(x)$. Then graph $g(x)$ on the same coordinate plane as the graph of $f(x)$ by applying the transformations to the asymptote $x = 0$ and to the reference points $(1, 0)$ and $(b, 1)$. Also state the domain and range of $g(x)$ using set notation.

2. $g(x) = \frac{1}{2} \log_2 (x + 1) + 2$

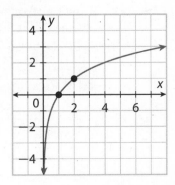

⚙ Explain 2 Writing, Graphing, and Analyzing a Logarithmic Model

You can obtain a logarithmic model for real-world data either by performing logarithmic regression on the data or by finding the inverse of an exponential model if one is available.

Example 2 **A biologist studied a population of foxes in a forest preserve over a period of time. The table gives the data that the biologist collected.**

Years Since Study Began	Fox Population
0	55
2	72
3	99
5	123
8	151
12	234
15	336
18	475

From the data, the biologist obtained the exponential model $P = 62(1.12)^t$ where P is the fox population at time t (in years since the study began). The biologist is interested in having a model that gives the time it takes the fox population to reach a certain level.

(A) One way to obtain the model that the biologist wants is to perform logarithmic regression on a graphing calculator using the data set but with the variables switched (that is, the fox population is the independent variable and time is the dependent variable). After obtaining the logarithmic regression model, graph it on a scatter plot of the data. Analyze the model in terms of whether it is increasing or decreasing as well as its average rate of change from $P = 100$ to $P = 200$, from $P = 200$ to $P = 300$, and from $P = 300$ to $P = 400$. Do the model's average rates of change increase, decrease, or stay the same? What does this mean for the fox population?

Using a graphing calculator, enter the population data into one list (L1) and the time data into another list (L2).

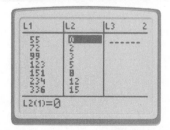

Perform logarithmic regression by pressing the [STAT] key, choosing the **CALC** menu, and selecting **9:LnReg**. Note that the calculator's regression model is a natural logarithmic function.

So, the model is $t = -35.6 + 8.66 \ln P$. Graphing this model on a scatter plot of the data visually confirms that the model is a good fit for the data.

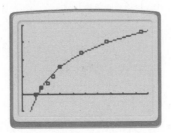

From the graph, you can see that the function is increasing. To find the model's average rates of change, divide the change in t (the dependent variable) by the change in P (the independent variable):

$$\text{Average rate of change} = \frac{t_2 - t_1}{P_2 - P_1}$$

Population	Number of Years to Reach That Population	Average Rate of Change
100	$t = -35.6 + 8.66 \ln 100 \approx 4.3$	
200	$t = -35.6 + 8.66 \ln 200 \approx 10.3$	$\dfrac{10.3 - 4.3}{200 - 100} = \dfrac{6.0}{100} = 0.060$
300	$t = -35.6 + 8.66 \ln 300 \approx 13.8$	$\dfrac{13.8 - 10.3}{300 - 200} = \dfrac{3.5}{100} = 0.035$
400	$t = -35.6 + 8.66 \ln 400 \approx 16.3$	$\dfrac{16.3 - 13.8}{400 - 300} = \dfrac{2.5}{100} = 0.025$

The model's average rates of change are decreasing. This means that as the fox population grows, it takes less time for the population to increase by another 100 foxes.

(B) Another way to obtain the model that the biologist wants is to find the inverse of the exponential model. Find the inverse model and compare it with the logarithmic regression model.

In order to compare the inverse of the biologist's model, $P = 62(1.12)^t$, with the logarithmic regression model, you must rewrite the biologist's model with base e so that the inverse will involve a natural logarithm. This means that you want to find a constant c such that $e^c = 1.12$. Writing the exponential equation $e^c = 1.12$ in logarithmic form gives $c = \ln 1.12$, so $c = \boxed{}$ to the nearest thousandth.

Replacing 1.12 with $e^{\boxed{}}$ in the biologist's model gives $P = 62 \left(e^{\boxed{}} \right)^t$, or $P = 62\, e^{\boxed{}\, t}$. Now find the inverse of this function.

Write the equation. $\qquad\qquad\qquad P = 62e^{\boxed{}\, t}$

Divide both sides by 62. $\qquad\qquad \dfrac{P}{62} = e^{\boxed{}\, t}$

Write in logarithmic form. $\qquad\qquad \ln \dfrac{P}{62} = \boxed{}\, t$

Divide both sides by $\boxed{}$. $\qquad \boxed{}\, \ln \dfrac{P}{62} = t$

So, the inverse of the exponential model is $t = \boxed{} \ln \dfrac{P}{62}$. To compare this model with the logarithmic regression model, use a graphing calculator to graph both $y = \boxed{} \ln \dfrac{x}{62}$ and $y = -35.6 + 8.66 \ln x$. You observe that the graphs [roughly coincide/significantly diverge], so the models are [basically equivalent/very different].

Reflect

3. **Discussion** In a later lesson, you will learn the quotient property of logarithms, which states that $\log_b \dfrac{m}{n} = \log_b m - \log_b n$ for any positive numbers m and n. Explain how you can use this property to compare the two models in Example 3.

_____

_____

_____

_____

Your Turn

4. Maria made a deposit in a bank account and left the money untouched for several years. The table lists her account balance at the end of each year.

Years Since the Deposit Was Made	Account Balance
0	$1000.00
1	$1020.00
2	$1040.40
3	$1061.21

a. Write an exponential model for the account balance as a function of time (in years since the deposit was made).

b. Find the inverse of the exponential model after rewriting it with a base of e. Describe what information the inverse gives.

c. Perform logarithmic regression on the data (using the account balance as the independent variable and time as the dependent variable). Compare this model with the inverse model from part b.

Elaborate

5. Which transformations of $f(x) = \log_b(x)$ change the function's end behavior (both as x increases without bound and as x decreases toward 0 from the right)? Which transformations change the location of the graph's x-intercept?

_____

_____

6. How are reference points helpful when graphing transformations of $f(x) = \log_b(x)$?

_____

7. What are two ways to obtain a logarithmic model for a set of data?

_____

_____

8. **Essential Question Check-In** Describe the transformations you must perform on the graph of $f(x) = \log_b(x)$ to obtain the graph of $g(x) = a\log_b(x - h) + k$.

_____

_____

_____

• Online Homework
• Hints and Help
• Extra Practice

1. Graph the logarithmic functions $f(x) = \log_2 x$, $f(x) = \log x$, and $f(x) = \ln x$ on the same coordinate plane. To distinguish the curves, label the point on each curve where the y-coordinate is 1.

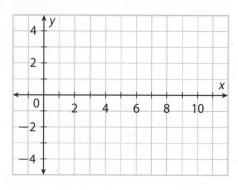

2. Describe the attributes that the logarithmic functions $f(x) = \log_2 x$, $f(x) = \log x$, and $f(x) = \ln x$ have in common and the attributes that make them different. Attributes should include domain, range, end behavior, asymptotes, intercepts, intervals where the functions are positive and where they are negative, intervals where the functions are increasing and where they are decreasing, and the average rate of change on an interval.

3. For each of the six functions, describe how its graph is a transformation of the graph of $f(x) = \log_2 x$. Also identify what attributes of $f(x) = \log_2 x$ change as a result of the transformation. Attributes to consider are the domain, the range, the end behavior, the vertical asymptote, the x-intercept, the intervals where the function is positive and where it is negative, and whether the function increases or decreases throughout its domain.

a. $g(x) = \log_2 x - 5$ *shifed up 5*

b. $g(x) = 4 \log_2 x$ *vertically stretned by a facr. 4*

c. $g(x) = \log_2 (x + 6)$ *Shifed left 6*

d. $g(x) = -\frac{3}{4} \log_2 x$ *verticall compesset by 3/4, reflected over x*

e. $g(x) = \log_2 x + 7$ *Shifted up 7*

f. $g(x) = \log_2 (x - 8)$ *Shifed piant 8*

Identify the transformations of the graph of $f(x) = \log_b x$ that produce the graph of the given function $g(x)$. Then graph $g(x)$ on the same coordinate plane as the graph of $f(x)$ by applying the transformations to the asymptote $x = 0$ and to the reference points $(1, 0)$ and $(b, 1)$. Also state the domain and range of $g(x)$ using set notation.

4. $g(x) = -4 \log_2 (x + 2) + 1$

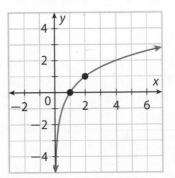

5. $g(x) = 3 \log (x - 1) - 1$

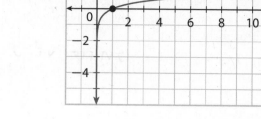

6. $f(x) = \frac{1}{2} \log_2 (x - 1) - 2$

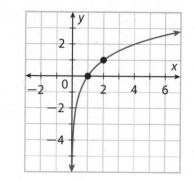

7. $g(x) = -4 \ln(x - 4) + 3$

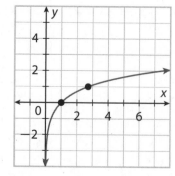

8. $g(x) = -2 \log(x + 2) + 5$

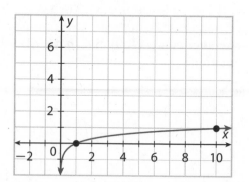

9. The radioactive isotope fluorine-18 is used in medicine to produce images of internal organs and detect cancer. It decays to the stable element oxygen-18. The table gives the percent of fluorine-18 that remains in a sample over a period of time.

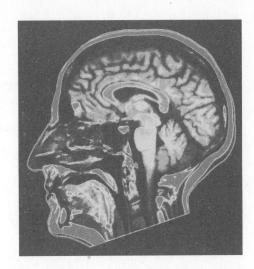

Time (hours)	Percent of Fluorine-18 Remaining
0	100
1	68.5
2	46.9
3	32.1

a. Write an exponential model for the percent of fluorine-18 remaining as a function of time (in hours).

b. Find the inverse of the exponential model after rewriting it with a base of e. Describe what information the inverse gives.

c. Perform logarithmic regression on the data (using the percent of fluorine-18 remaining as the independent variable and time as the dependent variable). Compare this model with the inverse model from part b.

10. During the period between 2001–2011, the average price of an ounce of gold doubled every 4 years. In 2001, the average price of gold was about $270 per ounce.

Year	Average Price of an Ounce of Gold
2001	$271.04
2002	$309.73
2003	$363.38
2004	$409.72
2005	$444.74
2006	$603.46
2007	$695.39
2008	$871.96
2009	$972.35
2010	$1224.53
2011	$1571.52

a. Use the fact that the average price of an ounce of gold doubled every 4 years to write an exponential model for the average price as a function of time (in years since 2001).

b. Find the inverse of the exponential model after rewriting it with a base of e. Describe what information the inverse gives.

c. Perform logarithmic regression on the data in the table (using the average price of an ounce of gold as the independent variable and time as the dependent variable). Compare this model with the inverse model from part b.

11. **Multiple Representations** For the function $g(x) = \log(x - h)$, what value of the parameter h will cause the function to pass through the point $(7, 1)$? Answer the question in two different ways: once by using the function's rule, and once by thinking in terms of the function's graph.

12. **Explain the Error** A student drew the graph of $g(x) = 2 \log_{\frac{1}{2}}(x - 2)$ as shown. Explain the error that the student made, and draw the correct graph.

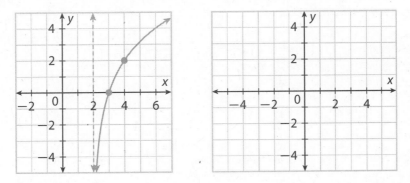

13. **Construct Arguments** Prove that $\log_{\frac{1}{b}} x = -\log_b x$ for any positive value of b not equal to 1. Begin the proof by setting $\log_{\frac{1}{b}} x$ equal to m and rewriting the equation in exponential form.

Lesson Performance Task

Given the following data about the heights of chair seats and table tops for children, make separate scatterplots of the ordered pairs (age of child, chair seat height) and the ordered pairs (age of child, table top height). Explain why a logarithmic model would be appropriate for each data set. Perform a logarithmic regression on each data set, and describe the transformations needed to obtain the graph of the model from the graph of the parent function $f(x) = \ln x$.

Age of Child (years)	Chair Seat Height (inches)	Table Top Height (inches)
1	5	12
1.5	6.5	14
2	8	16
3	10	18
5	12	20
7.5	14	22
11	16	25

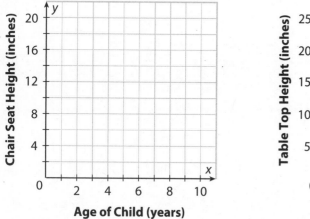

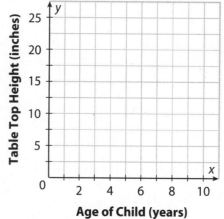

Logarithmic Functions

Essential Question: How can you use logarithmic functions to solve real-world problems?

Key Vocabulary
asymptote
  (asíntota)
common logarithm
  (logaritmo común)
logarithm
  (logaritmo)
logarithmic function
  (función logarítmica)
natural logarithm
  (logaritmo natural)

KEY EXAMPLE   *(Lesson 15.1)*

Evaluate $f(x) = \log_4 x$ when $x = 1024$.

$$f(1024) = \log_4 1024$$

$\quad 4^{f(1024)} = 1024 \qquad$ by definition of logarithm

$\quad 4^{f(1024)} = 4^5 \qquad\quad$ because $4^5 = 1024$

$\quad f(1024) = 5$

KEY EXAMPLE   *(Lesson 15.2)*

Graph $f(x) = 3 \log_2 (x + 1) - 4$.

The parameters for $f(x) = a \log_b (x - h) + k$ are $a = 3$, $b = 2$, $h = -1$, and $k = -4$.

Find reference points:

$$(1 + h, k) = (0, -4)$$
$$(b + h, a + k) = (2 - 1, 3 - 4) = (1, -1)$$

The two reference points are $(0, -4)$ and $(1, -1)$.

Find the asymptote:

$$x = h = -1$$

Plot the points and draw the asymptote. Connect the points with a curve that passes through the reference points and continually draws nearer the asymptote.

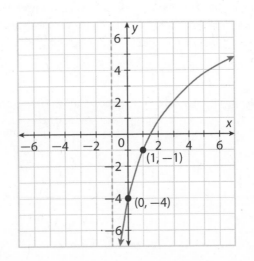

EXERCISES

Evaluate each logarithmic function for the given value. *(Lesson 15.1)*

1. $f(x) = \log_2 x$, for $f(256)$

2. $f(x) = \log_9 x$, for $f(6561)$

Graph each function. *(Lesson 15.2)*

3. $f(x) = 2 \log_3 (x - 2) + 1$

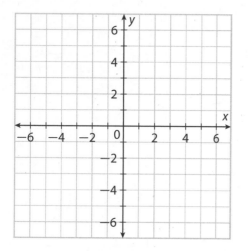

4. $f(x) = \log_5 (x + 1) - 1$

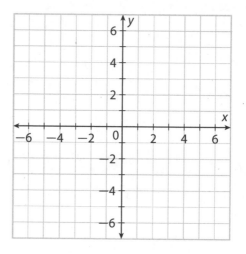

MODULE PERFORMANCE TASK

What's the Dosage?

Kira is a scientist working for a pharmaceutical lab and has developed a new drug. According to her research, 30% of the drug is eliminated from the bloodstream every 6 hours. Her initial dosage plan is to have the patient take a 1200 mg pill of the drug every 12 hours.

The patient needs to have at least 500 mg of the drug in the bloodstream at all times, but the total amount should never exceed 2500 mg. The drug should be taken for no more than 4 days. Does Kira's proposed dosage plan meet the medical requirements for the drug? Find a function that describes the amount of drug in the patient's bloodstream as a function of the number of doses.

Start by listing in the space below the information you will need to solve the problem. Then use your own paper to complete the task. Be sure to write down all your data and assumptions. Then use graphs, numbers, words, or algebra to explain how you reached your conclusion.

(Ready) to Go On?

15.1–15.2 Logarithmic Functions

- Online Homework
- Hints and Help
- Extra Practice

Rewrite the given equation in exponential format. *(Lesson 15.1)*

1. $\log_6 x = r$

2. $\log_{\frac{3}{4}} 12x = 35y$

Evaluate each logarithmic function for the given value. *(Lesson 15.1)*

3. $f(x) = \log_5 x$ for $f(125)$

4. $f(x) = \log_3 x$ for $f(729)$

Graph each function. *(Lesson 15.2)*

5. $f(x) = -3\log_e (x + 1) + 2$

6. $f(x) = 4\log_{10} (x + 4) - 3$

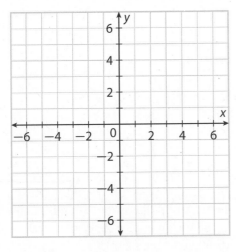

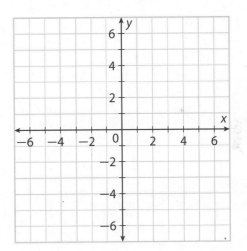

ESSENTIAL QUESTION

7. How is the graph of the logarithmic function $f(x) = \log_4 x$ related to the graph of the exponential function $g(x) = 4^x$?

© Houghton Mifflin Harcourt Publishing Company

Module 15

779

Study Guide Review

Assessment Readiness

1. Consider each function. Does the function show exponential decay?
   Select Yes or No for A–C.

   A. $f(x) = \left(\frac{1}{4}\right)^x$ ◯ Yes   ◯ No

   B. $f(x) = 1.6\left(\frac{3}{4}\right)^x$ ◯ Yes   ◯ No

   C. $f(x) = \frac{3}{5}(1.1)^x$ ◯ Yes   ◯ No

2. Consider the function $f(x) = \frac{1}{4}\log_5(x+3) - 2$. Choose True or False for each statement.

   A. The domain of this function is $\{x \mid x > -3\}$.   ◯ True   ◯ False

   B. There is no range to this function.   ◯ True   ◯ False

   C. The range of this function is $\{y \mid y > -2\}$ ◯ True   ◯ False

3. Shelby is canoeing in a river. She travels 4 miles upstream and 4 miles downstream in a total of 5 hours. In still water, Shelby can travel at an average speed of 2 miles per hour. To the nearest tenth, what is the average speed of the river's current? Explain.

4. Researchers have found that after 25 years of age, the average size of the pupil in a person's eye decreases. The relationship between pupil diameter d (in millimeters) and age a (in years) can be modeled by $d = -2.1158 \log_e a + 13.669$. What is the average diameter of a pupil for a person 25 years old? 50 years old? Explain how you got your answer.

Logarithmic Properties and Exponential Equations

Essential Question: How do the properties of logarithms allow you to solve real-world problems?

REAL WORLD VIDEO
Scientists use radiocarbon dating and other techniques to study the fossils of mastodons and other extinct species found at the La Brea Tar Pits.

MODULE PERFORMANCE TASK PREVIEW
How Old Is That Bone?

All living organisms contain carbon. Carbon has two main isotopes, carbon-12 and carbon-14. C-14 is radioactive and decays at a steady rate. Living organisms continually replenish their stores of carbon, and the ratio between C-12 and C-14 stays relatively constant. When the organism dies, this ratio changes at a known rate as C-14 decays. How can we use a logarithmic equation and carbon dating to determine the age of a mastodon bone? Let's find out!

Are YOU Ready?

Complete these exercises to review skills you will need for this module.

Exponents

Example 1 Simplify $\dfrac{40 \cdot x^6 y}{5x^2 y^5}$.

$\dfrac{40 \cdot x^6 y}{5x^2 y^5} = \dfrac{40}{5} \cdot x^{6-2} y^{1-5}$ Subtract exponents.

$= \dfrac{8x^4}{y^4}$ Simplify.

Simplify each expression.

1. $\dfrac{xy^2}{x^3 y^2}$

2. $\dfrac{18x^3 y^7}{2y^5}$

3. $\dfrac{12x^4}{8x^9 y}$

Multi-Step Equations

Example 2 Solve $3(5 - 2x) = -x$ for x.

$15 - 6x = -x$ Distribute the 3.

$15 = 5x$ Add $6x$ to both sides.

$3 = x$ Divide both sides by 5.

The solution is $x = 3$.

Solve.

4. $5(4x + 9) = 2x$

5. $3(x + 12) = 2(4 - 2x)$

6. $(x - 2)^2 = 4(x + 1)$

Equations Involving Exponents

Example 3 Solve $2x^{\frac{1}{3}} - 1 = 3$ for x.

$2x^{\frac{1}{3}} = 4$ Add 1 to both sides.

$x^{\frac{1}{3}} = 2$ Divide both sides by 2.

$\left(x^{\frac{1}{3}}\right)^3 = (2)^3$ Raise both sides to the power of 3.

$x = 8$ Simplify.

Solve.

7. $3x^{\frac{1}{4}} + 2 = 11$

8. $8x^{\frac{1}{2}} + 20 = 100$

9. $4x^{\frac{1}{3}} + 15 = 35$

16.1 Properties of Logarithms

Essential Question: What are the properties of logarithms?

Resource
Locker

 Explore 1 **Investigating the Properties of Logarithms**

You can use a scientific calculator to evaluate a logarithmic expression.

(A) Evaluate the expressions in each set using a scientific calculator.

Set A	Set B
$\log \frac{10}{e} \approx$ ____	$\frac{1}{\log e} \approx$ ____
$\ln 10 \approx$ ____	$1 + \log e \approx$ ____
$\log e^{10} \approx$ ____	$1 - \log e \approx$ ____
$\log 10e \approx$ ____	$10 \log e \approx$ ____

(B) Match the expressions in Set A to the equivalent expressions in Set B.

$\log \frac{10}{e} =$ ____

$\ln 10 =$ ____

$\log e^{10} =$ ____

$\log 10e =$ ____

Reflect

1. How can you check the results of evaluating the logarithmic expressions in Set A? Use this method to check each.

_____

_____

_____

_____

_____

_____

_____

2. Discussion How do you know that $\log e$ and $\ln 10$ are reciprocals? Given that the expressions are reciprocals, show another way to represent each expression.

_____

_____

⊘ Explore 2 Proving the Properties of Logarithms

A logarithm is the exponent to which a base must be raised in order to obtain a given number. So $\log_b b^m = m$. It follows that $\log_b b^0 = 0$, so $\log_b 1 = 0$. Also, $\log_b b^1 = 1$, so $\log_b b = 1$. Additional properties of logarithms are the Product Property of Logarithms, the Quotient Property of Logarithms, the Power Property of Logarithms, and the Change of Base Property of Logarithms.

Properties of Logarithms	
For any positive numbers a, m, n, b $(b \neq 1)$, and c $(c \neq 1)$, the following properties hold.	
Definition-Based Properties	$\log_b b^m = m \qquad \log_b 1 = 0 \qquad \log_b b = 1$
Product Property of Logarithms	$\log_b mn = \log_b m + \log_b n$
Quotient Property of Logarithms	$\log_b \dfrac{m}{n} = \log_b m - \log_b n$
Power Property of Logarithms	$\log_b m^n = n\log_b m$
Change of Base Property of Logarithms	$\log_c a = \dfrac{\log_b a}{\log_b c}$

Given positive numbers m, n, and b $(b \neq 1)$, prove the Product Property of Logarithms.

(A) Let $x = \log_b m$ and $y = \log_b n$. Rewrite the expressions in exponential form.

$m = \boxed{}$

$n = \boxed{}$

(B) Substitute for m and n.

$\log_b mn = \log_b \left(\boxed{} \right)$

(C) Use the Product of Powers Property of Exponents to simplify.

$\log_b \left(b^x \cdot b^y \right) = \log_b b^{\boxed{}}$

(D) Use the definition of a logarithm $\log_b b^m = m$ to simplify further.

$\log_b b^{x+y} = \boxed{}$

(E) Substitute for x and y.

$x + y = \boxed{}$

© Houghton Mifflin Harcourt Publishing Company

3. Prove the Power Property of Logarithms. Justify each step of your proof.

_____

_____

_____

_____

_____

_____

🔑 Explain 1 Using the Properties of Logarithms

Logarithmic expressions can be rewritten using one or more of the properties of logarithms.

Example 1 **Express each expression as a single logarithm. Simplify if possible. Then check your results by converting to exponential form and evaluating.**

(A) $\log_3 27 - \log_3 81$

$$\log_3 27 - \log_3 81 = \log_3\left(\frac{27}{81}\right) \qquad \text{Quotient Property of Logarithms}$$

$$= \log_3\left(\frac{1}{3}\right) \qquad \text{Simplify.}$$

$$= \log_3 3^{-1} \qquad \text{Write using base 3.}$$

$$= -1\log_3 3 \qquad \text{Power Property of Logarithms}$$

$$= -1 \qquad \text{Simplify.}$$

Check:

$$\log_3\left(\frac{1}{3}\right) = -1$$

$$\frac{1}{3} = 3^{-1}$$

$$\frac{1}{3} = \frac{1}{3}$$

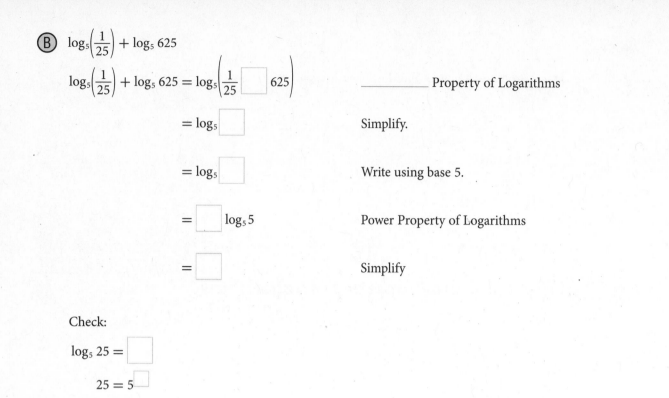

(B) $\log_5\left(\dfrac{1}{25}\right) + \log_5 625$

$\log_5\left(\dfrac{1}{25}\right) + \log_5 625 = \log_5\left(\dfrac{1}{25}\ \boxed{}\ 625\right)$ _____ Property of Logarithms

$= \log_5 \boxed{}$ Simplify.

$= \log_5 \boxed{}$ Write using base 5.

$= \boxed{}\ \log_5 5$ Power Property of Logarithms

$= \boxed{}$ Simplify

Check:

$\log_5 25 = \boxed{}$

$25 = 5^{\boxed{}}$

$25 = \boxed{}$

Your Turn

Express each expression as a single logarithm. Simplify if possible.

4. $\log_4 64^3$

5. $\log_8 18 - \log_8 2$

⚙ Explain 2   Rewriting a Logarithmic Model

There are standard formulas that involve logarithms, such as the formula for measuring the loudness of sounds. The loudness of a sound $L(I)$, in decibels, is given by the function $L(I) = 10\log\left(\dfrac{I}{I_0}\right)$, where I is the sound's intensity in watts per square meter and I_0 is the intensity of a barely audible sound. It's also possible to develop logarithmic models from exponential growth or decay models of the form $f(t) = a(1 + r)^t$ or $f(t) = a(1 - r)^t$ by finding the inverse.

Example 2 Solve the problems using logarithmic models.

(A) During a concert, an orchestra plays a piece of music in which its volume increases from one measure to the next, tripling the sound's intensity. Find how many decibels the loudness of the sound increases between the two measures.

Let I be the intensity in the first measure. So $3I$ is the intensity in the second measure.

Increase in loudness $= L(3I) - L(I)$	Write the expression.
$= 10\log\left(\dfrac{3I}{I_0}\right) - 10\log\left(\dfrac{I}{I_0}\right)$	Substitute.
$= 10\left(\log\left(\dfrac{3I}{I_0}\right) - \log\left(\dfrac{I}{I_0}\right)\right)$	Distributive Property
$= 10\left(\log 3 + \log\left(\dfrac{I}{I_0}\right) - \log\left(\dfrac{I}{I_0}\right)\right)$	Product Property of Logarithms
$= 10\log 3$	Simplify.
≈ 4.77	Evaluate the logarithm.

So the loudness of sound increases by about 4.77 decibels.

(B) The population of the United States in 2012 was 313.9 million. If the population increases exponentially at an average rate of 1% each year, how long will it take for the population to double?

The exponential growth model is $P = P_0(1 + r)^t$, where P is the population in millions after t years, P_0 is the population in 2012, and r is the average growth rate.

$P_0 = 313.9$

$P = 2P_0 = \boxed{}$

$r = 0.01$

Find the inverse model of $P = P_0(1 + r)^t$.

$P = P_0(1 + r)^t$	Exponential model
$\dfrac{P}{P_0} = (1 + r)^t$	Divide both sides by P_0.
$\log_{1+r}\left(\dfrac{P}{P_0}\right) = \log_{\boxed{}}(1 + r)^t$	Take the log of both sides.

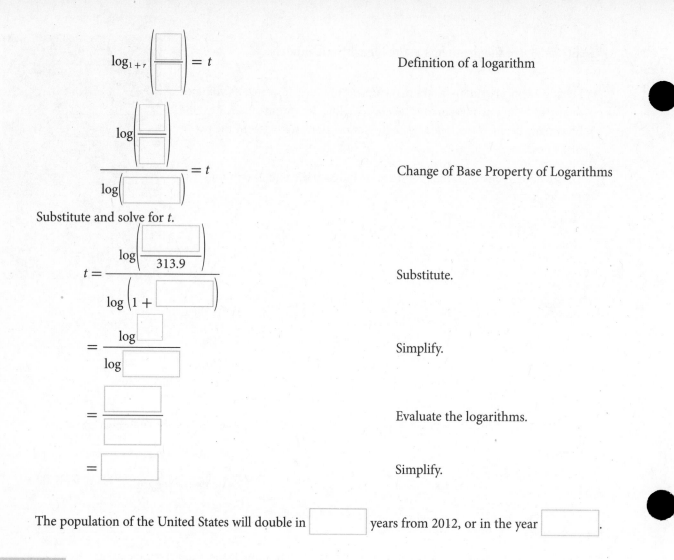

$$\log_{1+r}\left(\dfrac{\boxed{}}{\boxed{}}\right) = t \qquad \text{Definition of a logarithm}$$

$$\dfrac{\log\left(\dfrac{\boxed{}}{\boxed{}}\right)}{\log\left(\boxed{}\right)} = t \qquad \text{Change of Base Property of Logarithms}$$

Substitute and solve for t.

$$t = \dfrac{\log\left(\dfrac{\boxed{}}{313.9}\right)}{\log\left(1 + \boxed{}\right)} \qquad \text{Substitute.}$$

$$= \dfrac{\log\boxed{}}{\log\boxed{}} \qquad \text{Simplify.}$$

$$= \dfrac{\boxed{}}{\boxed{}} \qquad \text{Evaluate the logarithms.}$$

$$= \boxed{} \qquad \text{Simplify.}$$

The population of the United States will double in $\boxed{}$ years from 2012, or in the year $\boxed{}$.

Your Turn

6. A bank account earns 6% annual interest compounded annually. The balance B of the account after t years is given by the equation $B = B_0(1.06)^t$, where B_0 is the starting balance. If the account starts with a balance of $250, how long will it take to triple the balance of the account?

© Houghton Mifflin Harcourt Publishing Company

Elaborate

7. On what other properties do the proofs of the properties of logarithms rely?

8. What properties of logarithms would you use to rewrite the expression $\log_7 x + \log_7 4x$ as a single logarithm?

9. Explain how the properties of logarithms are useful in finding the inverse of an exponential growth or decay model.

10. **Essential Question Check-In** State each of the Product, Quotient, and Power Properties of Logarithms in a simple sentence.

⭐ Evaluate: Homework and Practice

Express each expression as a single logarithm. Simplify if possible.

1. $\log_9 12 + \log_9 546.75$

2. $\log_2 76.8 - \log_2 1.2$

3. $\log_{\frac{2}{5}} 0.0256^3$

4. $\log_{11} 11^{23}$

5. $\log_5 5^{x+1} + \log_4 256^2$

6. $\log\left(\log_7 98 - \log_7 2\right)^x$

7. $\log_{x+1}\left(x^2 + 2x + 1\right)^3$

8. $\log_4 5 + \log_4 12 - \log_4 3.75$

Solve the problems using logarithmic models.

9. **Geology** Seismologists use the Richter scale to express the energy, or magnitude, of an earthquake. The Richter magnitude of an earthquake M is related to the energy released in ergs E shown by the formula $M = \frac{2}{3}\log\left(\frac{E}{10^{11.8}}\right)$. In 1964, an earthquake centered at Prince William Sound, Alaska registered a magnitude of 9.2 on the Richter scale. Find the energy released by the earthquake.

10. **Astronomy** The difference between the apparent magnitude (brightness) m of a star and its absolute magnitude M is given by the formula $m - M = 5\log\frac{d}{10}$, where d is the distance of the star from the Earth, measured in parsecs. Find the distance d of the star Rho Oph from Earth, where Rho Oph has an apparent magnitude of 5.0 and an absolute magnitude -0.4.

11. The intensity of the sound of a conversation ranges from 10^{-10} watts per square meter to 10^{-6} watts per square meter. What is the range in the loudness of the conversation? Use $I_0 = 10^{-12}$ watts per square meter.

12. The intensity of sound from the stands of a football game is 25 times as great when the home team scores a touchdown as it is when the away team scores. Find the difference in the loudness of the sound when the two teams score.

13. Finance A stock priced at $40 increases at a rate of 8% per year. Write and evaluate a logarithmic expression for the number of years that it will take for the value of the stock to reach $50.

14. Suppose that the population of one endangered species decreases at a rate of 4% per year. In one habitat, the current population of the species is 143. After how long will the population drop below 30?

15. The population P of bacteria in a culture after t minutes is given by the equation $P = P_0 (1.12)^t$, where P_0 is the initial population. If the number of bacteria starts at 200, how long will it take for the population to increase to 1000?

16. Chemistry Most swimming pool experts recommend a pH of between 7.0 and 7.6 for water in a swimming pool. Use $pH = -\log[H^+]$ and write an expression for the difference in hydrogen ion concentration over this pH range.

17. Match the logarithmic expressions to equivalent expressions.

a. $\log_2 4x$ _____ $2x$

b. $\log_2 \dfrac{x}{4}$ _____ $2 + \log_2 x$

c. $\log_2 4^x$ _____ $\dfrac{\log x}{\log 2}$

d. $\log_2 x^4$ _____ $4\log_2 x$

e. $\log_2 x$ _____ $\log_2 x - 2$

18. Prove the Quotient Property of Logarithms. Justify each step of your proof.

19. Prove the Change of Base Property of Logarithms. Justify each step of your proof.

20. Multi-Step The radioactive isotope Carbon-14 decays exponentially at a rate of 0.0121% each year.

    a. How long will it take 250 g of Carbon-14 to decay to 100 g?

    b. The half-life for a radioactive isotope is the amount of time it takes for the isotope to reach half its initial value. What is the half-life of Carbon-14?

21. Explain the Error A student simplified the expression $\log_2 8 + \log_3 27$ as shown. Explain and correct the student's error.

$$\log_2 8 + \log_3 27 = \log(8 \cdot 27)$$
$$= \log(216)$$
$$\approx 2.33$$

22. Communicate Mathematical Ideas Explain why it is not necessary for a scientific calculator to have both a key for common logs and a key for natural logs.

23. Analyze Relationships Explain how to find the relationship between $\log_b a$ and $\log_{\frac{1}{b}} a$.

Lesson Performance Task

Given the population data for the state of Texas from 1920–2010, perform exponential regression to obtain an exponential growth model for population as a function of time (represent 1920 as Year 0).

Obtain a logarithmic model for time as a function of population two ways: (1) by finding the inverse of the exponential model, and (2) by performing logarithmic regression on the same set of data but using population as the independent variable and time as the dependent variable. Then confirm that the two expressions are equivalent by applying the properties of logarithms.

Year	U.S. Census Count
1920	4,663,228
1930	5,824,715
1940	6,414,824
1950	7,711,194
1960	9,579,677
1970	11,196,730
1980	14,229,191
1990	16,986,335
2000	20,851,820
2010	25,145,561

16.2 Solving Exponential Equations

Essential Question: What are some ways you can solve an equation of the form $ab^x = c$, where a and c are nonzero real numbers and b is greater than 0 and not equal to 1?

 Explore **Solving Exponential Equations Graphically**

One way to solve exponential equations is graphically. First, graph each side of the equation separately. The point(s) at which the two graphs intersect are the solutions of the equation.

(A) First, look at the equation $275e^{0.06x} = 1000$. To solve the equation graphically, split it into two separate equations.

$y_1 = $ [____]

$y_2 = $ [____]

(B) What will the graphs of y_1 and y_2 look like?

_____

_____

(C) Graph y_1 and y_2 using a graphing calculator.

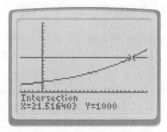

(D) The x-coordinate of the point of intersection is approximately [____].

(E) So, the solution of the equation is $x \approx$ [____].

(F) Now, look at the equation $10^{2x} = 10^4$. Split the equation into two separate equations.

$y_1 = $ [____]

$y_2 = $ [____]

G) What will the graphs of y_1 and y_2 look like?

_____

_____

H) Graph y_1 and y_2 using a graphing calculator.

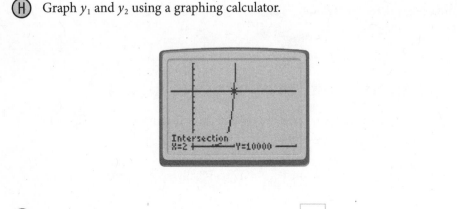

I) The x-coordinate of the point of intersection is [ ].

J) So, the solution of the equation is $x \approx$ [ ].

Reflect

1. How can you check the solution of an exponential equation after it is found graphically?

_____

_____

✏ Explain 1 Solving Exponential Equations Algebraically

In addition to solving exponential equations graphically, exponential equations can be solved algebraically. One way to solve exponential equations is to rewrite them in logarithmic form. Another way is to use the Property of Equality for Logarithmic Equations which states that for any positive numbers x, y, and b $(b \neq 1)$, $\log_b x = \log_b y$ if and only if $x = y$.

Example 1 **Solve the equations. Give the exact solution and an approximate solution to three decimal places.**

A) $10 = 5e^{4x}$

$10 = 5e^{4x}$ — Original equation

$2 = e^{4x}$ — Divide both sides by 5.

$\ln 2 = 4x$ — Rewrite in logarithmic form.

$\dfrac{\ln 2}{4} = \dfrac{4x}{4}$ — Divide both sides by 4.

$\dfrac{\ln 2}{4} = x$ — Simplify.

$0.173 \approx x$ — Evaluate. Round to three decimal places.

Ⓑ $5^x - 4 = 7$

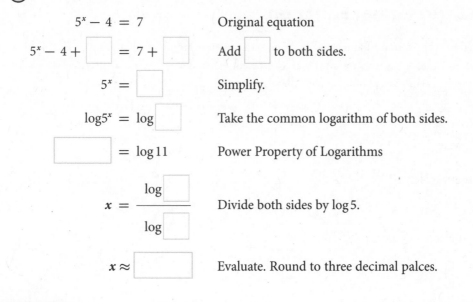

$5^x - 4 = 7$	Original equation
$5^x - 4 + \boxed{} = 7 + \boxed{}$	Add $\boxed{}$ to both sides.
$5^x = \boxed{}$	Simplify.
$\log 5^x = \log \boxed{}$	Take the common logarithm of both sides.
$\boxed{} = \log 11$	Power Property of Logarithms
$x = \dfrac{\log \boxed{}}{\log \boxed{}}$	Divide both sides by $\log 5$.
$x \approx \boxed{}$	Evaluate. Round to three decimal palces.

Reflect

2. Consider the equation $2^{x-3} = 85$. How can you solve this equation using logarithm base 2?

_____

_____

_____

_____

_____

_____

_____

3. Discussion When solving an exponential equation with base e, what is the benefit of taking the natural logarithm of both sides of the equation?

_____

Your Turn

Solve the equations. Give the exact solution and an approximate solution to three decimal places.

4. $2e^{x-1} + 5 = 80$

5. $6^{3x} = 12$

Solve a Real-World Problem by Solving an Exponential Equation

Suppose that \$250 is deposited into an account that pays 4.5% compounded quarterly. The equation $A = P\left(1 + \frac{r}{4}\right)^n$ gives the amount A in the account after n quarters for an initial investment P that earns interest at a rate r. Solve for n to find how long it will take for the account to contain at least \$500.

Analyze Information

Identify the important information.

- The initial investment P is \$ $\boxed{}$.

- The interest rate is $\boxed{}$ %, so r is $\boxed{}$.

- The amount A in the account after n quarters is \$ $\boxed{}$.

Formulate a Plan

Solve the equation for $A = P\left(1 + \frac{r}{4}\right)^n$ for $\boxed{}$ by substituting in the known information and using logarithms.

Solve

$$\boxed{} = \boxed{}\left(1 + \frac{\boxed{}}{4}\right)^n \qquad \text{Substitute.}$$

$$\boxed{} = \left(1 + \frac{0.045}{4}\right)^n \qquad \text{Divide both sides by 250.}$$

$$2 = \boxed{}^{\,n} \qquad \text{Evaluate the expression in parentheses.}$$

$$\log 2 = \log 1.01125^n \qquad \text{Take the common logarithm of both sides.}$$

$$\log 2 = \boxed{} \log \boxed{} \qquad \text{Power Property of Logarithms}$$

$$\frac{\log \boxed{}}{\log \boxed{}} = n \qquad \text{Divide both sides by } \log 1.01125.$$

$$\boxed{} \approx n \qquad \text{Evaluate.}$$

It will take about [ ] quarters, or about [ ] years, for the account to contain at least $500.

Check by substituting this value for *n* in the equation and solving for *A*.

$$A = 250\left(1 + \frac{0.045}{4}\right)^{\square} \qquad \text{Substitute.}$$

$$= 250\left(\boxed{}\right)^{61.96} \qquad \text{Evaluate the expression in parentheses.}$$

$$\approx 250\left(\boxed{}\right) \qquad \text{Evaluate the exponent.}$$

$$\approx \boxed{} \qquad \text{Multiply.}$$

So, the answer is reasonable.

Your Turn

6. How long will it take to triple a $250 initial investment in an account that pays 4.5% compounded quarterly?

Elaborate

7. Describe how to solve an exponential equation graphically.

_____

_____

8. **Essential Question Check-In** Describe how to solve an exponential equation algebraically.

_____

_____

Solve the equations graphically.

1. $4e^{0.1x} = 60$

2. $120e^{2x} = 75e^{3x}$

3. $5 = 625e^{0.02x}$

Solve the equations graphically. Then check your solutions algebraically.

4. $10e^{6x} = 5e^{-3x}$

5. $450e^{0.4x} = 2000$

Solve the equations. Give the exact solution and an approximate solution to three decimal places.

6. $6^{3x-9} - 10 = -3$

7. $7e^{3x} = 42$

8. $11^{6x+2} = 12$

9. $e^{\frac{2x-1}{3}} = 250$

10. $\left(10^x\right)^2 + 90 = 105$

11. $5^{\frac{x}{4}} = 30$

Solve.

12. The price P of a gallon of gas after t years is given by the equation $P = P_0(1 + r)^t$, where P_0 is the initial price of gas and r is the rate of inflation. If the price of a gallon of gas is currently $3.25, how long will it take for the price to rise to $4.00 if the rate of inflation is 10.5%?

13. Finance The amount A in a bank account after t years is given by the equation $A = A_0\left(1 + \frac{r}{6}\right)^{6t}$, where A_0 is the initial amount and r is the interest rate. Suppose there is $600 in the account. If the interest rate is 4%, after how many years will the amount triple?

14. A baseball player has a 25% chance of hitting a home run during a game. For how many games will the probability of hitting a home run in every game drop to 5%?

15. Meteorology In one part of the atmosphere where the temperature is a constant $-70\ °F$, pressure can be expressed as a function of altitude by the equation $P(h) = 128(10)^{-0.682h}$, where P is the atmospheric pressure in kilopascals (kPa) and h is the altitude in kilometers above sea level. The pressure ranges from 2.55 kPa to 22.9 kPa in this region. What is the range of altitudes?

16. You can choose a prize of either a $20,000 car or one penny on the first day, double that (2 cents) on the second day, and so on for a month. On what day would you receive at least the value of the car?

17. **Population** The population of a small coastal resort town, currently 3400, grows at a rate of 3% per year. This growth can be expressed by the exponential equation $P = 3400(1 + 0.03)^t$, where P is the population after t years. Find the number of years it will take for the population to reach 10,000.

$3400(1.03)^t \cdot 37$

32 years

18. A veterinarian has instructed Harrison to give his 75-lb dog one 325-mg aspirin tablet for arthritis. The amount of aspirin A remaining in the dog's body after t minutes can be expressed by $A = 325\left(\frac{1}{2}\right)^{\frac{t}{15}}$. How long will it take for the amount of aspirin to drop to 50 mg?

19. Agriculture The number of farms in Iowa (in thousands) can be modeled by $N(t) = 119(0.987)^t$, where t is the number of years since 1980. According to the model, when will the number of farms in Iowa be about 80,000?

20. Match the equations with the solutions.

    a. $9e^{3x} = 27$ _____ $x \approx 1.099$

    b. $9e^x = 27$ _____ $x \approx 1.022$

    c. $9e^{3x-4} = 27$ _____ $x \approx 0.366$

    d. $9e^{3x} + 2 = 27$ _____ $x \approx 1.700$

$$e^{3x} = 3 = e^{3x}$$
$$e^x = 3 = e^x$$
$$e^{3x-4} = 3 = e^{3x-4}$$
$$e^{3x} + 2 = 3 \qquad e^{3x} = 1$$

H.O.T. Focus on Higher Order Thinking

21. Explain the Error A student solved the equation $e^{4x} - 6 = 10$ as shown. Find and correct the student's mistake. Is there an easier way to solve the problem? Verify that both methods result in the same answer.

$$e^{4x} - 6 = 10$$
$$e^{4x} = 16$$
$$\log e^{4x} = \log 16$$
$$4x \log e = \log 16$$
$$4x(1) = \log 16$$
$$x = \frac{\log 16}{4}$$
$$x \approx 0.301$$

22. Multi-Step The amount A in an account after t years is given by the equation $A = Pe^{rt}$, where P is the initial amount and r is the interest rate.

a. Find an equation that models approximately how long it will take for the initial amount P in the account to double with the interest rate r. Write the equation in terms of the interest rate expressed as a percent.

b. The Rule of 72 states that you can find the approximate time it will take to double your money by dividing 72 by the interest rate. The rule uses 72 instead of 69 because 72 has more divisors, making it easier to calculate mentally. Use the Rule of 72 to find the approximate time it takes to double an initial investment of $300 with an interest rate of 3.75%. Determine that this result is reasonable by solving the equation $A = P_0(1.0375)^t$, where A is the amount after t years and P_0 is the initial investment.

23. Represent Real-World Problems Suppose you have an initial mass M_0 of a radioactive substance with a half-life of h. Then the mass of the parent isotopes at time t is $P(t) = M_0\left(\frac{1}{2}\right)^{\frac{t}{h}}$. Since the substance is decaying from the original parent isotopes into the new daughter isotopes while the mass of all the isotopes remains constant, the mass of the daughter isotopes at time t is $D(t) = M_0 - P(t)$. Find when the masses of the parent isotopes and daughter isotopes are equal. Explain the meaning of your answer and why it makes sense.

Lesson Performance Task

The frequency of a note on the piano, in Hz, is related to its position on the keyboard by the function $f(n) = 440 \cdot 2^{\frac{n}{12}}$, where n is the number of keys above or below the note concert A, concert A being the A key above middle C on the piano. Using this function, find the position n of the key that has a frequency of 110 Hz. Why is this number a negative value?

Logarithmic Properties and Exponential Equations

Essential Question: How do the properties of logarithms allow you to solve real-world problems?

Key Vocabulary
exponential equation
(ecuación exponencial)

KEY EXAMPLE (Lesson 16.1)

Simplify: $\log_5 5^{x+2} + \log_2 16^3$.

Apply properties of logarithms.

$$\log_5 5^{x+2} + \log_2 16^3 = (x+2)\log_5 5 + 3\log_2 16$$

$$= (x+2) + 3\log_2 (2^4)$$

$$= x + 2 + 3(4)$$

$$= x + 14$$

KEY EXAMPLE (Lesson 16.2)

Solve the equation: $4^{3x+1} = 6$.

$$4^{3x+1} = 6$$

$$\log 4^{3x+1} = \log 6 \qquad \text{Take the log of both sides.}$$

$$(3x+1)\log 4 = \log 6 \qquad \text{Bring down the exponent.}$$

$$3x + 1 = \frac{\log 6}{\log 4} \qquad \text{Rearrange to isolate } x.$$

$$3x = \frac{\log 6}{\log 4} - 1$$

$$x = \frac{1}{3}\left(\frac{\log 6}{\log 4} - 1\right) \approx 0.0975$$

EXERCISES

Use properties of logarithms to simplify. *(Lesson 16.1)*

1. $\log_{\frac{3}{5}} 0.216^4$

2. $\log_4 4^{x-2} + \log_3 243^2$

3. $\log_8 0.015625^x$

4. $\log 10^{2x+1} + \log_3 9$

Solve each equation. *(Lesson 16.2)*

5. $5^x = 50$

6. $6^{x+2} = 45$

7. $20^{2x+3} = 15$

8. $3^{5x+1} = 150$

MODULE PERFORMANCE TASK

How Old Is That Bone?

The La Brea Tar Pits in Los Angeles contain one of the best preserved collections of Pleistocene vertebrates, including over 660 species of organisms. An archeologist working at La Brea Tar Pits wants to assess the age of a mastodon bone fragment she discovered. She measures that the fragment has 22% as much carbon-14 as typical living tissue. Given that the half-life of carbon-14 is 5370 years, what is the bone fragment's age?

Start by listing in the space below the information you will need to solve the problem. Then use your own paper to complete the task. Be sure to write down all your data and assumptions. Then use graphs, numbers, words, or algebra to explain how you reached your conclusion.

(Ready) to Go On?

16.1–16.2 Logarithmic Properties and Exponential Equations

- Online Homework
- Hints and Help
- Extra Practice

Use properties of logarithms to simplify. *(Lesson 16.1)*

1. $\log_{\frac{6}{5}} 2.0736^5$

2. $\log_2 3.2 - \log_2 0.025$

3. $\log_7 7^{2x-1} + \log_3 81^2$

4. $\log_5 125 - \log 10^{5x}$

Solve each equation. Give the exact solution and an approximate solution to three decimal places. *(Lesson 16.2)*

5. $7^{2x} = 30$

6. $5^{2x-1} = 20$

7. $2^{0.5x+7} = 215$

8. $10^{3x-3} = 15$

ESSENTIAL QUESTION

9. How do you solve an exponential equation algebraically?

Assessment Readiness

1. For each function below, determine if the function has an inverse defined for all real numbers. Select Yes or No for **A–C.**

   A. $f(x) = 4x^3 - 1$ ⃝ Yes   ⃝ No

   B. $f(x) = \sqrt{3x} + 2$ ⃝ Yes   ⃝ No

   C. $f(x) = 4x^2 + 2$ ⃝ Yes   ⃝ No

2. Consider the equation $8^{x+1} = 12$. Choose True or False for each statement.

   A. After bringing down the exponent, the equation is $(x + 1)\log 8 = \log 12$.   ⃝ True   ⃝ False

   B. The equation cannot be solved because the bases are not the same.   ⃝ True   ⃝ False

   C. The approximate value of x is 0.195.   ⃝ True   ⃝ False

3. At a constant temperature, the pressure, P, of an enclosed gas is inversely proportional to the volume, V, of the gas. If $P = 50$ pounds per square inch when $V = 30$ cubic inches, how can you find the pressure when the volume is 125 cubic inches?

4. $A = P(1 + r)^n$ gives amount A in an account after n years after an initial investment P that earns interest at an annual rate r. How long will it take for $250 to increase to $500 at 4% annual interest? Explain how you got your answer.

Assessment Readiness

- Online Homework
- Hints and Help
- Extra Practice

1. Consider each sequence rule. Does the rule match the geometric sequence 5, 10, 20, 40, 80, … ? Select Yes or No for A–C.

   A. $a_n = 5(2)^n$ ◯ Yes   ◯ No

   B. $a_n = 10(2n)$ ◯ Yes   ◯ No

   C. $a_n = 5(2)^{n-1}$ ◯ Yes   ◯ No

2. Consider a situation where a population doubles every five years. Select True or False for each statement.

   A. The situation could be modeled with an exponential equation. ◯ True   ◯ False

   B. The situation could not be modeled with a quadratic equation. ◯ True   ◯ False

   C. The situation could be modeled with a linear equation. ◯ True   ◯ False

3. Consider the function $f(x) = \log_6 x$. Select True or False for each statement. What is $f(216)$?

   A. To evaluate $f(216)$, one way is to type it into the calculator as log 216 divided by log 6. ◯ True   ◯ False

   B. There is no way to evaluate $\log_6$ in the calculator, because the log function in the calculator has a base of 10. ◯ True   ◯ False

   C. When the function is evaluated for $x = 216$, $f(216) \approx 3$. ◯ True   ◯ False

4. Consider each equation. Is the equation the inverse function of $f(x) = 8x^3 + 2$?

   A. $f^{-1}(x) = \dfrac{\sqrt[2]{x-2}}{2}$ ◯ Yes   ◯ No

   B. $f^{-1}(x) = \dfrac{\sqrt[3]{x-2}}{2}$ ◯ Yes   ◯ No

   C. $f^{-1}(x) = \dfrac{\sqrt[3]{x-2}}{8}$ ◯ Yes   ◯ No

   D. $f^{-1}(x) = \dfrac{\sqrt[3]{x+2}}{2}$ ◯ Yes   ◯ No

5. In science class, Danny watched a video that talked about a type of spore that would have the following amount of spores in the petri dish each hour:

Hours	0	1	2	3	4
Spores	1	3	9	27	81

Danny wants to match the growth of the spores to a linear, quadratic, or exponential model. Using the information given, which model matches the spore growth? Explain.

6. A circular plot of land has a radius $3x - 1$. What is the polynomial representing the area of the land? Explain your answer.

7. The number of bacteria growing in a petri dish after n hours can be modeled by $b(t) = b_0 r^n$, where b_0 is the initial number of bacteria and r is the rate at which the bacteria grow. If the number of bacteria quadruples after 1 hour, how many hours will it take to produce 51,200 bacteria if there are initially 50 bacteria? Explain your answer.

Performance Tasks

★ **8.** The amount of freight transported by rail in the United States was about 580 billion *ton-miles* in 1960 and has been increasing at a rate of 2.32% per year since then.

   A. Write and graph a function representing the amount of freight, in billions of ton-miles, transported annually (1960 = year 0).

   B. In what year would you predict that the number of ton-miles would have exceeded or would exceed 1 trillion (1000 billion)?

★★★ **9.** In one part of the atmosphere where the temperature is a constant −70°F, from about 11 km to 25 km above sea level, pressure can be expressed as a function of altitude by the equation $P(h) = 128(10)^{-0.0682h}$, where P is the atmospheric pressure in kilopascals (kPa) and h is the altitude in kilometers above sea level.

    A. What is the altitude, to the nearest tenth of a kilometer, where the pressure is 5.54 kPa?

    B. A kilopascal is 0.145 psi. Would the model predict a sea-level pressure less than or greater than the actual sea-level pressure, 14.7 psi? Explain.

★★★ **10.** The loudness of sound is measured on a logarithmic scale according to the formula $L = 10\log\left(\dfrac{I}{I_0}\right)$, where L is the loudness of sound in decibels (dB), I is the intensity of sound, and I_0 is the intensity of the softest audible sound.

Sound	Intensity
Jet takeoff	$10^{15}I_0$
Jackhammer	$10^{12}I_0$
Hair dryer	$10^{7}I_0$
Whisper	$10^{3}I_0$
Leaves rustling	$10^{2}I_0$
Softest audible sound	I_0

    A. Find the loudness in decibels of each sound listed in the table.

    B. The sound at a rock concert is found to have a loudness of 110 decibels. Find the intensity of this sound. Where should this sound be placed in the table in order to preserve the order from least to greatest intensity?

    C. A decibel is $\dfrac{1}{10}$ of a bel. Is a jet plane louder than a sound that measures 20 bels? Explain.

Nuclear Medicine Technologist The radioactive properties of the isotope technetium-99m can be used in combination with a tin compound to map circulatory system disorders. Technetium-99m has a half-life of 6 hours.

a. Write an exponential decay function that models this situation. The function $p(t)$ should give the percent of the isotope remaining after t hours.

b. Describe domain, range, and the end behavior of $p(t)$ as t increases without bound for the function found in part a.

c. Write the inverse of the decay function. Use a common logarithm for your final function.

d. How long does it take until 5% of the technetium-99m remains? Round to the nearest tenth of an hour.

UNIT 7

Trigonometric Functions

MATH IN CAREERS

Boat Builder A boat builder builds and repairs all types of marine vessels, from sailboats to riverboats. Boat builders are responsible for drafting a boat's design; building the frame, hull, deck, and cabins; and fitting the engine. Boat builders often use computer technologies when designing a boat and must use geometry and trigonometry when interpreting blueprints and shaping and cutting materials to specified measurements. Boat builders need to be able to estimate and calculate costs of materials and labor and to understand mathematical models of different aspects of boats and boating.

If you are interested in a career as a boat builder, you should study these mathematical subjects:
- Geometry
- Algebra
- Trigonometry
- Business Math

Check out the career activity at the end of the unit to find out how **Boat Builders** use math.

© Houghton Mifflin Harcourt Publishing Company • ©Michael Interisano/Design Pics/Corbis

Reading Start-Up

Visualize Vocabulary

Use the ✔ words to complete the graphic.

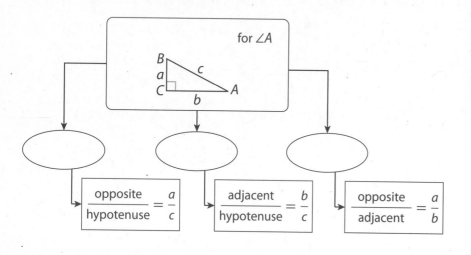

for ∠A

$$\frac{\text{opposite}}{\text{hypotenuse}} = \frac{a}{c}$$

$$\frac{\text{adjacent}}{\text{hypotenuse}} = \frac{b}{c}$$

$$\frac{\text{opposite}}{\text{adjacent}} = \frac{a}{b}$$

Vocabulary

Review Words

✔ cosine (coseno)

✔ sine (seno)

✔ tangent (tangente)

✔ trigonometric ratio (razón trigonométrica)

Preview Words

amplitude (amplitud)

angle of rotation (ángulo de referencia)

cosecant function (función cosecante)

cotangent function (función cotangente)

period (periodo)

periodic function (function periódica)

radian (radián)

reference angle (ángulo de rotación)

secant function (función secante)

Understand Vocabulary

To become familiar with some of the vocabulary terms in the module, consider the following. You may refer to the module, the glossary, or a dictionary.

1. An _____ is formed by a rotating ray, called the terminal side, and a stationary ray, called the initial side.

2. A _____ repeats exactly in regular intervals.

3. The _____ of a periodic function is half the difference of the maximum and minimum values and is always positive.

Active Reading

Layered Book Before beginning each module in this unit, create a layered book to help you summarize the information in each lesson. Each flap of the layered book can correspond to definitions and examples of the trigonometric functions, their graphs, and transformations. Write details of each function on the appropriate flap to create a summary of the module.

Unit-Circle Definition of Trigonometric Functions

Essential Question: How can the unit-circle definition of trigonometric functions help to solve real-world problems?

REAL WORLD VIDEO
How does a digital device like a smartphone display time on an analog clock? You may be surprised to learn that the answer involves trigonometry.

MODULE PERFORMANCE TASK PREVIEW

Telling Time with Trig

Imagine you are designing an analog clock widget that can be displayed on a variety of digital devices. You have to solve the problem of how to convert digital information about time into the corresponding positions of the hands of the clock. How can you use trigonometry to program your clock to display time accurately? It's time to find out!

© Houghton Mifflin Harcourt Publishing Company • Image Credits: ©Dacian G/ Shutterstock

Are (YOU) Ready?

Complete these exercises to review skills you will need for this module.

Pythagorean Theorem

• Online Homework
• Hints and Help
• Extra Practice

Example 1

Two sides of a right triangle measure 3 units and 1.5 units. Find the length of the third side. If possible, find the angle measures.

Use the Pythagorean Theorem $a^2 + b^2 = c^2$ to find the missing length.

The third side is either a leg or a hypotenuse.

If it's a hypotenuse, then it is c in the Pythagorean formula: $(1.5)^2 + 3^2 = c^2$, and $c = \sqrt{(1.5)^2 + 3^2} = \sqrt{2.25 + 9} = \sqrt{11.25} \approx 3.35$. The ratio of the side lengths is $1.5 : 3 : 3.35$, so this triangle is not a special right triangle.

If it's a leg, then it is a in the Pythagorean formula: $a^2 + 1.5^2 = 3^2$, and $a = \sqrt{3^2 - 1.5^2} = \sqrt{9 - 2.25} = 1.5\sqrt{3}$. Since the ratio of the sides $1.5 : 1.5\sqrt{3} : 3$ are in the form $a : a\sqrt{3} : 2a$, the triangle is a 30°-60°-90° special right triangle.

Two side lengths of a right triangle are given. Find the possible lengths of the missing side. When the sides form a special right triangle, find the angle measures of the triangle.

1. $4\sqrt{3}, 2\sqrt{3}$

2. $8, 15$

3. $3\sqrt{2}, 3$

Distance Formula

Example 2

Find the distance between the points $(7, -1)$ and $(16, 11)$.

$$d = \sqrt{(x_1 - x_2)^2 + (y_1 - y_2)^2} = \sqrt{(7 - 16)^2 + (-1 - 11)^2}$$
$$= \sqrt{81 + 144} = \sqrt{225} = 15$$

The distance is 15.

Find the distance between the given points.

4. $(-4, 20)$ and $(3, -4)$

5. $(8, 9)$ and $(0, -6)$

6. $(2.5, -2)$ and $(-5, 2)$

17.1 Angles of Rotation and Radian Measure

Essential Question: What is the relationship between the unit circle and radian measure?

⊘ Explore 1 Drawing Angles of Rotation and Finding Coterminal Angles

In trigonometry, an **angle of rotation** is an angle formed by the starting and ending positions of a ray that rotates about its endpoint. The angle is in *standard position* in a coordinate plane when the starting position of the ray, or *initial side* of the angle, is on the positive *x*-axis and has its endpoint at the origin. To show the amount and direction of rotation, a curved arrow is drawn to the ending position of the ray, or *terminal side* of the angle.

In geometry, you were accustomed to working with angles having measures between 0° and 180°. In trigonometry, angles can have measures greater than 180° and even less than 0°. To see why, think in terms of revolutions, or complete circular motions. Let θ be an angle of rotation in standard position.

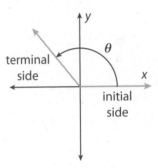

- If the rotation for an angle θ is less than 1 revolution in a counterclockwise direction, then the measure of θ is between 0° and 360°. An angle of rotation measured *clockwise* from standard position has a *negative* angle measure. **Coterminal angles** are angles that share the same terminal side. For example, the angles with measures of 257° and −103° are coterminal, as shown.

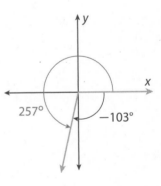

- If the rotation for θ is more than 1 revolution but less than 2 revolutions in a counterclockwise direction, then the measure of θ is between 360° and 720°, as shown. Because you can have any number of revolutions with an angle of rotation, there is a counterclockwise angle of rotation corresponding to any positive real number and a clockwise angle of rotation corresponding to any negative real number.

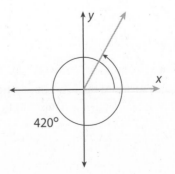

© Houghton Mifflin Harcourt Publishing Company

(A) Draw an angle of rotation of 310°. In what quadrant is the terminal side of the angle?

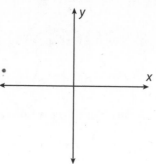

(B) On the same graph from the previous step, draw a positive coterminal angle. What is the angle measure of your angle?

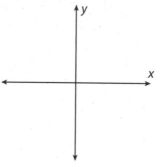

(C) On the same graph from the previous two steps, draw a negative coterminal angle. What is the angle measure of your angle?

Reflect

1. Is the measure of an angle of rotation in standard position completely determined by the position of its terminal side? Explain.

_____

_____

2. Find the measure between 720° and 1080° of an angle that is coterminal with an angle that has a measure of −30°. In addition, describe a general method for finding the measure of any angle that is coterminal with a given angle.

_____

_____

_____

Explore 2 Understanding Radian Measure

The diagram shows three circles centered at the origin. The arcs that are on the circle between the initial and terminal sides of the 225° central angle are called *intercepted arcs*.

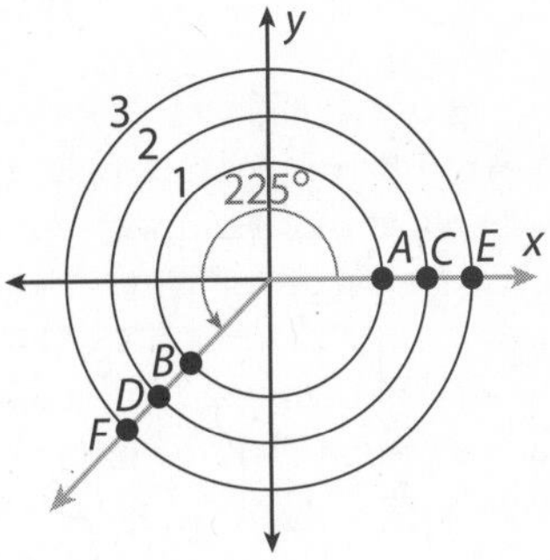

$\overset{\frown}{AB}$ is on a circle with radius 1 unit.

$\overset{\frown}{CD}$ is on a circle with radius 2 units.

$\overset{\frown}{EF}$ is on a circle with radius 3 units.

Notice that the intercepted arcs have different lengths, although they are intercepted by the same central angle of 225°. You will now explore how these arc lengths are related to the angle.

Ⓐ The angle of rotation is ☐ degrees counterclockwise.

There are ☐ degrees in a circle.

225° represents $\dfrac{\square}{\square}$ of the total number of degrees in a circle.

So, the length of each intercepted arc is $\dfrac{\square}{\square}$ of the total circumference of the circle that it lies on.

Ⓑ Complete the table. To find the length of the intercepted arc, use the fraction you found in the previous step. Give all answers in terms of π.

Radius, r	Circumference, C $(C = 2\pi r)$	Length of Intercepted Arc, s	Ratio of Arc Length to Radius, $\frac{s}{r}$
1			
2			
3			

Reflect

3. What do you notice about the ratios $\frac{s}{r}$ in the fourth column of the table?

_____

4. When the ratios of the values of a variable y to the corresponding values of another variable x all equal a constant k, y is said to be *proportional* to x, and the constant k is called the *constant of proportionality*. Because $\frac{y}{x} = k$, you can solve for y to get $y = kx$. In the case of the arcs that are intercepted by a 225° angle, is the arc length s proportional to the radius r? If so, what is the constant of proportionality, and what equation gives s in terms of r?

_____

5. Suppose that the central angle is 270° instead of 225°. Would the arc length s still be proportional to the radius r? If so, would the constant of proportionality still be the same? Explain.

_____

_____

Explain 1 Converting Between Degree Measure and Radian Measure

For a central angle θ that intercepts an arc of length s on a circle with radius r, the **radian measure** of the angle is the ratio $\theta = \frac{s}{r}$. In particular, on a *unit circle*, a circle centered at the origin with a radius of 1 unit, $\theta = s$. So, 1 *radian* is the angle that intercepts an arc of length 1 on a unit circle, as shown.

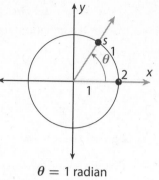

$\theta = 1$ radian

Recall that there are $360°$ in a full circle. Since the circumference of a circle of radius r is $s = 2\pi r$, the number of radians in a full circle is $\frac{2\pi r}{r} = 2\pi$. Therefore, $360° = 2\pi$ radians. So, $1° = \frac{2\pi}{360} = \frac{\pi}{180}$ radians and 1 radian $= \frac{360}{2\pi} = \frac{180}{\pi}$ degrees. This result is summed up in the following table.

CONVERTING DEGREES TO RADIANS	CONVERTING RADIANS TO DEGREES
Multiply the number of degrees by $\left(\frac{\pi \text{ radians}}{180°}\right)$.	Multiply the number of radians by $\left(\frac{180°}{\pi \text{ radians}}\right)$.

Example 1 Convert each measure from degrees to radians or from radians to degrees.

(A)

Degree measure	Radian measure
$20°$	$\frac{\pi}{180°} \cdot 20° = \frac{\pi}{9}$
$315°$	$\frac{\pi}{180°} \cdot 315° = \frac{7\pi}{4}$
$600°$	$\frac{\pi}{180°} \cdot 600° = \frac{10\pi}{3}$
$-60°$	$\frac{\pi}{180°} \cdot (-60°) = -\frac{\pi}{3}$
$-540°$	$\frac{\pi}{180°} \cdot (-540°) = -3\pi$

(B)

Radian measure	Degree measure
$\frac{\pi}{8}$	$\frac{180°}{\pi} \cdot \frac{\pi}{8} = \boxed{}$
$\frac{4\pi}{3}$	$\boxed{} \cdot \frac{4\pi}{3} = \boxed{}$
$\frac{9\pi}{2}$	
$-\frac{7\pi}{12}$	
$-\frac{13\pi}{6}$	

6. Which is larger, a degree or a radian? Explain.

_____

7. The unit circle below shows the measures of angles of rotation that are commonly used in trigonometry, with radian measures outside the circle and degree measures inside the circle. Provide the missing measures.

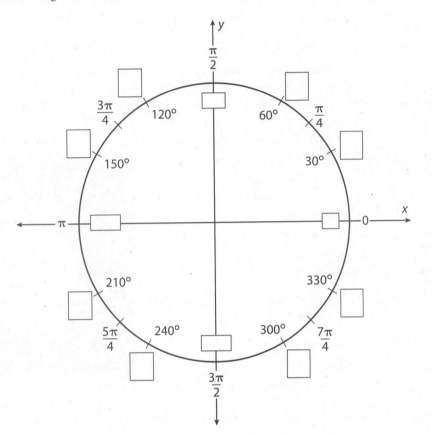

Convert each measure from degrees to radians or from radians to degrees.

8. −495°

9. $\dfrac{13\pi}{12}$

⚙ Explain 2 Solving a Real-World Problem Involving Arc Length

As you saw in the first Explain, for a central angle θ in radian measure, $\theta = \frac{s}{r}$ where s is the intercepted arc length. Multiplying both sides of the equation by r gives the arc length formula for a circle:

Arc Length Formula
For a circle of radius r, the arc length s intercepted by a central angle θ (measured in radians) is given by the following formula. $$s = r\theta$$

Many problems involving arc length also involve *angular velocity*, which is the angle measure through which an object turns in a given time interval. For example, the second hand of a clock has an angular velocity of 360° per minute, or 6° per second. Angular velocity may also be expressed in radians per unit of time. This makes finding the arc length traversed in an amount of time especially easy by using the arc length formula.

Ⓐ **The Sun** A point on the Sun's equator makes a full revolution once every 25.38 days. The Sun has a radius of about 432,200 miles at its equator. What is the angular velocity in radians per hour of a point on the Sun's equator? What distance around the Sun's axis does the point travel in one hour? How does this compare with the distance of about 1038 miles traveled by a point on Earth's equator in an hour?

One revolution is 2π radians. The angular velocity in radians per day is $\frac{2\pi}{25.38}$. Convert this to radians per hour.

$$\frac{2\pi \text{ radians}}{25.38 \text{ days}} \cdot \frac{1 \text{ day}}{24 \text{ hours}} = \frac{2\pi \text{ radians}}{25.38(24) \text{ hours}}$$
$$\approx 0.01032 \text{ radians/h}$$

The distance the point travels in an hour is the arc length it traverses in an hour.

$$s = r\theta$$
$$= 432{,}200(0.01032)$$
$$\approx 4460$$

The point travels about 4460 miles around the Sun's axis in an hour. This is more than 4 times farther than a point on Earth's equator travels in the same time.

Ⓑ **The Earth** Earth's equator is at a latitude of 0°. The Arctic circle is at a latitude of 66.52°N. The diameter of the equator is 7926 miles. The diameter of the Arctic circle is 3150 miles.

a. Find the angular velocity in degrees per minute of a point on the equator and of a point on the Arctic circle.

b. How far does a point on the Equator travel in 15 minutes?

c. How long will it take a point on the Arctic circle to travel this distance?

© Houghton Mifflin Harcourt Publishing Company • Image Credits: ©Markus Gann/Shutterstock

a. Every point on Earth completes 1 revolution of _____ degrees each 24 hours, so the angular velocities of the points will be the same. Convert the angular velocity to degrees per minute.

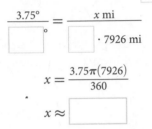

$$\frac{\boxed{}^{\circ}}{\boxed{}\ \text{h}} \cdot \frac{1\ \text{h}}{60\ \text{min}} = \frac{\boxed{}^{\circ}}{24(60)\ \text{min}} = \boxed{}^{\circ}/\text{min}$$

The angular velocity is $\boxed{}^{\circ}$/min.

b. Multiply the time by the angular velocity to find the angle through which a point rotates in 15 minutes.

$\boxed{}$ min $\cdot$ 0.25°/min = $\boxed{}^{\circ}$

Write a proportion to find the distance to the nearest tenth that this represents at the equator, where Earth's circumference is $\boxed{}$ $\cdot$ 7926 miles.

$$\frac{3.75^{\circ}}{\boxed{}^{\circ}} = \frac{x\ \text{mi}}{\boxed{} \cdot 7926\ \text{mi}}$$

$$x = \frac{3.75\pi(7926)}{360}$$

$$x \approx \boxed{}$$

A point at the equator travels about _____ miles in 15 minutes.

c. Write a proportion to find the angle of rotation to the nearest thousandth required to move a point 259.4 miles on the Arctic circle, where the circumference is $\boxed{}$ $\cdot$ 3150 miles.

$$\frac{259.4\ \text{mi}}{\boxed{} \cdot 3150\ \text{mi}} = \frac{x^{\circ}}{\boxed{}^{\circ}}$$

$$x = \frac{259.4(360)}{3150\pi}$$

$$x \approx \boxed{}$$

Use the angular velocity to find the time t to the nearest hundredth required for a point on the Arctic circle to move through an angle of rotation of 9.437°.

$$\left(\boxed{}^{\circ}/\text{min}\right)(t\ \text{min}) = 9.437^{\circ}$$

$$t \approx \boxed{}$$

It takes about _____ minutes for a point on the Arctic circle to travel the same distance that a point on the equator travels in 15 minutes.

10. How does using an angle of rotation to find the length of the arc on a circle intercepted by the angle differ when degrees are used from when radians are used?

_____

_____

_____

_____

11. **Astronomy** A neutron star (an incredibly dense collapsed star) in the Sagittarius Galaxy has a radius of 10 miles and completes a full revolution every 0.0014 seconds. Find the angular velocity of the star in radians per second, then use this velocity to determine how far a point on the equator of the star travels each second. How does this compare to the speed of light (about 186,000 mi/sec)?

12. **Geography** The northeastern corner of Maine is due north of the southern tip of South America in Chile. The difference in latitude between the locations is 103°. Using both degree measure and radian measure, and a north-south circumference of Earth of 24,860 miles, find the distance between the two locations.

💬 Elaborate

13. Given the measure of two angles of rotation, how can you determine whether they are coterminal without actually drawing the angles?

_____

_____

14. What is the conversion factor to go from degrees to radians? What is the conversion factor to go from radians to degrees? How are the conversion factors related?

_____

_____

_____

15. **Essential Question Check-In** An angle of rotation in standard position intercepts an arc of length 1 on the unit circle. What is the radian measure of the angle of rotation?

_____

_____

Personal
Math
Trainer

• Online Homework
• Hints and Help
• Extra Practice

Draw the indicated angle of rotation in standard position.

1. A positive angle coterminal
to 130°

2. A negative angle coterminal
to 130°

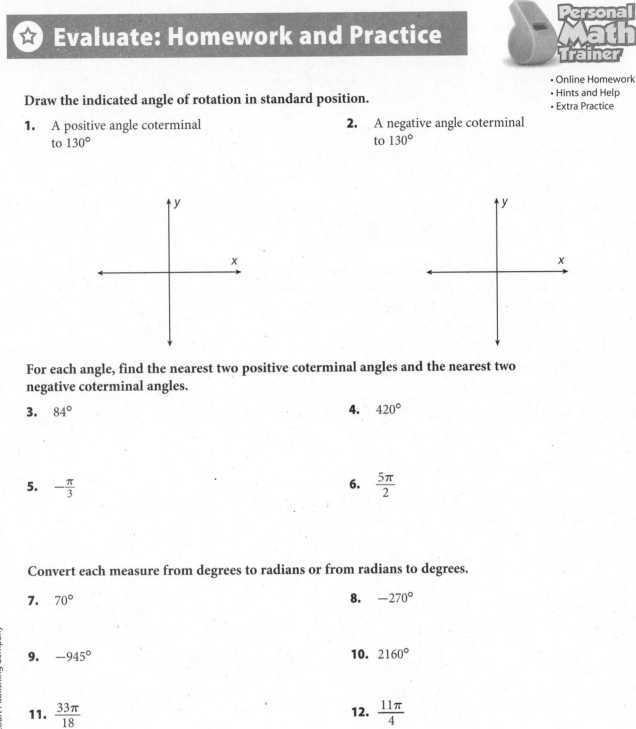

For each angle, find the nearest two positive coterminal angles and the nearest two negative coterminal angles.

3. 84°

4. 420°

5. $-\dfrac{\pi}{3}$

6. $\dfrac{5\pi}{2}$

Convert each measure from degrees to radians or from radians to degrees.

7. 70°

8. −270°

9. −945°

10. 2160°

11. $\dfrac{33\pi}{18}$

12. $\dfrac{11\pi}{4}$

13. $-\dfrac{5\pi}{3}$

14. $-\dfrac{7\pi}{2}$

15. Geography A student in the United States has an friend overseas with whom she corresponds by computer. The foreign student says, "If you write the latitude and longitude of my school in radians instead of degrees, you get the coordinates 0.6227 radians north latitude and 2.438 radians east longitude". Convert the coordinates back to degrees. Then use a globe, map, or app to identify the city.

16. Geography If a ship sailed due south from Iceland to Antarctica, it would sail through an angle of rotation of about 140° around Earth's center. Find this measure in radians. Then, using 3960 miles for Earth's radius, find how far the ship would travel.

17. Geography Acapulco, Mexico and Hyderabad, India both lie at 17° north latitude, and lie very nearly halfway around the world from each other in an east-west direction. The radius of Earth at a latitude of 17° is about 3790 miles. Suppose that you could fly from Acapulco directly west to Hyderabad or fly directly north to Hyderabad. Which way would be shorter, and by how much? Use 3960 miles for Earth's radius. (Hint: To fly directly north, you would go from 17° north latitude to 90° north latitude, and then back down to 17° north latitude.)

18. Planetary Exploration "Opportunity" and "Phoenix" are two of the robotic explorers on Mars. Opportunity landed at 2° south latitude, where Mars' radius is about 2110 miles. Phoenix landed at 68° north latitude, where Mars' radius is about 790 miles. Mars rotates on its axis once every 24.6 Earth-hours. How far does each explorer travel as Mars rotates by 1 radian? How many hours does it take Mars to rotate 1 radian? Using this answer, how fast is each explorer traveling around Mars' axis in miles per hour?

19. Earth's Rotation The 40th parallel of north latitude runs across the United States through Philadelphia, Indianapolis, and Denver. At this latitude, Earth's radius is about 3030 miles. The earth rotates with an angular velocity of $\frac{\pi}{12}$ radians (or 15°) per hour toward the east. If a jet flies due west with the same angular velocity relative to the ground at the equinox, the Sun as viewed from the jet will stop in the sky. How fast in miles per hour would the jet have to travel west at the 40th parallel for this to happen?

20. Our Galaxy It is about 30,000 light years from our solar system to the center of the Milky Way Galaxy. The solar system revolves around the center of the Milky Way with an angular velocity of about 2.6×10^{-8} radians per year.

    a. What distance does the solar system travel in its orbit each year?

    b. Given that a light year is about 5.88×10^{12} miles, how fast is the solar system circling the center of the galaxy in miles per hour?

21. Driving A windshield wiper blade turns through an angle of 135°. The bottom of the blade traces an arc with a 9-inch radius. The top of the blade traces an arc with a 23-inch radius. To the nearest inch, how much longer is the top arc than the bottom arc?

22. Cycling You are riding your bicycle, which has tires with a 30-inch diameter, at a steady 15 miles per hour. What is the angular velocity of a point on the outside of the tire in radians per second?

23. Select all angles that are coterminal with an angle of rotation of 300°.

    A. $-420°$

    B. $2100°$

    C. $-900°$

    D. $-\frac{\pi}{3}$ radians

    E. $\frac{23\pi}{3}$ radians

    F. $-\frac{7\pi}{3}$ radians

H.O.T. Focus on Higher Order Thinking

24. Explain the Error Lisa was told that a portion of the restaurant on the Space Needle in Seattle rotates at a rate of 8 radians per hour. When asked to find the distance through which she would travel if she sat at a table 40 feet from the center of rotation for a meal lasting 2 hours, she produced the following result:

$\theta = \frac{s}{r}$

$8 = \frac{s}{40}$

$320 = s$ The distance is 320 feet.

25. Represent Real-World Problems The minute hand on a clock has an angular velocity of 2π radians/hour, while the hour hand has an angular velocity of $\frac{\pi}{6}$ radians/hour. At 12:00, the hour and second hands both point straight up. The two hands will next come back together sometime after 1:00. At what exact time will this happen? (Hint: You want to find the next time when the angle of rotation made by the hour hand is coterminal with the angle made by the minute hand after it has first completed one full revolution.)

26. Critical Thinking Write a single rational expression that can be used to represent all angles that are coterminal with an angle of $\frac{5\pi}{8}$ radians.

27. Extension You know that the length s of the arc intercepted on a circle of radius r by an angle of rotation of θ radians is $s = r\theta$. Find an expression for the area of the sector of the circle with radius r that has a central angle of θ radians. Explain your reasoning.

Lesson Performance Task

At a space exploration center, astronauts are training on a human centrifuge that has a diameter of 70 feet.

a. The centrifuge makes 72 complete revolutions in 2 minutes. What is the angular velocity of the centrifuge in radians per second? What distance does an astronaut travel around the center each second?

b. Acceleration is the rate of change of velocity with time. An object moving at a constant velocity v in circular motion with a radius of r has an acceleration a of $a = \frac{v^2}{r}$. What is the astronaut's acceleration? (Note that the acceleration will have units of feet per second *squared*.)

c. One "g" is the acceleration caused on Earth's surface by gravity. This acceleration is what gives you your weight. Some roller coasters can produce an acceleration in a tight loop of 5 or even 6 g's. Earth's gravity produces an acceleration of 32 ft/s². How many g's is the astronaut experiencing in the centrifuge?

© Houghton Mifflin Harcourt Publishing Company

17.2 Defining and Evaluating the Basic Trigonometric Functions

Resource Locker

Essential Question: How does the unit circle allow the trigonometric functions to be defined for all real numbers instead of just for acute angles?

 **Explore** **Using Special Right Triangles in a Unit Circle**

In geometry, you learned that sine, cosine, and tangent are ratios of the lengths of the sides of a right triangle. In particular, if θ is an acute angle in a right triangle, then:

$$\sin \theta = \frac{\text{length of the opposite leg}}{\text{length of the hypotenuse}}$$

$$\cos \theta = \frac{\text{length of the adjacent leg}}{\text{length of the hypotenuse}}$$

$$\tan \theta = \frac{\text{length of the opposite leg}}{\text{length of the adjacent leg}}$$

You also studied two sets of special right triangles: those with angles of 45°—45°—90° and those with angles of 30° —60° —90°, and found a general relationship for the lengths of the three sides in each type of triangle:

The variable, a, can take any positive value. To see how these triangles and the values of sine, cosine, and tangent for their angles relate to the unit circle, the hypotenuse must have a length of 1. This corresponds to leg lengths of $\frac{\sqrt{2}}{2}$ for the 45° —45° —90° triangle, and leg lengths of $\frac{\sqrt{3}}{2}$ and $\frac{1}{2}$ for the 30° —60° —90° triangle.

(A) A 45° —45° —90° triangle has been inscribed inside a unit circle.

- Sketch the result of reflecting the triangle across the y-axis.

- Sketch the result of reflecting the triangle across the x-axis.

- Sketch the result of reflecting the triangle across both axes.

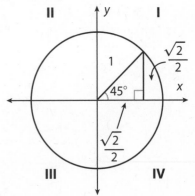

You should have a triangle in each of the four quadrants.

- For each triangle you drew, indicate the *signed* length of each leg. For example, a leg pointing left or down from the *x*- or *y*-axis should have a negative value.

Use the signed lengths of the legs and the ratios associated with the trigonometric functions to fill in the table.

	Quadrant I $0° < \theta < 90°$	Quadrant II $90° < \theta < 180°$	Quadrant III $180° < \theta < 270°$	Quadrant IV $270° < \theta < 360°$
Angle of rotation, θ	$45°$			
$\sin \theta$	$\frac{\sqrt{2}}{2}$			
$\cos \theta$	$\frac{\sqrt{2}}{2}$			
$\tan \theta$	1			

Ⓑ Repeat the process from Step A for the $30° - 60° - 90°$ triangle that has been inscribed in the unit circle.

- Sketch the three reflected triangles and label the signed lengths of the legs.

- Use the signed lengths of the legs and the ratios associated with the trigonometric functions to fill in the table.

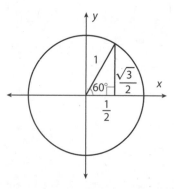

	Quadrant I $0° < \theta < 90°$	Quadrant II $90° < \theta < 180°$	Quadrant III $180° < \theta < 270°$	Quadrant IV $270° < \theta < 360°$
Angle of rotation, θ	$60°$			
$\sin \theta$	$\frac{\sqrt{3}}{2}$			
$\cos \theta$	$\frac{1}{2}$			
$\tan \theta$	$\sqrt{3}$			

(C) Repeat the process for this 30° −60° −90° triangle that has been inscribed in the unit circle.

- Sketch the three reflected triangles and label the signed lengths of the legs.

- Use the signed lengths of the legs and the ratios associated with the trigonometric functions to fill in the table.

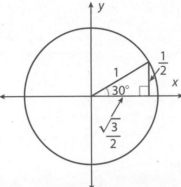

	Quadrant I $0° < \theta < 90°$	Quadrant II $90° < \theta < 180°$	Quadrant III $180° < \theta < 270°$	Quadrant IV $270° < \theta < 360°$
Angle of rotation, θ	30°			
$\sin\theta$	$\frac{1}{2}$			
$\cos\theta$	$\frac{\sqrt{3}}{2}$			
$\tan\theta$	$\frac{\sqrt{3}}{3}$			

Reflect

1. What do you observe about the absolute values of the trigonometric functions in any row of each table?

_____

2. Identify which quadrants have positive values for $\sin\theta$ and which quadrants have negative values. Do the same for $\cos\theta$ and $\tan\theta$.

_____

_____

_____

3. How do the signed lengths of the triangles' legs relate to the point where the triangle intersects the unit circle? Use this to relate the coordinates of the intersection points to the trigonometric functions of the angle θ.

_____

_____

_____

_____

Evaluating the Basic Trigonometric Functions for Special Angles

In the Explore, each of the reflected triangles has an interior angle with its vertex at the center of the circle whose measure is equal to the measure of the corresponding angle of the original triangle. These four angles serve as *reference angles* for the rotation angles listed in the table. This concept can be extended to any rotation angle.

The **reference angle** of a rotation angle is the acute angle from the terminal side of the rotation angle to the *x*-axis.

For rotation angles that represent less than one full revolution $\left(0° \le \theta < 360° \text{ or } 0 \le \theta < 2\pi\right)$ the measure of the reference angle can be found using a quadrant dependent formula. The quadrant also determines the signs of the trigonometric function. The formulas and signs are summarized in the table.

| Quadrant | Reference angle (θ') | | Sign | | |
	Degrees	Radians	Sin	Cos	Tan
I	$\theta' = \theta$	$\theta' = \theta$	+	+	+
II	$\theta' = 180° - \theta$	$\theta' = \pi - \theta$	+	−	−
III	$\theta' = \theta - 180°$	$\theta' = \theta - \pi$	−	−	+
IV	$\theta' = 360° - \theta$	$\theta' = 2\pi - \theta$	−	+	−

To find the values of the trigonometric functions of an angle θ you can use the ratios from the reference angle to find the absolute values of the function values, and then you can use the quadrant to determine the signs of the function values.

What about rotation angles larger than a full rotation? You have already observed that the values of cos θ and sin θ match the *x*- and *y*-coordinates where the terminal side of the angle intersects the circle.

Using this as the definition for sine and cosine, and including the definition of tangent as $\frac{y}{x}$, the trigonometric functions can be extended to any angle. Angles representing multiple revolutions, and negative angles give the same result for any trigonometric function as the coterminal angle between 0° and 360°.

Example 1   **Evaluate the trigonometric function by using the quadrant and the reference angle to determine the sign and absolute value of the function value.**

Ⓐ $\cos \dfrac{16\pi}{3}$

Identify the coterminal angle between 0 and 2π. $\dfrac{16}{3}\pi = 4\pi + \dfrac{4}{3}\pi$

Find the reference angle for Quadrant III. $\theta' = \dfrac{4}{3}\pi - \pi$

$\theta' = \dfrac{\pi}{3}$

Identify the special right triangle angle. $\theta' = \dfrac{\pi}{3} \times \dfrac{180°}{\pi} = 60°$

Use the sides of a 30° −60° −90° triangle. $\cos \theta' = \dfrac{1}{2}$

Apply the sign of cosine in Quadrant III. $\cos \dfrac{16}{3}\pi = -\cos\dfrac{\pi}{3}$

$= -\dfrac{1}{2}$

(B) $\tan \dfrac{11\pi}{4}$

Identify the coterminal angle between 0 and 2π.

Find the reference angle for Quadrant $\boxed{}$.

Identify the special right triangle angle.

Use the ratios of the sides of a $45° - 45° - 90°$ triangle.

Apply the sign of tangent in Quadrant II.

$\dfrac{11}{4}\pi = 2\pi + \boxed{}$

$\theta' = \boxed{} - \dfrac{3}{4}\pi$

$\theta' = \boxed{}$

$\theta' = \dfrac{\pi}{4} \times \boxed{} = 45°$

$\tan \theta' = \boxed{}$

$\tan \dfrac{11\pi}{4} = \boxed{}$

Reflect

4. Explain how defining sine, cosine, and tangent in terms of x- and y-coordinates instead of in terms of the sides of a right triangle also allows these functions to be evaluated at quadrantal angles.

_____

_____

_____

_____

Your Turn

Evaluate the trigonometric function by using the quadrant and the reference angle to determine the sign and absolute value of the function value.

5. $\sin \dfrac{5\pi}{6}$

6. $\cos 7\pi$

Evaluating the Basic Trigonometric Functions Using a Calculator

Using coordinates of points on the unit circle to define trigonometric functions, you can see that the sine and cosine functions can be defined for any angle measure. But because the ratio that describes the tangent function has the variable x as its denominator, the tangent function is not defined for any angle for which x is 0. This occurs at angles whose measures are $\cdots, -\frac{3\pi}{2}, -\frac{\pi}{2}, \frac{\pi}{2}, \frac{3\pi}{2}, \frac{5\pi}{2}, \cdots$, or $\left(\frac{2n+1}{2}\right)\pi$ for all integers n. These angle measures are not included in the domain of the tangent function.

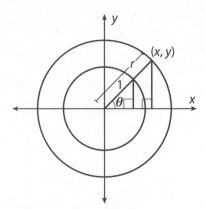

Because the values of the sine and cosine functions are coordinates of points on the unit circle, the output of the sine and cosine functions will always range from -1 to 1. The output of the tangent function, however, can be arbitrarily large because the denominator can become arbitrarily small (as long as it does not equal 0).

	Sine	**Cosine**	**Tangent**
Domain	$\left\{\theta \mid \theta \in \mathbb{R}\right\}$	$\left\{\theta \mid \theta \in \mathbb{R}\right\}$	$\left\{\theta \mid \theta \neq \dfrac{(2n+1)\pi}{2}, n \in \mathbb{Z}\right\}$
Range	$\left\{\theta \mid -1 \leq \theta \leq 1\right\}$	$\left\{\theta \mid -1 \leq \theta \leq 1\right\}$	$\left\{\theta \mid \theta \in \mathbb{R}\right\}$

Using trigonometric functions to find coordinates of any point on a circle as a function of an angle is useful for solving real-world applications.

The diagram shows two concentric circles with a single angle inscribed in both. The inner circle is a unit circle, and the outer circle has a radius of r. The two inscribed right triangles are similar —we know this because they have two angles of the same size—, and the coordinates of the outer point can be determined by using the ratios of the sides of similar triangles. The base and height of the inside triangle are $\cos\theta$ and $\sin\theta$ respectively. The ratio of outer and inner widths and outer and inner heights are the same as the ratio of outer and inner hypotenuses, or $\frac{r}{1}$. Thus, the x- and y-coordinates of any point on a circular arc of radius r and angle θ are given by $(r\cos\theta, r\sin\theta)$.

The trigonometric ratios can be expanded to the coordinates (x, y) of any point on a circle with radius r centered at the origin:

$$\sin\theta = \frac{y}{r} \qquad \cos\theta = \frac{x}{r} \qquad \tan\theta = \frac{y}{x}, x \neq 0$$

Example 2 Use trigonometric functions and a calculator to solve the problem.

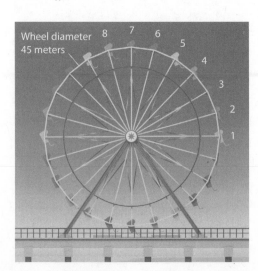

(A) A Ferris wheel with a diameter of 45 meters and 24 seats spread evenly around the outside wheel is stopped in the position shown in the diagram. Using the center of the Ferris wheel as the origin, what are the horizontal and vertical positions of Seat 8? How far above the bottom of the wheel is Seat 8? Solve the problem using radians. Give answers to the nearest tenth of a meter.

First check that your calculator is in radian mode. On a graphing calculator, the units for angle measure can be changed to radians by pressing ⬛MODE⬛ and selecting radians.

Determine the angle between two adjacent seats.

$$\theta_{\text{sep}} = \frac{2\pi}{24} = \frac{\pi}{12}$$

Determine how many seats there are from Seat 8 to Seat 1.

$$8 - 1 = 7$$

Find the rotation angle of Seat 8.

$$\theta = 7\left(\frac{\pi}{12}\right) = \frac{7\pi}{12}$$

Find the x- and y-coordinates.

$$
\begin{aligned}
(x, y) &= \left(r\cos\theta,\ r\sin\theta\right) \\
&= \left(\left(\frac{45}{2}\right)\cos\frac{7\pi}{12},\ \left(\frac{45}{2}\right)\sin\frac{7\pi}{12}\right) \\
&\approx (-5.8,\ 21.7)
\end{aligned}
$$

Seat 8 is about 5.8 meters to the left and 21.7 meters above the center of the wheel. The center is 22.5 meters above the bottom of the wheel, so Seat 8 is stopped 44.2 meters above the bottom of the wheel.

(B) An airplane begins to descend toward a runway 1 mile away at an angle of $-5°$ to the horizontal. What is its change in elevation after it flies 5000 feet horizontally towards the runway?

First check that your calculator is in degree mode. On a graphing calculator, the units for angle measure can be changed to degrees by pressing MODE and selecting degrees.

Using the beginning of the descent as the origin, the horizontal distance traveled by the plane should be treated as the ___-coordinate. The change in elevation is the ___-coordinate.

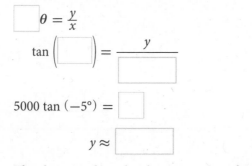

$$\boxed{}\ \theta = \frac{y}{x}$$

$$\tan\left(\boxed{}\right) = \frac{y}{\boxed{}}$$

$$5000 \tan(-5°) = \boxed{}$$

$$y \approx \boxed{}$$

The elevation drops by about _____ feet.

Reflect

7. How could you describe the position of Seat 8 in Example A with a negative angle measure?

_____

_____

© Houghton Mifflin Harcourt Publishing Company

8. How long a shadow does a 40-foot tall tree cast on the ground if the sun is at an angle of 0.5 radians relative to the horizon? Use a calculator to solve the problem.

 **Elaborate**

9. Explain the meaning of the message "ERR:DOMAIN" if you try to evaluate $\tan \frac{\pi}{2}$ on a graphing calculator. Why do you get this error message?

_____

_____

_____

_____

10. Explain why it is helpful to find coterminal and reference angles when evaluating trigonometric functions of large positive and negative angles without a calculator.

_____

_____

_____

_____

_____

_____

_____

11. **Essential Question Check-In** Explain how to define the sine and cosine of an angle in terms of a coordinate on the unit circle.

_____

_____

_____

_____

☆ Evaluate: Homework and Practice

1. A right triangle with an angle of approximately 53.1° is inscribed in the first quadrant of the unit circle, with a horizontal length of $\frac{3}{5}$ and a vertical length of $\frac{4}{5}$.

   Complete the table for the following trigonometric functions.

Angle of rotation, θ	53.1	126.9	233.1	306.9
$\sin\theta$				
$\cos\theta$				
$\tan\theta$				

Evaluate the trigonometric function without using a calculator. Angles are given in degrees.

2. $\cos 135°$

3. $\tan(-30°)$

4. $\sin 480°$

5. $\cos 720°$

Evaluate the trigonometric function without using a calculator. Angles are given in radians.

6. $\cos \dfrac{7\pi}{4}$

7. $\sin\left(-\dfrac{\pi}{2}\right)$

8. $\tan\left(-\dfrac{10\pi}{3}\right)$

9. $\tan\dfrac{16\pi}{3}$

Use a calculator to evaluate the trigonometric function of the angle given in degrees.

10. $\sin 132°$

11. $\cos\left(-203°\right)$

12. $\tan 43°$

13. $\cos 547°$

Use a calculator to evaluate the trigonometric function of the angle given in radians.

14. $\sin\left(\dfrac{5}{8}\pi\right)$

15. $\cos\left(1.2\pi\right)$

16. $\tan\left(10.5\right)$

17. $\sin\left(-3.7\right)$

Find a value or an expression for the coordinate on a circle centered at (0, 0) and at an angle θ from the x-axis.

18. radius $= 10$, $\theta = 135°$, x-coordinate

19. radius $= 5$, $\theta = 2.7$ radians, y-coordinate

20. radius $= r$, $\theta = \dfrac{17\pi}{4}$ radians , x-coordinate

21. radius $= 0.5$, $\theta = 2\phi$, y-coordinate

Use trigonometric functions to solve the real-world problems.

22. A swing hangs from a beam 10 feet high, with the seat hanging 2 feet above the ground. In motion, the swing moves back and forth from −130° to −50° to the horizontal. How far forward and back does the swing move along the ground at the extremes?

23. The Americans with Disabilities Act sets the maximum angle for a wheelchair ramp entering a business at 4.76°. Determine the horizontal distance needed to accommodate a ramp that goes up to a door 4 feet off the ground.

24. Jennifer is riding on a merry-go-round at a carnival that revolves at a speed of 3.3 revolutions per minute. She is sitting 7 feet from the center of the merry-go-round. If Jennifer's starting position is considered to be at 0 radians, what are her x- and y-coordinates after 57 seconds?

25. A car is traveling on a road that goes up a hill. The hill has an angle of 17° relative to horizontal. How high up the hill vertically will the car be after it has traveled 100 yards up the road?

26. Classify $f(\theta)$ of these trigonometric functions as less than, greater than, or equal to zero.

   A. $f(\theta) = \sin\theta$, θ is in quadrant III

   B. $f(\theta) = \tan\theta$, θ is in quadrant II

   C. $f(\theta) = \cos\theta$, θ is in quadrant IV

   D. $f(\theta) = \cos\theta$, $\theta = 180°$

   E. $f(\theta) = \tan\theta$, $\theta = 540°$

   F. $f(\theta) = \tan\theta$, θ in quadrant I

H.O.T. Focus on Higher Order Thinking

27. Explain the Error Sven used his calculator to find $\sin 10°$ and got an answer of approximately -0.5440, which seems wrong given that $10°$ is in the first quadrant. What did Sven do wrong? What is the correct answer?

28. Look for a Pattern Use the reference triangles and your calculator to make an observation about the rate of change of $\tan\theta$ over the interval 0 to 2π. Where does the rate of change increase? Where does it decrease? Are there any intervals where $\tan\theta$ is a decreasing function? Explain.

29. Analyze Relationships Use the unit circle and quadrant locations to prove that $\cos(-\theta) = \cos\theta$ for any angle, θ.

Lesson Performance Task

In Italy, there is a large circular test track that is used to test race cars and other high-speed automobiles.

a. Suppose a similar track has a radius of 6 kilometers. Find the circumference of the track.

b. While test-driving a new car on the similar track, a driver starts at the right-hand side of the circular track, travels in a counter-clockwise direction, and stops $\frac{3}{5}$ of the way around the track. Using the center of the track as the origin and the starting point as the intersection of the x-axis and the circle represented by the track, find the coordinates, to the nearest tenth, of the point where the driver stopped the car.

c. The driver continues in the same direction, but stops again approximately at the point $(5.2, 3.0)$. What is the car's position on the track relative to its starting point? Had the car made more or less than 1 revolution around the track when it stopped the second time? Explain.

d. If the car drove once around the track in 6 minutes and 48 seconds, what is its average velocity? Give your answer to the nearest tenth of a kilometer per hour.

17.3 Using a Pythagorean Identity

Essential Question: How can you use a given value of one of the trigonometric functions to calculate the values of the other functions?

Resource
Locker

🧭 Explore   Proving a Pythagorean Identity

In the previous lesson, you learned that the coordinates of any point (x, y) that lies on the unit circle where the terminal ray of an angle θ intersects the circle are $x = \cos\theta$ and $y = \sin\theta$, and that $\tan\theta = \frac{y}{x}$. Combining these facts gives the identity $\tan\theta = \frac{\sin\theta}{\cos\theta}$, which is true for all values of θ where $\cos\theta \neq 0$. In the following Explore, you will derive another identity based on the Pythagorean theorem, which is why the identity is known as a *Pythagorean identity*.

(A)   The terminal side of an angle θ intersects the unit circle at the point (a, b) as shown. Write a and b in terms of trigonometric functions involving θ.

$a =$ _____

$b =$ _____

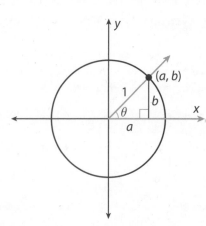

(B)   Apply the Pythagorean theorem to the right triangle in the diagram. Note that when a trigonometric function is squared, the exponent is typically written immediately after the name of the function. For instance, $(\sin\theta)^2 = \sin^2\theta$.

Write the Pythagorean Theorem. $a^2 + b^2 = c^2$

Substitute for a, b, and c. $\left(\boxed{}\right)^2 + \left(\boxed{}\right)^2 = \boxed{}^2$

Square each expression. $\boxed{} + \boxed{} = \boxed{}$

1. The identity is typically written with the sine function first. Write the identity this way, and explain why it is equivalent to the one in Step B.

_____

_____

2. Confirm the Pythagorean identity for $\theta = \frac{\pi}{3}$.

3. Confirm the Pythagorean identity for $\theta = \frac{3\pi}{4}$.

⚙ Explain 1 · Finding the Value of the Other Trigonometric Functions Given the Value of sin θ or cos θ

You can rewrite the identity $\sin^2\theta + \cos^2\theta = 1$ to express one trigonometric function in terms of the other. As shown, each alternate version of the identity involves both positive and negative square roots. You can determine which sign to use based on knowing the quadrant in which the terminal side of θ lies.

Solve for sin θ	Solve for cos θ
$\sin^2\theta + \cos^2\theta = 1$	$\sin^2\theta + \cos^2\theta = 1$
$\sin^2\theta = 1 - \cos^2\theta$	$\cos^2\theta = 1 - \cos^2\theta$
$\sin\theta = \pm\sqrt{1 - \cos^2\theta}$	$\cos\theta = \pm\sqrt{1 - \sin^2\theta}$

Example 1 Find the approximate value of each trigonometric function.

Ⓐ Given that $\sin\theta = 0.766$ where $0 < \theta < \frac{\pi}{2}$, find $\cos\theta$.

Use the identity to solve for $\cos\theta$. $\quad\quad\quad\quad\quad\quad \cos\theta = \pm\sqrt{1 - \sin^2\theta}$

Substitute for $\sin\theta$. $\quad\quad\quad\quad\quad\quad\quad\quad\quad\quad = \pm\sqrt{1 - (0.766)^2}$

Use a calculator, then round. $\quad\quad\quad\quad\quad\quad\quad \approx \pm 0.643$

The terminal side of θ lies in Quadrant I, where $\cos\theta > 0$. So, $\cos\theta \approx 0.643$.

(B) Given that $\cos\theta = -0.906$ where $\pi < \theta < \frac{3\pi}{2}$, find $\sin\theta$.

Use the identity to solve for $\sin\theta$. $\qquad\qquad \sin\theta = \pm\sqrt{1 - \cos^2\theta}$

Substitute for $\cos\theta$. $\qquad\qquad\qquad\qquad = \pm\sqrt{1 - \left(\boxed{}\right)^2}$

Use a calculator, then round. $\qquad\qquad\qquad \approx \pm\boxed{}$

The terminal side of θ lies in Quadrant $\boxed{}$, where $\sin\theta \boxed{}$ 0. So, $\sin\theta \approx \boxed{}$.

Reflect

4. Suppose that $\frac{\pi}{2} < \theta < \pi$ instead of $0 < \theta < \frac{\pi}{2}$ in part A of this Example. How does this affect the value of $\sin\theta$?

_____

_____

5. Suppose that $\frac{3\pi}{2} < \theta < 2\pi$ instead of $\pi < \theta < \frac{3\pi}{2}$ in part B of this Example. How does this affect the value of $\sin\theta$?

_____

_____

6. Explain how you would use the results of part A of this Example to determine the approximate value for $\tan\theta$. Then find it.

_____

_____

Your Turn

7. Given that $\sin\theta = -0.644$ where $\pi < \theta < \frac{3\pi}{2}$, find $\cos\theta$.

8. Given that $\cos\theta = -0.994$ where $\frac{\pi}{2} < \theta < \pi$, find $\sin\theta$. Then find $\tan\theta$.

✏ Explain 2   Finding the Value of Other Trigonometric Functions Given the Value of tanθ

If you multiply both sides of the identity $\tan\theta = \frac{\sin\theta}{\cos\theta}$ by $\cos\theta$, you get the identity $\cos\theta\tan\theta = \sin\theta$, or $\sin\theta \doteq \cos\theta\,\tan\theta$. Also, if you divide both sides of $\sin\theta = \cos\theta\,\tan\theta$ by $\tan\theta$, you get the identity $\cos\theta = \frac{\sin\theta}{\tan\theta}$. You can use the first of these identities to find the sine and cosine of an angle when you know the tangent.

Example 2   **Find the approximate value of each trigonometric function.**

Ⓐ   Given that $\tan\theta \approx -2.327$ where $\frac{\pi}{2} < \theta < \pi$, find the values of $\sin\theta$ and $\cos\theta$.

First, write $\sin\theta$ in terms of $\cos\theta$.

Use the identity $\sin\theta = \cos\theta\,\tan\theta$.	$\sin\theta = \cos\theta\,\tan\theta$
Substitute the value of $\tan\theta$.	$\approx -2.327\cos\theta$

Now use the Pythagorean Identity to find $\cos\theta$. Then find $\sin\theta$.

Use the Pythagorean Identity.	$\sin^2\theta + \cos^2\theta = 1$
Substitute for $\sin\theta$.	$(-2.327\cos\theta)^2 + \cos^2\theta \approx 1$
Square.	$5.415\cos^2\theta + \cos^2\theta \approx 1$
Combine like terms.	$6.415\cos^2\theta \approx 1$
Solve for $\cos^2\theta$.	$\cos^2\theta \approx 0.156$
Solve for $\cos\theta$.	$\cos\theta \approx \pm0.395$

The terminal side of θ lies in Quadrant II, where $\cos\theta < 0$. Therefore, $\cos\theta \approx -0.395$ and $\sin\theta \approx -2.327\cos\theta \approx 0.919$.

Ⓑ   Given that $\tan\theta \approx -4.366$ where $\frac{3\pi}{2} < \theta < 2\pi$, find the values of $\sin\theta$ and $\cos\theta$.

First, write $\sin\theta$ in terms of $\cos\theta$.

Use the identity $\sin\theta = \cos\theta\,\tan\theta$.	$\sin\theta = \cos\theta\,\tan\theta$
Substitute the value of $\tan\theta$.	$\approx \boxed{}\cos\theta$

Now use the Pythagorean Identity to find $\cos\theta$. Then find $\sin\theta$.

Use the Pythagorean Identity.	$\sin^2\theta + \cos^2\theta = 1$
Substitute for $\sin\theta$.	$\left(\boxed{}\cos\theta\right)^2 + \cos^2\theta \approx 1$
Square.	$\boxed{}\cos^2\theta + \cos^2\theta \approx 1$
Combine like terms.	$\boxed{}\cos^2\theta \approx 1$
Solve for $\cos^2\theta$.	$\cos^2\theta \approx \boxed{}$
Solve for $\cos\theta$.	$\cos\theta \approx \boxed{}$

The terminal side of θ lies in Quadrant $\boxed{}$, where $\cos\theta \boxed{}\, 0$. Therefore, $\cos\theta \approx \boxed{}$ and $\sin\theta \approx \boxed{}\cos\theta \approx \boxed{}$.

9. In part A of this Example, when you multiplied the given value of tanθ by the calculated value of cosθ in order to find the value of sinθ, was the product positive or negative? Explain why this is the result you would expect.

_____

10. If tan$\theta = 1$ where $0 < \theta < \frac{\pi}{2}$, show that you can solve for sinθ and cosθ exactly using the Pythagorean identity. Why is this so?

_____

_____

Your Turn

11. Given that tan$\theta \approx 3.454$ where $\pi < \theta < \frac{3\pi}{2}$, find the values of sin$\theta$ and cosθ.

Elaborate

12. What conclusions can you draw if you are given only the information that tan$\theta = -1$?

_____

_____

_____

_____

_____

13. Discussion Explain in what way the process of finding the sine and cosine of an angle from the tangent ratio is similar to the process of solving a linear equation in two variables by substitution.

_____

_____

_____

_____

_____

_____

_____

14. Essential Question Check-In If you know only the sine or cosine of an angle and the quadrant in which the angle terminates, how can you find the other trigonometric ratios?

_____

_____

_____

_____

☆ Evaluate: Homework and Practice

- Online Homework
- Hints and Help
- Extra Practice

Find the approximate value of each trigonometric function.

1. Given that $\sin\theta = 0.515$ where $0 < \theta < \frac{\pi}{2}$, find $\cos\theta$.

2. Given that $\cos\theta = 0.198$ where $\frac{3\pi}{2} < \theta < 2\pi$, find $\sin\theta$.

3. Given that $\sin\theta = -0.447$ where $\frac{3\pi}{2} < \theta < 2\pi$, find $\cos\theta$.

4. Given that $\cos\theta = -0.544$ where $\frac{\pi}{2} < \theta < 2\pi$, find $\sin\theta$.

5. Given that $\sin\theta = -0.908$ where $\pi < \theta < \frac{3\pi}{2}$, find $\cos\theta$.

6. Given that $\sin\theta = 0.313$ where $\frac{\pi}{2} < \theta < \pi$, find $\cos\theta$.

7. Given that $\cos\theta = 0.678$ where $0 < \theta < \frac{\pi}{2}$, find $\sin\theta$.

8. Given that $\cos\theta = -0.489$ where $\pi < \theta < \frac{3\pi}{2}$, find $\sin\theta$.

Find the approximate value of each trigonometric function.

9. Given that $\tan\theta \approx -3.966$ where $\frac{\pi}{2} < \theta < \pi$, find the values of $\sin\theta$ and $\cos\theta$.

10. Given that $\tan\theta \approx -4.580$ where $\frac{3\pi}{2} < \theta < 2\pi$, find the values of $\sin\theta$ and $\cos\theta$.

© Houghton Mifflin Harcourt Publishing Company

11. Given that $\tan\theta \approx 7.549$ where $0 < \theta < \frac{\pi}{2}$, find the values of $\sin\theta$ and $\cos\theta$.

12. Given that $\tan\theta \approx 4.575$ where $\pi < \theta < \frac{3\pi}{2}$, find the values of $\sin\theta$ and $\cos\theta$.

13. Given that $\tan\theta \approx -1.237$ where $\frac{3\pi}{2}, < \theta < 2\pi$ find the values of $\sin\theta$ and $\cos\theta$.

14. Given that $\tan\theta \approx 5.632$ where $\pi < \theta < \frac{3\pi}{2}$, find the values of $\sin\theta$ and $\cos\theta$.

15. Given that $\tan\theta \approx 6.653$ where $0 < \theta < \frac{\pi}{2}$, find the values of $\sin\theta$ and $\cos\theta$.

16. Given that $\tan\theta \approx -9.366$ where $\frac{\pi}{2}, < \theta < \pi$ find the values of $\sin\theta$ and $\cos\theta$.

17. Given the trigonometric function and the location of the terminal side of the angle, state whether the function value will be positive or negative.

    A. $\cos\theta$, Quadrant I

    B. $\sin\theta$, Quadrant IV

    C. $\tan\theta$, Quadrant II

    D. $\sin\theta$, Quadrant III

    E. $\tan\theta$, Quadrant III

18. Confirm the Pythagorean identity $\sin^2\theta + \cos^2\theta = 1$ for $\theta = \frac{7\pi}{4}$.

19. Recall that the equation of a circle with radius r centered at the origin is $x^2 + y^2 = r^2$. Use this fact and the fact that the coordinates of a point on this circle are $(x, y) = (r\cos\theta, r\sin\theta)$ for a central angle θ to show that the Pythagorean identity derived above is true.

20. **Sports** A ski supply company is testing the friction of a new ski wax by placing a waxed block on an inclined plane covered with wet snow. The inclined plane is slowly raised until the block begins to slide. At the instant the block starts to slide, the component of the weight of the block parallel to the incline, $mg\sin\theta$, and the resistive force of friction, $\mu mg\cos\theta$, are equal, where μ is the coefficient of friction. Find the value of μ to the nearest hundredth if $\sin\theta = 0.139$ at the instant the block begins to slide.

21. **Driving** Tires and roads are designed so that the coefficient of friction between the rubber of the tires and the asphalt of the roads is very high, which gives plenty of traction for starting, stopping, and turning. For a particular road surface and tire, the steepest angle for which a car could rest on the slope without starting to slide has a sine of 0.643. This value satisfies the equation $mg\sin\theta = \mu mg\cos\theta$ where μ is the coefficient of friction. Find the value of μ to the nearest hundredth.

22. Explain the Error Julian was given that $\sin\theta = -0.555$ where $\frac{3\pi}{2} < \theta < 2\pi$ and told to find $\cos\theta$. He produced the following work:

$$\cos\theta = \pm\sqrt{1 - \sin^2\theta}$$
$$= \pm\sqrt{1 - (-0.555^2)}$$
$$\approx \pm 1.144$$

Since $\cos\theta > 0$ when $\frac{3\pi}{2} < \theta < 2\pi$, $\cos\theta \approx 1.144$.

Explain his error and state the correct answer.

Critical Thinking **Rewrite each trigonometric expression in terms of $\cos\theta$ and simplify.**

23. $\dfrac{\sin^2\theta}{1 - \cos\theta}$

24. $\cos\theta + \sin\theta \cos\theta - \tan\theta + \tan\theta \sin^2\theta$ $\left(\text{Hint: Begin by factoring } \tan\theta \text{ from the last two terms.}\right)$

25. Critical Thinking To what trigonometric function does the expression $\dfrac{\sqrt{1 - \cos^2\theta}}{\sqrt{1 - \sin^2\theta}}$ simplify? Explain your answer.

Lesson Performance Task

A tower casts a shadow that is 160 feet long at a particular time one morning. With the base of the tower as the origin, east as the positive x-axis, and north as the positive y-axis, the shadow at this time is in the northwest quadrant formed by the axes. Also at this time, the tangent of the angle of rotation measured so that the shadow lies on the terminal ray is $\tan\theta = -2.545$. What are the coordinates of the tip of the shadow to the nearest foot, and what do they indicate?

Unit-Circle Definition of Trigonometric Functions

Essential Question: How can the unit-circle definition of trigonometric functions help to solve real-world problems?

KEY EXAMPLE   *(Lesson 17.1)*

A laboratory centrifuge with a diameter of 12 inches makes approximately 10,000 revolutions in 3 minutes. How long will it take for a test tube in the centrifuge to travel 360,000 degrees? How far will the test tube travel in inches?

$3 \text{ min} \cdot \dfrac{60 \text{ sec}}{1 \text{ min}} = 180 \text{ s}$ Convert minutes to seconds

$\dfrac{360°(10,000)}{180 \text{ sec}} = 20,000°/s$ Find the angular velocity in terms of degrees/s.

$\dfrac{360,000°}{\dfrac{20,000°}{1 \text{ sec}}} = 18 \text{ s}$ Divide the number of degrees by the velocity.

$360,000 \cdot \dfrac{\pi}{180} = 20,000\pi$ Convert degrees to radians.

$s = r\theta = 6 \cdot 2000\pi \approx 37,700$ Use the formula for the arc length to find the distance.

The test tube travels 360,000 degrees in 18 seconds, and travels approximately 37,700 inches.

KEY EXAMPLE   *(Lesson 17.2)*

Evaluate the trigonometric function $\cos \frac{13\pi}{3}$ by using the quadrant and the reference angle to determine the sign and absolute value.

$\dfrac{13\pi}{3} = 4\pi + \dfrac{\pi}{3}$ Identify the coterminal angle between 0 and 2π.

$\theta' = \dfrac{\pi}{3}$ Find the reference angle for quadrant I.

$\theta' = \dfrac{\pi}{3} \times \dfrac{180°}{\pi} = 60°$ Identify the special right triangle angle.

$\cos\theta' = \dfrac{1}{2}$ Use the sides of a 30°-60°-90° triangle.

$\cos \dfrac{13\pi}{3} = +\cos \dfrac{\pi}{3}$ Apply the sign of cosine in quadrant I.

$\cos \dfrac{13\pi}{3} = \dfrac{1}{2}$

EXERCISES

A merry-go-round with the given radius turns through the given angle. How far, in feet, will a child on the edge of the merry-go-round travel? *(Lesson 17.1)*

1. 4 feet; 270°

2. 6 feet; 310°

3. 2 feet; 720°

4. 3 feet; 90°

A child is riding a carousel at an amusement park. How long will it take for the child to travel through the given angle at the given angular velocity? *(Lesson 17.1)*

5. 3 rev/min; 270°

6. 5 rev/min; 310°

Evaluate the trigonometric function by using the quadrant and the reference angle to determine the sign and absolute value. *(Lesson 17.2)*

7. $\sin \frac{13\pi}{4}$

8. $\tan \frac{4\pi}{3}$

MODULE PERFORMANCE TASK

Telling Time with Trig

An analog clock displays time on a computer screen. It is based on a unit circle, so the programmer can use cosine and sine to specify the positions of the ends of the hands. Draw a clock face and label each of the hour marks with its coordinates. What are the coordinates of each hand at 4:30?

Start by listing in the space below the information you will need to solve the problem. Then use your own paper to complete the task. Be sure to write down all your data and assumptions. Then use graphs, numbers, words, or algebra to explain how you reached your conclusion.

(Ready) to Go On?

17.1–17.3 Unit-Circle Definition of Trigonometric Functions

- Online Homework
- Hints and Help
- Extra Practice

A coin has a radius of 10 mm. How long will it take the coin to roll through the given angle measure at the given angular velocity? How far will it travel in that time?

1. 180°; 5 rev/s

2. 360°; 7 rev/s

3. 540°; 6 rev/s

4. 1800°; 4 rev/s

Evaluate the trigonometric function by using the quadrant and the reference angle to determine the sign and absolute value.

5. $\cos \dfrac{17\pi}{4}$

6. $\sin 410°$

Find the approximate value of each trigonometric function.

7. Given $\sin \theta = 0.996$; find $\cos \theta$

8. Given $\cos \theta = 0.342$; find $\sin \theta$

ESSENTIAL QUESTION

9. How does using radian measure simplify finding distances around a circle compared to using degree measure?

Assessment Readiness

1. Consider the radian measure $\frac{16\pi}{5}$. Is the statement correct?

   Select Yes or No for A–C.

   A. $\cos \frac{16\pi}{5} \approx -0.809$ ◯ Yes   ◯ No

   B. $\tan \frac{16\pi}{5} \approx 0.727$ ◯ Yes   ◯ No

   C. $\sin \frac{16\pi}{5} \approx 0.588$ ◯ Yes   ◯ No

2. Consider a situation where a colored ring is 10 inches in diameter. Choose True or False for each statement.

   A. If the ring is rolling at a rate of 2 revolutions per second, it will take approximately 0.17 second to travel 120°.   ◯ True   ◯ False

   B. The angular velocity is needed to find the distance the ring will travel in rotating through 1080°.   ◯ True   ◯ False

   C. The radius is needed to find how long it will take the ring to rotate through 1080°.   ◯ True   ◯ False

3. Carlos wants to find the value of $\cos \theta$ given $\sin \theta = 0.707$, and he finds that $\cos \theta$ is the same value. Is this possible, or did he make a mistake? Explain.

4. Given the equation $y = x(x - 3)(2x + 7)$, find the rational roots. Explain how you determined your answer.

Graphing Trigonometric Functions

Essential Question: How can graphing trigonometric functions help to solve real-world problems?

REAL WORLD VIDEO
Check out how data about periodic phenomena such as tides and phases of the moon can be represented by a sine function.

© Houghton Mifflin Harcourt Publishing Company • Image Credits: ©Craig Tuttle/Corbis

MODULE PERFORMANCE TASK PREVIEW

What's Your Sine?

The moon is visible only because we see the sun's light reflecting from the moon's surface. Depending on where the moon is in its orbit around Earth, we see no moon, a full moon, or any fraction of the moon's surface in between. How can we use a sine function to figure out what fraction of the moon's surface will be lit on any given night? Let's find out!

Are YOU Ready?

Complete these exercises to review skills you will need for this module.

Stretching, Compressing, and Reflecting Quadratic Functions

Online Homework
- Hints and Help
- Extra Practice

Example 1   The graph of $g(x) = -2(x + 9)^2 - 4$ is vertically compressed by a factor of 0.5 and reflected over the y-axis. Write the new function.

Vertical compression:

$g'(x) = 0.5\left(-2(x + 9)^2 - 4\right) = -(x + 9)^2 - 2$

Reflection over the y-axis: $g''(x) = -(-x + 9)^2 - 2$

The new function is $g''(x) = -(-x + 9)^2 - 2$.

Write the new function for $f(x) = (x + 1)^2 - 2$ after the given transformation.

1.   reflection over x-axis

2.   horizontal compression, factor of 10

3.   vertical stretch, factor of 2

Combining Transformations of Quadratic Functions

Example 2   The graph of $f(x) = -2(x + 5)^2 + 1$ is transformed 3 units right and 2 units down. Write the new function.

The vertex is $(-5, 1)$. Its location after the transformation is $(-5 + 3, 1 - 2)$, or $(-2, -1)$.

The new function is $f'(x) = -2(x + 2)^2 - 1$.

Write the new function after the given transformation.

4. $p(x) = 0.1(x - 8)^2 + 9$
5 units left, 6 units down

5. $q(x) = -0.5(x + 2)^2 - 12$
1 unit right, 9 units up

6. $h(x) = 0.8(x - 8)^2 - 10$
7 units left, 4 units up

© Houghton Mifflin Harcourt Publishing Company

870

18.1 Stretching, Compressing, and Reflecting Sine and Cosine Graphs

Resource Locker

Essential Question: What are the key features of the graphs of the sine and cosine functions?

⊘ Explore 1 Graphing the Basic Sine and Cosine Functions

Recall that the points around the unit circle have coordinates (cos θ, sin θ) as shown.

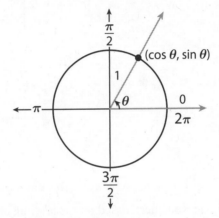

(A) Identify the following points on the graph of the sine function on the interval [0, 2π].

  A. the three points where *x*-intercepts occur

  B. the point of maximum value

  C. the point of minimum value

(B) Complete the table of values. Plot the points from the table, and draw a smooth curve through them.

θ	0	$\frac{\pi}{6}$	$\frac{\pi}{2}$	$\frac{5\pi}{6}$	π	$\frac{7\pi}{6}$	$\frac{3\pi}{2}$	$\frac{11\pi}{6}$	2π
$f(\theta) = \sin \theta$									

Identify the following points on the graph of the cosine function on the interval $[0, 2\pi]$.

A. the two points where x-intercepts occur

B. the two points of maximum value

C. the point of minimum value

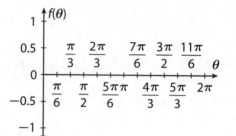

(D) Complete the table of values. Plot the points from the table, and draw a smooth curve through them.

θ	0	$\dfrac{\pi}{3}$	$\dfrac{\pi}{2}$	$\dfrac{2\pi}{3}$	π	$\dfrac{4\pi}{3}$	$\dfrac{3\pi}{2}$	$\dfrac{5\pi}{3}$	2π
$f(\theta) = \cos\theta$									

Reflect

1. Give a decimal approximation of $\sin\frac{\pi}{3}$. Check to see whether the curve that you drew passes through the point $\left(\frac{\pi}{3}, \sin\frac{\pi}{3}\right)$. What other points can you check based on the labeling of the θ–axis?

2. On the interval $0 \le \theta \le 2\pi$, where does the sine function have positive values? Where does it have negative values? Answer the same questions for cosine.

3. What are the minimum and maximum values of $f(\theta) = \sin\theta$ and $f(\theta) = \cos\theta$ on the interval $0 \le \theta \le 2\pi$? Where do the extreme values occur in relation to the θ–intercepts?

4. Describe a rotation that will map the graph of $f(\theta) = \sin\theta$ onto itself on the interval $0 \le \theta \le 2\pi$.

5. Recall that coterminal angles differ by a multiple of 2π and have the same sine value and the same cosine value. This means that the graphs of sine and cosine on the interval $0 \le \theta \le 2\pi$ represent one *cycle* of the complete graphs and that the cycles repeat every 2π radians. Use this fact to extend the graphs of $f(\theta) = \sin\theta$ and $f(\theta) = \cos\theta$ to the left and right by 1 cycle.

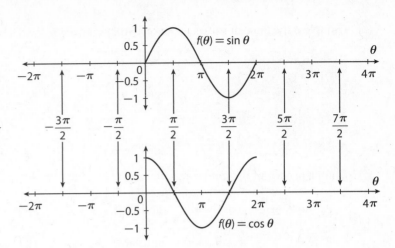

⊘ Explore 2 Graphing the Reciprocals of the Basic Sine and Cosine Functions

The **cosecant** and **secant** functions are the reciprocals of the sine and cosine functions, respectively.

$$\csc\theta = \frac{1}{\sin\theta} \qquad \sec\theta = \frac{1}{\cos\theta}$$

(A) Complete the table of values. Note that whenever $\sin\theta = 0$, $\csc\theta$ is undefined.

θ	0	$\frac{\pi}{6}$	$\frac{\pi}{2}$	$\frac{5\pi}{6}$	π	$\frac{7\pi}{6}$	$\frac{3\pi}{2}$	$\frac{11\pi}{6}$	2π
$f(\theta) = \sin\theta$	0	0.5	1	0.5	0	−0.5	−1	−0.5	0
$f(\theta) = \csc\theta$									

(B) Complete each of the following statements.

A. As $\theta \to 0^+$, $\sin\theta \to$ ☐ and $\csc\theta \to$ ☐ .

B. As $\theta \to 0^-$, $\sin\theta \to$ ☐ and $\csc\theta \to$ ☐ .

What does this behavior tell you about the graph of the cosecant function?

(C) Sketch the graph of $f(\theta) = \csc\theta$ over the interval $[0, 2\pi]$. Then, extend the graph to the left and right until the entire coordinate plane is filled. Note that the sine function has been plotted for ease of graphing.

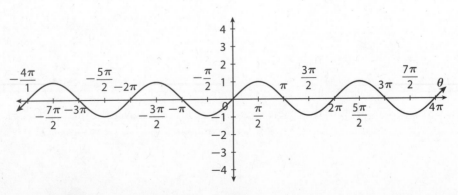

(D) Complete the table of values. Note that whenever $\cos \theta = 0$, $\sec \theta$ is undefined.

θ	0	$\dfrac{\pi}{3}$	$\dfrac{\pi}{2}$	$\dfrac{2\pi}{3}$	π	$\dfrac{4\pi}{3}$	$\dfrac{3\pi}{2}$	$\dfrac{5\pi}{3}$	2π
$f(\theta) = \cos \theta$	1	0.5	0	−0.5	−1	−0.5	0	0.5	1
$f(\theta) = \sec \theta$									

(E) Complete each of the following statements.

A. As $\theta \to \dfrac{\pi}{2}^{+}$, $\cos \theta \to \boxed{}$ and $\sec \theta \to \boxed{}$.

B. As $\theta \to \dfrac{\pi}{2}^{-}$, $\cos \theta \to \boxed{}$ and $\sec \theta \to \boxed{}$.

What does this behavior tell you about the graph of the cosecant function?

(F) Sketch the graph of $f(\theta) = \sec \theta$ over the interval $[0, 2\pi]$. Then, extend the graph to the left and right until the entire coordinate plane is filled. Note that the cosine function has been plotted for ease of graphing.

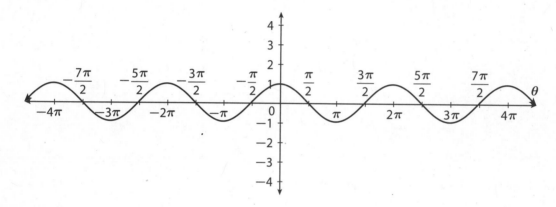

Reflect

6. How do the domain, range, maximum values, and minimum values compare between the sine and cosine functions and their reciprocals?

_____

_____

_____

_____

_____

_____

_____

7. Describe the vertical asymptotes of the cosecant and secant functions over the interval $[0, 2\pi]$.

_____

_____

Explain 1   Graphing $f(x) = a\,\sin\frac{1}{b}x$ or $f(x) = a\,\cos\frac{1}{b}x$

In Explore 1, you graphed the sine and cosine functions on the interval $0 \le \theta \le 2\pi$, which represents all of the angles of rotation within the first counterclockwise revolution that starts at 0. Your drawings are not the complete graphs, however. They are simply one *cycle* of the graphs.

The graphs of sine and cosine consist of repeated cycles that form a wave-like shape. When a function repeats its values over regular intervals on the horizontal axis as the sine and cosine functions do, the function is called **periodic**, and the length of the interval is called the function's **period**. In Explore 1, you saw that the basic sine and cosine functions each have a period of 2π.

The wave-like shape of the sine and cosine functions has a "crest" (where the function's maximum value occurs) and a "trough" (where the function's minimum value occurs). Halfway between the "crest" and the "trough" is the graph's **midline**. The distance that the "crest" rises above the midline or the distance that the "trough" falls below the midline is called the graph's **amplitude**. In Explore 1, you saw that the basic sine and cosine functions each have an amplitude of 1.

Note that for trigonometric functions, the angle θ is the independent variable, and the output $f(\theta)$ is the dependent variable. You can graph these functions on the familiar xy-coordinate plane by letting x represent the angle and y represent the value of the function.

Example 1 **For each trigonometric function, identify the vertical stretch or compression and the horizontal stretch or compression. Then, graph the function and identify its period.**

(A) $y = 3\,\sin 2x$

The equation has the general form $y = a\,\sin\frac{1}{b}\,x$. The value of a is 3. Since $\frac{1}{b} = 2$, the value of b is $\frac{1}{2}$. So, the graph of the parent sine function must be vertically stretched by a factor of 3 and horizontally compressed by a factor of $\frac{1}{2}$.

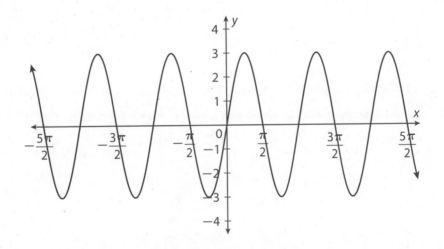

Horizontally stretching or compressing the parent function's graph by a factor of $|b|$ changes the period of the function. Since the parent function has a period of 2π, multiply 2π by $|b|$ to obtain the period of the transformed function.

Period: $2\pi \cdot |b| = 2\pi \cdot \frac{1}{2} = \pi$

(B) $y = -3 \cos \frac{x}{2}$

The equation has the general form $y = a \cos \frac{1}{b} x$. The value of a is _____. Since

$\frac{1}{b} = \boxed{}$, the value of b is _____.

So, the graph of the parent function must be vertically [stretched/compressed] by a factor of _____ and horizontally

[compressed/stretched] by a factor of _____.

Graph the function. Note that since a is negative, the graph will be reflected across the [x/y]-axis.

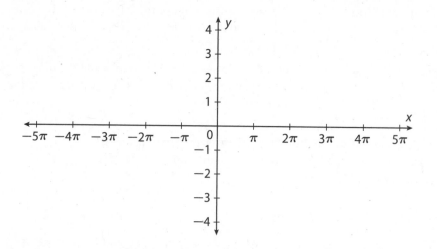

Find the function's period.

$2\pi \cdot |b| = 2\pi \cdot \boxed{} = \boxed{}$

Reflect

8. For the function $y = a \sin\frac{1}{b}x$ or $y = a \cos\frac{1}{b}x$, what is the amplitude, under what circumstances is the graph of the function reflected about the x-axis, and how is the period determined?

_____

_____

_____

Your Turn

Identify the vertical stretch or compression and the horizontal stretch or compression. Then, graph the function and identify its period.

9. $y = \frac{1}{2} \sin 4x$

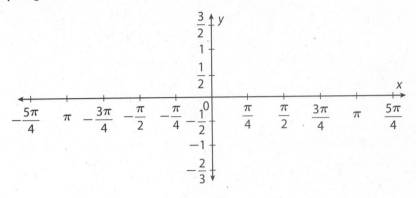

Explain 2 **Writing $f(x) = a \sin\frac{1}{b}x$ or $f(x) = a \cos\frac{1}{b}x$**

You can write the equation of a trigonometric function if you are given its graph.

Example 2 Write an equation for each graph.

(A) Because the graph's y-intercept is 0, the graph is a sine function.

Since the maximum and minimum values are 2 and -2, respectively, the graph is a vertical stretch of the parent sine function by a factor of 2. So, $a = 2$.

The period of the function is 2.

Use the equation $2\pi b = 2$ to find a positive value for $\frac{1}{b}$.

$$2\pi b = 2$$

$$b = \frac{2}{2\pi} = \frac{1}{\pi}$$

$$\frac{1}{b} = \pi$$

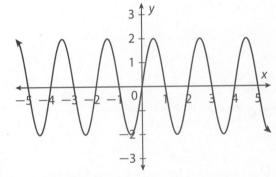

An equation for the graph is $y = 2 \sin \pi x$.

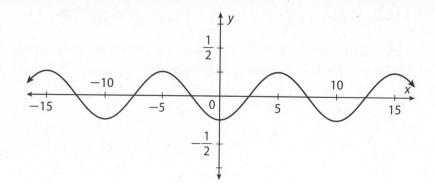

Because the graph's y-intercept is negative, the graph is a[sine/cosine]function reflected across the x-axis.

Since the maximum and minimum in the graph are ☐ and ☐ , respectively, the graph will be

vertical [stretch/compression] of the graph of the parent cosine function by a factor of ☐ .

The period of the function is ☐ .

Use the equation $2\pi b =$ ☐ to find a positive value for $\frac{1}{b}$.

$2\pi b =$ ☐

$b = \dfrac{\boxed{}}{2\pi} = \dfrac{\boxed{}}{\pi}$

$\dfrac{1}{b} = \dfrac{\pi}{\boxed{}}$

An equation for the graph is $y =$ ☐ $\cos$ ☐ x.

Your Turn

Write an equation for the graph.

10.

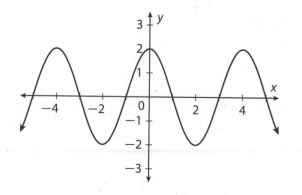

⚙ Explain 3 Modeling with Sine or Cosine Functions

Sine and cosine functions can be used to model real-world phenomena, such as sound waves. Different sounds create different waves. One way to distinguish sounds is to measure *frequency*. **Frequency** is the number of cycles in a given unit of time, so it is the reciprocal of the period of a function.

Hertz (Hz) is the standard measure of frequency and represents one cycle per second. For example, the sound wave made by a tuning fork for middle A has a frequency of 440 Hz. This means that the wave repeats 440 times in 1 second.

As a tuning fork vibrates, it creates fluctuations in air pressure. The maximum change in air pressure, typically measured in pascals, is the sound wave's amplitude.

Example 3   Graph each function, and then find its frequency. What do the frequency, amplitude, and period represent in the context of the problem?

(A) **Physics** Use a sine function to graph a sound wave with a period of 0.004 second and an amplitude of 4 pascals.

Graph the function.

$$\text{frequency} = \frac{1}{\text{period}} = \frac{1}{0.004} = 250 \text{ Hz}$$

The frequency represents the number of cycles of the sound wave every second. The amplitude represents the maximum change in air pressure. The period represents the amount of time it takes for the sound wave to repeat.

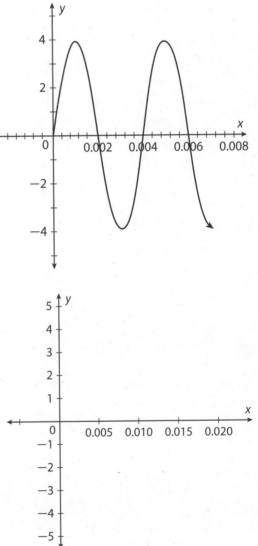

(B) **Physics** Use a cosine function to graph a sound wave with a period of 0.010 second and an amplitude of 3 pascals. Note that the recording of the sound wave started when the wave was at its maximum height.

Graph the function.

$$\text{frequency} = \frac{1}{\text{period}} = \frac{1}{\boxed{}} = \boxed{} \text{ Hz}$$

The frequency represents the number cycles of the sound wave every _____. The amplitude represents the maximum change in _____. The period represents the amount of time it takes for the sound wave to [end/repeat].

Graph the function, and then find its frequency. What do the frequency, amplitude, and period represent in the context of the problem?

11. A pendulum makes one back-and-forth swing every 1.5 seconds. Its horizontal displacement relative to its position at rest is measured in inches. Starting when the pendulum is 5 inches (its maximum displacement) to the right of its position at rest, use a cosine function to graph the pendulum's horizontal displacement over time.

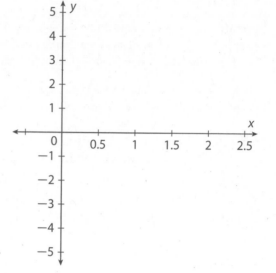

Elaborate

12. The graphs of sine and cosine are periodic functions. Refer to angles of rotation and the unit circle to explain why this is so.

_____

_____

_____

13. Referring to angles of rotation and the unit circle, explain why $\sin(-\theta) = -\sin\theta$, and why $\cos(-\theta) = \cos\theta$. Use the graphs of $\sin\theta$ and $\cos\theta$ for reference.

_____

_____

_____

14. How does the unit circle explain why the 2 in $y = \sin 2x$ results in a horizontal compression of the graph of $y = \sin x$?

_____

_____

_____

15. **Essential Question Check-In** What is one key difference between the graphs of the sine and cosine functions?

_____

_____

_____

☆ Evaluate: Homework and Practice

• Online Homework
• Hints and Help
• Extra Practice

For each trigonometric function, identify the vertical stretch or compression and the horizontal stretch or compression. Then, graph the function and identify its period.

1. $y = 4 \sin x$

2. $y = \frac{1}{2} \cos 2x$

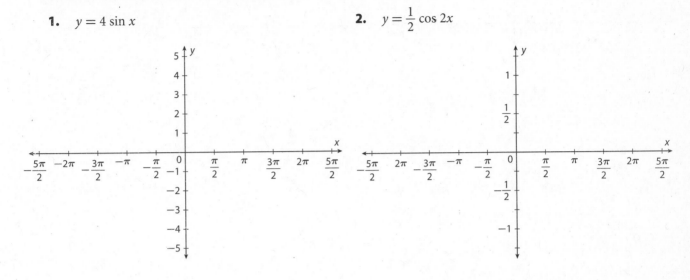

3. $y = -3 \sin \frac{1}{6}x$

4. $y = -2 \cos \frac{1}{3}x$

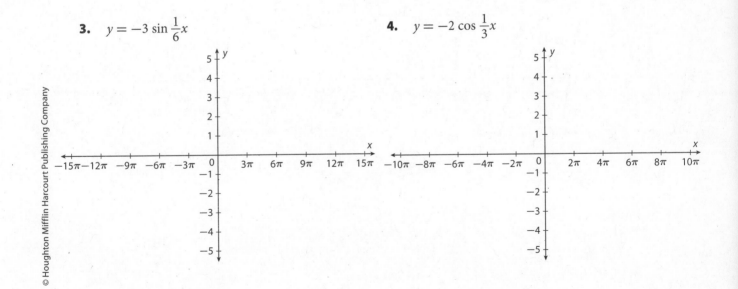

5. $y = \dfrac{1}{3} \sin 2x$

6. $y = -\dfrac{1}{4} \cos 3x$

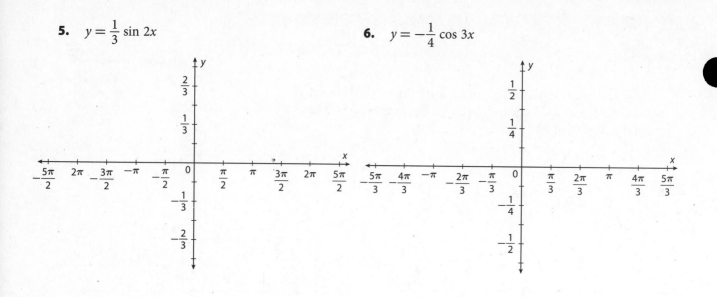

Write an equation for each graph.

7.

8.

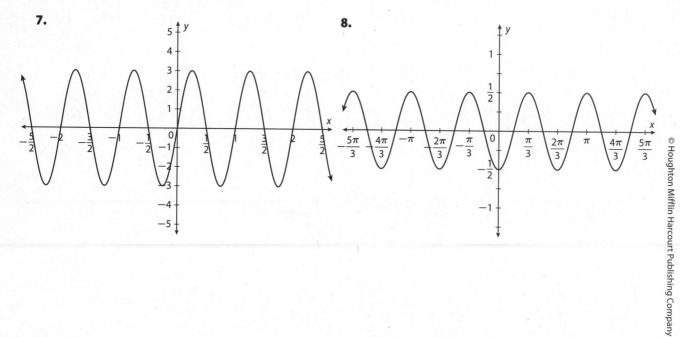

9.

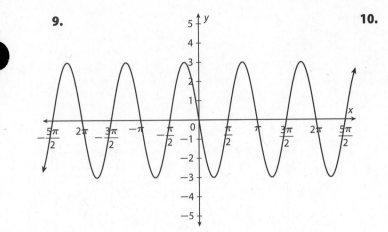

10.

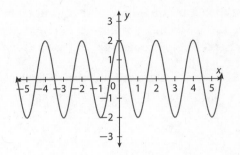

11. **12.**

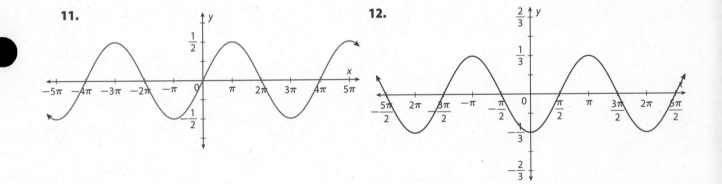

Graph each function, and then find its frequency. What do the frequency, amplitude, and period represent in the context of the problem?

13. **Physics** Use a sine function to graph a sound wave with a period of 0.003 second and an amplitude of 2 pascals.

14. **Physics** A mass attached to a spring oscillates up and down every 2 seconds. Draw a graph of the vertical displacement of the mass relative to its position at rest if the spring is stretched to a length of 15 cm before the mass is released.

15. **Physics** A pendulum is released at a point 5 meters to the right of its position at rest. Graph a cosine function that represents the pendulum's horizontal displacement relative to its position at rest if it completes one back-and-forth swing every π seconds.

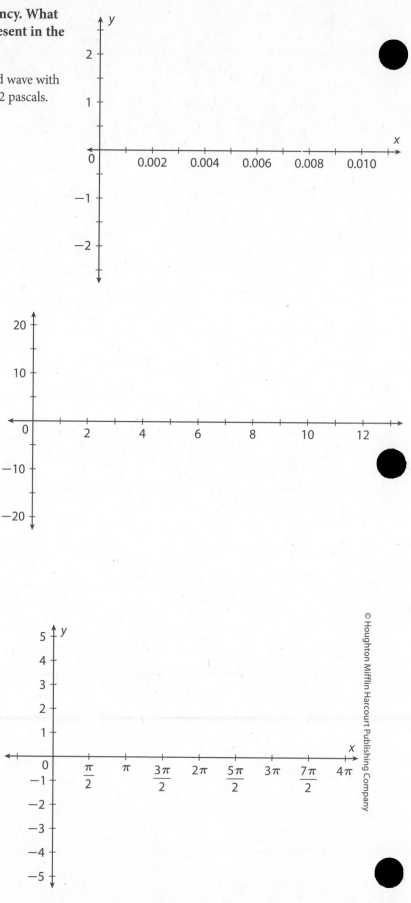

16. Automobiles Each piston in a car's engine moves up and down in a cylinder and causes a crankshaft to rotate. Suppose a piston starts at the midpoint of a stroke and has a maximum displacement from the midpoint of 50 mm. Also suppose the crankshaft is rotating at a rate of 3000 revolutions per minute (rpm). Use a sine function to graph the piston's displacement relative to the midpoint of its stroke.

(Note that 60 rpm = 1 revolution per second.)

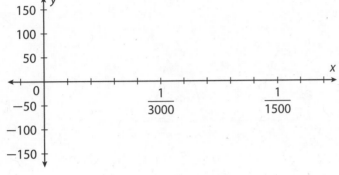

17. Identify the domain and range of each trigonometric function. State which functions have the same domain and which functions have the same range.

A. $y = \sin x$

B. $y = 2\cos x$

C. $y = -3\sin \frac{1}{2}x$

D. $y = -\frac{4}{5}\sin \pi x$

E. $y = 2\sin \frac{x}{4}$

18. Use Explore 1 for reference. State how the basic sine and cosine functions are similar and how they are different. How are the graphs of the functions geometrically related?

19. Describe the graphs of the cosecant and secant functions. Note any asymptotes, *x*-intercepts, and maximum or minimum values.

20. Compare the two sine functions in terms of their periods.

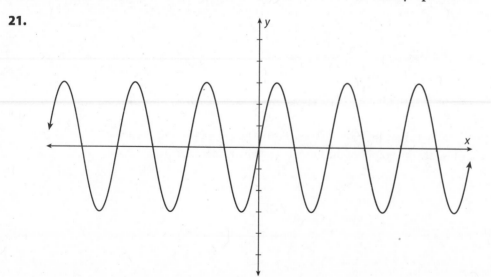

θ	0	$\dfrac{\pi}{6}$	$\dfrac{\pi}{2}$	$\dfrac{5\pi}{6}$	π	$\dfrac{7\pi}{6}$	$\dfrac{3\pi}{2}$	$\dfrac{11\pi}{6}$	2π
$f(\theta)$	0	1	2	1	0	−1	−2	−1	0

Sketch the graph of a cosecant or secant function, as appropriate, using the provided graph of a sine or cosine function as a reference. Be sure to include asymptotes.

21.

22.

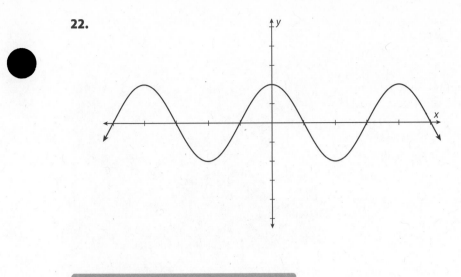

23. Critical Thinking Graph the basic sine and cosine functions together. Identify where $\sin \theta = \cos \theta$, and explain where these intersections occur in terms of the unit circle.

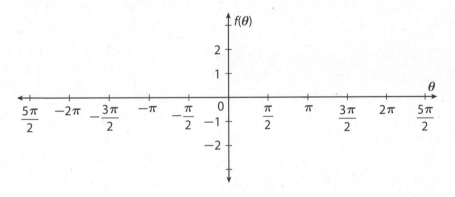

24. Explain the Error When instructed to write the equation of a sine function with a vertical stretch of 2 and a horizontal compression of $\frac{1}{2}$, Charles produced the answer $y = 2 \sin \frac{1}{2}x$. Explain his error, and state the correct answer.

25. Critical Thinking State the domain and range of the secant function on the interval $[0, 2\pi]$. Explain how the domain and range indicate that the graph of the secant function has vertical asymptotes.

© Houghton Mifflin Harcourt Publishing Company

Lesson Performance Task

A vuvuzela is a plastic horn about 2 feet long and is used during soccer matches in South Africa. If the sound level of the vuvuzela is 120 decibels from 1 meter away, the sound pressure is 20 pascals. A function of the sound pressure P in pascals from the sound wave of a vuvuzela as a function of time t in seconds is approximately $P(t) = 20 \sin(1464.612t)$.

a. Identify the amplitude and period of the sound wave. Explain your findings.

b. Use the period of the function to find the frequency of the sound in hertz (Hz). The table shows the notes and frequency of a section of a piano's keyboard. What is the note that the vuvuzela plays? Explain.

Note	Frequency (Hz)
Middle C	261.626
B	246.942
B-flat	233.082
A	220
A-flat	207.652
G	195.998
G-flat	184.997

c. A piano tuner strikes a tuning fork for middle A, which has a frequency 440 Hz, at 80 decibels from 1 meter away, or a sound pressure of 0.2 pascal. What is an equation that represents the sound pressure P in pascals as a function of time t in seconds? Show your work.

18.2 Stretching, Compressing, and Reflecting Tangent Graphs

Essential Question: What are the key features of the graph of the tangent function?

⊘ Explore **Graphing the Basic Tangent Function and Its Reciprocal**

Recall that the tangent of an angle can be found from the relationship $\tan\theta = \frac{\sin\theta}{\cos\theta}$. Using the coordinates of the position on the unit circle, $(x, y) = (\cos\theta, \sin\theta)$, the value of the tangent function can also be found from the ratio of y to x.

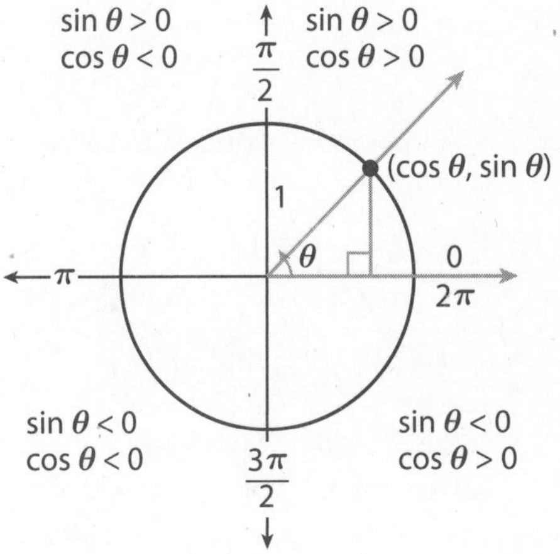

(A) The tangent of an angle is undefined when the denominator of the defining ratio is 0.

As θ increases from 0, the first angle (in radians) at which the

tangent becomes undefined is ⬚.

As θ decreases from 0, the first angle (in radians) at which the

tangent becomes undefined is ⬚.

The tangent is defined between these two angles. Use special triangles and the (x, y) coordinates of the unit circle to fill in the table of reference points (the x-intercept and the halfway points):

θ	$-\frac{\pi}{4}$	0	$\frac{\pi}{4}$
$\tan\theta$			

(B) Use your calculator to evaluate tangent as it approaches $\frac{\pi}{2} \approx 1.5708$ and $-\frac{\pi}{2} \approx -1.5708$.

θ	1.492	1.555	1.569	...	$\frac{\pi}{2} \approx 1.5708$
$\tan\theta$				...	Undefined

θ	−1.492	−1.555	−1.569	...	$-\frac{\pi}{2} \approx -1.5708$
$\tan\theta$				...	Undefined

The tangent function [increases/decreases] without bound as the angle approaches $\frac{\pi}{2}$ from below, and [increases/decreases] without bound as it approaches $-\frac{\pi}{2}$ from above. There are vertical _____ at $\frac{\pi}{2}$ and $-\frac{\pi}{2}$.

Diagram (right side):
$\sin\theta > 0$, $\cos\theta < 0$; $\frac{\pi}{2}$; $\sin\theta > 0$, $\cos\theta > 0$
$(\cos\theta, \sin\theta)$
1
π ; θ ; 0 ; 2π
$\sin\theta < 0$, $\cos\theta < 0$; $\frac{3\pi}{2}$; $\sin\theta < 0$, $\cos\theta > 0$

(C) Use the reference points from Step A and the asymptotic behavior observed in Step B to graph $f(\theta) = \tan\theta$ from $-\frac{\pi}{2}$ to $\frac{\pi}{2}$. Draw the vertical asymptotes.

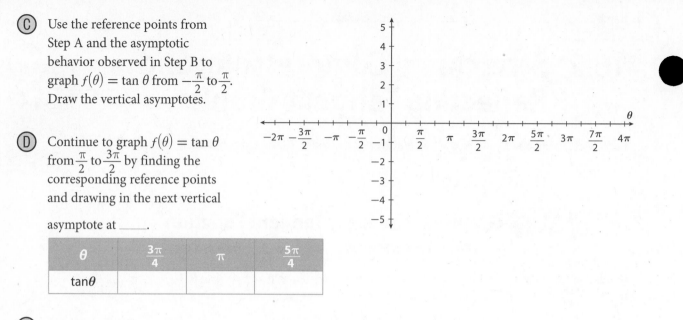

(D) Continue to graph $f(\theta) = \tan\theta$ from $\frac{\pi}{2}$ to $\frac{3\pi}{2}$ by finding the corresponding reference points and drawing in the next vertical asymptote at _____.

θ	$\frac{3\pi}{4}$	π	$\frac{5\pi}{4}$
$\tan\theta$			

(E) Use the same technique to complete the graph from -2π to 4π.

(F) The **cotangent** (or cot) is the reciprocal of the tangent. It can be found by inverting the ratio used to find the tangent of an angle:

$\cot\theta = \frac{1}{\tan\theta} = \frac{\cos\theta}{\sin\theta} = \frac{x}{y}$

Like the tangent function, the graph of cotangent has regular vertical asymptotes, but at angles where $\sin\theta$ is equal to 0. The first interval with positive angle measure and defined values of cotangent is bracketed by vertical asymptotes at $\theta =$ ☐ and $\theta =$ ☐ .

(G) Fill in the table of reference points for $\cot\theta$.

θ	$\frac{\pi}{4}$	$\frac{\pi}{2}$	$\frac{3\pi}{4}$
$\cot\theta$			

Cotangent is undefined everywhere tangent is equal to _____, and cotangent is equal to 1 or −1 when tangent is equal to _____ or _____, respectively.

(H) Sketch the asymptotes at 0 and π and use the reference points to sketch the first cycle of $f(\theta) = \cot\theta$. Then continue the graph to the left and right using the same pattern of repeating asymptotes and reference points that you used to plot $f(\theta) = \tan\theta$.

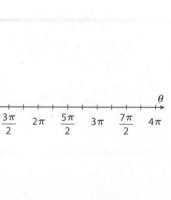

Reflect

1. Describe the behavior of the graph of the tangent function. Include where the function equals 0, where it has asymptotes, what the period is, and over what regions it is increasing and/or decreasing.

   _____

   _____

2. Describe the behavior of the graph of the cotangent function. Include where the function equals 0, where it has asymptotes, what the period is, and over what regions it is increasing and/or decreasing.

   _____

   _____

3. Use reference angles to explain why the graph of $f(\theta) = \tan \theta$ appears to show $f(-\theta) = -\tan \theta$.

   _____

   _____

   _____

   _____

⚙ Explain 1　Graphing $f(x) = a \tan\left(\frac{1}{b}x\right)$

Tangent functions can be graphed on the xy–coordinate plane by letting x represent the angle in radians and y represent the value of the function.

The plot of a transformed tangent function can be found from the transformation parameters, as you have done for other families of functions. The parameter a causes the graph to stretch (for $|a| > 1$), compress (for $|a| < 1$), and/or reflect across the x-axis (for $a < 0$). The parameter b controls the horizontal stretches and compressions of the function and the locations of the vertical asymptotes, with the asymptotes $x = \frac{-\pi}{2}$ and $x = \frac{\pi}{2}$ moving in or out to $x = -\frac{b\pi}{2}$ and $x = \frac{b\pi}{2}$. Use the asymptotes to guide your sketch by keeping the curve (or curves if drawing more than one cycle) inside the asymptotes. The other guide to the shape comes from the halfway points at $\left(-\frac{\pi b}{4}, -a\right)$ and $\left(\frac{\pi b}{4}, a\right)$, which correspond to the points $\left(-\frac{\pi}{4}, -1\right)$ and $\left(\frac{\pi}{4}, 1\right)$ in the parent function.

Example 1 Plot one cycle of the transformed tangent function $g(x)$ on the axes provided with the parent function $f(x) = \tan x$.

Ⓐ $g(x) = \frac{1}{2}\tan\frac{x}{3}$

Assign values to a and b from the function rule.

$a = \frac{1}{2}, b = 3$

Draw the vertical asymptotes at $x = -\frac{3\pi}{2}$ and $x = \frac{3\pi}{2}$.

Draw the reference points at $\left(-\frac{3\pi}{4}, -\frac{1}{2}\right)$, $(0, 0)$, $\left(\frac{3\pi}{4}, \frac{1}{2}\right)$.

Sketch the function.

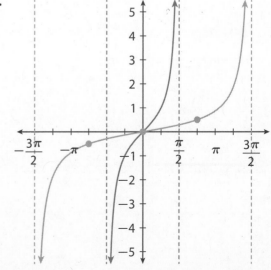

Ⓑ $g(x) = -2 \tan 2x$

Assign values to a and b from the function rule.

$a = \boxed{}$, $b = \boxed{}$

Draw the vertical asymptotes at $x = \boxed{}$

and $x = \boxed{}$.

Draw the reference points at $\left(\boxed{}, 2 \right)$,

$\left(\boxed{}, 0 \right), \left(\boxed{}, -2 \right)$.

Sketch the function.

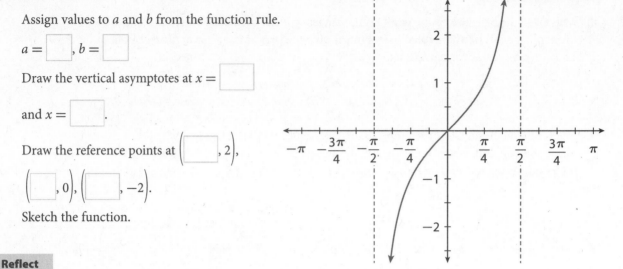

Reflect

4. Why is the vertical stretch parameter, a, referred to as the amplitude when transforming sine and cosine functions, but not tangent functions? If it is not the amplitude, how can it be used to help graph the function?

_____

_____

_____

_____

_____

5. **Make a Conjecture** Do transformed functions of the form $f(x) = a \tan \left(\frac{1}{b} x \right)$ have the same behavior seen in the parent function, that is, $f(-x) = -f(x)$? Explain your answer and how it helps to graph transformed functions.

_____

_____

_____

Your Turn

6. Graph $g(x) = -3 \tan \frac{x}{2}$.

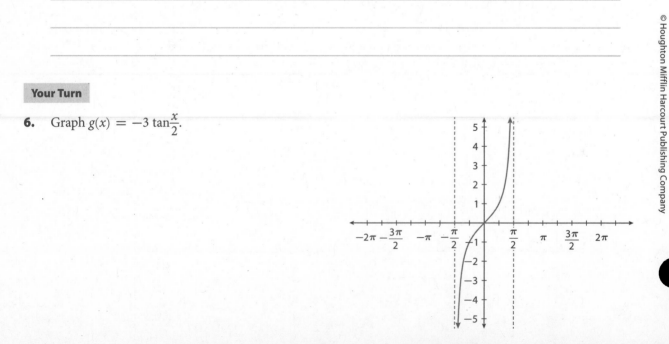

Writing $f(x) = a \tan\left(\frac{1}{b}x\right)$

To write the function rule for a graph of a transformed tangent function, identify the value of b from the spacing between the asymptotes. The asymptotes spread apart by a factor of $|b|$ if $|b| > 1$ or move inward if $|b| < 1$. The asymptotes are the points where the function is undefined, or $\frac{x}{b} = \frac{\pi}{2} + n\pi$, where n is an integer. The separation between any two consecutive asymptotes is $b\pi$.

The parameter a can be found by evaluating $\tan\frac{x}{b}$ at a known point. Finally, unless degrees are specified, the input to the tangent function should be assumed to be in radians, even if the x-axis of the graph is labeled with integers instead of multiples of π.

Example 2 Write the function rule for the transformed tangent function of the form $f(x) = a \tan\left(\frac{1}{b}x\right)$ from the graph.

(A) Find b from the distance between the asymptotes.

$\pi b = 1 - (-1)$, so $b = \frac{2}{\pi}$

Substitute the value of b into the function rule.

$$f(x) = a \tan\frac{\pi}{2}x$$

Use the point $\left(\frac{1}{2}, 2\right)$ to find a.

$$2 = a \tan\left(\frac{\pi}{2} \cdot \frac{1}{2}\right)$$

$$2 = a \tan\frac{\pi}{4}$$

$$2 = a$$

Write the function rule. $\qquad f(x) = 2 \tan\frac{\pi}{2}x$

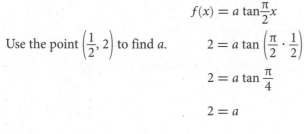

(B) Find b from the distance between the asymptotes.

$\pi b = \boxed{} - \left(\boxed{}\right)$

$\pi b = \boxed{}$

$b = \boxed{}$

Substitute the value of b.

$f(x) = a \tan\boxed{} x$

Use the point $\left(\frac{3\pi}{4}, -2\right)$ to find a.

$\boxed{} = a \tan\left(\frac{1}{3} \cdot \boxed{}\right)$

$-2 = a \tan\boxed{}$

$-2 = a$

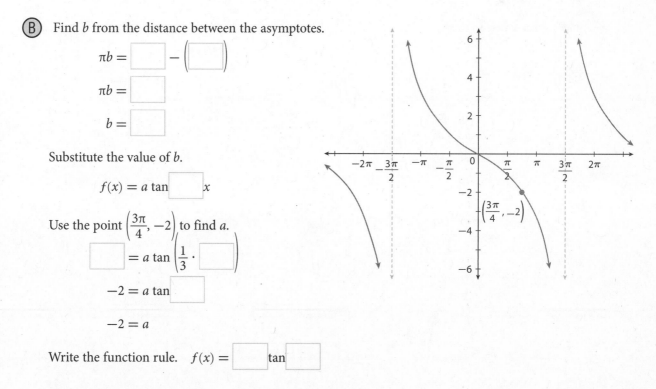

Write the function rule. $\quad f(x) = \boxed{} \tan\boxed{}$

7. Write the function rule for the transformed tangent function from its graph.

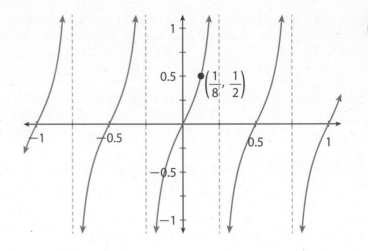

🎸 Explain 3 Comparing Tangent Functions

To compare tangent functions expressed in different forms such as graphs, tables, and equations, find the common elements that can be determined from each. Asymptotes are generally easy to recognize, and can be used to determine the period of the function.

Example 3 Compare the two tangent functions indicated by comparing their periods.

(A) $f(x)$ is shown in the graph; $g(x) = -\tan \frac{x}{3}$.

The period of $f(x)$ is $\pi - (-\pi) = 2\pi$.

The period of $g(x)$ is $\pi b = 3\pi$.

$g(x)$ has a greater period than $f(x)$.

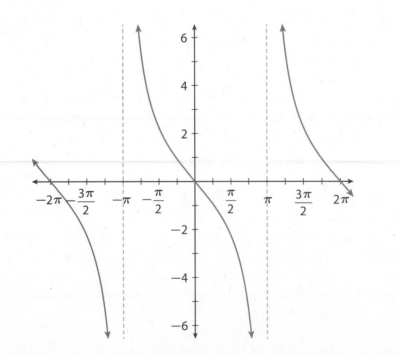

(B) $f(x)$ is shown in the graph; $g(x)$ is shown in the table.

x	g(x)
$-\dfrac{\pi}{4}$	Undefined
$-\dfrac{\pi}{8}$	-1
0	0
$\dfrac{\pi}{8}$	1
$\dfrac{\pi}{4}$	Undefined

The period of $f(x)$ is $\boxed{}-\left(\boxed{}\right)=\boxed{}$.

The asymptotes of $g(x)$ can be found where the function is _____.

The period of $g(x)$ is $\boxed{}-\left(\boxed{}\right)=\boxed{}$.

$g(x)$ has the same period as $f(x)$.

Your Turn

8. $f(x) = 3\tan\dfrac{\pi}{3}x$

x	g(x)
$-\dfrac{1}{6}$	Undefined
$-\dfrac{1}{12}$	-1
0	0
$\dfrac{1}{12}$	1
$\dfrac{1}{6}$	Undefined

© Houghton Mifflin Harcourt Publishing Company

✏ Explain 4   Modeling with Tangent Functions

Tangent functions can be used to model real-world situations that relate perpendicular measures (such as horizontal distance and height) to a changing angle.

Example 4   Read the description and use a tangent function to model the quantities. Use a calculator to make a table of points and graph the model. Describe the significance of the asymptote(s) and determine the domain over which the model works.

A climber is ascending the face of a 500-foot high vertical cliff at 5 feet per minute. Her climbing partner is observing from 150 feet away. Find the function that describes the amount of time climbing as a function of the angle of elevation of the observer's line-of-sight to the climber. Does the viewing angle ever reach 75 degrees?

🧩 Analyze Information

- The distance from the observer to the cliff base is 150 feet.
- The cliff is 500 feet high.
- The climber is climbing at 5 feet per minute.

🧩 Formulate a Plan

- A vertical line from the cliff base to the climber forms the second leg of a right triangle that can be used to find the appropriate trigonometric ratio.
- Use the right triangle to find a relationship between the height of the climber and the angle of elevation from which the observer is viewing.
- To find the time as a function of the angle, use the speed of the climber to rewrite the tangent expression.

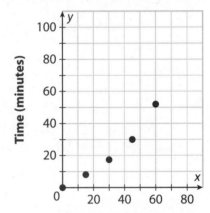

Time (minutes) vs **Elevation angle (degrees)**

🧩 Solve

The height as a function of viewing angle is $\tan \theta = \dfrac{\boxed{}}{\boxed{}}$.

The height of the climber is a function of time; $h = \boxed{}\, t$.

Substituting $\boxed{}$ for h in the second equation gives:

$\tan \theta = \dfrac{\boxed{}}{150}$

$\tan \theta = \dfrac{t}{\boxed{}}$

$t = \boxed{}$

θ	Time (minutes)
0	
15	
30	
45	
60	

Using the function to calculate time, a viewing angle of 75 degrees should be reached in _____ minutes. However, the height at that time would be _____ feet, which is higher than the cliff top This means that a viewing angle of 75 degrees is impossible.

Your Turn

9. You observe a model rocket launch from 20 feet away. Find the rule for the rocket's elevation as a function of the elevation angle, and graph it.

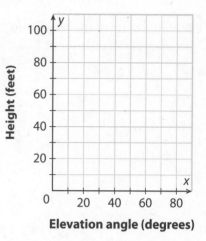

💬 **Elaborate**

10. If sine, cosine and tangent are all based on coordinates of the unit circle, why do sine and cosine have a domain of all real numbers while the tangent function does not?

_____

_____

_____

11. Why does the tangent function have a different period than the sine and cosine functions if they are all defined using the unit circle?

_____

_____

12. **Essential Question Check-in** How do the asymptotes and *x*-intercepts help in graphing the tangent function and its transformations?

_____

_____

_____

• Online Homework
• Hints and Help
• Extra Practice

1. Write the rules that describe all asymptotes of the functions $f(x) = \tan x$ and $f(x) = \cot x$.

Plot one cycle of the transformed tangent function $g(x)$ on the axes provided with the parent function $f(x) = \tan x$.

2. $g(x) = \tan 3x$

3. $g(x) = 3 \tan \dfrac{2}{3}x$

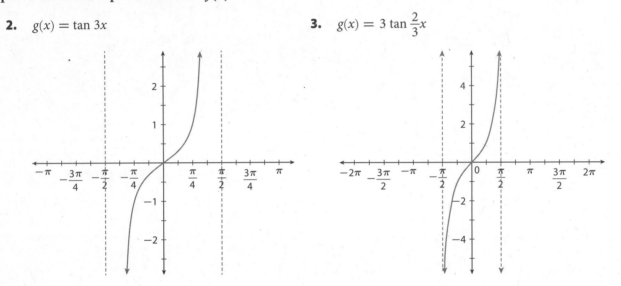

4. $g(x) = -\tan \dfrac{x}{3}$

5. $g(x) = -\dfrac{1}{4} \tan 4x$

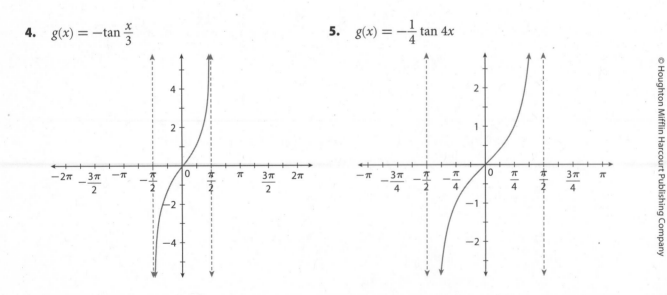

Write the function rule for the transformed tangent function of the form $g(x) = a \tan\left[\dfrac{1}{b}x\right]$ **from the graph.**

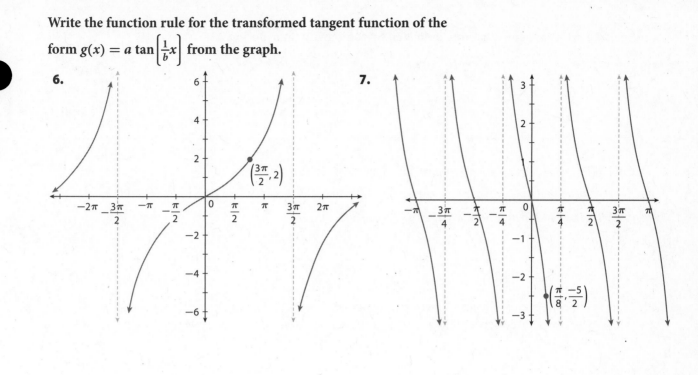

6.

$\left(\dfrac{3\pi}{2}, 2\right)$

7.

$\left(\dfrac{\pi}{8}, \dfrac{-5}{2}\right)$

8.

$\left(\dfrac{3}{4}, -1\right)$

9.

$(1, 4)$

Compare the two tangent functions indicated by comparing their periods.

10.

x	f(x)
−12	undefined
−6	−3
0	0
6	3
12	undefined

$g(x)$ is a tangent function with asymptotes at −10 and 10.

11. $f(x) = 3 \tan 4x$; $g(x)$ is a tangent function whose graph passes through points with x-coordinates $-\dfrac{\pi}{4}$ and $\dfrac{\pi}{4}$ that are halfway between the x-intercept at 0 and the nearest vertical asymptotes.

12. $f(x)$ is shown in the graph.

$g(x)$ is a tangent function stretched horizontally by a factor of 2.

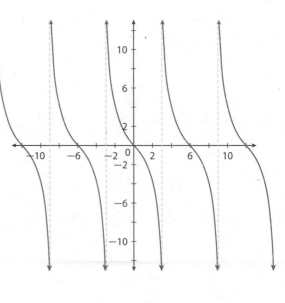

13. $f(x) = 3 \tan \pi x$

x	g(x)
−1	undefined
$-\dfrac{1}{2}$	2
0	0
$\dfrac{1}{2}$	−2
1	undefined

14. Sam is watching airplanes fly over his head at an airshow. The airplanes approach from the east at an altitude of 0.1 mile. Sam watches the airplanes approach and fly past. Measure angles from straight over Sam's head, with angles to the east being positive and angles to the west being negative. Find the horizontal position p of the planes from Sam as a function of the angle of Sam's view as the planes approach and fly over.

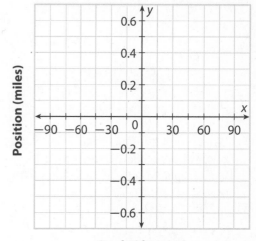

15. A police car stops in a long tunnel and parks 20 feet from the wall. The siren light makes a complete revolution once per second. Find the position p between the point where the center of the beam of light strikes the tunnel wall at time t and the point on the wall closest to the light's source. Graph the position as a function of time for $-0.25 < t < 0.25$ where at time $t = 0$ the beam is pointed directly at the wall.

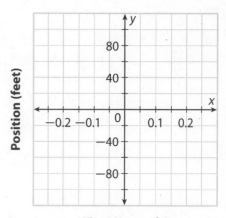

16. A security camera is mounted on the ceiling 10 feet above the floor at the midpoint of a long hallway. Find the position p along the hallway of the center of the camera's field of view as a function of the angle the camera makes relative to pointing straight down.

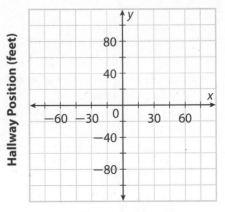

Center angle (degrees)

(y-axis label: Hallway Position (feet))

17. What positions of the planes correspond to the points on the graph whose x-coordinates are halfway between the graph's x-intercept and vertical asymptotes in the airshow example in Exercise 14?

18. What positions along the hallway are at the center of the view of the security camera when it is at the halfway points of the graph in Exercise 16?

19. At what time is the police siren light shining on the wall at a distance of 20 feet in a negative direction in Exercise 15? (Note that negative values for time indicate time before the light rotates to the closest point on the wall.)

20. Multiple Response The function $g(x) = -3 \tan \pi x$ has which of the following transformations compared to the parent function $f(x) = \tan x$?

A. a vertical stretch by a factor of 3

B. a vertical compression by a factor of 3

C. a horizontal stretch by a factor of π

D. a horizontal compression by a factor of $\frac{1}{\pi}$

E. a reflection over the x-axis

F. a translation up by 3

G. a translation down by 3

21. **Draw Conclusions** In the security camera model of Exercise 16, imagine that the camera has a field of view that is 20° wide (i.e. if the center of the image is looking at 40°, the total image views from 30° to 50°). What center angle views the shortest stretch of the hallway? What center angle views the longest stretch?

22. **Justify Reasoning** In the police siren example of Exercise 15, if the graph were extended to longer times and encompassed more periods of the tangent function, explain whether it would make sense to include all other periods of the tangent function.

23. **Communicate Mathematical Ideas** How could you sketch a graph of a tangent function on a coordinate plane with no grid lines (except the *x*- and *y*-axes) that is already showing the sine and cosine functions?

Lesson Performance Task

A community on the equator celebrates the equinox by having a festival at the town's sundial. Because the town is located at the equator, the sun rises directly in the east and sets directly in the west, passing directly overhead at solar noon, halfway through the 12 hours of daylight. The sundial rests on the ground, and its gnomon, the pointer that casts the shadow, is 4 feet above the ground. Let x be the angle of the sun from the sundial in degrees and let s be the length of the sundial's shadow in feet, as shown in the figure.

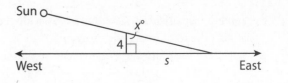

A. Write an equation that expresses the relationship between s and x, and then solve for s.

B. Let the angle off the sundial to the west be negative and the angle off the sundial to the east be positive. Write a function for the length of the sundial's shadow, s, in feet to the east as a function of time t hours after solar noon using the fact that the angle changes by 15° per hour.

C. Describe the graph of $s(t)$ from part B as a series of transformations from the parent function $f(t) = \tan t$. Also indicate the period of the function.

D. Since solar noon occurs at 12:15 p.m. local time, sunrise and sunset occur around 6:15 a.m. and 6:15 p.m., respectively. Complete the table to determine the values of t and $s(t)$, rounding to the nearest hundredth as needed. What is the meaning of the negative values for $s(t)$?

Local Time	t	$s(t)$
6:15 a.m.		
8:15 a.m.		
10:15 a.m.		
12:15 p.m.		
2:15 p.m.		
4:15 p.m.		
6:15 p.m.		

E. Do the values of $s(t)$ make sense at sunrise and sunset? Explain your reasoning.

18.3 Translating Trigonometric Graphs

Essential Question: How do the constants h and k in the functions $f(x) = a \sin\frac{1}{b}(x - h) + k$, $f(x) = a \cos\frac{1}{b}(x - h) + k$, and $f(x) = a \tan\frac{1}{b}(x - h) + k$ affect their graphs?

Resource
Locker

⊘ Explore   Translating the Graph of a Trigonometric Function

In previous lessons, you saw in what ways the graphs of $f(x) = a \sin\left(\frac{1}{b}\right)x$, $f(x) = a \cos\left(\frac{1}{b}\right)x$, and $f(x) = a \tan\left(\frac{1}{b}\right)x$ were vertical and horizontal shrinks and stretches of the graphs of their parent functions. You saw that the vertical stretches and shrinks changed the amplitude of sine and cosine graphs, but did not change the midline on the x-axis, and the horizontal stretches and compressions changed the period of all of the graphs.

As with other types of functions, you can indicate horizontal and vertical translations in the equations for trigonometric functions. Trigonometric functions in the form $f(x) = a \sin\frac{1}{b}(x - h) + k$, $f(x) = a \cos\frac{1}{b}(x - h) + k$, or $f(x) = a \tan\frac{1}{b}(x - h) + k$ indicate a vertical translation by k and a horizontal translation by h.

(A)   Answer the following questions about the graph of $f(x) = 0.5 \sin 3x$.

    a. What is the period of the graph?

    b. What are the first three x-intercepts for $x \geq 0$?

    c. What are the maximum and minimum values of the first cycle for $x \geq 0$, and where do they occur?

    d. What are the five key points of the graph that represent the values you found?

Use the key points to sketch one cycle of the graph.

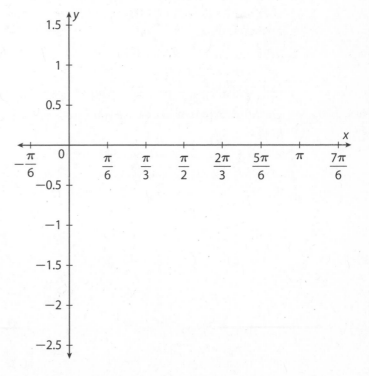

(B) Identify h and k for

$f(x) = 0.5 \sin 3\left(x - \frac{\pi}{3}\right) - 1.5$,

and tell what translations they indicate. Find the images of the key points of the graph in Step A. Finally, sketch the graph from Step A again, along with the graph of its image, after the indicated translations.

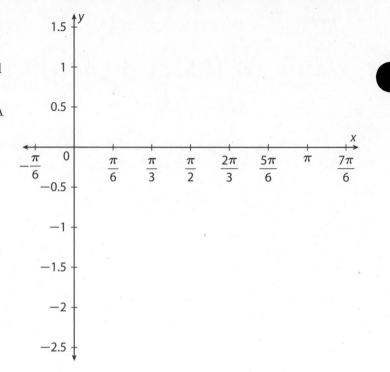

(C) Answer the following questions about the graph of $f(x) = 2\tan\frac{1}{2}x$.

a. What is the period of the graph?

b. What is the x-intercept of the graph at or nearest the origin? What are the asymptotes?

c. What are the halfway points on either side of the x-intercept that you found?

d. What are the three key points of the graph that represent the values you found?

Use the key points to sketch one cycle of the graph. Also show the asymptotes.

(D) Identify h and k for $f(x) = 2\tan\frac{1}{2}(x + \pi) + 3$, and tell what translations they indicate. Find the images of the key points of the graph in Step A, and the new asymptotes. Finally, sketch the graph from Step A again, along with the graph of its image after the indicated translations. (Note: Show the asymptotes for the translated graph, but not for the original graph.)

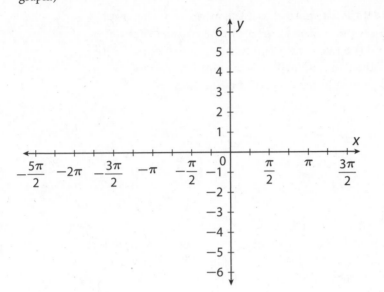

Reflect

1. Suppose that you are told to extend the graph of the translated function you graphed in Step B to the left and to the right. Without actually drawing the graph, explain how you would do this.

_____

_____

_____

_____

_____

2. What feature of the graphs of the trigonometric functions is represented by the value of the parameter k?

_____

_____

Explain 1   Graphing General Trigonometric Functions

Now you can combine all you have learned about the parameters a, b, h, and k in the equations for trigonometric functions to graph functions of the form $f(x) = a\sin\frac{1}{b}(x - h) + k$, $f(x) = a\cos\frac{1}{b}(x - h) + k$, or $f(x) = a\tan\frac{1}{b}(x - h) + k$ directly from their equations without first graphing parent functions.

Example 1   **For the function given, identify the period and the midline of the graph, and where the graph crosses the midline. For a sine or cosine function, identify the amplitude and the maximum and minimum values and where they occur. For a tangent function, identify the asymptotes and the values of the halfway points. Then graph one cycle of the function.**

(A) $f(x) = 3\sin(x - \pi) + 1$

Period: $\frac{1}{b} = 1$, so $b = 1$; period $= 2\pi \cdot 1 = 2\pi$

Midline: $y = k$, or $y = 1$

Amplitude: $a = 3$

The point $(0, 0)$ on the graph of the parent function $y = \sin x$ is translated $h = \pi$ units to the right and $k = 1$ unit up to $(\pi, 1)$. The graph also crosses the midline at the endpoint of the cycle , $(\pi + 2\pi, 1) = (3\pi, 1)$ and at the point halfway between $(\pi, 1)$ and $(3\pi, 1)$ or at $(2\pi, 1)$. So, the graph contains $(\pi, 1)$, $(2\pi, 1)$ and $(3\pi, 1)$.

Maximum: $a = 3$ units above the midline, or $k + a = 1 + 3 = 4$; occurs halfway between the first and second midline crossings, or at $x = \frac{\pi + 2\pi}{2} = \frac{3\pi}{2}$. So, the graph contains $\left(\frac{3\pi}{2}, 4\right)$.

Minimum: $a = 3$ units below the midline, or $k - a = 1 - 3 = -2$; occurs halfway between the second and third midline crossings, or at $x = \frac{2\pi + 3\pi}{2} = \frac{5\pi}{2}$. So, the graph contains $\left(\frac{5\pi}{2}, -2\right)$.

Plot the key points found and sketch the graph.

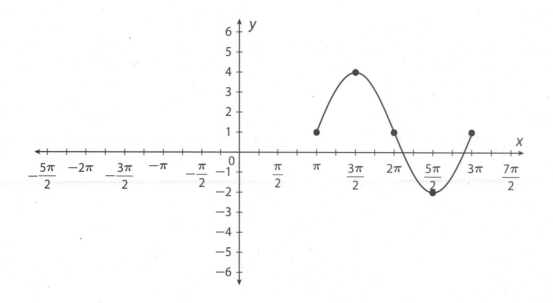

(B) $f(x) = -2\tan\frac{1}{2}(x - 2\pi) + 2$

Period: $\dfrac{1}{b} = \boxed{}$, so $b = \boxed{}$; period $= \boxed{} \cdot 2 = \boxed{}$

Midline: $y = k$, or $y = \boxed{}$

The point $(0, 0)$ on the graph of $y = \tan x$ is translated $h = \boxed{}$ units to the _____ and $k = \boxed{}$

units _____ to $\left(\boxed{}, \boxed{} \right)$. There are asymptotes half a cycle to the left and right of this point, or at

$x = 2\pi - \boxed{} = \boxed{}$ and $x = 2\pi + \boxed{} = \boxed{}$.

Halfway points occur halfway between the asymptotes and where the graph crosses its midline, or at

$x = \dfrac{\boxed{} + 2\pi}{2} = \dfrac{\boxed{}}{2}$ and $x = \dfrac{2\pi + \boxed{}}{2} = \dfrac{\boxed{}}{2}$.

The halfway points of $y = \tan x$ have y–values of -1 and 1. Because $a = \boxed{}$ in

$f(x) = -2\tan\frac{1}{2}(x - 2\pi) + 2$, the halfway points are reflected across the midline and stretched

vertically from it by a factor of $\boxed{}$. The halfway points are

$\left(\dfrac{3\pi}{2}, a\left(\boxed{} \right) + k \right) = \left(\dfrac{3\pi}{2}, -2\left(\boxed{} \right) + 2 \right) = \left(\dfrac{3\pi}{2}, \boxed{} \right)$ and

$\left(\dfrac{5\pi}{2}, a\left(\boxed{} \right) + k \right) = \left(\dfrac{5\pi}{2}, -2\left(\boxed{} \right) + 2 \right) = \left(\dfrac{5\pi}{2}, \boxed{} \right)$.

Plot the key points found and sketch the graph.

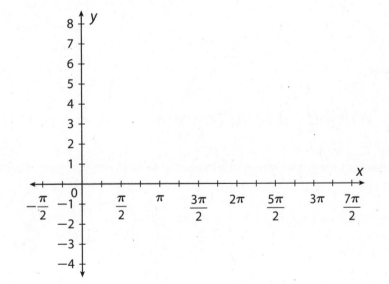

3. For $f(x) = 2\cos 2\left(x - \dfrac{\pi}{2}\right) + 1$, identify the period, the midline, where the graph crosses the midline, the amplitude, and the maximum and minimum values and where they occur. Then graph one cycle of the function.

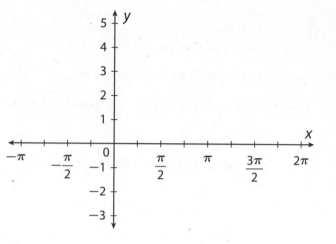

🗝 Explain 2 | Writing General Trigonometric Functions

Because the equations of $f(x) = a\sin\frac{1}{b}(x - h) + k$, $f(x) = a\cos\frac{1}{b}(x - h) + k$, or $f(x) = a\tan\frac{1}{b}(x - h) + k$ directly reflect the physical features of their graphs, it is straightforward to write an equation given a graph of one of these functions.

Example 2 | **Write an equation as indicated for the given graph.**

Ⓐ a cosine function

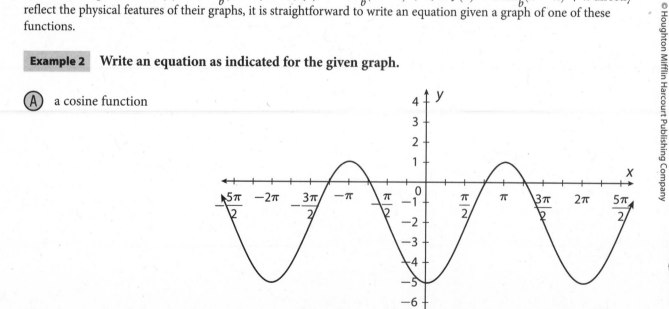

Amplitude: $a = \frac{1 - (-5)}{2} = 3$

Midline: $y = -2$, so $k = -2$.

Period: 2π; so, $2\pi \cdot b = 2\pi$, and $b = 1$.

You can obtain a local maximum at $x = -\pi$ by translating the graph of $y = \cos x$ to the left by π units. So, $h = -\pi$.

A cosine equation is $f(x) = 3\cos(x + \pi) - 2$. Notice that the equations $f(x) = 3\cos(x - \pi) - 2$ and $f(x) = -3\cos x - 2$ also represent the graph.

(B) a tangent function with midline and halfway points shown

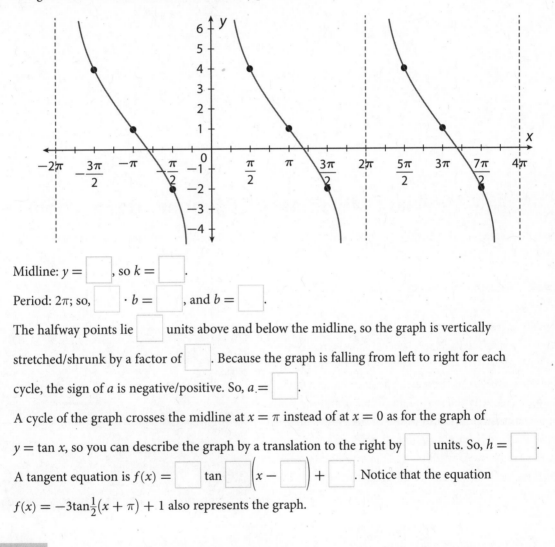

Midline: $y = \boxed{}$, so $k = \boxed{}$.

Period: 2π; so, $\boxed{} \cdot b = \boxed{}$, and $b = \boxed{}$.

The halfway points lie $\boxed{}$ units above and below the midline, so the graph is vertically

stretched/shrunk by a factor of $\boxed{}$. Because the graph is falling from left to right for each

cycle, the sign of a is negative/positive. So, $a = \boxed{}$.

A cycle of the graph crosses the midline at $x = \pi$ instead of at $x = 0$ as for the graph of

$y = \tan x$, so you can describe the graph by a translation to the right by $\boxed{}$ units. So, $h = \boxed{}$.

A tangent equation is $f(x) = \boxed{} \tan \boxed{} \left(x - \boxed{} \right) + \boxed{}$. Notice that the equation

$f(x) = -3\tan\frac{1}{2}(x + \pi) + 1$ also represents the graph.

Reflect

4. How could you write a sine function from the cosine function first described by Example 2A?

_____

_____

_____

_____

5. What is true in general about the graph of a tangent function of the form $f(x) = a\tan\frac{1}{b}(x - h) + k$ when $a > 0$? when $a < 0$?

_____

_____

Your Turn

6. Write a sine function for the graph.

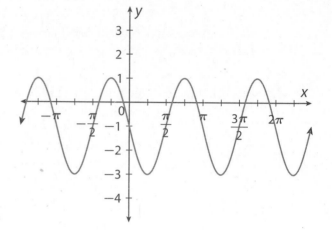

🗝 Explain 3 Modeling with General Trigonometric Functions

Many real-world phenomena, such as circular motion and wave motion, involve repeating patterns that are described by trigonometric functions.

Example 3 **Interpret values of trigonometric models.**

Ⓐ **Paddle Wheels** The motion of a point on the outer edge of a riverboat's paddle wheel blade is modeled by $h(t) = 8\sin\frac{\pi}{2}(t - 1) + 6$ where h is the height in feet measured from the water line and t is the time in seconds. Identify the period, midline, amplitude, and maximum and minimum values of the graph. For one cycle starting from $t = 0$, find all points where the graph intersects its midline and the coordinates of any local maxima and minima. Interpret these points in the context of the problem, and graph one cycle.

Period: $\frac{1}{b} = \frac{\pi}{2}$, so $b = \frac{2}{\pi}$, and $2\pi \cdot b = 4$; Midline: $k = 6$, so the midline is $h(t) = 6$.

Amplitude: $a = 8$; Maximum: $k + a = 6 + 8 = 14$; Minimum: $k - a = 6 - 8 = -2$

When $t = 0$, $h(t) = 8\sin\frac{\pi}{2}(0 - 1) + 6 = 8\sin\left(-\frac{\pi}{2}\right) + 6 = 8(-1) + 6 = -2$. So, $(0, -2)$ is on the graph. This is a minimum. There is a second minimum at the end of the cycle at $(0 + 4, -2) = (4, -2)$.

A maximum lies halfway between the x–values of the minima at $x = \frac{0 + 4}{2} = 2$. So, $(2, 14)$ is on the graph.

The graph crosses its midline halfway between each local maximum or minimum, or at $x = \frac{0+2}{2} = 1$ and $x = \frac{2+4}{2} = 3$. So, $(1, 6)$ and $(3, 6)$ are on the graph.

The point $(0, -2)$ means that the outer edge of the blade is 2 feet below the water's surface at time $t = 0$. One second later, it is at $(1, 6)$, or 6 feet above the water's surface—the height of the wheel's center. At $(2, 14)$, it reaches its maximum height of 14 feet, is back to the height of the center at $(3, 6)$, and at $(4, -2)$ returns to the lowest point 2 feet below the water at the end of one 4-second cycle.

(B) **Amusement Parks** The motion of a gondola car on the Ferris wheel at Navy Pier in Chicago can be modeled by $h(t) = 70\sin\frac{2\pi}{7}(t - 1.75) + 80$, where h is the height in feet and t is the time in minutes. Identify the period, midline, amplitude, and maximum and minimum values of the graph. For one cycle starting from $t = 0$, find all points where the graph intersects its midline and the coordinates of any local maxima and minima. Interpret these points in the context of the problem, and graph one cycle.

Period: $\frac{1}{b} = \boxed{}$, so $b = \boxed{}$, and $2\pi \cdot b = \boxed{}$;

Midline: $k = \boxed{}$, so the midline is $h(t) = \boxed{}$.

Amplitude: $a = \boxed{}$; Maximum: $k + a = \boxed{} + \boxed{} = \boxed{}$;

Minimum: $k - a = \boxed{} - \boxed{} = \boxed{}$

When $t = 0$, $h(t) = 70\sin\frac{2\pi}{7}\left(\boxed{} - 1.75\right) + 80 = 70\sin\left(-\frac{\pi}{\boxed{}}\right) + 80$

$= 70\left(\boxed{}\right) + 80 = \boxed{}$. So, $\left(0, \boxed{}\right)$ is on the graph. This is a minimum.

There is a second minimum at the end of the cycle at $\left(0 + \boxed{}, 10\right)$

$= \left(\boxed{}, 10.\right)$ A maximum lies halfway between the x-values of the minima

at $x = \frac{0 + \boxed{}}{2} = \boxed{}$. So, $\left(\boxed{}, \boxed{}\right)$ is on the graph.

The graph crosses its midline halfway between each local maximum or minimum, or at $x = \frac{0 + 3.5}{2} = 1.75$ and $x = \frac{3.5 + \boxed{}}{2} = \boxed{}$.

So, $\left(1.75, \boxed{}\right)$ and $\left(\boxed{}, \boxed{}\right)$ are on the graph.

The point $(0, 10)$ means that the gondola is ☐ feet above the ground at time $t = 0$.

After 1.75 minutes, it is at $\left(1.75, \boxed{}\right)$, or ☐ feet above the ground—the height

of the wheel's center. At $\left(3.5, \boxed{}\right)$ it reaches its maximum height of ☐ feet.

It is back to the height of the center at $(5.25, 80)$, and at $(7, 10)$ it returns to the lowest point, 10 feet above the ground, at the end of one 7-minute cycle.

Your Turn

7. **Amusement Parks** The height h in feet of a car on a different Ferris wheel can be modeled by $h(t) = -16\cos\frac{\pi}{45} t + 24$, where t is the time in seconds. Identify the period, midline, amplitude, and maximum and minimum values of the graph. For one cycle starting from $t = 0$, find all points where the graph intersects its midline and the coordinates of any local maxima and minima. Interpret these points in the context of the problem, and graph one cycle.

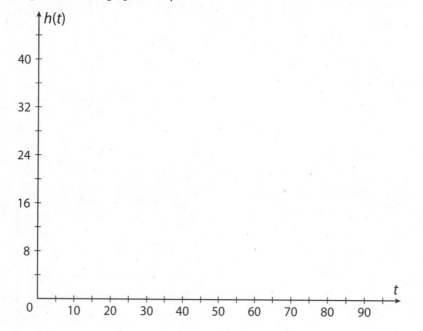

8. How can being given the first local maximum and local minimum of a cosine function $(a > 0)$ help you write its equation?

_____

_____

_____

_____

_____

9. **Essential Question Check-In** How do positive values of h affect the graph of a function in the form $f(x) = a \sin \frac{1}{b}(x - h) + k$? How do negative values of k affect the graph of this function?

_____

_____

⭐ Evaluate: Homework and Practice

- Online Homework
- Hints and Help
- Extra Practice

For each function, identify the period and the midline of the graph, and where the graph crosses the midline. For a sine or cosine function, identify the amplitude and the maximum and minimum values and where they occur. For a tangent function, identify the asymptotes and the values of the halfway points. Then graph one cycle.

1. $f(x) = -3\sin(x + \pi) + 1$

2. $f(x) = 2 \cos 3x + 1$

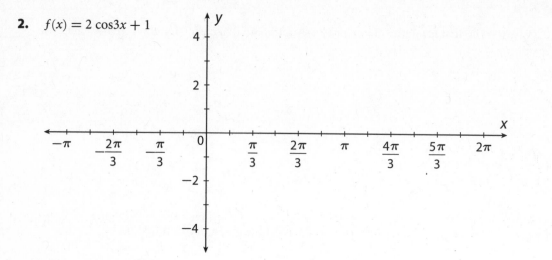

3. $f(x) = \tan\frac{1}{2}(x - \pi) + 3$

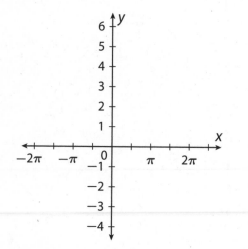

4. $f(x) = 3\sin\frac{\pi}{2}(x-2) + 3$

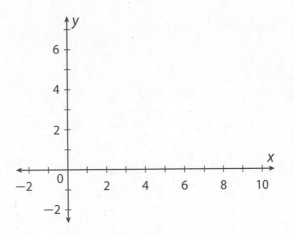

Write an equation as indicated for the given graph.

5. a sine function

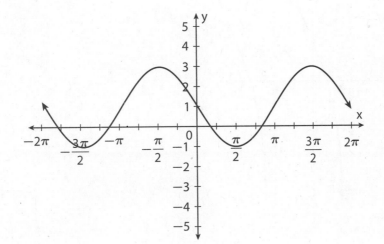

6. a cosine function

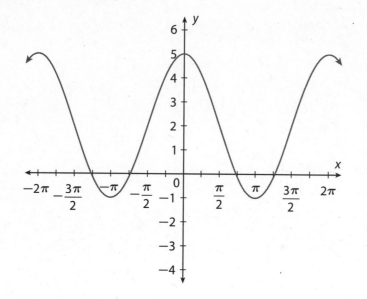

7. a tangent function

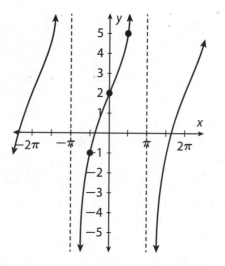

For the context described, identify the period, midline, amplitude, and maximum and minimum values of the graph. For one cycle starting from $t = 0$, find all points where the graph intersects its midline and the coordinates of any local maxima and minima. Interpret these points in the context of the problem, and graph one cycle.

8. **Historic Technology** Water turns a water wheel at an old mill. The water comes in at the top of the wheel through a wooden chute. The function $h(t) = 15\cos\frac{\pi}{5}t + 20$ models the height h in feet above the stream into which the water empties of a point on the wheel where t is the time in seconds.

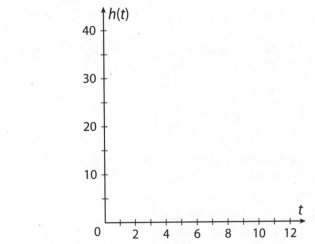

9. **Games** A toy is suspended 36 inches above the floor on a spring. A child reaches up, pulls the toy, and releases it. The function $h(t) = 10\sin\pi(x - 0.5) + 36$ models the toy's height h in inches above the floor after t seconds.

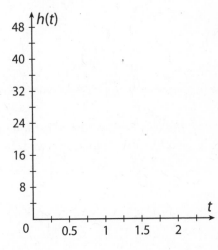

10. Match each sine function with the cosine function that has the same graph.

A. $y = \sin 2x$

B. $y = \frac{1}{2}\sin 3x$

C. $y = \frac{1}{2}\sin 4(x - 2)$

D. $y = \sin(x - \pi) + 1$

E. $y = \sin\left(x + \frac{\pi}{2}\right) + 4$

1. $y = \cos\left(x + \frac{\pi}{2}\right) + 1$

2. $y = \frac{1}{2}\cos 4\left(x - \frac{16 + \pi}{8}\right)$

3. $y = \cos 2\left(x - \frac{\pi}{4}\right)$

4. $y = \cos(x) + 4$

5. $y = \frac{1}{2}\cos 3\left(x - \frac{\pi}{6}\right)$

11. How do h and k affect the key points of the graphs of sine, cosine, and tangent functions?

H.O.T. **Focus on Higher Order Thinking**

12. Explain the Error Sage was told to write the equation of a sine function with a period of 2π, an amplitude of 5, a horizontal translation of 3 units right, and a vertical translation of 6 units up. She wrote the equation $f(x) = 5\sin 2\pi(x - 3) + 6$. Explain Sage's error and give the correct equation.

13. Critical Thinking Can any sine or cosine function graph be represented by a sine equation with a positive coefficient a? Explain your answer.

14. Make a Prediction What will the graph of the function $f(x) = \cos^2 x + \sin^2 x$ look like? Explain your answer and check it on a graphing calculator.

Lesson Performance Task

At a location off a pier on the Maine coastline, the function $d(t) = 4.36\cos(0.499t) + 8.79$ models the depth d in feet of the water t hours after the first high tide during a first quarter moon.

  a. Identify the amplitude and period of the function as well as the equation of the midline. Describe the graph of this function as a series of transformations of the parent function $y = \cos x$.

  b. Explain how you can use the cosine function from part A to write a sine function to model the depth of the water. Describe the graph of this function as a series of transformations of the parent function $y = \sin x$.

  c. The heights of astronomical tides are affected by the moon phase. A function that models the depth of the water at the same location after the first low tide during a new moon is $d(t) = 6.31\sin\left[0.503(t - 3.13)\right] + 8.75$. Identify the amplitude and period of the function as well as the equation of the midline. Describe the graph of this function as a series of transformations of the parent function $y = \sin x$.

(Continued on next page)

d. Explain how you can use the sine function from part C on the previous page to write a cosine function to model the height of the water. Describe the graph of this function as a series of transformations of the parent function $y = \cos x$.

e. Compare the functions from parts A and B with the functions from parts C and D. How do the tides during a new moon compare to the tides during a first quarter moon?

18.4 Fitting Sine Functions to Data

Essential Question: How can you model data using a sine function?

✎ Explore Roughly Fitting a Sine Function to Data

When the graph of a set of data has a wave-like pattern, you can model the data with a sine function of the form $y = a \sin \frac{1}{b}(x - h) + k$. While it is also possible to use a cosine function as a model, it's not necessary because the basic sine and cosine curves are identical apart from a horizontal translation due to the fact that $\cos x = \sin\left(x + \frac{\pi}{2}\right)$.

Consider Chicago's monthly average temperatures in degrees Fahrenheit.

Month	1	2	3	4	5	6	7	8	9	10	11	12
Average temperature (°F)	23.8	27.7	37.9	48.9	59.1	68.9	74.0	72.4	64.6	52.5	40.3	27.7

Ⓐ Graph the data.

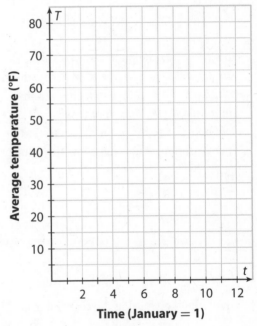

Time (January = 1)

Ⓑ You want to write a model of the form $y = a \sin \frac{1}{b}(x - h) + k$ where x represents time (in months, starting with 1 for January), y represents average monthly temperature (in degrees Fahrenheit), and a, b, h, and k are constants. Begin by finding the value of b.

You know that the parameter b produces a horizontal stretch or compression of the graph of $y = \sin x$ by a factor of b. You also know that the period of $y = \sin x$ is 2π, so the period of $y = a \sin \frac{1}{b}(x - h) + k$ is $2\pi b$. Use this information to find the value of b for the temperature data. Explain your reasoning. Then substitute the value of b into the model.

_____

_____

© Houghton Mifflin Harcourt Publishing Company

(C) You know that the parameter k produces a vertical translation of the graph of $y = \sin x$. You also know that the graph of $y = \sin x$ has $y = 0$ as its midline, so the graph of $y = a \sin \frac{1}{b}(x - h) + k$ has $y = k$ as its midline. The midline, which is a horizontal line, occurs halfway between the highest and lowest data points. Use this information to find the value of k for the temperature data. Explain your reasoning. Then substitute the value of k into the model.

_____

_____

_____

(D) You know that the parameter h produces a horizontal translation of the graph of $y = \sin x$. You also know that the graph of $y = \sin x$ crosses its midline at $x = 0$, so the graph of $y = a \sin \frac{1}{b}(x - h) + k$ crosses its midline at $x = h$. Use this information to find the value of h for the temperature data. Explain your reasoning. Then substitute the value of h into the model.

_____

_____

_____

(E) You know that the parameter a produces a vertical stretch or compression of the graph of $y = \sin x$ as well as a reflection across the midline when a is negative. You also know that the graph of $y = \sin x$ has an amplitude of 1, so the graph of $y = a \sin \frac{1}{b}(x - h) + k$ has an amplitude of $|a|$. The amplitude is half the vertical distance between the highest and lowest data points. Use this information to find the value of a for the temperature data. Explain your reasoning. Then substitute the value of a into the model.

_____

_____

_____

_____

(F) Graph the model using the coordinate grid from Step A.

Reflect

1. If the temperature data had been given in degrees Celsius rather than degrees Fahrenheit, how would the model change?

_____

_____

2. If you let t represent time and T represent temperature, what does the model become?

_____

3. If you define January as month 0 instead of month 1, how does the graph of the data change, and what does the model become?

_____

_____

🔑 Explain 1 **Fitting a Sine Function to Data Using Technology**

You can obtain a sine model for a set of data by performing sine regression using a graphing calculator in the same way as you would perform linear regression, exponential regression, and so on.

Ⓐ The table gives Chicago's monthly average temperatures as in the Explore. Use a graphing calculator to obtain a sine regression model for the data. Graph the regression model along with the model from the Explore, and compare the models visually.

Month	1	2	3	4	5	6	7	8	9	10	11	12
Average temperature (°F)	23.8	27.7	37.9	48.9	59.1	68.9	74.0	72.4	64.6	52.5	40.3	27.7

Step 1 Enter the data into lists L_1 and L_2. Then press the [STAT] key and select **C:SinReg** from the **CALC** menu.

So, the regression model is $y = 25.2 \sin(0.5x - 2) + 48.7$.

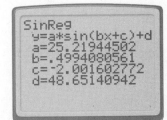

Step 2 Graph the data, the regression model, and the model $y = 25.1 \sin\frac{\pi}{6}(x - 4) + 48.9$ from the Explore. Visually compare the models.

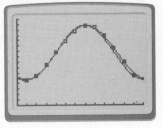

Both models appear to fit the data equally well from $x = 1$ to $x = 8$. For values of x greater than 8, the regression model fits the data better than the rough-fit model from the Explore does.

Ⓑ The table gives the monthly mean minimum temperature, in degrees Celsius, for Canberra, Australia. Roughly fit a sine model of the form $y = a \sin\frac{1}{b}(x - h) + k$ to the data. Then obtain a sine regression model using a graphing calculator. Finally, visually compare the two models in relation to the data.

Month	1	2	3	4	5	6	7	8	9	10	11	12
Minimum temperature (°C)	13.2	13.1	10.7	6.7	3.2	1.0	−0.1	1.0	3.3	6.1	8.8	11.4

© Houghton Mifflin Harcourt Publishing Company

Step 1 Roughly fit a sine model of the form $y = a \sin \frac{1}{b}(x - h) + k$.

- The period $2\pi b$ must equal 12, so $b =$ ☐ and $\frac{1}{b} =$ ☐.
- The horizontal midline is halfway between the highest and lowest data points, so
  $k = \frac{13.2 + (-0.1)}{2} =$ ☐.
- The first occurrence of a temperature close to 6.55 °C is in month ___, so $h =$ ☐.
- The amplitude is half the vertical distance between the highest and lowest data
  points, so $|a| = \frac{13.2 - (-0.1)}{2} =$ ☐. Because the temperatures are
  [increasing/decreasing] near $x = 4$, $a =$ ☐.

So, a sine model for the data is $y =$ ☐ $\sin$ ☐ $\left(x -$ ☐ $\right) +$ ☐.

Step 2 Enter the data into a graphing calculator and perform sine regression.

The sine regression model is $y =$ ☐ $\sin \left($ ☐ $x +$ ☐ $\right) +$ ☐.

Step 3 Visually compare the two models.

Both models appear to fit the data equally well from $x = 1$ to $x = 10$. For values of x greater than 10, the regression model fits the data [better/worse] than the rough-fit model.

Reflect

4. Rewrite the regression model in Part A so that it has the form $y = a \sin \frac{1}{b}(x - h) + k$. Then compare this form of the regression model with the rough-fit model from the Explore.

_____

_____

_____

_____

5. **Discussion** Rewrite the regression model in Part B so that it has the form $y = a \sin \frac{1}{b}(x - h) + k$. Then compare this form of the regression model with the rough-fit model in Part B. How can you reconcile any differences you observe?

_____

_____

_____

_____

_____

_____

_____

_____

6. The table gives the monthly mean maximum temperature, in degrees Celsius, for Canberra, Australia. Roughly fit a sine model of the form $y = a \sin \frac{1}{b}(x - h) + k$ to the data. Then obtain a sine regression model using a graphing calculator. Finally, visually compare the two models in relation to the data.

Month	1	2	3	4	5	6	7	8	9	10	11	12
Maximum temperature (°C)	28.0	27.1	24.5	20.0	15.6	12.3	11.4	13.0	16.2	19.4	22.7	26.1

⚙ Explain 2 Solving a Real-World Problem Using a Sine Model

You can use the graph of a sine model to determine when the model takes on a value of interest.

Example 2 The table gives the amount of daylight, in hours and minutes, in Chicago on the first day of every month. For what period of time during a year does Chicago get a minimum of 12 hours of daylight?

Day	Jan. 1	Feb. 1	Mar. 1	Apr. 1	May 1	June 1	July 1	Aug. 1	Sept. 1	Oct. 1	Nov. 1	Dec. 1
Amount of daylight (h:min)	9:12	10:03	11:15	12:43	14:02	15:01	15:10	14:24	13:08	11:45	10:22	9:22

🧩 Analyze Information

The independent variable in this situation is _____, given as calendar dates (the first day of every month).

The dependent variable is _____, measured in hours and minutes.

Formulate a Plan

You want a sine regression model for the data in order to find _____

_____ .

To obtain the model, you need to convert each of the given calendar dates

to _____ . You also need to
convert each corresponding amount of daylight from hours and minutes

to _____ .

Solve

You can use an online day-of-year calendar to convert the calendar dates to days since the start of the year (assuming it's not a leap year). Converting hours and minutes to decimal hours simply involves dividing the minutes by _____ and adding the result to the hours. Complete the table, giving decimal hours to the nearest hundredth if necessary.

Day	1	32	60	91	121	152	182	213	244	274	305	335
Amount of daylight (hours)												

Enter the data into a graphing calculator and perform sine regression. The sine

regression model is $y = \boxed{} \sin \left(\boxed{} x + \boxed{} \right) + \boxed{}$. Graph the

model along with the line $y = \boxed{}$. Use **5:intersect** from the **CALC** menu to determine the coordinates of each of the points of intersection of the sine curve and the line.

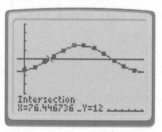
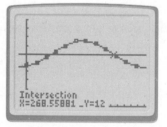

To the nearest whole number, the x-coordinate for the first point of intersection

is _____ , and the x-coordinate of the second point of intersection is _____ .
Using a day-of-year calendar, you find that 76 corresponds to _____ and 269
corresponds to _____ . Since the graph of the sine model is above the line
between those two dates, Chicago gets a minimum of 12 hours of daylight between

_____ and _____ .

Justify and Evaluate

Looking back at the table of data, you see that the first time the amount of daylight
is 12 hours or greater is _____ and the last time is _____ . These
dates fall within the interval you found using the sine regression model, which
confirms your answer.

Module 18

928

Lesson 4

© Houghton Mifflin Harcourt Publishing Company

Your Turn

7. The table gives the amount of daylight, in hours and minutes, in Sydney, Australia, on the first day of every month. For what period of time during a year does Sydney get a minimum of 12 hours of daylight?

Day	Jan. 1	Feb. 1	Mar. 1	Apr. 1	May 1	June 1	July 1	Aug. 1	Sept. 1	Oct. 1	Nov. 1	Dec. 1
Amount of daylight (h:min)	14:22	13:44	12:49	11:44	10:45	10:03	9:56	10:27	11:23	12:25	13:27	14:13

Data as ordered pairs with days of year and decimal hours: (1, 14.37), (32, 13.73), (60, 12.82), (91, 11.73), (121, 10.75), (152, 10.05), (182, 9.93), (213, 10.45), (244, 11.38), (274, 12.42), (305, 13.45), (335, 14.22)

Elaborate

8. What pattern must graphed data exhibit in order for a sine function to be an appropriate model for the data?

_____

9. When modeling data with the function $y = a \sin \frac{1}{b}(x - h) + k$, how do you use the data to identify a reasonable value for the parameter a?

_____

_____

_____

10. When you obtain both a rough-fit sine model and a sine regression model for a set of data, can you compare the constants in the two models directly? Explain.

_____

_____

_____

11. **Essential Question Check-In** One way to fit a sine model to data is to use the data to identify reasonable values for the parameters a, b, h, and k in $y = a \sin \frac{1}{b}(x - h) + k$. What is another way?

_____

For the situation described:

(a) Graph the data, roughly fit a sine model of the form
$y = a \sin \frac{1}{b}(x - h) + k$ to the data, and graph the model on the
same grid as the data.

(b) Obtain a sine regression model using a graphing calculator, and
then visually compare the two models in relation to the data.

1. The table gives the average monthly temperature in Nashville, Tennessee, in degrees
Fahrenheit.

Month	1	2	3	4	5	6	7	8	9	10	11	12
Average temperature (°F)	37.7	41.7	50.0	59.0	67.5	75.7	79.4	78.7	71.5	60.3	49.8	40.4

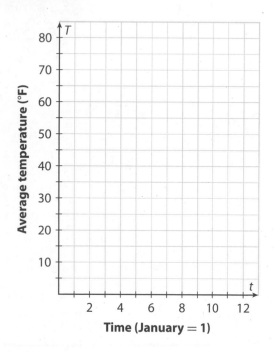

2. The table shows the approximate US residential monthly electricity consumption in billions of kilowatt-hours (kWh) for one year where $x = 1$ represents January.

Month	1	2	3	4	5	6	7	8	9	10	11	12
Consumption (billions of kWh)	136	116	106	91	94	114	137	138	115	98	92	124

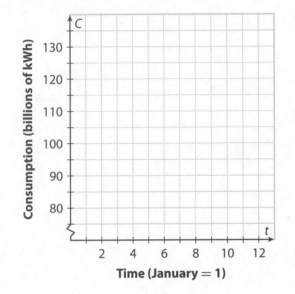

© Houghton Mifflin Harcourt Publishing Company · Image Credits: ©Radius Images/Alamy

For the situation described:

(a) Graph the data, roughly fit a sine model of the form $y = a \sin \frac{1}{b}(x - h) + k$ to the data, and graph the model on the same grid as the data.

(b) Obtain a sine regression model using a graphing calculator, and then visually compare the two models in relation to the data.

(c) Use a graphing calculator and the regression model to answer the question.

3. The table shows the amount of daylight (in minutes) from sunrise to sunset on the 21st day of each month (given as the day of the year) in Green Bay, Wisconsin, where January 1 = day 1.

Day of year	21	52	80	111	141	172	202	233	264	294	325	355
Amount of daylight (minutes)	565	646	732	826	901	933	902	826	733	643	563	530

For about how long each year is the amount of daylight at most 10 hours?

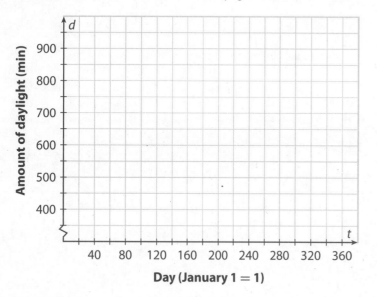

4. The table shows the decimal portion of the moon's surface illuminated from Earth's view at midnight from Washington, D.C., in March, 2014, where x represents the day of the month.

Day	1	3	5	7	9	11	13	15	17	19	21	23	25	27	29	31
Portion of moon illuminated	0.00	0.05	0.19	0.37	0.56	0.74	0.89	0.98	1.00	0.94	0.80	0.60	0.37	0.17	0.03	0.00

A "gibbous moon" refers to the moon phases when more than half of the moon is illuminated, but it is not a full moon. About how long is the period that the moon is either a gibbous moon or a full moon?

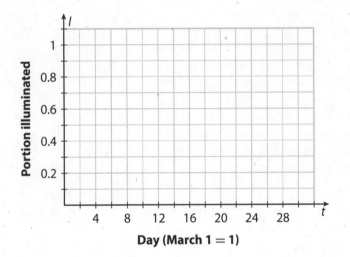

Day (March 1 = 1)

5. **Make a Conjecture** Why does it make sense that a graphing calculator has a sine regression option but not a cosine regression option?

6. **Critical Thinking** In a science class lab, a mass is suspended from a spring above a tabletop. The mass is pulled down and released. By examining frames from a video as the mass bobs up and down, the class obtains the model $d(t) = 5 \sin 4(t - 0.39)$ for the displacement d of the mass relative to its resting position at time t in seconds. Cassandra notices that after several seconds the mass is not bobbing up and down as far, but it still seems to take about the same time for a cycle. Graph $y = e^{-0.05x}\left[5 \sin 4(x - 0.39)\right]$ on a graphing calculator with the original model for $0 \leq x \leq 10$. Explain how this model differs from the original model, and how it might account for Cassandra's observation.

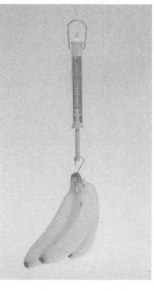

7. **Explain the Error** Given a set of data about the Sun's maximum angle θ (in degrees) above the horizon in Boston on any day of the year, Ryan uses his graphing calculator to obtain the regression model $\theta = 23.6 \sin (0.0168t - 1.32) + 47.4$ where t is the number of days since the start of a year. He concludes that the midline of the model's graph is $\theta = 47.4°$ and that the first time during the year that the Sun is reaches this maximum angle in Boston is $t = 1.32$, which corresponds to January 2. What is wrong with Ryan's conclusion? What is the correct conclusion?

Lesson Performance Task

For two years, a polling agency called a random sample of people every other month and asked them, "Do you think you have or are coming down with a cold or the flu today?" The percentage of those who responded "yes" to the pollsters is shown in the table.

Date	Percentage with cold or flu
January 15, 2012	9.3
March 15, 2012	6.4
May 15, 2012	4.2
July 15, 2012	3.1
September 15, 2012	5.2
November 15, 2012	7.9
January 15, 2013	10.8
March 15, 2013	7.1
May 15, 2013	4.7
July 15, 2013	3.0
September 15, 2013	5.3
November 15, 2013	7.7

a. Are the data periodic? If so, how many cycles do the data represent? Explain your reasoning.

b. When dealing with periodic phenomena, scientists often average corresponding data values from multiple cycles. For instance, for a given location, meteorologists often average the daily high temperatures and the daily low temperatures for corresponding days over a series of years. Why does it make sense to do so?

c. Complete the table by averaging the corresponding data values from the previous table. Also, replace the calendar dates in the cycle with the number of days since the start of a year (assuming it's not a leap year).

Days since start of year	Percentage with cold or flu

d. Roughly fit a sine model to the data in part c.

e. Use a graphing calculator to obtain a sine regression model for the data in part c. Visually compare this model with your rough-fit model.

f. Use the regression model to determine the period of time during the year when more than 6% of people have a cold or the flu.

Graphing Trigonometric Functions

Essential Question: How can graphing trigonometric functions help to solve real-world problems?

KEY EXAMPLE   *(Lesson 18.1)*

Find the amplitude and period of $f(x) = -\frac{1}{2}\cos 2x$.

$a = -\frac{1}{2}$

$\frac{1}{b} = 2$, so $b = \frac{1}{2}$

Identify a and b by comparing the function with the general equation $f(x) = a\cos\frac{1}{b}(x-h)+k$ or $f(x) = a\sin\frac{1}{b}(x-h)+k$.

$\text{amplitude} = |a| = \frac{1}{2}$ $\text{period} = 2\pi \cdot b = \frac{2\pi}{2} = \pi$

KEY EXAMPLE   *(Lesson 18.2)*

Find the period, x-intercepts, and asymptotes of $f(x) = \cot\frac{\pi}{2}x$.

$\frac{1}{b} = \frac{\pi}{2}$, so $b = \frac{2}{\pi}$

Identify b by comparing the function with the general equation $f(x) = \tan\frac{1}{b}x$ or $f(x) = \cot\frac{1}{b}x$.

period = 2

period $= \pi \cdot b = \pi \cdot \frac{2}{\pi} = 2$

The first x-intercept is at 1.

Identify the first x-intercept.

The x-intercepts are at $1 + 2n$.

Generalize the intercept locations (n = integer).

The first asymptote is at $x = 0$.

Identify the first asymptote.

The asymptotes are at $x = 2n$.

Generalize the asymptote locations.

KEY EXAMPLE   *(Lesson 18.3)*

Find the amplitude, period, horizontal and vertical shifts, maximum, minimum, and midline of $f(x) = 3\cos(x - \pi) - 1$.

$f(x) = 3 \qquad \cos 1(x \qquad -\pi) \qquad -1$

$\uparrow \qquad\qquad \uparrow \qquad\qquad \uparrow \qquad\qquad \uparrow$

$\text{amplitude} = |3| \quad \text{period } 2\pi \cdot 1 \quad \text{horizontal shift} \quad \text{vertical shift}$

$= 3 \qquad\quad = 2\pi \qquad\quad = \pi \qquad\quad = -1$

$\text{maximum} = \text{amplitude} + \text{vertical shift} = 3 + (-1) = 2 \rightarrow (\pi, 2); (3\pi, 2)$

$\text{minimum} = -\text{amplitude} + \text{vertical shift} = -3 + (-1) = -4 \rightarrow (2\pi, -4)$

$\text{midline: } y = \dfrac{\text{maximum} + \text{minimum}}{2} = \dfrac{2 + (-4)}{2} = -1$

The table gives information on tides at Canada's
Bay of Fundy. Assume that it takes 6.25 hours for
the tide to come in and another 6.25 hours for the
tide to retreat. Write a cosine function that models
the height of the tide over time.

Tides at the Bay of Fundy		
	Time (h)	Height (m)
High Tide	$t = 0$	16.3
Low Tide	$t = 6.25$	0

amplitude: $(0.5)16.3 = 8.15 = a$

period: $12.5 = 2\pi \cdot |b| \rightarrow b = \frac{25}{4\pi}$ vertical shift: $(0.5)16.3 = 8.15$

function: $f(x) = 8.15\cos\frac{4\pi}{25}t + 8.15$

EXERCISES

1. Identify the amplitude and period of $f(x) = \frac{\pi}{2}\sin \pi x$ *(Lesson 18.1)*

2. Identify the period, x-intercepts, and asymptotes of $f(x) = \tan \pi x$. *(Lesson 18.2)*

3. Find the amplitude, period, horizontal shift, maximum, minimum, and midline of
$f(x) = 2\sin\left(x - \frac{\pi}{2}\right) + 3$. *(Lesson 18.3)*

MODULE PERFORMANCE TASK

What's Your Sine?

During a new moon, 0% of the moon's surface visible from Earth is illuminated by the Sun.
At the full moon, 100% of the moon is lit. The moon cycles back and forth between these
extremes about every 29.5 days. The table gives the fraction of the moon that was lit on certain
days in January 2014.

Day	1	5	10	13	16	20	25	28	31
Fraction Lit	0.00	0.20	0.70	0.92	1.00	0.86	0.40	0.11	0.00

Use this information to find a sine function that models this phenomenon. Then use your
model to predict the fraction of the moon's visible surface that is lit on any given day in 2014.

Start by listing in the space below the information you will need to solve the problem. Then
complete the task on your own paper. Use graphs, numbers, words, or algebra to explain how
you reached your conclusion.

(Ready) to Go On?

18.1–18.4 Graphing Trigonometric Functions

1. Find the amplitude, period, horizontal shift, and x-intercepts of $f(x) = \sin\left(x - \frac{5\pi}{4}\right)$.

2. The displacement in inches of a mass attached to a spring is modeled by $y_1(t) = 3\sin\left(\frac{2\pi}{5}t + \frac{\pi}{2}\right)$, where t is the time in seconds.

   a. What is the amplitude of the motion?

   b. What is the period of the motion?

   c. What is the initial displacement when $t = 0$?

3. The paddle wheel of a ship is 11 feet in diameter, revolves 15 times per minute when moving at top speed, and is 2 feet below the water's surface at its lowest point. Using this speed and starting from a point at the very top of the wheel, write a model for the height h (in feet) of the end of the paddle relative to the water's surface as a function of time t (in minutes).

ESSENTIAL QUESTION

4. What are the key features of the graphs of a trigonometric function, and how can you use a trigonometric function to model real-world data?

© Houghton Mifflin Harcourt Publishing Company

Assessment Readiness

1. Consider the graph of the function $f(x) = \pi\cos\left(x + \frac{\pi}{2}\right) + 2$. Choose True or False for each statement.

    A. The period is π.   ○ True   ○ False

    B. The amplitude is 1.   ○ True   ○ False

    C. The horizontal shift is $-\frac{\pi}{2}$.   ○ True   ○ False

2. Does the given function have an amplitude of 4? Select Yes or No for A–C.

    A. $f(x) = 4\csc x$ ○ Yes   ○ No

    B. $f(x) = -4\sin \pi x$ ○ Yes   ○ No

    C. $f(x) = \sin 4x + 4$ ○ Yes   ○ No

3. A basketball is dropped from a height of 15 feet. Can the height of the basketball be modeled by a trigonometric function? If so, write the function. If not, explain why not.

4. In photosynthesis, a plant converts carbon dioxide and water to sugar and oxygen. This process is studied by measuring a plant's carbon assimilation C (in micromoles of CO_2 per square meter per second). For a bean plant, $C(t) = 1.2 \sin \frac{\pi}{12}(t - 6) + 7$, where t is time in hours starting at midnight.

    a. What is the period of the function?

    b. What is the maximum and at what time does it occur?

Assessment Readiness

1. Consider that $\sin \theta \approx 0.819$.

Select Yes or No to tell whether the statement is possible.

   A. $\cos \theta \approx 0.819$ ○ Yes   ○ No

   B. $\cos \theta \approx -0.574$ ○ Yes   ○ No

   C. $\cos \theta \approx 0.574$ ○ Yes   ○ No

2. Consider the graphs of the functions $f(x) = 0.25 \cos 4 \left(x - \frac{\pi}{2}\right) + 0.5$ and $g(x) = 0.25 \cos 4 \left(x + \frac{\pi}{2}\right) + 0.5$. Select True or False for each statement.

   A. Both graphs look exactly the same.   ○ True   ○ False

   B. $g(x)$ is translated up $\frac{\pi}{2}$, and $f(x)$ is translated down $\frac{\pi}{2}$.   ○ True   ○ False

   C. $g(x)$ is translated left $\frac{\pi}{2}$, and $f(x)$ is translated right $\frac{\pi}{2}$.   ○ True   ○ False

3. Consider a ball that has a diameter of 10 inches rolling at a rate of 20 revolutions per second. Select True or False for each statement.

   A. It will take 0.1 second to travel 7200 degrees.   ○ True   ○ False

   B. It will take 5 minutes to travel 7200 degrees.   ○ True   ○ False

   C. The ball will travel approximately 436 inches if it rolls through 5000 degrees.   ○ True   ○ False

4. Consider the radian measure $\frac{23\pi}{4}$. Is the statement correct?

Select Yes or No for A–C.

   A. $\cos \frac{23\pi}{4} \approx -0.707$ ○ Yes   ○ No

   B. $\tan \frac{23\pi}{4} = -1$ ○ Yes   ○ No

   C. $\sin \frac{23\pi}{4} \approx 0.707$ ○ Yes   ○ No

5. Hannah is graphing the functions $f(x) = 5\sin(x)$ and $g(x) = 5\csc(x)$ on the same coordinate plane. Explain what she should see if she graphs them correctly.

6. While completing an assignment in class, students were required to recognize the period and amplitude of a trigonometric function without graphing the function. Roland said that the function $f(x) = 4\sin\left(\frac{1}{2}x\right)$ has a period of 4 and an amplitude of $\frac{1}{2}$. Describe and correct his mistake.

7. Use two different methods to find the roots of the quadratic equation $h(x) = x^2 + 3x - 18$. Explain which methods you used, and why. Did you get the same roots?

Performance Tasks

★ 8. In women's fastpitch softball, the circular pitching motion occurs through about $1\frac{1}{2}$ arm revolutions. What radian measure does this represent? For a pitcher whose pitch radius is 2 feet, what circular distance does the ball travel during the pitching motion?

★★ **9.** A DVD's rotational speed varies from 1530 rpm (revolutions per minute) when the inner edge is being read to 630 rpm when the outer edge is being read.

A. What is the total rotation of the DVD in radians after 10 seconds, if the computer is reading data on the outer edge? Show how you got your answer.

B. In 10 seconds, what linear distance is covered by the part of the DVD that passes under the reader head from part A, which is about 6 cm from the center of the DVD?

C. If the computer is reading data on the inner edge (about 2.5 cm from the center of the DVD), what linear distance is covered by the part of the DVD that passes under the reader head in 10 seconds?

★★★**10.** Belinda recorded the dew point in her hometown in °F each day for a year (not a leap year) and entered the data into her graphing calculator, with $x = 0$ as January 1. She then performed a sinusoidal regression on her graphing calculator as shown.

```
SinReg
  y=a*sin(bx+c)+d
  a=25.00093178
  b=.0172134433
  c=-1.583656413
  d=39.99899918
```

A. What is the model function? What are the function's period and amplitude? (Answers can be rounded to 2 decimal places, but don't round when calculating.)

B. Use the model function to find the approximate dew point on February 20. Also, determine on what day(s) the model says the dew point was 55 °F by using your graphing calculator.

C. What is the horizontal shift of the model function? What would the horizontal shift have been if the cosine function had been used instead of the sine function in the model? Support your answer.

Boat Builder A side view of a riverboat's paddle wheel is shown. The paddle wheel has a diameter of 16 feet and rotates at a rate of 1 revolution every 4 seconds. Its lowest point is 2 feet below the water line. The function

$h(t) = 8\sin\left[\frac{\pi}{2}(t-1)\right] + 6$ models the motion of the paddle

point labeled P. The function gives the "height" (which is negative when the paddle is below the water line) at time t (in seconds).

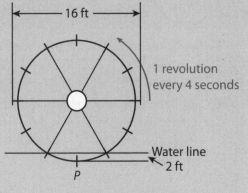

a. Graph the function on the interval $0 \le t \le 6$.

b. What is the significance of the graph's t-intercepts in the context of the situation?

c. What is the significance of the maximum and minimum values of h in the context of the situation?

d. If a point on the edge of the paddle travels a distance of 1 mile, through how many complete revolutions has the paddle wheel turned?

UNIT 8

Probability

MATH IN CAREERS

Epidemiologist Epidemiologists study infectious agents like viruses and bacteria and use the data they collect to prevent outbreaks from spreading. Using math, an epidemiologist can predict how fast an epidemic might spread.

If you're interested in a career as an epidemiologist, you should study these mathematical subjects:
- Algebra
- Statistics
- Linear Algebra

Research other careers that require the use of statistical modeling to understand real-world scenarios. Check out the career activity at the end of the unit to find out how **Epidemiologists** use math.

Reading Start-Up

Vocabulary

Review Words

✔ event (*evento*)

✔ outcome (*resultado*)

✔ probability (*probabilidad*)

✔ sample space (*muestra de espacio*)

✔ trial (*prueba*)

Preview Words

combination (*combinación*)

complement (*complementar*)

conditional probability (*probabilidad condicional*)

dependent events (*eventos dependientes*)

element (*elemento*)

empty set (*conjunto vacío*)

factorial (*factorial*)

independent events (*eventos independientes*)

intersection (*intersección*)

permutation (*permutación*)

set (*conjunto*)

subset (*subconjunto*)

union (*unión*)

Visualize Vocabulary

Match the review words to their descriptions to complete the chart.

Word	Description
	The measure of how likely an event is to occur
	All possible outcomes of an experiment
	Any set of outcomes
	A single repetition or observation of an experiment
	A result of an experiment

Understand Vocabulary

Complete the sentences using the preview words.

1. The _____ contains no elements.

2. If the occurrence of one event does not affect the occurrence of another event, then the events are called _____.

3. A(n) _____ is a group of objects in a particular order.

4. To find the _____ of a positive integer, find the product of the number and all of the positive integers less than the number.

Active Reading

Four-Corner Fold Before beginning the unit, create a four-corner fold for each module. Label each flap with lesson titles from the module. As you study each lesson, write important ideas such as vocabulary, diagrams, and formulas under the appropriate flap. Refer to your layered books as you complete exercises.

Introduction to Probability

Essential Question: How can you use probability to solve real-world problems?

REAL WORLD VIDEO
Check out how principles of probability are used to derive and interpret baseball players' statistics.

MODULE PERFORMANCE TASK PREVIEW
Baseball Probability

In this module, you will use concepts of probability to determine the chances of various outcomes for a baseball player at bat. To successfully complete this task, you'll need to calculate a theoretical probability for a real-world situation. Batter up!

Are (YOU) Ready?

Complete these exercises to review skills you will need for this module.

Probability of Simple Events

Example 1   Find the probability of rolling a 4 when using a normal six-sided die with each side having equal probability.

• Online Homework
• Hints and Help
• Extra Practice

Each of the six faces has equal probability, so the probability of any face being rolled is $\frac{1}{6}$.

There is only one face with a four on it, so the probability of rolling a four is also $\frac{1}{6}$.

Find each probability.

1. The probability of flipping a coin and getting a heads, given that the probability of getting a tails is the same, and there is no chance that the coin lands on its side.

   _____

2. The probability of drawing a Jack of Hearts from a 52-card deck given the deck is properly shuffled.

   _____

3. The probability of any particular day being Sunday.

   _____

Probability of Compound Events

Example 2   Find the probability of drawing a red card or a black card when the probability of either is $\frac{1}{4}$ and you only draw one card.

Only one card is drawn and either card has a $\frac{1}{4}$ probability, so the probability of drawing one or the other is the sum of their probabilities.

Probability of drawing a red card or black card $\frac{1}{4} + \frac{1}{4} = \frac{1}{2}$.

Find each probability.

4. The probability of rolling a twelve-sided die and getting a 4 or a 6 given the probability of getting a 4 is $\frac{1}{12}$ and is equal to the probability of getting a 6.

   _____

5. The probability of pulling a red or a blue marble from a jar given the probability of drawing a red marble is $\frac{1}{4}$ and the probability of pulling a blue marble is $\frac{1}{2}$ and you only pull one marble.

   _____

19.1 Probability and Set Theory

Essential Question: How are sets and their relationships used to calculate probabilities?

Resource Locker

Explore Working with Sets

A **set** is a collection of distinct objects. Each object in a set is called an **element** of the set. A set is often denoted by writing the elements in braces.

The set with no elements is the **empty set**, denoted by ∅ or { }.

The set of all elements under consideration is the **universal set**, denoted by U.

Identifying the number of elements in a set is important for calculating probabilities.

(A) Use set notation to identify each set described in the table and identify the number of elements in each set.

Set	Set Notation	Number of Elements in the Set
Set A is the set of prime numbers less than 10.	$A = \left\{ 2, 3, \boxed{}, 7 \right\}$	$n(A) = 4$
Set B is the set of even natural numbers less than 10.	$B = \left\{ \boxed{}, \boxed{}, \boxed{}, \boxed{} \right\}$	$n(B) = \boxed{}$
Set C is the set of natural numbers less than 10 that are multiples of 4.	$\boxed{} = \left\{ 4, \boxed{} \right\}$	$n(C) = \boxed{}$
The universal set is all natural numbers less than 10.	$U =$	$\boxed{} \left(\boxed{} \right) = 9$

The following table identifies terms used to describe relationships among sets. Use sets A, B, C, and U from the previous table. You will supply the missing Venn diagrams in the Example column, including the referenced elements of the sets, as you complete steps B–I following.

Term	Notation	Venn Diagram	Example
Set C is a **subset** of set B if every element of C is also an element of B.	$C \subset B$		
The **intersection** of sets A and B is the set of all elements that are in both A and B.	$A \cap B$	$A \cap B$ is the double-shaded region.	
The **union** of sets A and B is the set of all elements that are in A or B.	$A \cup B$	$A \cup B$ is the entire shaded region.	
The **complement** of set A is the set of all elements in the universal set U that are *not* in A.	A^C or $\sim A$	A^C is the shaded region.	

(B) Since C is a subset of B, every element of set C, which consists of the numbers _____ and _____, is located not only in oval C, but also within oval B. Set B includes the elements of C as well as the additional elements _____ and _____, which are located in oval B outside of oval C. The universal set includes the elements of sets B and C as well as the additional elements _____, _____, _____, _____, and _____, which are located in region U outside of ovals B and C.

(C) In the first row of the table, draw the corresponding Venn diagram that includes the elements of B, C, and U. _____

(D) To determine the intersection of A and B, first define the elements of set A and set B separately, then identify all the elements found in both sets A *and* B.

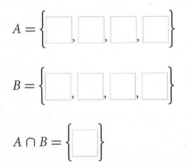

$A = \left\{ \boxed{}, \boxed{}, \boxed{}, \boxed{} \right\}$

$B = \left\{ \boxed{}, \boxed{}, \boxed{}, \boxed{} \right\}$

$A \cap B = \left\{ \boxed{} \right\}$

(E) In the second row of the table, draw the Venn diagram for $A \cap B$ that includes the elements of A, B, and U and the double-shaded intersection region. _____

(F) To determine the union of sets A and B, identify all the elements found in either set A or set B by combining all the elements of the two sets into the union set.

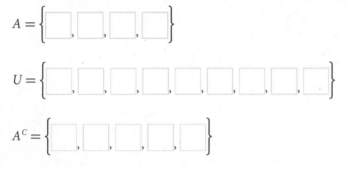

$A \cup B = \left\{ , , , , , \right\}$

(G) In the third row of the table, draw the Venn diagram for $A \cup B$ that includes the elements of A, B, and U and the shaded union region. _____

(H) To determine the complement of set A, first identify the elements of set A and universal set U separately, then identify all the elements in the universal set that are *not* in set A.

$A = \left\{ , , , \right\}$

$U = \left\{ , , , , , , , \right\}$

$A^C = \left\{ , , , \right\}$

(I) In the fourth row of the table, draw the Venn diagram for A^C that includes the elements of A and U and the shaded region that represents the complement of A. _____

Reflect

1. **Draw Conclusions** Do sets always have an intersection that is not the empty set? Provide an example to support your conclusion.

_____

_____

🗝 Explain 1 Calculating Theoretical Probabilities

A *probability experiment* is an activity involving chance. Each repetition of the experiment is called a *trial* and each possible result of the experiment is termed an *outcome*. A set of outcomes is known as an *event*, and the set of all possible outcomes is called the *sample space*.

Probability measures how likely an event is to occur. An event that is impossible has a probability of 0, while an event that is certain has a probability of 1. All other events have a probability between 0 and 1. When all the outcomes of a probability experiment are equally likely, the **theoretical probability** of an event A in the sample space S is given by

$$P(A) = \frac{\text{number of outcomes in the event}}{\text{number of outcomes in the sample space}} = \frac{n(A)}{n(S)}.$$

© Houghton Mifflin Harcourt Publishing Company

Example 1 Calculate $P(A)$, $P(A \cup B)$, $P(A \cap B)$, and $P(A^C)$ for each situation.

(A) You roll a number cube. Event A is rolling a prime number. Event B is rolling an even number.

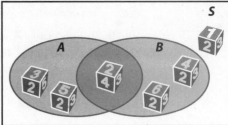

$S = \{1, 2, 3, 4, 5, 6\}$, so $n(S) = 6$. $A = \{2, 3, 5\}$, so $n(A) = 3$.

So, $P(A) = \dfrac{n(A)}{n(S)} = \dfrac{3}{6} = \dfrac{1}{2}$.

$A \cup B = \{2, 3, 4, 5, 6\}$, so $n(A \cup B) = 5$. So, $P(A \cup B) = \dfrac{n(A \cup B)}{n(S)} = \dfrac{5}{6}$.

$A \cap B = \{2\}$, so $n(A \cap B) = 1$. So, $P(A \cap B) = \dfrac{n(A \cap B)}{n(S)} = \dfrac{1}{6}$.

$A^C = \{1, 4, 6\}$, so $n(A^C) = 3$. So, $P(A^C) = \dfrac{n(A^C)}{n(S)} = \dfrac{3}{6} = \dfrac{1}{2}$.

(B) Your grocery basket contains one bag of each of the following items: oranges, green apples, green grapes, green broccoli, white cauliflower, orange carrots, and green spinach. You are getting ready to transfer your items from your cart to the conveyer belt for check-out. Event A is picking a bag containing a vegetable first. Event B is picking a bag containing a green food first. All bags have an equal chance of being picked first.

$S = \{\text{orange, apple, grape, broccoli, cauliflower, carrot, spinach}\}$, so $n(S) = \boxed{}$.

$A = \{\text{broccoli, cauliflower,} \underline{\hspace{1.5cm}}, \underline{\hspace{1.5cm}}\}$, so $n(A) = \boxed{}$. So $P(A) = \dfrac{n\left(\boxed{}\right)}{n\left(\boxed{}\right)} = \dfrac{\boxed{}}{\boxed{}}$.

$A \cup B = \{\text{broccoli,} \underline{\hspace{1.5cm}}, \underline{\hspace{1.5cm}}, \underline{\hspace{1.5cm}}, \underline{\hspace{1.5cm}}, \text{grape}\}$, so $n(A \cup B) = \boxed{}$.

$P(A \cup B) = \dfrac{\boxed{}\left(\boxed{}\right)}{\boxed{}\left(\boxed{}\right)} = \dfrac{\boxed{}}{\boxed{}}$

$A \cap B = \{\underline{\hspace{1.5cm}}, \underline{\hspace{1.5cm}}\}$, so $n(A \cap B) = \boxed{}$

$P(A \cap B) = \dfrac{\boxed{}\left(\boxed{}\right)}{\boxed{}\left(\boxed{}\right)} = \dfrac{\boxed{}}{\boxed{}}$

$P\left(\boxed{}\right) = \dfrac{\boxed{}\left(\boxed{}\right)}{\boxed{}\left(\boxed{}\right)} = \dfrac{\boxed{}}{\boxed{}}$

2. **Discussion** In Example 1B, which is greater, $P(A \cup B)$ or $P(A \cap B)$? Do you think this result is true in general? Explain.

_____

_____

_____

Your Turn

The numbers 1 through 30 are written on slips of paper that are then placed in a hat. Students draw a slip to determine the order in which they will give an oral report. Event A is being one of the first 10 students to give their report. Event B is picking a multiple of 6. If you pick first, calculate each of the indicated probabilities.

3. $P(A)$

4. $P(A \cup B)$

5. $P(A \cap B)$

6. $P(A^c)$

🔑 Explain 2 Using the Complement of an Event

You may have noticed in the previous examples that the probability of an event occurring and the probability of the event not occurring (i.e., the probability of the complement of the event) have a sum of 1. This relationship can be useful when it is more convenient to calculate the probability of the complement of an event than it is to calculate the probability of the event.

Probabilities of an Event and Its Complement	
$P(A) + P(A^c) = 1$	The sum of the probability of an event and the probability of its complement is 1.
$P(A) = 1 - P(A^c)$	The probability of an event is 1 minus the probability of its complement.
$P(A^c) = 1 - P(A)$	The probability of the complement of an event is 1 minus the probability of the event.

© Houghton Mifflin Harcourt Publishing Company

Example 2 Use the complement to calculate the indicated probabilities.

(A) You roll a blue number cube and a white number cube at the same time. What is the probability that you do not roll doubles?

Step 1 Define the events. Let A be that you do not roll doubles and A^c that you do roll doubles.

Step 2 Make a diagram. A two-way table is one helpful way to identify all the possible outcomes in the sample space.

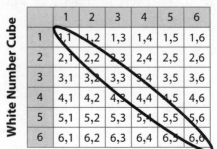

Blue Number Cube

	1	2	3	4	5	6
1	1,1	1,2	1,3	1,4	1,5	1,6
2	2,1	2,2	2,3	2,4	2,5	2,6
3	3,1	3,2	3,3	3,4	3,5	3,6
4	4,1	4,2	4,3	4,4	4,5	4,6
5	5,1	5,2	5,3	5,4	5,5	5,6
6	6,1	6,2	6,3	6,4	6,5	6,6

(White Number Cube labels the rows)

Step 3 Determine $P(A^c)$. Since there are fewer outcomes for rolling doubles, it is more convenient to determine the probability of rolling doubles, which is $P(A^c)$. To determine $n(A^c)$, draw a loop around the outcomes in the table that correspond to A^c and then calculate $P(A^c)$.

$$P(A^c) = \frac{n(A^c)}{n(S)} = \frac{6}{36} = \frac{1}{6}$$

Step 4 Determine $P(A)$. Use the relationship between the probability of an event and its complement to determine $P(A)$.

$$P(A) = 1 - P(A^c) = 1 - \frac{1}{6} = \frac{5}{6}$$

So, the probability of not rolling doubles is $\frac{5}{6}$.

(B) One pile of cards contains the numbers 2 through 6 in red hearts. A second pile of cards contains the numbers 4 through 8 in black spades. Each pile of cards has been randomly shuffled. If one card from each pile is chosen at the same time, what is the probability that the sum will be less than 12?

Step 1 Define the events. Let A be the event that the sum is less than 12 and A^c be the event that _____.

Step 2 Make a diagram. Complete the table to show all the outcomes in the sample space.

Step 3 Determine $P(A^c)$. Circle the outcomes in the table that correspond to A^c, then determine $P(A^c)$.

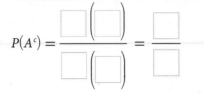

$$P(A^c) = \frac{\boxed{}\left(\boxed{}\right)}{\boxed{}\left(\boxed{}\right)} = \frac{\boxed{}}{\boxed{}}$$

Red Hearts ♥

	2	3	4	5	6
4	4+2	4+3			
5	5+2				
6					
7					
8					

(Black Spades ♠ labels the rows)

Step 4 Determine $P(A)$. Use the relationship between the probability of an event and its complement to determine $P(A^c)$.

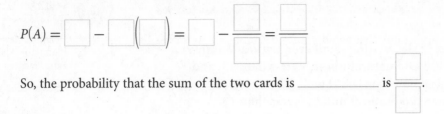

$$P(A) = \boxed{} - \boxed{}\left(\boxed{}\right) = \boxed{} - \dfrac{\boxed{}}{\boxed{}} = \dfrac{\boxed{}}{\boxed{}}$$

So, the probability that the sum of the two cards is _____ is $\dfrac{\boxed{}}{\boxed{}}$.

Reflect

7. Describe a different way to calculate the probability that the sum of the two cards will be less than 12.

_____

_____

Your Turn

One bag of marbles contains two red, one yellow, one green, and one blue marble. Another bag contains one marble of each of the same four colors. One marble from each bag is chosen at the same time. Use the complement to calculate the indicated probabilities.

8. Probability of selecting two different colors

9. Probability of not selecting a yellow marble

Elaborate

10. Can a subset of A contain elements of A^C? Why or why not?

_____

_____

_____

11. For any set A, what does $A \cap \emptyset$ equal? What does $A \cup \emptyset$ equal? Explain.

_____

_____

_____

12. Essential Question Check-In How do the terms *set*, *element*, and *universal set* correlate to the terms used to calculate theoretical probability?

_____

_____

_____

☆ Evaluate: Homework and Practice

Set A is the set of factors of 12, set B is the set of even natural numbers less than 13, set C is the set of odd natural numbers less than 13, and set D is the set of even natural numbers less than 7. The universal set for these questions is the set of natural numbers less than 13.

So, $A = \left\{1, 2, 3, 4, 6, 12\right\}$, $B = \left\{2, 4, 6, 8, 10, 12\right\}$,
$C = \left\{1, 3, 5, 7, 9, 11\right\}$, $D = \left\{2, 4, 6\right\}$, and
$U = \left\{1, 2, 3, 4, 5, 6, 7, 8, 9, 10, 11, 12\right\}$. Answer each question.

1. Is $D \subset A$? Explain why or why not.

2. Is $B \subset A$? Explain why or why not.

3. What is $A \cap B$?

4. What is $A \cap C$?

5. What is $A \cup B$?

6. What is $A \cup C$?

7. What is A^C?

8. What is B^C?

You have a set of 10 cards numbered 1 to 10. You choose a card at random. Event A is choosing a number less than 7. Event B is choosing an odd number. Calculate the probability.

9. $P(A)$

10. $P(B)$

11. $P(A \cup B)$

12. $P(A \cap B)$

13. $P(A^C)$

14. $P(B^C)$

Use the complement of the event to find the probability.

15. You roll a 6-sided number cube. What is the probability that you do not roll a 2?

16. You choose a card at random from a standard deck of cards. What is the probability that you do not choose a red king?

17. You spin the spinner shown. The spinner is divided into 12 equal sectors. What is the probability of not spinning a 2?

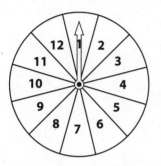

18. A bag contains 2 red, 5 blue, and 3 green balls. A ball is chosen at random. What is the probability of not choosing a red ball?

19. Cards numbered 1–12 are placed in a bag. A card is chosen at random. What is the probability of not choosing a number less than 5?

20. Slips of paper numbered 1–20 are folded and placed into a hat, and then a slip of paper is drawn at random. What is the probability the slip drawn has a number which is not a multiple of 4 or 5?

21. You are going to roll two number cubes, a white number cube and a red number cube, and find the sum of the two numbers that come up.

    a. What is the probability that the sum will be 6?

    b. What is the probability that the sum will not be 6?

22. You have cards with the letters A, B, C, D, E, F, G, H, I, J, K, L, M, N, O, P. Event U is choosing the cards A, B, C or D. Event V is choosing a vowel. Event W is choosing a letter in the word "APPLE". Find $P(U \cap V \cap W)$.

A standard deck of cards has 13 cards (2, 3, 4, 5, 6, 7, 8, 9, 10, jack, queen, king, ace) in each of 4 suits (hearts, clubs, diamonds, spades). The hearts and diamonds cards are red. The clubs and spades cards are black. Answer each question.

23. You choose a card from a standard deck of cards at random. What is the probability that you do not choose an ace? Explain.

24. You choose a card from a standard deck of cards at random. What is the probability that you do not choose a club? Explain.

25. You choose a card from a standard deck of cards at random. Event A is choosing a red card. Event B is choosing an even number. Event C is choosing a black card. Find $P(A \cap B \cap C)$. Explain.

26. You are selecting a card at random from a standard deck of cards. Match each event with the correct probability. Indicate a match by writing the letter of the event on the line in front of the corresponding probability.

A. Picking a card that is both red and a heart. _____ $\dfrac{1}{52}$

B. Picking a card that is both a heart and an ace. _____ $\dfrac{1}{4}$

C. Picking a card that is not both a heart and an ace. _____ $\dfrac{51}{52}$

H.O.T. Focus on Higher Order Thinking

27. Critique Reasoning A bag contains white tiles, black tiles, and gray tiles. Someone is going to choose a tile at random. $P(W)$, the probability of choosing a white tile, is $\frac{1}{4}$. A student claims that the probability of choosing a black tile, $P(B)$, is $\frac{3}{4}$ since $P(B) = 1 - P(W) = 1 - \frac{1}{4} = \frac{3}{4}$. Do you agree? Explain.

28. Communicate Mathematical Ideas A bag contains 5 red marbles and 10 blue marbles. You are going to choose a marble at random. Event A is choosing a red marble. Event B is choosing a blue marble. What is $P(A \cap B)$? Explain.

29. Critical Thinking Jeffery states that for a sample space S where all outcomes are equally likely, $0 \leq P(A) \leq 1$ for any subset A of S. Create an argument that will justify his statement or state a counterexample.

Lesson Performance Task

For the sets you've worked with in this lesson, membership in a set is binary: Either something belongs to the set or it doesn't. For instance, 5 is an element of the set of odd numbers, but 6 isn't

In 1965, Lofti Zadeh developed the idea of "fuzzy" sets to deal with sets for which membership is not binary. He defined a *degree* of membership that can vary from 0 to 1. For instance, a membership function $m_L(w)$ for the set L of large dogs where the degree of membership m is determined by the weight w of a dog might be defined as follows:

- A dog is a full member of the set L if it weighs 80 pounds or more. This can be written as $m_L(w) = 1$ for $w \geq 80$.

- A dog is not a member of the set L if it weighs 60 pounds or less. This can be written as $m_L(w) = 0$ for $w \leq 60$.

- A dog is a partial member of the set L if it weighs between 60 and 80 pounds. This can be written as $0 < m_L(w) < 1$ for $60 < w < 80$.

The "large dogs" portion of the graph shown displays the membership criteria listed above. Note that the graph shows only values of $m(w)$ that are positive.

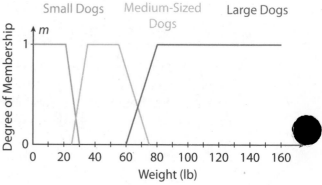

1. Using the graph, give the approximate weights for which a dog is considered a full member, a partial member, and not a member of the set S of small dogs.

2. The union of two "fuzzy" sets A and B is given by the membership rule $m_{A \cup B}(x) = \text{maximum}\big(m_A(x), m_B(x)\big)$. So, for a dog of a given size, the degree of its membership in the set of small or medium-sized dogs $(S \cup M)$ is the greater of its degree of membership in the set of small dogs and its degree of membership in the set of medium-sized dogs.

   The intersection of A and B is given by the membership rule $m_{A \cap B}(x) = \text{minimum}\big(m_A(x), m_B(x)\big)$. So, for a dog of a given size, the degree of its membership in the set of dogs that are both small and medium-sized $(S \cap M)$ is the lesser of its degree of membership in the set of small dogs and its degree of membership in the set of medium-sized dogs.

   Using the graph above and letting S be the set of small dogs, M be the set of medium-sized dogs, and L be the set of large dogs, draw the graph of each set.

   a. $S \cup M$

   b. $M \cap L$

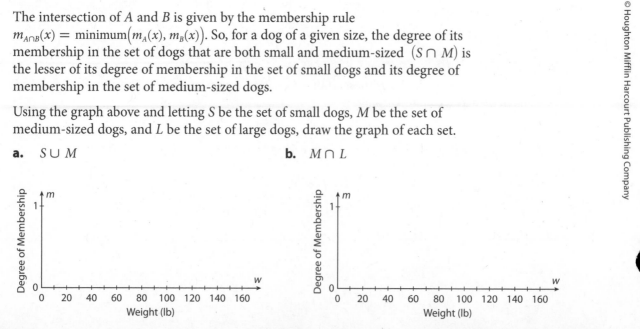

19.2 Permutations and Probability

Resource Locker

Essential Question: When are permutations useful in calculating probability?

Explore   Finding the Number of Permutations

A **permutation** is a selection of objects from a group in which order is important. For example, there are 6 permutations of the letters A, B, and C.

ABC	ACB	BAC	BCA	CAB	CBA

You can find the number of permutations with the **Fundamental Counting Principle**.

Fundamental Counting Principle

If there are n items and a_1 ways to choose the first item, a_2 ways to select the second item after the first item has been chosen, and so on, there are $a_1 \times a_2 \times \ldots \times a_n$ ways to choose n items.

There are 7 members in a club. Each year the club elects a president, a vice president, and a treasurer.

(A) What is the number of permutations of all 7 members of the club?

There are _____ different ways to make the first selection.

Once the first person has been chosen, there are _____ different ways to make the second selection.

Once the first two people have been chosen, there are _____ different ways to make the third selection.

Continuing this pattern, there are _____ permutations of all the members of the club.

(B) The club is holding elections for a president, a vice president, and a treasurer. How many different ways can these positions be filled?

There are _____ different ways the position of president can be filled.

Once the president has been chosen, there are _____ different ways the position of vice president can be filled. Once the president and vice president have been chosen, there are _____ different ways the position of treasurer can be filled.

So, there are _____ different ways that the positions can be filled.

© Houghton Mifflin Harcourt Publishing Company

(C) What is the number of permutations of the members of the club who were not elected as officers?

After the officers have been elected, there are _____ members remaining. So there are _____ different ways to make the first selection.

Once the first person has been chosen, there are _____ different ways to make the second selection.

Continuing this pattern, there are _____ permutations of the unelected members of the club.

(D) Divide the number of permutations of all the members by the number of permutations of the unelected members.

There are _____ permutations of all the members of the club.

There are _____ permutations of the unelected members of the club.

The quotient of these two values is _____.

Reflect

1. How does the answer to Step D compare to the answer to Step B?

_____

2. **Discussion** Explain the effect of dividing the total number of permutations by the number of permutations of items not selected.

_____

_____

⚷ Explain 1 Finding a Probability Using Permutations

The results of the Explore can be generalized to give a formula for permutations. To do so, it is helpful to use *factorials*. For a positive integer n, n **factorial**, written $n!$, is defined as follows.

$$n! = n \times (n - 1) \times (n - 2) \times \ldots \times 3 \times 2 \times 1$$

That is, $n!$ is the product of n and all the positive integers less than n. Note that $0!$ is defined to be 1.

In the Explore, the number of permutations of the 7 objects taken 3 at a time is

$$7 \times 6 \times 5 = \frac{7 \times 6 \times 5 \times 4 \times 3 \times 2 \times 1}{4 \times 3 \times 2 \times 1} = \frac{7!}{4!} = \frac{7!}{(7-3)!}$$

This can be generalized as follows.

Permutations
The number of permutations of n objects taken r at a time is given by $_nP_r = \dfrac{n!}{(n-r)!}$.

© Houghton Mifflin Harcourt Publishing Company

Example 1 Use permutations to find the probabilities.

 A research laboratory requires a four-digit security code to gain access to the facility. A security code can contain any of the digits 0, 1, 2, 3, 4, 5, 6, 7, 8, and 9, but no digit is repeated. What is the probability that a scientist is randomly assigned a code with the digits 1, 2, 3, and 4 in any order?

The sample space S consists is the number of permutations of 4 digits selected from 10 digits.

$$n(S) = {}_{10}P_4 = \frac{10!}{(10-4)!} = \frac{10!}{6!} = 5040$$

Event A consists of permutations of a security code with the digits 1, 2, 3, and 4.

$$n(A) = {}_4P_4 = \frac{4!}{(4-4)!} = \frac{4!}{0!} = 24$$

The probability of getting a security code with the digits 1, 2, 3, and 4 is

$$P(A) = \frac{n(A)}{n(S)} = \frac{24}{5040} = \frac{1}{210}.$$

(B) A certain motorcycle license plate consists of 5 digits that are randomly selected. No digit is repeated. What is the probability of getting a license plate consisting of all even digits?

The sample space S consists of permutations of _____ selected from _____.

$$n(S) = \square P \square = \frac{\square}{\square} = \boxed{}$$

Event A consists of permutations of a license plate with _____.

$$n(A) = \square P \square \frac{\square}{\square} = \boxed{}$$

The probability of getting a license plate with _____ is

$$P(A) = \frac{n(A)}{n(S)} = \frac{\square}{\square} = \frac{\square}{\square}.$$

Your Turn

There are 8 finalists in the 100-meter dash at the Olympic Games. Suppose 3 of the finalists are from the United States, and that all finalists are equally likely to win.

3. What is the probability that the United States will win all 3 medals in this event?

4. What is the probability that the United States will win no medals in this event?

⚙ Explain 2 Finding the Number of Permutations with Repetition

Up to this point, the problems have focused on finding the permutations of distinct objects. If some of the objects are repeated, this will reduce the number of permutations that are distinguishable.

For example, here are the permutations of the letters A, B, and C.

| ABC | ACB | BAC | BCA | CAB | CBA |

Next, here are the permutations of the letters M, O, and M. Bold type is used to show the different positions of the repeated letter.

| **M**O**M** | **MOM** | **MM**O | M**M**O | O**MM** | O**MM** |

Shown without the bold type, here are the permutations of the letters M, O, and M.

| MOM | MOM | MMO | MMO | OMM | OMM |

Notice that since the letter M is repeated, there are only 3 distinguishable permutations of the letters. This can be generalized with a formula for permutations with repetition.

Permutations with Repetition

The number of different permutations of *n* objects where one object repeats *a* times, a second object repeats *b* times, and so on is

$$\frac{n!}{a! \times b! \times \ldots}$$

Example 2 Find the number of permutations.

Ⓐ How many different permutations are there of the letters in the word ARKANSAS?

There are 8 letters in the word, and there are 3 A's and 2 S's, so the number of permutations

of the letters in ARKANSAS is $\frac{8!}{3!2!} = 3360$.

Ⓑ One of the zip codes for Anchorage, Alaska, is 99522. How many permutations are there of the numbers in this zip code?

There are _____ digits in the zip code, and there are _____, and _____ in the zip code, so the number of permutations of the zip code is

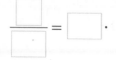

Your Turn

5. How many different permutations can be formed using all the letters in MISSISSIPPI?

6. One of the standard telephone numbers for directory assistance is 555–1212. How many different permutations of this telephone number are possible?

Finding a Probability Using Permutations with Repetition

Permutations with repetition can be used to find probablilities.

 Example 3 **The school jazz band has 4 boys and 4 girls, and they are randomly lined up for a yearbook photo.**

(A) Find the probability of getting an alternating boy-girl arrangement.

The sample space S consists of permutations of 8 objects, with 4 boys and 4 girls.

$$n(S) \frac{8!}{4!4!} = 70$$

Event A consists of permutations that alternate boy-girl or girl-boy. The possible permutations are BGBGBGBG and GBGBGBGB.

$$n(A) = 2$$

The probability of getting an alternating boy-girl arrangement is $P(A) = \frac{n(A)}{n(S)} = \frac{2}{70} = \frac{1}{35}$.

(B) Find the probability of getting all of the boys grouped together.

The sample space S consists of permutations of _____, with _____.

$$n(S) = \frac{\boxed{}}{\boxed{}} = \boxed{}$$

Event A consists of permutations with _____. The possible permutations are BBBBGGGG, GBBBBGGG, _____.

$$n(A) = \boxed{}$$

The probability of getting all the boys grouped together is $P(A) = \frac{n(A)}{n(S)} = \frac{\boxed{}}{\boxed{}} = \frac{\boxed{}}{\boxed{}}$.

Your Turn

7. There are 2 mystery books, 2 romance books, and 2 poetry books to be randomly placed on a shelf. What is the probability that the mystery books are next to each other, the romance books are next to each other, and the poetry books are next to each other?

8. What is the probability that a random arrangement of the letters in the word APPLE will have the two P's next to each other?

Elaborate

9. If $_nP_a = {_nP_b}$, what is the relationship between a and b? Explain your answer.

_____

10. It was observed that there are 6 permutations of the letters A, B, and C. They are ABC, ACB, BAC, BCA, CAB, and CBA. If the conditions are changed so that the order of selection does not matter, what happens to these 6 different groups?

_____

_____

11. Essential Question Check-In How do you determine whether choosing a group of objects involves permutations?

_____

☆ Evaluate: Homework and Practice

• Online Homework
• Hints and Help
• Extra Practice

1. An MP3 player has a playlist with 12 songs. You select the shuffle option, which plays each song in a random order without repetition, for the playlist. In how many different orders can the songs be played?

2. There are 10 runners in a race. Medals are awarded for 1st, 2nd, and 3rd place. In how many different ways can the medals be awarded?

3. There are 9 players on a baseball team. In how many different ways can the coach choose players for first base, second base, third base, and shortstop?

4. A bag contains 9 tiles, each with a different number from 1 to 9. You choose a tile without looking, put it aside, choose a second tile without looking, put it aside, then choose a third tile without looking. What is the probability that you choose tiles with the numbers 1, 2, and 3 in that order?

5. There are 11 students on a committee. To decide which 3 of these students will attend a conference, 3 names are chosen at random by pulling names one at a time from a hat. What is the probability that Sarah, Jamal, and Mai are chosen in any order?

6. A clerk has 4 different letters that need to go in 4 different envelopes. The clerk places one letter in each envelope at random. What is the probability that all 4 letters are placed in the correct envelopes?

7. A swim coach randomly selects 3 swimmers from a team of 8 to swim in a heat. What is the probability that she will choose the three strongest swimmers?

8. How many different sequences of letters can be formed using all the letters in ENVELOPE?

9. Yolanda has 3 each of red, blue, and green marbles. How many possible ways can the 9 marbles be arranged in a row?

10. Jane has 16 cards. Ten of the cards look exactly the same and have the number 1 on them. The other 6 cards look exactly the same and have the number 2 on them. Jane is going to make a row containing all 16 cards. How many different ways can she order the row?

11. Ramon has 10 cards, each with one number on it. The numbers are 1, 2, 3, 4, 4, 6, 6, 6, 6, 6. Ramon is going to make a row containing all 10 cards. How many different ways can he order the row?

12. A grocer has 5 apples and 5 oranges for a window display. The grocer makes a row of the 10 pieces of fruit by choosing one piece of fruit at random, making it the first piece in the row, choosing a second piece of fruit at random, making it the second piece in the row, and so on. What is the probability that the grocer arranges the fruits in alternating order? (Assume that the apples are not distinguishable and that the oranges are not distinguishable.)

13. The letters G, E, O, M, E, T, R, Y are on 8 tiles in a bag, one letter on each tile. If you select tiles randomly from the bag and place them in a row from left to right, what is the probability the tiles will spell out GEOMETRY?

14. There are 11 boys and 10 girls in a classroom. A teacher chooses a student at random and puts that student at the head of a line, chooses a second student at random and makes that student second in the line, and so on, until all 21 students are in the line. What is the probability that the teacher puts them in a line alternating boys and girls? where no two of the same gender stand together?

15. There are 4 female and 4 male kittens are sleeping together in a row. Assuming that the arrangement is a random arrangement, what is the probability that all the female kittens are together, and all the male kittens are together?

16. If a ski club with 12 members votes to choose 3 group leaders, what is the probability that Marsha, Kevin, and Nicola will be chosen in any order for President, Treasurer, and Secretary?

17. There are 7 books numbered 1–7 on the summer reading list. Peter randomly chooses 2 books. What is the probability that Peter chooses books numbered 1 and 2, in either order?

18. On an exam, students are asked to list 5 historical events in the order in which they occurred. A student randomly orders the events. What is the probability that the student chooses the correct order?

19. A fan makes 6 posters to hold up at a basketball game. Each poster has a letter of the word TIGERS. Six friends sit next to each other in a row. The posters are distributed at random. What is the probability that TIGERS is spelled correctly when the friends hold up the posters?

20. The 10 letter tiles S, A, C, D, E, E, M, I, I, and O are in a bag. What is the probability that the letters S-A-M-E will be drawn from the bag at random, in that order?

21. If three cards are drawn at random from a standard deck of 52 cards, what is the probability that they will all be 7s? (There are four 7s in a standard deck of 52 cards.)

22. A shop classroom has ten desks in a row. If there are 6 students in shop class and they choose their desks at random, what is the probability they will sit in the first six desks?

23. Match each event with its probability. All orders are chosen randomly.

 A. There are 15 floats that will be in a town parade. Event A: The mascot float is chosen to be first and the football team float is chosen to be second.

 B. Beth is one of 10 students performing in a school talent show. Event B: Beth is chosen to be the fifth performer and her best friend is chosen to be fourth.

 C. Sylvester is in a music competition with 14 other musicians. Event C: Sylvester is chosen to be last, and his two best friends are chosen to be first and second.

  _____ $\dfrac{1}{1365}$

  _____ $\dfrac{1}{210}$

  _____ $\dfrac{1}{90}$

H.O.T. **Focus on Higher Order Thinking**

24. Explain the Error Describe and correct the error in evaluating the expression.

$$_5P_3 = \frac{5!}{3!} = \frac{5 \times 4 \times \cancel{3!}}{\cancel{3!}} = 20$$

25. Make a Conjecture If you are going to draw four cards from a deck of cards, does drawing four aces from the deck have the same probability as drawing four 3s? Explain.

26. Communicate Mathematical Ideas Nolan has Algebra, Biology, and World History homework. Assume that he chooses the order that he does his homework at random. Explain how to find the probability of his doing his Algebra homework first.

27. Explain the Error A student solved the problem shown. The student's work is also shown. Explain the error and provide the correct answer.

A bag contains 6 tiles with the letters A, B, C, D, E, and F, one letter on each tile. You choose 4 tiles one at a time without looking and line them up from left to right as you choose them. What is the probability that your tiles spell BEAD?

Let S be the sample space and let A be the event that the tiles spell BEAD.

$$n(S) = {}_6P_4 = \frac{6!}{(6-4)!} = \frac{6!}{2!} = 360$$

$$n(A) = {}_4P_4 = \frac{4!}{(4-4)!} = \frac{4!}{0!} = 24$$

$$P(A) = \frac{n(A)}{n(S)} = \frac{24}{360} = \frac{1}{5}$$

Lesson Performance Task

How many different ways can a blue card, a red card, and a green card be arranged? The diagram shows that the answer is six.

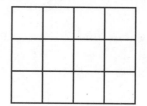

1. Now solve this problem: What is the least number of colors needed to color the pattern shown here, so that no two squares with a common boundary have the same color? Draw a sketch to show your answer.

2. Now try this one. Again, find the least number of colors needed to color the pattern so that no two regions with a common boundary have the same color. Draw a sketch to show your answer.

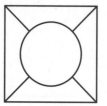

3. In 1974, Kenneth Appel and Wolfgang Haken solved a problem that had confounded mathematicians for more than a century. They proved that no matter how complex a map is, it can be colored in a maximum of four colors, so that no two regions with a common boundary have the same color. Sketch the figure shown here. Can you color it in four colors? Can you color it in three colors?

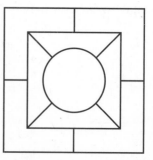

19.3 Combinations and Probability

Essential Question: What is the difference between a permutation and a combination?

Resource
Locker

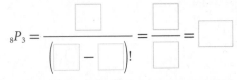 **Finding the Number of Combinations**

A **combination** is a selection of objects from a group in which order is unimportant. For example, if 3 letters are chosen from the group of letters A, B, C, and D, there are 4 different combinations.

ABC	ABD	ACD	BCD

A restaurant has 8 different appetizers on the menu, as shown in the table. They also offer an appetizer sampler, which contains any 3 of the appetizers served on a single plate. How many different appetizer samplers can be created? The order in which the appetizers are selected does not matter.

Appetizers	
Nachos	Chicken Wings
Chicken Quesadilla	Vegetarian Egg Rolls
Potato Skins	Soft Pretzels
Beef Chili	Guacamole Dip

(A) Find the number appetizer samplers that are possible if the order of selection does matter. This is the number of permutations of 8 objects taken 3 at a time.

$$_8P_3 = \frac{\boxed{}}{\left(\boxed{} - \boxed{}\right)!} = \frac{\boxed{}}{\boxed{}} = \boxed{}$$

(B) Find the number of different ways to select a particular group of appetizers. This is the number of permutations of 3 objects.

$$_3P_3 = \frac{\boxed{}}{\left(\boxed{} - \boxed{}\right)!} = \frac{\boxed{}}{\boxed{}} = \boxed{}$$

© Houghton Mifflin Harcourt Publishing Company • ©Tom Henderson/The Food Passionates/Corbis

To find the number of possible appetizer samplers if the order of selection does not matter, divide the answer to part A by the answer to part B.

So the number of appetizer samplers that can be created is $\dfrac{\boxed{}}{\boxed{}} = \boxed{}$.

Reflect

1. Explain why the answer to Part A was divided by the answer to Part B.

_____

_____

_____

2. On Mondays and Tuesdays, the restaurant offers an appetizer sampler that contains any 4 of the appetizers listed. How many different appetizer samplers can be created?

_____

3. In general, are there more ways or fewer ways to select objects when the order does not matter? Why?

_____

_____

Explain 1   Finding a Probability Using Combinations

The results of the Explore can be generalized to give a formula for combinations. In the Explore, the number of combinations of the 8 objects taken 3 at a time is

$$_8P_3 \div {_3P_3} = \frac{8!}{(8-3)!} \div \frac{3!}{(3-3)!} = \frac{8!}{(8-3)!} \cdot \frac{0!}{3!} = \frac{8!}{(8-3)!} \cdot \frac{1}{3!} = \frac{8!}{3!(8-3)!}$$

This can be generalized as follows.

Combinations
The number of combinations of n objects taken r at a time is given by $$_nC_r = \frac{n!}{r!(n-r)!}$$

Example 1   Find each probability.

(A) There are 4 boys and 8 girls on the debate team. The coach randomly chooses 3 of the students to participate in a competition. What is the probability that the coach chooses all girls?

The sample space S consists of combinations of 3 students taken from the group of 12 students.

$n(S) = {_{12}C_3} = \dfrac{12!}{3!9!} = 220$

Event A consists of combinations of 3 girls taken from the set of 8 girls.

$n(A) = {_8C_3} = \dfrac{8!}{3!5!} = 56$

The probability that the coach chooses all girls is $P(A) = \dfrac{n(A)}{n(S)} = \dfrac{56}{220} = \dfrac{14}{55}$.

B There are 52 cards in a standard deck, 13 in each of 4 suits: clubs, diamonds, hearts, and spades. Five cards are randomly drawn from the deck. What is the probability that all five cards are diamonds?

The sample space S consists of combinations of _____ cards drawn from 52 cards.

$$n(S) = {}_\square C_\square = \frac{\boxed{}}{\boxed{}} = \boxed{}$$

Event A consists of combinations of 5 cards drawn from the _____ diamonds.

$$n(A) = {}_\square C_\square = \frac{\boxed{}}{\boxed{}} = \boxed{}$$

The probability of randomly selecting _____ cards that are diamonds is

$$P(A) = \frac{n(A)}{n(S)} = \frac{\boxed{}}{\boxed{}} = \frac{\boxed{}}{\boxed{}}.$$

Your Turn

4. A coin is tossed 4 times. What is the probability of getting exactly 3 heads?

5. A standard deck of cards is divided in half, with the red cards (diamonds and hearts) separated from the black cards (spades and clubs). Four cards are randomly drawn from the red half. What is the probability they are all diamonds?

🔑 Explain 2　Finding a Probability Using Combinations and Addition

Sometimes, counting problems involve the phrases "at least" or "at most." For these problems, combinations must be added.

For example, suppose a coin is flipped 3 times. The coin could show heads 0, 1, 2, or 3 times. To find the number of combinations with at least 2 heads, add the number of combinations with 2 heads and the number of combinations with 3 heads $\left({}_3C_2 + {}_3C_3\right)$.

Example 2　Find each probability.

(A)　A coin is flipped 5 times.
What is the probability that the result is heads at least 4 of the 5 times?

The number of outcomes in the sample space S can be found by using the Fundamental Counting Principle since each flip can result in heads or tails.

$$n(S) = 2 \cdot 2 \cdot 2 \cdot 2 \cdot 2 = 2^5 = 32$$

Let A be the event that the coin shows heads at least 4 times. This is the sum of 2 events, the coin showing heads 4 times and the coin showing heads 5 times. Find the sum of the combinations with 4 heads from 5 coins and with 5 heads from 5 coins.

$$n(A) = {}_5C_4 + {}_5C_5 = \frac{5!}{4!1!} + \frac{5!}{5!0!} = 5 + 1 = 6$$

The probability that the coin shows at least 4 heads is $P(A) = \dfrac{n(A)}{n(S)} = \dfrac{6}{32} = \dfrac{3}{16}$.

(B)　Three number cubes are rolled and the result is recorded. What is the probability that at least 2 of the number cubes show 6?

The number of outcomes in the sample space S can be found by using the Fundamental Counting Principle since each roll can result in 1, 2, 3, 4, 5, or 6.

$$n(S) = \boxed{} = \boxed{}$$

Let A be the event that at least 2 number cubes show 6. This is the sum of 2 events,

_____ or _____. The event of getting

6 on 2 number cubes occurs _____ since there are _____ possibilities for the other

number cube.

$$n(A) = \boxed{} + \boxed{} = \boxed{} + \boxed{} = \boxed{} + \boxed{} = \boxed{}$$

The probability of getting a 6 at least twice in 3 rolls is $P(A) = \dfrac{n(A)}{n(S)} = \dfrac{\boxed{}}{\boxed{}} = \dfrac{\boxed{}}{\boxed{}}$.

6. A math department has a large database of true-false questions, half of which are true and half of which are false, that are used to create future exams. A new test is created by randomly selecting 6 questions from the database. What is the probability the new test contains at most 2 questions where the correct answer is "true"?

7. There are equally many boys and girls in the senior class. If 5 seniors are randomly selected to form the student council, what is the probability the council will contain at least 3 girls?

💬 Elaborate

8. **Discussion** A coin is flipped 5 times, and the result of heads or tails is recorded. To find the probability of getting tails at least once, the events of 1, 2, 3, 4, or 5 tails can be added together. Is there a faster way to calculate this probability?

_____

_____

9. If $_nC_a = {_nC_b}$, what is the relationship between a and b? Explain your answer.

_____

10. **Essential Question Check-In** How do you determine whether choosing a group of objects involves combinations?

_____

1. A cat has a litter of 6 kittens. You plan to adopt 2 of the kittens. In how many ways can you choose 2 of the kittens from the litter?

2. An amusement park has 11 roller coasters. In how many ways can you choose 4 of the roller coasters to ride during your visit to the park?

3. Four students from 30-member math club will be selected to organize a fundraiser. How many groups of 4 students are possible?

4. A school has 5 Spanish teachers and 4 French teachers. The school's principal randomly chooses 2 of the teachers to attend a conference. What is the probability that the principal chooses 2 Spanish teachers?

5. There are 6 fiction books and 8 nonfiction books on a reading list. Your teacher randomly assigns you 4 books to read over the summer. What is the probability that you are assigned all nonfiction books?

6. A bag contains 26 tiles, each with a different letter of the alphabet written on it. You choose 3 tiles from the bag without looking. What is the probability that you choose the tiles with the letters A, B, and C?

7. You are randomly assigned a password consisting of 6 different characters chosen from the digits 0 to 9 and the letters A to Z. As a percent, what is the probability that you are assigned a password consisting of only letters? Round your answer to the nearest tenth of a percent.

8. A bouquet of 6 flowers is made up by randomly choosing between roses and carnations. What is the probability the bouquet will have at most 2 roses?

9. A bag of fruit contains 10 pieces of fruit, chosen randomly from bins of apples and oranges. What is the probability the bag contains at least 6 oranges?

10. You flip a coin 10 times. What is the probability that you get at most 3 heads?

11. You flip a coin 8 times. What is the probability you will get at least 5 heads?

12. You flip a coin 5 times. What is the probability that every result will be tails?

13. There are 12 balloons in a bag: 3 each of blue, green, red, and yellow. Three balloons are chosen at random. Find the probability that all 3 balloons are green.

14. There are 6 female and 3 male kittens at an adoption center. Four kittens are chosen at random. What is the probability that all 4 kittens are female?

There are 21 students in your class. The teacher wants to send 4 students to the library each day. The teacher will choose the students to go to the library at random each day for the first four days from the list of students who have not already gone. Answer each question.

15. What is the probability you will be chosen to go on the first day?

16. If you have not yet been chosen to go on days 1–3, what is the probability you will be chosen to go on the fourth day?

17. Your teacher chooses 2 students at random to represent your homeroom. The homeroom has a total of 30 students, including your best friend. What is the probability that you and your best friend are chosen?

There are 12 peaches and 8 bananas in a fruit basket. You get a snack for yourself and three of your friends by choosing four of the pieces of fruit at random. Answer each question.

18. What is the probability that all 4 are peaches?

19. What is the probability that all 4 are bananas?

20. There are 30 students in your class. Your science teacher will choose 5 students at random to create a group to do a project. Find the probability that you and your 2 best friends in the science class will be chosen to be in the group.

21. On a television game show, 9 members of the studio audience are randomly selected to be eligible contestants.

    a. Six of the 9 eligible contestants are randomly chosen to play a game on the stage. How many combinations of 6 players from the group of eligible contestants are possible?

    b. You and your two friends are part of the group of 9 eligible contestants. What is the probability that all three of you are chosen to play the game on stage? Explain how you found your answer.

© Houghton Mifflin Harcourt Publishing Company

22. Determine whether you should use permutations or combinations to find the number of possibilities in each of the following situations. Select the correct answer for each lettered part.

a. Selecting a group of 5 people
from a group of 8 people ○ permutation ○ combination

b. Finding the number of combinations
for a combination lock ○ permutation ○ combination

c. Awarding first and second place ribbons
in a contest ○ permutation ○ combination

d. Choosing 3 books to read in any order
from a list of 7 books ○ permutation ○ combination

H.O.T. **Focus on Higher Order Thinking**

23. Communicate Mathematical Ideas Using the letters A, B, and C, explain the difference between a permutation and a combination.

24. a. Draw Conclusions Calculate $_{10}C_6$ and $_{10}C_4$.

b. What do you notice about these values? Explain why this makes sense.

c. Use your observations to help you state a generalization about combinations.

25. Justify Reasoning Use the formula for combinations to make a generalization about $_nC_n$. Explain why this makes sense.

26. Explain the Error Describe and correct the error in evaluating $_9C_4$.

$$_9C_4 = \frac{9!}{(9-4)!} = \frac{9!}{5!} = 3024$$

Lesson Performance Task

1. In the 2012 elections, there were six candidates for the United States Senate in Vermont. In how many different orders, from first through sixth, could the candidates have finished?

2. The winner of the Vermont Senatorial election received 208,253 votes, 71.1% of the total votes cast. The candidate coming in second received 24.8% of the vote. How many votes did the second-place candidate receive? Round to the nearest ten.

3. Following the 2012 election there were 53 Democratic, 45 Republican, and 2 Independent senators in Congress.

    a. How many committees of 5 Democratic senators could be formed?

    b. How many committees of 48 Democratic senators could be formed?

    c. Explain how a clever person who knew nothing about combinations could guess the answer to (b) if the person knew the answer to (a).

4. Following the election, a newspaper printed a circle graph showing the make-up of the Senate. How many degrees were allotted to the sector representing Democrats, how many to Republicans, and how many to Independents?

19.4 Mutually Exclusive and Overlapping Events

Essential Question: How are probabilities affected when events are mutually exclusive or overlapping?

⊙ Explore 1 Finding the Probability of Mutually Exclusive Events

Two events are **mutually exclusive events** if they cannot both occur in the same trial of an experiment. For example, if you flip a coin it cannot land heads up and tails up in the same trial. Therefore, the events are mutually exclusive.

A number dodecahedron has 12 sides numbered 1 through 12. What is the probability that you roll the cube and the result is an even number or a 7?

(A) Let A be the event that you roll an even number. Let B be the event that you roll a 7. Let S be the sample space.

Complete the Venn diagram by writing all outcomes in the sample space in the appropriate region.

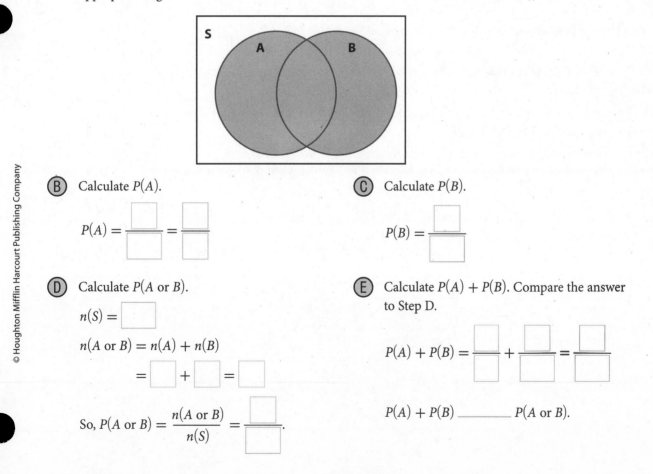

(B) Calculate $P(A)$.

$$P(A) = \frac{\boxed{}}{\boxed{}} = \frac{\boxed{}}{\boxed{}}$$

(C) Calculate $P(B)$.

$$P(B) = \frac{\boxed{}}{\boxed{}}$$

(D) Calculate $P(A \text{ or } B)$.

$n(S) = \boxed{}$

$n(A \text{ or } B) = n(A) + n(B)$

$\qquad = \boxed{} + \boxed{} = \boxed{}$

So, $P(A \text{ or } B) = \dfrac{n(A \text{ or } B)}{n(S)} = \dfrac{\boxed{}}{\boxed{}}$.

(E) Calculate $P(A) + P(B)$. Compare the answer to Step D.

$$P(A) + P(B) = \frac{\boxed{}}{\boxed{}} + \frac{\boxed{}}{\boxed{}} = \frac{\boxed{}}{\boxed{}}$$

$P(A) + P(B)$ _____ $P(A \text{ or } B)$.

1. **Discussion** How would you describe mutually exclusive events to another student in your own words? How could you use a Venn diagram to assist in your explanation?

_____

_____

_____

2. Look back over the steps. What can you conjecture about the probability of the union of events that are mutually exclusive?

_____

_____

_____

_____

⊘ Explore 2   Finding the Probability of Overlapping Events

The process used in the previous Explore can be generalized to give the formula for the probability of mutually exclusive events.

Mutually Exclusive Events

If A and B are mutually exclusive events, then $P(A \text{ or } B) = P(A) + P(B)$.

Two events are **overlapping events** (or inclusive events) if they have one or more outcomes in common.

What is the probability that you roll a number dodecahedron and the result is an even number or a number greater than 7?

(A) Let A be the event that you roll an even number. Let B be the event that you roll a number greater than 7. Let S be the sample space.

Complete the Venn diagram by writing all outcomes in the sample space in the appropriate region.

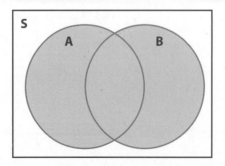

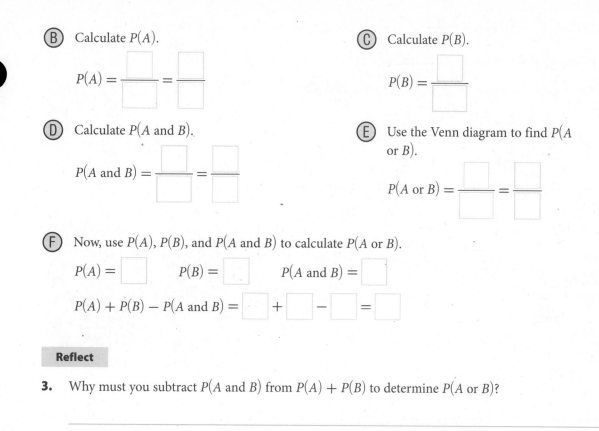

Ⓑ Calculate $P(A)$.

$$P(A) = \frac{\square}{\square} = \frac{\square}{\square}$$

Ⓒ Calculate $P(B)$.

$$P(B) = \frac{\square}{\square}$$

Ⓓ Calculate $P(A \text{ and } B)$.

$$P(A \text{ and } B) = \frac{\square}{\square} = \frac{\square}{\square}$$

Ⓔ Use the Venn diagram to find $P(A \text{ or } B)$.

$$P(A \text{ or } B) = \frac{\square}{\square} = \frac{\square}{\square}$$

Ⓕ Now, use $P(A)$, $P(B)$, and $P(A \text{ and } B)$ to calculate $P(A \text{ or } B)$.

$$P(A) = \boxed{} \qquad P(B) = \boxed{} \qquad P(A \text{ and } B) = \boxed{}$$

$$P(A) + P(B) - P(A \text{ and } B) = \boxed{} + \boxed{} - \boxed{} = \boxed{}$$

Reflect

3. Why must you subtract $P(A \text{ and } B)$ from $P(A) + P(B)$ to determine $P(A \text{ or } B)$?

_____

_____

_____

4. Look back over the steps. What can you conjecture about the probability of the union of two events that are overlapping?

_____

_____

🖉 Explain 1 Finding a Probability From a Two-Way Table of Data

The previous Explore leads to the following rule.

The Addition Rule
$P(A \text{ or } B) = P(A) + P(B) - P(A \text{ and } B)$

Example 1 Use the given two-way tables to determine the probabilities.

Ⓐ $P(\text{senior or girl})$

	Freshman	Sophomore	Junior	Senior	TOTAL
Boy	98	104	100	94	396
Girl	102	106	96	108	412
Total	200	210	196	202	808

To determine $P(\text{senior or girl})$, first calculate $P(\text{senior})$, $P(\text{girl})$, and $P(\text{senior and girl})$.

$P(\text{senior}) = \frac{202}{808} = \frac{1}{4}$; $P(\text{girl}) = \frac{412}{808} = \frac{103}{202}$ $P(\text{senior and girl}) = \frac{108}{808} = \frac{27}{202}$

Use the addition rule to determine $P(\text{senior or girl})$.

$P(\text{senior or girl}) = P(\text{senior}) + P(\text{girl}) - P(\text{senior and girl})$

$$= \frac{1}{4} + \frac{103}{202} - \frac{27}{202}$$

$$= \frac{253}{404}$$

Therefore, the probability that a student is a senior or a girl is $\frac{253}{404}$.

Ⓑ $P\left((\text{domestic or late})^c\right)$

	Late	On Time	Total
Domestic Flights	12	108	120
International Flights	6	54	60
Total	18	162	180

To determine $P\left((\text{domestic or late})^c\right)$, first calculate $P(\text{domestic or late})$.

$P(\text{domestic}) = \dfrac{\boxed{}}{\boxed{}} = \dfrac{\boxed{}}{\boxed{}}$; $P(\text{late}) = \dfrac{\boxed{}}{\boxed{}} = \dfrac{\boxed{}}{\boxed{}}$; $P(\text{domestic and late}) = \dfrac{\boxed{}}{\boxed{}} = \dfrac{\boxed{}}{\boxed{}}$

Use the addition rule to determine $P(\text{domestic or late})$.

$P(\text{domestic or late}) = P(\text{domestic}) + P(\text{late}) - P(\text{domestic and late})$

$$= \dfrac{\boxed{}}{\boxed{}} + \dfrac{\boxed{}}{\boxed{}} - \dfrac{\boxed{}}{\boxed{}} = \dfrac{\boxed{}}{\boxed{}}$$

Therefore, $P\left((\text{domestic or late})^c\right) = 1 - P(\text{domestic or late})$

$$= 1 - \dfrac{\boxed{}}{\boxed{}}$$

$$= \dfrac{\boxed{}}{\boxed{}}$$

5. Use the table to determine P(headache or no medicine).

	Took Medicine	No Medicine	TOTAL
Headache	12	15	27
No Headache	48	25	73
TOTAL	60	40	100

💬 Elaborate

6. Give an example of mutually exclusive events and an example of overlapping events.

_____

_____

_____

_____

7. **Essential Question Check-In** How do you determine the probability of mutually exclusive events and overlapping events?

_____

_____

_____

☆ Evaluate: Homework and Practice

- Online Homework
- Hints and Help
- Extra Practice

1. A bag contains 3 blue marbles, 5 red marbles, and 4 green marbles. You choose one without looking. What is the probability that it is red or green?

© Houghton Mifflin Harcourt Publishing Company

2. A number icosahedron has 20 sides numbered 1 through 20. What is the probability that the result of a roll is a number less than 4 or greater than 11?

3. A bag contains 26 tiles, each with a different letter of the alphabet written on it. You choose a tile without looking. What is the probability that you choose a vowel (a, e, i, o, or u) or a letter in the word GEOMETRY?

4. **Persevere in Problem Solving** You roll two number cubes at the same time. Each cube has sides numbered 1 through 6. What is the probability that the sum of the numbers rolled is even or greater than 9? (*Hint:* Create and fill out a probability chart.)

© Houghton Mifflin Harcourt Publishing Company

The table shows the data for car insurance quotes for 125 drivers made by an insurance company in one week.

	Teen	Adult (20 or over)	Total
0 accidents	15	53	68
1 accident	4	32	36
2+ accidents	9	12	21
Total	28	97	125

You randomly choose one of the drivers. Find the probability of each event.

5. The driver is an adult.

6. The driver is a teen with 0 or 1 accident.

7. The driver is a teen.

8. The driver has 2+ accidents.

9. The driver is a teen and has 2+ accidents.

10. The driver is a teen or a driver with 2+ accidents.

Use the following information for Exercises 11–16. The table shown shows the results of a customer satisfaction survey for a cellular service provider, by location of the customer. In the survey, customers were asked whether they would recommend a plan with the provider to a friend.

	Arlington	Towson	Parkville	Total
Yes	40	35	41	116
No	18	10	6	34
Total	58	45	47	150

One of the customers that was surveyed was chosen at random.
Find the probability of each event.

11. The customer was from Towson and said No. **12.** The customer was from Parkville.

13. The customer said Yes. **14.** The customer was from Parkville and said Yes.

15. The customer was from Parkville or said Yes.

16. Explain why you cannot use the rule $P(A \text{ or } B) = P(A) + P(B)$ in Exercise 15.

Use the following information for Exercises 17–21. Roberto is the owner of a car dealership. He is assessing the success rate of his top three salespeople in order to offer one of them a promotion. Over two months, for each attempted sale, he records whether the salesperson made a successful sale or not. The results are shown in the chart.

	Successful	Unsuccessful	Total
Becky	6	6	12
Raul	4	5	9
Darrell	6	9	15
Total	16	20	36

Roberto randomly chooses one of the attempted sales.

17. Find the probability that the sale was one of Becky's or Raul's successful sales.

18. Find the probability that the sale was one of the unsuccessful sales or one of Raul's successful sales.

19. Find the probability that the sale was one of Darrell's unsuccessful sales or one of Raul's unsuccessful sales.

20. Find the probability that the sale was an unsuccessful sale or one of Becky's attempted sales.

21. Find the probability that the sale was a successful sale or one of Raul's attempted sales.

22. You are going to draw one card at random from a standard deck of cards. A standard deck of cards has 13 cards (2, 3, 4, 5, 6, 7, 8, 9, 10, jack, queen, king, ace) in each of 4 suits (hearts, clubs, diamonds, spades). The hearts and diamonds cards are red. The clubs and spades cards are black. Which of the following have a probability of less than $\frac{1}{4}$? Choose all that apply.

   a. Drawing a card that is a spade and an ace

   b. Drawing a card that is a club or an ace

   c. Drawing a card that is a face card or a club

   d. Drawing a card that is black and a heart

   e. Drawing a red card and a number card from 2–9

H.O.T. **Focus on Higher Order Thinking**

23. Draw Conclusions A survey of 1108 employees at a software company finds that 621 employees take a bus to work and 445 employees take a train to work. Some employees take both a bus and a train, and 321 employees take only a train. To the nearest percent, find the probability that a randomly chosen employee takes a bus or a train to work. Explain.

24. **Communicate Mathematical Ideas** Explain how to use a Venn diagram to find the probability of randomly choosing a multiple of 3 or a multiple of 4 from the set of numbers from 1 to 25. Then find the probability.

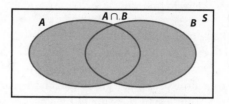

25. **Explain the Error** Sanderson attempted to find the probability of randomly choosing a 10 or a diamond from a standard deck of playing cards. He used the following logic:

Let S be the sample space, A be the event that the card is a 10, and B be the event that the card is a diamond.

There are 52 cards in the deck, so $n(S) = 52$.

There are four 10s in the deck, so $n(A) = 4$.

There are 13 diamonds in the deck, so $n(B) = 13$.

One 10 is a diamond, so $n(A \cap B) = 1$.

$$P(A \cup B) = \frac{n(A \cup B)}{n(S)} = \frac{n(A) \cdot n(B) - n(A \cap B)}{n(S)} = \frac{4 \cdot 13 - 1}{52} = \frac{51}{52}$$

Describe and correct Sanderson's mistake.

Lesson Performance Task

What is the smallest number of randomly chosen people that are needed in order for there to be a better than 50% probability that at least two of them will have the same birthday? The astonishing answer is 23. Follow these steps to find why.

1. Can a person have a birthday on two different days? Use the vocabulary of this lesson to explain your answer.

Looking for the probability that two or more people in a group of 23 have matching birthdays is a challenge. Maybe there is one match but maybe there are five matches or seven or fourteen. A much easier way is to look for the probability that there are *no* matches in a group of 23. In other words, all 23 have different birthdays. Then use that number to find the answer.

2. There are 365 days in a non-leap year.

   a. Write an expression for the number of ways you can assign different birthdays to 23 people. (Hint: Think of the people as standing in a line, and you are going to assign a different number from 1 to 365 to each person.)

   b. Write an expression for the number of ways you can assign any birthday to 23 people. (Hint: Now think about assigning any number from 1 to 365 to each of 23 people.)

   c. How can you use your answers to (a) and (b) to find the probability that no people in a group of 23 have the same birthday? Use a calculator to find the probability to the nearest ten-thousandth.

   d. What is the probability that at least two people in a group of 23 have the same birthday? Explain your reasoning.

Introduction to Probability

Essential Question: How can you use probability to solve real-world problems?

Key Vocabulary

set *(conjunto, juego)*

element *(elemento)*

empty set *(conjunto vacío)*

universal set *(conjunto universal)*

subset *(subconjunto)*

intersection *(intersección)*

union *(unión)*

complement *(complementar)*

theoretical probability *(probabilidad teórica)*

permutation *(permutación)*

Fundamental Counting Principle *(principio fundamental de conteo)*

factorial *(factorial)*

combination *(combinación)*

KEY EXAMPLE   *(Lesson 19.1)*

When rolling two fair number cubes, what is the probability that the sum of the two cubes will not be even or prime?

The sum of two number cubes can be any integer from 2 through 12. Of these, the only possible sum that is not even or prime is 9. There are 36 possible outcomes for rolling two number cubes. Of these, the only ones that sum to 9 are (3, 6), (6, 3), (4, 5), and (5, 4). So, P(sum is not even or prime) $= \frac{4}{36} = \frac{1}{9}$.

KEY EXAMPLE   *(Lesson 19.2)*

Ten marbles are placed in a jar. Of the 10 marbles, 3 are blue, 2 are red, 3 are green, 1 is orange, and 1 is yellow. The 10 marbles are randomly placed in a line. What is the probability that all marbles of the same color are next to each other?

Marbles of the same color are indistinguishable objects. The sample space S consists of permutations of 10 objects, with 3 of one type, 3 of another type, and 2 of a third type.

$$n(S) = \frac{10!}{3!3!2!} = 50{,}400.$$

Event A consists of permutations that have all marbles of the same color next to each other, so it is the number of ways of ordering the 5 colors.

$$n(A) = 5! = 120$$

The probability that all marbles of the same color are next to each other is

$$P(A) = \frac{n(A)}{n(S)} = \frac{120}{50{,}400} = \frac{1}{420}.$$

KEY EXAMPLE   *(Lesson 19.3)*

A class of 15 boys and 15 girls is putting together a random group of 3 students to do classroom chores. What is the probability that at least 2 of the students are boys?

The sample space S consists of combinations of three student groups.

$$n(S) = \frac{30!}{3!27!} = 4060.$$

Event A consists of combinations that have 2 boys or 3 boys in the group. The event of getting 2 boys in the group occurs 15 times, once for each individual girl in the class.

$$n(A) = 15 \cdot {}_{15}C_2 + {}_{15}C_3 = 15 \cdot \frac{15!}{2!13!} + \frac{15!}{3!12!} = 2030$$

The probability that there will be at least 2 boys in the group is $P(A) = \frac{n(A)}{n(S)} = \frac{2030}{4060} = \frac{1}{2}.$

EXERCISES

Use the sets below to find the indicated set for problems 1–4. *(Lesson 19.1)*

$U = \{1, 2, 3, 4, 5, 6, 7, 8, 9\}$

$A = \{1, 3, 5, 7, 9\}$

$B = \{2, 4, 6, 8\}$

$C = \{1, 2, 4, 5, 7, 9\}$

1. $A \cup C$ _____

2. $B \cap C$ _____

3. A^C _____

4. $A \cap B$ _____

5. A computer password can use all digits (0–9) and all letters (*a–z*) that are case sensitive (upper and lower). How many different permutations of 5-figure passwords are there if there is no repeated input? *(Lesson 19.2)*

6. Brandon is rolling a 10-sided number cube 5 times. What is the probability that he will roll at least two 7s? *(Lesson 19.3)*

Determine if the given events are mutually exclusive. If not, explain why. *(Lesson 19.4)*

7. Rolling a 3 or a 4 on a regular number cube

8. Drawing a queen or a red card from a standard deck of 52 cards

9. Flipping a coin and having it land on heads or tails

10. Rolling an even number or a prime number on a number cube

MODULE PERFORMANCE TASK

Baseball Probability

A baseball player will be batting three times during today's game. So far this season, the player has gotten an average of 1 hit in every 3 times at bat. Based on this data, what is the probability that the player will get exactly one hit in today's game? Is that outcome more or less likely than getting no hits?

Start by making notes in the space below about your plan for solving the problem. Then use your own paper to complete the task, using words, numbers, or diagrams to explain how your reached your conclusions.

(Ready) to Go On?

19.1–19.4 Introduction to Probability

• Online Homework
• Hints and Help
• Extra Practice

Find the probabilities.

1. Twenty-six tiles with the letters A through Z are placed face down on a table and mixed. (For the purpose of this exercise assume that the letter Y is a vowel.) Five tiles are drawn in order. Compute the probability that only consonants are selected.

2. The two-way table shows the results of a poll in a certain country that asked voters, sorted by political party, whether they supported or opposed a proposed government initiative. Find the given probabilities.

	Party A	Party B	Other Party	No Party	Total
Support	97	68	8	19	192
Oppose	32	81	16	11	140
Undecided	9	23	10	26	68
Total	138	172	34	56	400

   a. $P(\text{no party or undecided})$

   b. $P\left((\text{party A or support})^c\right)$

ESSENTIAL QUESTION

3. A teacher is assigning 32 presentation topics to 9 students at random. Each student will get 3 topics, and no topic will be repeated. Somil is very interested in 5 topics. What is the probability that Somil will be assigned at least one of his preferred topics? Explain how you arrived at your answer.

© Houghton Mifflin Harcourt Publishing Company

Assessment Readiness

1. Jonah is arranging books on a shelf. The order of the books matters to him. There are 336 ways he can arrange the books. Choose True or False for each statement.

   A. He might be arranging 3 books from a selection of 8 different books. ◯ True ◯ False

   B. He might be arranging 4 books from a selection of 8 different books. ◯ True ◯ False

   C. He might be arranging 5 books from a selection of 8 different books. ◯ True ◯ False

2. Decide whether the probability of tossing the given sum with two dice is $\frac{5}{36}$. Select Yes or No for A–C.

   A. A sum of 6. ◯ Yes ◯ No

   B. A sum of 7. ◯ Yes ◯ No

   C. A sum of 8. ◯ Yes ◯ No

3. Let H be the event that a coin flip lands with heads showing, and let T be the event that a flip lands with tails showing. (Note that $P(H) = P(T) = 0.5$.) What is the probability that you will get heads at least once if you flip the coin ten times? Explain your reasoning.

4. There are 8 girls and 6 boys on the student council. How many committees of 3 girls and 2 boys can be formed? Show your work.

Conditional Probability and Independence of Events

Essential Question: How can you use conditional probability and independence of events to solve real-world problems?

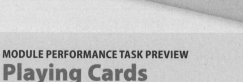

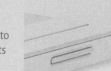

REAL WORLD VIDEO
Check out how principles of conditional probability are used to understand the chances of events in playing cards.

MODULE PERFORMANCE TASK PREVIEW
Playing Cards

In this module, you will use concepts of conditional probability to determine the chance of drawing a hand of cards with a certain property. To successfully complete this task you'll need to master these skills:

- Distinguish between independent and dependent events.
- Apply the conditional probability formula to a real-world situation.
- Use the Multiplication Rule appropriately.

© Houghton Mifflin Harcourt Publishing Company • Image Credits: ©Sergey Nivens/Shutterstock

Are (YOU) Ready?

Complete these exercises to review skills you will need for this module.

Probability of Compound Events

Example 1

Find the probability of rolling a pair of six-sided dice and the sum of their faces being even or equal to 3.

3 is not even, so the two probabilities are mutually exclusive. The probability is equal to the sums of the probabilities of rolling an even sum or rolling a sum of 3.

Probability of rolling an even sum $= \frac{18}{36}$ Count the number of outcomes for the first event.

Probability of rolling a sum of 3 $= \frac{2}{36}$ Count the number of outcomes for the second event.

Probability of rolling an even sum or a sum of 3 $= \frac{18}{36} + \frac{2}{36} = \frac{20}{36} = \frac{5}{9}$

Find each probability.

1. The probability of rolling two dice at the same time and getting a 4 with either die or the sum of the dice is 6. _____

2. The probability of rolling two dice at the same time and getting a 4 with either die and the sum of the dice is 6. _____

3. The probability of pulling red or blue marbles (or both) from a jar of only red and blue marbles when you pull out two marbles given that pulling red and pulling blue are equally likely events. _____

4. The probability of pulling a red marble and a blue marble from a jar of only red and blue marbles when you pull out two marbles given that pulling red and pulling blue are equally likely events. _____

5. The probability of flipping a coin three times and getting exactly two heads or at least one tails given the probability of getting a heads is $\frac{1}{2}$ and the probability of getting a tails is $\frac{1}{2}$. _____

6. The probability of flipping a coin three times and getting exactly two heads and at least one tails given the probability of getting a heads is $\frac{1}{2}$ and the probability of getting a tails is $\frac{1}{2}$. _____

7. The probability of flipping a coin three times and getting at least two heads or at least one tails given the probability of getting a heads is $\frac{1}{2}$ and the probability of getting a tails is $\frac{1}{2}$. _____

20.1 Conditional Probability

Essential Question: How do you calculate a conditional probability?

⊘ Explore 1 **Finding Conditional Probabilities from a Two-Way Frequency Table**

The probability that event A occurs given that event B has already occurred is called the **conditional probability** of A given B and is written $P(A \mid B)$.

One hundred migraine headache sufferers participated in a study of a new medicine. Some were given the new medicine, and others were not. After one week, participants were asked if they had experienced a headache during the week. The two-way frequency table shows the results.

	Took medicine	No medicine	Total
Headache	11	13	24
No headache	54	22	76
Total	65	35	100

Let event A be the event that a participant did not get a headache. Let event B be the event that a participant took the medicine.

(A) To the nearest percent, what is the probability that a participant who took the medicine did not get a headache?

_____ participants took the medicine.

Of these, _____ did not get a headache.

So, $P(A \mid B) = \dfrac{\boxed{}}{\boxed{}} \approx \boxed{}$ %.

(B) To the nearest percent, what is the probability that a participant who did not get a headache took the medicine?

_____ participants did not get a headache.

Of these, _____ took the medicine.

So, $P(B \mid A) = \dfrac{\boxed{}}{\boxed{}} \approx \boxed{}$ %.

(C) Let $n(A)$ be the number of participants who did not get a headache, $n(B)$ be the number of participants who took the medicine, and $n(A \cap B)$ be the number of participants who took the medicine and did not get a headache.

$n(A) = \boxed{}$ $n(B) = \boxed{}$ $n(A \cap B) = \boxed{}$

Express $P(A \mid B)$ and $P(B \mid A)$ in terms of $n(A)$, $n(B)$, and $n(A \cap B)$.

$P(A \mid B) = \dfrac{\boxed{}}{\boxed{}}$ $P(B \mid A) = \dfrac{\boxed{}}{\boxed{}}$

1. For the question "What is the probability that a participant who did not get a headache took the medicine?", what event is assumed to have already occurred?

2. In general, does it appear that $P(A|B) = P(B|A)$? Why or why not?

Explore 2 Finding Conditional Probabilities from a Two-Way Relative Frequency Table

You can develop a formula for $P(A|B)$ that uses relative frequencies (which are probabilities) rather than frequencies (which are counts).

	Took medicine	No medicine	Total
Headache	11	13	24
No headache	54	22	76
Total	65	35	100

(A) To obtain relative frequencies, divide every number in the table by 100, the total number of participants in the study.

	Took medicine	No medicine	Total
Headache			
No headache			
Total			1

(B) Recall that event A is the event that a participant did not get a headache and that event B is the event that a participant took the medicine. Use the relative frequency table from Step A to find $P(A)$, $P(B)$, and $P(A \cap B)$.

(C) In the first Explore, you found the conditional probabilities $P(A|B) \approx 83\%$ and $P(B|A) \approx 71\%$ by using the frequencies in the two-way frequency table. Use the relative frequencies from the table in Step A to find the equivalent conditional probabilities.

$$P(A|B) = \frac{P(A \cap B)}{P(B)} = \frac{\boxed{}}{\boxed{}} \approx \boxed{}\%$$
$$P(B|A) = \frac{P(A \cap B)}{P(A)} = \frac{\boxed{}}{\boxed{}} \approx \boxed{}\%$$

Ⓓ Generalize the results by using $n(S)$ as the number of elements in the sample space (in this case, the number of participants in the study). For instance, you can write $P(A) = \frac{n(A)}{n(S)}$. Write each of the following probabilities in a similar way.

$$P(B) = \frac{\boxed{}}{\boxed{}} \qquad P(A \cap B) = \frac{\boxed{}}{\boxed{}} \qquad P(A|B) = \frac{\overset{n(A \cap B)}{\boxed{}}}{\underset{n(B)}{\boxed{}}} = \frac{P(A \cap B)}{\boxed{}}$$

Reflect

3. Why are the two forms of $P(A \cap B)$, $\frac{n(A \cap B)}{n(B)}$ and $\frac{P(A \cap B)}{P(B)}$, equivalent?

_____

4. What is a formula for $P(B|A)$ that involves probabilities rather than counts? How do you obtain this formula from the fact that $P(B|A) = \frac{n(A \cap B)}{n(A)}$?

_____

🖉 Explain 1 Using the Conditional Probability Formula

In the previous Explore, you discovered the following formula for conditional probability.

Conditional Probability

The conditional probability of A given B (that is, the probability that event A occurs given that event B occurs) is as follows:

$$P(A|B) = \frac{P(A \cap B)}{P(B)}$$

Example 1 Find the specified probability.

Ⓐ For a standard deck of playing cards, find the probability that a red card randomly drawn from the deck is a jack.

Step 1 Find $P(R)$, the probability that a red card is drawn from the deck.

There are 26 red cards in the deck of 52 cards, so $P(R) = \frac{26}{52}$.

Step 2 Find $P(J \cap R)$, the probability that a red jack is drawn from the deck.

There are 2 red jacks in the deck, so $P(J \cap R) = \frac{2}{52}$.

Step 3 Substitute the probabilities from Steps 1 and 2 into the formula for conditional probability.

$$P(J|R) = \frac{P(J \cap R)}{P(R)} = \frac{\frac{2}{52}}{\frac{26}{52}}$$

Step 4 Simplify the result.

$$P(J|R) = \frac{\frac{2}{52} \cdot 52}{\frac{26}{52} \cdot 52} = \frac{2}{26} = \frac{1}{13}$$

(B) For a standard deck of playing cards, find the probability that a jack randomly drawn from the deck is a red card.

Step 1 Find $P(J)$, the probability that a jack is drawn from the deck.

There are _____ jacks in the deck of 52 cards, so $P(J) = \frac{\square}{52}$.

Step 2 Find $P(J \cap R)$, the probability that a red jack is drawn from the deck.

There are _____ red jacks in the deck, so $P(J \cap R) = \frac{\square}{52}$.

Step 3 Substitute the probabilities from Steps 1 and 2 into the formula for conditional probability.

$$P(R|J) = \frac{P(J \cap R)}{P(J)} = \frac{\frac{\square}{52}}{\frac{\square}{52}}$$

Step 4 Simplify the result.

$$P(R|J) = \frac{\frac{\square}{52} \cdot 52}{\frac{\square}{52} \cdot 52} = \frac{\square}{\square} = \frac{1}{\square}$$

Your Turn

5. For a standard deck of playing cards, find the probability that a face card randomly drawn from the deck is a king. (The ace is *not* a face card.)

6. For a standard deck of playing cards, find the probability that a queen randomly drawn from the deck is a diamond.

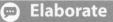 **Elaborate**

7. When calculating a conditional probability from a two-way table, explain why it doesn't matter whether the table gives frequencies or relative frequencies.

_____

_____

8. **Discussion** Is it possible to have $P(B|A) = P(A|B)$ for some events A and B? What conditions would need to exist?

_____

_____

9. **Essential Question Check-In** In a two-way frequency table, suppose event A represents a row of the table and event B represents a column of the table. Describe how to find the conditional probability $P(A|B)$ using the frequencies in the table.

_____

_____

⭐ Evaluate: Homework and Practice

• Online Homework
• Hints and Help
• Extra Practice

In order to study the relationship between the amount of sleep a student gets and his or her school performance, a researcher collected data from 120 students. The two-way frequency table shows the number of students who passed and failed an exam and the number of students who got more or less than 6 hours of sleep the night before. Use the table to answer the questions in Exercises 1–3.

	Passed exam	Failed exam	Total
Less than 6 hours of sleep	12	10	22
More than 6 hours of sleep	90	8	98
Total	102	18	120

1. To the nearest percent, what is the probability that a student who failed the exam got less than 6 hours of sleep?

2. To the nearest percent, what is the probability that a student who got less than 6 hours of sleep failed the exam?

© Houghton Mifflin Harcourt Publishing Company

3. To the nearest percent, what is the probability that a student got less than 6 hours of sleep and failed the exam?

4. You have a standard deck of playing cards from which you randomly select a card. Event D is getting a diamond, and event F is getting a face card (a jack, queen, or king).

Show that $P(D|F) = \dfrac{n(D \cap F)}{n(F)}$ and $P(D|F) = \dfrac{P(D \cap F)}{P(F)}$ are equal.

The table shows data in the previous table as relative frequencies (rounded to the nearest thousandth when necessary). Use the table for Exercises 5–7.

	Passed exam	Failed exam	Total
Less than 6 hours of sleep	0.100	0.083	0.183
More than 6 hours of sleep	0.750	0.067	0.817
Total	0.850	0.150	1.000

5. To the nearest percent, what is the probability that a student who passed the exam got more than 6 hours of sleep?

6. To the nearest percent, what is the probability that a student who got more than 6 hours of sleep passed the exam?

7. Which is greater, the probability that a student who got less than 6 hours of sleep passed the exam or the probability that a student who got more than 6 hours of sleep failed the exam? Explain.

You randomly draw a card from a standard deck of playing cards. Let A be the event that the card is an ace, let B be the event that the card is black, and let C be the event that the card is a club. Find the specified probability as a fraction.

8. $P(A|B)$

9. $P(B|A)$

10. $P(A|C)$

11. $P(C|A)$

12. $P(B|C)$

13. $P(C|B)$

14. A botanist studied the effect of a new fertilizer by choosing 100 orchids and giving 70% of these plants the fertilizer. Of the plants that got the fertilizer, 40% produced flowers within a month. Of the plants that did not get the fertilizer, 10% produced flowers within a month.

    a. Use the given information to complete the two-way frequency table.

	Received fertilizer	Did not receive fertilizer	Total
Did not flower in one month			
Flowered in one month			
Total			

    b. To the nearest percent, what is the probability that an orchid that produced flowers got fertilizer?

    c. To the nearest percent, what is the probability that an orchid that got fertilizer produced flowers?

15. At a school fair, a box contains 24 yellow balls and 76 red balls. One-fourth of the balls of each color are labeled "Win a prize." Match each description of a probability with its value as a percent.

    A. The probability that a randomly selected ball labeled "Win a prize" is yellow   _____ 76%

    B. The probability that a randomly selected ball labeled "Win a prize" is red   _____ 25%

    C. The probability that a randomly selected ball is labeled "Win a prize" and is red   _____ 24%

    D. The probability that a randomly selected yellow ball is labeled "Win a prize"   _____ 19%

16. A teacher gave her students two tests. If 45% of the students passed both tests and 60% passed the first test, what is the probability that a student who passed the first test also passed the second?

17. You randomly select two marbles, one at a time, from a pouch containing blue and green marbles. The probability of selecting a blue marble on the first draw and a green marble on the second draw is 25%, and the probability of selecting a blue marble on the first draw is 56%. To the nearest percent, what is the probability of selecting a green marble on the second draw, given that the first marble was blue?

You roll two number cubes, one red and one blue. The table shows the probabilities for events based on whether or not a 1 is rolled on each number cube. Use the table to find the specified conditional probability, expressed as a fraction. Then show that the conditional probability is correct by listing the possible outcomes as ordered pairs of the form (number on red cube, number on blue cube) and identifying the successful outcomes.

	Rolling a 1 on the red cube	Not rolling a 1 on the red cube	Total
Rolling a 1 on the blue cube	$\frac{1}{36}$	$\frac{5}{36}$	$\frac{1}{6}$
Not rolling a 1 on the blue cube	$\frac{5}{36}$	$\frac{25}{36}$	$\frac{5}{6}$
Total	$\frac{1}{6}$	$\frac{5}{6}$	1

18. P(not rolling a 1 on the blue cube | rolling a 1 on the red cube)

19. P(not rolling a 1 on the blue cube | not rolling a 1 on the red cube)

20. The table shows the results of a quality-control study at a computer factory.

	Shipped	Not shipped	Total
Defective	3	7	10
Not defective	89	1	90
Total	92	8	100

a. To the nearest tenth of a percent, what is the probability that a shipped computer is not defective?

b. To the nearest tenth of a percent, what is the probability that a defective computer is shipped?

21. Analyze Relationships In the Venn diagram, the circles representing events A and B divide the sample space S into four regions: the overlap of the circles, the part of A not in the overlap, the part of B not in the overlap, and the part of S not in A or B. Suppose that the area of each region is proportional to the number of outcomes that fall within the region. Which conditional probability is greater: $P(A|B)$ or $P(B|A)$? Explain.

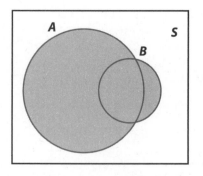

22. **Explain the Error** A student was asked to use the table shown to find the probability, to nearest percent, that a participant in a study of a new medicine for migraine headaches did not take the medicine, given that the participant reported no headaches.

	Took medicine	No medicine	Total
Headache	11	13	24
No headache	54	22	76
Total	65	35	100

The student made the following calculation.

$P(\text{no medicine} \mid \text{no headache}) = \dfrac{22}{35} \approx 0.63 = 63\%$

Explain the student's error, and find the correct probability.

23. **Communicate Mathematical Ideas** Explain how a conditional probability based on a two-way frequency table effectively reduces it to a one-way table. In your explanation, refer to the two-way table shown, which lists frequencies for events A, B, and their complements. Highlight the part of the table that supports your explanation.

	A	Not A	Total
B	$n(A \cap B)$	$n(\text{not } A \cap B)$	$n(B)$
Not B	$n(A \cap \text{not } B)$	$n(\text{not } A \cap \text{not } B)$	$n(\text{not } B)$
Total	$n(A)$	$n(\text{not } A)$	$n(S)$

Lesson Performance Task

The two-way frequency table gives the results of a survey that asked students this question: Which of these would you most like to meet: a famous singer, a movie star, or a sports star?

	Famous singer	Movie star	Sports star	Total
Boys	20	15	55	
Girls	40	50	20	
Total				

a. Complete the table by finding the row totals, column totals, and grand total.

b. To the nearest percent, what is the probability that a student who chose "movie star" is a girl?

c. To the nearest percent, what is the probability that a student who chose "famous singer" is a boy?

d. To the nearest percent, what is the probability that a boy chose "sports star"?

e. To the nearest percent, what is the probability that a girl chose "famous singer"?

f. To the nearest percent, what is the probability that a student who chose either "famous singer" or "movie star" is a boy?

g. To the nearest percent, what is the probability that a girl did not choose "sports star"?

20.2 Independent Events

Essential Question: What does it mean for two events to be independent?

Resource
Locker

⊘ Explore   Understanding the Independence of Events

Suppose you flip a coin and roll a number cube. You would expect the probability of getting heads on the coin to be $\frac{1}{2}$ regardless of what number you get from rolling the number cube. Likewise, you would expect the probability of rolling a 3 on the number cube to be $\frac{1}{6}$ regardless of whether of the coin flip results in heads or tails.

When the occurrence of one event has no effect on the occurrence of another event, the two events are called **independent events**.

Ⓐ A jar contains 15 red marbles and 17 yellow marbles. You randomly draw a marble from the jar. Let R be the event that you get a red marble, and let Y be the event that you get a yellow marble.

Since the jar has a total of _____ marbles, $P(R) = \dfrac{\square}{\square}$ and $P(Y) = \dfrac{\square}{\square}$.

Ⓑ Suppose the first marble you draw is a red marble, and you put that marble back in the jar before randomly drawing a second marble. Find $P(Y|R)$, the probability that you get a yellow marble on the second draw after getting a red marble on the first draw. Explain your reasoning.

Since the jar still has a total of _____ marbles and _____ of them are yellow, $P(Y|R) = \dfrac{\square}{\square}$.

Ⓒ Suppose you *don't* put the red marble back in the jar before randomly drawing a second marble. Find $P(Y|R)$, the probability that you get a yellow marble on the second draw after getting a red marble on the first draw. Explain your reasoning.

Since the jar now has a total of _____ marbles and _____ of them are yellow, $P(Y|R) = \dfrac{\square}{\square}$.

Reflect

1. In one case you replaced the first marble before drawing the second, and in the other case you didn't. For which case was $P(Y|R)$ equal to $P(Y)$? Why?

   _____

   _____

2. In which of the two cases would you say the events of getting a red marble on the first draw and getting a yellow marble on the second draw are independent? What is true about $P(Y|R)$ and $P(Y)$ in this case?

   _____

   _____

Determining if Events are Independent

To determine the independence of two events A and B, you can check to see whether $P(A|B) = P(A)$ since the occurrence of event A is unaffected by the occurrence of event B if and only if the events are independent.

Example 1   The two-way frequency table gives data about 180 randomly selected flights that arrive at an airport. Use the table to answer the question.

	Late Arrival	On Time	Total
Domestic Flights	12	108	120
International Flights	6	54	60
Total	18	162	180

(A) Is the event that a flight is on time independent of the event that a flight is domestic?

Let O be the event that a flight is on time. Let D be the event that a flight is domestic. Find $P(O)$ and $P(O|D)$. To find $P(O)$, note that the total number of flights is 180, and of those flights, there are 162 on-time flights. So, $P(O) = \frac{162}{180} = 90\%$.

To find $P(O|D)$, note that there are 120 domestic flights, and of those flights, there are 108 on-time flights.

So, $P(O|D), = \frac{108}{120} = 90\%$.

Since $P(O|D) = P(O)$, the event that a flight is on time is independent of the event that a flight is domestic.

(B) Is the event that a flight is international independent of the event that a flight arrives late?

Let I be the event that a flight is international. Let L be the event that a flight arrives late. Find $P(I)$ and $P(I|L)$. To find $P(I)$, note that the total number of flights is 180, and of those

flights, there are ____ international flights. So, $P(I) = \dfrac{\boxed{}}{180} = \boxed{}$ %.

To find $P(I|L)$, note that there are ____ flights that arrive late, and of those flights, there are ____

international flights. So, $P(I|L) = \dfrac{\boxed{}}{\boxed{}} = \boxed{}$ %.

Since $P(I|L) \boxed{} P(I)$, the event that a flight is international [is/is not] independent of the

event that a flight arrives late.

Your Turn

The two-way frequency table gives data about 200 randomly selected apartments in a city. Use the table to answer the question.

	1 Bedroom	2+ Bedrooms	Total
Single Occupant	64	12	76
Multiple Occupants	26	98	124
Total	90	110	200

3. Is the event that an apartment has a single occupant independent of the event that an apartment has 1 bedroom?

_____

_____

_____

4. Is the event that an apartment has 2 or more bedrooms independent of the event that an apartment has multiple occupants?

_____

_____

_____

⚙ Explain 2   Finding the Probability of Independent Events

From the definition of conditional probability you know that $P(A|B) = \dfrac{P(A \cap B)}{P(B)}$ for any events A and B. If those

events happen to be independent, you can replace $P(A|B)$ with $P(A)$ and get $P(A) = \dfrac{P(A \cap B)}{P(B)}$. Solving the last

equation for $P(A \cap B)$ gives the following result.

> **Probability of Independent Events**
>
> Events A and B are independent if and only if $P(A \cap B) = P(A) \cdot P(B)$.

Example 2   Find the specified probability.

(A) Recall the jar with 15 red marbles and 17 yellow marbles from the Explore. Suppose you randomly draw one marble from the jar. After you put that marble back in the jar, you randomly draw a second marble. What is the probability that you draw a yellow marble first and a red marble second?

Let Y be the event of drawing a yellow marble first. Let R be the event of drawing a red marble second. Then $P(Y) = \frac{17}{32}$ and, because the first marble drawn is replaced before the second marble is drawn, $P(R|Y) = P(R) = \frac{15}{32}$. Since the events are independent, you can multiply their probabilities: $P(Y \cap R) = P(Y) \cdot P(R) = \frac{17}{32} \cdot \frac{15}{32} = \frac{255}{1024} \approx 25\%$.

© Houghton Mifflin Harcourt Publishing Company

B You spin the spinner shown two times. What is the probability that the spinner stops on an even number on the first spin, followed by an odd number on the second spin?

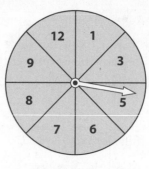

Let E be the event of getting an even number on the first spin. Let O be the event of getting an odd

number on the second spin. Then $P(E) = \dfrac{\square}{8}$ and, because the first spin has no effect on the second

spin, $P(O|E) = P(O) = \dfrac{\square}{8}$. Since the events are independent, you can multiply their probabilities:

$P(E \cap O) = P(E) \cdot P(O) = \dfrac{\square}{8} \cdot \dfrac{\square}{8} = \dfrac{\square}{64} \approx \boxed{} \%.$

Reflect

5. In Part B, what is the probability that the spinner stops on an odd number on the first spin, followed by an even number on the second spin? What do you observe? What does this tell you?

_____

_____

_____

_____

Your Turn

6. You spin a spinner with 4 red sections, 3 blue sections, 2 green sections, and 1 yellow section. If all the sections are of equal size, what is the probability that the spinner stops on green first and blue second?

7. A number cube has the numbers 3, 5, 6, 8, 10, and 12 on its faces. You roll the number cube twice. What is the probability that you roll an odd number on both rolls?

⚙ Explain 3 Showing That Events Are Independent

So far, you have used the formula $P(A \cap B) = P(A) \cdot P(B)$ when you knew that events A and B are independent. You can also use the formula to determine whether two events are independent.

Example 3 **Determine if the events are independent.**

(A) The two-way frequency table shows data for 120 randomly selected patients who have the same doctor. Determine whether a patient who takes vitamins and a patient who exercises regularly are independent events.

	Takes Vitamins	No Vitamins	Total
Regular Exercise	48	28	76
No regular Exercise	12	32	44
Total	60	60	120

Let V be the event that a patient takes vitamins. Let E be the event that a patient exercises regularly.

Step 1 Find $P(V)$, $P(E)$, and $P(V \cap E)$. The total number of patients is 120.

There are 60 patients who take vitamins, so $P(V) = \frac{60}{120} = \frac{1}{2}$.

There are 76 patients who exercise regularly, so $P(B) = \frac{76}{120} = \frac{19}{30}$.

There are 48 patients who take vitamins and exercise regularly, so $P(V \cap E) = \frac{48}{120} = 40\%$.

Step 2 Compare $P(V \cap E)$ and $P(V) \cdot P(E)$.

$P(V) \cdot P(E) = \frac{1}{2} \cdot \frac{19}{30} = \frac{19}{60} \approx 32\%$

Because $P(V \cap E) \neq P(V) \cdot P(E)$, the events are not independent.

(B) The two-way frequency table shows data for 60 randomly selected children at an elementary school. Determine whether a child who knows how to ride a bike and a child who knows how to swim are independent events.

	Knows how to Ride a Bike	Doesn't Know how to Ride a Bike	Total
Knows how to Swim	30	10	40
Doesn't Know how to Swim	15	5	20
Total	45	15	60

Let B be the event a child knows how to ride a bike. Let S be the event that a child knows how to swim.

Step 1 Find $P(B)$, $P(S)$, and $P(B \cap S)$. The total number of children is 60.

There are _____ children who know how to ride a bike, so $P(B) = \frac{\boxed{}}{60} = \frac{\boxed{}}{4}$.

There are _____ children who know how to swim, so $P(S) = \frac{\boxed{}}{60} = \frac{\boxed{}}{3}$.

There are _____ children who know how to ride a bike and swim, so $P(B \cap S) = \frac{\boxed{}}{60} = \frac{\boxed{}}{2}$.

© Houghton Mifflin Harcourt Publishing Company

Module 20   **1019**   Lesson 2

Step 2 Compare $P(B \cap S)$ and $P(B) \cdot P(S)$.

$$P(B) \cdot P(S) = \frac{\boxed{}}{4} \cdot \frac{\boxed{}}{3} = \frac{\boxed{}}{2}$$

Because $P(B \cap S)\ \boxed{}\ P(B) \cdot P(S)$, the events [are/are not] independent.

Your Turn

8. A farmer wants to know if an insecticide is effective in preventing small insects called aphids from damaging tomato plants. The farmer experiments with 80 plants and records the results in the two-way frequency table. Determine whether a plant that was sprayed with insecticide and a plant that has aphids are independent events.

	Has Aphids	No Aphids	Total
Sprayed with Insecticide	12	40	52
Not Sprayed with Insecticide	14	14	28
Total	26	54	80

9. A student wants to know if right-handed people are more or less likely to play a musical instrument than left-handed people. The student collects data from 250 people, as shown in the two-way frequency table. Determine whether being right-handed and playing a musical instrument are independent events.

	Right-Handed	Left-Handed	Total
Plays a Musical Instrument	44	6	50
Does not Play a Musical Instrument	176	24	200
Total	220	30	250

10. What are the ways that you can show that two events *A* and *B* are independent?

_____

_____

11. How can you find the probability that two independent events *A* and *B* both occur?

_____

12. **Essential Question Check-In** Give an example of two independent events and explain why they are independent.

_____

_____

_____

_____

☆ Evaluate: Homework and Practice

Personal Math Trainer

• Online Homework
• Hints and Help
• Extra Practice

1. A bag contains 12 red and 8 blue chips. Two chips are separately drawn at random from the bag.

   a. Suppose that a single chip is drawn at random from the bag. Find the probability that the chip is red and the probability that the chip is blue.

   b. Suppose that two chips are separately drawn at random from the bag and that the first chip is returned to the bag before the second chip is drawn. Find the probability that the second chip drawn is blue given the first chip drawn was red.

   c. Suppose that two chips are separately drawn at random from the bag and that the first chip is not returned to the bag before the second chip is drawn. Find the probability that the second chip drawn is blue given the first chip drawn was red.

   d. In which situation—the first chip is returned to the bag or not returned to the bag—are the events that the first chip is red and the second chip is blue independent? Explain.

2. Identify whether the events are independent or not independent.

a. Flip a coin twice and get tails both times. ○ Independent ○ Not Independent

b. Roll a number cube and get 1 on the first roll and 6 on the second. ○ Independent ○ Not Independent

c. Draw an ace from a shuffled deck, put the card back and reshuffle the deck, and then draw an 8. ○ Independent ○ Not Independent

d. Rotate a bingo cage and draw the ball labeled B-4, set it aside, and then rotate the cage again and draw the ball labled N-38. ○ Independent ○ Not Independent

Answer the question using the fact that $P(A|B) = P(A)$ only when events A and B are independent.

3. The two-way frequency table shows data for 80 randomly selected people who live in a metropolitan area. Is the event that a person prefers public transportation independent of the event that a person lives in the city?

	Prefers to Drive	Prefers Public Transportation	Total
Lives in the City	12	24	36
Lives in the Suburbs	33	11	44
Total	45	35	80

4. The two-way frequency table shows data for 120 randomly selected people who take vacations. Is the event that a person prefers vacationing out of state independent of the event that a person is a woman?

	Prefers Vacationing Out of State	Prefers Vacationing in State	Total
Men	48	32	80
Women	24	16	40
Total	72	48	120

A jar contains marbles of various colors as listed in the table. Suppose you randomly draw one marble from the jar. After you put that marble back in the jar, you randomly draw a second marble. Use this information to answer the question, giving a probability as a percent and rounding to the nearest tenth of percent when necessary.

Color of Marble	Number of Marbles
Red	20
Yellow	18
Green	12
Blue	10

5. What is the probability that you draw a blue marble first and a red marble second?

6. What is the probability that you draw a yellow marble first and a green marble second?

7. What is the probability that you draw a yellow marble both times?

8. What color marble for the first draw and what color marble for the second draw have the greatest probability of occurring together? What is that probability?

© Houghton Mifflin Harcourt Publishing Company

You spin the spinner shown two times. Each section of the spinner is the same size. Use this information to answer the question, giving a probability as a percent and rounding to the nearest tenth of a percent when necessary.

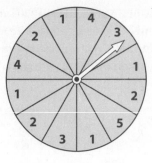

9. What is the probability that the spinner stops on 1 first and 2 second?

10. What is the probability that the spinner stops on 4 first and 3 second?

11. What is the probability that the spinner stops on an odd number first and an even number second?

12. What first number and what second number have the least probability of occurring together? What is that probability?

13. Find the probability of getting heads on every toss of a coin when the coin is tossed 3 times.

14. You are randomly choosing cards, one at a time and with replacement, from a standard deck of cards. Find the probability that you choose an ace, then a red card, and then a face card. (Remember that face cards are jacks, queens, and kings.)

Determine whether the given events are independent using the fact that $P(A \cap B) = P(A) \cdot P(B)$ only when events A and B are independent.

15. The manager of a produce stand wants to find out whether there is a connection between people who buy fresh vegetables and people who buy fresh fruit. The manager collects data on 200 randomly chosen shoppers, as shown in the two-way frequency table. Determine whether buying fresh vegetables and buying fresh fruit are independent events.

	Bought Vegetables	No Vegetables	Total
Bought Fruit	56	20	76
No Fruit	49	75	124
Total	105	95	200

16. The owner of a bookstore collects data about the reading preferences of 60 randomly chosen customers, as shown in the two-way frequency table. Determine whether being a female and preferring fiction are independent events.

	Prefers Fiction	Prefers Nonfiction	Total
Female	15	10	25
Male	21	14	35
Total	36	24	60

17. The psychology department at a college collects data about whether there is a relationship between a student's intended career and the student's like or dislike for solving puzzles. The two-way frequency table shows the collected data for 80 randomly chosen students. Determine whether planning for a career in a field involving math or science and a like for solving puzzles are independent events.

	Plans a Career in a Math/Science Field	Plans a Career in a Non-Math/Science Field	Total
Likes Solving Puzzles	35	15	50
Dislikes Solving Puzzles	9	21	30
Total	44	36	80

18. A local television station surveys some of its viewers to determine the primary reason they watch the station. The two-way frequency table gives the survey data. Determine whether a viewer is a man and a viewer primarily watches the station for entertainment are independent events.

	Primarily Watches for Information (News, Weather, Sports)	Primarily Watches for Entertainment (Comedies, Dramas)	Total
Men	28	12	40
Women	35	15	50
Total	63	27	90

19. Using what you know about independent events, complete the two-way frequency table in such a way that any event from a column will be independent of any event from a row. Give an example using the table to demonstrate the independence of two events.

	Women	Men	Total
Prefers Writing with a Pen			100
Prefers Writing with a Pencil			50
Total	60	90	150

20. Make a Prediction A box contains 100 balloons. The balloons come in two colors: 80 are yellow and 20 are green. The balloons are also either marked or unmarked: 50 are marked "Happy Birthday!" and 50 are not. A balloon is randomly chosen from the box. How many yellow "Happy Birthday!" balloons must be in the box if the event that a balloon is yellow and the event that a balloon is marked "Happy Birthday!" are independent? Explain.

© Houghton Mifflin Harcourt Publishing Company

21. Construct Arguments Given that events A and B are independent, prove that the complement of event A, A^c, is also independent of event B.

22. Multi-Step The two-way frequency table shows two events, A and B, and their complements, A^c and B^c. Let $P(A) = a$ and $P(B) = b$. Using a, b, and the grand total T, form the products listed in the table to find the number of elements in $A \cap B$, $A \cap B^c$, $A^c \cap B$, and $A^c \cap B^c$.

	A	A^c	Total
B	abT	$(1-a)bT$	
B^c	$a(1-b)T$	$(1-a)(1-b)T$	
Total			T

a. Find the table's missing row and column totals in simplest form.

b. Show that events A and B are independent using the fact that $P(A|B) = P(A)$ only when events A and B are independent.

c. Show that events A and B^c are independent.

d. Show that events A^c and B are independent.

e. Show that events A^c and B^c are independent.

Lesson Performance Task

Before the mid-1800s, little was known about the way that plants pass along characteristics such as color and height to their offspring. From painstaking observations of garden peas, the Austrian monk Gregor Mendel discovered the basic laws of heredity. The table shows the results of three of Mendel's experiments. In each experiment, he looked at a particular characteristic of garden peas by planting seeds exclusively of one type.

Characteristic	Type Planted	Results in Second Generation
Flower color	100% violet	705 violet, 224 white
Seed texture	100% round	5474 round, 1850 wrinkled
Seed color	100% yellow	6022 yellow, 2011 green

1. Suppose you plant garden peas with violet flowers and round, yellow seeds. Estimate the probability of obtaining second-generation plants with violet flowers, the probability of obtaining second-generation plants with round seeds, and the probability of obtaining second-generation plants with yellow seeds. Explain how you made your estimates.

Mendel saw that certain traits, such as violet flowers and round seeds, seemed stronger than others, such white flowers and wrinkled seeds. He called the stronger traits "dominant" and the weaker traits "recessive." Both traits can be carried in the genes of a plant, because a gene consists of two *alleles*, one received from the mother and one from the father. (For plants, the "father" is the plant from which the pollen comes, and the "mother" is the plant whose pistil receives the pollen.) When at least one of the alleles has the dominant trait, the plant exhibits the dominant trait. Only when both alleles have the recessive trait does the plant exhibit the recessive trait.

You can use a 2 × 2 Punnett square, like the one shown, to see the results of crossing the genes of two parent plants. In this Punnett square, V represents the dominant flower color violet and v represents the recessive flower color white. If each parent's genes contain both V and v alleles, the offspring may receive, independently and with equal probability, either a V allele or a v allele from each parent.

	V	v
V	VV	Vv
v	vV	vv

2. After planting a first generation of plants exhibiting only dominant traits, Mendel observed that the second generation consisted of plants with a ratio of about 3:1 dominant-to-recessive traits. Does the Punnett square support or refute Mendel's observation? Explain.

3. Draw a 4 × 4 Punnett square for finding the results of crossing two violet-flower-and-round-seed parent plants. Let V and R represent the dominant traits violet flowers and round seeds, respectively. Let v and r represent the recessive traits white flowers and wrinkled seeds, respectively. Each column heading and row heading of your Punnett square should contain a two-letter combination of V or v and R or r. Each cell of your Punnett square will then contain four letters. Use the Punnett square to find the probability that a second-generation plant will have white flowers and round seeds. Explain your reasoning.

© Houghton Mifflin Harcourt Publishing Company

20.3 Dependent Events

Essential Question: How do you find the probability of dependent events?

Resource Locker

Explore   Finding a Way to Calculate the Probability of Dependent Events

You know two tests for the independence of events *A* and *B*:

1. If $P(A|B) = P(A)$, then *A* and *B* are independent.

2. If $P(A \cap B) = P(A) \cdot P(B)$, then *A* and *B* are independent.

Two events that fail either of these tests are **dependent events** because the occurrence of one event affects the occurrence of the other event.

Ⓐ The two-way frequency table shows the results of a survey of 100 people who regularly walk for exercise. Let *O* be the event that a person prefers walking outdoors. Let *M* be the event that a person is male. Find $P(O)$, $P(M)$, and $P(O \cap M)$ as fractions. Then determine whether events *O* and *M* are independent or dependent.

	Prefers walking outdoors	Prefers walking on a treadmill	Total
Male	40	10	50
Female	20	30	50
Total	60	40	100

_____

_____

Ⓑ Calculate the conditional probabilities $P(O|M)$ and $P(M|O)$.

$$P(O|M) = \frac{n(O \cap M)}{n(M)} = \frac{\boxed{}}{\boxed{}} = \frac{\boxed{}}{5}$$

$$P(M|O) = \frac{n(O \cap M)}{n(O)} = \frac{\boxed{}}{\boxed{}} = \frac{\boxed{}}{3}$$

Complete the multiplication table using the fractions for $P(O)$ and $P(M)$ from Step A and the fractions for $P(O|M)$ and $P(M|O)$ from Step B.

x	$P(O)$	$P(M)$
$P(O\|M)$		
$P(M\|O)$		

(D) Do any of the four products in Step C equal $P(O \cap M)$, calculated in Step A? If so, which of the four products?

_____

Reflect

1. In a previous lesson you learned the conditional probability formula $P(B|A) = \frac{P(A \cap B)}{P(A)}$. How does this formula explain the results you obtained in Step D?

_____

_____

_____

2. Let F be the event that a person is female. Let T be the event that a person prefers walking on a treadmill. Write two formulas you can use to calculate $P(F \cap T)$. Use either one to find the value of $P(F \cap T)$, and then confirm the result by finding $P(F \cap T)$ directly from the two-way frequency table.

_____

_____

_____

🔑 Explain 1   Finding the Probability of Two Dependent Events

You can use the Multiplication Rule to find the probability of dependent events.

Multiplication Rule

$P(A \cap B) = P(A) \cdot P(B|A)$ where $P(B|A)$ is the conditional probability of event B, given that event A has occurred.

Example 1   There are 5 tiles with the letters A, B, C, D, and E in a bag. You choose a tile without looking, put it aside, and then choose another tile without looking. Use the Multiplication Rule to find the specified probability, writing it as a fraction.

(A) Find the probability that you choose a vowel followed by a consonant.

Let V be the event that the first tile is a vowel. Let C be the event that the second tile is a consonant. Of the 5 tiles, there are 2 vowels, so $P(V) = \frac{2}{5}$.

Of the 4 remaining tiles, there are 3 consonants, so $P(C|V) = \frac{3}{4}$.

By the Multiplication Rule, $P(V \cap C) = P(V) \cdot P(V|C) = \frac{2}{5} \cdot \frac{3}{4} = \frac{6}{20} = \frac{3}{10}$.

(B) Find the probability that you choose a vowel followed by another vowel.

Let $V1$ be the event that the first tile is a vowel. Let $V2$ be the event that the second tile is also a vowel. Of the 5 tiles, there are ____ vowels, so $P(V1) = \frac{\square}{5}$.

Of the 4 remaining tiles, there is ____ vowel, so $P(V2|V1) = \frac{\square}{4}$.

By the Multiplication Rule, $P(V1 \cap V2) = P(V1) \cdot P(V2|V1) = \frac{\square}{5} \cdot \frac{\square}{4} = \frac{\square}{20} = \frac{\square}{10}$.

Your Turn

A bag holds 4 white marbles and 2 blue marbles. You choose a marble without looking, put it aside, and choose another marble without looking. Use the Multiplication Rule to find the specified probability, writing it as a fraction.

3. Find the probability that you choose a white marble followed by a blue marble.

4. Find the probability that you choose a white marble followed by another white marble.

You can extend the Multiplication Rule to three or more events. For instance, for three events A, B, and C, the rule becomes $P(A \cap B \cap C) = P(A) \cdot P(B|A) \cdot P(C|A \cap B)$.

Example 2 **You have a key ring with 7 different keys. You're attempting to unlock a door in the dark, so you try keys one at a time and keep track of which ones you try.**

Ⓐ Find the probability that the third key you try is the right one.

Let $W1$ be the event that the first key you try is wrong. Let $W2$ be the event that the second key you try is also wrong. Let R be the event that the third key you try is right.

On the first try, there are 6 wrong keys among the 7 keys, so $P(W1) = \frac{6}{7}$.

On the second try, there are 5 wrong keys among the 6 remaining keys, so $P(W2|W1) = \frac{5}{6}$.

On the third try, there is 1 right key among the 5 remaining keys, so $P(R|W2 \cap W1) = \frac{1}{5}$.

By the Multiplication Rule, $P(W1 \cap W2 \cap R) = P(W1) \cdot P(W2|W1) \cdot P(R|W1 \cap W2) = \frac{6}{7} \cdot \frac{5}{6} \cdot \frac{1}{5} = \frac{1}{7}$.

Ⓑ Find the probability that one of the first three keys you try is right.

There are two ways to approach this problem:

1. You can break the problem into three cases: (1) the first key you try is right; (2) the first key is wrong, but the second key is right; and (3) the first two keys are wrong, but the third key is right.

2. You can use the complement: The complement of the event that one of the first three keys is right is the event that *none* of the first three keys is right.

Use the second approach.

Let $W1$, $W2$, and $W3$ be the events that the first, second, and third keys, respectively, are wrong.

From Part A, you already know that $P(W1) = \dfrac{\square}{7}$ and $P(W2|W1) = \dfrac{\square}{6}$.

On the third try, there are 4 wrong keys among the 5 remaining keys, so $P(W3|W2 \cap W1) = \dfrac{\square}{5}$.

By the Multiplication Rule,

$P(W1 \cap W2 \cap W3) = P(W1) \cdot P(W2|W1) \cdot P(W3|W1 \cap W2) = \dfrac{\square}{7} \cdot \dfrac{\square}{6} \cdot \dfrac{\square}{5} = \dfrac{\square}{\square}$.

The event $W1 \cap W2 \cap W3$ is the complement of the one you want. So, the probability that one of

the first three keys you try is right is $1 - P(W1 \cap W2 \cap W3) = 1 - \dfrac{\square}{\square} = \dfrac{\square}{\square}$.

5. In Part B, show that the first approach to solving the problem gives the same result.

_____

_____

_____

_____

_____

_____

_____

_____

_____

6. In Part A, suppose you don't keep track of the keys as you try them. How does the probability change? Explain.

_____

_____

_____

_____

Your Turn

Three people are standing in line at a car rental agency at an airport. Each person is willing to take whatever rental car is offered. The agency has 4 white cars and 2 silver ones available and offers them to customers on a random basis.

7. Find the probability that all three customers get white cars.

8. Find the probability that two of the customers get the silver cars and one gets a white car.

Elaborate

9. When are two events dependent?

_____

_____

10. Suppose you are given a bag with 3 blue marbles and 2 red marbles, and you are asked to find the probability of drawing 2 blue marbles by drawing one marble at a time and not replacing the first marble drawn. Why does not replacing the first marble make these events dependent? What would make these events independent? Explain.

_____

_____

_____

_____

_____

_____

11. Essential Question Check-In According to the Multiplication Rule, when finding $P(A \cap B)$ for dependent events A and B, you multiply $P(A)$ by what?

_____

© Houghton Mifflin Harcourt Publishing Company

1. Town officials are considering a property tax increase to finance the building of a new school. The two-way frequency table shows the results of a survey of 110 town residents.

	Supports a property tax increase	Does not support a property tax increase	Total
Lives in a household with children	50	20	70
Lives in a household without children	10	30	40
Total	60	50	110

a. Let C be the event that a person lives in a household with children. Let S be the event that a person supports a property tax increase. Are the events C and S independent or dependent? Explain.

b. Find $P(C|S)$ and $P(S|C)$. Which of these two conditional probabilities can you multiply with $P(C)$ to get $P(C \cap S)$? Which of the two can you multiply with $P(S)$ to get $P(C \cap S)$?

2. A mall surveyed 120 shoppers to find out whether they typically wait for a sale to get a better price or make purchases on the spur of the moment regardless of price. The two-way frequency table shows the results of the survey.

	Waits for a Sale	Buys on Impulse	Total
Woman	40	10	50
Man	50	20	70
Total	90	30	120

a. Let W be the event that a shopper is a woman. Let S be the event that a shopper typically waits for a sale. Are the events W and S independent or dependent? Explain.

b. Find $P(W|S)$ and $P(S|W)$. Which of these two conditional probabilities can you multiply with $P(W)$ to get $P(W \cap S)$? Which of the two can you multiply with $P(S)$ to get $P(W \cap S)$?

There are 4 green, 10 red, and 6 yellow marbles in a bag. Each time you randomly choose a marble, you put it aside before choosing another marble at random. Use the Multiplication Rule to find the specified probability, writing it as a fraction.

3. Find the probability that you choose a red marble followed by a yellow marble.

4. Find the probabilty that you choose one yellow marble followed by another yellow marble.

5. Find the probability that you choose a red marble, followed by a yellow marble, followed by a green marble.

6. Find the probability that you choose three red marbles.

The table shows the sums that are possible when you roll two number cubes and add the numbers. Use this information to answer the questions.

+	1	2	3	4	5	6
1	2	3	4	5	6	7
2	3	4	5	6	7	8
3	4	5	6	7	8	9
4	5	6	7	8	9	10
5	6	7	8	9	10	11
6	7	8	9	10	11	12

7. Let A be the event that you roll a 2 on the number cube represented by the row labeled 2. Let B be the event that the sum of the numbers on the cubes is 7.

   a. Are these events independent or dependent? Explain.

   b. What is $P(A \cap B)$?

8. Let A be the event that you roll a 3 on the number cube represented by the row labeled 3. Let B be the event that the sum of the numbers on the cubes is 5.

   a. Are these events independent or dependent? Explain.

   b. What is $P(A \cap B)$?

9. A cooler contains 6 bottles of apple juice and 8 bottles of grape juice. You choose a bottle without looking, put it aside, and then choose another bottle without looking. Match each situation with its probability. More than one situation can have the same probability.

   a. Choose apple juice and then grape juice. _____ $\frac{4}{13}$

   b. Choose apple juice and then apple juice. _____ $\frac{24}{91}$

   c. Choose grape juice and then apple juice. _____ $\frac{15}{91}$

   d. Choose grape juice and then grape juice.

10. Jorge plays all tracks on a playlist with no repeats. The playlist he's listening to has 12 songs, 4 of which are his favorites.

  a. What is the probability that the first song played is one of his favorites, but the next two songs are not?

  b. What is the probability that the first three songs played are all his favorites?

  c. Jorge can also play the tracks on his playlist in a random order with repeats possible. If he does this, how does your answer to part b change? Explain why.

11. You are playing a game of bingo with friends. In this game, balls are labeled with one of the letters of the word BINGO and a number. Some of these letter-number combinations are written on a bingo card in a 5 × 5 array, and as balls are randomly drawn and announced, players mark their cards if the ball's letter-number combination appears on the cards. The first player to complete a row, column, or diagonal on a card says "Bingo!" and wins the game. In the game you're playing, there are 20 balls left. To complete a row on your card, you need N-32 called. To complete a column, you need G-51 called. To complete a diagonal, you need B-6 called.

  a. What is the probability that the next two balls drawn do not have a letter-number combination you need, but the third ball does?

  b. What is the probability that none of the letter-number combinations you need is called from the next three balls?

12. You are talking with 3 friends, and the conversation turns to birthdays.

    a. What is the probability that no two people in your group were born in the same month?

    b. Is the probability that at least two people in your group were born in the same month greater or less than $\frac{1}{2}$? Explain.

    c. How many people in a group would it take for the probability that at least two people were born in the same month to be greater than $\frac{1}{2}$? Explain.

13. Construct Arguments Show how to extend the Multiplication Rule to three events A, B, and C.

14. Make a Prediction A bag contains the same number of red marbles and blue marbles. You choose a marble without looking, put it aside, and then choose another marble. Is there a greater-than-50% chance or a less-than-50% chance that you choose two marbles with different colors? Explain.

Lesson Performance Task

To prepare for an accuracy landing competition, a team of skydivers has laid out targets in a large open field. During practice sessions, team members attempt to land inside a target.

Two rectangular targets are shown on each field. Assuming a skydiver lands at random in the field, find the probabilities that the skydiver lands inside the specified target(s).

1. Calculate the probabilities using the targets shown here.

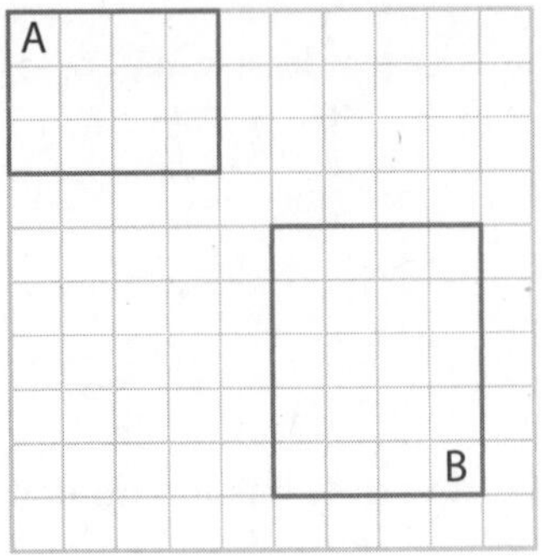

   a. $P(A)$

   b. $P(B)$

   c. $P(A \cap B)$

   d. $P(A \cup B)$

   e. $P(A|B)$

   f. $P(B|A)$

2. Calculate the probabilities using the targets shown here.

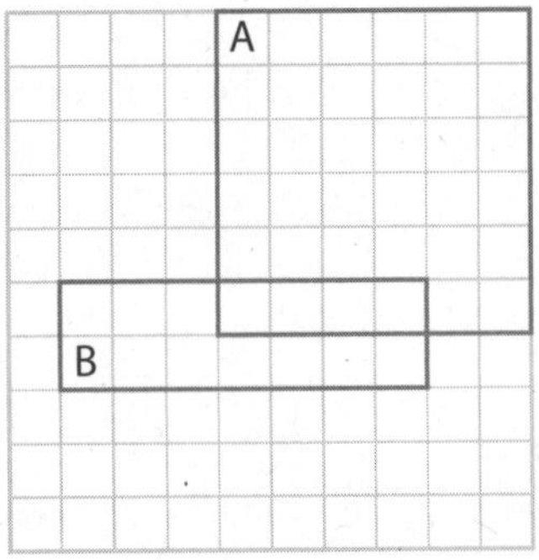

   a. $P(A)$

   b. $P(B)$

   c. $P(A \cap B)$

   d. $P(A \cup B)$

   e. $P(A|B)$

   f. $P(B|A)$

3. Calculate the probabilities using the targets shown here.

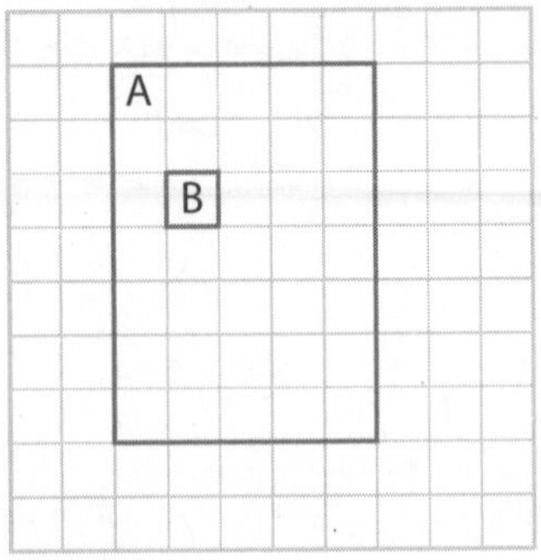

   a. $P(A)$

   b. $P(B)$

   c. $P(A \cap B)$

   d. $P(A \cup B)$

   e. $P(A|B)$

   f. $P(B|A)$

Essential Question: How can you use conditional probability and independence of events to solve real-world problems?

KEY EXAMPLE   *(Lesson 20.1)*

Find the probability that a black card drawn from the deck is a queen. (The deck is a standard one of 52 cards.)

The deck has 52 cards and 26 of them are black, so the probability of

drawing a black card is $P(B) = \frac{26}{52}$. There are 2 black queens in the deck, so the probability of drawing

one of them from the deck is $P(Q \cap B) = \frac{2}{52} = \frac{1}{26}$. Using the formula for conditional probability,

$P(Q \mid B) = \frac{P(Q \cap B)}{P(B)} = \frac{\frac{2}{52}}{\frac{26}{52}} = \frac{1}{13}$.

KEY EXAMPLE   *(Lesson 20.2)*

Jim rolled a set of two number cubes. If these are standard 6-sided number cubes, what is the probability of obtaining 12? (That means the values of the top faces add up to 12.)

The only way to get 12 is for both of the top sides of the number cubes to be 6. The events of obtaining 6s are independent. Each of these events has the probability of $\frac{1}{6}$ (1 out of 6 options), so the probability of getting 12 is $\frac{1}{6} \cdot \frac{1}{6} = \frac{1}{36}$ by the multiplication rule.

KEY EXAMPLE   *(Lesson 20.3)*

What is the probability of selecting 2 blue marbles out of a jar of 20, half of them blue? How did you obtain it?

Let event A be selecting a blue marble on the first pick. Let event B be selecting a blue marble on the second one. The first marble is not replaced, so these are dependent events. Of the 20 marbles, half of them are blue, so $P(A) = \frac{1}{2}$. Of the remaining 19 marbles, 9 of them are blue, so the probability of selecting one is $P(B) = \frac{9}{19}$. Thus, the probability of selecting 2 blue marbles is $P(A \text{ and } B) = \frac{1}{2} \cdot \frac{9}{19} = \frac{9}{38}$, using the multiplication rule.

Exercises

Determine the conditional probability. *(Lesson 20.1)*

1. What is the probability that a diamond that is drawn from the deck is a queen?

2. What is the probability that a queen drawn is a diamond?

Show that the following situation refers to independent events. *(Lesson 20.2)*

3. Isabelle believes that right- and left-footed soccer players are equally likely to score goals. She collected data from 260 players from a local soccer league. Using the following two-way frequency table, show that being right-footed and scoring goals are independent events.

	Right-Footed	Left-Footed	Total
Has scored a goal	39	13	52
Has not scored a goal	156	52	208
TOTAL	195	65	260

Identify whether a situation involves independent or dependent events. *(Lesson 20.3)*

4. Jim has 2 blue, 2 green, and 2 black socks in his drawer. He picks out 2 socks, one after the other. Determine the probability of him getting a matching pair of blue socks.

MODULE PERFORMANCE TASK

Drawing Aces

You have a standard deck of 52 playing cards. You pick three cards in a row without replacement. What is the probability that all three are aces?

Now you replace the three cards, shuffle, and pick four cards in a row without replacement. What is the probability that none are aces?

Begin by making notes in the space below about your plan for approaching this problem. Then complete the task on your own paper, using words, numbers, or diagrams to explain how you reached your conclusions.

(Ready) to Go On?

20.1–20.3 Conditional Probability and Independence of Events

• Online Homework
• Hints and Help
• Extra Practice

Compute the requested probability and explain how you obtained it.

1. A farmer wants to know if a particular fertilizer can cause blackberry shrubs to produce fruit early. Using the following two-way table, compute the probability of a plant producing fruit early without receiving fertilizer.

	Early Fruit	No Fruit	Total
Received Fertilizer	37	3	40
Did not receive fertilizer	19	21	40
TOTAL	56	24	80

2. Lisa flipped the same coin twice. Determine the probability of the coin landing on tails on the second try.

3. Lisa flipped the same coin three times. What is the probability she obtained all tails?

ESSENTIAL QUESTION

4. A jar contains 12 pennies, 5 nickels, and 18 quarters. You select 2 coins at random, one after the other.

   Does selecting a nickel affect the probability of selecting another nickel? Does not selecting a dime affect the probability of selecting a nickel? Describe how you would find the probability of selecting 2 nickels.

© Houghton Mifflin Harcourt Publishing Company

Assessment Readiness

1. Are the events independent? Choose Yes or No for each situation.

   A. Picking a penny and a marble out of a
   jar of pennies and a jar of marbles. ◯ Yes   ◯ No

   B. Drawing cards from a deck to form a
   4-card hand. ◯ Yes   ◯ No

   C. Choosing a color for a new shirt from a
   choice of red, yellow, or purple. ◯ Yes   ◯ No

2. Of the boys running for School President, 2 are juniors and 3 are seniors. Of the girls who are running, 4 are juniors and 1 is a senior. Decide whether the situation has a probability of $\frac{2}{5}$. Select Yes or No for A–C.

   A. A girl wins. ◯ Yes   ◯ No
   B. A candidate who is a boy is a junior. ◯ Yes   ◯ No
   C. A candidate who is a junior is a boy. ◯ Yes   ◯ No

3. You shuffle a standard deck of playing cards and deal one card. What is the probability that you deal an ace or a club? Explain your reasoning.

4. Claude has 2 jars of marbles. Each jar has 10 blue marbles and 10 green marbles. He selects 2 marbles from each jar. What is the probability they are all blue? Explain your reasoning.

Probability and Decision Making

Essential Question: How can you use probability to solve real-world problems?

REAL WORLD VIDEO
Physicians today use many sophisticated tests and technologies to help diagnose illnesses, but they must still consider probability in their diagnoses and decisions about treatment.

MODULE PERFORMANCE TASK PREVIEW

What's the Diagnosis?

The science of medicine has come a long way since surgeries were performed by the neighborhood barber, and leeches were used to treat just about every ailment. Nevertheless, modern medicine isn't perfect, and widely used tests for diagnosing illnesses aren't always 100 percent accurate. In this module you'll learn how probability can be used to measure the reliability of tests, and then use what you learned to evaluate decisions about a diagnosis.

Are (YOU) Ready?

Complete these exercises to review skills you will need for this module.

Probability of Simple Events

• Online Homework
• Hints and Help
• Extra Practice

Example 1

Two 6-sided conventional number cubes are tossed.
What is the probability that their sum is greater than 8?

+	1	2	3	4	5	6
1	2	3	4	5	6	7
2	3	4	5	6	7	8
3	4	5	6	7	8	9
4	5	6	7	8	9	10
5	6	7	8	9	10	11
6	7	8	9	10	11	12

There are 10 values greater than 8 and a total number of 36 values.

$$\frac{\text{number of favorable outcomes}}{\text{total number of outcomes}} = \frac{10}{36} = \frac{5}{18}$$

The probability that the sum of the two number cubes is greater than 8 is $\frac{5}{18}$.

Two number cubes are tossed. Find each probability.

1. The sum is prime. _____   **2.** The product is prime._____   **3.** The product is a perfect square._____

Making Predictions with Probability

Example 2

A fly lands on the target shown. What is the probability that the fly landed on red?

The area of the entire target is 6^2, or 36 units^2.

Red area is: $A = \pi r^2 = \pi(1)^2 = \pi$.

$$\frac{\text{number of favorable outcomes}}{\text{total number of outcomes}} = \frac{\pi}{36} \approx 8.7\%$$

Use the target to find the percent probability, to the nearest tenth.

4. Blue _____   **5.** Yellow or red _____   **6.** Not within a circle _____

21.1 Using Probability to Make Fair Decisions

Essential Question: How can you use probability to help you make fair decisions?

⊘ Explore Using Probabilities When Drawing at Random

You are sharing a veggie supreme pizza with friends. There is one slice left and you and a friend both want it. Both of you have already had two slices. What is a fair way to solve this problem?

Ⓐ Suppose you both decide to have the same amount of pizza. This means that the last slice will be cut into two pieces. Describe a fair way to split this last piece.

_____

_____

Ⓑ Suppose instead you decide that one of you will get the whole slice. Complete the table so that the result of each option gives a fair chance for each of you to get the last slice. Why do each of these possibilities give a fair chance?

Option	Result (you get last slice)	Result (friend gets last slice)
Flip a coin	Heads	
Roll a standard die		1, 3, 5
Play Rock, Paper, Scissors	You win.	You _____.
Draw lots using two straws of different lengths		Short straw

_____

_____

Reflect

1. Suppose, when down to the last piece, you tell your friend, "I will cut the last piece, and I will choose which piece you get." Why is this method unfair?

_____

_____

2. Your friend suggests that you shoot free throws to decide who gets the last piece. Use probability to explain why this might not be a fair way to decide.

_____

_____

🔑 Explain 1   Awarding a Prize to a Random Winner

Suppose you have to decide how to award a prize to a person at an event. You might want every person attending to have the same chance of winning, or you might want people to do something to improve their chance of winning. How can you award the prize fairly?

Example 1   **Explain whether each method of awarding a prize is fair.**

Ⓐ The sponsor of an event wants to award a door prize to one attendee. Each person in attendance is given a ticket with a unique number on it. All of the numbers are placed in a bowl, and one is drawn at random. The person with the matching number wins the prize.

The method of awarding a door prize is fair. Each number has the same chance of being chosen, so each attendee has an equal probability of winning the prize. If n attendees are at the event, then the probability of winning the prize is $\frac{1}{n}$ for each attendee.

Ⓑ A fundraiser includes a raffle in which half of the money collected goes to a charity, and the other half goes to one winner. Tickets are sold for $5 each. Copies of all the tickets are placed in a box, and one ticket is drawn at random. The person with the matching ticket wins the raffle.

The method of choosing a raffle winner is fair/not fair because

each _____ has an equal probability of being drawn.

Reflect

3. In Example 1B, the probability may not be the same for each person to win the raffle. Explain why the method is still fair.

_____

_____

Your Turn

4. Each month, a company wants to award a special parking space to an employee at random. Describe a fair way to do this. Include a way to ensure that a person doesn't win a second time before each employee has won once.

_____

_____

_____

© Houghton Mifflin Harcourt Publishing Company • Image Credits: ©Bill Oxford/iStockPhoto.com

Explain 2 · Solving Real-World Problems Fairly

You can use a random number generator to choose a winner of a prize.

Example 2   Use a problem solving plan.

A class of 24 students sold 65 magazine subscriptions to raise money for a trip. The table shows three of the students and the number of subscriptions each sold. As an incentive to participate, you will award a prize to one student in the class. Describe a method of awarding the prize fairly. Use probabilities to explain why your method is fair for the students listed.

Student	Subscriptions Sold
Miri	5
Liam	2
Madison	0

Analyze Information

Identify the important information.

- There are _____ students.
- They sold _____ magazine subscriptions.
- There is one prize, so there will be one winner.

Formulate a Plan

To be fair, students who sold more subscriptions should have a better chance of winning the prize than the students who sold fewer.

Find a method of assigning outcomes so that the chance of winning is proportional to the number of subscriptions sold.

Solve

The class sold 65 subscriptions, so assign the numbers 1–65 to the students. Each student gets as many numbers as the number of subscriptions he or she sold.

Student	Subscriptions Sold	Numbers Assigned	Probability of Winning
Miri	5	1–5	$\frac{\Box}{65} \approx 7.7\%$
Liam	2	6, 7	$\frac{\Box}{65} \approx 3.1\%$
Madison	0	none	$\frac{\Box}{65} = 0\%$

Then use a calculator to find a random integer from 1 to 65 (randInt(1, 65)). Then, for instance, if the result is 7, Liam wins the prize.

Justify and Evaluate

This method seems fair/unfair because it gives everyone who sold subscriptions a chance of winning. You could award a prize to the student who sold the most subscriptions, but this might not be possible if multiple students all sold the same number, and it might not seem fair if some students have better access to buyers than others.

© Houghton Mifflin Harcourt Publishing Company

5. A student suggests that it would be better to assign the numbers to students randomly rather than in numerical order. Would doing this affect the probability of winning?

_____

_____

6. A charity is giving a movie ticket for every 10 coats donated. Jacob collected 8 coats, Ben collected 6, and Ryan and Zak each collected 3. They decide to donate the coats together so that they will get 2 movie tickets. Describe how to use a random number generator to decide which 2 boys get a ticket.

_____

_____

_____

_____

Explain 3   Solving the Problem of Points

The decision-making process that you will apply in this example is based on the "Problem of Points" that was studied by the French mathematicians Blaise Pascal and Pierre de Fermat in the 17th century. Their work on the problem launched the branch of mathematics now known as probability.

Example 3   Two students, Lee and Rory, find a box containing 100 baseball cards. To determine who should get the cards, they decide to play a game with the rules shown.

Game Rules
• One of the students repeatedly tosses a coin.
• When the coin lands heads up, Lee gets a point.
• When the coin lands tails up, Rory gets a point.
• The first student to reach 20 points wins the game and gets the baseball cards.

As Lee and Rory are playing the game, they are interrupted and unable to continue. How should the 100 baseball cards be divided between the students given that the game was interrupted at the described moment?

(A)   When they are interrupted, Lee has 19 points and Rory has 17 points.

At most, 3 coin tosses would have been needed for someone to win the game.

Make a list of all possible results using H for heads and T for tails. Draw boxes around the outcomes in which Lee wins the game.

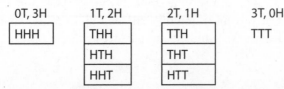

0T, 3H	1T, 2H	2T, 1H	3T, 0H
HHH	THH	TTH	TTT
	HTH	THT	
	HHT	HTT	

© Houghton Mifflin Harcourt Publishing Company

There are 8 possible results. Lee wins in 7 of them and Rory wins in 1 of them.

The probability of Lee winning is $\frac{7}{8}$, so he should get $\frac{7}{8}$ of the cards which is 87.5 cards. The probability of Rory winning is $\frac{1}{8}$, so he should get $\frac{1}{8}$ of the cards which is 12.5 cards. Rather than split a card into two, they might decide to flip a coin for that card or let Lee have it because he was more likely to win it.

(B) When they are interrupted, Lee has 18 points and Rory has 17 points.

At most, _____ more coin tosses would have been needed.

List all possible results. Draw boxes around the outcomes in which Lee wins.

0T, 4H   1T, 3H   2T, 2H   3T, 1H   4T, 0H

There are _____ possible results. Lee wins in _____ of them and Rory wins

in _____ of them.

The probability of Lee winning is _____ , so he should get _____ cards.

The probability of Rory winning is _____ , so he should get _____ cards.

Reflect

7. **Discussion** A student suggests that a better way to divide the cards in Example 3B would be to split the cards based on the number of points earned so far. Which method do you think is better?

_____

_____

_____

Your Turn

8. Describe a situation where the game is interrupted, resulting in the cards needing to be divided evenly between the two players.

9. **Discussion** In the situation described in the Explore, suppose you like the crust and your friend does not. Is there a fair way to cut the slice of pizza that might not result in two pieces with the same area?

_____

_____

_____

10. How would the solution to Example 2 need to change if there were two prizes to award? Assume that you do not want one student to win both prizes.

_____

_____

_____

_____

_____

_____

11. **Essential Question Check-In** Describe a way to use probability to make a fair choice of a raffle winner.

_____

_____

_____

☆ Evaluate: Homework and Practice

Personal Math Trainer
• Online Homework
• Hints and Help
• Extra Practice

1. You and a friend split the cost of a package of five passes to a climbing gym. Describe a way that you could fairly decide who gets to use the fifth pass.

2. In addition to prizes for first, second, and third place, the organizers of a race have a prize that they want each participant to have an equal chance of winning. Describe a fair method of choosing a winner for this prize.

Decide whether each method is a fair way to choose a winner based on whether each person has an equal chance of winning. Explain your answer by calculating each person's probability of winning.

3. Roll a standard die. Meri wins if the result is less than 3. Riley wins if the result is greater than 3.

4. Draw a card from a standard deck of cards. Meri wins if the card is red. Riley wins if the card is black.

5. Flip a coin. Meri wins if it lands heads. Riley wins if it lands tails.

6. Meri and Riley both jump as high as they can. Whoever jumps higher wins.

7. Roll a standard die. Meri wins if the result is even. Riley wins if the result is odd.

8. Randomly draw a stone from a box that contains 5 black stones and 4 white stones. Meri wins if the stone is black. Riley wins if the stone is white.

9. A chess club has received a chess set to give to one of its members. The club decides that everyone should have a chance of winning the set based on how many games they have won this season. Describe a fair method to decide who wins the set. Find the probability that each member will win it.

Member	Games Won	Probability of Winning	Member	Games Won	Probability of Winning
Kayla	30		Hailey	12	
Noah	23		Gabe	12	
Ava	18		Concour	5	

10. Owen, Diego, and Cody often play a game of chance during lunch. When they can't finish, they calculate the probability that each will win given the current state of the game and assign partial wins. Today, when they had to stop, they calculated that there were 56 possibilities for how the game could be completed. Owen was the winner in 23 of the possibilities, Diego was the winner in 18 of them, and Cody was the winner in 15. To two decimal places, how should they assign partial wins?

© Houghton Mifflin Harcourt Publishing Company • Image Credits: ©T. Grimm/ vario images GmbH & Co.KG/Alamy

Represent Real-World Problems Twenty students, including Paige, volunteer to work at the school banquet. Each volunteer worked a nonzero whole number of hours. Paige worked 4 hours. The students worked a total of 45 hours. The organizers would like to award a prize to one of the volunteers.

11. Describe a process for awarding the prize so that each volunteer has an equal chance of winning. Find the probability that Paige wins.

12. Describe a process for awarding the prize so that each volunteer's chance of winning is proportional to how many hours the volunteer worked. Find the probability that Paige wins.

There are 10,000 seats available in a sports stadium. Each seat has a package beneath it, and 20 of the seats have an additional prize-winning package with a family pass for the entire season.

13. Under what circumstances is this method of choosing winners of the family passes fair?

14. Assuming that the method of choosing winners is fair, what is the probability of winning a family pass if you attend the game?

15. What is the probability of not winning a family pass if you attend the game?

A teacher tells students, "For each puzzle problem you complete, I will assign you an entry number for a prize giveaway." In all, 10 students complete 53 puzzle problems. Leon completed 7. To award the prize, the teacher uses a calculator to generate a random integer from 1 to 53. Leon is assigned the numbers 18 to 24.

16. What is the probability that a particular number is chosen?

17. What is the probability that one of Leon's numbers will be chosen?

18. What is the probability that one of Leon's numbers will not be chosen?

19. Is this fair to Leon according to the original instructions? Explain.

20. **Make a Conjecture** Two teams are playing a game against one another in class to earn 10 extra points on an assignment. The teacher said that the points will be split fairly between the two teams, depending on the results of the game. If Team A earned 1300 points and Team B earned 2200 points, describe one way the teacher could split up the 10 extra points. Explain.

21. **Persevere in Problem Solving** Alexa and Sofia are at a yard sale, and they find a box of 20 collectible toys that they both want. They can't agree about who saw it first, so they flip a coin until Alexa gets 10 heads or Sofia gets 10 tails. When Alexa has 3 heads and Sofia has 6 tails, they decide to stop and divide the toys proportionally based on the probability each has of winning under the original rules. How should they divide the toys?

Lesson Performance Task

Three games are described below. For each game, tell whether it is fair (all players are equally likely to win) or unfair (one player has an advantage). Explain how you reached your decision, being sure to discuss how probability entered into your decision.

1. You and your friend each toss a quarter. If two heads turn up, you win. If a head and a tail turn up, your friend wins. If two tails turn up, you play again.

2. You and your friend each roll a number cube. If the sum of the numbers is odd, you get 1 point. If the sum is even, your friend gets 1 point.

3. You and your friend each roll a number cube. If the product of the numbers is odd, you get 1 point. If the product is even, your friend gets 1 point.

21.2 Analyzing Decisions

Essential Question: How can conditional probability help you make real-world decisions?

Resource
Locker

✏ Explore 1 Analyzing a Decision Using Probability

Suppose scientists have developed a test that can be used at birth to determine whether a baby is right-handed or left-handed. The test uses a drop of the baby's saliva and instantly gives the result. The test has been in development long enough for the scientists to track the babies as they grow into toddlers and to see whether their test is accurate. About 10% of babies turn out to be left-handed.

The scientists have learned that when children are left-handed, the test correctly identifies them as left-handed 92% of the time. Also, when children are right-handed, the test correctly identifies them as right-handed 95% of the time.

(A) In the first year on the market, the test is used on 1,000,000 babies. Complete the table. Begin with the grand total (lower-right table cell) and the row totals, and use those to help you fill in the four "Actually" versus "Tests" cells and then the two column totals.

	Tests Left-handed	Tests Right-handed	Total
Actually Left-handed			
Actually Right-handed			
Total			

(B) What is the probability that a baby who tests left-handed actually is left-handed? _____

(C) What is the probability that a baby who tests right-handed actually is right-handed? _____

Reflect

1. Is the test a good test of right-handedness?

_____

2. A baby is tested, and the test shows the baby will be left-handed. The parents decide to buy a left-handed baseball glove for when the baby is old enough to play baseball. Is this a reasonable decision?

_____

_____

3. Discussion Describe two ways in which the test can become a more reliable indicator of left-handedness.

_____

_____

_____

⊘ Explore 2 Deriving Bayes' Theorem

Bayes' Theorem gives a formula for calculating an unknown conditional probability from other known probabilities. You can use Bayes' Theorem to calculate conditional probabilities like those in Steps B and C in Explore 1.

(A) Complete the steps to derive Bayes' Theorem.

    (1)   Write the formula for $P(B|A)$. _____

    (2)   Solve for $P(A \cap B)$. _____

    (3)   Write the formula for $P(A|B)$. _____

    (4)   Substitute the expression for $P(A \cap B)$ in step (2) into the formula for $P(A|B)$ in

        step (3). _____

(B) Complete the equations at the bottom of the tree diagram. Use the fact that the probability shown along each branch is the probability of the single event to which that branch leads. Each product of probabilities listed at the bottom of the tree diagram is the probability that two events occur together.

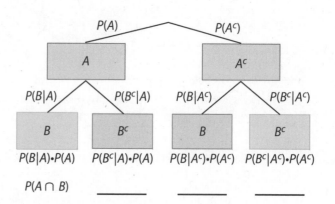

(C) Complete the explanation for finding $P(B)$ using the tree diagram in Step B.

Because events A and A^c are mutually exclusive, the events $A \cap B$ and _____ are

mutually exclusive. Since the union of $A \cap B$ and _____ is _____,

$P(B) = P(A \cap B) + $ _____ $ = P(A) \cdot P(B|A) + $ _____.

(D) Use your result from Step C to rewrite your final expression from Step A to get another form of Bayes' Theorem.

4. Explain in words what each expression means in the context of Explore 1.

$P(A)$ is the probability of actually being left-handed.

$P(B)$ is the probability of testing left-handed.

$P(A|B)$ is _____.

$P(B|A)$ is _____.

5. Use Bayes' Theorem to calculate the probability that a baby actually is left-handed, given that the baby tests left-handed. Explain what this probability means.

_____

_____

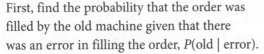 **Explain 1** **Using Bayes' Theorem**

Bayes' Theorem is a useful tool when you need to make or analyze decisions.

Bayes' Theorem
Given two events A and B with $P(B) \neq 0$, $P(A|B) = \dfrac{P(A) \cdot P(B|A)}{P(B)}$.
Another form is $P(A|B) = \dfrac{P(A) \cdot P(B|A)}{P(A) \cdot P(B|A) + P(A^c) \cdot P(B|A^c)}$.

Example 1 **Suppose Walter operates an order-filling machine that has an error rate of 0.5%. He installs a new order-filling machine that has an error rate of only 0.1%. The new machine takes over 80% of the order-filling tasks.**

(A) One day, Walter gets a call from a customer complaining that her order wasn't filled properly. Walter blames the problem on the old machine. Was he correct in doing so?

First, find the probability that the order was filled by the old machine given that there was an error in filling the order, $P(\text{old} \mid \text{error})$.

$$P(\text{old}|\text{error}) = \frac{P(\text{old}) \cdot P(\text{error}|\text{old})}{P(\text{error})}$$

$$= \frac{(0.20) \cdot 0.005}{0.001 + 0.0008} = \frac{0.001}{0.0018} = \frac{5}{9} \approx 0.56$$

Given that there is a mistake, the probability is about 56% that the old machine filled the order. The probability that the new machine filled the order is $1 - 0.56 = 44\%$. The old machine is only slightly more likely than the new machine to have filled the order. Walter shouldn't blame the old machine.

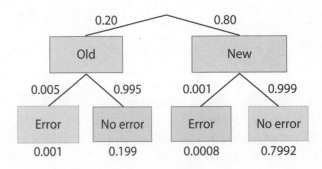

B Walter needs to increase capacity for filling orders so he increases the number of orders being filled by the old machine to 30% of the total orders. What percent of errors in filled orders are made by the old machine? Is Walter unreasonably increasing the risk of shipping incorrectly filled orders?

Find the probability that _____

given that _____,

$P(\underline{\quad} \mid \underline{\quad})$.

Use Bayes' Theorem.

_____

_____

Describe the result of making this change.

_____

_____

_____

_____

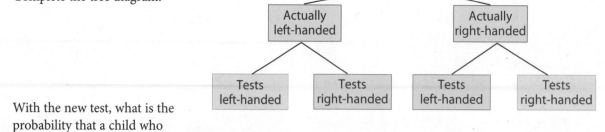

> Old
> New
> Error   No error   Error   No error

6. Given that the old machine fills so few orders, how can it be responsible for more than half of the errors?

_____

In the situation described in Explore 1, suppose the scientists have changed the test so that now it correctly identifies left-handed babies 100% of the time, and still correctly identifies right-handed babies 95% of the time.

7. Complete the tree diagram.

> Actually left-handed   Actually right-handed
> Tests left-handed   Tests right-handed   Tests left-handed   Tests right-handed

8. With the new test, what is the probability that a child who tests left-handed will be left-handed? How does this compare to the original test?

9. With the new test, what is the probability that a child who tests right-handed will be right-handed? How does this compare to the original test?

© Houghton Mifflin Harcourt Publishing Company

10. **Discussion** Compare the probabilities you found in Explore 1 and Your Turn 8 and 9. Why did the probability that a baby who tests right-handed actually is right-handed become 100%?

_____

_____

_____

11. **Essential Question Check-In** How can you use probability to help you analyze decisions?

_____

_____

_____

⭐ **Evaluate: Homework and Practice**

• Online Homework
• Hints and Help
• Extra Practice

1. A factory manager is assessing the work of two assembly-line workers. Helen has been on the job longer than Kyle. Their production rates for the last month are in the table. Based on comparing the number of defective products, the manager is considering putting Helen on probation. Is this a good decision? Why or why not?

	Helen	Kyle	Total
Defective	50	20	70
Not defective	965	350	1,315
Total	1,015	370	1,385

2. **Multiple Step** A reporter asked 150 voters if they plan to vote in favor of a new library and a new arena. The table shows the results. If you are given that a voter plans to vote no for the new arena, what is the probability that the voter also plans to vote no for the new library?

	Yes for Library	No for Library	Total
Yes for Arena	21	30	51
No for Arena	57	42	99
Total	78	72	150

3. You want to hand out coupons for a local restaurant to students who live off campus at a rural college with a population of 10,000 students. You know that 10% of the students live off campus and that 98% of those students ride a bike. Also, 62% of the students who live on campus do not have a bike. You decide to give a coupon to any student you see who is riding a bike. Complete the table. Then explain whether this a good decision.

	Bike	No bike	Total
On campus			
Off campus			
Total			

4. A test for a virus correctly identifies someone who has the virus (by returning a positive result) 99% of the time. The test correctly identifies someone who does not have the virus (by returning a negative result) 99% of the time. It is known that 0.5% of the population has the virus. A doctor decides to treat anyone who tests positive for the virus. Complete the two-way table assuming a total population of 1,000,000 people have been tested. Is this a good decision?

	Tests Positive	Tests Negative	Total
Virus			
No virus			
Total			

5. It is known that 2% of the population has a certain allergy. A test correctly identifies people who have the allergy 98% of the time. The test correctly identifies people who do not have the allergy 95% of the time. A website recommends that anyone who tests positive for the allergy should begin taking anti-allergy medication. Complete the two-way table. Do you think this is a good recommendation? Why or why not?

	Test Positive	Test Negative	Total
Total			10,000

The copyright notice on the side.

6. Use the tree diagram shown.

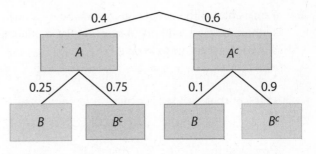

  a. Find $P(A^c) \cdot P(B|A^c)$.

  b. Find $P(B)$.

  c. Use Bayes's Theorem to find $P(A^c|B)$.

7. The probabilities of drawing lemons and limes from a
bag are shown in the tree diagram. Find the probability
of drawing the two pieces of fruit randomly from the bag.

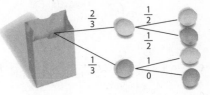

  a. two lemons   **b.** two limes

  c. lime then lemon   **d.** lemon then lime OR lime then lemon

8. **Multiple Step** A school principal plans a school picnic for June 2. A few days before
the event, the weather forecast predicts rain for June 2, so the principal decides to
cancel the picnic. Consider the following information.

  • In the school's town, the probability that it rains on any day in June is 3%.
  • When it rains, the forecast correctly predicts rain 90% of the time.
  • When it does not rain, the forecast incorrectly predicts rain 5% of the time.

  a. Find $P(\text{prediction of rain}|\text{rains})$ and $P(\text{rains})$.

  b. Complete the tree diagram, and find $P(\text{prediction of rain})$.

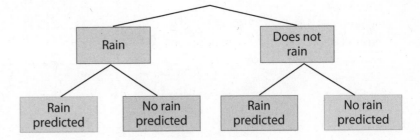

  c. Find $P(\text{rains}|\text{ prediction of rain})$.

  d. Is the decision to cancel the picnic reasonable?

9. Pamela has collected data on the number of students in the sophomore class who play a sport or play a musical instrument. She has learned the following.

- 42.5% of all students in her school play a musical instrument.

- 20% of those who play a musical instrument also play a sport.

- 40% of those who play no instrument also play no sport.

Complete the tree diagram. Would it be reasonable to conclude that a student who doesn't play a sport plays a musical instrument?

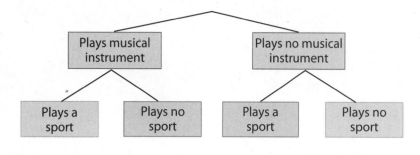

10. Interpret the Answer Company X supplies 35% of the phones to an electronics store and Company Y supplies the remainder. The manager of the store knows that 25% of the phones in the last shipment from Company X were defective, while only 5% of the phones from Company Y were defective. The manager chooses a phone at random and finds that it is defective. The manager decides that the phone must have come from Company X. Do you think this is a reasonable conclusion? Why or why not?

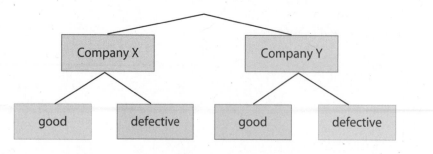

11. Suppose that strep throat affects 2% of the population and a test to detect it produces an accurate result 99% of the time. Create a tree diagram and use Bayes' Theorem to find the probability that someone who tests positive actually has strep throat.

12. **Fundraising** A hand-made quilt is first prize in a fund-raiser raffle. The table shows information about all the ticket buyers. Given that the winner of the quilt is a man, what is the probability that he resides in Sharonville?

	Men	Women	Total
Forestview	35	45	80
Sharonville	15	25	40

13. Recall that the Multiplication Rule says that $P(A \cap B) = P(A) \cdot P(B|A)$. If you switch the order of events A and B, then the rule becomes $P(B \cap A) = P(B) \cdot P(A|B)$. Use the Multiplication Rule and the fact that $P(B \cap A) = P(A \cap B)$ to prove Bayes' Theorem. (Hint: Divide each side by $P(B)$.)

14. **Sociology** A sociologist collected data on the types of pets in 100 randomly selected households. Suppose you want to offer a service to households that own both a cat and a dog. Complete the table. Based on the data in the table, would it be more effective to hand information to people walking dogs or to people buying cat food?

		Owns a Cat		
		Yes	No	
Owns a Dog	Yes	15	24	
	No	18	43	

© Houghton Mifflin Harcourt Publishing Company

15. **Interpret the Answer** It is known that 1% of all mice in a laboratory have a genetic mutation. A test for the mutation correctly identifies mice that have the mutation 98% of the time. The test correctly identifies mice that do not have the mutation 96% of the time. A lab assistant tests a mouse and finds that the mouse tests positive for the mutation. The lab assistant decides that the mouse must have the mutation. Is this a good decision? Complete the tree diagram and explain your answer.

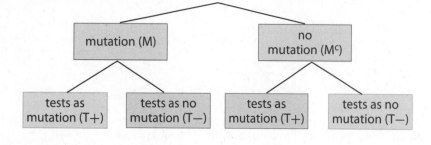

16. **Interpret the Answer** It is known that 96% of all dogs do not get trained. One professional trainer claims that 54% of trained dogs will sit on one of the first four commands to sit and that no other dogs will sit on command. A condominium community wants to impose a restriction on dogs that are not trained. They want each dog owner to show that his or her dog will sit on one of the first four commands. Assuming that the professional trainer's claim is correct, is this a fair way to identify dogs that have not been trained? Explain.

17. **Multiple Steps** Tomas has a choice of three possible routes to work. On each day, he randomly selects a route and keeps track of whether he is late. Based on this 40-day trial, which route makes Tomas least likely to be late for work?

	Late	Not Late
Route A	IIII	HHt HHt
Route B	III	HHt II
Route C	IIII	HHt HHt II

18. Critique Reasoning When Elisabeth saw this tree diagram, she said that the calculations must be incorrect. Do you agree? Justify your answer.

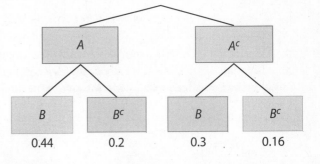

19. Multiple Representations The Venn diagram shows how many of the first 100 customers of a new bakery bought either bread or cookies, both, or neither. Taryn claims that the data indicate that a customer who bought cookies is more likely to have bought bread than a customer who bought bread is likely to have bought cookies. Is she correct?

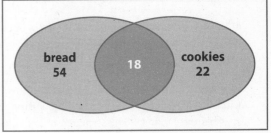

20. Persevere in Problem Solving At one high school, the probability that a student is absent today, given that the student was absent yesterday, is 0.12. The probability that a student is absent today, given that the student was present yesterday, is 0.05. The probability that a student was absent yesterday is 0.1. A teacher forgot to take attendance in several classes yesterday, so he assumed that attendance in his class today is the same as yesterday. If there were 40 students in these classes, how many errors would you expect by doing this?

Lesson Performance Task

You're a contestant on a TV quiz show. Before you are three doors. Behind two of the doors, there's a goat. Behind one of the doors, there's a new car. You are asked to pick a door. After you make your choice, the quizmaster opens one of the doors you *didn't* choose, revealing a goat.

Door 1   Door 2   Door 3

Now there are only two doors. You can stick with your original choice or you can switch to the one remaining door. Should you switch?

Intuition tells most people that, with two doors left, there's a 50% probability that they're right and a 50% probability that they're wrong. They conclude that it doesn't matter whether they switch or not.

Does it? Using Bayes' Theorem, it can be shown mathematically that you're much better off switching! You can reach the same conclusion using logical reasoning skills. Assume that the car is behind Door 1. (The same reasoning can be applied if the car is behind one of the other doors.) You've decided to switch your choice after the first goat is revealed. There are three possibilities based on which door you choose first. Describe each possibility and what happens when you switch. Based on the three possibilities, what is the probability that you win the car? Explain how you obtain the probability..

© Houghton Mifflin Harcourt Publishing Company • Image Credits: (l) ©Henrik5000/iStockPhoto.com; (m) ©Photodisc/Getty Images; (r) ©Photodisc/Getty Images

Probability and Decision Making

Essential Question: How can you use probability to solve real-world problems?

KEY EXAMPLE   (Lesson 21.1)

Determine whether the method of awarding a prize is fair. Explain.

A festival has a baked goods fundraising raffle in which tickets are drawn for winners. The tickets are sold for $2 each, and the purchaser of the ticket places his or her name on the ticket before placing the ticket into a fishbowl on a table. There are 20 cakes for prizes. A ticket is drawn at random from the fishbowl for each cake.

The method of awarding the prize is fair. This is because each ticket has an equal probability of being drawn. For each of n tickets bought, that ticket has a $\frac{1}{n}$ chance of being drawn. The more tickets someone buys, the better chance they have of winning a cake.

KEY EXAMPLE   (Lesson 21.2)

Suppose Rhonda's Block Warehouse operates a block-making machine that has an error rate of 0.7%. Then Rhonda installs a new block-making machine that has an error rate of only 0.3%. The new machine takes over 75% of the block-making tasks. One day, Rhonda gets a call from a customer complaining that his block is not made properly. Rhonda blames the problem on the old machine. Was she correct in doing so?

Find the probability that the block was made by the old machine given that the block is bad, $P(\text{old}|\text{bad})$.

$$P(\text{old}|\text{bad}) = \frac{P(\text{old}) \cdot P(\text{bad}|\text{old})}{P(\text{old}) \cdot P(\text{bad}|\text{old}) + P(\text{new}) \cdot P(\text{bad}|\text{new})} \qquad \text{Bayes' Theorem}$$

$$= \frac{0.25 \cdot 0.7}{0.25 \cdot 0.7 + 0.75 \cdot 0.3} \qquad \text{Substitute known probabilities}$$

$$= 0.4375, \text{ or } 43.75\%$$

Given that the probability that a bad block is made by the old machine is less than 50%, Rhonda should not blame the old machine for the bad block.

EXERCISES

Determine whether the method of awarding a prize is fair. Explain. If it is not fair, describe a way that would be fair. *(Lesson 21.1)*

1. A teacher gives a ticket to each student who earns a 90 or above on any homework assignment. At the end of each week, the teacher draws from the ticket jar and gives the winning student a free homework pass for the next week.

Suppose that a card dealing machine has a probability of 23% of dealing a face card. An older machine has a 14% chance of dealing a face card. Use Bayes's Theorem to find the probability. *(Lesson 21.2)*

2. If each machine is used 50% of the time, and a face card is the next card dealt, what is the probability the new machine dealt the card?

MODULE PERFORMANCE TASK

What's the Diagnosis?

Lenny works in a factory that makes cleaning products. Lately he has been suffering from headaches. He asks his doctor if the chemicals used in the factory might be responsible for his headaches. The doctor performs a blood test that is routinely used to diagnose the kind of illness Lenny is concerned about.

Use the following facts to gauge the probability that Lenny has the illness if he tests positive:

1. The test has a reliability rate of 85 percent.

2. The test has a false positive rate of 8 percent.

3. The illness affects 3 percent of people who are Lenny's age and who work in conditions similar to those he works in.

Start by listing on your own paper the information you will need to solve the problem. Then complete the task. Use numbers, words, or algebra to explain how you reached your conclusion.

© Houghton Mifflin Harcourt Publishing Company

(Ready) to Go On?

• Online Homework
• Hints and Help
• Extra Practice

Determine whether the method of awarding a prize is fair. Explain briefly.

1. Prize to every 500th customer

2. Ticket to every customer; drawing

3. Choose number 1–10; draw number

4. Ticket to all cars; two to red cars

Rodney's Repair Service has a lug nut tightening machine that works well 89% of the time. They got a new machine that works well 98% of the time. Each machine is used 50% of the time. Use Bayes's Theorem to find each probability.

5. new machine given malfunctioned

6. old machine given malfunctioned

7. old machine given worked well

8. new machine given worked well

ESSENTIAL QUESTION

9. How can probability and decision making help the organizer of a raffle?

© Houghton Mifflin Harcourt Publishing Company

Assessment Readiness

1. Consider the situation. Is the method of awarding the prize fair?

   Select Yes or No for **A–C.**

   A. Ticket for every $10 spent, random drawing ◯ Yes ◯ No

   B. Prize to the person who can press a buzzer
   the quickest ◯ Yes ◯ No

   C. Pair of number cubes is tossed; finalist
   A wins if the sum is 2–7 and finalist B wins
   if the sum is 8–12 ◯ Yes ◯ No

2. Consider the situation of having four tiles in a bag spelling M-A-T-H drawn randomly
   without replacement. Choose True or False for each statement.

   A. There is one way to draw all 4 tiles
   from the bag, if order doesn't matter. ◯ True ◯ False

   B. There are six ways to draw 2 tiles from the
   bag, if order matters. ◯ True ◯ False

   C. There are twenty four ways to draw 3 tiles
   from the bag if order matters. ◯ True ◯ False

3. The band class has two trumpet players. Of the two, the first trumpet player plays a
   wrong note 4% of the time, and the second trumpet player plays a wrong note 9%
   of the time. If one song has the first trumpet player playing 75% of the song, and the
   second trumpet player playing the rest, use Bayes' Theorem to find the probability that
   a particular wrong note was played by the second trumpet player. Explain why your
   answer makes sense.

4. Gerald says that the sequence 4, 16, 64, 256,… can be described by the rule
   $2 \cdot 2^n = 4^n$. Describe and correct his mistake.

Assessment Readiness

1. Figure *ABCDE* is similar to figure *LMNOP*. Select True or False for each mathematical statement.

   A. $\frac{BC}{AE} = \frac{MN}{OP}$ ○ True ○ False

   B. $\frac{AB}{DE} = \frac{LM}{OP}$ ○ True ○ False

   C. $\frac{BD}{AE} = \frac{MN}{LP}$ ○ True ○ False

2. The transformation $(x, y) \rightarrow (x - 2, y + 1)$ is applied to $\triangle XYZ$. Select True or False for each statement.

   A. The area of $\triangle X'Y'Z'$ is the same as the area of $\triangle XYZ$. ○ True ○ False

   B. The distance from X to X' is equal to the distance from Z to Z'. ○ True ○ False

   C. The transformation is a rotation. ○ True ○ False

3. Does each scenario describe independent events? Select Yes or No for each situation.

   A. Drawing one card and then another from a standard deck of cards and having both be aces ○ Yes ○ No

   B. Rolling a fair number cube twice and getting 6 on both rolls ○ Yes ○ No

   C. Rolling a 3 on a fair number cube and flipping tails on a fair coin ○ Yes ○ No

4. Each student in a class has been assigned at random to draw a parallelogram, a rectangle, a rhombus, or a square. Select True or False for each statement about the likelihood that the quadrilateral that the student draws will be a parallelogram.

   A. It is unlikely, but not certain, because the probability is less than 0.5. ○ True ○ False

   B. It is likely, but not certain, because the probability is more than 0.5. ○ True ○ False

   C. It is impossible for it not to happen because the probability is 1. ○ True ○ False

5. The events A and B are independent. Select True or False for each statement.

   A. $P(A \mid B) = P(B \mid A)$ ○ True ○ False

   B. $P(A \text{ and } B) = P(B) \cdot P(A)$ ○ True ○ False

   C. $P(A) = P(B)$ ○ True ○ False

6. Vera needs to place 15 student volunteers at a local fire station. Five students will wash fire trucks, 7 will be assigned to paint, and 3 will be assigned to wash windows. What is the number of possible job assignments expressed using factorials and as a simplified number?

7. The table below shows the number of days that a meteorologist predicted it would be sunny and the number of days it was sunny. Based on the data in the table, what is the conditional probability that it will be sunny on a day when the meteorologist predicts it will be sunny? Show your work.

	Sunny	Not Sunny	Total
Predicts Sunny	570	20	590
Does Not Predict Sunny	63	347	410
Total	633	367	1000

8. Complete the two-way table below. Then find the fraction of red cards in a standard 52-card deck that have a number on them and find the fraction of numbered cards that are red.

	Red	Black	Total
Number			
No Number			
Total			

Performance Tasks

★ 9. Sixteen cards numbered 1 through 16 are placed face down, and Stephanie chooses one at random. What is the probability that the number on Stephanie's card is less than 5 or greater than 10? Show your work.

★★**10.** Students in 4 different classes are surveyed about their favorite movie type. What is the probability that a randomly selected student in class B prefers comedies? What is the probability that a randomly selected student who prefers comedies is in class B? Explain why the two probabilities are not the same. Show your work.

	A	B	C	D
Action	12	9	8	11
Comedy	13	11	15	4
Drama	6	11	7	18

★★★**11.** A Chinese restaurant has a buffet that includes ice cream for dessert. The table shows the selections made last week.

	Chocolate	Vanilla	Strawberry
Cone	24	18	12
Dish	12	21	15

A. Which flavor is the most popular? Which serving method? Is the combination of the most popular flavor and serving method the most popular dessert choice overall? Explain.

B. Which of the following is more likely? Explain.
   • A customer chooses vanilla, given that the customer chose a cone.
   • A customer chooses a cone, given that the customer chose vanilla?

C. A class of 24 students gets the buffet for lunch. If they all get ice cream, about how many will get a cone or vanilla? Explain.

Epidemiologist An epidemiologist is aiding in the treatment of a community plagued by two different infectious agents, X and Z. Each infectious agent must be treated differently with a new treatment if the patient has been infected by both agents. The community has a total population of 15,000 people, where 5% are healthy and 60% are afflicted by the X infection. The same incident happened to 10 other communities with similar results as the first. What is the probability that people will be healthy? have the X affliction? have the Z affliction? have both afflictions?

Statistics

MATH IN CAREERS

Pharmaceutical Scientist
Pharmaceutical scientists work in a variety of capacities, such as inventing and synthesizing new drugs, creating dosage delivery systems, and studying how a particular drug interacts in a living organism. They also design and conduct clinical trials to test the efficacy of novel medications. Pharmaceutical scientists make use of algebra, calculus, and differential equations to model and interpret the effects of a drug and the drug's rate of decay in the body. They also use statistics to help make informed decisions about a medication's usefulness.

If you are interested in a career as a pharmaceutical scientist, you should study these mathematical subjects:
- Algebra
- Statistics
- Calculus
- Differential Equations

Check out the career activity at the end of the unit to find out how **Pharmaceutical Scientists** use math.

© Houghton Mifflin Harcourt Publishing Company • ©Erik Isakson/Blend Images/Corbis

Reading Start-Up

Vocabulary

Review Words

✔ binomial experiment
(experimento binomial)

✔ binomial probability
(probabilidad binomial)

✔ normal distribution
(distribución normal)

Preview Words

biased sample *(muestra no representativa)*

margin of error *(margen de error)*

null hypothesis *(hipótesis nula)*

observational study *(estudio de observación)*

population *(población)*

probability distribution *(distribución de probabilidad)*

sample *(muestra)*

standard normal value *(valor normal estándar)*

statistic *(estadística)*

Visualize Vocabulary

Match the review words to their descriptions to complete the chart.

Word	Description
	A probability experiment with a fixed number of independent trials in which each outcome falls into exactly one of two categories
	A bell shaped probability distribution
	In a binomial experiment, the probability of r successes $(0 \leq r \leq n)$ is $p(r) = {}_nC_r \cdot p^r q^{n-r}$, with probability of success p and probability of failure q and $p + q = 1$

Understand Vocabulary

To become familiar with some of the vocabulary terms in the module, consider the following. You may refer to the module, the glossary, or a dictionary.

1. A number that describes a sample is a _____ .

2. A _____ does not fairly represent the population.

3. A _____ is a part of the population.

4. The _____ is an assumption in statistics that there is no difference between the two groups being tested.

Active Reading

Key-Term Fold Before beginning each module in this unit, create a key-term fold to help you learn the definitions in each lesson. Each tab can contain a key term on one side and its definition on the other. When possible, include an example with the definition. Use the key-term fold to quiz yourself on the definitions of the key terms in the unit.

Gathering and Displaying Data

Essential Question: How can gathering and displaying data help to solve real-world problems?

REAL WORLD VIDEO
Unlike packaged foods, fresh fruit and vegetables do not have nutrition labels. Check out some ways we can gather and analyze nutrition data for fresh produce.

MODULE PERFORMANCE TASK PREVIEW

Fruit Nutrition Data

Good nutrition is especially important while you are still growing. You can achieve good nutrition by monitoring the nutrients that you eat. You already know to eat plenty of fruits and vegetables, but how do the nutrients in, say, a pear compare with those of a peach? You've heard that you can't compare apples and oranges, but later on, that's exactly what we'll be doing!

Are (YOU) Ready?

Complete these exercises to review skills you will need for this module.

Two-Way Tables

• Online Homework
• Hints and Help
• Extra Practice

Example 1

The table shows the number of tickets sold for seats in the four areas of the local playhouse for showings in a three-day period. What percent of the tickets sold for the Saturday showing were for orchestra level seating?

Saturday is the second to last column. The total tickets sold for the Saturday performance were $4 + 891 + 540 + 695$, which is a total of 2130 tickets. The percent of those tickets that were orchestra level is $\frac{891}{2130} \cdot 100$, or about 42%.

	Friday	Saturday	Sunday
Box	12	4	2
Orchestra	856	891	773
Loge	492	540	411
Balcony	712	695	359

Use the table shown to find each percent.

1. What percent of all the loge tickets sold were for the Friday showing?

_____

2. What percent of all tickets sold were for the Sunday showing?

_____

3. What percent of all tickets sold were for seats at either the loge or balcony level?

_____

Box Plots

Example 2

A box plot shows the least and greatest data items, the upper and lower quartiles, and the median of all the data. Find the lower quartile of these data:

20, 25, 8, 1, 17, 2, 9, 23, 21, 2, 16, 12

Order the data:

1, 2, 2, 8, 9, 12, 16, 17, 20, 21, 23, 25

The lower quartile is the median of the first half of the data: 1, 2, 2, 8, 9, 12. The median is halfway between 2 and 8, which is 5.

Use the data in the example to find each measure.

4. Median _____

5. Upper quartile _____

6. Range _____

22.1 Data-Gathering Techniques

Essential Question: Under what circumstances should a sample statistic be used as an estimator of a population parameter?

Resource Locker

 Explore **Finding the Mean of Samples Obtained from Various Sampling Methods**

You collect data about a **population** by surveying or studying some or all of the individuals in the population. When *all* the individuals in a population are surveyed or studied, the data-gathering technique is called a **census**. A **parameter** is a number that summarizes a characteristic of the population. When only some of the individuals in a population are surveyed or studied, the data-gathering technique is called **sampling**. A **statistic** is a number that summarizes a characteristic of a sample. Statistics can be used to estimate parameters.

Consider the following table, which lists the salaries (in thousands of dollars) of all 30 employees at a small company. In this Explore, you will take samples from this population and compute the mean (the sum of the data divided by the sample size).

Salaries at a Small Company									
21	24	26	28	30	32	33	35	37	41
44	46	47	49	50	51	52	54	55	57
58	62	62	64	64	65	70	71	73	80

(A) Suppose the employees whose salaries are 51, 57, 58, 65, 70, and 73 volunteer to be in the sample. This is called a *self-selected sample*. Compute the sample's mean, rounding to the nearest whole number.

_____

(B) Suppose the six salaries in the first two columns of the table are chosen. This is called a *convenience sample* because the data are easy to obtain. Record the salaries, and then compute the sample's mean, rounding to the nearest whole number.

_____

(C) Suppose every fifth salary in the list, reading from left to right in each row, is chosen. This is called a *systematic sample*. Record the salaries, and then compute the sample's mean, rounding to the nearest whole number.

_____

Ⓓ Label the data in the table with the identifiers 1–10 for the first row, 11–20 for the second row, and 21–30 for the third row. Then use a graphing calculator's random integer generator to generate six identifiers between 1 and 30, as shown. (If any identifiers are repeated, simply generate replacements for them until you have six unique identifiers.) This is called a *simple random sample*. Record the corresponding salaries, and then compute the sample's mean, rounding to the nearest whole number.

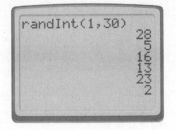

_____

_____

Reflect

1. Compute the mean of the population. Then list the four samples from best to worst in terms of how well each sample mean estimates the population mean.

_____

_____

2. With the way the table is organized, both the convenience sample and the systematic sample have means that are not too far from the population mean. Why?

_____

_____

_____

_____

🔑 Explain 1 Distinguishing Among Sampling Methods

The goal of sampling is to obtain a **representative sample**, because the statistic obtained from the sample is a good estimator of the corresponding population parameter. Some sampling methods can result in **biased samples** that may not be representative of the population and can produce statistics that lead to inaccurate conclusions about the corresponding population parameters.

Sampling Method	Description
Simple random sample	Each individual in the population has an equal chance of being selected.
Self-selected sample	Individuals volunteer to be part of the sample.
Convenience sample	Individuals are selected based on how accessible they are.
Systematic sample	Members of the sample are chosen according to a rule, such as every nth individual in the population.
Stratified sample	The population is divided into groups, and individuals from each group are selected (typically through a random sample within each group).
Cluster sample	The population is divided into groups, some of the groups are randomly selected, and either all the individuals in the selected groups are selected or just some of the individuals from the selected groups are selected (typically through a random sample within each selected group).

© Houghton Mifflin Harcourt Publishing Company

The Explore showed that simple random samples are likely to be representative of a population (as are other sampling methods that involve randomness) and are therefore preferred over sampling methods that don't involve randomness.

Example 1 **Identify the population, classify the sampling methods, and decide whether the sampling methods could result in a biased sample. Explain your reasoning.**

(A) The officials of the National Football League (NFL) want to know how the players feel about some proposed changes to the NFL rules. They decide to ask a sample of 100 players.

   a. The officials choose the first 100 players who volunteer their opinions.

   b. The officials randomly choose 3 or 4 players from each of the 32 teams in the NFL.

   c. The officials have a computer randomly generate a list of 100 players from a database of all NFL players.

The population consists of the players in the NFL.

a. This is a self-selected sample because the players volunteer their opinions. This could result in a biased sample because the players who feel strongly about the rules would be the first ones to volunteer and get their opinions counted.

b. This is a stratified sample because the players are separated by team and randomly chosen from each team. This is not likely to be biased since the players are chosen randomly and are taken from each team.

c. This is a simple random sample because each player has an equally likely chance of being chosen. This is not likely to be biased since the players are chosen randomly.

(B) Administrators at your school want to know if students think that more vegetarian items should be added to the lunch menu.

   a. The administrators survey every 25th student who enters the cafeteria during the lunch period.

   b. The administrators survey the first 50 students who get in the lunch line to buy lunch.

   c. The administrators use a randomly generated list of 50 students from a master list of all students.

The population consists of _____.

a. This is a _____ sample because _____. This method [is/isn't] likely to result in a biased sample because _____

b. This is a _____ sample because _____. This method [is/isn't] likely to result in a biased sample because _____.

c. This is a _____ sample because _____

_____. This method [is/isn't] likely to result in a biased sample because

_____.

Identify the population, classify the sampling methods, and decide whether the sampling methods could result in a biased sample. Explain your reasoning.

3. A local newspaper conducts a survey to find out if adult residents of the city think the use of hand-held cell phones while driving in the city should be banned.

  a. The newspaper sends a text message to a random selection of 1000 subscribers whose cell phones are listed in the paper's subscription database.

  b. Using the 10 neighborhoods into which the city is divided, the newspaper randomly contacts 100 adults living in each of the neighborhoods.

🖋 Explain 2   Making Predictions from a Random Sample

In statistics, you work with data. Data can be **numerical**, such as heights or salaries, or **categorical**, such as eye color or political affiliation. While a statistic like the mean is appropriate for numerical data, an appropriate statistic for categorical data is a **proportion**, which is the relative frequency of a category.

Example 2   A community health center surveyed a small random sample of adults in the community about their exercise habits. The survey asked whether the person engages in regular cardio exercise (running, walking, swimming, or other) and, if so, what the duration and frequency of exercise are. Of the 25 people surveyed, 10 said that they do engage in regular cardio exercise. The table lists the data for those 10 people. Calculate statistics from the sample, and use the statistics to make predictions about the exercise habits of the approximately 5000 adults living in the community.

Type of exercise	Duration (minutes spent exercising)	Frequency (times per week)
Running	30	4
Walking	20	5
Running	40	3
Running	60	6
Swimming	40	4
Other	90	2
Running	30	3
Walking	20	5
Running	30	4
Other	120	1

(A) Calculate the proportion of adults who get regular cardio exercise and the proportion of runners among those who get regular cardio exercise. Use the proportions to predict the number of runners among all adults living in the community.

Proportion of adults who get regular cardio exercise: $\frac{10}{25} = 0.4$ or 40%

Proportion of runners among those who get regular cardio exercise: $\frac{5}{10} = 0.5$ or 50%

To predict the number of runners in the community, multiply the number of adults in the community by the proportion of adults who get regular cardio exercise and then by the proportion of runners among those who get regular cardio exercise.

Predicted number of runners in the community: $5000 \cdot 0.4 \cdot 0.5 = 1000$

(B) Calculate the mean duration of exercise for those who get regular cardio exercise and the mean frequency of exercise for those who get regular cardio exercise. Use the means to predict, for those who get regular cardio exercise, the number of hours spent exercising each week. Show your calculations and include units.

Mean duration of exercise for those who get regular cardio exercise: _____ minutes

Mean frequency of exercise for those who get regular cardio exercise: _____ times per week

To predict the number of hours spent exercising, multiply the mean duration of exercise (in minutes) for those who get regular cardio exercise by the mean frequency of exercise (in times per week) for those who get regular cardio exercise. This product will be in minutes per week. To convert to hours per week, also multiply by the conversion factor $\frac{1 \text{ hour}}{60 \text{ minutes}}$.

Predicted time spent exercising: ☐ minutes · ☐ /week · $\frac{1 \text{ hour}}{60 \text{ minutes}} \approx$ ☐ hours/week

Reflect

4. **Discussion** How much confidence do you have in the predictions made from the results of the survey? Explain your reasoning.

_____

_____

Your Turn

5. A ski resort uses the information gained from scanning season ski passes in lift lines to determine how many days out of each season the pass holders ski and how many lift rides they take each day. The table lists the data for a random sample of 16 pass holders. Calculate the mean number of days skied and the mean number of lift rides taken per day. Use the means to predict the number of lift rides taken per season by a pass holder.

Number of days	10	5	2	14	27	3	18	5
Number of lift rides	12	15	6	18	10	6	15	9
Number of days	4	16	7	12	19	14	25	13
Number of lift rides	11	13	14	10	8	6	15	18

© Houghton Mifflin Harcourt Publishing Company

6. Name a sampling method that is more likely to produce a representative sample and a sampling method that is more likely to produce a biased sample.

_____

_____

7. Why are there different statistics for numerical and categorical data?

_____

_____

_____

_____

8. **Essential Question Check-In** Explain the difference between a parameter and a statistic.

_____

_____

☆ Evaluate: Homework and Practice

- Online Homework
- Hints and Help
- Extra Practice

1. A student council wants to know whether students would like the council to sponsor a mid-winter dance or a mid-winter carnival this year. Classify each sampling method.

   a. Survey every tenth student on the school's roster.

   b. Survey all students in three randomly selected homerooms.

   c. Survey 20 randomly selected freshmen, 20 randomly selected sophomores, 20 randomly selected juniors, and 20 randomly selected seniors.

   d. Survey those who ask the council president for a questionnaire.

   e. Survey a random selection of those who happen to be in the cafeteria at noon.

2. The officers of a neighborhood association want to know whether residents are interested in beautifying the neighborhood and, if so, how much money they are willing to contribute toward the costs involved. The officers are considering two methods for gathering data:

Method A: Call and survey every tenth resident on the association's roster.

Method B: Randomly select and survey 10 residents from among those who come to the neighborhood block party.

   a. Identify the population.

b. Which sampling method is most likely to result in a representative sample of the population? Explain.

c. Describe another sampling method that is likely to result in a representative sample of the population.

d. Describe the categorical and numerical data that the officers of the neighborhood association want to gather.

Decide whether the sampling method could result in a biased sample. Explain your reasoning.

3. On the first day of school, all of the incoming freshmen attend an orientation program. Afterward, the principal wants to learn the opinions of the freshmen regarding the orientation. She decides to ask 25 freshmen as they leave the auditorium to complete a questionnaire.

4. The members of the school drama club want to know how much students are willing to pay for a ticket to one of their productions. They decide that each member of the drama club should ask 5 of his or her friends what they are each willing to pay.

5. A medical conference has 500 participating doctors. The table lists the doctors' specialties. A researcher wants to survey a sample of 25 of the doctors to get their opinions on proposed new rules for health care providers. Explain why it may be better for the researcher to use a stratified sample rather than a simple random sample.

Specialty	Number of Doctors
Dermatology	40
Geriatrics	120
Oncology	140
Pediatrics	100
Surgery	100

6. A researcher wants to conduct a face-to-face survey of 100 farmers in a large agricultural state to get their opinions about the risks and rewards of farming. The researcher has limited time and budget. Explain why it may be better for the researcher to use a cluster sample based on counties in the state rather than a simple random sample.

© Houghton Mifflin Harcourt Publishing Company

Identify the population and the sampling method.

7. A quality control inspector at a computer assembly plant needs to estimate the number of defective computers in a group of 250 computers. He tests 25 randomly chosen computers.

8. The manager of a movie theater wants to know how the movie viewers feel about the new stadium seating at the theater. She asks every 30th person who exits the theater each Saturday night for a month.

9. Eric is interested in purchasing a used sports car. He selects the make and model of the car at a website that locates all used cars of that make and model for sale within a certain distance of his home. The website delivers a list of 120 cars that meet his criteria. Eric randomly selects 10 of those cars and records what type of engine and transmission they have, as shown in the table.

Engine (L = liter)	Transmission
3.6 L V6	Manual
3.6 L V6	Automatic
6.2 L V8	Manual
3.6 L V6	Manual
6.2 L Supercharged V8	Manual
3.6 L V6	Automatic
6.2 L V8	Manual
3.6 L V6	Automatic
3.6 L V6	Manual
6.2 L V8	Automatic

  a. If Eric can only drive cars with automatic transmissions, predict the number of such cars on the website's list. Show your calculations.

  b. Eric knows that the 3.6 L V6 engine takes regular gasoline, but the 6.2 L V8 engine requires premium gasoline. To minimize his fuel costs, he wants a car with the 3.6 L V6 engine. Predict the number of such cars on the website's list. Show your calculations.

  c. Predict the number of cars that have a 3.6 L V6 engine and an automatic transmission. Show your calculations.

© Houghton Mifflin Harcourt Publishing Company

10. A community theater association plans to produce three plays for the upcoming season. The association surveys a random sample of the approximately 7000 households in the community to see if an adult member of the household is interested in attending plays and, if so, what type of plays the person prefers (comedy, drama, or musical), how many members of the household (including the person surveyed) might attend plays, and how many of the three plays those household members might attend. Of the 50 adults surveyed, 12 indicated an interest in attending plays. The table lists the data for those 12 people.

Preferred Type of Play	Number of People Attending	Number of Plays Attending
Comedy	2	1
Musical	3	2
Musical	1	2
Drama	2	3
Comedy	3	2
Comedy	2	3
Musical	4	1
Drama	2	3
Comedy	2	2
Musical	2	3
Comedy	5	1
Drama	1	2

a. Describe the categorical and numerical data gathered in the survey.

b. Calculate the proportion of adults who indicated an interest in attending plays and calculate the proportion of adults who prefer dramas among those who are interested in attending plays. If approximately 15,000 adults live in the community, predict the number of adults who are interested in attending plays that are dramas. Show your calculations.

c. For an adult with an interest in attending plays, calculate the mean number of household members who might attend plays and the mean number of plays that those household members might attend. Round each mean to the nearest tenth. If the theater association plans to sells tickets to the plays for $40 each, predict the amount of revenue from ticket sales. Show your calculations and include units.

11. Match each description of a sample on the left with a sampling technique on the right.

A. A television reporter asks people walking by on the street to answer a question about an upcoming election.

_____ Simple random sample

B. A television reporter randomly selects voting precincts and then contacts voters randomly chosen from a list of registered voters residing in those precincts to ask about an upcoming election.

_____ Self-selected sample

C. A television reporter contacts voters randomly chosen from a complete list of registered voters to ask about an upcoming election.

_____ Convenience sample

D. A television reporter contacts every 100th voter from a complete list of registered voters to ask about an upcoming election.

_____ Systematic sample

E. A television reporter contacts registered voters randomly chosen from every voting precinct to ask about an upcoming election.

_____ Stratified sample

F. A television reporter asks viewers to call in their response to a question about an upcoming election.

_____ Cluster sample

H.O.T. Focus on Higher Order Thinking

12. Critical Thinking A reporter for a high school newspaper asked all members of the school's track team how many miles they run each week.

a. What type of data did the reporter gather?

b. Was the reporter's data-gathering technique a census or a sample? Explain.

c. Are the data representative of the entire student body? Why or why not?

13. Communicate Mathematical Ideas Categorical data can be nominal or ordinal. *Nominal data* refer to categories that do not have any "natural" ordering, while *ordinal data* refer to categories that do have an order. Similarly, numerical data can be discrete or continuous. *Discrete data* are typically counts or scores (which cannot be made more precise), while *continuous data* are typically measurements (which can be made more precise). For each description of a set of data, identify whether the data are nominal, ordinal, discrete, or continuous. Explain your reasoning. Also give another example of the same type of data.

a. A researcher records how many people live in a subject's household.

b. A researcher records the gender of each subject.

c. A researcher records the amount of time each subject spends using an electronic device during a day.

d. A researcher records whether each subject is a young adult, a middle-aged adult, or a senior.

14. Analyze Relationships The grid represents the entire population of 100 trees in an apple orchard. The values in the grid show the number of kilograms of apples produced by each tree during one year. Given the data, obtain three random samples of size 20 from the population and find the mean of each sample. Discuss how the means of those samples compare with the population mean, which is 68.9.

109	52	62	72	110	61	51	50	100	50
54	104	54	111	74	73	77	68	65	66
108	53	27	75	52	117	76	60	64	67
73	36	103	71	67	60	59	26	80	61
38	63	35	112	75	68	51	72	79	62
58	105	55	53	118	57	101	66	116	31
29	57	74	33	102	69	28	71	30	58
39	55	34	120	64	114	70	113	78	63
107	37	56	25	76	70	69	77	30	115
56	40	106	32	119	65	80	78	79	59

© Houghton Mifflin Harcourt Publishing Company

Lesson Performance Task

Think about your school's cafeteria and the food it serves. Suppose you are given the opportunity to conduct a survey about the cafeteria.

    a. Identify the population to be surveyed.

    b. Write one or more survey questions. For each question, state whether it will generate numerical data or categorical data.

    c. Assuming that you aren't able to conduct a census of the population, describe how you could obtain a representative sample of the population.

    d. Suppose you asked a random sample of 25 students in your school whether they were satisfied with cafeteria lunches and how often in a typical week they brought their own lunches. The tables give the results of the survey. If the school has 600 students, use the results to predict the number of students who are satisfied with cafeteria lunches and the number of lunches brought to school in a typical week.

Satisfied with cafeteria lunches?	
Response	**Number**
Yes	18
No	7

Bring own lunches how often in a week?	
Response	**Number**
5 times	2
4 times	1
3 times	4
2 times	2
1 time	4
0 times	12

22.2 Shape, Center, and Spread

Essential Question: Which measures of center and spread are appropriate for a normal distribution, and which are appropriate for a skewed distribution?

⊘ Explore 1 Seeing the Shape of a Distribution

"Raw" data values are simply presented in an unorganized list. Organizing the data values by using the frequency with which they occur results in a **distribution** of the data. A distribution may be presented as a frequency table or as a data display. Data displays for numerical data, such as line plots, histograms, and box plots, involve a number line, while data displays for categorical data, such as bar graphs and circle graphs, do not. Data displays reveal the shape of a distribution.

The table gives data about a random sample of 20 babies born at a hospital.

Baby	Birth Month	Birth Weight (kg)	Mother's Age
1	5	3.3	28
2	7	3.6	31
3	11	3.5	33
4	2	3.4	35
5	10	3.7	39
6	3	3.4	30
7	1	3.5	29
8	4	3.2	30
9	7	3.6	31
10	6	3.4	32

Baby	Birth Month	Birth Weight (kg)	Mother's Age
11	9	3.6	33
12	10	3.5	29
13	11	3.4	31
14	1	3.7	29
15	6	3.5	34
16	5	3.8	30
17	8	3.5	32
18	9	3.6	30
19	12	3.3	29
20	2	3.5	28

(A) Make a line plot for the distribution of birth months.

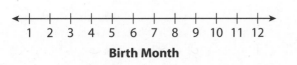

Birth Month

B Make a line plot for the distribution of birth weights.

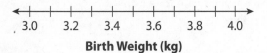
Birth Weight (kg)

C Make a line plot for the distribution of mothers' ages.

27 28 29 30 31 32 33 34 35 36 37 38 39 40
Mother's Age

Reflect

1. Describe the shape of the distribution of birth months.

_____

2. Describe the shape of the distribution of birth weights.

_____

3. Describe the shape of the distribution of mothers' ages.

_____

⊙ Explore 2 Relating Measures of Center and Spread to the Shape of a Distribution

As you saw in the previous Explore, data distributions can have various shapes. Some of these shapes are given names in statistics.

• A distribution whose shape is basically level (that is, it looks like a rectangle) is called a **uniform distribution**.

• A distribution that is mounded in the middle with symmetric "tails" at each end (that is, it looks bell-shaped) is called a **normal distribution**.

• A distribution that is mounded but not symmetric because one "tail" is much longer than the other is called a **skewed distribution**. When the longer "tail" is on the left, the distribution is said to be *skewed left*. When the longer "tail" is on the right, the distribution is said to be *skewed right*.

The figures show the general shapes of normal and skewed distributions.

Skewed left

Symmetric

Skewed right

Shape is one way of characterizing a data distribution. Another way is by identifying the distribution's center and spread. You should already be familiar with the following measures of center and spread:

- The *mean* of n data values is the sum of the data values divided by n. If $x_1, x_2, ..., x_n$ are data values from a sample, then the mean $\bar{x}$ is given by:

$$\bar{x} = \frac{x_1 + x_2 + \cdots + x_n}{n}$$

- The *median* of n data values written in ascending order is the middle value if n is odd, and is the mean of the two middle values if n is even.

- The *standard deviation* of n data values is the square root of the mean of the squared deviations from the distribution's mean. If $x_1, x_2, ..., x_n$ are data values from a sample, then the standard deviation s is given by:

$$s = \sqrt{\frac{(x_1 - \bar{x})^2 + (x_2 - \bar{x})^2 + \cdots + (x_n - \bar{x})^2}{n}}$$

- The *interquartile range*, or IQR, of data values written in ascending order is the difference between the median of the upper half of the data, called the *third quartile* or Q_3, and the median of the lower half of the data, called the *first quartile* or Q_1. So, IQR $= Q_3 - Q_1$.

To distinguish a population mean from a sample mean, statisticians use the Greek letter mu, written μ, instead of $\bar{x}$. Similarly, they use the Greek letter sigma, written σ, instead of s to distinguish a population standard deviation from a sample standard deviation.

(A) Use a graphing calculator to compute the measures of center and the measures of spread for the distribution of baby weights and the distribution of mothers' ages from the previous Explore. Begin by entering the two sets of data into two lists on a graphing calculator as shown.

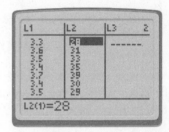

(B) Calculate the "1-Variable Statistics" for the distribution of baby weights. Record the statistics listed. (Note: Your calculator may report the standard deviation with a denominator of $n - 1$ as "s_x" and the standard deviation with a denominator of n as "σ_x." In statistics, when you want to use a sample's standard deviation as an estimate of the population's standard deviation, you use s_x, which is sometimes called the "corrected" sample standard deviation. Otherwise, you can just use σ_x, which you should do in this lesson.)

$\bar{x} = $ _____   Median $= $ _____

$s \approx $ _____   IQR $= Q_3 - Q_1 = $ _____

(C) Calculate the "1-Variable Statistics" for the distribution of mothers' ages. Record the statistics listed.

$\bar{x} = $ _____   Median $= $ _____

$s \approx $ _____   IQR $= Q_3 - Q_1 = $ _____

4. What do you notice about the mean and median for the symmetric distribution (baby weights) as compared with the mean and median for the skewed distribution (mothers' ages)? Explain why this happens.

_____

_____

_____

5. The standard deviation and IQR for the skewed distribution are significantly greater than the corresponding statistics for the symmetric distribution. Explain why this makes sense.

_____

_____

6. Which measures of center and spread would you report for the symmetric distribution? For the skewed distribution? Explain your reasoning.

_____

_____

_____

⊙ Explain 1   Making and Analyzing a Histogram

You can use a graphing calculator to create a histogram of numerical data using the viewing window settings Xmin (the least *x*-value), Xmax (the greatest *x*-value), and Xscl (the width of an interval on the *x*-axis, which becomes the width of the histogram).

Example 1   Use a graphing calculator to make a histogram of the given data and then analyze the graph.

Ⓐ **a.** Make a histogram of the baby weights from Explore 1. Based on the shape of the distribution, identify what type of distribution it is.

Begin by turning on a statistics plot, selecting the histogram option, and entering the list where the data are stored.

Set the viewing window. To obtain a histogram that looks very much like the line plot that you drew for this data set, use the values shown. Xscl determines the width of each bar, so when Xscl = 0.1 and Xmin = 3.15, the first bar covers the interval $3.15 \le x < 3.25$, which captures the weight 3.2 kg.

Draw the histogram by pressing 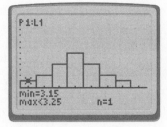 GRAPH. You can obtain the heights of the bars by pressing TRACE and using the arrow keys.

The distribution has a central mound and symmetric tails, so it is a normal distribution.

b. By examining the histogram, determine the percent of the data that are within 1 standard deviation ($s \approx 0.14$) of the mean ($\bar{x} = 3.5$). That is, determine the percent of the data in the interval $3.5 - 0.14 < x < 3.5 + 0.14$, or $3.36 < x < 3.64$. Explain your reasoning.

The bars for x-values that satisfy $3.36 < x < 3.64$ have heights of 4, 6, and 4, so 14 data values out of 20, or 70% of the data, are in the interval.

c. Suppose one of the baby weights is chosen at random. By examining the histogram, determine the probability that the weight is more than 1 standard deviation above the mean. That is, determine the probability that the weight is in the interval $x > 3.5 + 0.14$, or $x > 3.64$. Explain your reasoning.

The bars for x-values that satisfy $x > 3.64$ have heights of 2 and 1, so the probability that the weight is in the interval is $\frac{3}{20} = 0.15$ or 15%.

(B) The table gives the lengths (in inches) of the random sample of 20 babies from Explore 1.

Baby	Baby Length (in.)	Baby	Baby Length (in.)	Baby	Baby Length (in.)
1	17	8	18	15	20
2	21	9	21	16	23
3	20	10	19	17	20
4	19	11	21	18	21
5	22	12	20	19	18
6	19	13	19	20	20
7	20	14	22		

a. Make a histogram of the baby lengths. Based on the shape of the distribution, identify what type of distribution it is.

The distribution has a central mound and symmetric tails, so it is a _____ distribution.

b. By examining the histogram, determine the percent of the data that are within 2 standard deviations ($s \approx 1.4$) of the mean ($\bar{x} = 20$). Explain your reasoning.

The interval for data that are within 2 standard deviations of the mean is

[   ] $< x <$ [   ]. The bars for x-values that satisfy [   ] $< x <$ [   ] have heights

of _____, so ____ data values out of 20, or ____% of the data, are in the interval.

c. Suppose one of the baby lengths is chosen at random. By examining the histogram, determine the probability that the length is less than 2 standard deviations below the mean. Explain your reasoning.

The interval for data that are less than 2 standard deviations below the mean is

$x < \boxed{}$. The only bar for x-values that satisfy $x < \boxed{}$ has a height of _____ , so the

probability that the length is in the interval is $\dfrac{\boxed{}}{20} =$ _____ or _____%.

Your Turn

7. The table lists the test scores of a random sample of 22 students who are taking the same math class.

Student	Math test scores	Student	Math test scores	Student	Math test scores
1	86	9	90	16	83
2	78	10	85	17	83
3	95	11	83	18	70
4	83	12	99	19	73
5	83	13	81	20	79
6	81	14	75	21	85
7	87	15	85	22	83
8	81				

a. Use a graphing calculator to make a histogram of the math test scores. Based on the shape of the distribution, identify what type of distribution it is.

b. By examining the histogram, determine the percent of the data that are within 2 standard deviations $(s \approx 6.3)$ of the mean $(\bar{x} \approx 83)$. Explain your reasoning.

c. Suppose one of the math test scores is chosen at random. By examining the histogram, determine the probability that the test score is less than 2 standard deviations below the mean. Explain your reasoning.

⚙ Explain 2 **Making and Analyzing a Box Plot**

A box plot, also known as a box-and-whisker plot, is based on five key numbers: the minimum data value, the first quartile of the data values, the median (second quartile) of the data values, the third quartile of the data values, and the maximum data value. A graphing calculator will automatically compute these values when drawing a box plot. A graphing calculator also gives you two options for drawing box plots: one that shows outliers and one that does not. For this lesson, choose the second option.

Example 2 Use a graphing calculator to make a box plot of the given data and then analyze the graph.

(A) **a.** Make a box plot of the mothers' ages from Explore 1. How does the box plot show that this skewed distribution is skewed right?

Begin by turning on a statistics plot, selecting the second box plot option, and entering the list where the data are stored.

Set the viewing window. Use the values shown.

Draw the box plot by pressing GRAPH . You can obtain the box plot's five key values by pressing TRACE and using the arrow keys.

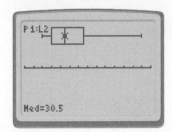

The part of the box to the right of the median is slightly wider than the part to the left, and the "whisker" on the right is much longer than the one on the left, so the distribution is skewed right.

b. Suppose one of the mothers' ages is chosen at random. Based on the box plot and not the original set of data, what can you say is the approximate probability that the age falls between the median, 30.5, and the third quartile, 32.5? Explain your reasoning.

The probability is about 25%, or 0.25, because Q_1, the median, and Q_3 divide the data into four almost-equal parts.

(B) The list gives the ages of a random sample of 16 people who visited a doctor's office one day.

80, 52, 78, 64, 70, 80, 78, 35, 78, 74, 82, 73, 80, 75, 62, 80

a. Make a box plot of the ages. How does the box plot show that this skewed distribution is skewed left?

The part of the box to the _____ of the median is slightly wider than the part to

the _____ and the "whisker" on the _____ is much longer than the one

on the _____, so the distribution is skewed left.

© Houghton Mifflin Harcourt Publishing Company

b. Suppose one of the ages is chosen at random. Based on the box plot and not the original set of data, what can you say is the approximate probability that the age falls between the first quartile, 67, and the third quartile, 80? Explain your reasoning.

The probability is about _____%, or _____, because Q_1, the median, and Q_3

divide the data into _____ almost-equal parts and there are two parts that each

represent about _____% of the data between the first and third quartiles.

Your Turn

8. The list gives the starting salaries (in thousands of dollars) of a random sample of 18 positions at a large company. Use a graphing calculator to make a box plot and then analyze the graph.

40, 32, 27, 40, 34, 25, 37, 39, 40, 37, 28, 39, 35, 39, 40, 43, 30, 35

a. Make a box plot of the starting salaries. How does the box plot show that this skewed distribution is skewed left?

b. Suppose one of the starting salaries is chosen at random. Based on the box plot and not the original set of data, what can you say is the approximate probability that the salary is less than the third quartile, 40? Explain your reasoning.

⊙ Elaborate

9. Explain the difference between a normal distribution and a skewed distribution.

_____

_____

_____

_____

10. Discussion Describe how you can use a line plot, a histogram, and a box plot of a set of data to answer questions about the percent of the data that fall within a specified interval.

_____

_____

_____

_____

_____

_____

_____

11. Essential Question Check-In Why are the mean and standard deviation not appropriate statistics to use with a skewed distribution?

_____

_____

_____

_____

⭐ Evaluate: Homework and Practice

• Online Homework
• Hints and Help
• Extra Practice

1. Make a line plot of the data. Based on the shape of the distribution, identify what type of distribution it is.

a. Ages of children: 4, 9, 12, 8, 7, 8, 7, 10, 8, 9, 6, 8

```
3  4  5  6  7  8  9  10 11 12
```

b. Scores on a test: 80, 78, 70, 77, 75, 77, 76, 66, 77, 76, 75, 77

```
66 67 68 69 70 71 72 73 74 75 76 77 78 79 80
```

c. Salaries (in thousands of dollars) of employees: 35, 35, 36, 40, 37, 36, 37, 35, 35, 38, 36, 34

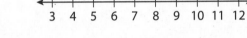

```
32 33 34 35 36 37 38 39 40
```

In Exercises 2–3, use the data in the table. The table gives the heights and weights of a random sample of 14 college baseball players.

Height (in.)	Weight (lb)
70	160
69	165
72	170
70	170
68	150
71	175
70	160
69	165
71	165
70	170
67	155
69	165
71	165
73	185

2. **a.** Find the mean, median, standard deviation, and IQR of the height data.

b. Use a graphing calculator to make a histogram of the height data. Based on the shape of the distribution, identify what type of distribution it is.

c. By examining the histogram of the height distribution, determine the percent of the data that fall within 1 standard deviation of the mean. Explain your reasoning.

d. Suppose one of the heights is chosen at random. By examining the histogram, determine the probability that the height is more than 1 standard deviation above the mean. Explain your reasoning.

3. **a.** Find the mean, median, standard deviation, and IQR of the weight data.

b. Use a graphing calculator to make a histogram of the weight data. Based on the shape of the distribution, identify what type of distribution it is.

c. By examining the histogram, determine the percent of the weight data that are within 2 standard deviations of the mean. Explain your reasoning.

d. Suppose one of the weights is chosen at random. By examining the histogram, determine the probability that the weight is less than 1 standard deviation above the mean. Explain your reasoning.

4. The line plot shows a random sample of resting heart rates (in beats per minute) for 24 adults.

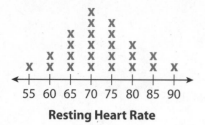

Resting Heart Rate

a. Find the mean, median, standard deviation, and IQR of the heart rates.

b. By examining the line plot, determine the percent of the data that are within 1 standard deviation of the mean. Explain your reasoning.

c. Suppose one of the heart rates is chosen at random. By examining the line plot, determine the probability that the heart rate is more than 1 standard deviation below the mean. Explain your reasoning.

5. The list gives the prices (in thousands of dollars) of a random sample of houses for sale in a large town.

175, 400, 325, 350, 500, 375, 350, 375, 400, 375, 250, 400, 200, 375, 400, 400, 375, 325, 400, 350

a. Find the mean, median, standard deviation, and IQR of the house prices. How do these statistics tell you that the distribution is not symmetric?

b. Use a graphing calculator to make a box plot of the house prices. How does the box plot show that this skewed distribution is skewed left?

c. Suppose one of the house prices is chosen at random. Based on the box plot and not the original set of data, what can you say is the approximate probability that the price falls between the first and the third quartiles? Explain your reasoning.

6. The line plot shows a random sample of the amounts of time (in minutes) that an employee at a call center spent on the phone with customers.

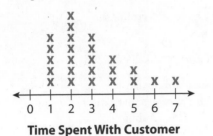

Time Spent With Customer

a. Do you expect the mean to be equal to, less than, or greater than the median? Explain.

b. Find the mean, median, standard deviation, and IQR of the time data. Do these statistics agree with your answer for part a?

c. Use a graphing calculator to make a box plot of the time data. How does the box plot show that the distribution is skewed right?

d. Suppose one of the times spent with a customer is chosen at random. Based on the box plot and not the original set of data, what can you say is the approximate probability that the time is greater than the third quartile? Explain your reasoning.

7. Classify each description as applying to a normal distribution or a skewed distribution.

A. Histogram is mound-shaped with two symmetric tails. ◯ Normal ◯ Skewed

B. Mean and median are equal or almost equal. ◯ Normal ◯ Skewed

C. Box plot has one "whisker" longer than the other. ◯ Normal ◯ Skewed

D. Histogram is mounded with one tail longer than the other. ◯ Normal ◯ Skewed

E. Box plot is symmetric with respect to the median. ◯ Normal ◯ Skewed

F. Mean and median are significantly different. ◯ Normal ◯ Skewed

8. **Explain the Error** A student was given the following data and asked to determine the percent of the data that fall within 1 standard deviation of the mean.

    20, 21, 21, 22, 22, 22, 22, 23, 23, 23, 23, 24, 24, 24, 24, 24, 25, 25, 25, 26, 26, 26, 27, 27, 28

    The student gave this answer: "The interval for data that are within 1 standard deviation of the mean is $24 - 3.5 < x < 24 + 3.5$, or $21.5 < x < 27.5$. The bars for x-values that satisfy $21.5 < x < 27.5$ have heights of 4, 4, 5, 3, 3, and 2, so 21 data values out of 25, or about 84% of the data, are in the interval." Find and correct the student's error.

9. **Analyze Relationships** The list gives the number of siblings that a child has from a random sample of 10 children at a daycare center.

    5, 2, 3, 1, 0, 2, 3, 1, 2, 1

    a. Use a graphing calculator to create a box plot of the data. Does the box plot indicate that the distribution is normal or skewed? Explain.

    b. Find the mean, median, standard deviation, and IQR of the sibling data. What is the relationship between the mean and median?

    c. Suppose that an 11th child at the daycare is included in the random sample, and that child has 1 sibling. How does the box plot change? How does the relationship between the mean and median change?

    d. Suppose that a 12th child at the daycare is included in the random sample, and that child also has 1 sibling. How does the box plot change? How does the relationship between the mean and median change?

e. What is the general rule about the relationship between the mean and median when a distribution is skewed right? What has your investigation of the sibling data demonstrated about this rule?

10. **Draw Conclusions** Recall that a graphing calculator may give two versions of the standard deviation. The population standard deviation, which you can also use for the "uncorrected" sample standard deviation, is $\sigma_x = \sqrt{\dfrac{(x_1 - \bar{x})^2 + (x_2 - \bar{x})^2 + \cdots + (x_n - \bar{x})^2}{n}}$.

The "corrected" sample standard deviation is $s_x = \sqrt{\dfrac{(x_1 - \bar{x})^2 + (x_2 - \bar{x})^2 + \cdots + (x_n - \bar{x})^2}{n - 1}}$.

Write and simplify the ratio $\dfrac{\sigma_x}{s_x}$. Then determine what this ratio approaches as n increases without bound. What does this result mean in terms of finding standard deviations of samples?

Lesson Performance Task

The table gives data about a random sample of 16 cats brought to a veterinarian's office during one week.

Sex	Weight (pounds)	Age (years)
Male	12	11
Female	9	2
Female	8	12
Male	10	15
Female	10	10
Male	11	10
Male	10	11
Male	11	7

Sex	Weight (pounds)	Age (years)
Female	9	5
Male	12	8
Female	7	13
Male	11	11
Female	10	13
Male	13	9
Female	8	12
Female	9	16

a. Find the mean, median, standard deviation, and IQR of the weight data. Do the same for the age data.

b. Use a graphing calculator to make a histogram of the weight data and a separate histogram of the age data. Based on the shape of each distribution, identify what type of distribution it is. Explain your reasoning.

c. By examining the histogram of the weight distribution, determine the percent of the data that fall within 1 standard deviation of the mean. Explain your reasoning.

d. For the age data, $Q_1 = 8.5$ and $Q_3 = 12.5$. By examining the histogram of the age distribution, find the probability that the age of a randomly chosen cat falls between Q_1 and Q_3. Why does this make sense?

e. Investigate whether being male or female has an impact on a cat's weight and age. Do so by calculating the mean weight and age of female cats and the mean weight and age of male cats. For which variable, weight or age, does being male or female have a greater impact? How much of an impact is there?

Essential Question: How can gathering and displaying data help solve real-world problems?

KEY EXAMPLE   *(Lesson 22.1)*

A local community center surveyed a small random sample of people in the community about their time spent volunteering. The survey asked whether the person engaged in regular volunteer work (food kitchen, hospital, community center, or other) and, if so, the duration and frequency of the volunteer work.

Of the 20 people surveyed, 8 said they do engage in regular volunteer work. The table lists the data for those 8 people.

Type of Work	Duration (hours)	Days per Week
Food Kitchen	2	5
Hospital	3	3
Hospital	2	4
Food Kitchen	5	3
Comm. Center	4	5
Hospital	2	4
Other	3	5
Comm. Center	2	4

Key Vocabulary

population *(población)*
census *(censo)*
parameter *(parámetro)*
sample *(muestra)*
sampling statistic *(estadística)*
representative sample
   (muestra representantiva)
biased sample *(muestra no*
   representantiva)
numerical data *(datos*
   numéricos)
categorical data
   (datos categóricos)
proportion *(proporción)*
distribution *(distribución)*
uniform distribution
   (distribución uniforme)
normal distribution
   (distribución normal)
skewed distribution
   (distribución asimétrica)

Calculate statistics from the sample, and use the statistics to make predictions about the volunteering habits of the approximately 10,000 people living in the community.

Proportion of adults who volunteer $= \dfrac{8}{20} = 0.4 = 40\%$

Proportion of hospital volunteers $= \dfrac{3}{8} = 0.375 = 37.5\%$

Use proportion and a verbal model to predict the number of hospital volunteers among all people living in the community.

Total hospital volunteers = Community × Prop. of Volunteers × Prop. of Hospital Volunteers
$$= 10{,}000 \times 0.4 \times 0.375 = 1500$$

KEY EXAMPLE   *(Lesson 22.2)*

Using the volunteer table, make a line plot for the distribution of hours, and a line plot for the distribution of frequency (days per week).

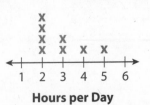

Hours per Day

This line plot is skewed right.

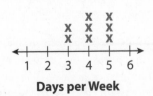

Days per Week

This line plot has a nearly uniform distribution.

A local high school surveys a random sample of students out of a total of approximately 2500 students to see if a student is interested in attending sporting events and, if so, what type of sporting events the person prefers (football, baseball, volleyball, or track), how many friends they would bring along, and how many events they would be willing to attend a year.

Of the 25 students surveyed, 10 indicated an interest in attending sporting events. The table lists the data for those 10 people.

Sporting Event	Number of Friends	Number of Events
Football	3	5
Football	0	6
Baseball	2	4
Volleyball	2	8
Football	5	7
Track	1	3
Football	3	4
Volleyball	2	5
Baseball	4	2
Track	3	3

1. Using the statistics from the sample, create a verbal model to predict the number of students likely to attend a track meet, then predict the total attendance when they bring their friends. *(Lesson 22.1)*

Fruit Nutrition Data

The table compares the nutritional values of ten fruits. Specifically, the table shows how much of the recommended daily allowance of three different nutrients is met by a serving of each fruit.

You want to display the data so you can pick up a piece of fruit and know how it compares nutritionally to the other nine fruits. Make appropriate data representations and use them to describe the distributions for each of these data sets. Then, pick one fruit and use your data representations to compare it with the other fruits.

Start on your own paper by listing information you will need to solve the problem. Then use graphs, numbers, tables, words, or algebra to explain how you reached your conclusion.

Fruit	Percentage of Daily Value		
	Potassium	Fiber	Vitamin C
Apple	7	20	8
Banana	13	12	15
Cantaloupe	7	4	80
Cherries	10	4	15
Orange	7	12	130
Peach	7	8	15
Pear	5	24	10
Pineapple	3	4	50
Strawberries	5	8	160
Watermelon	8	4	25

(Ready) to Go On?

23.1–23.2 Gathering and Displaying Data

- Online Homework
- Hints and Help
- Extra Practice

Use the table for exercises 1–4.

A local business surveys a random sample of about 500 employees to see if they are working overtime and, if so, how many hours per week and how many weeks per month. The company has four types of employees: sales, engineer, manager, and clerical.

The 40 employees surveyed were evenly split between the four employment categories. Ten worked overtime last month. The table lists the data for those 10 people.

Employee	Avg. Overtime/Week	Weeks/Month
Manager	8	3
Manager	10	2
Sales	3	1
Engineer	2	1
Manager	8	2
Clerical	8	2
Sales	4	3
Engineer	3	1
Manager	7	3
Sales	2	2

1. Predict the number of managers working overtime out of the employees of the company.

2. Predict the number of sales people working overtime out of the employees of the company.

3. Create the line plot for the number of weeks per month the sample of employees works overtime.

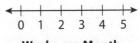

Weeks per Month

ESSENTIAL QUESTION

4. How can gathering and displaying data help a business owner?

Assessment Readiness

1. Consider the equation $y = \frac{3x - 2}{x + 2}$. Is the function defined for the value of x?
   Select Yes or No for A–C.

   A. $x = 2$ ○ Yes   ○ No

   B. $x = -2$ ○ Yes   ○ No

   C. $x = 0$ ○ Yes   ○ No

2. Consider the distribution of data on line plots. Choose True or False for each statement.

   A. A distribution that is "skewed" has
   most of the data in the middle
   with two tails on each side.   ○ True   ○ False

   B. A "uniform" distribution has a data
   distribution that is basically level, though
   it doesn't have to be exactly level.   ○ True   ○ False

   C. A distribution that is "normal"
   looks bell-shaped.   ○ True   ○ False

3. The junior class at a local school would like to survey students to pick a theme for the junior-senior prom. They are considering the following survey methods:

   • Survey every tenth student in the junior and senior classes on the school roster.

   • Survey every fifteenth student on the school roster for freshman through seniors.

   • Survey those who happen to be standing around outside in the morning before the first bell rings.

   Which sampling method would most likely result in a theme that would please those attending the prom? Explain.

4. Solve the equation $2x^2 + 6x + 10 = 0$ for all values of x. Explain the method you used, and why.

Data Distributions

Essential Question: How can you use data distributions to solve real-world problems?

REAL WORLD VIDEO
Regular, vigorous exercise is an important part of maintaining a healthy body weight. Check out some ways we can display and analyze data distributions for body weight in a population.

MODULE PERFORMANCE TASK PREVIEW

BMI and Obesity

Health experts use a variety of statistics to measure the overall health of a population. One of these is body mass index (BMI), which uses a person's weight and height to produce a number that describes whether he or she is overweight, underweight, or normal. How many people are within the normal range? How many are obese? These are weighty questions! An ounce of curiosity is all we will need to figure them out at the end of the module.

Complete these exercises to review skills you will need for this module.

Measures of Center and Spread

• Online Homework
• Hints and Help
• Extra Practice

Example 1   Find the median, mean, and range of these ordered data.

8, 15, 15, 26, 33, 49, 50, 54

Median: $\dfrac{26 + 33}{2} = 29.5$

Mean: $\dfrac{8 + 15 + 15 + 26 + 33 + 49 + 50 + 54}{8} = 31.25$

Range: $54 - 8 = 46$

Find the median, mean, and range.

1.   16, 38, 12, 19, 40

2.   14, 4, 10, 6, 16, 9, 1, 2, 5, 3

3.   15, 8, 12, 1, 10, 2

Normal Distributions

Example 2   The graph shows a normal distribution of Intelligence Quotient (IQ) scores. What percent of the population has an IQ score greater than the mean?

The curve is symmetrical about an IQ score of 100, which is the mean. So 50% of the population has an IQ score greater than the mean.

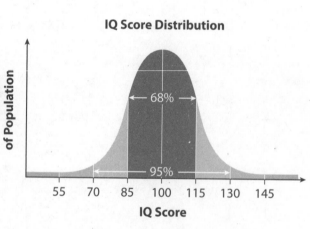

IQ Score Distribution

68%

95%

55 70 85 100 115 130 145

IQ Score

Use the graph to answer the questions.

4.   What percent of the population has an IQ score above 130?

5.   What percent of the population has an IQ score above 115?

6.   What percent of the population has an IQ score between 70 and 85?

23.1 Probability Distributions

Essential Question: What is a probability distribution for a discrete random variable, and how can it be displayed?

Resource Locker

🧭 Explore   Using Simulation to Obtain an Empirical Probability Distribution

A **random variable** is a variable whose value is determined by the outcome of a probability experiment. For example, when you roll a number cube, you can use the random variable X to represent the number you roll. The possible values of X are 1, 2, 3, 4, 5, and 6.

A **probability distribution** is a data distribution that gives the probabilities of the values of a random variable. A probability distribution can be represented by a histogram in which the values of the random variable—that is, the possible outcomes—are on the horizontal axis, and probabilities are on the vertical axis. The probability distribution for rolling a number cube is shown. Notice that it is a uniform distribution.

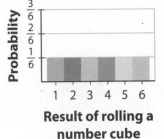

Result of rolling a number cube

When the values of a random variable are discrete, as is the case for rolling a number cube, a histogram for the probability distribution typically shows bars that each have a width of 1 and are centered on a value of the variable. The area of each bar therefore equals the probability of the corresponding outcome, and the combined areas of the bars are the sum of the probabilities, which is 1.

A **cumulative probability** is the probability that a random variable is less than or equal to a given value. You can find cumulative probabilities from a histogram by adding the areas of the bars for all outcomes less than or equal to the given value.

Suppose you flip a coin 5 times in a row. Use a simulation to determine the probability distribution for the number of times the coin lands heads up.

Ⓐ When you flip a coin, the possible outcomes are heads and tails. Use a graphing calculator to generate the integers 0 and 1 randomly, associating each 0 with tails and each 1 with heads.

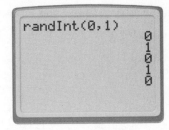

To do the simulation, press MATH and then select the probability (**PRB**) menu. Choose **5:randInt** and enter a 0, a comma, a 1, and a closing parenthesis. Now press ENTER 5 times to generate a group of 0s and 1s. This simulates one trial (that is, one set of 5 coin flips).

Carry out 4 trials and record your results in the table.

Trial	1	2	3	4
Number of heads				

© Houghton Mifflin Harcourt Publishing Company

Ⓑ Report your results to your teacher in order to combine everyone's results. Use the combined class data to complete the table. To find the relative frequency for an outcome, divide the frequency of the outcome by the total number of trials in the class and round to the nearest hundredth.

Number of heads	0	1	2	3	4	5
Frequency						
Relative frequency						

Ⓒ Enter the outcomes (0 through 5) into your calculator as list L_1. Enter the relative frequencies as list L_2. Make a histogram by turning on a statistics plot, selecting the histogram option, and using L_1 for Xlist and L_2 for Freq as shown. Then set the viewing window as shown. Finally, press GRAPH to obtain a histogram like the one shown. Describe the shape of the probability distribution.

_____

_____

1. **Discussion** If you flipped a coin 5 times and got 5 heads, would this cause you to question whether the coin is fair? Why or why not?

_____

_____

⚙ Explain 1   Displaying and Analyzing a Theoretical Probability Distribution

Recall that a binomial experiment involves repeated trials where each trial has only two outcomes: success or failure. The probability of success on each trial is p, and the probability of failure on each trial is $q = 1 - p$. The binomial probability of r successes in n trials is given by $P(X = r) = {}_nC_r \, p^r q^{n-r}$.

> **Example 1**   Calculate all the theoretical probabilities for the given binomial experiment. Then draw a histogram of the probability distribution, observe its shape, and use it to find the specified probabilities.

(A)   A binomial experiment consists of flipping a fair coin for 5 trials where getting heads is considered a success. Find the probability of getting 3 or more heads and the probability of getting at least 1 head.

To calculate the probabilities, set n equal to 5 and let r range from 0 to 5 in ${}_nC_r \, p^r q^{n-r}$. Since the coin is fair, $p = \frac{1}{2}$ and $q = \frac{1}{2}$.

Number of heads	0	1	2	3	4	5
Theoretical probability	$\frac{1}{32}$	$\frac{5}{32}$	$\frac{10}{32}$	$\frac{10}{32}$	$\frac{5}{32}$	$\frac{1}{32}$

Create a histogram.

The distribution is mounded and has symmetric tails, so it is a normal distribution.

The probability of getting 3 or more heads is:

$$P(X \geq 3) = P(X = 3) + P(X = 4) + P(X = 5)$$
$$= \frac{10}{32} + \frac{5}{32} + \frac{1}{32}$$
$$= \frac{16}{32} = 0.5$$

The probability of getting at least 1 head is:

$$P(X \geq 1) = 1 - P(X = 0)$$
$$= 1 - \frac{1}{32}$$
$$= \frac{31}{32} \approx 0.969$$

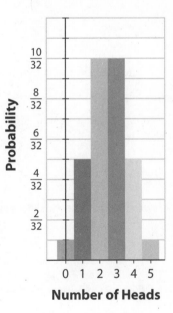

(B) A binomial experiment consists of flipping a biased coin for 5 trials where getting heads is considered a success. The coin lands heads up 75% of the time. Find the probability of getting 3 or more heads and the probability of getting at least 1 head.

To calculate the probabilities, set n equal to 5 and let r range from 0 to 5 in $_nC_r\, p^r q^{n-r}$.

Since the coin is biased such that it lands heads up 75% of the time, $p = \frac{3}{4}$ and $q = \boxed{}$.

Number of heads	0	1	2	3	4	5
Theoretical probability						

Create a histogram.

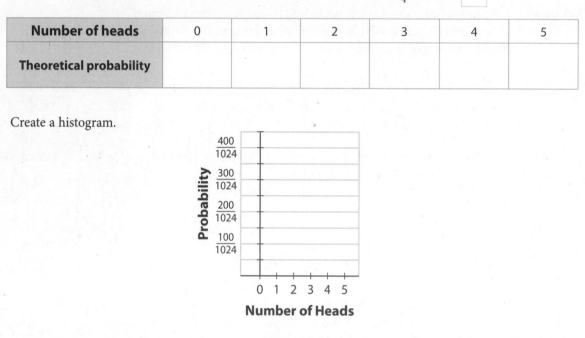

The distribution is mounded and has a tail to the left, so the distribution is skewed _____.

The probability of getting 3 or more heads is:

$$P(X \geq 3) = P(X = 3) + P(X = 4) + P(X = 5)$$

$$= \frac{\boxed{}}{\boxed{}} + \frac{\boxed{}}{\boxed{}} + \frac{\boxed{}}{\boxed{}}$$

$$= \frac{\boxed{}}{\boxed{}} \approx \boxed{}$$

The probability of getting at least 1 head is:
$$P(X \geq 1) = 1 - P(X = 0)$$

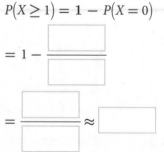

$$= 1 - \frac{\boxed{}}{\boxed{}}$$

$$= \frac{\boxed{}}{\boxed{}} \approx \boxed{}$$

2. Why are the probabilities in the histogram you made in the Explore different from the probabilities given in the histogram from Part A?

_____

_____

3. For which coin, the fair coin in Part A or the biased coin in Part B, is flipping a coin 5 times and getting 5 heads more likely to occur? Explain.

_____

_____

_____

4. Discussion Can you definitively conclude whether a coin that results in repeated heads when flipped is fair or biased? What might make you favor one conclusion over the other?

_____

_____

_____

Your Turn

Calculate all the theoretical probabilities for the given binomial experiment. Then draw a histogram of the probability distribution, observe its shape, and use it to find the specified probabilities.

5. A binomial experiment consists of flipping a biased coin for 4 trials where getting heads is considered a success. The coin lands heads up 40% of the time. Find the probability of getting 2 or more heads and the probability of getting fewer than 4 heads.

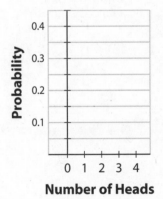

Number of heads	0	1	2	3	4
Theoretical probability					

6. A binomial experiment consists of flipping a biased coin for 4 trials where getting tails is considered a success. The coin lands heads up 40% of the time. Find the probability of getting 2 or more tails and the probability of getting fewer than 4 tails.

Number of heads	0	1	2	3	4
Theoretical probability					

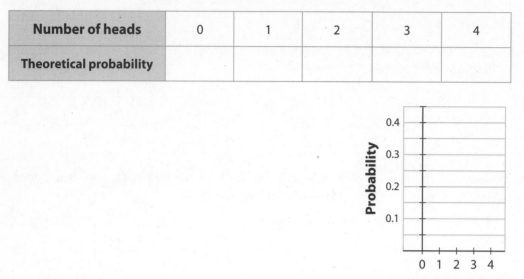

Elaborate

7. What is a random variable, and what makes a random variable discrete?

_____

_____

_____

8. How can a histogram for a probability distribution be used to calculate a cumulative probability?

_____

_____

_____

9. **Essential Question Check-In** What is a probability distribution for a discrete random variable?

_____

_____

_____

☆ Evaluate: Homework and Practice

• Online Homework
• Hints and Help
• Extra Practice

1. A spinner has three equal sections, labeled 1, 2, and 3. You spin the spinner twice and find the sum of the two numbers the spinner lands on.

   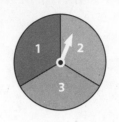

   a. Let X be a random variable that represents the sum of the two numbers. What are the possible values of X?

   b. Complete the table.

Sum					
Probability					

   c. Make a histogram of the probability distribution.

   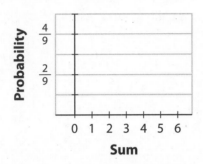

   d. What is the probability that the sum is not 2? How is this probability represented in the histogram?

2. You roll two number cubes at the same time. Let X be a random variable that represents the absolute value of the difference of the numbers rolled.

a. What are the possible values of X?

b. Complete the table.

Absolute difference					
Probability					

c. Is this probability distribution symmetric? Why or why not?

d. Find the probability of getting a difference greater than 3.

3. A trick coin is designed to land heads up with a probability of 80%. You flip the coin 7 times.

a. Complete the table?

Number of heads							
Theoretical probability							

b. Make a histogram of the probability distribution.

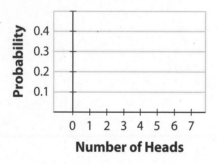

c. What is the probability of getting 6 or 7 heads?

d. What is the probability of getting 4 or more heads?

e. Which is greater, the probability of getting an even number of heads or the probability of getting an odd number of heads?

f. Suppose you flip a coin 7 times and get 7 heads. Based on what you know now, would you question whether the coin is fair? Why or why not?

4. You flip a coin 4 times in a row. The histogram shows the theoretical probability distribution for this situation.

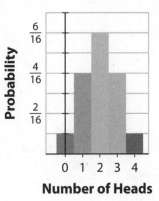

a. What is the probability of getting 3 or more heads?

b. What is the probability of getting at most 2 heads?

c. How do you know that the coin is fair?

5. A spinner has 4 equal sections that are labeled 1, 2, 3, and 4. You spin the spinner twice and find the sum of the 2 numbers it lands on. Let X be a random variable that represents the sum of the 2 numbers.

a. Complete the table.

Sum	2	3	4	5	6	7	8
Frequency	1	2	3	4	3	2	1
Probability							

b. Make a histogram of the probability distribution.

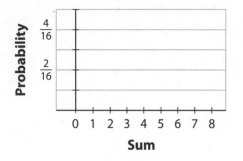

c. What is the probability of getting a sum of 6 or more?

d. Without actually calculating any probabilities, determine the relationship between $P(X > 5)$ and $P(X < 5)$. Explain your reasoning.

6. You roll 2 number cubes at the same time. Let X be a random variable that represents the sum of the numbers rolled.

a. Complete the table to show the sums that are possible. In the table, the row heads are the numbers that are possible on one number cube, and the column heads are the numbers that are possible on the other number cube.

	1	2	3	4	5	6
1						
2						
3						
4						
5						
6						

b. Complete the second row of the table to show the number of ways that you can get each sum. Then find the probability of each sum to complete the third row.

Sum	2	3	4	5	6	7	8	9	10	11	12
Frequency	1										
Probability	$\frac{1}{36}$										

c. Make a histogram of the probability distribution.

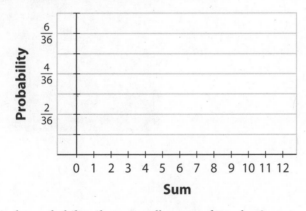

d. What is the probability that you roll a sum of 5 or less?

e. What is the probability that you roll a sum of 12 four times in a row? If this happened, would you question whether the number cubes are fair?

7. A fair coin is flipped 6 times. Match each specified probability on the left with its value on the right. (A value on the right may apply to more than one specified probability on the left.)

A. The probability of getting at least 4 heads

B. The probability of getting no more than 1 head

C. The probability of getting 1 or 2 heads

D. The probability of getting no more than 2 heads

E. The probability of getting an even number of heads

F. The probability of getting an odd number of heads

$$\frac{7}{64}$$

$$\frac{21}{64}$$

$$\frac{11}{32}$$

$$\frac{1}{2}$$

H.O.T. Focus on Higher Order Thinking

8. Represent Real-World Situations About 19.4% of the U.S. population that is 25 years old and over have a bachelor's degree only, and 10.5% have an advanced degree.

a. Find the probability that of 6 randomly selected people who are 25 years old or over, 4 have at least a bachelor's degree.

b. Find the probability that of 6 randomly selected people who are 25 years old or over, 4 do not have even a bachelor's degree.

c. Suppose all 6 of 6 randomly selected people have advanced degrees. Would you question the probability model? Explain.

9. **Justify Reasoning** Describe a way to get fair results from a coin that you suspect is biased. Explain how you know that the process is fair.

10. **Construct Arguments** Use the formula $P(X = r) = {}_nC_r \, p^r \, q^{n-r}$ for a binomial experiment to explain why the probability distribution for the number of heads obtained when a fair coin is flipped n times is symmetric.

Lesson Performance Task

According to the U.S. Census, in 2010 the number of people 18 years old or over in the U.S. was 229.1 million, and of those people, 129.5 million were married.

    a. Find the probability that of 10 randomly selected people 18 years old or over, 6 are married.

    b. Consider a survey where all 10 of the people surveyed are married. What conclusion might you draw about that survey?

© Houghton Mifflin Harcourt Publishing Company

23.2 Normal Distributions

Essential Question: How do you find percents of data and probabilities of events associated with normal distributions?

Resource Locker

⊘ Explore 1   Substituting a Normal Curve for a Symmetric Histogram

The table below gives the mass (in kilograms) of 20 babies at birth. You know that there are 20 babies, because that is the sum of the frequencies. You also know that the masses are normally distributed because the mass with the greatest frequency occurs at the center of the distribution and the other frequencies taper off symmetrically from that center. The mean of the data is 3.5 kg, and the standard deviation is 0.14 kg.

You can use a graphing calculator to draw a smooth bell-shaped curve, called a *normal curve*, that captures the shape of the histogram. A normal curve has the property that the area under the curve (and above the x-axis) is 1. This means that you must adjust the heights of the bars in the histogram so that the sum of the areas of the bars is 1.

(A) Find the relative frequency of each mass.

Mass (kg)	3.2	3.3	3.4	3.5	3.6	3.7	3.8
Frequency	1	2	4	6	4	2	1
Relative frequency	$\frac{1}{20} = 0.05$						
Adjusted bar height	$\frac{0.05}{0.1} = 0.5$						

(B) What is the sum of the relative frequencies? _____

(C) For a given mass, the relative frequency is the area that you want the bar to have. Since you used a bar width of 0.1 when you created the histogram, the area of the bar is $0.1h$ where h is the height of the bar. You want $0.1h$ to equal the relative frequency f, so solve $0.1h = f$ for h to find the adjusted bar height. Complete this row in the table.

(D) Enter each mass from the table into L_1 on your graphing calculator. Then enter each adjusted bar height into L_2.

(E) Turn on a statistics plot and select the histogram option. For Xlist, enter L_1. For Freq, enter L_2. Set the graphing window as shown. Then press GRAPH.

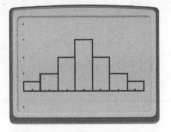

(F) Your calculator has a built-in function called a *normal probability density function*, which you can access by pressing 2nd VARS and selecting the first choice from the DISTR (distribution) menu. When entering this function to be graphed, you must include the mean and standard deviation of the distribution by entering **normalpdf(X, 3.5, 0.14)**. When you press GRAPH, the calculator will draw a normal curve that fits the histogram.

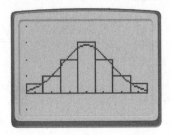

Reflect

1. Describe the end behavior of the normal probability density function.

_____

2. **Discussion** If the area under the normal curve is 1, then what is the area under the curve to the left of the mean, 3.5? Describe how to obtain this area using the bars in the histogram. Show that your method gives the correct result.

_____

_____

3. Explain how you can use the bars in the histogram to estimate the area under the curve within 1 standard deviation of the mean, which is the interval from $3.5 - 0.14 = 3.36$ to $3.5 + 0.14 = 3.64$ on the x-axis. Then find the estimate.

_____

_____

4. Explain how you can use the bars in the histogram to estimate the area under the curve within 2 standard deviations of the mean, which is the interval from $3.5 - 2(0.14) = 3.22$ to $3.5 + 2(0.14) = 3.78$ on the x-axis. Then find the estimate.

_____

_____

⏺ Explain 1 Finding Areas Under a Normal Curve

All normal curves have the following properties, sometimes collectively called the 68–95–99.7 rule:

- 68% of the data fall within 1 standard deviation of the mean.
- 95% of the data fall within 2 standard deviations of the mean.
- 99.7% of the data fall within 3 standard deviations of the mean.

A normal curve's symmetry allows you to separate the area under the curve into eight parts and know the percent of the data in each part.

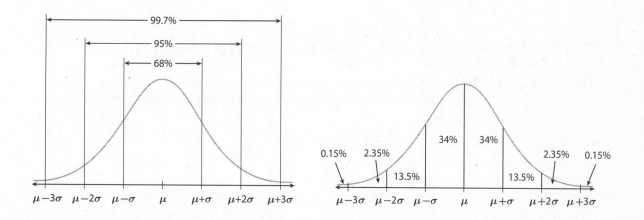

Example 1 **Suppose the heights (in inches) of men (ages 20–29) years old in the United States are normally distributed with a mean of 69.3 inches and a standard deviation of 2.92 inches. Find each of the following.**

(A) The percent of men who are between 63.46 inches and 75.14 inches tall.

63.46 inches is 5.84 inches, or 2 standard deviations, below the mean.

75.14 inches is 5.84 inches, or 2 standard deviations, above the mean.

95% of the data in a normal distribution fall within 2 standard deviations of the mean.

So, 95% of males are between 63.46 inches and 75.14 inches tall.

(B) The percent of men who are taller than 72.22 inches.

72.22 inches is ☐ inches, or _____ standard deviation(s), above the mean.

When the area under a normal curve is separated into eight parts, the parts that satisfy the condition that the height will be greater than 72.22 inches have percents of _____ .

The sum of these percents is ____%.

So, ☐ % of males are taller than 72.22 inches.

Suppose the heights (in inches) of men (ages 20–29) in the United States are normally distributed with a mean of 69.3 inches and a standard deviation of 2.92 inches. Find each of the following.

5. The percent of men who are between 60.54 inches and 78.06 inches tall.

6. The percent of men who are shorter than 60.54 inches.

⚙ Explain 2 Using the Standard Normal Distribution

The **standard normal distribution** has a mean of 0 and a standard deviation of 1. A data value x from a normal distribution with mean μ and standard deviation σ can be standardized by finding its **z-score** using the formula $z = \frac{x - \mu}{\sigma}$.

Areas under the standard normal curve to the left of a given z-score have been computed and appear in the standard normal table below. This table allows you to find a greater range of percents and probabilities than you can using μ and multiples of σ. For example, the area under the curve to the left of the z-score 1.3 is 0.9032. (In the table, "0.0000+" means slightly more than 0, and "1.0000−" means slightly less than 1.)

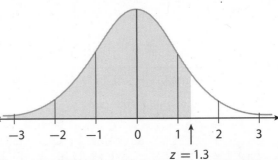

$z = 1.3$

Standard Normal Table										
z	.0	.1	.2	.3	.4	.5	.6	.7	.8	.9
−3	0.0013	0.0010	0.0007	0.0005	0.0003	0.0002	0.0002	0.0001	0.0001	0.0000+
−2	0.0228	0.0179	0.0139	0.0107	0.0082	0.0062	0.0047	0.0035	0.0026	0.0019
−1	0.1587	0.1357	0.1151	0.0968	0.0808	0.0668	0.0548	0.0446	0.0359	0.0287
−0	0.5000	0.4602	0.4207	0.3821	0.3446	0.3085	0.2743	0.2420	0.2119	0.1841
0	0.5000	0.5398	0.5793	0.6179	0.6554	0.6915	0.7257	0.7580	0.7881	0.8159
1	0.8413	0.8643	0.8849	0.9032	0.9192	0.9332	0.9452	0.9554	0.9641	0.9713
2	0.9772	0.9821	0.9861	0.9893	0.9918	0.9938	0.9953	0.9965	0.9974	0.9981
3	0.9987	0.9990	0.9993	0.9995	0.9997	0.9998	0.9998	0.9999	0.9999	1.000−

Example 2 Suppose the heights (in inches) of women (ages 20–29) in the United States are normally distributed with a mean of 64.1 inches and a standard deviation of 2.75 inches. Find the percent of women who are no more than 65 inches tall and the probability that a randomly chosen woman is between 60 inches and 63 inches tall.

🧩 Analyze Information

The mean of the heights is _____ inches.

The standard deviation of the heights is _____ inches.

Formulate a Plan

Convert the heights to _____ and use the _____ to find the probabilities needed.

Solve

First, find the percent of women who are no more than 65 inches tall.

Convert 65 to a z-score (to the nearest tenth): $z_{65} = \dfrac{65 - \mu}{\sigma} = \dfrac{65 - \boxed{}}{\boxed{}} \approx \boxed{}$

Recognize that the phrase "no more than 65 inches" means that $z \le z_{65}$. Read the decimal from the appropriate row and column of the standard normal table: _____

Write the decimal as a percent: _____

Next, find the probability that a randomly chosen woman is between 60 inches and 63 inches tall.

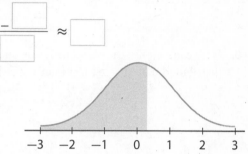

Convert 60 to a z-score: $z_{60} = \dfrac{60 - \mu}{\sigma} = \dfrac{60 - \boxed{}}{\boxed{}} \approx \boxed{}$

Convert 63 to a z-score: $z_{63} = \dfrac{63 - \mu}{\sigma} = \dfrac{63 - \boxed{}}{\boxed{}} = \boxed{}$

Because the standard normal table gives areas under the standard normal curve to the left of a given z-score, you find $P(z_{60} \le z \le z_{63})$ by subtracting $P(z \le z_{60})$ from $P(z \le z_{63})$. Complete the following calculation using the appropriate values from the table:

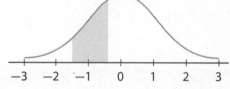

$P(z_{60} \le z \le z_{63}) = P(z \le z_{63}) - P(z \le z_{60}) =$ _____

Write the decimal as a percent: _____

Justify and Evaluate

65 inches is slightly _____ than the mean height. Since all the heights up to the mean represent _____ % of the data, it makes sense that all the heights up to 65 inches are slightly _____ than 50%. Heights from 60–63 inches are within the area for heights less than 65 inches but there are fewer, so it makes sense that the probability is _____ than 50%.

Your Turn

Suppose the heights (in inches) of adult females (ages 20–29) in the United States are normally distributed with a mean of 64.1 inches and a standard deviation of 2.75 inches.

7. Find the percent of women who are at least 66 inches tall.

8. Find the percent of women who are less than or equal to 61.6 inches tall.

9. Explain how you know that the area under a normal curve between $\mu + \sigma$ and $\mu + 2\sigma$ represents 13.5% of the data if you know that the percent of the data within 1 standard deviation of the mean is 68% and the percent of the data within 2 standard deviations of the mean is 95%.

_____

_____

_____

10. How can you use the 68-95-99.7 rule and the symmetry of a normal curve to find the percent of normally distributed data that are less than 1 standard deviation above the mean?

_____

_____

_____

_____

11. **Essential Question Check-In** Explain what a z-score is and how it's used.

_____

_____

_____

⭐ Evaluate: Homework and Practice

• Online Homework
• Hints and Help
• Extra Practice

1. The first calculator screen shows the probability distribution when 6 coins are flipped and the number of heads is counted. The second screen shows the probability distribution of the number of correct answers given by a group of people on a 6-question quiz. For which distribution is it reasonable to use a normal curve as an approximation? Why?

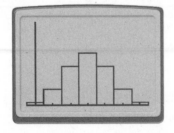

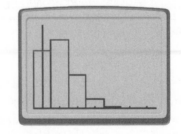

A college-entrance exam is designed so that scores are normally distributed with a mean of 500 and a standard deviation of 100.

2. What percent of exam scores are between 400 and 600?

3. What is the probability that a randomly chosen exam score is above 600?

4. What is the probability that a randomly chosen exam score is less than 300 or greater than 700?

5. What is the probability that a randomly chosen exam score is above 300?

Flight 202's arrival time is normally distributed with a mean arrival time of 4:30 p.m. and a standard deviation of 15 minutes. Find the probability that a randomly chosen arrival time is within the given time period.

6. After 4:45 p.m.

7. Between 4:15 p.m. and 5:00 p.m.

8. Between 3:45 p.m. and 4:30 p.m.

9. By 4:45 p.m.

Suppose the scores on a test given to all juniors in a school district are normally distributed with a mean of 74 and a standard deviation of 8. Find each of the following using the standard normal table.

10. Find the percent of juniors whose score is no more than 90.

11. Find the percent of juniors whose score is between 58 and 74.

12. Find the percent of juniors whose score is at least 74.

13. Find the probability that a randomly chosen junior has a score above 82.

14. Find the probability that a randomly chosen junior has a score between 66 and 90.

15. Find the probability that a randomly chosen junior has a score below 74.

Graphing Calculator On a graphing calculator, you can use the function normalcdf(lower bound, upper bound, μ, σ) on the DISTR menu to find the area under a normal curve for values of x between a specified lower bound and a specified upper bound. You can use $-1\text{E}99$ as the lower bound to represent negative infinity and $1\text{E}99$ as the upper bound to represent positive infinity. Suppose that cans of lemonade mix have amounts of lemonade mix that are normally distributed with a mean of 350 grams and a standard deviation of 4 grams. Use this information and a graphing calculator to answer each question.

16. What percent of cans have less than 338 grams of lemonade mix?

17. What is the probability that a randomly chosen can has between 342 grams and 350 grams of lemonade mix?

18. What is the probability that a randomly chosen can has less than 342 grams or more than 346 grams of lemonade mix?

Spreadsheet In a spreadsheet, you can use the function NORM DIST(upper bound, μ, σ, TRUE) to find the area under a normal curve for values of x less than or equal to a specified upper bound. Suppose the heights of all the children in a state are normally distributed with a mean of 45 inches and a standard deviation of 6 inches. Use this information and a spreadsheet to answer each question.

19. What is the probability that a randomly chosen child is less than 40 inches tall?

20. What is the probability that a randomly chosen child is greater than 47 inches tall?

21. What percent of children are between 50 and 53 inches tall?

22. What is the probability that a randomly chosen child is less than 38 inches tall or more than 51 inches tall?

23. Explain the Error A student was asked to describe the relationship between the area under a normal curve for all x-values less than a and the area under the normal curve for all x-values greater than a. The student's response was "Both areas are 0.5 because the curve is symmetric." Explain the student's error.

24. Make a Conjecture A local orchard packages apples in bags. When full, the bags weigh 5 pounds each and contain a whole number of apples. The weights are normally distributed with a mean of 5 pounds and a standard deviation of 0.25 pound. An inspector weighs each bag and rejects all bags that weigh less than 5 pounds. Describe the shape of the distribution of the weights of the bags that are not rejected.

25. Analyze Relationships A biologist is measuring the lengths of frogs in a certain location. The lengths of 20 frogs are shown. If the mean is 7.4 centimeters and the standard deviation is 0.8 centimeter, do the data appear to be normally distributed? Complete the table and explain.

Length (cm)				
7.5	5.8	7.9	7.6	8.1
7.9	7.1	5.9	8.4	7.3
7.1	6.4	8.3	8.4	6.7
8.1	7.8	5.9	6.8	8.1

z	Area $\leq z$	x	Values $\leq x$	
			Projected	Actual
−2	0.02	5.8	$0.02 \cdot 20 = 0.4 \approx 0$	1
−1	0.16	6.6		
0	0.5			
1	0.84	8.2		
2	0.98			

© Houghton Mifflin Harcourt Publishing Company • Image Credits: ©Irina Schmidt/Shutterstock

Lesson Performance Task

Suppose a nurse records the temperatures of healthy men and women. The table represents the means and standard deviations of the data.

	Women	Men
°F	98.4 ± 0.7 °F	98.1 ± 0.7 °F
°C	36.9 ± 0.4 °C	36.7 ± 0.4 °C

A. What is the range of temperatures for 1, 2, and 3 standard deviations for both women and men?

(Give temperatures in both degrees Fahrenheit and degrees Celsius.)

B. Assuming a normal distribution, find the probability that a randomly selected man's temperature is between 96.7 °F and 97.4 °F.

C. A fever is considered medically significant if body temperature reaches 100.4 °F (38 °C). What can you observe about this temperature?

23.3 Sampling Distributions

Essential Question: How is the mean of a sampling distribution related to the corresponding population mean or population proportion?

Explore 1 Developing a Distribution of Sample Means

The tables provide the following data about the first 50 people to join a new gym: member ID number, age, and sex.

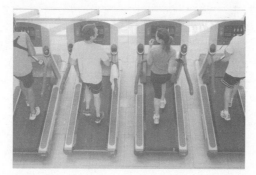

ID	Age	Sex	ID	Age	Sex	ID	Age	Sex	ID	Age	Sex	ID	Age	Sex
1	30	M	11	38	F	21	74	F	31	32	M	41	46	M
2	48	M	12	24	M	22	21	M	32	28	F	42	34	F
3	52	M	13	48	F	23	29	F	33	35	M	43	44	F
4	25	F	14	45	M	24	48	M	34	49	M	44	68	M
5	63	F	15	28	F	25	37	M	35	18	M	45	24	F
6	50	F	16	39	M	26	52	F	36	56	F	46	34	F
7	18	F	17	37	F	27	25	F	37	48	F	47	55	F
8	28	F	18	63	F	28	44	M	38	38	F	48	39	M
9	72	M	19	20	M	29	29	F	39	52	F	49	40	F
10	25	F	20	81	F	30	66	M	40	33	F	50	30	F

(A) Enter the age data into a graphing calculator and find the mean age μ and standard deviation σ for the population of the gym's first 50 members. Round each statistic to the nearest tenth.

_____

(B) Use a graphing calculator's random number generator to choose a sample of 5 gym members. Find the mean age $\overline{x}$ for your sample. Round to the nearest tenth.

_____

(C) Report your sample mean to your teacher. As other students report their sample means, create a class histogram. To do so, shade a square above the appropriate interval as each sample mean is reported. For sample means that lie on an interval boundary, shade a square on the interval to the *right*. For instance, if the sample mean is 39.5, shade a square on the interval from 39.5 to 40.5.

Make your own copy of the class histogram using the grid shown.

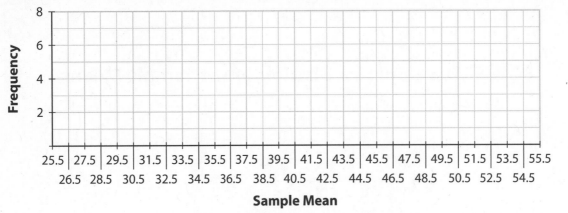

Sample Mean

(D) Calculate the mean of the sample means, $\mu_{\bar{x}}$, and the standard deviation of the sample means, $\sigma_{\bar{x}}$.

_____

(E) Now use a graphing calculator's random number generator to choose a sample of 15 gym members. Find the mean for your sample. Round to the nearest tenth.

_____

(F) Report your sample mean to your teacher. As other students report their sample means, create a class histogram and make your own copy of it.

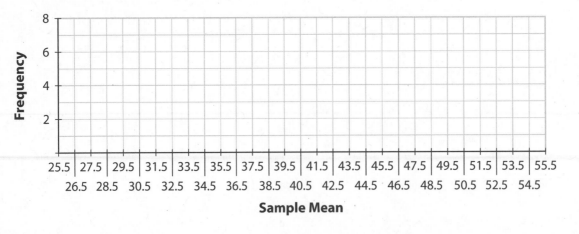

Sample Mean

(G) Calculate the mean of the sample means, $\mu_{\bar{x}}$, and the standard deviation of the sample means, $\sigma_{\bar{x}}$.

_____

1. In the class histograms, how does the mean of the sample means compare with the population mean?

   _____

2. What happens to the standard deviation of the sample means as the sample size increases?

   _____

3. What happens to the shape of the histogram as the sample size increases?

   _____

Explore 2 Developing a Distribution of Sample Proportions

Use the tables of gym membership data from Explore 1. This time you will develop a sampling distribution based on a sample proportion rather than a sample mean.

Ⓐ Find the proportion p of female gym members in the population.

   _____

Ⓑ Use a graphing calculator's random number generator to choose a sample of 5 gym members. Find the proportion $\hat{p}$ of female gym members for your sample.

   _____

Ⓒ Report your sample proportion to your teacher. As other students report their sample proportions, create a class histogram and make your own copy of it.

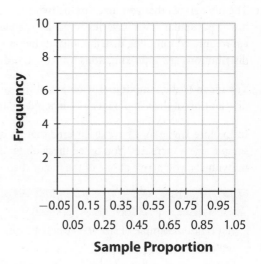

Ⓓ Calculate the mean of the sample proportions, $\mu_{\hat{p}}$, and the standard deviation of the sample proportions, $\sigma_{\hat{p}}$. Round to the nearest hundredth.

   _____

Ⓔ Now use your calculator's random number generator to choose a sample of 10 gym members. Find the proportion of female members $\hat{p}$ for your sample.

   _____

(F) Report your sample proportion to your teacher. As other students report their sample proportions, create a class histogram and make your own copy of it.

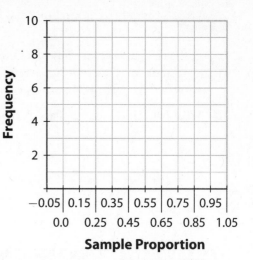

(G) Calculate the mean of the sample proportions, $\mu_{\hat{p}}$, and the standard deviation of the sample proportions, $\sigma_{\hat{p}}$. Round to the nearest hundredth.

_____

Reflect

4. In the class histograms, how does the mean of the sample proportions compare with the population proportion?

_____

5. What happens to the standard deviation of the sample proportions as the sample size increases?

_____

🔑 Explain 1 Using the Sampling Distribution of the Sample Mean

The histograms that you made in the two Explores are *sampling distributions*. A **sampling distribution** shows how a particular statistic varies across all samples of n individuals from the same population. In Explore 1, you approximated sampling distributions of the sample mean, $\bar{x}$, for samples of size 5 and 15. (The reason your sampling distributions are approximations is that you did not find *all* samples of a given size.)

The mean of the sampling distribution of the sample mean is denoted $\mu_{\bar{x}}$. The standard deviation of the sampling distribution of the sample mean is denoted $\sigma_{\bar{x}}$ and is also called the **standard error of the mean**.

In Explore 1, you may have discovered that $\mu_{\bar{x}}$ is close to $\bar{x}$ regardless of the sample size and that $\sigma_{\bar{x}}$ decreases as the sample size n increases. You based these observations on simulations. When you consider all possible samples of n individuals, you arrive at one of the major theorems of statistics.

Properties of the Sampling Distribution of the Sample Mean

If a random sample of size n is selected from a population with mean μ and standard deviation σ, then

1. $\mu_{\bar{x}} = \mu$,

2. $\sigma_{\bar{x}} = \dfrac{\sigma}{\sqrt{n}}$, and

3. The sampling distribution of the sample mean is normal if the population is normal; for all other populations, the sampling distribution of the mean approaches a normal distribution as n increases.

The third property stated above is known as the Central Limit Theorem.

Example 1 Boxes of Cruncho cereal have a mean mass of 323 grams with a standard deviation of 20 grams.

(A) For random samples of 36 boxes, what interval centered on the mean of the sampling distribution captures 95% of the sample means?

Write the given information about the population and a sample.

$$\mu = 323 \qquad \sigma = 20 \qquad n = 36$$

Find the mean of the sampling distribution of the sample mean and the standard error of the mean.

$$\mu_{\bar{x}} = \mu = 323 \qquad \sigma_{\bar{x}} = \frac{\sigma}{\sqrt{n}} = \frac{20}{\sqrt{36}} = \frac{20}{6} \approx 3.3$$

The sampling distribution of the sample mean is approximately normal. In a normal distribution, 95% of the data fall within 2 standard deviations of the mean.

$$\mu_{\bar{x}} - 2\sigma_{\bar{x}} = 323 - 2(3.3) = 316.4 \qquad \mu_{\bar{x}} + 2\sigma_{\bar{x}} = 323 + 2(3.3) = 329.6$$

So, for random samples of 36 boxes, 95% of the sample means fall between 316.4 grams and 329.6 grams.

(B) What is the probability that a random sample of 25 boxes has a mean mass of at most 325 grams?

Write the given information about the population and the sample.

$$\mu = \boxed{} \qquad \sigma = \boxed{} \qquad n = \boxed{}$$

Find the mean of the sampling distribution of the sample mean and the standard error of the mean.

$$\mu_{\bar{x}} = \mu = \boxed{} \qquad \sigma_{\bar{x}} = \frac{\sigma}{\sqrt{n}} = \frac{\boxed{}}{\sqrt{\boxed{}}} = \frac{\boxed{}}{\boxed{}} = \boxed{}$$

The sampling distribution of the sample mean is approximately normal. Use a graphing calculator to find $P(\bar{x} \leq 325)$.

$$P(\bar{x} \leq 325) = \text{normalcdf}\left(-1\text{E}99, \boxed{}, \boxed{}, \boxed{}\right) \approx \boxed{}$$

So, the probability that the random sample has a mean mass of at most 325 grams is about _____.

Your Turn

Boxes of Cruncho cereal have a mean mass of 323 grams with a standard deviation of 20 grams.

6. For random samples of 50 boxes, what interval centered on the mean of the sampling distribution captures 99.7% of the sample means?

7. What is the probability that a random sample of 100 boxes has a mean mass of at least 320 grams?

Using the Sampling Distribution of the Sample Proportion

When you work with the sampling distribution of a sample proportion, p represents the proportion of individuals in the population that have a particular characteristic (that is, the proportion of "successes") and $\hat{p}$ is the proportion of successes in a sample. The mean of the sampling distribution of the sample proportion is denoted $\mu_{\hat{p}}$. The standard deviation of the sampling distribution of the sample proportion is denoted $\sigma_{\hat{p}}$ and is also called the **standard error of the proportion**.

Properties of the Sampling Distribution of the Sample Proportion

If a random sample of size n is selected from a population with proportion p of successes, then

1. $\mu_{\hat{p}} = p,$

2. $\sigma_{\hat{p}} = \sqrt{\dfrac{p(1-p)}{n}},$ and

3. if both np and $n(1-p)$ are at least 10, then the sampling distribution of the sample proportion is approximately normal.

Example 2 **40% of the students at a university live off campus. When sampling from this population, consider "successes" to be students who live off campus.**

(A) For random samples of 50 students, what interval centered on the mean of the sampling distribution captures 95% of the sample proportions?

Write the given information about the population and a sample.

$p = 0.4 \qquad n = 50$

Find the mean of the sampling distribution of the sample proportion and the standard error of the proportion.

$\mu_{\hat{p}} = p = 0.4 \qquad\qquad \sigma_{\hat{p}} = \sqrt{\dfrac{p(1-p)}{n}} = \sqrt{\dfrac{0.4(1-0.4)}{50}} \approx 0.069$

Check that np and $n(1-p)$ are both at least 10.

$np = 50 \cdot 0.4 = 20 \qquad\qquad n(1-p) = 50 \cdot 0.6 = 30$

Since np and $n(1-p)$ are both greater than 10, the sampling distribution of the sample proportion is approximately normal. In a normal distribution, 95% of the data fall within 2 standard deviations of the mean.

$\mu_{\hat{p}} - 2\sigma_{\hat{p}} = 0.4 - 2(0.069) = 0.262 \qquad \mu_{\hat{p}} + 2\sigma_{\hat{p}} = 0.4 + 2(0.069) = 0.538$

So, for random samples of 50 students, 95% of the sample proportions fall between 26.2% and 53.8%.

(B) What is the probability that a random sample of 25 students has a sample proportion of at most 37%?

Write the given information about the population and the sample, where a success is a student who lives off campus.

$p = \boxed{}$ $n = \boxed{}$

Find the mean of the sampling distribution of the sample proportion and the standard error of the proportion.

$$\mu_{\hat{p}} = p = \boxed{} \qquad \sigma_{\hat{p}} = \sqrt{\frac{p(1-p)}{n}} = \sqrt{\frac{\boxed{}\left(1 - \boxed{}\right)}{\boxed{}}} = \boxed{}$$

Check that np and $n(1-p)$ are both at least 10.

$$np = \boxed{} \cdot \boxed{} = \boxed{} \qquad n(1-p) = \boxed{} \cdot \boxed{} = \boxed{}$$

Since np and $n(1-p)$ are greater than or equal to 10, the sampling distribution of the sample proportion is approximately normal. Use a graphing calculator to find $P(\hat{p} \leq 0.37)$.

$$P(\hat{p} \leq 0.37) = \text{normalcdf}\left(-1\text{E}99, \boxed{}, \boxed{}, \boxed{}\right) \approx \boxed{}$$

So, the probability that the random sample has a sample proportion of at most 37% is about _____.

YourTurn

40% of the students at a university live off campus. When sampling from this population, consider "successes" to be students who live off campus.

8. For random samples of 80 students, what interval centered on the mean of the sampling distribution captures 68% of the sample proportions?

9. What is the probability that a random sample of 60 students includes more than 18 students who live off campus?

Elaborate

10. What is a sampling distribution?

_____

_____

11. What allows you to conclude that 95% of the sample means in a sampling distribution are within 2 standard deviations of the population mean?

_____

_____

_____

_____

_____

12. When finding a sample mean or a sample proportion, why is using the greatest sample size possible (given constraints on the cost and time of sampling) a desirable thing to do?

_____

_____

_____

13. **Essential Question Check-In**   When you repeatedly take random samples of the same size from a population, what does the mean of the samples approximate?

_____

_____

© Houghton Mifflin Harcourt Publishing Company

1. The general manager of a multiplex theater took random samples of size 10 from the audiences attending the opening weekend of a new movie. From each sample, the manager obtained the mean age and the proportion of those who said they liked the movie. The sample means and sample proportions are listed in the tables.

Sample number	Sample mean (age)	Sample proportion (liked the movie)
1	22.1	0.6
2	25.7	0.9
3	24.8	0.7
4	24.3	0.7
5	23.9	0.8
6	23.3	0.6
7	22.8	0.5
8	24.0	0.8
9	25.1	0.7
10	23.6	0.7

Sample number	Sample mean (age)	Sample proportion (liked the movie)
11	24.2	0.5
12	26.4	0.6
13	25.9	0.7
14	23.8	0.8
15	21.1	0.7
16	24.4	0.7
17	23.9	0.6
18	25.1	0.7
19	24.7	0.9
20	22.9	0.6

a. Based on the 20 samples, what is the best estimate for the mean age of all the people who saw the movie? Explain.

b. Based on this sample, what is the best estimate for the proportion of all the people who saw the movie and liked it? Explain.

c. What could the manager have done to improve the accuracy of both estimates?

On a standardized science test, the seniors at Fillmore High School have a mean score of 425 with a standard deviation of 80.

2. For random samples of 30 seniors, what interval centered on the mean of the sampling distribution captures 95% of the mean scores?

3. For random samples of 100 seniors, what interval centered on the mean of the sampling distribution captures 68% of the mean scores?

4. What is the probability that a random sample of 50 seniors has a mean score of at most 415?

5. What is the probability that a random sample of 25 seniors has a mean score of at least 430?

For Exercises 6–9, use the following information: The safety placard on an elevator states that up to 8 people (1200 kilograms) can ride the elevator at one time. Suppose the people who work in the office building where the elevator is located have a mean mass of 80 kilograms with a standard deviation of 25 kilograms.

6. For random samples of 8 people who work in the office building, what interval centered on the mean of the sampling distribution captures 95% of the mean masses?

7. For random samples of 8 people who work in the office building, what interval centered on the mean of the sampling distribution captures 99.7% of the mean masses?

8. What is the probability that a random sample of 8 people who work in the office building has a mean mass of at most 90 kilograms?

9. Based on the elevator's safety placard, what is the maximum mean mass of 8 people who can ride the elevator at one time? What is the probability that a random sample of 8 people who work in the office building exceeds this maximum mean mass?

A popcorn manufacturer puts a prize in 25% of its bags of popcorn. When sampling from this population, consider "successes" to be bags of popcorn containing a prize.

10. For random samples of 100 bags of popcorn, what interval centered on the mean of the sampling distribution captures 95% of the sample proportions?

© Houghton Mifflin Harcourt Publishing Company

11. For random samples of 80 bags of popcorn, what interval centered on the mean of the sampling distribution captures 68% of the sample proportions?

12. What is the probability that a random sample of 120 bags of popcorn has prizes in at most 30% of the bags?

13. What is the probability that a random sample of 60 bags has prizes in more than 12 bags?

About 28% of students at a large school play varsity sports. When sampling from this population, consider "successes" to be students who play varsity sports.

14. For random samples of 75 students, what interval centered on the mean of the sampling distribution captures 95% of the sample proportions?

15. For random samples of 100 students, what interval centered on the mean of the sampling distribution captures 99.7% of the sample proportions?

16. What is the probability that a random sample of 45 students includes more than 18 students who play varsity sports?

17. What is the probability that a random sample of 60 students includes from 12 to 24 students who play varsity sports?

18. Among the 450 seniors in a large high school, 306 plan to be in college in the fall following high school graduation. Suppose random samples of 100 seniors are taken from this population in order to obtain sample proportions of seniors who plan to be college in the fall. Which of the following are true statements? Select all that apply.

a. Every sample proportion is 0.68.

b. The mean of the sampling distribution of the sample proportion is 0.68.

c. The standard error of the proportion is about 0.047.

d. The standard error of the proportion is about 0.0047.

e. The sampling distribution of the sample proportion is skewed.

f. The sampling distribution of the sample proportion is approximately normal.

19. Explain the Error A student was told that a population has a mean of 400 and a standard deviation of 25. The student was asked to find the probability that a random sample of size 45 taken from the population has a mean of at most 401. The student entered normalcdf $(-1\text{E}99, 401, 400, 25)$ on a graphing calculator and got a probability of about 0.516. What did the student do wrong? Show how to find the correct answer.

20. Draw Conclusions Amanda plans to use random sampling to estimate the percent of people who are truly ambidextrous (that is, they do not have a dominant right or left hand). She suspects that the percent is quite low, perhaps as low as 1%. If she wants the sampling distribution of the sample proportion to be approximately normal, what minimum sample size should she use? Explain.

21. Check for Reasonableness Given that about 90% of people are right-handed, you are interested in knowing what percent of people put their right thumb on top when they clasp their hands. Having no other information to go on, you assume that people who put their right thumb on top when they clasp their hands are those who are also right-handed. You then take a random sample of 100 people and find that 60 put their right thumb on top when they clasp their hands. Does this result lead you to question your assumption? Explain why or why not.

Lesson Performance Task

Among the data that the U.S. Census Bureau collects are the sizes of households, as shown in the table.

Number of people in household	Number of households	Number of people
1	31,886,794	
2	38,635,170	
3	18,044,529	
4	15,030,350	
5	6,940,508	
6	2,704,873	
7 or more	1,749,501	

a. In the table above, assume that you can simply use 7 as the number of people in households with 7 or more people. Complete the third column of the table. Then use that column to approximate the population mean μ (that is, the mean number of people in a household). Explain your reasoning.

b. Is the actual population mean greater than or less than the mean that you calculated? Explain.

c. Given that $\mu \approx 2.49$ and $\sigma \approx 1.42$, find the probability that a random sample of 100 households in the United States has a mean size of 2.3 people or less.

d. Given that $\mu \approx 2.49$ and $\sigma \approx 1.42$, find the probability that a random sample of 100 households in the United States has a mean size of 2.6 people or more.

Data Distributions

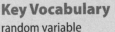
Essential Question: How can data distributions help solve real-world problems?

© Houghton Mifflin Harcourt Publishing Company

Key Vocabulary

random variable
(variable aleatoria)
probability distribution
(distribución de probabilidad)
cumulative probability
(probabilidad acumulativa)
sampling distribution
(distribución muestral)
standard error of the mean
(error típico de la media)

KEY EXAMPLE   *(Lesson 23.1)*

A spinner has four equal sections that are labeled 1, 2, 3, and 4. A number cube has six sides labeled 1, 2, 3, 4, 5, and 6. You spin the spinner and roll the number cube, then find the sum of the two numbers. Let x be a random variable that represents the sum of the two numbers. Make a histogram of the probability distribution of x.

First, complete the table. Then, make a histogram of the probability distribution.

Sum	2	3	4	5	6	7	8	9	10
Frequency	1	2	3	4	4	4	3	2	1
Probability	$\frac{1}{24}$	$\frac{2}{24}$	$\frac{3}{24}$	$\frac{4}{24}$	$\frac{4}{24}$	$\frac{4}{24}$	$\frac{3}{24}$	$\frac{2}{24}$	$\frac{1}{24}$

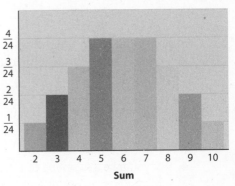

KEY EXAMPLE   *(Lesson 23.2)*

Suppose the heights (in feet) of oak trees in the United States are normally distributed with a mean of 68.5 feet and a standard deviation of 12 feet. Find the percent of trees that are no more than 72 feet tall.

$z_{72} = \dfrac{72 - \mu}{\sigma} = \dfrac{72 - 68.5}{12} \approx 0.3$ Convert 72 to a z–score

$P(z \le z_{72}) = 0.6179$ Read from standard normal table.

62%   Write decimal as percent.

KEY EXAMPLE   *(Lesson 23.2)*

Suppose the average birth weight of a full-term newborn is approximately 7.5 pounds with a standard deviation of 2 pounds. You choose a random sample at the hospital of 20 newborn weights. What is the probability that your sample has a mean weight of up to 7.75 pounds?

$\mu = 7.5,\ \sigma = 2,\ n = 20$ Write the given information.

$\mu_x = \mu = 7.5,\ \sigma_{\bar{x}} = \dfrac{\sigma}{\sqrt{20}} = \dfrac{2}{\sqrt{20}} \approx 0.447$ Find the mean of the sampling distribution and the standard error.

$z_{7.25} = \dfrac{7.75 - 7.5}{0.447} \approx 0.6$ Convert 7.75 to a z–score.

$P(z \le z_{7.25}) = 0.7257 = 73\%$ Use the standard normal table.

Complete the frequency table, then create the histogram of the probability distribution.

1. A spinner has five equal sections labeled 1, 2, 3, 4, and 5. You spin the spinner twice, then find the sum of the two numbers. *(Lesson 23.1)*

Sum	2	3	4	5	6	7	8	9	10
Frequency									
Probability									

Suppose the mean weight (in pounds) of a newborn elephant is 200 pounds with a standard deviation of 23 pounds. *(Lesson 23.2)*

2. Find the percent of elephants that are no more than 212 pounds.

3. Find the percent of elephants that are no more than 205 pounds.

4. If you take a sampling of 15 elephants, what is the probability that your sample has a mean weight of up to 198?

MODULE PERFORMANCE TASK

BMI and Obesity

You can calculate your BMI (body mass index) by dividing your weight in kilograms by the square of your height in meters. A person with a BMI from 18.5 to 24.9 is considered to have a healthy weight. An overweight adult has a BMI from 25.0 to 29.9. An obese person has a BMI greater than 29.9.

The BMI of 18-year-old males is approximately normally distributed with a mean of 24.2 and a standard deviation of 5.1. What percent of 18-year-old males are overweight? What percentage are obese?

Start on your own paper by listing information you will need to solve the problem. Then use graphs, numbers, tables, words, or algebra to explain how you reached your conclusion.

(Ready) to Go On?

23.1–23.3 Data Distributions

• Online Homework
• Hints and Help
• Extra Practice

At a local company, the ages of all new employees hired during the last 10 years are normally distributed. The mean age is 35 years old, with a standard deviation of 10 years.

1. Find the percent of new employees that are no more than 27 years old.

2. Find the percent of new employees that are no more than 39 years old.

3. Find the percent of new employees that are at least 27 years old.

4. If you were to take a sampling of 10 employees, what is the probability that the mean age of the sample will be at least 32?

5. If you were to take a sampling of 10 employees, what is the probability that the mean age of the sample will be at least 38?

ESSENTIAL QUESTION

6. How could data distributions help a doctor do his or her job? Give an example.

Assessment Readiness

1. Consider the histogram. Does the statement correctly describe the histogram? Select Yes or No for **A–C**.

   A. There are 16 data values. ○ Yes ○ No

   B. Data is spread among 5 sums. ○ Yes ○ No

   C. Each sum is equally likely. ○ Yes ○ No

2. Consider the shape of a histogram with a normal distribution. Choose True or False for each statement.

   A. A histogram with normal distribution increases, but never decreases. ○ True ○ False

   B. A histogram with normal distribution makes a bell curve. The bell could be wide or tall. ○ True ○ False

   C. A histogram with normal distribution has the same shape as a line plot with normal distribution. ○ True ○ False

3. A local zoo plans to add a new animal display according to the desires of the community members who spend the most time at the zoo. They are considering the following survey methods:

   • Put a survey up on their website and solicit responses from those visiting the site.

   • Survey every 12th customer buying a ticket for the zoo.

   • Survey every annual zoo pass purchaser.

   Which sampling method would most likely result in a theme that would please those who spend the most time at the zoo? Explain.

4. Suppose the average time a student spends on homework at a certain school is 3.75 hours a night, with a standard deviation of 1.5 hours. You choose a random sample of 20 students. What is the probability that your sample has a mean time of up to 4.25 hours? Explain.

Making Inferences from Data

Essential Question: How can making inferences from data help to solve real-world problems?

REAL WORLD VIDEO
Competitive athletes train hard and are always looking for training techniques that might give them an advantage over their competitors. How can we use data to make judgments about the effectiveness of various training strategies?

MODULE PERFORMANCE TASK PREVIEW

Sports Nutrition

The greatest sports players have to be in their best health in order to play at a high level. They exercise regularly and avoid unhealthy habits. Coaches tell them what to eat and what not to eat to play a good game. But really, how necessary is good nutrition for great athletic performance? By the end of this module, you'll have the means to answer this question.

Are (YOU) Ready?

Complete these exercises to review skills you will need for this module.

Trend Lines and Predictions

Example 1   A pet store asked loyal customers the weight of their dog and monthly budgeted expenses for owning it. The scatter plot shows the results of this survey with a line of best fit. Approximate the monthly cost of a dog weighing 40 pounds.

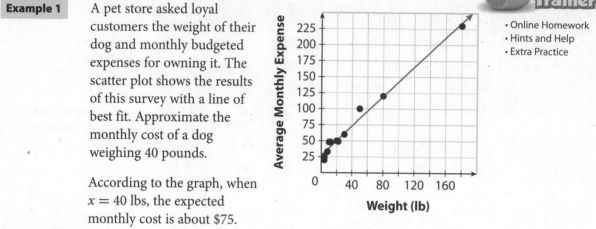

According to the graph, when $x = 40$ lbs, the expected monthly cost is about $75.

Find the expected monthly cost of owning a dog at the given weight.

1.   60 lb

2.   100 lb

3.   150 lb

Making Inferences From a Random Sample

Example 2   A product quality engineer takes a random sample of 200 widgets and finds that 15 of them are defective. At this factory, the rule is if the defect rate is greater than 8.5%, the assembly line needs to be shut down for retooling. Should the engineer shut down the assembly line?

No. In the sample, only $\frac{15}{200} = 7.5\%$ of the widgets were defective.

For each sample size and number of defective widgets, should the engineer close down the assembly line or not? Explain.

4.   Sample size = 5; defective widgets = 1

5.   Sample size = 150; defective widgets = 27

24.1 Confidence Intervals and Margins of Error

Essential Question: How do you calculate a confidence interval and a margin of error for a population proportion or population mean?

⊘ Explore   Identifying Likely Population Proportions

In a previous lesson, you took samples from a population whose parameter of interest is known in order to see how well a sample statistic estimated that parameter. In this lesson, you will estimate a population parameter using a statistic obtained from a random sample, and you will quantify the accuracy of that estimate.

Suppose you survey a random sample of 50 students at your high school and find that 40% of those surveyed attended the football game last Saturday. Although you cannot survey the entire population of students, you would still like to know what population proportions are reasonably likely in this situation.

(A) Suppose the proportion p of the population that attended last Saturday's game is 30%. Find the reasonably likely values of the sample proportion $\hat{p}$.

In this case, $p = \boxed{}$ and $n = \boxed{}$.

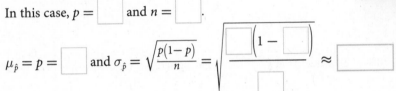

$$\mu_{\hat{p}} = p = \boxed{} \text{ and } \sigma_{\hat{p}} = \sqrt{\frac{p(1-p)}{n}} = \sqrt{\frac{\boxed{}\left(1-\boxed{}\right)}{\boxed{}}} \approx \boxed{}$$

(B) The reasonably likely values of $\hat{p}$ fall within 2 standard deviations of $\mu_{\hat{p}}$.

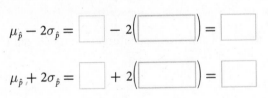

$$\mu_{\hat{p}} - 2\sigma_{\hat{p}} = \boxed{} - 2\left(\boxed{}\right) = \boxed{}$$

$$\mu_{\hat{p}} + 2\sigma_{\hat{p}} = \boxed{} + 2\left(\boxed{}\right) = \boxed{}$$

(C) On the graph, draw a horizontal line segment at the level of 0.3 on the vertical axis to represent the interval of likely values of $\hat{p}$ you found in Step B.

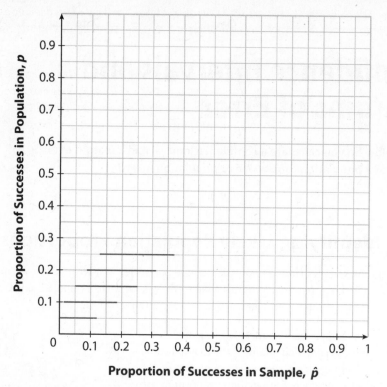

Proportion of Successes in Population, *p*

Proportion of Successes in Sample, $\hat{p}$

(D) Now repeat the process for $p = 0.35, 0.4, 0.45$, and so on to complete the graph in Step C. You may wish to divide up the work with other students and pool your findings.

(E) Draw a vertical line at 0.4 on the horizontal axis. This represents $\hat{p} = 0.4$. The line segments that this vertical line intersects are the population proportions for which a sample proportion of 0.4 is reasonably likely.

Reflect

1. **Discussion** Is it possible that 30% of all students at your school attended last Saturday's football game? Is it likely? Explain.

_____

_____

2. **Discussion** Is it possible that 60% of all students at your school attended last Saturday's football game? Is it likely? Explain.

_____

_____

3. **Discussion** Based on your graph, which population proportions do you think are reasonably likely? Why?

_____

_____

⚙ Explain 1 **Finding a Confidence Interval for a Population Proportion**

A **confidence interval** is an approximate range of values that is likely to include an unknown population parameter. The *level* of a confidence interval, such as 95%, gives the probability that the interval includes the true value of the parameter.

Recall that when data are normally distributed, 95% of the values fall within 2 standard deviations of the mean. Using this idea in the Explore, you found a 95% confidence interval for the proportion of all students who attended the football game last Saturday.

The graph that you completed in the Explore is shown. You can see from the graph that when the horizontal line segment at $p = 0.4$ is rotated 90° about the point $(0.4, 0.4)$, it becomes a vertical line segment that captures all of the likely population proportions. Since you already know the interval on the horizontal axis that defines the horizontal segment, you can find the interval on the vertical axis that defines the vertical segment by using the fact that $\mu_{\hat{p}} = p$ and interchanging the variables $\hat{p}$ on the horizontal axis) and p (on the vertical axis). So, the horizontal axis interval $\mu_{\hat{p}} - 2\sigma_{\hat{p}} \leq \hat{p} \leq \mu_{\hat{p}} + 2\sigma_{\hat{p}}$ becomes the vertical axis interval as follows:

Replace $\mu_{\hat{p}}$ with p. $\qquad p - 2\sigma_{\hat{p}} \leq \hat{p} \leq p + 2\sigma_{\hat{p}}$

Interchange $\hat{p}$ and p. $\qquad \hat{p} - 2\sigma_{\hat{p}} \leq p \leq \hat{p} + 2\sigma_{\hat{p}}$

In this case, the vertical axis interval is the 95% confidence interval for p. This result can be generalized to a $c\%$ confidence interval for p.

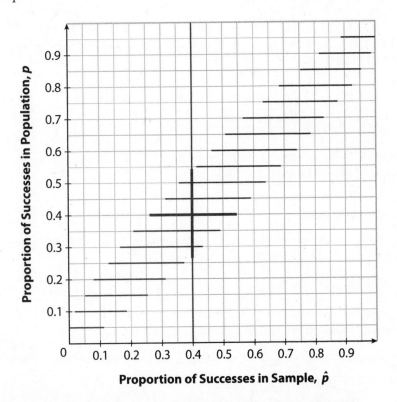

Proportion of Successes in Population, p (vertical axis)

Proportion of Successes in Sample, $\hat{p}$ (horizontal axis)

A Confidence Interval for a Population Proportion

A $c\%$ confidence interval for the proportion p of successes in a population is given by $\hat{p} - z_c \sqrt{\frac{\hat{p}(1-\hat{p})}{n}} \leq p \leq \hat{p} + z_c \sqrt{\frac{\hat{p}(1-\hat{p})}{n}}$, where $\hat{p}$ is the sample proportion, n is the sample size, and z_c depends upon the desired degree of confidence.

In order for this interval to describe the value of p reasonably accurately, three conditions must be met:

1. There are only two possible outcomes associated with the parameter of interest. The population proportion for one outcome is p, and the proportion for the other outcome is $1 - p$.

2. $n\hat{p}$ and $n(1 - \hat{p})$ must both be at least 10.

3. The size of the population must be at least 10 times the size of the sample, and the sample must be random.

Use the values in the table for z_c. Note that you should use 1.96 rather than 2 for $z_{95\%}$ for greater accuracy.

Desired degree of confidence	90%	95%	99%
Value of z_c	1.645	1.96	2.576

Example 1 **In a random sample of 100 four-year-old children in the United States, 76 were able to write their name. Find the specified confidence interval for the proportion p of four-year-olds in the United States who can write their name.**

 Find a 95% confidence interval.

Identify the sample size n, the proportion $\hat{p}$ of four-year-olds in the sample who can write their name, and the value of z_c for a 95% confidence interval.

$n = 100$ $\hat{p} = 0.76$ $z_c = 1.96$

Substitute the values of n, $\hat{p}$, and z_c into the formulas for the endpoints of the confidence interval. Simplify and round to two decimal places.

$$\hat{p} - z_c\sqrt{\frac{\hat{p}(1-\hat{p})}{n}} = 0.76 - 1.96\sqrt{\frac{0.76(1-0.76)}{100}} \approx 0.68$$

$$\hat{p} + z_c\sqrt{\frac{\hat{p}(1-\hat{p})}{n}} = 0.76 + 1.96\sqrt{\frac{0.76(1-0.76)}{100}} \approx 0.84$$

So, you can state with 95% confidence that the proportion of all four-year-olds in the United States who can write their name lies between 68% and 84%.

(B) Find a 99% confidence interval.

Identify the sample size n, the proportion $\hat{p}$ of four-year-olds in the sample who can write their name, and the value of z_c for a 99% confidence interval.

$n = \boxed{}$ $\hat{p} = \boxed{}$ $z_c = \boxed{}$

Substitute the values of n, $\hat{p}$, and z_c into the formulas for the endpoints of the confidence interval. Simplify and round to two decimal places.

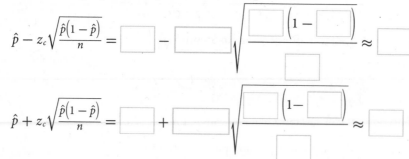

So, you can state with 99% confidence that the proportion of all four-year-olds in the United States who can write their name lies between _____ and _____.

4. **Discussion** Do the data from the sample of four-year-old children satisfy the three conditions for using the confidence interval formula? Explain.

_____

_____

_____

5. **Discussion** Does increasing the value of c increase or decrease the range of values for a confidence interval of a population proportion? Explain why it happens mathematically and why it makes sense.

_____

_____

_____

_____

6. Isabelle surveys a random sample of 80 voters in her large town and finds that 46 support raising property taxes in order to build a new library. Find a 95% confidence interval for the proportion p of all voters in Isabelle's town who support raising property taxes in order to build a new library.

⚷ Explain 2   Finding a Confidence Interval for a Population Mean

You can use reasoning similar to the argument in the Explore to develop a formula for a confidence interval for a population mean.

> ### A Confidence Interval for a Population Mean
>
> A $c\%$ confidence interval for the mean μ in a normally distributed population is given by $\bar{x} - z_c \dfrac{\sigma}{\sqrt{n}} \leq \mu \leq \bar{x} + z_c \dfrac{\sigma}{\sqrt{n}}$, where $\bar{x}$ is the sample mean, n is the sample size, σ is the population standard deviation, and z_c depends upon the desired degree of confidence.

Note that it is assumed that the population is normally distributed and that you know the population standard deviation σ. In a more advanced statistics course, you can develop a confidence interval that does not depend upon a normally distributed population or knowing the population standard deviation.

Example 2 **For the given situation, find the specified confidence interval for the population mean.**

Ⓐ In a random sample of 20 students at a large high school, the mean score on a standardized test is 610. Given that the standard deviation of all scores at the school is 120, find a 99% confidence interval for the mean score among all students at the school.

© Houghton Mifflin Harcourt Publishing Company

Identify the sample size n, the sample mean $\bar{x}$, the population standard deviation σ, and the value of z_c for a 99% confidence interval.

$n = 20$ $\bar{x} = 610$ $\sigma = 120$ $z_c = 2.576$

Substitute the values of n, $\bar{x}$, σ, and z_c into the formulas for the endpoints of the confidence interval. Simplify and round to the nearest whole number.

$$\bar{x} - z_c \frac{\sigma}{\sqrt{n}} = 610 - 2.576 \cdot \frac{120}{\sqrt{20}} \approx 541 \qquad \bar{x} + z_c \frac{\sigma}{\sqrt{n}} = 610 + 2.576 \cdot \frac{120}{\sqrt{20}} \approx 679$$

So, you can state with 99% confidence that the mean score among all students lies between 541 and 679.

(B) In a random sample of 30 students at a large high school, the mean score on a standardized test is 1514. Given that the standard deviation of all scores at the school is 141, find a 95% confidence interval for the mean score among all students at the school.

Identify the sample size n, the sample mean $\bar{x}$, the population standard deviation σ, and the value of z_c for a 95% confidence interval.

$n = \boxed{}$ $\bar{x} = \boxed{}$ $\sigma = \boxed{}$ $z_c = \boxed{}$

Substitute the values of n, $\bar{x}$, σ, and z_c into the formulas for the endpoints of the confidence interval. Simplify and round to the nearest whole number.

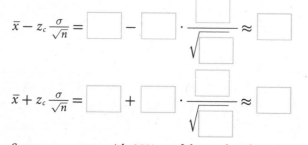

So, you can state with 95% confidence that the mean score among all students at the school lies between _____ and _____.

Reflect

7. What must you assume about the test scores of all students to use the formula for the confidence interval?

_____

Your Turn

8. In a random sample of 42 employees in a large company, the mean weekly number of minutes spent exercising is 86. Given that the standard deviation of all employees is 22.4, find a 99% confidence interval for the mean weekly number of minutes spent exercising among all employees in the company.

✏️ Explain 3 Choosing a Sample Size

In Part B of Example 2, you found the 95% confidence interval $1464 \leq \bar{x} \leq 1564$, which is a range of values centered at $\bar{x} = 1514$. You can write the confidence interval as 1514 ± 50, where 50 is called the *margin of error*. The **margin of error** is half the length of a confidence interval.

Margin of Error for a Population Proportion

The margin of error E for the proportion of successes in a population with sample proportion $\hat{p}$ and sample size n is given by $E = z_c \sqrt{\dfrac{\hat{p}(1-\hat{p})}{n}}$, where z_c depends on the degree of the confidence interval.

Margin of Error for a Population Mean

The margin of error E for the mean in a normally distributed population with standard deviation σ, sample mean $\bar{x}$, and sample size n is given by $E = z_c \dfrac{\sigma}{\sqrt{n}}$, where z_c depends on the degree of the confidence interval.

From the formulas you can see that the margin of error decreases as the sample size n increases. This suggests using a sample that is as large as possible. However, it is often more practical to determine a margin of error that is acceptable and then calculate the required sample size.

Example 3 Find the appropriate sample size for the given situation.

(A) A researcher wants to know the percent of teenagers in the United States who have social networking profiles. She is aiming for a 90% confidence interval and a margin of error of 4%. What sample size n should she use?

Step 1 Rewrite the margin-of-error formula for a population proportion by solving for n.

$E = z_c \sqrt{\dfrac{\hat{p}(1-\hat{p})}{n}}$ Write the formula.

$E^2 = z_c^2 \cdot \dfrac{\hat{p}(1-\hat{p})}{n}$ Square both sides.

$nE^2 = z_c^2 \cdot \hat{p}(1-\hat{p})$ Multiply both sides by n.

$n = z_c^2 \cdot \dfrac{\hat{p}(1-\hat{p})}{E^2}$ Divide both sides by E^2.

Step 2 Estimate the value of $\hat{p}$.

The researcher has not conducted the survey and is trying to find $\hat{p}$. So, she must estimate $\hat{p}$ as 0.5, which is the value of $\hat{p}$ that makes the expression $\hat{p}(1-\hat{p})$ as large as possible.

Step 3 Identify the values of E and z_c.

E is the margin of error written as a decimal and z_c is the z-score that corresponds to a 90% confidence interval. So, $E = 0.04$ and $z_c = 1.645$.

Step 4 Substitute the values of $\hat{p}$, E, and z_c in the rewritten margin-of-error formula from Step 1.

$n = z_c^2 \cdot \dfrac{\hat{p}(1-\hat{p})}{E^2} = \dfrac{(1.645)^2 \cdot 0.5\,(1-0.5)}{(0.04)^2} \approx 423$

So, the researcher should survey a random sample of 423 teenagers.

(B) Caleb is a restaurant manager and wants to know the mean number of seconds it takes to complete a customer's order. He is aiming for a 95% confidence interval and a margin of error of 6 seconds. Based on past experience, Caleb estimates the population standard deviation to be 21 seconds. What sample size n should he use?

Step 1 Rewrite the margin-of-error formula for a population mean by solving for n.

$E = z_c \dfrac{\sigma}{\sqrt{n}}$ Write the formula.

$E^2 = $ _____   Square both sides.

$nE^2 = $ _____   Multiply both sides by n.

$n = $ _____   Divide both sides by E^2.

Step 2 Identify the values of E, σ, and z_c.

E is the margin of error, σ is the population standard deviation, and z_c is the z–score that corresponds to a 95% confidence interval. So, $E = $ _____, $\sigma = $ _____ and $z_c = $ _____.

Substitute the values of E, σ, and z_c in the margin of error for a population mean formula that was solved for n.

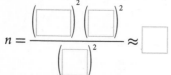

$$n = \dfrac{\left(\Box\right)^2 \left(\Box\right)^2}{\left(\Box\right)^2} \approx \Box$$

So, Caleb should survey a random sample of _____ orders.

Reflect

9. **Discussion** In Part A, do you expect the sample size to increase or decrease if the researcher decides she wants a smaller margin of error? Explain using the margin-of-error formula for a population proportion.

_____

_____

_____

10. **Discussion** In Part B, do you expect the sample size to increase or decrease if Caleb decides he wants a 99% confidence interval instead of a 95% confidence interval? Explain using the margin-of-error formula for a population mean.

_____

_____

_____

11. Zoe is an editor of a newspaper in a state capital and wants to know the percent of residents in her state who are in favor of banning the use of handheld cell phones while driving, a bill that is being considered in the state legislature. After researching similar polls conducted in other states, she estimates that $\hat{p} = 0.35$. She is aiming for a 95% confidence interval and a margin of error of 5%. What sample size n should Zoe use?

Elaborate

12. How can an interval that captures 95% of the sample proportions in a sampling distribution be used to find a 95% confidence interval for a population proportion?

13. Describe how increasing the sample size affects the confidence interval of a population mean.

14. **Essential Question Check-in** What is the relationship between a confidence interval and a margin of error for a population proportion or population mean?

Identify the values of the sample proportion $\hat{p}$ that fall within 2 standard deviations of the given population proportion p for each situation.

1. Suppose that 44% of all employees at a large company attended a recent company function. Alannah plans to survey a random sample of 32 employees to estimate the population proportion. What are the values of $\hat{p}$ that she is likely to obtain?

2. Suppose the proportion p of a school's students who oppose a change to the school's dress code is 73%. Nicole surveys a random sample of 56 students to find the percent of students who oppose the change. What are the values of $\hat{p}$ that she is likely to obtain?

For the given situation, find the specified confidence interval for the population proportion.

3. Hunter surveys a random sample of 64 students at his community college and finds that 37.5% of the students saw a film at the local movie theater in the last 30 days. Find a 90% confidence interval for the proportion p of all students at the community college who saw a film at the movie theater in the last 30 days.

4. In a random sample of 300 U.S. households, 111 households have a pet dog. Find a 99% confidence interval for the proportion p of all U.S. households that have a pet dog.

5. A quality control team at a company that manufactures digital utility meters randomly selects 320 meters and finds 12 to be defective. Find a 95% confidence interval for the proportion p of all digital utility meters that the company manufactures and are defective.

6. In a random sample of 495 four-year-olds in a state, 54.7% can provide the first and last name of at least one parent or guardian. Find a 99% confidence interval for the proportion p of all four-year-olds in the state who can provide the first and last name of at least one parent or guardian.

© Houghton Mifflin Harcourt Publishing Company • Image Credits: ©Javier Brosch/Shutterstock

For the given situation, find the specified confidence interval for the population mean.

7. An online website that tracks gas prices surveys a random sample of 73 gas stations in a state and finds that the mean price of 1 gallon of regular gasoline is $3.576. If the website estimates from past surveys that the population standard deviation is $0.117, find a 95% confidence interval for the mean price of regular gasoline in the state.

8. Caiden manages the security team at a large airport and surveys a random sample of 149 travelers. He finds that the mean amount of time that it takes passengers to clear security is 28.3 minutes. From past experience, Caiden estimates that the population standard deviation is 6.4 minutes. Find a 90% confidence interval for the mean amount of time that it takes passengers to clear security.

9. A quality control team at a company that manufactures smartphones measures the battery life of 24 randomly selected smartphones and finds that the mean amount of continuous video playback from a full charge is 12.70 hours. Given that the population standard deviation is 0.83 hour, find a 99% confidence interval for the mean amount of continuous video playback from a full charge.

© Houghton Mifflin Harcourt Publishing Company

10. Stephen surveys 53 randomly selected students at his large high school and finds that the mean amount of time spent on homework per night is 107.9 minutes. Given that the population standard deviation is 22.7 minutes, find a 90% confidence interval for the mean amount of time students at the school spend on homework per night.

Find the appropriate sample size for the given situation.

11. Executives at a health insurance company want to know the percent of residents in a state who have health insurance. Based on data from other states, they estimate that $\hat{p} = 0.8$. They are aiming for a 99% confidence interval and a margin of error of 1.5%. What sample size n should they use?

12. Tyler is a manager at a utility company and wants to know the mean amount of electricity that residential customers consume per month. He is aiming for a 90% confidence interval and a margin of error of 10 kilowatt-hours (kWh). From past experience, Tyler estimates that the population standard deviation is 91.1 kWh. What sample size n should he use?

13. Teneka is a restaurant owner and wants to know the mean amount of revenue per day. She is aiming for a 95% confidence interval and a margin of error of $200. Given that the population standard deviation is $870, what sample size should Teneka use?

14. Biology Miranda is a biologist who is measuring the lengths of randomly selected frogs of the same species from two locations.

a. Miranda measures the lengths of 25 frogs from location A and finds that the mean length is 7.35 cm. Given that the population standard deviation is 0.71 cm, find a 95% confidence interval for the mean length of frogs from location A.

b. Miranda measures the lengths of 20 frogs from location B and finds that the mean length is 7.17 cm. Given that the population standard deviation is 0.69 cm, find a 95% confidence interval for the mean length of frogs from location B.

c. Is it clear that the mean length of frogs from one location is greater than the mean length of frogs from the other location? Explain your reasoning.

15. Which of the following sets of desired margin of error E, desired confidence level c, and given sample proportion $\hat{p}$ or population standard deviation σ require a sample size of at least 100? Select all that apply.

A. $E = 0.1, c = 95\%, \hat{p} = 0.5$

B. $E = 1000, c = 99\%, \sigma = 4000$

C. $E = 0.04, c = 90\%, \hat{p} = 0.9$

D. $E = 4, c = 95\%, \sigma = 18.6$

E. $E = 0.06, c = 99\%, \hat{p} = 0.3$

F. $E = 50, c = 90\%, \sigma = 309$

16. Multiple Representations The margin of error E for the proportion of successes in a population may be estimated by $\frac{1}{\sqrt{n}}$, where n is the sample size. Explain where this estimate comes from. Assume a 95% confidence interval.

17. Draw Conclusions In the Explore, you wrote an interval of the form $\mu_{\hat{p}} - 2\sigma_{\hat{p}} < \hat{p} < \mu_{\hat{p}} + 2\sigma_{\hat{p}}$ that captures 95% of the sample proportions. You know that $\mu_{\hat{p}} = p$, so you can rewrite the interval as $p - 2\sigma_{\hat{p}} < \hat{p} < p + 2\sigma_{\hat{p}}$. Solve this compound inequality for p. What does this result tell you?

18. Explain the Error A quality assurance team for an LED bulb manufacturer tested 400 randomly selected LED bulbs and found that 6 are defective. A member of the team performed the following calculations to obtain a 95% confidence interval for the proportion p of LED bulbs that are defective. Explain the error.

$n = 400 \qquad \hat{p} = \frac{6}{400} = 0.015 \qquad z_c = 1.96$

$\hat{p} - z_c\sqrt{\frac{\hat{p}(1-\hat{p})}{n}} = 0.015 - 1.96\sqrt{\frac{0.015(1-0.015)}{400}} \approx 0.003$

$\hat{p} + z_c\sqrt{\frac{\hat{p}(1-\hat{p})}{n}} = 0.015 + 1.96\sqrt{\frac{0.015(1-0.015)}{400}} \approx 0.027$

With 95% confidence, the proportion of LED bulbs that are defective lies between 0.3% and 2.7%.

Lesson Performance Task

Between 2010 and 2011, a research group conducted a survey of young working women and men, ages 18 to 34. Of the 610 women surveyed, 66% indicated that being successful in a high-paying career is either "one of the most important things" or "very important" in their lives. Of the 703 men surveyed, only 59% replied that they attach such importance to career.

  a. Find a 95% confidence interval for each sample proportion.

  b. Find the margin of error for each result at the 95% confidence level.

  c. Is it possible that the population proportions could actually be equal? Explain.

24.2 Surveys, Experiments, and Observational Studies

Essential Question: What kinds of statistical research are there, and which ones can establish cause-and-effect relationships between variables?

⊙ Explore   Recognizing Different Forms of Statistical Research

Statistical research takes various forms depending on whether the purpose of the research is to measure a variable in a population, to see if there is evidence of an association between two variables, or to determine whether one variable actually influences another variable.

Suppose a graduate school researcher is considering three studies related to math and music. One study involves asking a random sample of high school students in a large school district whether they listen to music while doing math homework. A second study involves asking a random sample of students at a large university whether they are majoring in math and whether they also play a musical instrument or sing. A third study involves a group of adult participants where half will be randomly assigned either to listen to classical music for 15 minutes before taking a logical reasoning test or to listen to white noise for 15 minutes before taking the same test.

(A) Which study appears to look for an association between two variables without actively manipulating either one? What are those variables?

_____

_____

_____

_____

(B) Which study appears to be looking for evidence that one variable actually influences another variable? What are those variables, and which one is manipulated to see if it influences the other?

_____

_____

_____

_____

_____

Ⓒ Which study appears to be simply measuring a variable in a population? What is that variable?

_____

_____

_____

Reflect

1. **Discussion** Describe the type of result or conclusion the researcher might obtain from each study.

_____

_____

_____

_____

_____

_____

🔑 Explain 1 Detecting Errors in Surveys

A survey measures characteristics of interest about a population using a sample selected from the population. As you saw in a previous lesson, a sample needs to be representative of the population in order for the measurements obtained from the sample to be accurate. Random sampling is generally the best way to ensure representation.

Even when random sampling is used, a survey's results can have errors. Some of the sources of errors are:

- *Biased questions:* The wording of questions in a survey can influence the way people respond to questions. Survey questions need to be worded in a neutral, unbiased way.

- *Interviewer effect:* If an interviewer asks the questions in a survey, the person being interviewed may give inaccurate responses to avoid being embarrassed.

- *Nonresponse:* Some people may be difficult to contact, or they may simply refuse to participate once contacted. If nonresponse rates are higher for certain subgroups of a population, then those subgroups will be underrepresented in the survey results.

Example 1 **Explain why the results of each survey are likely to be inaccurate, and then suggest a way to improve the accuracy of the survey.**

Ⓐ The owner of a business, conducts interviews with a random sample of employees to have them rate how satisfied they are with their jobs.

Since the interviewer is the owner of the business, the employees may not be completely open about any job dissatisfaction they may have. The employees may feel that their job security is at stake. A better survey would involve a neutral interviewer or allow the employees to respond anonymously.

© Houghton Mifflin Harcourt Publishing Company • Image Credits: ©Minerva Studio/Shutterstock

(B) In a random sample of town residents, a survey asks, "Are you in favor of a special tax levy to renovate the dilapidated town hall?"

The question is biased because _____

_____

A better survey would _____

_____

Reflect

2. Even if the survey question in Part B is revised to avoid being biased, do the people surveyed have enough information to give an informed and accurate response? Explain.

_____

_____

_____

Your Turn

Explain why the results of the survey are likely to be inaccurate, and then suggest a way to improve the accuracy of the survey.

3. A teacher conducts one-on-one interviews with a random sample of her students to get feedback on her teaching methods.

⚙ Explain 2   Distinguishing Between Observational Studies and Experiments

In an **observational study**, researchers determine whether an existing condition, called a *factor*, in a population is related to a characteristic of interest. For instance, an observational study might be used to find the incidence of heart disease among those who smoke. In the study, being a smoker is the factor, and having heart disease is the characteristic of interest.

In an **experiment**, researchers create a condition by imposing a treatment on some of the subjects of the experiment. For instance, an experiment might be conducted by having some people with eczema take a vitamin E pill daily, and then observing whether their symptoms improve. In the experiment, taking the vitamin E pill is the treatment, and improvement of symptoms is the characteristic of interest.

Generally, an experiment is preferred over an observational study because an experiment allows researchers to manipulate one variable to see its effect on another. However, there may be practical or unethical reasons against performing an experiment. For example, it would be unethical to ask people to smoke in order to study the effects of smoking on their health. Instead, an observational study should be performed using people who already smoke.

Example 2 Determine whether each research study is an observational study or an experiment. Identify the factor if it is an observational study or the treatment if is an experiment. Also identify the characteristic of interest.

(A) Researchers measure the cholesterol of 50 subjects who report that they eat fish regularly and 50 subjects who report that they do not eat fish regularly.

This research study is an observational study. The factor is whether people eat fish regularly, and the characteristic of interest is cholesterol level.

(B) Researchers have 100 subjects with high cholesterol take fish oil pills daily for two months. They monitor the cholesterol of the subjects during that time.

This research study is an _____. The factor/treatment is _____

_____. The characteristic of interest is _____.

Reflect

4. **Discussion** Suppose the researchers in Part A find that considerably more people who eat fish regularly have normal cholesterol levels than those who do not eat fish regularly. Is it reasonable to conclude that eating fish regularly has an effect on cholesterol? Explain.

_____

_____

_____

Your Turn

Determine whether the research study is an observational study or an experiment. Identify the factor if it is an observational study or the treatment if is an experiment. Also identify the characteristic of interest.

5. Researchers monitor the driving habits of 80 subjects in their twenties and 80 subjects in their fifties for one month by using a GPS device that tracks location and speed.

🖉 **Explain 3** **Identifying Control Groups and Treatment Groups in Experiments**

Whether a study is observational or experimental, it should be comparative in order to establish a connection between the factor or treatment and the characteristic of interest. For instance, determining the rate of car accidents among people who talk on cell phones while driving is not instructive unless you compare it with the rate of car accidents among people who don't talk on cell phones while driving and find that it is significantly different.

© Houghton Mifflin Harcourt Publishing Company • Image Credits: ©greatstockimages/Shutterstock

While a comparative observational study can suggest a relationship between two variables, such as cell phone use while driving and car accidents, it cannot establish a cause-and-effect relationship because there can be *confounding variables* (also called *lurking variables*) that influence the results. For instance, perhaps people who talk on cell phones while driving are more likely to drive aggressively, so it is the aggressive driving (not the cell phone use) that leads to a higher rate of car accidents.

In an experiment, randomization can remove the problem of a confounding variable by distributing the variable among the groups being compared so that its influence on the groups is more or less equal. Therefore, the best way to establish a cause-and-effect relationship between two variables is through a **randomized comparative experiment** where subjects are randomly divided into two groups: the *treatment group*, which is given the treatment, and the *control group*, which is not.

Example 3 Identify the treatment, characteristic of interest, control group, and treatment group for the given experiment. Assume all subjects of the research are selected randomly.

Ⓐ To see whether zinc has an effect on the duration of a cold, researchers have half of the subjects take tablets containing zinc at the onset of cold symptoms and the other half take tablets without any zinc. The durations of the colds are then recorded.

The treatment is having subjects take tablets that contain zinc at the onset of cold symptoms.
The characteristic of interest is the duration of the cold.
The control group consists of subjects who took tablets without zinc.
The treatment group consists of subjects who took tablets containing zinc.

Ⓑ To see whether regular moderate exercise has an effect on blood pressure, researchers have half of the subjects set aside 30 minutes daily for walking and the other half not do any walking beyond their normal daily routines. The subjects also take and record their blood pressure at the same time each day.

The treatment is having subjects _____.

The characteristic of interest is _____.

The control group consists of subjects who _____

_____.

The treatment group consists of subjects who _____.

Your Turn

6. Identify the treatment, characteristic of interest, control group, and treatment group for the following experiment. Assume all subjects of the research are selected randomly.

To see whether reviewing for a test with a classmate improves scores, researchers ask half of the subjects to study with a classmate and the other half to study alone. The test scores are then recorded.

Evaluating a Media Report of Statistical Research

When you encounter media reports of statistical research in your daily life, you should judge any reported conclusions on the basis of how the research was conducted. Among the questions you should consider are the following:

- Is the research a survey, an observational study, or an experiment? In broad terms, a survey simply measures variables, an observational study attempts to find an association between variables, and an experiment attempts to establish a cause-and-effect relationship between variables.

- Was randomization used in conducting the research? As you know, random sampling is considered the best way to obtain a representative sample from a population and therefore get accurate results. Randomization also helps to dilute the effects of confounding variables.

- Does the report include the details of the research, such as sample size, statistics, and margins of error? The details help you judge how much confidence to have in the results of the research or how much importance to place on the results.

Example 4   **Evaluate the article by answering the following questions.**

- Is this a survey, an observational study, or an experiment? How do you know?
- Was randomization used in the research? If so, how?
- What details of the research does the article include? Is any important information missing?

Ⓐ

> ## Caring Doctors Shorten and Ease
> ## the Common Cold
>
> Researchers have found that among patients with colds, those who gave their doctors perfect scores on a questionnaire measuring empathy have colds that did not last as long and were less severe. Empathy on the part of doctors included making patients feel at ease, listening to their concerns, and showing compassion.
>
> A total of 350 subjects who were experiencing the onset of a cold were randomly assigned to one of three groups: no doctor-patient interaction, standard interaction, and enhanced interaction. Only subjects in the third group saw doctors who had been coached on being empathetic.

- Is this a survey, an observational study, or an experiment? How do you know?
  This study is an experiment because treatments were imposed on two groups of patients: those who had a standard interaction with a doctor and those who had an enhanced interaction with a doctor.

- Was randomization used in the research? If so, how?
  Randomization was used by randomly assigning subjects to a control group or one of two treatment groups.

- What details of the research does the article include? Is any important information missing?
  The report includes the number of subjects but no statistics, such as measures of cold duration or severity.

Ⓑ

Fitness in Teen Years May Guard Against Heart Trouble Later

A study of almost 750,000 Swedish men suggests people who are aerobically fit as teenagers are less likely to have a heart attack later in life. Each 15 percent increase in the level of aerobic fitness as a teenager is associated with an 18 percent reduced risk of a heart attack 30 years later. Overall, teens and young adults who participate in regular cardiovascular training have a 35 percent reduced risk of a heart attack later in life.

The researchers analyzed medical data from men drafted into the nation's army, which requires a test of aerobic fitness at the time of induction. National health registers provided information on heart attacks the men had later in life.

- Is this a survey, an observational study, or an experiment? How do you know?

_____

_____

_____

- Was randomization used in the research? If so, how?

_____

_____

_____

- What details of the research does the article include? Is any important information missing?

_____

_____

_____

_____

_____

_____

_____

Reflect

7. **Discussion** What conclusion do you draw from the report in Part A? How much confidence do you have in that conclusion? Why?

_____

_____

_____

_____

8. Evaluate the article by answering the following questions.

- Is this a survey, an observational study, or an experiment? How do you know?
- Was randomization used in the research? If so, how?
- What details of the research does the article include? Is any important information missing?

> ## Study Finds One in Seven Would Fail Kitchen Inspection
>
> Research suggests that at least one in seven home kitchens would flunk a health inspection that is given to restaurants. Only 61 percent of home kitchens would get an A or B if put through a restaurant inspection, compared with 98 percent of Los Angeles County restaurants. At least 14 percent of home kitchens would fail. The results are based on a questionnaire about food safety administered on the Internet and taken by about 13,000.

Elaborate

9. What are some sources of errors in a survey? Why should these errors be avoided?

_____

_____

10. Describe the difference between a factor in an observational study and a treatment in an experiment.

_____

_____

_____

11. Explain what confounding variables are and describe how they are handled in a randomized experiment.

_____

_____

_____

_____

12. **Essential Question Check-in** How do the three kinds of statistical research discussed in this lesson study a characteristic of interest in a population?

_____

_____

_____

1. Members of a research team are considering three studies related to sleep and learning. The first study involves comparing the scores on a post-study test of learning from two groups of randomly chosen adults, with one group getting at least 7 hours of sleep per night for a week and the other group getting at most 6 hours of sleep per night for a week. A second study involves asking a random sample of students at a large university to report the average number of hours of sleep they get each night and their college grade point average. A third study involves asking a random sample of high school students in a large school district whether they feel they get enough sleep to stay alert throughout the school day.

   a. Which study appears to look for an association between two variables without actively manipulating either one? What are those variables?

   b. Which study appears to be looking for evidence that one variable actually influences another variable? What are those variables, and which one is manipulated to see if it influences the other?

   c. Which study appears to be simply measuring a variable in a population? What is that variable?

Explain why the results of each survey are likely to be inaccurate and then suggest a way to improve the accuracy of the survey.

2. A store offers its customers a chance to win a cash prize if they call a toll-free number on a receipt and participate in a customer satisfaction survey.

© Houghton Mifflin Harcourt Publishing Company

3. A reporter for a local newspaper asks a random sample of people attending a holiday parade, "Since this holiday parade is so popular, do you support having the city provide the support for a larger parade next year?"

Determine whether each research study is an observational study or an experiment. Identify the factor if it is an observational study or the treatment if is an experiment. Also identify the characteristic of interest.

4. Researchers found that of patients who had been taking a bone-loss drug for more than five years, a high percentage of patients also had an uncommon type of fracture in the thigh bone.

5. Researchers found that when patients with chronic illnesses were randomly divided into two groups, the group that got regular coaching by phone from health professionals to help them manage their illnesses had lower monthly medical costs than the group that did not get the coaching.

6. A caretaker at a zoo is studying the effect of a new diet on the health of the zoo's elephants. She continues to feed half of the elephants their existing food, switches the other half to a new diet, and then monitors the health of the elephants.

7. A school district wants to know whether there is a relationship between students' standardized test scores and the amount of time they spend on extracurricular activities. The school board surveys students from each school in the system to gather data about the average number of hours per week spent on extracurricular activities and each student's most recent test scores.

8. Researchers want to know the effect of vitamin C as a dietary supplement on blood pressure. Half of the randomly assigned subjects take one 1000-milligram tablet of vitamin C daily for six months while the other half of the subjects take one placebo tablet daily for six months. The blood pressure of all subjects is taken weekly.

Identify the treatment, characteristic of interest, control group, and treatment group for the given experiment. Assume all subjects of the research are selected randomly.

9. A restaurant manager wants to know whether to keep using orange slices as a garnish or to change to tangerine slices. All of the subjects are blindfolded. Half of the subjects are asked to eat orange slices, and the other half are asked to eat tangerine slices. All subjects are asked whether they like the taste of the fruit.

10. A pharmaceutical company wants to know about the side effects of a new cholesterol medication. Out of 400 randomly selected volunteers who currently take the existing cholesterol medication, the researchers switch the old drug with the new drug for 200 of them, and continue to give the other 200 the old drug. They then monitor the two groups for side effects.

11. A park service wants to determine whether reintroducing a particular species of underwater plant to the lakes in the park system would be beneficial to a particular species of fish living in the lakes. The researchers reintroduce the plant in one lake. One year later, they study the health of the fish population in the lake where the plant was reintroduced, as well as in an ecologically similar lake without the plant.

12. A research team wants to know whether a new formula for a laundry detergent is more effective than the existing formula. The team members first wash a variety of fabrics with a variety of stains using the detergent with the new formula, and then they wash the same pairings of fabrics and stains using the detergent with the existing formula. They then compare the extent to which the stains have been eliminated.

Evaluate each article by answering the following questions.

- Is this a survey, an observational study, or an experiment? How do you know?
- Was randomization used in the research? If so, how?
- What details of the research does the article include? Is any important information missing?

13.

> ## Doctors Work When Sick
>
> Doctors know that they can get sick from their patients, but when they are sick themselves, do they stay away from their patients? Researchers asked 537 doctors-in-training to anonymously report whether they had worked while sick during the past year. The researchers found that 58% said they had worked once while sick and 31% said they had worked more than once while sick.

14.

> ## Antibiotic Use Tied to Asthma and Allergies
>
> Antibiotic use in infants is linked to asthma and allergies, according to a study involving 1401 children. Researchers asked mothers how many doses of antibiotics their children received before 6 months of age as well as whether their children had developed asthma or allergies by age 6. Children who received just one dose of antibiotics were 40% more likely to develop asthma or allergies. The risk jumped to 70% for children who received two doses.

15. Which of the following research topics are best addressed through an observational study? Select all that apply.

   A. Does listening to loud music with headphones affect a person's hearing?

   B. Does second-hand smoke affect the health of pets?

   C. Does a particular medication make seasonal allergy symptoms less severe?

   D. Does increasing the number of stoplights per mile on a road decrease the number of car accidents on the road?

   E. Does drinking sports drinks before and while playing a game of baseball increase the number of runs scored?

   F. Does a certain toothpaste prevent cavities in children better than another toothpaste?

H.O.T. Focus on Higher Order Thinking

16. **Draw Conclusions** Randomly assigning subjects to the control group or the treatment group for an experiment means that if a difference between the two groups is observed at the conclusion of the experiment, then the difference must be due either to chance or to the treatment. How do you think a researcher can conclude that the difference is due to the treatment?

17. **Critique Reasoning** Consider the following experiment: Mr. Jones wants to know what the condition of his deck would be if he did not continue to reapply wood sealant to it every spring to protect it. This spring, he uses the sealant on the entire deck except for several adjacent boards. He then observes how exposure to the weather affects those boards in relation to the rest of the deck.

   Lindsay claims that the part of the deck to which the sealant is applied constitutes the treatment group because that is the part that is actually "treated." Is she correct? Explain.

18. **Persevere in Problem Solving** Give an example of a question that could be better answered by gathering data in an observational study than it could by gathering data in an experiment. Explain why an observational study would be more appropriate. Then describe an observational study that would answer the question.

© Houghton Mifflin Harcourt Publishing Company

Lesson Performance Task

Using an online search engine, look for a research-based article that interests you about teen health, teen fitness, or teen nutrition using the search terms "teen health articles," "teen fitness articles," or "teen nutrition articles." Print the article to give to your teacher, and include your analysis of the research on which the article is based. Your analysis should address the following points:

- On what type of research study is the article based? How do you know?

- Was randomization used in conducting the research? If so, how?

- What details about the research does the article include? Are there any details that appear to be missing?

- What is your overall evaluation of the research? How much importance do you place on the conclusions drawn from the research? Explain.

24.3 Determining the Significance of Experimental Results

Essential Question: In an experiment, when is an observed difference between the control group and treatment group likely to be caused by the treatment?

⊘ Explore 1   Formulating the Null Hypothesis

You can think of every randomized comparative experiment as a test of a *null hypothesis*. The **null hypothesis** states that any difference between the control group and the treatment group is due to chance. In other words, the null hypothesis is the assumption that the treatment has no effect.

An unusual experimental result may be *statistically significant*. The determination of **statistical significance** is based on the probability of randomly getting a result that is the same as, or more extreme than, the result obtained from the experiment under the assumption that the null hypothesis is true. A low probability of getting the result, or a more extreme result, by chance is evidence in favor of rejecting the null hypothesis.

A statistically significant result does not prove that the treatment has an effect; the null hypothesis may still be true, and a rare event may simply have occurred. Nevertheless, standard practice in statistics is to reject the null hypothesis in favor of the *alternative hypothesis* that the result is, in fact, due to the treatment.

(A)   Suppose 10 people with colds are treated with a new formula for an existing brand of cold medicine, and 10 other people with colds are treated with the original formula. The mean recovery times for the two groups are compared.

     The null hypothesis is that the mean recovery times for the two groups will be [very different/ about the same].

(B)   Suppose that the mean recovery time for both groups is 5 days. Does the result of the experiment appear to be statistically significant? Explain your reasoning.

_____

_____

(C)   Suppose a potential growth agent is sprayed on the leaves of 12 emerging ferns twice a week for a month. Another 12 emerging ferns are not sprayed with the growth agent. The mean stalk lengths of the two groups of ferns are compared after a month.

     State the null hypothesis.

_____

_____

© Houghton Mifflin Harcourt Publishing Company

(D) Suppose that the treated ferns had a mean stalk length that is twice the mean stalk length of the untreated ferns. Does the result of the experiment appear to be statistically significant? Explain your reasoning.

_____

_____

Reflect

1. **Discussion** In the U.S. legal system, a defendant is assumed innocent until guilt is proved beyond a reasonable doubt. How is what happens with a null hypothesis like what happens with a defendant?

_____

_____

_____

2. Does the experimental result in Step B prove that the new formula is no more effective than the original formula? Explain.

_____

_____

3. Does the experimental result in Step D prove that the growth agent works? Explain.

_____

_____

⊘ Explore 2 Simulating a Resampling Distribution

Suppose a company that offers a college entrance exam prep course wants to demonstrate that its course raises test scores. The company recruits 20 students and randomly assigns half of them to a treatment group, where subjects take the course before taking the college entrance exam, and half to a control group, where subjects do not take the course before taking the exam. The table shows the exam scores of the 10 students in each group. How can you tell whether the course actually improved the scores of the students in the treatment group?

	College Entrance Exam Scores				
Treatment group	1440	1610	1430	1700	1690
	1570	1480	1620	1780	2010
Control group	1150	1500	1050	1600	1460
	1860	1350	1750	1680	1330

One thing you could do is compute the mean exam score for each group to see if the means are different. Obviously, the company expects the treatment group's mean to be greater than the control group's mean. But even if that is the case, how do you know that the difference in the means can be attributed to the treatment and not to chance? In other words, how do you know if the difference is statistically significant?

© Houghton Mifflin Harcourt Publishing Company • Image Credits: ©Constantine Pankin/Shutterstock

The null hypothesis for this experiment is that the college entrance exam prep course has no effect on a student's score. Under this assumption, it doesn't matter whether a student is in the treatment group or the control group. Since each group is a sample of the students, the means of the two samples should be about equal. In fact, any random division of the 20 students into two groups of 10 should result in two means whose difference is relatively small and a matter of chance. This technique of scrambling the data, called *resampling*, allows you to create a *resampling distribution* of the differences of means for every possible pairing of groups with 10 students in each. You can test the null hypothesis by using the resampling distribution to find the likelihood, given that the null hypothesis is true, of getting a difference of means at least as great as the actual experimental difference. The test is called a **permutation test**, also known as a *randomization test*.

Use the table of exam scores to construct a resampling distribution for the difference of means, assuming that the null hypothesis is true. Then determine the significance of the actual experimental result.

(A) State the null hypothesis in terms of the difference of the two group means.

_____

(B) Calculate the mean score for the treatment group, $\bar{x}_T$, and the mean score for the control group, $\bar{x}_C$. Then find the difference of the means.

_____

(C) Label the data in the table with the identifiers 1 through 20. Then follow these steps to complete each of the following tables.

- Use a graphing calculator's random integer generator to generate a list of 10 identifiers between 1 and 20 with no identifiers repeated.

- Record the scores that correspond to those identifiers as the scores for Group A. Record the remaining 10 scores as the scores for Group B.

- Find $\bar{x}_A$, $\bar{x}_B$, and $\bar{x}_A - \bar{x}_B$, and record them in the table.

	Resampling 1					Means	Difference of means
Group A						$\bar{x}_A =$	
							$\bar{x}_A - \bar{x}_B =$
Group B						$\bar{x}_B =$	

	Resampling 2				Means	Difference of means
Group A					$\bar{x}_A =$	$\bar{x}_A - \bar{x}_B =$
Group B					$\bar{x}_B =$	

	Resampling 3				Means	Difference of means
Group A					$\bar{x}_A =$	$\bar{x}_A - \bar{x}_B =$
Group B					$\bar{x}_B =$	

D Report the differences of means that you found for simulations 1–3 to your teacher so that your teacher can create a frequency table and histogram of the class results. You should make your own copy of the frequency table and histogram using the table and grid shown.

Interval	Frequency
$-320 \leq x < -240$	
$-240 \leq x < -160$	
$-160 \leq x < -80$	
$-80 \leq x < 0$	
$0 \leq x < 80$	
$80 \leq x < 160$	
$160 \leq x < 240$	
$240 \leq x < 320$	

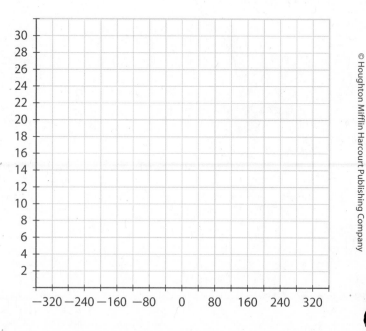

4. **Discussion** Would you say that the resampling distribution provides sufficient evidence to reject the null hypothesis? Explain your reasoning.

_____

_____

_____

Explain 1 Performing a Permutation Test

Once you use the resampling distribution to calculate the probability, called the *P–value*, of randomly getting a result that is the same as, or more extreme than, the result obtained from the experiment under the assumption that the null hypothesis is true, you can determine the significance of the result. Statisticians commonly use the following levels of significance:

- When $P > 0.10$, the result is *not significant*. The null hypothesis is not rejected.
- When $0.05 < P \leq 0.10$, the result is *marginally significant*. You can reject the null hypothesis at the 10% significance level.
- When $0.01 < P \leq 0.05$, the result is *significant*. You can reject the null hypothesis at the 5% significance level.
- When $P \leq 0.01$, the result is *highly significant*. You can reject the null hypothesis at the 1% significance level.

Example 1 Determine the experimental result's significance and state a conclusion.

(A) The histogram shows 90 resamples from Explore 2. Recall that the result obtained from the experiment was a difference of means of 160.

Step 1 Calculate the *P*-value.

Divide the sum of the frequencies for the intervals $160 \leq x < 240$ and $240 \leq x < 320$ by the sum of all frequencies (the total number of resamples). So, $P(x \geq 160) = \frac{2+1}{90} \approx 0.03$.

Step 2 Determine the significance. Because the *P*-value is between 0.05 and 0.01, the experimental result is significant. Reject the null hypothesis that the exam prep course has no effect in favor of the alternative hypothesis that the course has a positive effect.

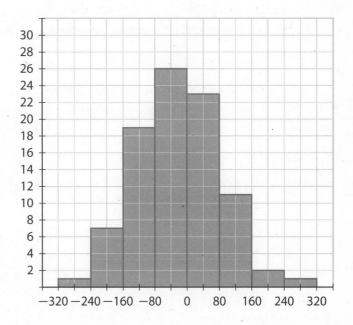

© Houghton Mifflin Harcourt Publishing Company

(B) A textbook company has created an electronic version of one of its books and wants to know what effect, if any, using the e-book has on student learning. A teacher who has two classes that already use the textbook agrees, with the permission of the school district, to participate in a research study. One of the classes uses the e-book for the next unit of instruction while the other class continues to use the print version of the book. After teaching the unit, the teacher gives the same test to both classes. The mean score for the class using the e-book is 82.3, while the mean score for the class using the print book is 78.2.

The resampling distribution for the difference of mean test scores, given that the null hypothesis is true, is normal with a mean of 0 and a standard error of 2. The distribution is shown.

Step 1 State the null hypothesis in terms of the difference of the mean test scores.

_____

Step 2 Identify the treatment group and its mean test score, $\bar{x}_T$, as well as the control group and its mean test score, $\bar{x}_C$. Then find $\bar{x}_T - \bar{x}_C$.

Treatment group: _____

$\bar{x}_C = \boxed{}$

Control group: _____

$\bar{x}_C = \boxed{}$

$\bar{x}_T - \bar{x}_C = \boxed{}$

Step 3 Use the resampling distribution to determine the significance of the experimental result.

The interval $-2\left(\boxed{}\right) \leq x \leq 2\left(\boxed{}\right)$, or $\boxed{} \leq x \leq \boxed{}$, captures the middle 95% of the differences of the means in the resampling distribution.

The experimental result is [significant/not significant] because it falls [inside/outside] the interval. [Reject/Don't reject] the null hypothesis that the e-book had no effect on student learning. [Accept/Don't accept] the alternative hypothesis that the e-book had an effect on student learning.

Reflect

5. Which part of this example, Part A or Part B, involves a *one-tailed* test and which part involves a *two-tailed* test? Explain your reasoning.

_____

_____

_____

_____

_____

Your Turn

Determine the experimental result's significance and state a conclusion.

6. In another experiment for the same company that offers the college entrance exam prep course, $\bar{x}_T = 1632$, $\bar{x}_C = 1370$, and the resampling distribution is normal with a mean of 0 and a standard error of 83.

7. Suppose a teacher at a different school agrees to participate in the same research study using the e-book. For this school, the mean score for the class using the e-book is 81.7, while the mean score for the class using the print book is 77.9. The resampling distribution for this school is the same as the resampling distribution for the first school.

💬 Elaborate

8. Describe how to obtain a resampling distribution given the data from an experiment.

_____

_____

_____

_____

9. Describe how to perform a permutation test using a resampling distribution.

_____

_____

_____

_____

10. **Essential Question Check-In** To what does the null hypothesis attribute any difference between the control group and the treatment group? To what does the alternative hypothesis attribute a difference?

_____

_____

© Houghton Mifflin Harcourt Publishing Company

1. A research dietitian is investigating whether the consumption of fish improves the strength of bones in older adults. Two hundred older adults are recruited for an experiment in which half are asked to eat fish at least three times per week while the other half maintains their regular diet. The dietitian measures the bone density of the subjects at the beginning and end of the experiment and calculates the mean change in bone density for the two groups.

a. State the null hypothesis for this experiment.

b. If the dietitian finds that the difference of the mean changes in bone density for the two groups is not statistically significant, how does the dietitian interpret the results of the experiment?

2. An agricultural researcher investigates a new fertilizer by planting a field of corn using the new fertilizer and another field using standard fertilizer. At the end of the growing season, the researcher measures the corn yield from each plant in each field and then calculates the mean corn yields for both fields.

a. State the null hypothesis for this experiment.

b. If the researcher finds that the mean corn yield for the field with the new fertilizer is greater than the mean corn yield for the field with standard fertilizer and that the difference of the mean yields is statistically significant, how does the researcher interpret the results of the experiment?

In Exercises 3 and 4, follow these steps for creating a resampling distribution using a combination of a spreadsheet and a graphing calculator. (The steps assume 10 data values for the control group and 10 for the treatment group. You will need to make adjustments for different numbers of data values.)

Step 1 Enter the original data from the experiment in column A of a spreadsheet. List all the treatment group's data first, followed by all the control group's data. Then calculate the difference of the means by entering = **AVERAGE(A1:A10) − AVERAGE(A11:A20)**in cell A21. ·

Step 2 In cell B1, enter = **RAND()** and fill down to cell B20.

Step 3 Select the rows containing the data and choose **Sort...** from the **Data** drop-down menu. In the dialog box, indicate that you want the data sorted on **Column B**.

Step 4 Clicking OK in the dialog box puts the random numbers in numerical order and rearranges the data from the experiment at the same time. The first 10 data values become the new treatment group, and the last 10 become the new control group. Notice that the difference of the means in cell A21 is also recalculated.

Step 5 Enter the difference of the means in List 1 of a graphing calculator. Then return to the spreadsheet, highlight cell B1, and fill down to the last data value. Doing so creates a new list of random numbers in column B.

Step 6 Repeat Steps 3–5 as many times as desired. Then use the graphing calculator to obtain a histogram of the simulated resampling distribution and use trace to obtain the frequencies of the bars in the histogram in order to perform a permutation test.

3. A psychology researcher is testing whether it's possible to reduce test anxiety and improve test performance by having people write about their thoughts and feelings before taking a test. The researcher recruits 20 people, randomly assigning half to the control group, who sit quietly for 15 minutes before taking a test of general knowledge, and the other half to the treatment group, who write about their thoughts and feelings for 15 minutes before taking the same test. The table lists the scores on the test.

Control group	88	72	75	63	81	77	68	78	82	66
Treatment group	89	82	74	83	78	76	71	80	88	69

a. State the null hypothesis for the experiment.

b. Calculate the mean score for the treatment group, $\bar{x}_T$, and the mean score for the control group, $\bar{x}_C$. Then find the difference of the means.

c. Use a spreadsheet and a calculator to obtain at least 50 resamples of the data.

Interval	Frequency
$-8 \leq x < -4$	
$-4 \leq x < 0$	
$0 \leq x < 4$	
$4 \leq x < 8$	

d. Calculate the P-value.

e. Determine the experimental result's significance and state a conclusion.

4. A medical researcher is testing a new gel coating for a pill and wants to know if it improves absorption into the bloodstream. The 12 subjects in the control group are asked to take the pill with the original coating, and the 12 subjects in the treatment group are asked to take the pill with the new coating. Blood samples are drawn from each subject 1 hour after ingesting a pill. The measured drug levels, in micrograms per milliliter, are listed in the table.

Control group	34	26	33	27	36	29	39	33	25	34	37	31
Treatment group	35	36	37	35	29	31	33	40	37	36	20	39

a. State the null hypothesis for the experiment.

b. Calculate the mean drug level for the treatment group, $\bar{x}_T$, and the mean drug level for the control group, $\bar{x}_C$. Then find the difference of the means.

c. Use a spreadsheet and a calculator to obtain at least 50 resamples of the data.

Interval	Frequency
$-6 \leq x < -4$	
$-4 \leq x < -2$	
$-2 \leq x < 0$	
$0 \leq x < 2$	
$2 \leq x < 4$	
$4 \leq x < 6$	

d. Calculate the P-value.

e. Determine the experimental result's significance and state a conclusion.

5. A research gerontologist is interested in finding ways to help seniors who suffer from insomnia. She conducts an experiment in which 50 elderly volunteers are randomly assigned to two groups, one that receives informational brochures about insomnia and one that receives two in-person therapy sessions and two follow-up phone calls on how to overcome insomnia. Both groups are monitored for the amount of sleep they get each night. After 1 month, the mean change in the amount of sleep that each group gets is calculated and found to be 0.2 hour for the group that gets brochures and 1.4 hours for the group that gets therapy sessions and phone calls.

   a. State the null hypothesis for the experiment.

   b. Identify the treatment group and its mean amount of sleep, $\bar{x}_T$, as well as the control group and its mean amount of sleep, $\bar{x}_C$. Then find $\bar{x}_T - \bar{x}_C$.

   c. The resampling distribution for the difference of the mean change in the amount of sleep, given that the null hypothesis is true, is normal with a mean of 0 and a standard error of 0.5. What interval captures 95% of the differences of the means in the resampling distribution?

   d. Determine the experimental result's significance and state a conclusion.

© Houghton Mifflin Harcourt Publishing Company

6. A public health researcher is interested in knowing whether the calories that teenagers consume at fast food restaurants is affected by listing calorie counts on restaurant menu boards. He recruits 50 teenagers each from two localities, one where fast food restaurants are not required to post calorie counts and one where they are. The teenagers are asked to keep the receipt each time they eat at a fast food restaurant so that the researcher can determine the calorie count for the meal. The researcher finds that the mean calorie count for the teenagers living where restaurants do not post calorie counts is 554, while the mean calorie count for the teenagers living where restaurants do post calorie counts is 486.

a. State the null hypothesis for the experiment.

b. Identify the treatment group and its mean calorie count, $\bar{x}_T$, as well as the control group and its mean calorie count, $\bar{x}_C$. Then find $\bar{x}_T - \bar{x}_C$.

c. The resampling distribution for the difference of the mean calorie counts, given that the null hypothesis is true, is normal with a mean of 0 and a standard error of 40. What interval captures 95% of the differences of means in the resampling distribution?

d. Determine the experimental result's significance and state a conclusion.

7. A research botanist is investigating the health of plants that have been genetically engineered to be more disease resistant. The botanist measures the nitrogen levels in two groups of plants, ones that have been genetically engineered and ones that have not. Using the data from the experiment, the botanist creates the resampling distribution shown. The random variable X represents the difference of the mean nitrogen level for the genetically engineered plants and the mean nitrogen level for the standard plants. Use the resampling distribution to classify the significance of each value of X.

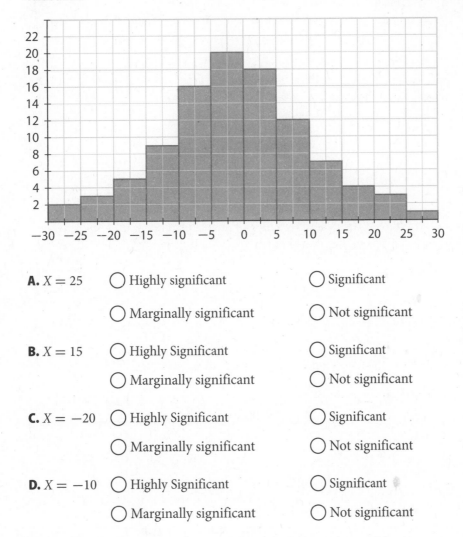

A. $X = 25$
- ◯ Highly significant
- ◯ Marginally significant
- ◯ Significant
- ◯ Not significant

B. $X = 15$
- ◯ Highly Significant
- ◯ Marginally significant
- ◯ Significant
- ◯ Not significant

C. $X = -20$
- ◯ Highly Significant
- ◯ Marginally significant
- ◯ Significant
- ◯ Not significant

D. $X = -10$
- ◯ Highly Significant
- ◯ Marginally significant
- ◯ Significant
- ◯ Not significant

8. **Draw Conclusions** The reason that the statistical test you used in this lesson is called a *permutation* test is that the process of resampling assigns different permutations of the labels "treatment" and "control" to the data from an experiment. Although the number of permutations of n distinct objects is $n!$, the objects in this case are some number of "treatment" labels and some number of "control" labels, so the objects are not distinct. When a set of n objects contains n_1 copies of the first object, n_2 copies of the second object, ..., and n_L copies of the last object, then the formula for the number of permutations of the n objects becomes $\dfrac{n!}{n_1! \cdot n_2! \cdot \ldots \cdot n_L!}$.

   a. Recall that in Explore 2, you had a control group with 10 students and a treatment group of 10 students. How many permutations of the "treatment" and "control" labels are possible? Did your class generate all possible resamples?

   b. Suppose your class had generated all possible resamples. Explain why the resampling distribution would be perfectly symmetric and centered on 0.

9. **Communicate Mathematical Ideas** The table shows measurements obtained from an experiment involving 3 subjects in the control group and 3 subjects in the treatment group.

Control group	2	4	3
Treatment group	9	10	5

   a. How many distinct resamples of the data are possible? Explain your reasoning.

   b. Calculate the difference of the means for the given treatment and control groups. Is this difference significant at the 5% level using a one-tailed test? Explain why or why not.

10. Explain the Error A student was given the resampling distribution shown and asked to determine the P-value when the actual difference of means for the treatment and control groups from an experiment is 30. The student gave the answer $\frac{4}{77} \approx 0.052$. Is the student correct? Explain.

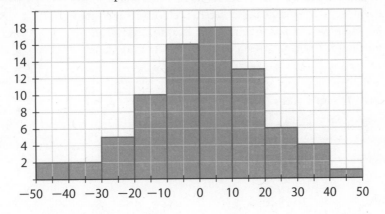

Lesson Performance Task

Researchers conducted an experiment where 12 teenage subjects were asked to use a driving simulator. At random intervals, a signal changed from green to red. Subjects were told to press a "brake" button as soon as they noticed that the signal changed to red. Each subject used the simulator under two conditions: while talking on a cell phone with a friend (the treatment) and while music was playing from a radio (the control). The table gives the data from the experiment.

Subject	Reaction Time (milliseconds)	
	Cell Phone (Treatment)	Radio (Control)
A	565	471
B	585	544
C	564	529
D	581	613
E	604	531
F	567	597
G	523	535
H	549	556
I	561	474
J	551	508
K	610	551
L	579	462

a. Calculate the mean reaction time for the treatment, $\bar{x}_T$, and the mean reaction time for the control, $\bar{x}_C$. Then find the difference of the means.

b. Because this experiment involved obtaining both the control data and the treatment data from the same subjects, resampling the data involves maintaining the pairing of the data but randomizing the order of the data within pairs. The table shows one resample where a coin was flipped for each of the 12 subjects. If the coin landed heads up, then the subject's reaction times were kept as they are. However, if the coin landed tails up, then the subject's reaction times were swapped. Using the data for the resample, find $\bar{x}_T$, $\bar{x}_C$, and $\bar{x}_T - \bar{x}_C$. How does the difference of the means for the resample compare with the difference of the means you obtained in part a?

Subject	Treatment Reaction Time (milliseconds)	Control Reaction Time (milliseconds)	Treatment Reaction Time for Resample	Control Reaction Time for Resample
A	565	471	565	471
B	585	544	544	585
C	564	529	564	529
D	581	613	581	613
E	604	531	531	604
F	567	597	567	597
G	523	535	535	523
H	549	556	549	556
I	561	474	474	561
J	551	508	551	508
K	610	551	551	610
L	579	462	462	579

c. State the null hypothesis for the experiment.

d. Under the assumption that the null hypothesis is true, researchers resampled the data 1000 times and obtained the resampling distribution shown in the table. Use the table to find the probability that a difference of the means from the resampling distribution is at least as great as the difference of the means that you found in part a.

Interval	Frequency
$-61 \leq x < -41$	5
$-41 \leq x < -21$	89
$-21 \leq x < -1$	390
$-1 \leq x < 19$	408
$19 \leq x < 39$	102
$39 \leq x < 59$	6

e. Using the *P*-value you obtained in part d, state the significance of the experimental result and the conclusion you can draw from the permutation test.

Essential Question: How can making inferences from data help to solve real-world problems?

KEY EXAMPLE   (Lesson 24.1)

In a random sample of 100 clothing buyers at a particular clothing store, 64 bought a pair of jeans. Find a 90% confidence interval for the proportion p of clothing buyers at that particular store who will buy jeans.

$n = 100$

$\hat{p} = 0.64$

$z_c = 1.645$

Determine the sample size n, the proportion $\hat{p}$, and the value of z_c for a 90% confidence interval.

Substitute into the formulas for the endpoints of the confidence interval.

$$\hat{p} - z_c \sqrt{\frac{\hat{p}(1-\hat{p})}{n}} = 0.64 - 1.645\sqrt{\frac{0.64(1-0.64)}{100}} \approx 0.56$$

$$\hat{p} + z_c \sqrt{\frac{\hat{p}(1-\hat{p})}{n}} = 0.64 + 1.645\sqrt{\frac{0.64(1-0.64)}{100}} \approx 0.72$$

So, you can state with 90% confidence that the proportion of people that will buy jeans at that particular store lies between 0.56 and 0.72.

KEY EXAMPLE   (Lesson 24.2)

Explain why the results of the survey are likely to be inaccurate, and then suggest a way to improve the accuracy of the survey.

Mr. Culberson, the owner of a sporting goods company, conducts one-on-one interviews with a random sample of employees to have them rate how satisfied they are with the quality of the goods they sell.

Because the person conducting the survey is the owner of the company, the employees may not be completely open about their feelings of the products. Some employees may not even buy the products. A better survey would involve a neutral interviewer, allow employees to respond anonymously, or to interview customers instead of employees.

In a random sample of town residents, a survey asks, "Are you in favor of a special tax levy to renovate the sad state of the city park?"

The question is biased because the words "sad state" suggest that the park is in such a state that it needs to be fixed, which makes it seem that the tax levy is necessary. The question should begin with a factual list of improvements, and then a question like, "Are you in favor of a tax levy to make improvements to the park?"

Key Vocabulary

confidence interval
  (intervalo de confianza)

margin of error
  (margen de error)

survey *(estudio)*

observational study *(estudio de observación)*

experiment *(experimento)*

randomized comparative
  experiment *(experimenta
  comparativa aleatorizado)*

null hypothesis
  (hipótesis nula)

statistically significant
  *(estadísticamente
  significativa)*

resampling *(remuestro)*

permutation test *(prueba de
  permutación)*

EXERCISES

In a random sample of 50 parfait buyers at Yo-Gurt Shop, 37 used vanilla frozen yogurt for their parfait. Find the proportion. *(Lesson 24.1)*

1. Find a 99% confidence interval for the population proportion p of parfait purchasers who will use vanilla frozen yogurt.

2. If the survey were expanded to 100 buyers, and 89 used vanilla frozen yogurt, find a 90% confidence interval for the population proportion p of parfait purchasers who will use vanilla frozen yogurt.

Explain why the results of the survey are likely to be inaccurate. *(Lesson 24.2)*

3. A survey of favorite sports for the school is taken after football practice.

MODULE PERFORMANCE TASK

Sports Nutrition

Twenty-four athletes training for the Olympics were randomly assigned to one of two groups for a sports nutrition study. The treatment group received a daily dosage of a particular nutritional supplement for 6 weeks. The control group received a placebo. Each athlete's power output was tested before and after the 6-week training period. Researchers reported the following gains for each athlete in watts per kilogram of body mass.

	Increase in Power (watts/kg of body mass)			
Treatment Group	0.52	0.21	0.38	0.36
	0.39	0.30	0.46	0.33
	0.41	0.53	0.27	0.40
Control Group	0.32	0.39	0.25	0.29
	0.28	0.41	0.18	0.28
	0.19	0.42	0.33	0.26

What is the difference in means between the treatment and control groups? Is this difference statistically significant? Start on your own paper by listing information you will need to solve the problem. Be sure to write down all your data and assumptions. Then use graphs, numbers, tables, words, or algebra to explain how you reached your conclusion.

(Ready) to Go On?

25.1–25.3 Making Inferences from Data

State the null hypothesis.

1. Ten plants are given a new plant food once a week, in addition to regular watering. Ten other plants are only watered regularly. After one month, the mean heights of the two groups of plants are compared.

2. A sample group of patients suffering from frequent headaches are given a new medicine designed to significantly reduce the number of headaches per month. Another group of patients also suffering from frequent headaches are given a sugar pill. After 6 months, the mean numbers of headaches are compared for the two groups.

Find the proportion.

3. A local school took a random sample of 500 students, in which 378 carried backpacks. Find the proportion of students who carry backpacks with a 95% confidence interval.

ESSENTIAL QUESTION

4. How can making inferences from data help a test-prep writer?

Assessment Readiness

1. A local band took a survey of 100 local music listeners about their favorite type of music. The results are as follows: 36 stated they preferred rock, 32 stated they preferred country, 25 stated they preferred hip-hop, and 7 stated they had no preference. Any probability uses a 95% confidence interval.

   Select Yes or No for A–C.

   A. The data have a normal distribution.   ◯ Yes   ◯ No

   B. probability of country: between 0.23 and 0.41   ◯ Yes   ◯ No

   C. probability of rock: between 0.27 and 0.45   ◯ Yes   ◯ No

2. Consider the situation where a company is testing a new pair of shoes. They give 20 runners a pair of their redesigned shoes and 20 runners a pair of the previous model of shoes. After one month, they will be testing the amount of wear on the shoes. Choose True or False for each statement.

   A. The null hypothesis would be that both shoes wear the same amount.   ◯ True   ◯ False

   B. A potential problem with the test is not knowing how much each runner runs in a week. This cannot be avoided.   ◯ True   ◯ False

   C. The desired hypothesis for the shoe company would be that the older shoes worked better than the redesigned ones.   ◯ True   ◯ False

3. A local political group is taking surveys of potential voters in the next election. They are calling voters registered in the Democratic Party to see which candidate is most likely to win the election for mayor. Explain why the results of the survey are likely to be inaccurate, and then suggest a way to improve the accuracy of the survey.

4. What type of function is illustrated by the points $(-1, 16)$, $(0, 4)$ $(1, 1)$, $\left(2, \frac{1}{4}\right)$ and $\left(3, \frac{1}{16}\right)$? Explain your answer.

Assessment Readiness

Personal
Math
Trainer

• Online Homework
• Hints and Help
• Extra Practice

1. Consider a survey to pick a new sport to add to the school. Is the suggested sampling method likely to result in an accurate result?

   Select Yes or No for A–C.

   A. survey every 10 attendees at a football game ○ Yes ○ No

   B. survey every teacher ○ Yes ○ No

   C. survey every 20 students on the school roster ○ Yes ○ No

2. Consider a situation where a pizza company wants to improve its sauce. They give each of 15 testers two unlabeled samples of pizza; one with the new sauce and one with the old sauce.

   Select True or False for each statement.

   A. The null result would be both sauces tasting the same. ○ True ○ False

   B. The desired result would be the customers preferring the new sauce. ○ True ○ False

   C. The undesired result would be that the customers cannot tell between the two sauces. ○ True ○ False

3. Consider the survey where a company owner, Ms. Baker, takes a random sample of her customers' names and their opinion about the quality of her product in return for a free donut.

   Select True or False for each statement.

   A. The survey is biased because the customers may not be honest to the owner of the company since they have to give their names. ○ True ○ False

   B. The survey would be more accurate if Ms. Baker would allow customers to survey anonymously. ○ True ○ False

   C. All customers will be honest if they get a free donut for completing the survey. ○ True ○ False

4. Consider each equation. Does the equation have at least 2 real roots?

   Select Yes or No for A–C.

   A. $f(x) = x^2 - 6$ ○ Yes ○ No

   B. $f(x) = x^2 + 2$ ○ Yes ○ No

   C. $f(x) = (x^2 - 2)(x + 2)(x - 4)$ ○ Yes ○ No

5. Describe the difference between a normal distribution and a uniform distribution.

6. Suppose the average time a student spends traveling to school via walking, car, or bus is 22 minutes, with a standard deviation of 12 minutes. You choose a random sample of 100 students. What is the probability that your sample has a mean time up to 24.4 minutes? Explain.

7. Karissa solved the absolute value equation $5 = 2|x - 3| + 2$ as shown. Describe and correct Karissa's mistake(s).

$5 = 2|x - 3| + 2$	Subtract 2 from both sides.
$3 = 2|x - 3|$	Divide both sides by 2.
$1.5 = |x - 3|$	Separate equation into two equations.
$1.5 = x - 3$ and $-1.5 = x - 3$	Solve for x.
$x = -1.5$ and $x = -4.5$	

Performance Tasks

★ **8.** Samples of the ages of members of two different athletic clubs in Smithville are shown.

Membership Information	
Power-Pump Gym	24, 28, 44, 50, 31, 20, 25, 54, 27, 19, 23, 37, 42, 25, 29, 40
Smithville Racket Club	14, 49, 30, 17, 28, 71, 64, 29, 12, 28, 60, 51, 23, 59, 66, 23

A. Determine the mean and standard deviation for each data set. Round to the nearest age.

B. What do the samples say about the age of a typical member at each club? Explain.

★★ **9.** A cable company wants to know if customers that pay for DVR service (to record shows) would cancel it if the ads in the shows could not be skipped when shows are viewed. A report from a survey shows that only 12% of customers that pay for DVR would cancel it.

   A. Name at least three aspects of the survey that you would want to know more about to help determine if the report is valid.

   B. The cable company ultimately wants more of its customers to pay for DVR service, since only 29% of customers currently subscribe to this service. How might this information affect the company's decision to disable fast-forwarding of ads? Write 3 statements about your reasoning.

★★★**10.** The United States Association of Table Tennis (USATT) uses a rating system for members. The ratings are normally distributed with a mean of 1400 and a standard deviation of 490.

   A. Ernesto says that about a third of all members have a rating between 900 and 1400. Is this correct? Explain.

   B. An "expert" player is considered to have a rating of at least 1900. About what percent of members are *not* "experts"?

   C. A USATT club in New York has 73 members. The club has an average member rating of 1870. Explain why the members of the club do not reflect the distribution of all USATT members.

Pharmaceutical Scientist A pharmaceutical scientist is testing whether a certain medication for raising glucose levels is more effective at higher doses. In a random trial, the fasting glucose levels of 5 patients being treated at a normal dose (Group A) and 5 patients being tested at a high dose (Group B) were recorded. The glucose levels in mmol/L are shown in the table.

A	5.4	5.7	4.8	4.3	4.6
B	5.5	5.1	4.2	5.9	4.9

a. State the null hypothesis for the experiment.

b. Compare the results for the control group and the treatment group using box plots.

c. Do you think that the researcher has enough evidence to reject the null hypothesis?

© Houghton Mifflin Harcourt Publishing Company

Glossary/Glosario

A

ENGLISH	SPANISH	EXAMPLES
absolute value of a complex number The absolute value of $a + bi$ is the distance from the origin to the point (a, b) in the complex plane and is denoted $\lvert a + bi \rvert = \sqrt{a^2 + b^2}$.	**valor absoluto de un número complejo** El valor absoluto de $a + bi$ es la distancia desde el origen hasta el punto (a, b) en el plano complejo y se expresa $\lvert a + bi \rvert = \sqrt{a^2 + b^2}$.	$\lvert 2 + 3i \rvert = \sqrt{2^2 + 3^2} = \sqrt{13}$
absolute value of a real number The absolute value of x is the distance from zero to x on a number line, denoted $\lvert x \rvert$. $\lvert x \rvert = \begin{cases} x & \text{if } x \geq 0 \\ -x & \text{if } x < 0 \end{cases}$	**valor absoluto de un número real** El valor absoluto de x es la distancia desde cero hasta x en una recta numérica y se expresa $\lvert x \rvert$. $\lvert x \rvert = \begin{cases} x & \text{si } x \geq 0 \\ -x & \text{si } x < 0 \end{cases}$	$\lvert 3 \rvert = 3$ $\lvert -3 \rvert = 3$
absolute-value function A function whose rule contains absolute-value expressions.	**función de valor absoluto** Función cuya regla contiene expresiones de valor absoluto.	*(graph with $f(x) = \lvert x \rvert$)*
amplitude The amplitude of a periodic function is half the difference of the maximum and minimum values (always positive).	**amplitud** La amplitud de una función periódica es la mitad de la diferencia entre los valores máximo y mínimo (siempre positivos).	*(graph with maximum: 3, minimum: −3)* $\text{amplitude} = \frac{1}{2}\big[3 - (-3)\big] = 3$
angle of depression The angle formed by a horizontal line and a line of sight to a point below.	**ángulo de depresión** Ángulo formado por una recta horizontal y una línea visual a un punto inferior.	*(diagram)*
angle of elevation The angle formed by a horizontal line and a line of sight to a point above.	**ángulo de elevación** Ángulo formado por una recta horizontal y una línea visual a un punto superior.	*(diagram)*
angle of rotation An angle formed by a rotating ray, called the terminal side, and a stationary reference ray, called the initial side.	**ángulo de rotación** Ángulo formado por un rayo en rotación, denominado lado terminal, y un rayo de referencia estático, denominado lado inicial.	*(diagram with Terminal side, 135°, 45°, Initial side)*

ENGLISH	SPANISH	EXAMPLES
arithmetic sequence A sequence whose successive terms differ by the same nonzero number d, called the *common difference*.	**sucesión aritmética** Sucesión cuyos términos sucesivos difieren en el mismo número distinto de cero d, denominado *diferencia común*.	4, 7, 10, 13, 16, ... $+3 +3 +3 +3$ $d = 3$
arithmetic series The indicated sum of the terms of an arithmetic sequence.	**serie aritmética** Suma indicada de los términos de una sucesión aritmética.	$4 + 7 + 10 + 13 + 16 + ...$
asymptote A line that a graph approaches as the value of a variable becomes extremely large or small.	**asíntota** Línea recta a la cual se aproxima una gráfica a medida que el valor de una variable se hace sumamente grande o pequeño.	
augmented matrix A matrix that consists of the coefficients and the constant terms in a system of linear equations.	**matriz aumentada** Matriz formada por los coeficientes y los términos constantes de un sistema de ecuaciones lineales.	System of equations Augmented matrix $3x + 2y = 5$ $2x - 3y = 1$ $\begin{bmatrix} 3 & 2 & 5 \\ 2 & -3 & 1 \end{bmatrix}$
average rate of change The ratio of the change in the function values, $f(x_2) - f(x_1)$ to the change in the x-values, $x_2 - x_1$.	**tasa de cambio promedio** Razón entre el cambio en los valores de la función, $f(x_2) - f(x_1)$ y el cambio en los valores de x, $x_2 - x_1$.	
axis of symmetry A line that divides a plane figure or a graph into two congruent reflected halves.	**eje de simetría** Línea que divide una figura plana o una gráfica en dos mitades reflejadas congruentes.	

B

ENGLISH	SPANISH	EXAMPLES
base of an exponential function The value of b in a function of the form $f(x) = ab^x$, where a and b are real numbers with $a \neq 0$, $b > 0$, and $b \neq 1$.	**base de una función exponencial** Valor de b en una función del tipo $f(x) = ab^x$, donde a y b son números reales con $a \neq 0$, $b > 0$, y $b \neq 1$.	$f(x) = 5(2)^x$ base
biased sample A sample that does not fairly represent the population.	**muestra no representativa** Muestra que no representa adecuadamente una población.	
binomial A polynomial with two terms.	**binomio** Polinomio con dos términos.	$x + y$ $2a^2 + 3$ $4m^3n^2 + 6mn^4$

Glossary/Glosario

ENGLISH	SPANISH	EXAMPLES
binomial experiment A probability experiment consists of n identical and independent trials whose outcomes are either successes or failures, with a constant probability of success p and a constant probability of failure q, where $q = 1 - p$ or $p + q = 1$.	**experimento binomial** Experimento de probabilidades que comprende n pruebas idénticas e independientes cuyos resultados son éxitos o fracasos, con una probabilidad constante de éxito p y una probabilidad constante de fracaso q, donde $q = 1 - p$ o $p + q = 1$.	A multiple-choice quiz has 10 questions with 4 answer choices. The number of trials is 10. If each question is answered randomly, the probability of success for each trial is $\frac{1}{4} = 0.25$ and the probability of failure is $\frac{3}{4} = 0.75$.
binomial probability In a binomial experiment, the probability of r successes $(0 \le r \le n)$ is $P(r) = {}_nC_r \cdot p^r q^{n-r}$.	**probabilidad binomial** En un experimento binomial, la probabilidad de r éxitos $(0 \le r \le n)$ es $P(r) = {}_nC_r \cdot p^r q^{n-r}$.	In the binomial experiment above, the probability of randomly guessing 6 problems correctly is $P = {}_{10}C_6 (0.25)^6 (0.75)^4 \approx 0.016$.
Binomial Theorem For any positive integer n, $(x + y)^n = {}_nC_0 x^n y^0 + {}_nC_1 x^{n-1} y^1 + {}_nC_2 x^{n-2} y^2 + \ldots + {}_nC_{n-1} x^1 y^{n-1} + {}_nC_n x^0 y^n$.	**Teorema de los binomios** Dado un entero positivo n, $(x + y)^n = {}_nC_0 x^n y^0 + {}_nC_1 x^{n-1} y^1 + {}_nC_2 x^{n-2} y^2 + \ldots + {}_nC_{n-1} x^1 y^{n-1} + {}_nC_n x^0 y^n$.	$(x + 2)^4 = {}_4C_0 x^4 2^0 + {}_4C_1 x^3 2^1 + {}_4C_2 x^2 2^2 + {}_4C_3 x^1 2^3 + {}_4C_4 x^0 2^4 = x^4 + 8x^3 + 24x^2 + 32x + 16$
branch of a hyperbola One of the two symmetrical parts of the hyperbola.	**rama de una hipérbola** Una de las dos partes simétricas de la hipérbola.	

C

categorical data Data that represent observations or attributes that can be sorted into groups or categories.	**datos categóricos** Datos que representan observaciones o atributos que pueden ser clasificados en grupos o categorías.	
census A survey of an entire population.	**censo** Estudio de una población entera.	
closure A set of numbers is said to be closed, or to have closure, under a given operation if the result of the operation on any two numbers in the set is also in the set.	**cerradura** Se dice que un conjunto de números es cerrado, o tiene cerradura, respecto de una operación determinada, si el resultado de la operación entre dos numerous cualesquiera del conjunto también está en el conjunto.	The natural numbers are closed under addition because the sum of two natural numbers is always a natural number.
coefficient matrix The matrix of the coefficients of the variables in a linear system of equations.	**matriz de coeficientes** Matriz de los coeficientes de las variables en un sistema lineal de ecuaciones.	System of equations Coefficient matrix $2x + 3y = 11$ $5x - 4y = 16$ $\begin{bmatrix} 2 & 3 \\ 5 & -4 \end{bmatrix}$

ENGLISH	SPANISH	EXAMPLES
combination A selection of a group of objects in which order is *not* important. The number of combinations of r objects chosen from a group of n objects is denoted $_nC_r$.	**combinación** Selección de un grupo de objetos en la cual el orden *no* es importante. El número de combinaciones de r objetos elegidos de un grupo de n objetos se expresa así: $_nC_r$.	For 4 objects A, B, C, and D, there are $_4C_2 = 6$ different combinations of 2 objects: AB, AC, AD, BC, BD, CD.
common difference In an arithmetic sequence, the nonzero constant difference of any term and the previous term.	**diferencia común** En una sucesión aritmética, diferencia constante distinta de cero entre cualquier término y el término anterior.	In the arithmetic sequence 3, 5, 7, 9, 11, ..., the common difference is 2.
common logarithm A logarithm whose base is 10, denoted $\log_{10}$ or just log.	**logaritmo común** Logaritmo de base 10, que se expresa $\log_{10}$ o simplemente log.	$\log 100 = \log_{10} 100 = 2$, since $10^2 = 100$.
common ratio In a geometric sequence, the constant ratio of any term and the previous term.	**razón común** En una sucesión geométrica, la razón constante r entre cualquier término y el término anterior.	In the geometric sequence 32, 16,18, 4, 2 ..., the common ratio is $\frac{1}{2}$.
complement of an event All outcomes in the sample space that are not in an event E, denoted $\bar{E}$.	**complemento de un suceso** Todos los resultados en el espacio muestral que no están en el suceso E y se expresan $\bar{E}$.	In the experiment of rolling a number cube, the complement of rolling a 3 is rolling a 1, 2, 4, 5, or 6.
completing the square A process used to form a perfect-square trinomial. To complete the square of $x^2 + bx$, add $\left(\frac{b}{2}\right)^2$.	**completar el cuadrado** Proceso utilizado para formar un trinomio cuadrado perfecto. Para completar el cuadrado de $x^2 + bx$, hay que sumar $\left(\frac{b}{2}\right)^2$.	$x^2 + 6x + \blacksquare$ Add $\left(\frac{6}{2}\right)^2 = 9$. $x^2 + 6x + 9$ $(x + 3)^2$ is a perfect square.
complex conjugate The complex conjugate of any complex number $a + bi$, denoted $\overline{a + bi}$, is $a - bi$.	**conjugado complejo** El conjugado complejo de cualquier número complejo $a + bi$, expresado como $\overline{a + bi}$, es $a - bi$.	$\overline{4 + 3i} = 4 - 3i$ $\overline{4 - 3i} = 4 + 3i$
complex fraction A fraction that contains one or more fractions in the numerator, the denominator, or both.	**fracción compleja** Fracción que contiene una o más fracciones en el numerador, en el denominador, o en ambos.	$\dfrac{\frac{1}{2}}{1 + \frac{2}{3}}$
complex number Any number that can be written as $a + bi$, where a and b are real numbers and $i = \sqrt{-1}$.	**número complejo** Todo número que se puede expresar como $a + bi$, donde a y b son números reales e $i = \sqrt{-1}$.	$4 + 2i$ $5 + 0i = 5$ $0 - 7i = -7i$
complex plane A set of coordinate axes in which the horizontal axis is the real axis and the vertical axis is the imaginary axis; used to graph complex numbers.	**plano complejo** Conjunto de ejes cartesianos en el cual el eje horizontal es el eje real y el eje vertical es el eje imaginario; se utiliza para representar gráficamente números complejos.	Imaginary axis $2i$ $0 + 0i$ Real axis -2 2 $-2i$

composition of functions The composition of functions f and g, written as $(f \circ g)(x)$ and defined as $f(g(x))$ uses the output of $g(x)$ as the input for $f(x)$.

composición de funciones La composición de las funciones f y g, expresada como $(f \circ g)(x)$ y definida como $f(g(x))$ utiliza la salida de $g(x)$ como la entrada para $f(x)$.

If $f(x) = x^2$ and $g(x) = x + 1$, the composite function $(f \circ g)(x) = (x + 1)^2$.

---

compound event An event made up of two or more simple events.

suceso compuesto Suceso formado por dos o más sucesos simples.

In the experiment of tossing a coin and rolling a number cube, the event of the coin landing heads and the number cube landing on 3.

---

compound interest Interest earned or paid on both the principal and previously earned interest, found using the formula $A(t) = P\left(1 + \dfrac{r}{n}\right)^{nt}$ where A is the final amount, P is the principal, r is the interest rate given as a decimal, n is the number of times interest is compounded, and t is the time.

interés compuesto Interés ganado o pagado tanto sobre el capital inicial como sobre el interés previamente ganado. Se halla usando la fórmula $A(t) = P\left(1 + \dfrac{r}{n}\right)^{nt}$, donde A es la cantidad final, P es el capital inicial, r es la tasa de interés indicada en forma de número decimal, n es el número de veces que se reinvierte el interés y t es el tiempo.

---

compression A transformation that pushes the points of a graph horizontally toward the y-axis or vertically toward the x-axis.

compresión Transformación que desplaza los puntos de una gráfica horizontalmente hacia el eje y o verticalmente hacia el eje x.

---

conditional probability The probability of event B, given that event A has already occurred or is certain to occur, denoted $P(B \mid A)$; used to find probability of dependent events.

probabilidad condicional Probabilidad del suceso B, dado que el suceso A ya ha ocurrido o es seguro que ocurrirá, expresada como $P(B \mid A)$; se utiliza para calcular la probabilidad de sucesos dependientes.

---

confidence interval An approximate range of values that is likely to include an unknown population parameter.

intervalo de confianza Un rango aproximado de valores que probablemente incluirá un parámetro de población desconocido.

---

conic section A plane figure formed by the intersection of a double right cone and a plane. Examples include circles, ellipses, hyperbolas, and parabolas.

sección cónica Figura plana formada por la intersección de un cono regular doble y un plano. Algunos ejemplos son círculos, elipses, hipérbolas y parábolas.

Circle   Ellipse   Parabola   Hyperbola

---

conjugate axis The axis of symmetry of a hyperbola that separates the two branches of the hyperbola.

eje conjugado Eje de simetría de una hipérbola que separa las dos ramas de la hipérbola.

Conjugate axis

Glossary/Glosario

Glossary/Glosario

constraint One of the inequalities that define the feasible region in a linear-programming problem.

restricción Una de las desigualdades que definen la región factible en un problema de programación lineal.

Constraints:
$x > 0$
$y > 0$
$x + y \leq 8$
$3x + 5y \leq 30$

Feasible region

---

continuous function A function whose graph is an unbroken line or curve with no gaps or breaks.

función continua Función cuya gráfica es una línea recta o curva continua, sin espacios ni interrupciones.

---

contradiction An equation that has no solutions.

contradicción Ecuación que no tiene soluciones.

$x + 1 = x$
$1 = 0 \, x$

---

correlation A measure of the strength and direction of the relationship between two variables or data sets.

correlación Medida de la fuerza y dirección de la relación entre dos variables o conjuntos de datos.

Positive correlation

No correlation

Negative correlation

---

correlation coefficient A number r, where $-1 \leq r \leq 1$, that describes how closely the points in a scatter plot cluster around the least–squares line.

coeficiente de correlación Número r, donde $-1 \leq r \leq 1$, que describe a qué distancia de la recta de mínimos cuadrados se agrupan los puntos de un diagrama de dispersión.

An r–value close to 1 describes a strong positive correlation.
An r–value close to 0 describes a weak correlation or no correlation.
An r–value close to -1 describes a strong negative correlation.

---

cosecant In a right triangle, the cosecant of angle A is the ratio of the length of the hypotenuse to the length of the side opposite A. It is the reciprocal of the sine function.

cosecante En un triángulo rectángulo, la cosecante del ángulo A es la razón entre la longitud de la hipotenusa y la longitud del cateto opuesto a A. Es la inversa de la función seno.

A
opposite
hypotenuse

$$\csc A = \frac{\text{hypotenuse}}{\text{opposite}} = \frac{1}{\sin A}$$

---

cosine In a right triangle, the cosine of angle A is the ratio of the length of the side adjacent to angle A to the length of the hypotenuse. It is the reciprocal of the secant function.

coseno En un triángulo rectángulo, el coseno del ángulo A es la razón entre la longitud del cateto adyacente al ángulo A y la longitud de la hipotenusa. Es la inversa de la función secante.

hypotenuse
A
adjacent

$$\cos A = \frac{\text{adjacent}}{\text{hypotenuse}} = \frac{1}{\sec A}$$

ENGLISH	SPANISH	EXAMPLES

cotangent In a right triangle, the cotangent of angle A is the ratio of the length of the side adjacent to A to the length of the side opposite A. It is the reciprocal of the tangent function. | **cotangente** En un triángulo rectángulo, la cotangente del ángulo A es la razón entre la longitud del cateto adyacente a A y la longitud del cateto opuesto a A. Es la inversa de la función tangente. |

$$\cot A = \frac{\text{adjacent}}{\text{opposite}} = \frac{1}{\tan A}$$

coterminal angles Two angles in standard position with the same terminal side. | **ángulos coterminales** Dos ángulos en posición estándar con el mismo lado terminal. |

critical values Values that separate the number line into intervals that either contain solutions or do not contain solutions. | **valores críticos** Valores que separan la recta numérica en intervalos que contienen o no contienen soluciones. |

cube-root function The function $f(x) = \sqrt[3]{x}$. | **función de raíz cúbica** La función $f(x) = \sqrt[3]{x}$. |

cubic function A polynomial function of degree 3. | **función cúbica** Función polinomial de grado 3. |

cumulative probability The probability that a random variable is less than or equal to a given value. | **probabilidad acumulada** La probabilidad de que una variable aleatoria sea menor o igual que un valor determinado. |

cycle of a periodic function The shortest repeating part of a periodic graph or function. | **ciclo de una función periódica** La parte repetida más corta de una gráfica o función periódica. |

D

decay factor The base $1 - r$ in an exponential expression. | **factor decremental** Base $1 - r$ en una expresión exponencial. |

$$2(0.93)^t$$

decay factor (representing $1 - 0.07$)

decay rate The constant percent decrease, in decimal form, in an exponential decay function. | **tasa de disminución** Disminución porcentual constante, en forma decimal, en una función de disminución exponencial. |

In the function $f(t) = a(1 - 0.2)^t$, 0.2 is the decay rate.

Glossary/Glosario

Glossary/Glosario

ENGLISH	SPANISH	EXAMPLES

decreasing A function is decreasing on an interval if $f(x_1) > f(x_2)$ when $x_1 > x_2$ for any x-values x_1 and x_2 from the interval.

decreciente Una función es decreciente en un intervalo si $f(x_1) > f(x_2)$ cuando $x_1 > x_2$ dados los valores de x, x_1 y x_2, pertenecientes al intervalo.

$f(x)$ is decreasing on the interval $x < 0$.

degree of a monomial The sum of the exponents of the variables in the monomial.

grado de un monomio Suma de los exponentes de las variables del monomio.

$4x^2y^5z^3$ Degree: $2+5+3=10$
5 Degree: $0\ (5=5x^0)$

degree of a polynomial The degree of the term of the polynomial with the greatest degree.

grado de un polinomio Grado del término del polinomio con el grado máximo.

$3x^2y^2 + 4xy^5 - 12x^3y^2$ Degree 6
Degree 4 Degree 6 Degree 5

dependent events Events for which the occurrence or nonoccurrence of one event affects the probability of the other event.

sucesos dependientes Dos sucesos son dependientes si el hecho de que uno de ellos se cumpla o no afecta la probabilidad del otro.

From a bag containing 3 red marbles and 2 blue marbles, drawing a red marble, and then drawing a blue marble without replacing the first marble.

dependent system A system of equations that has infinitely many solutions.

sistema dependiente Sistema de ecuaciones que tiene infinitamente muchas soluciones.

$\begin{cases} x+y=3 \\ 2x+2y=6 \end{cases}$

difference of two squares A polynomial of the form $a^2 - b^2$, which may be written as the product $(a+b)(a-b)$.

diferencia de dos cuadrados Polinomio del tipo $a^2 - b^2$, que se puede expresar como el producto $(a+b)(a-b)$.

$x^2 - 4 = (x+2)(x-2)$

directrix A fixed line used to define a *parabola*. Every point on the parabola is equidistant from the directrix and a fixed point called the *focus*.

directriz Línea fija utilizada para definir una *parábola*. Cada punto de la parábola es equidistante de la directriz y de un punto fijo denominado *foco*.

F Directrix
$P_1D_1 = P_1F\ P_2D_2 = P_2F$

discontinuous function A function whose graph has one or more jumps, breaks, or holes.

función discontinua Función cuya gráfica tiene uno o más saltos, interrupciones u hoyos.

discriminant The discriminant of the quadratic equation $ax^2 + bx + c = 0$ is $b^2 - 4ac$.

discriminante El discriminante de la ecuación cuadrática $ax^2 + bx + c = 0$ es $b^2 - 4ac$.

The discriminant of $2x^2 - 5x - 3 = 0$ is $(-5)^2 - 4(2)(-3) = 25 + 24 = 49$.

distribution A set of numerical data that you can graph using a data display that involves a number line, such as a line plot, histogram, or box plot.

distribución Un conjunto de datos numéricos que se pueden representar gráficamente mediante una representación de datos que incluye una recta numérica, como un diagrama de puntos, un histograma o un diagrama de cajas.

GL8

E

elementary row operations *See* row operations.

operaciones elementales de fila *Véase* operaciones de fila.

---

elimination A method used to solve systems of equations in which one variable is eliminated by adding or subtracting two equations of the system.

eliminación Método utilizado para resolver sistemas de ecuaciones por el cual se elimina una variable sumando o restando dos ecuaciones del sistema.

---

empty set A set with no elements.

conjunto vacío Conjunto sin elementos.

The solution set of $|x| < 0$ is the empty set, $\{\ \}$, or $\emptyset$.

---

end behavior The trends in the *y*-values of a function as the *x*-values approach positive and negative infinity.

comportamiento extremo Tendencia de los valores de *y* de una función a medida que los valores de *x* se aproximan al infinito positivo y negativo.

End behavior: $f(x) \rightarrow \infty$ as $x \rightarrow \infty$
$f(x) \rightarrow -\infty$ as $x \rightarrow -\infty$

---

even function A function in which $f(-x) = f(x)$ for all x in the domain of the function.

función par Función en la que para todos los valores de x dentro del dominio de la función.

$f(x) = |x|$ is an even function.

---

event An outcome or set of outcomes in a probability experiment.

suceso Resultado o conjunto de resultados en un experimento de probabilidad.

In the experiment of rolling a number cube, the event "an odd number" consists of the outcomes 1, 3, and 5.

---

expected value The weighted average of the numerical outcomes of a probability experiment.

valor esperado Promedio ponderado de los resultados numéricos de un experimento de probabilidad.

The table shows the probability of getting a given score by guessing on a three-question quiz.

Score	0	1	2	3
Probability	0.42	0.42	0.14	0.02

The expected value is a score of
$0\,(0.42) + 1\,(0.42) + 2\,(0.14) + 3\,(0.02)$
$= 0.76.$

---

experiment An operation, process, or activity in which outcomes can be used to estimate probability.

experimento Una operación, proceso o actividad cuyo resultado se puede usar para estimar la probabilidad.

Tossing a coin 10 times and noting the number of heads.

---

experimental probability The ratio of the number of times an event occurs to the number of trials, or times, that an activity is performed.

probabilidad experimental Razón entre la cantidad de veces que ocurre un suceso y la cantidad de pruebas, o veces, que se realiza una actividad.

Kendra made 6 of 10 free throws. The experimental probability that she will make her next free throw is

$P(\text{free throw}) = \dfrac{\text{number made}}{\text{number attempted}} = \dfrac{6}{10}.$

Glossary/Glosario

explicit formula A formula that defines the *n*th term a_n, or general term, of a sequence as a function of *n*.

fórmula explícita Fórmula que define el enésimo término a_n, o término general, de una sucesión como una función de *n*.

Sequence: 4, 7, 10, 13, 16, 19, ...
Explicit formula: $a_n = 1 + 3n$

---

exponential decay An exponential function of the form $f(x) = ab^x$ in which $0 < b < 1$. If *r* is the rate of decay, then the function can be written $y = a(1 - r)^t$, where *a* is the initial amount and *t* is the time.

decremento exponencial Función exponencial del tipo $f(x) = ab^x$ en la cual $0 < b < 1$. Si *r* es la tasa decremental, entonces la función se puede expresar como $y = a(1 - r)^t$, donde *a* es la cantidad inicial y *t* es el tiempo.

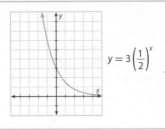

$y = 3\left(\dfrac{1}{2}\right)^x$

---

exponential equation An equation that contains one or more exponential expressions.

ecuación exponencial Ecuación que contiene una o más expresiones exponenciales.

$2^{x+1} = 8$

---

exponential function A function of the form $f(x) = ab^x$, where *a* and *b* are real numbers with $a \neq 0$, $b > 0$, and $b \neq 1$.

función exponencial Función del tipo $f(x) = ab^x$, donde *a* y *b* son números reales con $a \neq 0$, $b > 0$ y $b \neq 1$.

$f(x) = 2^x$

---

exponential growth An exponential function of the form $f(x) = ab^x$ in which $b > 1$. If *r* is the rate of growth, then the function can be written $y = a(1 + r)^t$, where *a* is the initial amount and *t* is the time.

crecimiento exponencial Función exponencial del tipo $f(x) = ab^x$ en la que $b > 1$. Si *r* es la tasa de crecimiento, entonces la función se puede expresar como $y = a(1 + r)^t$, donde *a* es la cantidad inicial y *t* es el tiempo.

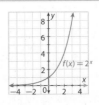

$f(x) = 2^x$

---

exponential regression A statistical method used to fit an exponential model to a given data set.

regresión exponencial Método estadístico utilizado para ajustar un modelo exponencial a un conjunto de datos determinado.

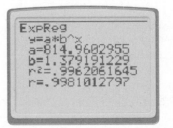

---

extraneous solution A solution of a derived equation that is not a solution of the original equation.

solución extraña Solución de una ecuación derivada que no es una solución de la ecuación original.

To solve $\sqrt{x} = -2$, square both sides; $x = 4$.
Check $\sqrt{4} = -2$ is false; so 4 is an extraneous solution.

F

Factor Theorem For any polynomial $P(x)$, $(x - a)$ is a factor of $P(x)$ if and only if $P(a) = 0$.

Teorema del factor Dado el polinomio $P(x)$, $(x - a)$ es un factor de $P(x)$ si y sólo si $P(a) = 0$.

$(x - 1)$ is a factor of $P(x) = x^2 - 1$ because $P(1) = 1^2 - 1 = 0$.

ENGLISH	SPANISH	EXAMPLES
factorial If n is a positive integer, then n factorial, written $n!$, is $n \cdot (n-1) \cdot (n-2) \cdot \ldots \cdot 2 \cdot 1$. The factorial of 0 is defined to be 1.	**factorial** Si n es un entero positivo, entonces el factorial de n, expresado como $n!$, es $n \cdot (n-1) \cdot (n-2) \cdot \ldots \cdot 2 \cdot 1$ Por definición, el factorial de 0 será 1.	$7! = 7 \cdot 6 \cdot 5 \cdot 4 \cdot 3 \cdot 2 \cdot 1 = 5040$ $0! = 1$
Fibonacci sequence The infinite sequence of numbers beginning with 1, 1 such that each term is the sum of the two previous terms.	**sucesión de Fibonacci** Sucesión infinita de números que comienza con 1, 1 de forma tal que cada término es la suma de los dos términos anteriores.	$1, 1, 2, 3, 5, 8, 13, 21, \ldots$
finite geometric series A geometric series in which the sum of a finite number of terms of a geometric sequence is found.	**serie geométrica finita** Una serie geométrica en la que se halla la suma de un número finito de términos de una secuencia geométrica.	
finite sequence A sequence with a finite number of terms.	**sucesión finita** Sucesión con un número finito de términos.	$1, 2, 3, 4, 5$
finite set A set with a definite, or finite, number of elements.	**conjunto finito** Conjunto con un número de elementos definido o finito.	$\{2, 4, 6, 8, 10\}$
first differences The differences between y-values of a function for evenly spaced x-values.	**primeras diferencias** Diferencias entre los valores de y de una función para valores de x espaciados uniformemente.	<table><tr><td>x</td><td>0</td><td>1</td><td>2</td><td>3</td></tr><tr><td>y</td><td>3</td><td>7</td><td>11</td><td>15</td></tr></table> first differences +4 +4 +4
focus (pl. foci) of a parabola A fixed point F used with a *directrix* to define a *parabola*.	**foco de una parábola** Punto fijo F utilizado con una *directriz* para definir una *parábola*.	Focus $\cdot F$
frequency of a data value The number of times the value appears in the data set.	**frecuencia de un valor de datos** Cantidad de veces que aparece el valor en un conjunto de datos.	In the data set 5, 6, 6, 6, 8, 9, the data value 6 has a frequency of 3.
frequency of a periodic function The number of cycles per unit of time. Also the reciprocal of the period.	**frecuencia de una función periódica** Cantidad de ciclos por unidad de tiempo. También es la inversa del periodo.	The function $y = \sin(2x)$ has a period of π and a frequency of $\frac{1}{\pi}$.
function rule An algebraic expression that defines a function.	**regla de función** Expresión algebraica que define una función.	$f(x) = 2x^2 + 3x - 7$ function rule

ENGLISH	SPANISH	EXAMPLES
Fundamental Counting Principle For *n* items, if there are m_1 ways to choose a first item, m_2 ways to choose a second item after the first item has been chosen, and so on, then there are $m_1 \cdot m_2 \cdot \ldots \cdot m_n$ ways to choose *n* items.	**Principio fundamental de conteo** Dados *n* elementos, si existen m_1 formas de elegir un primer elemento, m_2 formas de elegir un segundo elemento después de haber elegido el primero, y así sucesivamente, entonces existen $m_1 \cdot m_2 \cdot \ldots \cdot m_n$ formas de elegir *n* elementos.	If there are 4 colors of shirts, 3 colors of pants, and 2 colors of shoes, then there are $4 \cdot 3 \cdot 2 = 24$ possible outfits.

G

Gaussian Elimination An algorithm for solving systems of equations using matrices and row operations to eliminate variables in each equation in the system.	**Eliminación Gaussiana** Algoritmo para resolver sistemas de ecuaciones mediante matrices y operaciones de fila con el fin de eliminar variables en cada ecuación del sistema.	
general form of a conic section $Ax^2 + Bxy + Cy^2 + Dx + Ey + F = 0$, where *A* and *B* are not both 0.	**forma general de una sección cónica** $Ax^2 + Bxy + Cy^2 + Dx + Ey + F = 0$, donde *A* y *B* no son los dos 0.	A circle with a vertex at $(1, 2)$ and radius 3 has the general form $x^2 + y^2 - 2x - 4y - 4 = 0$.
geometric mean In a geometric sequence, a term that comes between two given nonconsecutive terms of the sequence. For positive numbers *a* and *b*, the geometric mean is $\sqrt{ab}$.	**media geométrica** En una sucesión geométrica, un término que se encuentra entre dos términos no consecutivos dados de la sucesión. Dados los números positivos *a* y *b*, la media geométrica es $\sqrt{ab}$.	The geometric mean of 4 and 9 is $\sqrt{4(9)} = \sqrt{36} = 6$.
geometric probability A form of theoretical probability determined by a ratio of geometric measures such as lengths, areas, or volumes.	**probabilidad geométrica** Una forma de la probabilidad teórica determinada por una razón de medidas geométricas, como longitud, área o volumen.	The probability of the pointer landing the 80° angle is $\frac{2}{9}$.
geometric sequence A sequence in which the ratio of successive terms is a constant *r*, called the common ratio, where $r \neq 0$ and $r \neq 1$.	**sucesión geométrica** Sucesión en la que la razón de los términos sucesivos es una constante *r*, denominada razón común, donde $r \neq 0$ y $r \neq 1$.	1, 2, 4, 8, 16, … $\cdot 2 \cdot 2 \cdot 2 \cdot 2 \qquad r = 2$
geometric series The indicated sum of the terms of a geometric sequence.	**serie geométrica** Suma indicada de los términos de una sucesión geométrica.	$1 + 2 + 4 + 8 + 16 + \ldots$

ENGLISH	SPANISH	EXAMPLES

greatest-integer function
A function denoted by $f(x) = [x]$ or $f(x) = \lfloor x \rfloor$ in which the number x is rounded down to the greatest integer that is less than or equal to x.

función de entero mayor
Función expresada como $f(x) = [x]$ o $f(x) = \lfloor x \rfloor$ en la cual el número x se redondea hacia abajo hasta el entero mayor que sea menor que o igual a x.

$\lfloor 4.98 \rfloor = 4$
$\lfloor -2.1 \rfloor = -3$

---

growth factor The base $1 + r$ in an exponential expression.

factor de crecimiento La base $1 + r$ en una expresión exponencial.

$12{,}000(1 + 0.14)^t$

↑

growth factor

---

growth rate The constant percent increase, in decimal form, in an exponential growth function.

tasa de crecimiento Aumento porcentual constante, en forma decimal, en una función de crecimiento exponencial.

In the function $f(t) = a(1 + 0.3)^t$, 0.3 is the growth rate.

H

Heron's Formula A triangle with side lengths a, b, and c has area $A = \sqrt{s(s-a)(s-b)(s-c)}$, where s is one-half the perimeter, or $s = \frac{1}{2}(a + b + c)$.

fórmula de Herón Un triángulo con longitudes de lado a, b y c tiene un área $A = \sqrt{s(s-a)(s-b)(s-c)}$, donde s es la mitad del perímetro ó $s = \frac{1}{2}(a + b + c)$.

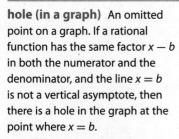

$s = \frac{1}{2}(3 + 6 + 7) = 8$
$A = \sqrt{8(8-3)(8-6)(8-7)}$
$= \sqrt{80} = 4\sqrt{5}$ square units

---

hole (in a graph) An omitted point on a graph. If a rational function has the same factor $x - b$ in both the numerator and the denominator, and the line $x = b$ is not a vertical asymptote, then there is a hole in the graph at the point where $x = b$.

hoyo (en una gráfica) Punto omitido en una gráfica. Si una función racional tiene el mismo factor $x - b$ tanto en el numerador como en el denominador, y la línea $x = b$ no es una asíntota vertical, entonces hay un hoyo en la gráfica en el punto donde $x = b$.

$f(x) = \dfrac{(x-2)(x+2)}{(x+2)}$ has a hole at $x = -2$.

---

hypothesis testing A type of testing used to determine whether the difference in two groups is likely to be caused by chance.

comprobación de hipótesis Tipo de comprobación que sirve para determinar si el azar es la causa probable de la diferencia entre dos grupos.

I

imaginary axis The vertical axis in the complex plane, it graphically represents the purely imaginary part of complex numbers.

eje imaginario Eje vertical de un plano complejo. Representa gráficamente la parte puramente imaginaria de los números complejos.

ENGLISH	SPANISH	EXAMPLES
imaginary number The square root of a negative number, written in the form bi, where b is a real number and i is the imaginary unit, $\sqrt{-1}$. Also called a *pure imaginary number*.	**número imaginario** Raíz cuadrada de un número negativo, expresado como bi, donde b es un número real e i es la unidad imaginaria, $\sqrt{-1}$. También se denomina *número imaginario puro*.	$\sqrt{-16} = \sqrt{16} \cdot \sqrt{-1} = 4i$
imaginary unit The unit in the imaginary number system, $\sqrt{-1}$.	**unidad imaginaria** Unidad del sistema de números imaginarios, $\sqrt{-1}$.	$\sqrt{-1} = i$
inconsistent system A system of equations or inequalities that has no solution.	**sistema inconsistente** Sistema de ecuaciones o desigualdades que no tiene solución.	$\begin{cases} y = 2.5x + 5 \\ y = 2.5x - 5 \end{cases}$ is inconsistent.
Increasing A function is increasing on an interval if $f(x_1) < f(x_2)$ when $x_1 < x_2$ for any x-values x_1 and x_2 from the interval.	**creciente** Una función es creciente en un intervalo si $f(x_1) < f(x_2)$ cuando $x_1 < x_2$ dados los valores de x, x_1 y x_2, pertenecienlos al intervalo.	$f(x) = |x|$ $f(x)$ is increasing on the interval $x > 0$.
independent events Events for which the occurrence or non-occurrence of one event does not affect the probability of the other event.	**sucesos independientes** Dos sucesos son independientes si el hecho de que se produzca o no uno de ellos no afecta la probabilidad del otro suceso.	From a bag containing 3 red marbles and 2 blue marbles, drawing a red marble, replacing it, and then drawing a blue marble.
independent system A system of equations that has exactly one solution.	**sistema independiente** Sistema de ecuaciones que tiene exactamente una solución.	$\begin{cases} y = -x + 4 \\ y = x + 2 \end{cases}$ Solution: $(1, 3)$
independent variable The input of a function; a variable whose value determines the value of the output, or dependent variable.	**variable independiente** Entrada de una función; variable cuyo valor determina el valor de la salida, o variable dependiente.	$y = 2x + 1$ independent variable
initial side The ray that lies on the positive x-axis when an angle is drawn in standard position.	**lado inicial** El rayo que se encuentra en el eje positivo x cuando se traza un ángulo en la posición estándar.	Terminal side 135° 45° 0 Initial side

ENGLISH	SPANISH	EXAMPLES

interval notation A way of writing the set of all real numbers between two endpoints. The symbols [and] are used to include an endpoint in an interval, and the symbols (and) are used to exclude an endpoint from an interval.

notación de intervalo Forma de expresar el conjunto de todos los números reales entre dos extremos. Los símbolos [y] se utilizan para incluir un extremo en un intervalo y los símbolos (y) se utilizan para excluir un extremo de un intervalo.

Interval notation	Set-builder notation
(a, b)	$\{x \mid a < x < b\}$
$(a, b]$	$\{x \mid a < x \le b\}$
$[a, b)$	$\{x \mid a \le x < b\}$
$[a, b]$	$\{x \mid a \le x \le b\}$

inverse function The function that results from exchanging the input and output values of a one-to-one function. The inverse of $f(x)$ is denoted $f^{-1}(x)$.

función inversa Función que resulta de intercambiar los valores de entrada y salida de una función uno a uno. La función inversa de $f(x)$ se expresa $f^{-1}(x)$

inverse relation The inverse of the relation consisting of all ordered pairs (x, y) is the set of all ordered pairs (y, x). The graph of an inverse relation is the reflection of the graph of the relation across the line $y = x$.

relación inversa La inversa de la relación que consta de todos los pares ordenados (x, y) es el conjunto de todos los pares ordenados (y, x). La gráfica de una relación inversa es el reflejo de la gráfica de la relación sobre la línea $y = x$.

irreducible factor A factor of degree 2 or greater that cannot be factored further.

factor irreducible Factor de grado 2 o mayor que no se puede seguir factorizando.

$x^2 + 7x + 1$

J

joint relative frequency The ratio of the frequency in a particular category divided by the total number of data values.

frecuencia relativa conjunta La razón de la frecuencia en una determinada categoría dividida entre el número total de valores.

L

Law of Cosines For $\triangle ABC$ with side lengths a, b, and c,
$a^2 = b^2 + c^2 - 2bc \cos A$
$b^2 = a^2 + c^2 - 2ac \cos B$
$c^2 = a^2 + b^2 - 2ab \cos C.$

Ley de cosenos Dado $\triangle ABC$ con longitudes de lado a, b y c,
$a^2 = b^2 + c^2 - 2bc \cos A$
$b^2 = a^2 + c^2 - 2ac \cos B$
$c^2 = a^2 + b^2 - 2ab \cos C$

$b^2 = 7^2 + 5^2 - 2(7)(5)\cos 100°$
$b^2 \approx 86.2$
$b \approx 9.3$

Law of Sines For $\triangle ABC$ with side lengths a, b, and c,
$\frac{\sin A}{a} = \frac{\sin B}{b} = \frac{\sin C}{c}.$

Ley de senos Dado $\triangle ABC$ con longitudes de lado a, b y c,
$\frac{\operatorname{sen}A}{a} = \frac{\operatorname{sen}B}{b} = \frac{\operatorname{sen}C}{c}.$

$\frac{\sin 49°}{r} = \frac{\sin 40°}{20}$
$r = \frac{20 \sin 49°}{\sin 40°} \approx 23.5$

Glossary/Glosario

Glossary/Glosario

ENGLISH	SPANISH	EXAMPLES
leading coefficient The coefficient of the first term of a polynomial in standard form.	**coeficiente principal** Coeficiente del primer termino de un polinomio en forma estandar	$3x^2 + 7x - 2$ ↑ Leading coefficient
limit For an infinite arithmetic series that converges, the number that the partial sums approach.	**límite** Para un serie que coverge, el número que se aproximan las sumas.	The series $\frac{1}{2} + \frac{1}{4} + \frac{1}{8} + \frac{1}{16} + \ldots$ has a limit of 1.
line of best fit The line that comes closest to all of the points in a data set.	**línea de mejor ajuste** Línea que más se acerca a todos los puntos de un conjunto de datos.	
linear equation in three variables An equation with three distinct variables, each of which is either first degree or has a coefficient of zero.	**ecuación lineal en tres variables** Ecuación con tres variables diferentes, sean de primer grado o tengan un coeficiente de cero.	$5 = 3x + 2y + 6z$
linear regression A statistical method used to fit a linear model to a given data set.	**regresión lineal** Método estadístico utilizado para ajustar un modelo lineal a un conjunto de datos determinado.	
linear system A system of equations containing only linear equations.	**sistema lineal** Sistema de ecuaciones que contiene sólo ecuaciones lineales.	$\begin{cases} y = 2x + 1 \\ x + y = 8 \end{cases}$
local maximum For a function f, $f(a)$ is a local maximum if there is an interval around a such that $f(x) < f(a)$ for every x-value in the interval except a.	**máximo local** Dada una función f, $f(a)$ es el máximo local si hay un intervalo en a tal que $f(x) < f(a)$ para cada valor de x en el intervalo excepto a.	
local minimum For a function f, $f(a)$ is a local minimum if there is an interval around a such that $f(x) > f(a)$ for every x-value in the interval except a.	**mínimo local** Dada una función f, $f(a)$ es el mínimo local si hay un intervalo en a tal que $f(x) > f(a)$ para cada valor de x en el intervalo excepto a.	
logarithm The exponent that a specified base must be raised to in order to get a certain value.	**logaritmo** Exponente al cual debe elevarse una base determinada a fin de obtener cierto valor.	$\log_2 8 = 3$, because 3 is the power that 2 is raised to in order to get 8; or $2^3 = 8$.
logarithmic equation An equation that contains a logarithm of a variable.	**ecuación logarítmica** Ecuación que contiene un logaritmo de una variable.	$\log x + 3 = 7$

logarithmic function A function of the form $f(x) = \log_b x$, where $b \neq 1$ and $b > 0$, which is the inverse of the exponential function $f(x) = b^x$.

función logarítmica Función del tipo $f(x) = \log_b x$, donde $b \neq 1$ y $b > 0$, que es la inversa de la función exponencial $f(x) = b^x$.

$f(x) = \log_4 x$

logarithmic regression A statistical method used to fit a logarithmic model to a given data set.

regresión logarítmica Método estadístico utilizado para ajustar un modelo logarítmico a un conjunto de datos determinado.

M

margin of error In a random sample, it defines an interval, centered on the sample percent, in which the population percent is most likely to lie.

margen de error En una muestra aleatoria, define un intervalo, centrado en el porcentaje de muestra, en el que es más probable que se encuentre el porcentaje de población.

matrix A rectangular array of numbers.

matriz Arreglo rectangular de números.

$$\begin{bmatrix} 1 & 0 & 3 \\ -2 & 2 & -5 \\ 7 & -6 & 3 \end{bmatrix}$$

maximum value of a function The y-value of the highest point on the graph of the function.

máximo de una función Valor de y del punto más alto en la gráfica de la función.

Maximum value

midline For the graph of a sine or cosine function, the horizontal line halfway between the maximum and minimum values of the curve; for the graph of a tangent function, the horizontal line through the point of each cycle that is midway between the asymptotes.

línea media En la gráfica de una función seno o coseno, la línea horizontal a medio camino entre los valores máximo y mínimo de la curva; en la gráfica de una función tangente, la línea horizontal que atraviesa el punto de cada ciclo que está a medio camino entre las asíntotas.

minimum value of a function The y-value of the lowest point on the graph of the function.

mínimo de una función Valor de y del punto más bajo en la gráfica de la función.

Minimum value

monomial A number or a product of numbers and variables with whole-number exponents, or a polynomial with one term.

monomio Número o producto de números y variables con exponentes de números cabales, o polinomio con un término.

$8x$, 9, $3x^2y^4$

Glossary/Glosario

ENGLISH	SPANISH	EXAMPLES

multiple root A root r is a multiple root when the factor $(x - r)$ appears in the equation more than once.

raíz múltiple Una raíz r es una raíz múltiple cuando el factor $(x - r)$ aparece en la ecuación más de una vez.

3 is a multiple root of
$P(x) = (x - 3)^2$.

multiplicity If a polynomial $P(x)$ has a multiple root at r, the multiplicity of r is the number of times $(x - r)$ appears as a factor in $P(x)$.

multiplicidad Si un polinomio $P(x)$ tiene una raíz múltiple en r, la multiplicidad de r es la cantidad de veces que $(x - r)$ aparece como factor en $P(x)$.

For $P(x) = (x - 3)^2$, the root 3 has a multiplicity of 2.

mutually exclusive events Two events are mutually exclusive if they cannot both occur in the same trial of an experiment.

sucesos mutuamente excluyentes Dos sucesos son mutuamente excluyentes si ambos no pueden ocurrir en la misma prueba de un experimento.

In the experiment of rolling a number cube, rolling a 3 and rolling an even number are mutually exclusive events.

N

natural logarithm A logarithm with base e, written as ln.

logaritmo natural Logaritmo con base e, que se escribe ln.

$\ln 5 = \log_e 5 \approx 1.6$

natural logarithmic function The function $f(x) = \ln x$, which is the inverse of the natural exponential function $f(x) = e^x$. Domain is $\{x \mid x > 0\}$; range is all real numbers

función logarítmica natural Función $f(x) = \ln x$, que es la inversa de la función exponencial natural $f(x) = e^x$. El dominio es $\{x \mid x > 0\}$; el rango es todos los números reales.

nonlinear system of equations A system in which at least one of the equations is not linear.

sistema no lineal de ecuaciones Sistema en el cual por lo menos una de las ecuaciones no es lineal.

$$\begin{cases} y = 2x^2 \\ y = -3^2 + 5 \end{cases}$$

normal distribution A distribution that is mounded in the middle with symmetric "tails" at each end, forming a bell shape.

distribución normal Una distribución que está elevada en el centro con "colas" simétricas en los extremos, lo que forma la figura de una campana.

nth root The nth root of a number a, written as $\sqrt[n]{a}$ or $a^{\frac{1}{n}}$, is a number that is equal to a when it is raised to the nth power.

enésima raíz La enésima raíz de un número a, que se escribe como $\sqrt[n]{a}$ or $a^{\frac{1}{n}}$, es un número igual a a cuando se eleva a la enésima potencia.

$\sqrt[5]{32} = 2$, because $2^5 = 32$.

null hypothesis The assumption made that any difference between the control group and the treatment group in an experiment is due to chance, and not to the treatment.

hipótesis nula La suposición de que cualquier diferencia entre el grupo de control y el grupo de tratamiento en un experimento se debe al azar, no al tratamiento.

numerical data Data that represent quantities or observations that can be measured.

datos numéricos Datos que representan cantidades u observaciones que pueden medirse.

O

observational study A study that observes individuals and measures variables without controlling the individuals or their environment in any way.

estudio de observación Estudio que permite observar a individuos y medir variables sin controlar a los individuos ni su ambiente.

odd function A function in which $f(-x) = -f(x)$ for all x in the domain of the function.

función impar Función en la que $f(-x) = -f(x)$ para todos los valores de x dentro del dominio de la función

$f(x) = x^3$ is an odd function.

one-to-one function A function in which each y-value corresponds to only one x-value. The inverse of a one-to-one function is also a function.

función uno a uno Función en la que cada valor de y corresponde a sólo un valor de x. La inversa de una función uno a uno es también una función.

ordered triple A set of three numbers that can be used to locate a point (x, y, z) in a three-dimensional coordinate system.

tripleta ordenada Conjunto de tres números que se pueden utilizar para ubicar un punto (x, y, z) en un sistema de coordenadas tridimensional.

$(2, -1, 3)$

overlapping events Events in the sample space of a probability experiment that have one or more outcomes in common.

eventos solapados Eventos en el espacio muestral de un experimento de probabilidad que tienen uno o más resultados en común.

P

parabola The shape of the graph of a quadratic function. Also, the set of points equidistant from a point F, called the focus, and a line d, called the *directrix*.

parábola Forma de la gráfica de una función cuadrática. También, conjunto de puntos equidistantes de un punto F, denominado *foco*, y una línea d, denominada *directriz*.

Focus

Directrix

parameter One of the constants in a function or equation that may be changed. Also the third variable in a set of parametric equations.

parámetro Una de las constantes en una función o ecuación que se puede cambiar. También es la tercera variable en un conjunto de ecuaciones paramétricas.

$y = (x - h)^2 + k$

parameters

parent cube root function The function $f(x) = \sqrt[3]{x}$.

función madre de la raíz cúbica Función del tipo $f(x) = \sqrt[3]{x}$.

$f(x) = \sqrt[3]{x}$

Glossary/Glosario

parent function The simplest function with the defining characteristics of the family. Functions in the same family are transformations of their parent function.

función madre La función más básica con las características de la familia. Las funciones de la misma familia son transformaciones de su función madre.

$f(x) = x^2$ is the parent function for $g(x) = x^2 + 4$ and $h(x) = 5(x + 2)^2 - 3$.

---

parent square root function The function $f(x) = \sqrt{x}$, where $x \geq 0$.

función madre de la raíz cuadrada Función del tipo $f(x) = \sqrt{x}$, donde $x \geq 0$.

$f(x) = \sqrt{x}$

---

partial sum Indicated by $S_n = \sum_{i=1}^{n} a_i$, the sum of a specified number of terms n of a sequence whose total number of terms is greater than n.

suma parcial Expresada por $S_n = \sum_{i=1}^{n} a_i$, la suma de un número específico n de términos de una sucesión cuyo número total de términos es mayor que n.

For the sequence $a_n = n^2$, the fourth partial sum of the infinite series $\sum_{k=1}^{\infty} k^2$ is

$$\sum_{k=1}^{4} k^2 = 1^2 + 2^2 + 3^2 + 4^2 = 30.$$

Pascal's triangle A triangular arrangement of numbers in which every row starts and ends with 1 and each other number is the sum of the two numbers above it.

triángulo de Pascal Arreglo triangular de números en el cual cada fila comienza y termina con 1 y cada uno de los demás números es la suma de los dos números que están encima de él.

```
        1
      1   1
    1   2   1
  1   3   3   1
1   4   6   4   1
```

---

perfect-square trinomial A trinomial whose factored form is the square of a binomial. A perfect-square trinomial has the form $a^2 - 2ab + b^2 = (a - b)^2$ or $a^2 + 2ab + b^2 = (a + b)^2$.

trinomio cuadrado perfecto Trinomio cuya forma factorizada es el cuadrado de un binomio. Un trinomio cuadrado perfecto tiene la forma $a^2 - 2ab + b^2 = (a - b)^2$ o $a^2 + 2ab + b^2 = (a + b)^2$.

$x^2 + 6x + 9$ is a perfect square trinomial, because $x^2 + 6x + 9 = (x + 3)^2$.

---

period of a periodic function The length of a cycle measured in units of the independent variable (usually time in seconds). Also the reciprocal of the frequency.

periodo de una función periódica Longitud de un ciclo medido en unidades de la variable independiente (generalmente el tiempo en segundos). También es la inversa de la frecuencia.

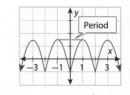

---

periodic function A function that repeats exactly in regular intervals, called *periods*.

función periódica Función que se repite exactamente a intervalos regulares denominados *periodos*.

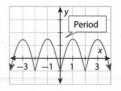

---

permutation An arrangement of a group of objects in which order is important. The number of permutations of r objects from a group of n objects is denoted $_nP_r$.

permutación Arreglo de un grupo de objetos en el cual el orden es importante. El número de permutaciones de r objetos de un grupo de n objetos se expresa $_nP_r$.

For 4 objects A, B, C, and D, there are $_4P_2 = 12$ different permutations of 2 objects: AB, AC, AD, BC, BD, CD, BA, CA, DA, CB, DB, and DC.

permutation test A significance test performed on the results of an experiment by forming every possible regrouping of all the data values taken from the control and treatment groups into two new groups, finding the distribution of the differences of the means for all of the new group pairings, and then finding the likelihood, given that the null hypothesis is true, of getting a difference of means at least as great as the original experimental difference.

prueba de permutación Una prueba de significancia realizada sobre los resultados de un experimento al formar todos los reagrupamientos posibles de todos los valores de datos tomados de los grupos de control y de tratamiento en dos nuevos grupos, hallar la distribución de las diferencias de las medias para todos los emparejamientos nuevos, y luego hallar la probabilidad, suponiendo que la hipótesis nula es verdadera, de obtener una diferencia de medias al menos tan grande como la diferencia experimental original.

---

phase shift A horizontal translation of a periodic function.

cambio de fase Traslación horizontal de una función periódica.

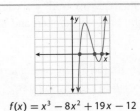

g is a phase shift of f $\frac{\pi}{2}$ units left.

---

piecewise function A function that is a combination of one or more functions.

función a trozos Función que es una combinación de una o más funciones.

$$f(x) = \begin{cases} -4 & \text{if } x \leq 0 \\ x+1 & \text{if } x > 0 \end{cases}$$

---

polynomial A monomial or a sum or difference of monomials.

polinomio Monomio o suma o diferencia de monomios.

$$2x^2 + 3x - 7$$

---

polynomial function A function whose rule is a polynomial.

función polinomial Función cuya regla es un polinomio.

$$f(x) = x^3 - 8x^2 + 19x - 12$$

---

polynomial identity A mathematical relationship equating one polynomial quantity to another.

identidad de polinomios Relación matemática que iguala una cantidad polinomial con otra.

$$(x^4 - y^4) = (x^2 + y^2)(x^2 - y^2)$$

---

population The entire group of objects or individuals considered for a survey.

población Grupo completo de objetos o individuos que se desea estudiar.

In a survey about the study habits of high school students, the population is all high school students.

---

probability A number from 0 to 1 (or 0% to 100%) that is the measure of how likely an event is to occur.

probabilidad Número entre 0 y 1 (o entre 0% y 100%) que describe cuán probable es que ocurra un suceso.

A bag contains 3 red marbles and 4 blue marbles. The probability of choosing a red marble is $\frac{3}{7}$.

ENGLISH	SPANISH	EXAMPLES

probability distribution for an experiment The function that pairs each outcome with its probability.

distribución de probabilidad para un experimento Función que asigna a cada resultado su probabilidad.

A number cube is rolled 10 times. The results are shown in the table.

Outcome	1	2	3	4	5	6
Probability	$\frac{1}{10}$	$\frac{1}{5}$	$\frac{1}{5}$	0	$\frac{3}{10}$	$\frac{1}{5}$

probability sample A sample in which every member of the population being sampled has a nonzero probability of being selected.

muestra de probabilidad Muestra en la que cada miembro de la población que se estudia tiene una probabilidad distinta de cero de ser elegido.

pure imaginary number *See* imaginary number.

número imaginario puro Ver número imaginario.

$3i$

Q

quadratic equation An equation that can be written in the form $ax^2 + bx + c = 0$, where a, b, and c are real numbers and $a \neq 0$.

ecuación cuadrática Ecuación que se puede expresar como $ax^2 + bx + c = 0$, donde a, b y c son números reales y $a \neq 0$.

$x^2 + 3x - 4 = 0$
$x^2 - 9 = 0$

Quadratic Formula The formula $x = \frac{-b \pm \sqrt{b^2 - 4ac}}{2a}$, which gives solutions, or roots, of equations in the form $ax^2 + bx + c = 0$, where $a \neq 0$.

fórmula cuadrática La fórmula $x = \frac{-b \pm \sqrt{b^2 - 4ac}}{2a}$, que da soluciones, o raíces, para las ecuaciones del tipo $ax^2 + bx + c = 0$, donde $a \neq 0$.

The solutions of $2x^2 - 5x - 3 = 0$ are given by
$$x = \frac{-(-5) \pm \sqrt{(-5)^2 - 4(2)(-3)}}{2(2)}$$
$$= \frac{5 \pm \sqrt{25 + 24}}{4} = \frac{5 \pm 7}{4};$$
$x = 3$ or $x = -\frac{1}{2}$.

quadratic function A function that can be written in the form $f(x) = ax^2 + bx + c$, where a, b, and c are real numbers and $a \neq 0$, or in the form $f(x) = a(x - h)^2 + k$, where a, h, and k are real numbers and $a \neq 0$.

función cuadrática Función que se puede expresar como $f(x) = ax^2 + bx + c$, donde a, b y c son números reales y $a \neq 0$, o como $f(x) = a(x - h)^2 + k$, donde a, h y k son números reales y $a \neq 0$.

$f(x) = x^2 - 6x + 8$

quadratic model A quadratic function used to represent a set of data.

modelo cuadrático Función cuadrática que se utiliza para representar un conjunto de datos.

x	4	6	8	10
$f(x)$	27	52	89	130

A quadratic model for the data is $f(x) = x^2 + 3.3x - 2.6$.

quadratic regression A statistical method used to fit a quadratic model to a given data set.

regresión cuadrática Método estadístico utilizado para ajustar un modelo cuadrático a un conjunto de datos determinado.

R

radian A unit of angle measure based on arc length. In a circle of radius r, if a central angle has a measure of 1 radian, then the length of the intercepted arc is r units.

2π radians $= 360°$
1 radian $\approx 57°$

radián Unidad de medida de un ángulo basada en la longitud del arco. En un círculo de radio r, si un ángulo central mide 1 radián, entonces la longitud del arco abarcado es r unidades.

2π radianes $= 360°$
1 radián $\approx 57°$

(circle with radius r, center O, and angle θ = 1 radian)

---

radical An indicated root of a quantity.

radical Raíz indicada de una cantidad.

$\sqrt{36} = 6,\ \sqrt[3]{27} = 3$

---

radical equation An equation that contains a variable within a radical.

ecuación radical Ecuación que contiene una variable dentro de un radical.

$\sqrt{x + 3} + 4 = 7$

---

radical function A function whose rule contains a variable within a radical.

función radical Función cuya regla contiene una variable dentro de un radical.

(graph with points (0,0), (1,1), (4,2), (9,3))

$f(x) = \sqrt{x}$

---

radicand The expression under a radical sign.

radicando Número o expresión debajo del signo de radical.

$\sqrt{x + 3} - 2$

Radicand

---

random variable A variable whose value is determined by the outcome of a probability experiment.

variable aleatoria Una variable cuyo valor viene determinado por el resultado de un experimento de probabilidad.

---

randomized comparative experiment An experiment in which the individuals are assigned to the control group or the treatment group at random, in order to minimize bias.

experimento comparativo aleatorizado Experimento en el que se elige al azar a los individuos para el grupo de control o para el grupo experimental, a fin de minimizar el sesgo.

---

range of a function or relation The set of output values of a function or relation.

rango de una función o relación Conjunto de los valores desalida de una función o relación.

The range of $y = x^2$ is $\left\{ y \mid y \geq 0 \right\}$.

---

rational equation An equation that contains one or more rational expressions.

ecuación racional Ecuación que contiene una o más expresiones racionales.

$\dfrac{x + 2}{x^2 + 3x - 1} = 6$

---

rational exponent An exponent that can be expressed as $\frac{m}{n}$ such that if m and n are integers, then $b^{\frac{m}{n}} = \sqrt[n]{b^m} = \left(\sqrt[n]{b}\right)^m$.

exponente racional Exponente quese puede expresar como $\frac{m}{n}$ tal que, si m y n son números enteros, entonces
$b^{\frac{m}{n}} = \sqrt[n]{b^m} = \left(\sqrt[n]{b}\right)^m$

$4^{\frac{2}{2}} = \sqrt{4^3} = \sqrt{64} = 8$
$4^{\frac{2}{2}} = \left(\sqrt{4}\right)^3 = 2^3 = 8$

rational expression An algebraic expression whose numerator and denominator are polynomials and whose denominator has a degree ≥ 1.

expresión racional Expresión algebraica cuyo numerador y denominador son polinomios y cuyo denominador tiene un grado ≥ 1.

$$\frac{x+2}{x^2 + 3x - 1}$$

rational function A function whose rule can be written as a rational expression.

función racional Función cuya regla se puede expresar como una expresión racional.

$$f(x) = \frac{x+2}{x^2 + 3x - 1}$$

real axis The horizontal axis in the complex plane; it graphically represents the real part of complex numbers.

eje real Eje horizontal de un plano complejo. Representa gráficamente la parte real de los números complejos.

recursive rule A rule for a sequence in which one or more previous terms are used to generate the next term.

Regla recurrente Regla para una sucesión en la cual uno o más términos anteriores se utilizan para generar el término siguiente.

For the sequence 5, 7, 9, 11, ..., a recursive rule is $a_1 = 5$ and $a_n = a_{n-1} + 2$.

reduced row-echelon form A form of an augmented matrix in which the coefficient columns form an identity matrix.

forma escalonada reducida por filas Forma de matriz aumentada en la que las columnas de coeficientes forman una matriz de identidad.

$$\begin{bmatrix} 1 & 0 & \vdots & -1 \\ 0 & 1 & \vdots & 3 \end{bmatrix}$$

reference angle For an angle in standard position, the reference angle is the positive acute angle formed by the terminal side of the angle and the x-axis.

ángulo de referencia Dado un ángulo en posición estándar, el ángulo de referencia es el ángulo agudo positivo formado por el lado terminal del ángulo y el eje x.

reflection A transformation that reflects, or "flips," a graph or figure across a line, called the line of reflection, such that each reflected point is the same distance from the line of reflection but is on the opposite side of the line.

reflexión Transformación que refleja, o invierte, una gráfica o figura sobre una línea, llamada la línea de reflexión, de manera tal que cada punto reflejado esté a la misma distancia de la línea de reflexión pero que se encuentre en el lado opuesto de la línea.

regression The statistical study of the relationship between variables.

regresión Estudio estadístico de la relación entre variables.

Remainder Theorem If the polynomial function $P(x)$ is divided by $x - a$, then the remainder r is $P(a)$.

Teorema del resto Si la función polinomial $P(x)$ se divide entre $x - a$, entonces, el residuo r será $P(a)$.

representative sample A sample that is a good estimator for its corresponding population parameter.

muestra representativa Una muestra que es un buen estimador para su parámetro de población correspondiente.

Glossary/Glosario

Glossary/Glosario

rotation A transformation that rotates or turns a figure about a point called the center of rotation.

rotación Transformación que hace rotar o girar una figura sobre un punto llamado centro de rotación.

row operation An operation performed on a row of an augmented matrix that creates an equivalent matrix.

operación por filas Operación realizada en una fila de una matriz aumentada que crea una matriz equivalente.

$$\begin{bmatrix} 2 & 0 & \vdots & -2 \\ 0 & 1 & \vdots & 3 \end{bmatrix} = \begin{bmatrix} \frac{1}{2}(2) & \frac{1}{2}(0) & \vdots & \frac{1}{2}(-2) \\ 0 & 1 & \vdots & 3 \end{bmatrix}$$
$$= \begin{bmatrix} 1 & 0 & \vdots & -1 \\ 0 & 1 & \vdots & 3 \end{bmatrix}$$

row-reduction method The process of performing elementary row operations on an augmented matrix to transform the matrix to reduced row echelon form.

método de reducción por filas Proceso por el cual se realizan operaciones elementales de filas en una matriz aumentada para transformar la matriz en una forma reducida de filas escalonadas.

$$\begin{bmatrix} 2 & 0 & \vdots & -2 \\ 0 & 1 & \vdots & 3 \end{bmatrix} = \begin{bmatrix} \frac{1}{2}(2) & \frac{1}{2}(0) & \vdots & \frac{1}{2}(-2) \\ 0 & 1 & \vdots & 3 \end{bmatrix}$$
$$= \begin{bmatrix} 1 & 0 & \vdots & -1 \\ 0 & 1 & \vdots & 3 \end{bmatrix}$$

S

sample A part of the population.

muestra Una parte de la población.

In a survey about the study habits of high school students, a sample is a survey of 100 students.

sample space The set of all possible outcomes of a probability experiment.

espacio muestral Conjunto de todos los resultados posibles en un experimento de probabilidades.

In the experiment of rolling a number cube, the sample space is 1, 2, 3, 4, 5, 6.

sampling distribution A distribution that shows how a particular statistic varies across all samples of n individuals from the same population.

distribución de muestreo Una distribución que muestra de qué manera una determinada estadística varía a lo largo de todas las muestras de n individuos de la misma población.

second-degree equation in two variables An equation constructed by adding terms in two variables with powers no higher than 2.

ecuación de segundo grado en dos variables Ecuación compuesta por la suma de términos en dos variables con potencias no mayores a 2.

$$ax^2 + by^2 + cx + dy + e = 0$$

second differences Differences between first differences of a function.

segundas diferencias Diferencias entre las primerasdiferencias de una función.

x	0	1	2	3
y	1	4	9	16

first differences   +3   +5   +7
second differences   +2   +2

self-selected sample A sample in which members volunteer to participate.

muestra de voluntarios Muestra en la que los miembros se ofrecen voluntariamente para participar.

sequence A list of numbers that often form a pattern.

sucesión Lista de números que generalmente forman un patrón.

1, 2, 4, 8, 16, ...

series The indicated sum of the terms of a sequence.

serie Suma indicada de los términos de una sucesión.

$1 + 2 + 4 + 8 + 16 + ...$

---

set A collection of items called elements.

conjunto Grupo de componentes denominados elementos.

$\{1, 2, 3\}$

---

set-builder notation A notation for a set that uses a rule to describe the properties of the elements of the set.

notación de conjuntos Notación para un conjunto que se vale de una regla para describir las propiedades de los elementos del conjunto.

$\{x | x > 3\}$ read, "The set of all x such that x is greater than 3."

---

simple event An event consisting of only one outcome.

suceso simple Suceso que contiene sólo un resultado.

In the experiment of rolling a number cube, the event consisting of the outcome 3 is a simple event.

---

simulation A model of an experiment, often one that would be too difficult or time-consuming to actually perform.

simulación Modelo de un experimento; generalmente se recurre a la simulación cuando realizar dicho experimento sería demasiado difícil o llevaría mucho tiempo.

A random number generator is used to simulate the roll of a number cube.

---

sine In a right triangle, the ratio of the length of the side opposite $\angle A$ to the length of the hypotenuse.

seno En un triángulo rectángulo, razón entre la longitud del cateto opuesto a $\angle A$ y la longitud de la hipotenusa.

$\sin A = \dfrac{\text{opposite}}{\text{hypotenuse}}$.

---

skewed distribution A distribution that is mounded but not symmetric because one "tail" is much longer than the other.

distribución sesgada Una distribución que está elevada pero no es simétrica porque una de las "colas" es mucho más larga que la otra.

---

square-root function A function whose rule contains a variable under a square-root sign.

función de raíz cuadrada Función cuya regla contiene una variable bajo un signo de raíz cuadrada.

$f(x) = \sqrt{x}$

---

standard deviation A measure of dispersion of a data set. The standard deviation σ is the square root of the variance.

desviación estándar Medida de dispersión de un conjunto de datos. La desviación estándar σ es la raíz cuadrada de la varianza.

Data set: $\{6, 7, 7, 9, 11\}$
Mean: $\dfrac{6 + 7 + 7 + 9 + 11}{5} = 8$
Variance: $\frac{1}{5}(4 + 1 + 1 + 1 + 9) = 3.2$
Standard deviation: $\sigma = \sqrt{3.2} \approx 1.8$

---

standard error of the mean The standard deviation of the sampling distribution of the sample mean, denoted $\sigma_{\bar{x}}$.

error estándar de la media La desviación estándar de la distribución de muestreo de la media de la muestra, que se indica así: $\sigma_{\bar{x}}$.

Glossary/Glosario

ENGLISH	SPANISH	EXAMPLES
standard error of the proportion The standard deviation of the sampling distribution of the sample proportion, denoted σ_p.	**error estándar de la proporción** La desviación estándar de la distribución de muestreo de la proporción de la muestra, que se indica así: σ_p.	
standard form of a polynomial A polynomial in one variable is written in standard form when the terms are in order from greatest degree to least degree.	**forma estándar de un polinomio** Un polinomio de una variable se expresa en forma estándar cuando los términos se ordenan de mayor a menor grado.	$3x^3 - 5x^2 + 6x - 7$
standard form of a quadratic equation $ax^2 + bx + c = 0$, where a, b, and c are real numbers and $a \neq 0$.	**forma estándar de una ecuación** cuadrática $ax^2 + bx + c = 0$, donde a, b y c son números reales y $a \neq 0$.	$2x^2 + 3x - 1 = 0$
standard normal distribution A normal distribution that has a mean of 0 and a standard deviation of 1.	**distribución normal estándar** Una distribución normal que tiene una media de 0 y una desviación estándar de 1.	
standard normal value A value that indicates how many standard deviations above or below the mean a particular value falls, given by the formula $z = \frac{x - \mu}{\sigma}$, where z is the standard normal value, x is the given value, μ is the mean, and σ is the standard deviation of a standard normal distribution.	**valor normal estándar** Valor que indica a cuántas desviaciones estándar por encima o por debajo de la media se encuentra un determinado valor, dado por la fórmula $z = \frac{x - \mu}{\sigma}$, donde z es el valor normal estándar, x es el valor dado, μ es la media y σ es la desviación estándar de una distribución normal estándar.	
standard position An angle in standard position has its vertex at the origin and its initial side on the positive x–axis.	**osición estándar** Ángulo cuyo vértice se encuentra en el origen y cuyo lado inicial se encuentra sobre el eje x.	
statistic A number that describes a sample.	**estadística** Número que describe una muestra.	
statistical significance A determination that the likelihood that an experimental result occurred by chance is so low that a conclusion in favor of rejecting the null hypothesis is justified.	**significación estadística** Una determinación de que la probabilidad de que un resultado experimental ocurriera por azar es tan reducida que está justificada una conclusión a favor de rechazar la hipótesis nula.	
step function A piecewise function that is constant over each interval in its domain.	**función escalón** Función a trozos que es constante en cada intervalo en su dominio.	

Glossary/Glosario

ENGLISH	SPANISH	EXAMPLES
stretch A transformation that pulls the points of a graph horizontally away from the y–axis or vertically away from the x–axis.	**estiramiento** Transformación que desplaza los puntos de una gráfica en forma horizontal alejándolos del eje y o en forma vertical alejándolos del eje x.	
summation notation A method of notating the sum of a series using the Greek letter $\sum$ (capital *sigma*).	**notación de sumatoria** Método de notación de la suma de una serie que utiliza la letra griega $\sum$ (SIGMA mayúscula).	$\displaystyle\sum_{n=1}^{5}3k = 3 + 6 + 9 + 12 + 15 = 45$
survey A data collection tool that uses questions to measure characteristics of interest about a population using a sample selected from the population.	**encuesta** Una herramienta para recopilar datos que usa preguntas para medir las características de interés sobre una población mediante una muestra seleccionada de entre la población.	
synthetic division A shorthand method of dividing by a linear binomial of the form $(x - a)$ by writing only the coefficients of the polynomials.	**división sintética** Método abreviado de división que consiste en dividir por un binomio lineal del tipo $(x - a)$ escribiendo sólo los coeficientes de los polinomios.	$(x^3 - 7x + 6) \div (x - 2)$ $\underline{2\rfloor}\quad 1 \quad 0 \quad -7 \quad 6$ $\qquad\qquad 2 \quad 4 \quad 6$ $\overline{\qquad 1 \quad 2 \quad -3 \rfloor 0}$ $(x^3 - 7x + 6) \div (x - 2) = x^2 + 2x - 3$
synthetic substitution The process of using synthetic division to evaluate a polynomial $p(x)$ when $x = c$.	**sustitución sintética** Proceso que consiste en usar la división sintética para evaluar un polinomio $p(x)$ cuando $x = c$.	
system of equations A set of two or more equations that have two or more variables.	**sistema de ecuaciones** Conjunto de dos o más ecuaciones que contienen dos o más variables.	$\begin{cases} 2x + 3y = -1 \\ x^2 = 4 \end{cases}$
system of linear inequalities A system of inequalities in two or more variables in which all of the inequalities are linear.	**sistema de desigualdades lineales** Sistema de desigualdades en dos o más variables en el que todas las desigualdades son lineales.	$\begin{cases} 2x + 3y \geq -1 \\ x - 3y < 4 \end{cases}$

T

term of a sequence An element or number in the sequence.	**término de una sucesión** Elemento o número de una sucesión.	5 is the third term in the sequence 1, 3, 5, 7, ...
terminal side For an angle in standard position, the ray that is rotated relative to the positive x–axis.	**lado terminal** Dado un ángulo en una posición estándar, el rayo que rota en relación con el eje positivo x.	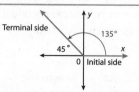

Glossary/Glosario

theoretical probability The ratio of the number of equally likely outcomes in an event to the total number of possible outcomes.

probabilidad teórica Razón entre el número de resultados igualmente probables de un suceso y el número total de resultados posibles.

The theoretical probability of rolling an odd number on a number cube is $\frac{3}{6} = \frac{1}{2}$.

---

three-dimensional coordinate system A space that is divided into eight regions by an x–axis, a y–axis, and a z–axis. The locations, or coordinates, of points are given by ordered triples.

sistema de coordenadas tridimensional Espacio dividido en ocho regiones por un eje x, un eje y y un eje z. Las ubicaciones, o coordenadas, de los puntos son dadas por tripletas ordenadas.

---

transformation A change in the position, size, or shape of a figure or graph.

transformación Cambio en la posición, tamaño o forma de una figura o gráfica.

---

translation A transformation that shifts or slides every point of a figure or graph the same distance in the same direction.

traslación Transformación en la que todos los puntos de una figura se mueven la misma distancia en la misma dirección.

---

trial In probability, a single repetition or observation of an experiment.

prueba En probabilidad, una sola repetición u observación de un experimento.

In the experiment of rolling a number cube, each roll is one trial.

---

trigonometric function A function whose rule is given by a trigonometric ratio.

función trigonométrica Función cuya regla es dada por una razón trigonométrica.

$f(x) = \sin x$

---

trigonometric ratio Ratio of the lengths of two sides of a right triangle.

razón trigonométrica Razón entre dos lados de un triángulo rectángulo.

$\sin A = \frac{a}{c}, \cos A = \frac{b}{c}, \tan A = \frac{a}{b}$

---

trigonometry The study of the measurement of triangles and of trigonometric functions and their applications.

trigonometría Estudio de la medición de los triángulos y de las funciones trigonométricas y sus aplicaciones.

---

trinomial A polynomial with three terms.

trinomio Polinomio con tres términos.

$4x^2 + 3xy - 5y^2$

© Houghton Mifflin Harcourt Publishing Company

Glossary/Glosario

ENGLISH	SPANISH	EXAMPLES

turning point A point on the graph of a function that corresponds to a local maximum (or minimum) where the graph changes from increasing to decreasing (or vice versa).

punto de inflexión Punto de la gráfica de una función que corresponde a un máximo (o mínimo) local donde la gráfica pasa de ser creciente a decreciente (o viceversa).

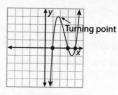

U

uniform distribution A distribution that is basically level, forming a shape that looks like a rectangle.

distribución uniforme Una distribución que es básicamente llana, formando una figura similar a un rectángulo.

unit circle A circle with a radius of 1, centered at the origin.

círculo unitario Círculo con un radio de 1, centrado en el origen.

Unit circle

V

variance The average of squared differences from the mean. The square root of the variance is called the *standard deviation*.

varianza Promedio de las diferencias cuadráticas en relación con la media. La raíz cuadrada de la varianza se denomina *desviación estándar*.

Data set: is $\{6, 7, 7, 9, 11\}$

Mean: $\dfrac{6 + 7 + 7 + 9 + 11}{5} = 8$

Variance: $\frac{1}{5}(4 + 1 + 1 + 1 + 9) = 3.2$

vertex form of a quadratic function A quadratic function written in the form $f(x) = a(x - h)^2 + k$, where a, h, and k are constants and (h, k) is the vertex.

forma en vértice de una función cuadrática Una función cuadrática expresada en la forma $f(x) = a(x - h)^2 + k$, donde a, h y k son constantes y (h, k) es el vértice.

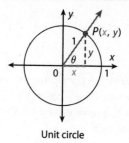

$f(x) = (x - 2)^2 + 2$

vertex of an absolute-value graph The point where the axis of symmetry intersects the graph.

vértice de una gráfica de valor absoluto Punto donde en el eje de simetría interseca la gráfica.

Vertex

$f(x) = |x|$

If $x < 0$, $f(x) = -x$

If $x > 0$, $f(x) = x$

vertex of a parabola The highest or lowest point on the parabola.

vértice de una parábola Punto más alto o más bajo de una parábola.

Vertex

Z

z-axis The third axis in a three-dimensional coordinate system.

eje z Tercer eje en un sistema de coordenadas tridimensional.

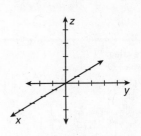

z-score A standardized data value from a normal distribution with mean μ and standard deviation σ found by using the formula $z = \frac{x - \mu}{\sigma}$ where x is the original data value.

puntaje z Un valor de datos estandarizado de una distribución normal con una media μ y una desviación estándar σ que se halla usando la fórmula $z = \frac{x - \mu}{\sigma}$, donde x es el valor de datos original.

zero of a function For the function f, any number x such that $f(x) = 0$.

cero de una función Dada la función f, todo número x tal que $f(x) = 0$.

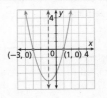

The zeros of $f(x) = x^2 + 2x - 3$ are -3 and 1.

Index

Index locator numbers are in Module. Lesson form. For example, 2.1 indicates Module 2, Lesson 1 as listed in the Table of Contents.

Index

Index

Index

© Houghton Mifflin Harcourt Publishing Company

Table of Measures

LENGTH

1 inch = 2.54 centimeters

1 meter = 39.37 inches

1 mile = 5,280 feet

1 mile = 1760 yards

1 mile = 1.609 kilometers

1 kilometer = 0.62 mile

MASS/WEIGHT

1 pound = 16 ounces

1 pound = 0.454 kilograms

1 kilogram = 2.2 pounds

1 ton = 2000 pounds

CAPACITY

1 cup = 8 fluid ounces

1 pint = 2 cups

1 quart = 2 pints

1 gallon = 4 quarts

1 gallon = 3.785 liters

1 liter = 0.264 gallons

1 liter = 1000 cubic centimeters

Symbols

$\neq$	is not equal to	π	pi: (about 3.14)
$\approx$	is approximately equal to	$\perp$	is perpendicular to
10^2	ten squared; ten to the second power	$\parallel$	is parallel to
		$\overleftrightarrow{AB}$	line AB
$2.\overline{6}$	repeating decimal 2.66666...	$\overrightarrow{AB}$	ray AB
$\lvert -4 \rvert$	the absolute value of negative 4	$\overline{AB}$	line segment AB
$\sqrt{}$	square root	$m\angle A$	measure of $\angle A$

Formulas

Triangle	$A = \frac{1}{2}bh$	Pythagorean Theorem	$a^2 + b^2 = c^2$
Parallelogram	$A = bh$	Quadratic Formula	$x = \dfrac{-b \pm \sqrt{b^2 - 4ac}}{2a}$
Circle	$A = \pi r^2$	Arithmetic Sequence	$a_n = a_1 + (n-1)d$
Circle	$C = \pi d$ or $C = 2\pi r$	Geometric Sequence	$a_n = a_1 r^{n-1}$
General Prisms	$V = Bh$	Geometric Series	$S_n = \dfrac{a_1 - a_1 r^n}{1 - r}$ where $r \neq 1$
Cylinder	$V = \pi r^2 h$	Radians	$1\ radian = \frac{180}{\pi}\ degrees$
Sphere	$V = \frac{4}{3}\pi r^3$	Degrees	$1\ degree = \frac{\pi}{180}\ radians$
Cone	$V = \frac{1}{3}\pi r^2 h$	Exponential Growth/Decay	$A = A_0\, e^{k(t - t_0)} + B_0$
Pyramid	$V = \frac{1}{3}Bh$		